THE GREAT EXEGESIS

al-Tafsīr al-Kabīr

FAKHR AL-DĪN AL-RĀZĪ

THE GREAT EXEGESIS

al-Tafsīr al-Kabīr

Volume I: The *Fātiḥa*

مفاتيح الغيب

Translated with notes by
Sohaib Saeed

Foreword by M.A.S. Abdel Haleem

THE ROYAL AAL AL-BAYT INSTITUTE
FOR ISLAMIC THOUGHT
and
THE ISLAMIC TEXTS SOCIETY

This first edition published 2018 by
The Royal Aal al-Bayt Institute for Islamic Thought &
The Islamic Texts Society
Miller's House
Kings Mill Lane
Great Shelford
Cambridge CB22 5EN, UK.

Reprinted 2024

British Library Cataloguing-in-Publication Data.
A catalogue record for this book is
available from the British Library.

ISBN: 978 1911141 21 1

CONTENTS

Acknowledgements vii
Foreword: M.A.S. Abdel Haleem ix
Translator's Introduction xi

THE GREAT EXEGESIS
Volume 1: The *Fātiḥa*

Introduction 1

BOOK I: Sciences Derived from the *Isti^cādha*

PART ONE: Literary Aspects of the *Isti^cādha*

Chapter One: The Word (*Kalima*) and its Like 17
Chapter Two: Sounds, Letters and their Rulings 40
Chapter Three: Nouns, Verbs and Particles 46
Chapter Four: Various Categorisations of the Noun 58
Chapter Five: Rulings Concerning Genus Nouns and Derived Nouns 64
Chapter Six: Inflected and Uninflected Nouns 66
Chapter Seven: Inflection of Verbs 82

PART TWO: Narrated and Rational Exegesis of the *Isti^cādha*

Chapter Eight: Juristic Issues Connected to the *Isti^cādha* 89
Chapter Nine: Rational Enquiries Concerning the *Isti^cādha* 98
Chapter Ten: Spiritual Allusions of the *Isti^cādha* 137
Chapter Eleven: Further Enquiries Associated with the *Isti^cādha* 146

BOOK II: The *Basmala*

Chapter One: Introductory Enquiries 157
Chapter Two: Concerning the Recitation and Writing of the *Basmala* 161
Chapter Three: Concerning the Name (*Ism*) 169
Chapter Four: Names Denoting Actual Attributes 183
Chapter Five: Names Denoting Relative Attributes 211
Chapter Six: Names Denoting Eliminative Attributes 215
Chapter Seven: Names Denoting Combinations of Actual and Relative Attributes 218

Chapter Eight: Remaining Issues Pertaining to Divine Names 236
Chapter Nine: The Name *Allāh* 243
Chapter Ten: The Names *al-Raḥmān* and *al-Raḥīm* 255
Chapter Eleven: Spiritual Allusions of the *Basmala* 259

BOOK III: The *Fātiḥa*

Chapter One: Names of this *Sūra* 271
Chapter Two: Virtues of this *Sūra* 277
Chapter Three: Rational Wisdoms Derived from this *Sūra* 281
Chapter Four: Juristic Issues Connected to this *Sūra* 295
Chapter Five: Exegesis of *Sūrat al-Fātiḥa* [Verse by Verse] 345
All praise is for God... 345
Lord of the worlds (Q.1.2) 360
The Compassionate, the Merciful (Q.1.3) 366
Master of the Day of Judgment (Q.1.4) 371
You we worship... 380
And from You we seek help (Q.1.5) 394
Guide us upon the straight path (Q.1.6) 397
The path of those on whom You have bestowed favour... 403
Not of those who incur wrath, nor of those who are astray (Q.1.7) 407
Chapter Six: Exegesis of *Sūrat al-Fātiḥa* as a Whole 412
Rational Subtleties Derived from this *Sūra* 412
The Approaches of Satan 415
How the *Fātiḥa* Contains All the Requisite Knowledge of the Beginning, the Middle and the End 417
God's Division of the Prayer into Two Halves 419
The Prayer is the Ascension of the Gnostics 428
On Divine Superiority and Greatness 434
Subtleties Concerning *All praise is for God* and the Five Divine Names in this *Sūra* 441
The Reason for the *Basmala* Containing the Three Names 448
The Reason for the *Fātiḥa* Containing the Five Names 449
Concluding Observation 450

Appendix: Persons Cited in the Text 453
Bibliography 467
Index 473

ACKNOWLEDGMENTS

I extend my thanks—after Almighty God—to all who made this possible: to HRH Prince Ghazi bin Muhammad for entrusting me with this tremendous task; to Aftab Ahmed for coordinating the project in its early stages; and to Fatima Azzam and colleagues at the Islamic Texts Society for their diligence and professionalism, not least Andrew Booso for his editorial eye at the final hurdle. I thank my family for their unfailing support, my mentor Professor Abdel Haleem for contributing the Foreword, and all those who shared pointers or simply shared my excitement at translating this great *Imām*.

Sohaib Saeed
Ramaḍān 1439 / May 2018

FOREWORD

Translation of the Qur'ān into English started in the 17th century CE and gained impetus over the last 50 years, so that there are now scores of such translations. In contrast, very little attention indeed has been given to the *tafsīr* (exegesis) of the Qur'ān. Over the last 25 years or so, a number of translations from Arabic *tafsīr* works, including part of Ṭabarī, Ibn Kathīr, Suyūṭī and Sayyid Qutb, have appeared, but no one has attempted until now to translate what I consider the single most important *tafsīr*, that of Fakhr al-Dīn al-Rāzī (d. 606 AH/1210 CE). This is perhaps due to the fact that it has been seen as a more difficult and complex task than any of the above: Rāzī's *al-Tafsīr al-Kabīr* is indeed great, both in its size and worth. The editions of Rāzī available until recently were prohibitive, up to eight large volumes with no indexing. The material covered by the *Tafsīr* was also more difficult: Rāzī was a great scholar of philosophy, theology, jurisprudence and an accomplished preacher in both Arabic and Persian, engaged in *taṣawwuf*, with a very fine spiritual sensibility. In addition, he was a top-class linguist in all aspects of the Arabic language: he raised and discussed questions about the language of the Qur'ān which only now, with our modern linguistic thinking, have begun to be noticed.

Because he included, in his *Tafsīr*, elements of all these subjects, especially philosophy, physics and astronomy, this led to the notion, which gained popularity, that his *Tafsīr* included everything except *tafsīr*. In my view, it is correct to say that the '*Great Exegesis*' includes all elements of *tafsīr*, plus other things. Rāzī's expertise in all the subjects he mastered, his great holistic vision of the text of the Qur'ān, his sharp power of analysis and, above all, his linguistic skills, distinguish his *Tafsīr*. If I was given the choice to take only one *tafsīr* to rely on, I would readily take Rāzī's.

All this makes translation of Rāzī more difficult and explains why translators have not come forward to take on this task. Translating Rāzī requires understanding and appreciation for the many disciplines that appear in the *Tafsīr*, an intimate knowledge of Arabic at the level used by Rāzī, in addition to mastery of the English language.

Sohaib Saeed has had the courage to attempt the daunting task of translating Rāzī, for which he is well qualified. He had his education in the UK, with a BA and MSc in Philosophy, then a BA in Theology from al-Azhar University, Cairo, and a PhD in *tafsīr* from London University. He appreciates the importance of *al-Tafsīr al-Kabīr* and has started his translation of the work by translating the *tafsīr* of the first *sūra*, *al-Fātiḥa*, recognising its importance to all Muslims.

Sohaib has not simply summarised but has translated the whole text on the *Fātiḥa* and this is what makes this work particularly important: scholars should be able to read a translation of the real text of *al-Tafsīr al-Kabīr* rather than what someone selects from it. In addition to translating, Sohaib has corrected some longstanding errors in the Arabic editions of the text and has added his own comments as necessary.

Sohaib should be highly complimented for undertaking this very important and difficult task. His translation is faithful, accurate, and effective; it sets the paradigm for himself and other translators who may come forward to contribute to this enormous enterprise of translating *al-Tafsīr al-Kabīr*, long-awaited by English-speaking Muslim and other readers.

Scholars of the Qur'ān will always be indebted to The Royal Aal al-Bayt Institute of Islamic Thought in Jordan and the Islamic Texts Society in Cambridge who inspired and facilitated this major work of translation. With their support it can be hoped that the whole of *al-Tafsīr al-Kabīr* will be published in English. But, thanks are of course particularly due to Sohaib Saeed, for his great efforts in producing the actual translation. I have pleasure in recommending this translation highly to readers of the Qur'ān and *tafsīr*.

Muhammad Abdel Haleem
King Fahd Professor of Islamic Studies
University of London

TRANSLATOR'S INTRODUCTION

This translation is of the first volume of the magnum opus of the celebrated Sunni Imām Muḥammad b. ᶜUmar al-Rāzī, known as Fakhr al-Dīn (544/1149–606/1210), a prolific author and independent-minded proponent of the Ashᶜarī school of theology and the Shāfiᶜī school of Law.[1] His Qur'ān commentary, *al-Tafsīr al-kabīr* ('The Great Exegesis')—also known as *Mafātīḥ al-ghayb* ('Keys to the Unseen')—is universally acknowledged to be one of the core works of the genre which, despite the uniqueness of its approach to the Qur'ān and the universe, drew from the earlier tradition and provided rich materials for subsequent exegetes. It is a compendium not only of Qur'ānic sciences and meanings, but also Arabic linguistics, comparative jurisprudence, Aristotelian and Islamic philosophy, dialectic theology (*ᶜilm al-kalām*) and Sufism (*taṣawwuf*).[2]

Rāzī was born in the Persian city of Rayy to a family that claimed lineage to the Arabian tribe of Quraysh. He began his studies under his father, Ḍiyā' al-Dīn ᶜUmar. On account of his father's position at the main mosque of the town, Rāzī became known as 'Ibn Khaṭīb al-Rayy' ('son of the preacher of Rayy'). Among his early teachers was al-Majd al-Jīlī, with whom Rāzī travelled to Azerbaijan, where he specialised in philosophy, Ashᶜarī theology and Shāfiᶜī jurisprudence. After a period in Khwarezm in which he debated leading Muᶜtazilīs, he set

1 Ceylan writes on Rāzī's willingness to differ with the eponymous founders of both schools. Despite Rāzī's writings possessing a Sufi influence, little is known of his Sufi affiliations, if any, although some biographers considered him to be a conventional Sufi. See Yasin Ceylan, 'Theology and *Tafsīr* in the Major Works of Fakhr al-Dīn al-Rāzī', PhD thesis, University of Edinburgh, 1980, pp. 18 and 21–22. [A. Booso, ed.]

2 There is a tendency among Muslim scholars to classify this work as *tafsīr bi'l-ra'y*, i.e. rational-based exegesis, which is then called 'valid/praiseworthy' when it conforms to Sunni orthodoxy, and 'blameworthy' otherwise; see Muḥammad Ḥusayn al-Dhahabī, *al-Tafsīr wa'l-mufassirūn*, 3 vols., Cairo: Dār al-Ḥadīth 2005, vol. 1, p. 247. This is made to contrast with tradition-based exegesis (*tafsīr bi'l-ma'thūr*) in which sayings of the Prophet and first generations are presented without much elaboration or exploration of new questions. Some traditions are explicit in their condemnation of explaining the Qur'ān according to *ra'y*, but this is understood to describe ignorant speculation. In reality, the boundary between the two approaches is unclear, and mainstream exegesis in general depends upon multiple sources, including traditions, Arabic language/rhetoric and contemporary sciences.

out for Bukhara and travelled around Transoxiana, leading a life full of interesting encounters, debates and writings. The last twelve years of his life were spent on his *Tafsīr*, among other works, and it was this grand commentary which most gathered the fruits of his mastery of the rational sciences. By the time of his death in Herat—allegedly due to poisoning by members of the Karrāmī sect—he was known by his followers as *Shaykh al-Islām*, the pre-eminent scholar of his age. During his final sickness, he dictated a famous testament in which he declared the superiority of the Qur'ān over the rational sciences.[1]

Modern scholarship has taken a great interest in the thought and writings of Rāzī, and numerous books and papers have been published in Arabic, English and other languages concerning the place of his philosophical, theological and scientific writings in Islamic intellectual history. Nearly one hundred books and treatises can reasonably be attributed to Rāzī: many are lost or unpublished, and few have received any serious editorial attention, let alone translation in full. As well as facilitating scholarly engagement with the author's views and methods, this translation of his *Tafsīr* is a long-awaited contribution to the library of English-language Qur'ān commentary for the Muslim and non-Muslim reader alike.[2] The reader will discover dimensions of interpretation and reflection which build on narrated exegesis and go further, without departing altogether into the esoteric realms of Sufi commentary: consequently, the work can be characterised as both highly spiritual and intellectual.

While Rāzī's general authorship of *The Great Exegesis* is a matter of agreement, there has been much scholarly discussion about whether it was unfinished at the time of his death and completed by a student or later scholar: the names of Khuwayyī (d. 637/1239) and Qāmūlī

1 I have drawn biographical details mainly from Tariq Jaffer, *Rāzī: Master of Qur'ānic Interpretation and Theological Reasoning*, New York: Oxford University Press, 2015; Ṭāhā Jābir al-ʿAlwānī, *al-Imām Fakhr al-Dīn al-Rāzī wa-muṣannafātuh*, Cairo: Dār al-Salām, 2010. On the dangers of misconstruing the 'last will and testament', see Tony Street, 'Concerning the Life and Works of Fakhr al-Dīn al-Rāzī', in Peter Riddell & Tony Street, eds., *Islam: Essays on Scripture, Thought and Society*, Leiden: Brill, 1997, pp. 135–146.

2 This volume is to be followed by another which will span five chapters of the Qur'ān: *Yūsuf* (XII), *al-Kahf* (XVIII), *al-Naml* (XXVII), *Yā-Sīn* (XXXVI) and *al-Mulk* (LXVII). Volume I (the *Fātiḥa*) has recently been translated into French by a Senegalese specialist in Islamic thought. Time did not allow me to draw from his work at all or to investigate the differences in our translations beyond one juncture which interested me (see Rāzī's Introduction below). However, I note that Cissé's translation is barely annotated, and that he has collapsed the overall structure into two 'Books' rather than the actual three. See *Le Commentaire de Faḫr d-Dīn r-Rāzī sur la Fātiha*, trans. Alphousseyni Cissé, Paris: L'Harmattan, 2017.

(d. 727/1327) are mooted in this connection. Whereas some claims are based on biographical remarks which are open to interpretation, others appeal to the content and style of specific commentaries which seemingly differ from parts that have been attributed to Rāzī with certainty. For example, Ibrāhīm Rufayda argues that both the ranges from *al-ʿAnkabūt* to *Yā-Sīn* (Q.xxix–xxxvi) and from *Qāf* to *al-Wāqiʿa* (Q.l–lvi) were compiled by another author upon the style of Rāzī.[1] Other scholars, such as Ṭāhā al-ʿAlwānī and Muḥsin ʿAbd al-Ḥamīd, have dismissed such claims and argued that any minor divergences in style—and indeed references in the text to Fakhr al-Dīn in the third person—can be attributed to an editorial process applied to a work that had already been completed.[2] An important step to resolve this debate will be to compare extant manuscripts so as to produce a critical edition.

Although there is no dispute that Rāzī authored the exegesis of *Sūrat al-Fātiḥa*, I have raised several points in the footnotes which may have some bearing on questions of authorship. These indicate that it was probably composed later than various other parts of the exegesis. I detected some signs of editorial involvement, as well as discrepancies between opinions presented in the *Fātiḥa* commentary and elsewhere. I also highlight that the last chapter of Book I has all the appearance of being unfinished.

The Structure of this Volume

The Great Exegesis in its overall structure resembles other lengthy *tafsīrs*, in that it follows the order of the Qur'ān and presents commentary on one or more verses at a time. However, the structure of enquiry within this scheme is reminiscent of his philosophical writings, in that the commentary is divided into units which Rāzī calls 'Enquiries' (*masā'il*, sing. *mas'ala*). There are divisions and categories above and below this basic unit, through which the author explores the issues raised by, and connected to, the verses. Such arguments may include extended lists of proofs for various points of view, which he may respond to summarily or at length.

The present volume represents an exception in terms of structure, as Rāzī has presented his extensive commentary on *Sūrat al-Fātiḥa* in three

1 Ibrāhīm Rufayda, *al-Naḥw wa-kutub al-tafsīr*, 2 vols., Misrata: al-Dār al-Jamāhīriyya, 1990, vol. ii, pp. 827–843. In his detailed study of the issue, Muʿallimī included three more *sūras* in the second insertion, making it from *Muḥammad* (hence Q.xlvii), and argued for a third insertion from *al-Mumtaḥana* to *al-Taḥrīm* (Q.lx–lxvi). See ʿAbd al-Raḥmān al-Muʿallimī, *al-Majmūʿ*, ed. Mājid al-Ziyadī, Mecca: al-Maktaba al-Makkiyya, 1996, pp. 101–134.

2 See ʿAlwānī, *al-Imām Fakhr al-Dīn*, pp. 151–164.

'Books' (*kutub*, sing. *kitāb*).[1] The first of these is concerned with the formula of seeking refuge, the *istiʿādha*, after introductions loosely connected to this topic.[2] Book II discusses the *basmala*, the formula invoking God's Name at the outset of the *Fātiḥa* and other *sūras*. This book is largely concerned with theological issues related to God's Names and Attributes. Book III contains, as it were, the exegesis proper, after four introductory chapters—the last of which is dedicated to juristic issues. These introductions are followed by a chapter which I have divided into two: Chapter Five, which discusses the remaining verses of the *Fātiḥa* in turn; and Chapter Six, a series of thematic reflections upon the whole *sūra*. I trust that the reader will find this adjustment intuitive and helpful.[3]

I have provided cross references throughout the text to assist the reader in connecting related discussions and benefiting from the complete text as a commentary upon the most important *sūra* of the Qur'ān. While intending to keep as close as possible to Rāzī's intended structure, I have taken some liberties to relabel and introduce a number of additional headings and subheadings (placed between square brackets). The norm in the Arabic text is for lists (or sequential subheadings) to be labelled as 'first, second'—even for lists within lists. To make this much clearer, I have usually rendered such sequences using letters or numbers, such that *awwal* may be called 'A' or '1' rather than translated literally as 'first'. The choice of label follows this rationale for the most part: 'A, B, C etc.' for lists of alternative opinions on a matter; '1, 2, 3 etc.' for evidences of one side or another in a debate, as well as generic lists; and 'a, b, c etc.' (lower case) for general points, sometimes within the aforementioned categories. Moreover, questions, objections or problems are introduced with 'OBJECTION' etc., together with 'RESPONSE' to make the sequence of arguments clearer than can be found in any edition before now.

It is a matter of tremendous regret that this celebrated work has

1 ʿAlwānī notes that a distinct commentary on the *Fātiḥa* was attributed to Rāzī and known as *Mafātīḥ al-ʿulūm* ('Keys to the Sciences'); see ʿAlwānī, *al-Imām Fakhr al-Dīn*, p. 147. It is possible that it stood alone before being integrated into *al-Tafsīr al-kabīr*, just as the reverse has occurred. Early print editions bound it together with *al-Baqara* and subsequent *sūras*, but the thirty-two volume editions made the *Fātiḥa* commentary into Volume I by itself.

2 Rāzī's *Tafsīr* has been famously characterised as containing 'everything but exegesis'. Although this is obvious hyperbole, the reader may find this ringing true from the outset of Book I with its linguistic explorations. However, it should be kept in mind that the author intended to lay certain foundations at the outset of the work. His Introduction outlines his theory that an infinite number of sciences—religious and natural—may be derived from, or grounded in, the Qur'ān.

3 Aside from this, the biggest structural adjustment was to Book I: its last four chapters (Part Two) were renumbered to maintain continuity with Part One. This makes Book I easier to navigate.

not been published in a critical edition, but instead has been reproduced numerous times with the same typographical errors. As such, I selected a typical modern print[1] for the first draft of the translation, noting errors in order to compare them later with earlier prints, especially the Amīriyya (Būlāq) edition of 1862.[2] Latterly, I had the opportunity to compare the text with a digitised manuscript from 1823, spanning the contents of Book III only, located at the University of Michigan.[3] This process led me to confirm the correct reading of certain words, but there are many more corrections I have made based on a close reading of the text itself, together with external sources. As well as references and clarifications in the footnotes, I have taken the liberty—as a critical reader before anything else—of offering my own comments and observations, sometimes referring to later exegetes. No doubt, our modern age requires a balanced approach which builds upon tradition without treating it as ossified.

Qur'ān and *Ḥadīth* References

For the most part, I have taken Abdullah Yusuf Ali's translation as the basis for translated verses throughout this volume; adaptations were necessary for numerous reasons, especially to ensure that the quotation fitted the purpose of the author who cited it. However, as I explain in a note at the beginning of the author's Introduction below, the translation of the *Fātiḥa* was adapted from that in *The Study Quran*.[4]

Before describing the *ḥadīth*-related challenges presented by this book and my approach to solving them, a few words about the complex and subtle sciences of *ḥadīth* verification and referencing are in order. Cognisant of the seriousness of attributing statements to the Prophet Muḥammad (may God bless him and grant him peace)—especially as source-texts for legal rulings etc.—Muslim scholars developed methods of inspecting, critiquing, categorising and compiling such reports. An acceptable (*maqbūl*) report is one which is traced through a connected chain of narrators deemed honest and reliable, such that one may state confidently that it originated with the Prophet, whether at the higher grading of 'authentic' (*ṣaḥīḥ*) or just below it as 'fair' (*ḥasan*).

1 Ed. Sayyid ʿImrān, 16 vols., Cairo: Dār al-Ḥadīth, 2012.

2 Ed. Naṣr al-Hūrīnī, 6 vols., Būlāq: al-Maṭbaʿa al-Amīriyya, 1862.

3 *Tafsīr Sūrat al-Fātiḥah nuqila min Tafsīr al-kabīr*, provided by the Hathi Trust Digital Library.

4 Seyyed H. Nasr, Caner Dagli et al., eds., *The Study Quran*, New York: HarperOne, 2015. Translations of the *Fātiḥa*'s verses are generally in italics without quotation marks, whereas other Qur'ānic references are set in roman within quotation marks.

On the opposite end of the spectrum are reports which are rejected (*mardūd*) due to the presence within the chain of any narrator suspected of forgery. As well as the 'fabricated' (*mawḍūʿ*) category, this includes reports for which a chain cannot be found, though this could theoretically be remedied by its discovery. The point is that one cannot attribute statements to the Prophet (may God bless him and grant him peace) on this basis. Between these, yet technically within the rejected category, are the 'weak' (*ḍaʿīf*) narrations which ought not to be attributed to the Prophet without indicating their doubtful provenance. Nevertheless, Islamic scholarship—including the work of Qur'ānic exegetes—has made extensive use of these reports and deemed them acceptable within a range of contexts, essentially when their utilisation does not establish or contradict a major point of law or creed.[1]

In this volume, Imām Rāzī cites over 200 *ḥadīth*s attributed to the Prophet, as well as others from the first generations: these are used in various contexts and to different ends. To engage in a thorough investigation of the reports would be far beyond the scope of a translator, and this is yet another thing which is awaited from a critical edition—may God hasten it! Instead, I referred at first to notes provided in the Dār al-Ḥadīth edition (Sayyid ʿImrān),[2] which cover some *ḥadīth*s but miss out many. A fuller coverage and more thorough analysis is provided by a 2016 Master's thesis by Rashā Sulaymān,[3] but even she misses around thirty *ḥadīth*s. More concerning are the deficiencies in their treatment of the specific wordings and variants cited by Rāzī, which has led them, in places, to faulty conclusions. Therefore, I checked their statements using print and electronic resources, and credited each (with the initials 'S.I.' and 'R.S.') in straightforward cases. Whenever Rāzī himself references his source, I suffice with that, sometimes providing a print reference, or an alternative source if the former is not readily available.[4]

1 For an overview of historical approaches and attitudes, see Jonathan A. C. Brown, *Hadith: Muhammad's Legacy in the Medieval and Modern World*, 2nd ed., London: Oneworld Academic, 2018, pp. 104–113.

2 Given the notorious practices of some Arab publishers, one cannot assume that an actual editor by this name exists.

3 Rashā Ṭāriq Shafīq Sulaymān, *al-Riwāyāt al-wārida fī tafsīr Sūrat al-Fātiḥa min Tafsīr al-Rāzī*, Master's thesis, An-Najah National University (Nablus), 2016.

4 The footnotes are minimalistic and do not meet the full standards of *takhrīj* referencing. My purpose is to direct the researcher to a source that possesses the general wording of the *ḥadīth*, not necessarily the specific narration quoted by Imām Rāzī.

I have generally remained silent on the grading of the *ḥadīth*s, mainly because there are different opinions in many cases. The experienced reader will recognise that certain sources—such as Bukhārī and Muslim—are guarantees of authenticity in the Islamic tradition, while others confer no such guarantee. I have likewise remained silent regarding weak narrations, except when they reach the level of 'very weak' (*ḍaʿīf jiddan*) as stated by one of my sources. I also point out 'fabricated' reports and others which I could not source. Given the ease with which a multitude of references can be accessed in the modern age, the inability to trace such reports should be deemed sufficient cause to abandon them. My plain advice is to exercise caution when reading *ḥadīth*s in even the best scholarly works outside that field of specialism.

THE GREAT EXEGESIS

INTRODUCTION

In the Name of God, the Compassionate, the Merciful. All praise is for God, Who has enabled us to perform the best of obedient deeds, shown us the means of attaining perfect felicity and guided us to say 'I seek refuge in God from the rejected Satan' against every sin and evil.

In the Name of God, the Compassionate, the Merciful we commence every virtuous and commanded act. *All praise is for God* to Whom belongs all that is in the heavens; *Lord of the worlds* with all their entities and attributes; *the Compassionate, the Merciful* to all possessors of needs; *Master of the Day of Judgment* Who assigns the righteous to lofty grades and confines the wicked to lowly states. *You we worship and from You we seek help* in fulfilling all our duties. *Guide us upon the straight path* with every form of guidance: *the path of those on whom You have bestowed favour* in every condition and station, *not of those who incur wrath, nor of those who are astray*, the people of ignorance and misguidance.[1]

May God bless and grant peace to Muḥammad, who was supported with the greatest signs and miracles, and to his family and Companions as long as the signs unfold.

As to what follows: this is a book laying out some of what Almighty God has bestowed upon me of sciences of the Opening *sūra*. I beseech Him to grant me the ability to complete it, and to make me deserving of His bounty and generosity in both worlds; indeed He is the best to guide, support and grant succour to the seekers.

This work comprises an introduction and chapters. What follows are the sections of the introduction.

1 For the translation of the *Fātiḥa*—which the author incorporated here into a rhyming introduction—I have used Nasr, Dagli et al., eds., *The Study Quran*, and adapted it for consistency with the opinions of Rāzī himself. Thus, in place of *Praise be to God*, I have rendered it *All praise is for God*. To reflect the centrality of divine favour (*niʿma*) in Rāzī's discourse, I changed *The path of those whom Thou hast blest*. I also replaced the archaic language preferred by the *Study Quran* editors.

Section 1: Summary of the Sciences of this *Sūra*[1]

I have stated at various times that it is possible to extract as many as 10,000 enquiries (*mas'ala*) from the precious and subtle teachings of this noble *sūra*. Yet this was considered fanciful by certain people harbouring envy, ignorance, delusion and obstinacy, who interpreted it in light of their own practice of making meaningless pronouncements.[2] Therefore, I have prefaced this book with an introduction which makes clear that what I have claimed is indeed very possible; and so I begin, seeking success from God.

[The *Istiʿādha*][3]

Our saying 'I seek refuge in God from the rejected Satan' (*aʿūdhu bi'Llāhi min al-shayṭān al-rajīm*) undoubtedly entails seeking divine refuge from all forbidden things, which in turn divide into the categories of beliefs and external actions.

In regards to BELIEFS, the famous *ḥadīth* from the Prophet (may God bless him and grant him peace) says: 'My nation will divide into seventy-three sects, all of them in the Fire except one.'[4] This implies that the remaining seventy-two suffer from corrupted beliefs and stances, which would not be confined to a single creedal issue. Rather, it may occur in numerous branches such as the essence of God, His Attributes, judgments, actions and Names; in matters of free will and preordainment; in attribution of justice and oppression (*taʿdīl wa-tajwīr*);[5] in reward, resurrection, promises and threats, names, rulings and leadership (*imāma*). If we were to

1 This refers to the categories of knowledge which can be derived from the *sūra*, as well as branches of study required in order to understand it comprehensively.

2 Cf. Jaffer, *Rāzī*, p. 33, in which this is read, not as a point about the psychology of projection, but instead as a criticism of earlier exegetes. Jaffer goes on to build upon this reading (which ignores the import of the phrase *alifūhu min anfusihim*) his argument for the novelty of Rāzī's approach. As for the French translation of this volume, it takes the key phrase to refer to the critics' own writings ('qu'ils ont écrit eux-mêmes'), perhaps mistaking *alifū* for *allafū*; see Cissé, *Le Commentaire de Faḫr d-Dīn r-Rāzī*, p. 48. Both have overlooked the fact that if the critics assumed that Rāzī was referring to the 'words whose kernels and foundations were empty of verification' (per Jaffer) in existing works of exegesis, then they would have little cause to object to his claim to gather 10,000 such items.

3 This is the verbal noun meaning 'the seeking of refuge', and is often used here to refer to the specific formula which is explained throughout Book I.

4 The first clause from this portion of the *ḥadīth* is well attested, the latter less so. This wording is found in Ṭabarānī (*Awsaṭ*) and elsewhere, and accepted by numerous scholars.

5 This is a reference to Muʿtazilī categories discussed extensively in *kalām* theology—see Ayman Shihadeh, *The Teleological Ethics of Fakhr al-Dīn al-Rāzī*, Leiden: Brill, 2006, p. 45. NB: the printed editions have *tajwīz*.

multiply the seventy-two misguided sects by this plethora of issues, the result would be a tremendous number.

If that is so for the misguidance among sects within this nation, then it is well known that the misguided sects outside this nation number close to 700. If their various types of error in conceiving questions of Divinity, essences and Attributes should be added to the preceding number, the sum would be multitudinous indeed.

Without doubt, saying 'I seek refuge in God' encompasses all these types of misguidance, and one cannot seek refuge in something unless one knows that thing and also recognises its falsity and unseemliness. It is therefore apparent that 'I seek refuge in God' comprises thousands of definite and genuine areas of enquiry.

As for wrong ACTIONS, these consist of every prohibited thing in the Qur'ān; *ḥadīths* which are either mass-transmitted (*mutawātir*) or solitary reports (*āḥād*); the consensus of the Muslims; or based on correct analogy. These certainly number in the thousands, or more, and saying 'I seek refuge in God' refers to all of them.

It follows that 'I seek refuge in God' comprises 10,000 significant areas of enquiry, more or less.

[The *Basmala*][1]

This divine statement can be looked at here in two ways:

THE FIRST: it is widely said by the scholars that Almighty God has 1001 pure and holy Names to be found in the Qur'ān and *Sunna*. Seeking out each of these Names is undoubtedly a noble and lofty pursuit. Moreover, knowledge of the Name does not obtain without prior knowledge of that which is named; and seeking to establish the reality of the named [Essence and Attributes] and their proofs, as well as the false contentions directed towards them—all this comprises many enquiries which number above the thousands.

THE SECOND: the *bā'* in the words *bi'smi 'Llāh* is for attachment (*ilṣāq*)[2] and is connected to a verb, i.e. 'In the Name of God *I commence my acts of obedience*.' This meaning is only known in such an abbreviated form once the various types of obedience—true beliefs and pure actions—are realised

1 This term refers to the formula 'In the Name of God' (or its fuller expression), and is 'carved' from the words *bi'smi 'Llāh* by a process called *naḥt*. In addition to the author's own use of the term (along with the word *tasmiya*, 'the naming'), I have sometimes—as here—used this word for brevity.

2 See Chapter Seven below for details on this particle.

with reference to their proofs and contentions to them are responded to, all of which would therefore perhaps exceed 10,000 enquiries.

A SUBTLE POINT: 'I seek refuge in God' indicates the disavowal of improper beliefs and actions, while 'In the Name of God' points to the desired beliefs and actions. As such, the latter does not become known until all correct beliefs and pure actions are recognised, and this [stated] order is in accordance with sound reason and explicit truth.

[Verse 2][1]

All praise is for God—know that praise (*ḥamd*) is only based on a favour (*niʿma*)[2] and therefore depends upon knowledge of that favour. However, the types of divine favours are beyond definition and enumeration, as God has said: 'If you should count the favours of God, you will never enumerate them' (Q.xiv.34).

Let us consider one example. The rational person must ponder upon his own self, which comprises both body and soul (*nafs*). Of these, the lesser aspect in terms of status and benefit is surely the body. Nevertheless, anatomists have discovered around 5,000 types of benefit which God has planned with perfect wisdom in the creation of the human body.[3] Yet whoever comes across these types in the books of anatomy will realise that what has been discovered and recorded is like a drop in the vast ocean compared to what has yet to be disclosed. It is thus apparent that knowing the manifestations of divine wisdom in the creation of human beings consists of 10,000 enquiries or more.

If we should add to this account the manifestations of divine wisdom in creating the Throne (*ʿarsh*) and the Footstool (*kursī*), and the levels of the heavens and their illuminated bodies set in place and in motion, each accorded its proportion and hue, together with the manifestations of divine wisdom in creating elements and their constituent beings in the inanimate world as well as the plant and animal kingdoms, with all their types and situations, then it will be established that this collection comprises one million (*alf alf*) enquiries, or less, or more.

Indeed, He has drawn attention to the fact that most of these things have been created for the benefit of humankind, as in: 'He has subjected

1 This labelling follows the view that the *basmala* is the first verse of the *sūra*: see Book III, Chapter Four, Enquiry 6 for the debate on this point.

2 See Book III, Chapter Five for a discussion of the word *ḥamd* in comparison to *madḥ*.

3 Rāzī was writing this nearly eight centuries ago. Cf. 'ten thousand' in a later passage: Book II, Chapter Eight, Enquiry 3.

to you what is in the heavens and on earth' (Q.XLV.13). Therefore, His saying *All praise is for God* encompasses a million enquiries, give or take.

As for His saying *Lord of the worlds*, this consists of a noun and its annexed genitive (i.e. *rabb* and *al-ʿālamīn*). Knowledge of this annexed construct (*iḍāfa*) depends on knowledge of its constituent parts, i.e. to know that He is Lord of the worlds is impossible without understanding both 'Lord' and 'the worlds'.

Al-ʿālamīn refers to every existent other than Almighty God, comprising three categories: [substances which are either] spatial (*mutaḥayyiz*) or separate[1] (*mufāriq*), and attributes (*ṣifāt*). Spatial things are either simple (*basīṭ*)[2] or composite (*murakkab*). The former is represented by the heavenly spheres (*aflāk*) and bodies (*kawākib*), and the elements (*ummahāt*), while the latter is represented by 'the three generated [kingdoms]' (*al-mawālīd al-thalātha*).[3]

Know that there is no proof of bodies[4] being restricted to these three categories; rather, it is proven that beyond the world[5] there is a void without bounds, and that the Almighty is capable of all possible things. As such, He could create a million worlds external to [our] world, each greater and more expansive than ours, and each containing the same in terms of Throne, Footstool, heavens, earths, sun and moon. The philosophers' proofs for the world being only one are flimsy and built upon faulty premises. Said Abū al-ʿAlāʾ al-Maʿarrī:

> O people, how many celestial spheres belong to God,
> through which the stars run with the sun and the moon!
> Trifling it is for God [to create] our past and our future,
> so we have no idea what lies beyond.

Evidently, seeking out all these types of bodies which we have mentioned would consist of thousands of thousands of enquiries. Indeed, if one were to focus solely on encompassing the wonders of the minerals that emerge from the mountains, such as metals, ores, brimstone, arsenic

1 I.e. immaterial.

2 This refers to bodies that are made of only one substance: sometimes called *basīṭ ʿurfī*.

3 I.e. animal, vegetable and mineral (see below). Compare this paragraph with that on *Lord of the worlds* in Book III, Chapter Five, under Verse 2.

4 Or perhaps what is intended here are *existents*.

5 I.e. the universe. This is an interesting contention in the light of modern cosmological theories which postulate a multiplicity of parallel universes, often termed the 'multi-verse'. See Adi Setia, 'Fakhr Al-Din Al-Razi on Physics and the Nature of the Physical World: A Preliminary Survey', *Islam & Science*, vol. II, no. 2, 2004, pp. 177–178.

compounds and salts, and knowing the various types of plant life, such as flowers, blossoms and fruits, as well as the species of animal life—from cattle to wild animals, and from birds to insects—then one's entire life would have been expended whilst barely scratching the surface. God said: 'If all the trees on earth were pens, and the sea were replenished by seven seas behind, the words of God would never be exhausted' (Q.xxxi.27). All of this is entirely subsumed within *Lord of the worlds*.

[Verse 3]

The Compassionate, the Merciful—know that mercy (*raḥma*) means to remove flaws and deliver goodness to those in need. The former aspect cannot be known without knowing the types of harms, the abundance of which is known only to God. To gain an appreciation of a small quantity of these, look at the books of medicine to encounter the diseases which take root in each limb and organ. Then ponder how God has guided the intellects of His creation to know that which is nutritious and medicinal from among minerals, plants and animals, and you will find this thought process to be an ocean without end.

Galen[1] related that when he composed his work on the benefits in the components of the eye, he said: 'I have held back from mentioning to people God's wisdom in making the hollow nerves meet at one place.' In his sleep, he saw an angel descending from heaven, saying: 'O Galen, your God is asking: Why have you held back from My servants in mentioning My wisdom?' Upon this, he became alert and wrote a book on the subject.[2] He further related: 'My spleen became inflamed so I treated it in every way I knew, but to no avail. Then, in the temple, I saw what appeared as an angel descending from heaven and commanding me to bleed between my small and ring fingers.'

Most significant medical discoveries originate at some point in such forms of inspiration. If a person were to come to know of such things, he

1 A Greek physician, surgeon and philosopher in the second century CE. Biographies of scholars from the Islamic era onwards are provided in the Appendix.

2 See Galen, *Peri Chreias Morion*, trans. M. T. May as *Galen on the Usefulness of the Parts of the Body*, 2 vols., Ithaca: Cornell University Press, 1968, pp. 490–491. In it, Galen says: 'I have explained nearly everything pertaining to the eyes with the exception of one point which I had intended to omit lest many of my readers be annoyed with the obscurity of the explanations and the length of the treatment...But afterward I dreamed that I was being censured because I was unjust to the most godlike of the instruments and was behaving impiously toward the Creator in leaving unexplained a great work of his providence for animals, and so I felt impelled to take up again what I had omitted and add it to the end of this book.' Rāzī cites this again (with slightly different wording) in Book II, Chapter Eight, Enquiry 3.

would realise that the mercy of God upon His servants is so multifarious that it cannot be known comprehensively.

[Verse 4]

Know that the human being in this world is like a traveller, with his years being as leagues, his months as miles and each breath a step, as he strives towards the world of the Hereafter in which the everlasting rewards are achieved. So if he should witness, while on the path, these various wonders in the dominion of the heavens and the earth, then let him consider the bliss, joy and delight of the wonders of the Hereafter!

With that in mind, *Master of the Day of Judgment* points towards all matters of the Hereafter, resurrection and gathering. These are of two categories:

1. Those which are purely dealt with by the intellect: for example, to say that it is possible for this world to be obliterated then recreated, and that it is possible for the human to be resurrected. This area of enquiry is dependent on seeking the reality of the soul (*nafs*), its states and characteristics, how it can outlive the body, the causes of its felicity or its misery, and how God is most able to restore it. These complex intellectual enquiries would number close to 500.
2. Those which are known by transmission (*samʿiyyāt*), comprising three types:
   a. What takes place [before][1] the coming of the Day of Judgment, of which there are minor signs as well as the ten major signs which we shall mention and explain.[2]
   b. What takes place upon the establishment of the Day of Judgment, namely the blowing of the trumpet, the death of all creatures, the collapse of the heavens and stars, and the death of every spiritual and corporeal being.
   c. What takes place after the Day of Judgment commences and how the people stand [before God], which includes: how they are brought to stand and what they experience there; the manner in which the angels and Prophets are brought, the judgment takes place, deeds are weighed, one party proceeds to the Garden, and the other to the Fire. Then, what are the characteristics of each party, what they experience once they reach the Garden or the Fire, and the words they utter and actions they perform.

1 The printed editions have *ʿinda* here as in the point following.

2 These are mentioned at scattered junctures. The *ḥadīth* mentioning all ten is cited under Rāzī's comments on Q.vi.158.

It is likely that these intellectual and transmitted enquiries number in the thousands, all of which fall under *Master of the Day of Judgment*.

[Verse 5]

You we worship and from You we seek help—know that worship (*ʿibāda*) means to perform a commanded action in such a way as to glorify the commander. It is therefore not possible to fulfil the implications of *You we worship* unless it is shown with proof that this world has a single, omnipotent, omniscient Deity Who is free of all needs and has obligated His servants with certain things and forbidden them from others, and that it is incumbent on creatures to obey Him and comply.

After establishing the aforementioned, one must detail the categories of duties (*taklīf*) and the types of commands and prohibitions. Everything written in the genre of positive law (*fiqh*) falls under the duties enjoined by God. Then beyond this specific [Muḥammadan] Law (*sharīʿa*), it encompasses the duties which He revealed upon the earlier Prophets in their respective dispensations, as well as the duties He has enjoined upon the heavenly angels ever since they were created and dedicated to devotion and service.

Just as the books of positive law are concerned with duties that are enjoined upon the limbs, the duties upon the heart—which are greater and nobler—are contained in the books of character (*akhlāq*) and practical philosophy (*siyāsāt*) according to the traditions of various religions and nations.

When a person looks at all these enquiries and realises that they are all subsumed in *You we worship*, he will consider the knowledge within this verse to be a tremendous ocean of which the intellects can only appreciate a small portion.

[Verse 6]

Guide us upon the straight path is a request for guidance (*hidāya*), which is attained through two methods: seeking knowledge via evidence and proof; and cleansing and disciplining one's inner self.

The EVIDENTIAL METHODS are in fact without limit, in that every single atom of creation from top to bottom bears testament to His perfect Divinity, might and supremacy. It has thus been said [poetically]: 'In everything there is a sign, pointing to the fact that He is One.'[1]

To explain: bodies in the universe are equal with respect to the fact of

1 This is a line of Abū al-ʿAtāhiya.

corporeality, but they differ in their attributes: colours, places and states. It cannot be that the variations between them are due to corporeality or its concomitants, because in that case everything would be identical; therefore, they must be due to an entity which particularises (*takhṣīṣ*) and plans (*tadbīr*). If this should be another body, then the same problem will apply to it, so it must be that the opposite is true. Then, if this entity operates through emanation (*fayḍ*) and disposition (*ṭabʿ*) as opposed to being living, knowledgeable and powerful, then this too would result in all things being identical. Therefore, it must be living, knowledgeable and powerful. Once you know this, it is apparent that every single particle in the heavens and on earth witnesses truly and testifies audibly to the existence of the powerful, wise and knowledgeable God.

My father, the Shaykh and Imām Ḍiyā' al-Dīn ʿUmar (may God have mercy on him), used to say: 'In every singular essence there are infinite types of evidence for the divine power, wisdom and mercy. This is because each atomic substance could be in an infinite number of alternative positions, and it could also have any of an infinite[1] number of attributes. Each one of these permutations, if it should obtain, would demonstrate the need for the wise and merciful Creator.' All of this goes to show that this field of enquiry is limitless.

As for seeking guidance through CLEANSING AND DISCIPLINE, then that is a sea without a shore. Each traveller on the path to Almighty God has his own method and approach, as God has said: 'To each is a direction to which he turns' (Q.II.148). The intellects are unable to penetrate these secrets, and minds have no way of grasping these sources of illumination. Nonetheless, the expert gnostics have discovered profound enquiries in this field, and subtle secrets which the majority are unlikely to appreciate.

[Verse 7]

The path of those on whom You have bestowed favour, not of those who incur wrath, nor of those who are astray. How majestic are these stations, and how great these levels! Whoever reads the explanations we have mentioned will be able to grasp the principles of all these conditions, for it has been shown above that this *sūra* contains an unlimited quantity of enquiries and secrets. As such, one who says that it contains 10,000 enquiries [is actually understating the case] in order for one's listeners to understand.

1 Some editions have dropped the word *mutanāhiya* here.

Section II: Another Approach to Demonstrate the Possibility of Deriving Many Enquiries from a Few Words[1]

Let us discuss our saying *aʿūdhu bi'Llāh* ('I seek refuge in God'). *Aʿūdhu* is an imperfect verb, which is a species of verbs. The particle *bā'* is for attachment (*ilṣāq*) and is a preposition, which is a species of particles. As for the Name *Allāh*, it is either a proper name or a derived name, according to the two opinions on the matter. Both proper and derived names are species of nouns.

It is known in the field of logic that knowledge of a species (*nawʿ*) is not possible without knowledge of its genus (*jins*), because the genus forms part of the identity of the species, and knowledge of the unit necessarily has priority over knowledge of the construction. As such, it is not possible to attain proper knowledge of 'I seek refuge in God' unless [the genera of] nouns, verbs and particles are known first, which entails identifying their definitions and characteristics.

Then one must divide the noun (*ism*) into proper nouns, derived nouns and generic nouns, defining each with its technical or practical definitions and characteristics. Thereafter, one is to discuss the word *Allāh*: is it a proper name or derived? If the latter, then derived from what? The many opinions advanced should be mentioned here.[2]

One must also investigate the verb (*fiʿl*) in general, followed by its categories, including the imperfect verb, with mention made of its definition, characteristics and types. This is followed by a detailed discussion of *aʿūdhu* in particular.

Likewise, one must investigate the particle (*ḥarf*) in general, and then discuss in particular prepositions with their definitions, characteristics and rulings, followed by the definition and characteristics of the *bā'* of attachment.

This would complete the linguistic enquiries surrounding 'I seek refuge in God,' and it is clear that what I have just alluded to contains very many enquiries.

Then the FOURTH LEVEL[3] [of enquiry] is to say: nouns, verbs and particles are all species of the genus 'word' (*kalima*). One must therefore investigate the nature, definition and characteristics of the word [in gen-

1 This section provides a rough outline of the topics addressed in the coming chapters, i.e. those that comprise the linguistic introduction.

2 See Book II, Chapter Nine.

3 Apparently, the preceding levels concerned nouns, verbs and particles, respectively. In what follows, the enquiries ascend into increasing levels of abstraction.

eral]. Then there are terms similar to *kalima*, namely *kalām*, *qawl*, *lafẓ*, *lugha* and *ʿibāra* which must also be clarified: are they synonymous or distinct, and if the latter, what is the detailed distinction between them?

THE FIFTH LEVEL is to note that all these words undoubtedly consist of sounds and letters, which leads us necessarily to enquire about the nature of sound and the causes of its existence. Certainly the voices of animals emerge due to breath escaping the chest, which leads us to investigate the nature of breath and the wisdom behind humans being made dependent upon breathing. Also, since the sounds follow from the intake or exhalation of air, we need to investigate the condition of the heart and lungs as well as the diaphragm from which the sound first originates, and the rest of the moving parts of the thorax, throat, tongue and lips.

As for the 'letter' (*ḥarf*), one needs to clarify whether it is the same as the sound (*ṣawt*) itself, or rather a condition present within the latter while distinct from it. Also, it is known that the letters are formed through the interruption of the sound at specific articulation points (*makhārij*) of the throat, tongue, teeth and lips. It is therefore necessary to investigate these trapping points as well as the organs which enable animals to produce a wide variety of [sounds], which, in turn, depends upon the study of anatomy.

THE SIXTH LEVEL of enquiry is to say: letters and sounds are perceived by the sense of hearing, whereas colours and lights are perceived by sight, and flavours by taste, and so on. Is it therefore accurate to say that these perceptions fall under a single genus with distinct quiddities (*tamām al-māhiyya*), and that their only commonality is their external concomitants (*lawāzim*), or is this not accurate?

THE SEVENTH LEVEL is to say that sensory qualities (*kayfiyyāt maḥsūsa*) are generally considered a species of qualities (*kayf*), in which case it is necessary to define 'quality' and then establish whether or not its relation to what comes under it is that of a genus to its species.

THE EIGHTH LEVEL is to note that the quality (*kayf*), quantity (*kam*) and relation (*nisba*) are all accidents (*ʿaraḍ*), which leads to investigating the accident and its categories, rulings, concomitants and implications.

THE NINTH LEVEL is that accident and substance (*jawhar*) both fall under the category of the contingent (*mumkin*), which in turn, along with the necessary (*wājib*), falls under that which exists (*mawjūd*). Therefore, one must investigate the consequents of existence and non-existence—is the relationship of existence to both the necessary and possible that of a genus to its species, or is it that of concomitants to their subject (*mawṣūfāt*)?—and so on in this regard.

THE TENTH LEVEL is to say that the categories of that which is known (*maʿlūm*) and mentioned (*madhkūr* and *mukhbar ʿanhu*) certainly encompass both the existent and the non-existent, so how is it possible for anything to be more universal than existence? Some even say that the supposed (*maẓnūn*) is even broader than the known. Moreover, if we should consider the known to be the broadest category, then its opposite would be the unknown. However, as long as the reality of something is not known, one cannot conclude that it is the opposite of anything, so the fact that we have designated the unknown as the opposite of the known necessitates that the unknown is, in fact, known! This entails that the opposite of the known is known, which is absurd.

[In conclusion,] whoever applies these ten levels to every existent being will find infinite doors of enquiry opened to him, of which his intellect cannot encompass even the smallest portion. This demonstrates how multitudinous sciences can be deduced from a small number of words.

Section III: Another Approach to Demonstrate our Claim Regarding the Many Enquiries Derived from this *Sūra*

Know that in this book, if we mention a single enquiry (*mas'ala*) and then provide ten arguments to establish its verity, then each of these arguments is an enquiry in its own right. If I should quote, for example, five counter-arguments, then each one is an enquiry in itself; likewise, if I provide two or three responses to each, then these are all independent enquiries. If I should say, for example, that such-and-such words have come in the Arabic language in sixty forms, and then provide those in detail, then this represents, in reality, sixty enquiries.[1] This is so because an enquiry is nothing more than a point of question and clarification; since that applies to each of these individual points, they are considered enquiries in their own right.

If that subtle point is clear, then I say: if we should consider the enquiries surrounding nouns and verbs; then descend to consider the division of verbs [or actions] into known and mentioned, existent and non-existent, necessary and contingent; and those pertaining to substances and accidents, as well as qualities and how these divide into the perceived and imperceptible; and those concerning sounds and letters,

1 This is not necessarily reflected in the headings provided in the book.

and their production and anatomical mechanisms—then we will find the matter most tremendous and expansive.

However, we shall commence in this book with the study of *kalima*, *kalām*, *qawl*, *lafẓ* and *ʿibāra*, then descend to study nouns, verbs and particles, and then to their respective sub-categories, and finally the types present in *aʿūdhu bi'Llāh*. We appeal to God's all-encompassing grace to grant us success in reaching this noble goal.

BOOK I

Sciences Derived from the *Istiʿādha*

The sciences derived from 'I seek refuge in God from the rejected Satan' are of two categories:

1. Those pertaining to language and grammar.
2. Those pertaining to theology (*uṣūl*) and Islamic law (*furūʿ*).

The first of these categories consists of [seven] chapters.[1]

1 The second part of Book I consists of four chapters, which we have relabelled, for greater clarity, as Chapter Eight onwards.

PART ONE: LITERARY ASPECTS OF THE *ISTIʿĀDHA*[1]

Chapter One
THE WORD (*KALIMA*) AND ITS LIKE

This contains a number of enquiries:

Enquiry 1
[Types of Derivation][2]

The best method to define the meanings of terms is [the science of] derivation (*ishtiqāq*), which is two types: minor (*aṣghar*) and major (*akbar*). The former refers, for example, to deriving the past or future forms from the verbal noun (*maṣdar*), or to deriving the active or passive participles from it.

As for major derivation,[3] it is based on the fact that the letters that make up any word can be re-ordered in various ways. To start with, a word made up simply of two letters can only be ordered in two ways, i.e. *m-n* can become *n-m*.

As for words made up of three letters—for example, *ḥ-m-d*—they

1 See Kees Versteegh, 'The linguistic introduction to Rāzī's *Tafsīr*', in Petr Zemánek, ed., *Studies in Near Eastern Languages and Literatures: Memorial Volume of Karel Petráček*, Prague: Academy of Sciences of the Czech Republic, 1996, pp. 589–603. He notes the influence of the Muʿtazilīs in defining the issues under examination, although our author is frequently disputing their arguments and conclusions. Overall, Versteegh characterises these linguistic chapters as 'a unique treatise by an *uṣūlī* writer who was interested in linguistic matters in a way that differed from his fellow *uṣūliyyūn*' (p. 598). One might have expected this chapter to be called 'Linguistic Aspects', but the author has used the word *adabiyya*, which translates as 'Literary'.

2 I have added such descriptions in parenthesis for ease of navigation. If an enquiry follows its predecessor closely, I may not provide a descriptive title. In some cases, the heading (not in parenthesis) is taken from the text.

3 This type of manipulation of roots and seeking common meanings is described as 'major' derivation because it affects the root more radically. However, it is not included in more precise definitions of *ishtiqāq*. See Muḥammad Ḥasan Jabal, *ʿIlm al-ishtiqāq naẓariyyan wa-taṭbīqan*, Cairo: Maktabat al-Ādāb, 2012, p. 41.

accept six permutations. This is because each of the letters can be made the first of the word, and then the remaining two letters can be ordered in two different ways—as three multiplied by two gives six, any word consisting of three letters has these six permutations.

A word of four letters—such as *ʿ-q-r-b* or *th-ʿ-l-b*—has twenty-four permutations: each of the four letters can be placed at the beginning and the remaining three letters have six permutations, and four multiplied by six gives twenty-four.

A word of five letters—for example, *s-f-r-j-l*—has 120 permutations because each of the five can come first, followed by the twenty-four permutations of the remaining four letters, as previously explained, and five times twenty-four is 120.

The rule in this regard[1] is that if you know the possible permutations of the lower integer and you wish to know them for the integer above, then multiply the higher integer by the number of permutations for the lower integer. And God knows best.

Enquiry 2

Dealing with the minor derivation is straightforward and familiar, whereas it is difficult to deal properly with the major derivation. It seems impossible beyond the three-letter roots which have no more than six permutations. As four- and five-letter roots have so many permutations—of which the majority are in fact unused—this form of derivation can only be applied to them in rare cases.

Indeed, it is unusual to find three-letter roots in which all the possible constructions are meaningful, as in most cases there are both used and unused permutations. Even so, whatever is possible falls within the ultimate extent of these linguistic investigations.

Enquiry 3
Explaining the *Kalima*

The possible permutations of *k-l-m* contain meanings of strength (*quwwa*) and severity (*shidda*); five of these are relevant, while one is unused:

1. *k-l-m*, from which comes: *kalām* (speech), as it strikes and impacts upon the hearing, and impacts the mind in the sense of delivering meaning; *kalm*, meaning 'a wound', which entails severity; and *kilām*, meaning 'a rough and severe piece of land'.
2. *k-m-l*, as the perfect (*kāmil*) is stronger than the deficient.

1 These are known in mathematics as factorials.

3. *l-k-m*, and the meaning of severity in 'the punch' (*lakm*) is obvious.
4. *m-k-l*—a well is *makūl* if it has little water, which would make drawing from it unappealing due to severe difficulty.
5. *m-l-k*—you say that you have *malakta* some dough if you have kneaded it thoroughly until it becomes strong. This applies to a person's ownership (*milk*), which is a type of power; and you say that 'you sold' (*amlakta*) a slave-girl because her master has power over her.[1]

Enquiry 4

The term *kalima* may be used for a single word or a greater quantity of interconnected words. By way of illustration: [the Arabs] applied it to a complete poem; we refer to the Word [i.e. formula] of Testimony [of faith] (*kalimat al-shahāda*) and say that 'the goodly word is a charity'.[2]

Since metaphor (*majāz*) is given preference [as an explanation] over homonymy (*ishtirāk*), we conclude that referring to multiple words as *kalima* is metaphorical, in two ways:[3] first, as the construction is made up of individual words, referring to it as *kalima* is using the name of the part for the whole; and second, lengthy speech which is interconnected attains a unity which makes it similar to a single word in that respect. Similarity (*mushābaha*) is a factor in effective metaphor,[4] so the word *kalima* is used for lengthy speech for that reason.

Enquiry 5

The word *kalima* has appeared in the Qur'ān with two other meanings. Firstly, Jesus (on whom be peace) is referred to as the 'word' of God,[5] either because he came into existence by His saying 'Be!' (*kun*) or because he came into being in a short space of time in the manner of a word. Secondly, the actions of God are described as 'words'; for example, 'Say: If the ocean were ink (wherewith to write out) the words of my Lord, sooner would the ocean be exhausted than would the words of my Lord' (Q.xviii.109). The explanations are the same two provided [for Jesus]. And God knows best.

1 It should be understood that slavery remained commonplace in the author's time and functioned as a convenient example of juristic principles pertaining to transactions, as well as linguistic usages such as this.

2 This is from a hadith in Bukhārī and Muslim—S.I.

3 That is, two types of Arabic *majāz* are in play with this usage.

4 Such would generally be categorised as *tashbīh* in contradistinction to *majāz*.

5 See Q.iv.171.

Enquiry 6
Explaining the Term *Qawl* (Statement)

The six permutations of this root entail movement (*ḥaraka*) and lightness (*khiffa*), as follows:

1. *q-w-l*, from which we have *qawl*, because that is easy upon the tongue.
2. *q-l-w*, from which comes: *qilw* for 'a wild donkey', due to its lightness of movement; *qalawta*, meaning 'to bake', for example, wheat or barley, because when something is baked it becomes dry and light, and is quicker to move; and *qalūlī*, meaning 'the light and frivolous one'.
3. *w-q-l*—*waql* means 'a mountain goat', due to its movement. In addition, one is said to *tawaqqal fī* a mountain if one ascends it.
4. *w-l-q*—the verb *walaqa* means 'to hasten'. The verse [i.e. Q.xxiv.15] was recited with *taliqūnahu*, i.e. 'you take it lightly and hasten [to spread it]'.[1]
5. *l-w-q* appears in the *ḥadīth* 'I do not eat food unless it has been softened (*luwwiqa*) for me,'[2] i.e. the hand has worked it with movements until it is edible. Also *lūqa* is 'butter', because of its lightness and quick movement as it does not have the firmness of cheese or whey.
6. *l-q-w*, from which comes *liqwa*, meaning 'an eagle', due to its lightness and fast flight. In addition there is *laqwa*, meaning 'an affliction on the face which affects its appearance', so it is as though there is a lightness upon it. *Laqwa* also denotes 'a camel which becomes pregnant quickly'.

Enquiry 7
[Explaining the term *Lugha* (Language)]

Ibn Jinnī (may God have mercy upon him) said: '*Lugha* is derived from [the verb] *laghawta*, meaning 'to speak'. Its original form is *lughwa*, similar to *kura* and *qula*—their final radicals are all *w*. This is evidenced by one's saying *karawtu bi'l-kura* and *qalawtu bi'l-qula*. [The verb] is vocalised also as *laghiya/yalghā*, meaning "to talk nonsense". This is found in the verse: "And, if they pass by futility (*laghw*), they pass by it with honourable (avoidance)" (Q.xxv.72).'[3]

1 This non-canonical reading was attributed to ʿĀ'isha, Ibn ʿAbbās and others. See ʿAbd al-Laṭīf al-Khaṭīb, *Muʿjam al-qirā'āt*, 10 vols., Damascus: Dār Saʿd al-Dīn, 2009, vol. vi, p. 238.

2 This was attributed to the Companion ʿUbāda b. al-Ṣāmit in Bayhaqī's *Shuʿab al-īmān*—S.I.

3 The points concerning *kalima* and *qawl* have been summarised from Ibn Jinnī, *al-Khaṣā'iṣ* (ed. Muḥammad ʿAlī al-Najjār, 3 vols., Cairo: al-Maktaba al-ʿIlmiyya, 1952, vol i, pp. 5–17). This quote is found in vol i, p. 33.

Ibn Jinnī had taken the major derivation into account when considering *kalima* and *qawl*, but he did not do so in this case, despite its relevance. [Hereunder are the permutations:]

1. *l-gh-w*, from which comes *lugha*, as well as vain (*laghw*) speech or action.
2. *l-w-gh*, which should be looked up.[1]
3. *gh-l-w*, from which we say that a person exhibits *ghulū* (excessiveness) in something. Also there is *ghalwa* [meaning 'the farthest reach of the arrow'].
4. *gh-w-l*, as has come in the verse: 'Free from headiness (*ghawl*)' (Q.xxxvii.47).
5. *w-gh-l*, from which we say that a person has *awghala* (gone in-depth) into something.
6. *w-l-gh*, from which comes a dog's salivating in a vessel.

It appears that the common factor between all the above is the performing of an action thoroughly and fully.

Enquiry 8
Lafẓ (Utterance)

I believe that the usage of *lafẓ* [literally 'to throw'] for these sounds and letters is a metaphorical one, on the basis that they occur upon the exhaling of breath from the chest. When a person exhales air from his chest, he traps it in specific places and then releases it, so these letters emerge at the end of the time of trapping and the beginning of the time of release.

Lafẓ means 'to throw' (*ramy*), which is present in these sounds and letters in two respects: first, the person throws the breath from within to without, and this throwing is the cause (*sabab*) for the words to be formed, so the term *lafẓ* is used for the words for this reason. Second, since the letters are formed by this throwing of air from within to without, this is similar to throwing the letters themselves out: and similarity (*mushābaha*) is [another] factor in metaphor (*majāz*).

Enquiry 9
ʿIbāra (Expression)

This is made up of *ʿ-b-r*, which in their six permutations have the meaning of passage (*ʿubūr*) and transition (*intiqāl*):

1 It is not clear to me why the explanation is not presented here. Dictionaries such as *Tāj al-ʿarūs* and *Lisān al-ʿArab* explain *lawgh* as 'circulating words in the mouth before uttering them', which would perhaps fit the overall theme suggested by Rāzī below.

1. ʿ-*b*-*r*, from which comes *ʿibāra*, in that a person is not able to pronounce it without the transition from one letter to the next. One can also say that the *ʿibāra* has the effect of transferring meaning from one's own mind to that of the listener. There is also: *ʿabra* (teardrop), which moves from within the eye to without; *ʿibra* (lesson), because a person makes the transition from an actual [occurrence] to hypothetical [scenarios]; *maʿbar* (crossing), because a person uses it for transition between two sides of the sea; and *taʿbīr* (dream interpretation), because it takes one from the visions in one's sleep to the hidden meanings.
2. ʿ-*r*-*b*—the Arabs are so called because of their many transitions and travels in winter and summer. It is said that someone *aʿraba* (expressed) in his speech because before this the word was unknown, but when expressed it transfers to the sphere of knowledge and clarity.
3. *b*-*r*-ʿ—someone is said to have *baraʿa* in something if he has perfected it and reached a high state.
4. *b*-ʿ-*r*, from which comes *baʿr* (dung), because it makes the transition from within to without.
5. *r*-ʿ-*b*—fear is called *ruʿb* because it represents a person's transition from one state to another.
6. *r*-*b*-ʿ—the *rabʿ* (spring dwelling) is so called because people transfer to and from it.

Enquiry 10
[The Difference between *Kalima* and *Kalām*]

The majority of grammarians said that the *kalima* does not mean the same as *kalām*, as the former refers to a single word, whereas the latter refers to a meaningful sentence. The majority of theologians (*uṣūliyyūn*)[1] stated that there is no difference between them, as each can refer to a single word or a construction. Ibn Jinnī supported the view of the grammarians and disputed that of the theologians (*mutakallimūn*); however, I have not found him to have any strong evidence concerning the distinction, other than a quote via Sībawayh implying that *kalām* is specific to the meaningful sentence, along with some other claims which are extremely weak.[2]

1 *Uṣūliyyūn* is used also for scholars of jurisprudence (*uṣūl al-fiqh*), which includes such linguistic inquiries. However, the subsequent mention of the *mutakallimūn* made me opt for 'theologians'. The majority approach in *uṣūl al-fiqh* is known as 'the method of the theologians' (*ṭarīqat al-mutakallimīn*), indicating the overlap between these fields.

2 See Ibn Jinnī, *al-Khaṣaʾiṣ*, vol. 1, pp. 16–17 and 25–32.

The theologians argued their case in the following ways:

a. Rational people agree that *kalām* (speech) is the opposite of muteness and silence; therefore, inasmuch as even pronouncing a single word negates muteness and silence, it constitutes *kalām*.
b. The word is derived from *kalm*, meaning 'to wound and impact'. Since anyone who hears a single word will understand its meaning and be impacted by it, it must be considered *kalām*.
c. It is correct to say that someone 'spoke (*takallama*) a single word', as it is correct to say that he did not speak except with this single word. All this indicates that the single word is indeed *kalām*, as otherwise it would not be correct to say these things.
d. It is correct to say that someone 'spoke with an incomplete *kalām*', which indicates that complete meaning is not a condition of something being *kalām*.

Enquiry II
[Legal Implications]

The aforementioned divergence of opinions leads to a juristic issue which is the first in the Book of Oaths in *al-Jāmiʿ al-kabīr* by Muḥammad b. al-Ḥasan (may God have mercy upon him). If a man says to his wife prior to consummation 'If I speak to you (*in kallamtuki*) then you are divorced' three times, then the question is raised: when he says this the second time, she is divorced one time; but does this second time count as an effective divorce?

Abū Ḥanīfa and his two companions said that it is effected, whereas Zufar said it does not. Zufar's argument is that when the man says, the second time, 'If I speak to you', that much is sufficient to fulfil the condition. This is because *kalām* is anything that delivers a meaning, whether that meaning is complete or not. With the fulfillment of the protasis, its apodosis takes effect, and this occurs upon his saying 'If I speak to you' [the second time]. As such, the remainder of his statement—'then you are divorced'—occurs when he no longer possesses a complete marital right, so it is unconnected to that and must not take effect.

As for Abū Ḥanīfa, his argument is that the protasis—'If I speak to you'—is incomplete, whereas *kalām* refers to a complete sentence. As such, divorce is not effected until he has completed his sentence: 'If I speak to you then you are divorced.'

The core of the dispute is that if we say that the term *kalām* can refer to a single word, then Zufar is correct, whereas if we say that it is specific to a whole sentence, then Abū Ḥanīfa is correct. Zufar's opinion is supported by the fact that if the man said on the second occasion 'If I speak to you' and stopped there without adding 'then you are divorced', then she would indeed be divorced; if this portion were not *kalām* then that would not be so.

Abū Ḥanīfa's view is supported by the fact that if the man said 'Whenever (*kullamā*) I speak to you, you are divorced' and then repeated it a second time, then—because the word *kullamā* entails repetition, and on the assumption that a single word counts as *kalām*—it would be necessary to say that she is divorced three times [i.e. the maximum] upon his saying the second 'Whenever I speak to you', even without adding 'you are divorced'. This is because this portion alone contains numerous words, each of which would effect divorce. It is possible that Zufar would assent to this.

Enquiry 12

The above dispute should only pertain to the wording 'If I speak to you then you are divorced,' whereas if he should say 'If I speak to you *with a single word* then you are divorced,' or 'If I pronounce (*naṭaqtu*) [anything],' or 'If I pronounce a word (*lafẓa*)' or 'If I say a word (*qawl*)'—then the correct opinion would be that of Zufar in every case. And God knows best.

Enquiry 13
[The Limits of *Kalām*]

Do the terms *kalima* and *kalām* include incoherent (*muhmal*) utterances? Some said that they do, because one may say that there is meaningful and meaningless speech, and also one may say that someone 'spoke incomprehensibly'. This is because even the incoherent impacts the hearing so the meaning of impact inherent to *kalām* is present.

On the other hand, some said that *kalima* and *kalām* only refer to the meaningful, because otherwise one would have to conclude that birdsong comprises words and speech.

Enquiry 14

If some sounds were constructed such that they convey meaning, but this construction is natural rather than conventional, would these sounds be referred to as words? For example, a person might say *akh* upon relaxing or feeling pain, and might cough like this: *aḥ*, *aḥ*.[1] These are constructed

1 The latter sounds are descriptive of coughing. The word *akh* also has the meaning of 'brother', but that does not seem to be the point here.

sounds and letters which indicate specific meanings, but this indication is by nature, not convention. Are they then considered words? Another example is the sound of the *qaṭā* (sand grouse) which seems to say *qaṭā*, and the *laqlaq* (stork) which seems to say *laq laq*—are such sounds considered words?

There are two opinions, but I have not found convincing proofs on either side. The relevance of the question would be if someone said 'If I hear a word, then my servant is free' —is he obliged to fulfil or expiate if he hears these types of utterance, or not?

Enquiry 15
[*Kalām* and *Qawl*]

Ibn Jinnī stated[1] that the term *qawl* applies in a literal sense to both complete sentences and single words, whereas *kalām* is specific to complete sentences and *kalima* to single words.

This distinction implies that, if we explain that the letters of *qawl* indicate lightness and ease, this must apply to the single word. The letters of *kalām* indicate impact, which only obtains with the complete sentence—but this is contradicted by the word *kalima*.

Something which may be adduced as evidence [for the above] is the poetic line: 'I said to her: "Stop!" (*qifī*), and she said "Qāf,"' in which her pronouncing only the letter *qāf* was described as a *qawl*.

Enquiry 16

He also said[2] that the term *qawl* may be used metaphorically with respect to beliefs and opinions; for example, 'So-and-so says (*yaqūlu*) what Abū Ḥanīfa says, or adopts the statement (*qawl*) of Mālik,' meaning that he believes what they used to opine and state. Do you not see that if you were to ask a man whether Almighty God may be seen, and he replied that seeing Him is not possible, you would say 'That is the *qawl* of the Muᶜtazilīs'? You could not say 'That is the *kalām* of the Muᶜtazilīs' without sounding awkward.

It is said that this metaphor is appropriate because beliefs are only understood via something else; since the two are similar in this respect, this is the explicative factor for the metaphor.[3]

1 Ibn Jinnī, *al-Khaṣa'iṣ*, vol. 1, p. 17.

2 Ibid., pp. 17–18.

3 Since *kalām* denotes complete sentences but a *qawl* may be a fragment, the point here is that a *qawl* may depend upon additional words to complete it and become intelligible. Likewise, beliefs depend upon verbal expression in order to be known. See Ibn Sīdah al-Mursī, *al-Muḥkam wa'l-muḥīṭ al-aᶜẓam*, ed. ᶜAbd al-Ḥamīd Hindāwī, Beirut: Dār al-Kutub al-ᶜIlmiyya, 2000, vol. VI, p. 561.

Enquiry 17

The verb *qāla* (to say) may be used in the absence of [literal] speech; for example, in the poem of Abū al-Najm: 'The birds said to him (*qālat lahu*): "Proceed..."' Another [poet] said: 'The two eyes said (*qālat*) to him: "We hear and obey"...' Furthermore, [there is the poetic verse]: 'The basin filled up and said (*qāla*): "That is enough..."'

There is a saying: 'The wall said to the stake: "Why are you splitting me?" [The stake] replied: "Ask the one who is hammering me, for the one behind me has not allowed me to stay behind."' Along these lines are the verses: 'When We will anything (to exist), We but say "Be!" and it is' (Q.xvi.40); and 'He said to [the sky] and to the earth: "Come together, willingly or unwillingly." They said: "We do come (together), in willing obedience"' (Q.xli.11).

Enquiry 18

Those who deny [the existence of] internal speech (*kalām al-nafs*) agreed that *kalām* and *qawl* refer to these [external] words. As for those who affirm internal speech, they agree that this internal (*nafsānī*) meaning can be described as *kalām* and *qawl*, citing in support of this view from the Qur'ān, narration and poetry:

THE QUR'ĀN: 'God bears witness that the hypocrites are indeed liars' (Q.lxiii.1)—it is obvious that their actual words were not untruthful, as they declared that Muḥammad is the Messenger of God and were truthful in that respect. Thus it must be said that they were lying in some speech other than that which was uttered, and that can only be the internal speech.

One might argue, on the contrary, that they were lying in their external speech, because rather than declaring that Muḥammad is the Messenger of God, they were merely stating that they bear witness to this: 'We bear witness that you are indeed the Messenger of God' (Q.lxiii.1). Bearing witness depends upon knowledge, which they lacked, so it follows that they were lying in what they expressed with their tongues.[1]

NARRATION (*ATHAR*): it is reported that ʿUmar said on the day of al-Saqīfa:[2] 'I had prepared some speech within myself, then Abū Bakr preceded me to it.'

POETRY: al-Akhṭal said: 'Speech (*kalām*) [resides] in the heart (*fu'ād*), while the tongue has only been made a guide to [what is in] the heart.'

1 This is an example of the author choosing not to reply to an objection.

2 This refers to the gathering in a building known as Saqīfat Banī Sāʿida, in which the decision was made to appoint Abū Bakr as caliph.

Those who dispute that what resides within should be called *kalām* point out that as long as someone does not utter anything or pronounce any letters, it can only be said that he has not spoken. Moreover, issues of fulfilment and expiation [of oaths] are connected with such [external] words. Some of our companions[1] have said that the terms *qawl* and *kalām* are shared by internal and external speech.

Enquiry 19
[Other Relevant Terms]

These words and expressions can also be referred to as *aḥādīth* [sing. *ḥadīth*], as God said: 'Let them produce a statement (*ḥadīth*) like it' (Q.LII.34). The reason for this nomenclature is that the words are made up of letters in immediate succession, so each one occurs (*yaḥduthu*) right after its companion. It may also be because hearing the words creates (*yuḥdithu*) knowledge and meaning in the hearts. And God knows best.[2]

Enquiry 20

There are many terms in this connection, namely *kalima*, *kalām*, *qawl*, *lafẓ*, *ʿibāra* and *ḥadīth*; we have explained all six of these. The seventh is *nuṭq*, for which it is necessary to investigate its derivation and whether it is synonymous with any of the above or distinct from them. If it is distinct, then what is the difference?[3]

Enquiry 21
Definition of *Kalima*

Zamakhsharī stated in the beginning of *al-Mufaṣṣal*: 'The *kalima* is an utterance (*lafẓa*) which denotes a single meaning by convention.' This definition is unsuitable, because a perfect tense [verb] is a *kalima* even though it does not indicate [only] a single meaning by convention. Rather, this [verb] contains two meanings: an event and a time; the same can be said of verb-nouns (*asmāʾ al-afʿāl*) such as *mah* and *ṣah*.[4] The cause of the error is that he should have attached the adjective 'single' to 'utterance' rather than 'meaning'.[5]

1 This must refer to Ashʿarī and/or Shāfiʿī scholars.

2 The term is also used for a 'report', especially sayings and actions etc. attributed to the Prophet (may God bless him and grant him peace) or the early generations.

3 The author has left this unanswered.

4 These mean 'stop' and 'hush' respectively, and—like ordinary imperatives—refer to the immediate future. It seems the author intended to include all verbs (perfect, imperfect and imperative) in this argument.

5 See Enquiry 24 below.

Enquiry 22
[Used and Unused Words]

A word (*lafẓ*) may be unused (*muhmal*)—and this [phenomenon] is known—or it may be used (*mustaʿmal*), which falls into three categories:

a. No portion of it conveys any meaning [by itself]—this is known as the 'singular' (*mufrad*), such as *faras* (horse) and *jamal* (camel).
b. No portion of it conveys any meaning while it is a portion, but in other situations, the portion(s) do convey meaning. An example is *ʿAbd Allāh* ('servant of God'): when considered as a personal name, no individual portion of it conveys a separate meaning; but when analysed as two portions of a possessive construct, each refers to another meaning. This category is known as the 'construct' (*murakkab*).
c. Each of its two portions conveys a separate meaning in every situation; for example, *al-ʿālamu ḥādithun* ('the world is created'), *al-samā'u kuratun* ('the sky is a sphere') and *Zaydun munṭaliqun* ('Zayd is departing'). This is known as the 'compound' (*mu'allaf*).

Enquiry 23

Meaningful expressions (*al-masmūʿ al-mufīd*) fall into four [conceptual] categories:

a. The words are compound and so is the meaning; for example, *al-insānu ḥayawānun* ('man is an animate being') and *ghulāmu Zaydin* ('Zayd's servant').
b. The word is singular and so is the meaning; for example, *waḥda* (unity), *nuqṭa* (point) and indeed *Allāh* (glorified is He).
c. The word is singular but the meaning is compound; for example, *insān* (human), which is a singular word denoting a quiddity consisting of many things.
d. The word is compound but the meaning is singular—but this is impossible.

Enquiry 24
[Better Definition of *Kalima*]

The *kalima* is a single word (*lafẓa*) which denotes a meaning by convention. This definition comprises four clauses: it is an utterance (*lafẓ*) and it is single (*mufrad*)—these are both familiar to you; it has a denotation, and this distinguishes it from the unused (*muhmal*); and this denotation is by convention (*iṣṭilāḥ*). I shall present the proof that the meanings of words are by coinage (*waḍʿ*) and are not inherent.[1]

1 See Enquiries 28–32 below.

Enquiry 25

The *kalima* has also been defined as 'a single sound (*ṣawt*) denoting a meaning by convention'; but Abū ʿAlī b. Sīnā said in *al-Awsaṭ*: 'This is unacceptable because sound is a material (*mādda*) whereas the word (*lafẓ*) is a genus, and citing the genus is preferable to the material.' He has a nuanced explanation of the difference between *material* and *genus*, which is, nevertheless, weak, as I explain in my philosophical works.

In my opinion, the reason [this definition] is unacceptable is that sounds include those of animals and others; the sounds of humans include those issuing from the throat along with other sounds; and sounds from the throat include those produced in specific ways such as these letters, and others such as those associated with pain, relief, coughing and so on. Therefore, *ṣawt* is a distant genus while *lafẓ* is proximate, and the latter has precedence over the former.

Enquiry 26

The Muʿtazilīs said that the condition for a word to be meaningful is that it be composed of two or more letters. This was countered by the likes of *qi* and *ʿi*.[1] The response to this is that there are additional letters hypothetically, i.e. these are originally *qī* and *ʿī* [with final *yāʾ*], as evidenced by the fact that their duals are *qiyā* and *ʿiyā*. The reply, in turn, is that the hypothetical does not change the fact that the words do consist of a single letter.

Further counters [to the original contention of the Muʿtazilīs] are the *lām* of the definite article [*al-*], the *nūn* of nunation (*tanwīn*) and [genitive pronouns] of annexation (*iḍāfa*), as all of these are meaningful letters. The letter is a species (*nawʿ*) under the genus of the word, and wherever the species is present, so is the genus; these letters are words despite not being constructed.

Enquiry 27

It is better to say: anything which is pronounced (*manṭūq bihi*)[2] and conveys [a meaning] by convention is a word. This [definition] encompasses the singular and the construct, while 'pronounced' excludes lines and gestures.

1 These are imperatives meaning 'save' and 'understand', from the verb roots *w-q-y* and *w-ʿ-y* respectively: the initial and final weak letters are removed in the imperative, leaving only the middle radical with its vowel. When pronounced in isolation, they would be provided a final /h/, i.e. *qih* and *ʿih*.

2 This must include the 'potentially pronounced', i.e. the written word, whereas 'lines' could include drawings.

Enquiry 28
[Meanings Are Not Inherent]

Contrary to ʿAbbād [b. Sulaymān], we say that the denotation of words is not inherent and real, as evidenced by the fact that denotations change with time and place: this is not the case with inherent things.

[OBJECTION:] ʿAbbād's argument is that, if there were no [inherent] relationships between particular words and particular meanings, then each relationship would involve the preponderance of one possibility without any preponderator, which is impossible.

RESPONSE: we counter with the fact that the world has been created at a particular time, rather than prior or subsequent [to that point], because otherwise it would not be preponderant.[1] [His opinion] is also problematic when one considers that each human being has his own particular name.

Enquiry 29
[Onomatopoeia]

Sometimes words are appropriate to their meanings; for example, naming the *qaṭā* and the *laqlaq*[2] such that the name of each resembles its sound.

The [Arabs] also used the word *khaḍm* for eating moist things such as watermelon and cucumber, and *qaḍm* for dry things; for example, 'The beast ate (*qaḍamat*) its barley.' This is because the letter *khā'* resembles the sound of eating something moist, while *qāf* resembles the sound of eating something dry. There are many examples of this kind cited by Ibn Jinnī in *al-Khaṣā'iṣ*.

Enquiry 30

We cannot be certain that the denotations of words are of divine designation (*tawqīf*). However, some have asserted this, citing reason and texts as proof:

FROM REASON: coining a word for a specific meaning is only possible through a statement (*qawl*), and if that statement depends on another coinage from the people, this entails that every coinage is preceded by another coinage *ad infinitum*, and this is impossible. Therefore it is necessary to end [the causal chain] at something established by God's decision.

TEXTUAL PROOF: 'He taught Adam the names of all things' (Q.II.31).

1 This response is unclear to me. The idea may be that people of various linguistic communities decide on the relationships between words and meanings, just as the Almighty decided the point at which the world should be originated.

2 See Enquiry 14.

RESPONSE TO THE FORMER: why should it not be possible that coinages are established by gestures?

RESPONSE TO THE LATTER: can the intended meaning of 'teaching' here not be inspiration (*ilhām*)?[1] Additionally, these languages may have belonged to peoples (*aqwām*) preceding Adam (on whom be peace), then God taught them to Adam.[2]

Enquiry 31

It is [also] impossible to be certain that words were coined by convention (*iṣṭilāḥ*), contra the Muʿtazilīs, who argued [that divine designation is impossible] on the basis that necessary knowledge of a description entails necessary knowledge of the described. As such, if God created the knowledge in the heart of a rational person to the effect that He has coined this word for that meaning, then God would Himself be known necessarily, and this makes responsibility (*taklīf*) meaningless.

RESPONSE: why can it not be that God creates necessary knowledge in the heart to the effect that someone has coined this word for that meaning, without specifying that the coiner is God Himself? This resolves the contention.

Enquiry 32

Due to the fact that the [preceding] evidences are all weak, we consider it possible for all languages to be divinely inspired, or all conventional, or for some to fall into either category.[3]

Enquiry 33
[More on Denotation]

[PROBLEM:] the single word does not denote its referent in and of itself, because it does not denote anything without it being known that it was coined for that meaning. However, this knowledge of the word being coined for that meaning obtains via the specific relationship between the word and the meaning, and knowledge of a relationship between two things must be preceded by [knowledge of] each of the two things. As such, if knowledge of the meaning is derived from that word, this leads to circularity, which is absurd.

1 I.e. inspiring man to coin names rather than direct designation.

2 Some traditions suggest the existence of earth-dwelling jinns before humans arrived.

3 See an extended discussion in Fakhr al-Dīn al-Rāzī, *al-Maḥṣūl fī ʿilm uṣūl al-fiqh*, ed. Ṭāhā al-ʿAlwānī, 6 vols., Beirut: Mu'assasat al-Risāla, 1992, vol 1, pp. 181–192.

RESPONSE: it is possible that when the juxtaposition of the specific word and specific meaning is established in the mind's eye, then the mind goes from perceiving the word to [conceiving] the meaning. This resolves the circularity.

Enquiry 34[1]

The aforementioned problem concerns the single word but not constructed [speech], because denotation in the former is conventional, while in the latter it is rational. Necessarily, when the mind hears these words, it takes into account their formation and, on that rational basis, attains knowledge of the constructed [meaning]. The difference is clear.

Enquiry 35

The denotations of words pertain to [meanings] in the mind, not [external] specifics. This is why it is said that words denote meanings, which are what the [speaker] means, and this is a matter of the mind. The proof of this is from two angles:

a. If we were to see a body from a distance and believe it were a rock, we would call it 'rock'. If we drew closer, observed its movement and thought it to be a bird, we would say 'bird'. If then we drew even closer and realised that it is a person, we would say 'person'. These different names pertaining to different conceptions in the mind demonstrate that the referent is a mental image, not the external reality.
b. If words denoted external existents [directly], it would follow if one person said 'The world is eternal' and another said 'The world is created' that the world is both eternal and created, which is impossible. However, if we say that the words denote mental meanings, then each of these statements only denotes what that speaker believes, and there is no contradiction.

Enquiry 36
[The Limits of Words]

It is impossible for every reality to be described by a word, because realities are endless, and endless things cannot be completely comprehended. Anything which is not comprehended cannot have a word coined for it.

Enquiry 37

A meaning which has a greater need of being expressed is more likely to

1 Versteegh says this and the following enquiry provide a retort to the Muʿtazilīs. See Versteegh, 'The linguistic introduction to Rāzī's *Tafsīr*', p. 598.

have a word coined for it, such as the forms for command, prohibition, general and specific. The proof of this is that [such things] are in great need of being expressed, so the motivation to coin a word is complete, and there is no impediment to that. When the motivation is strong and there is no impediment, the action follows necessarily.

Enquiry 38

Meanings which are obscure to the majority of people cannot be described by a well-known word. For example, 'movement' (*ḥaraka*) is a word for the transfer of a body from one side to another, which is known by everyone. On the other hand, the theory advanced by some theologians (*mutakallimūn*)[1] concerning the abstract reality (*maʿnā*) which gives rise to that transfer is an obscure concept only conceivable by the elite. As such, it must be said that 'movement' is the name of the transfer itself—not that which gives rise to it. Likewise, 'knowledge' (*ʿilm*) must refer to being knowledgeable in itself (*ʿālimiyya*), and 'power' (*qudra*) to being powerful (*qādiriyya*), rather than to the abstract realities which give rise to one being knowledgeable and powerful.

Enquiry 39[2]

'Meaning' is the name for the mental conception, not external existents, because 'meaning' is an expression for what the [speaker] means and intends. This applies directly (*bi'l-dhāt*) to the mental conceptions, and indirectly (*bi'l-ʿaraḍ*) to the external objects. Thus if it is said that a speaker 'intended this meaning by that utterance', then this means that he intended by uttering that word to make known that conceived thing.

Enquiry 40

It could be said of some meanings that it is impossible to express them in words. One example is the difference which we necessarily perceive between the sweetness present in plants and that present in sugar (*ṭabarzadh*), yet which cannot possibly be distinguished in words. Another is the internal states which some people may experience but cannot put into words or define.

1 When applied to *ʿilm and qudra*, the reference to inherent Divine Attributes is an Ashʿarī strategy in contrast to the Muʿtazila; see Enquiry 43 below. It appears that Rāzī did not adopt this for 'movement' in objects. The main point here concerns the use of labels for clear meanings; I assume that he means that the terms *ʿilm* and *qudra* should not be *reserved* for the abstract concepts.

2 This is similar to Enquiry 35 above.

Regarding the FIRST TYPE, the reason behind [the difficulty] is that the distinguishing factor between the sweetness of plants and that of sugar did not have a word coined for it in the language. Thus it is necessary to describe each in this relational way, i.e. 'the sweetness of plants' and 'the sweetness of sugar'. Insofar as no word was coined for the distinction, describing it with a word is not possible. If they had coined a word for it, it would have been possible.

As for the SECOND TYPE, namely a person experiencing a particular feeling which others have not, so it is impossible for him to define it in words: this is because the listener, if he does not know the referent in the first place, cannot comprehend that a certain word has been allocated to it. As long as people have not conceived of those meanings, they are unable to conceive that those words correspond to them, let alone to define them. On the other hand, if we suppose that a community conceived of these meanings and coined words for them, then it would be possible to define the experiences verbally. This is how the claim that many meanings are 'ineffable' should be understood.

Enquiry 41
Wisdom Behind Words Denoting Meaning

Since the human being was created such that he cannot meet all his needs by himself, he has needed to express what is in himself in order to seek the help of others. This expression requires a method, of which there are many, such as writing, gestures, hand clapping and other bodily movements; however, the easiest and best is to express what is in one's heart and mind using words, for the following reasons:

a. The emergence of breath creates sounds, and the interruption of these sounds produces the various letters, all of which occurs with no effort or difficulty, unlike writing, gestures etc.
b. These sounds disappear almost as soon as they are produced, so they exist when they are needed and cease when the need is over.
c. The various interruptions of sound in the articulation points produces numerous letters, which—based on their plentiful arrangements—give rise to an almost infinite quantity of words. If we then gave a word to each meaning, the distribution would occur without any confusion, unlike the case with gestures and clapping.

These three reasons have led sound minds to conclude that words are the best method of expressing what is in the hearts.

Enquiry 42
[Production of Words on the Scale of Purposes]

The perfection of a human being is in knowing truth for its own sake, and [knowing] good in order to act upon it. The essence of the self (*nafs*) upon creation is devoid of these two perfections, which it can only seek by means of the body. As such, the creation of the body is for this purpose.

The interests of the body cannot be achieved without the heart being a wellspring of innate heat; but the intensity of this heat requires that there be a way for it to cool so that it remains moderate. Therefore, the wise and merciful Creator designed for the heart an ability to expand and thus draw cool air to itself from outside the body; when this air remains in the heart for a moment, it becomes extremely heated so the heart must expel it once more. This is its contraction: it squeezes the air out so it exits the body. This is the wisdom behind animals being made to breathe.[1]

Thus the primary purpose is for the essential self to attain perfection by knowledge and action, from which followed the creation of the body on the second level, then the creation of the heart as a wellspring of innate heat on the third level, then the ability of the heart to expand and draw in goodly air from outside to cool off on the fourth level, and then its ability to contract and expel the scorching air on the fifth level. The passing of this air upon being expelled by the contracting heart to [the centres of] the voice falls on the sixth level [of purpose]; and then the wise and merciful Planner made this—on the seventh level— a means for sound to be produced, and created trapping points for articulation in the throat and on the tongue, teeth and lips. As a result, these various letters are generated; and from them, unlimited words. Then, into this pronunciation and speech were placed lofty wisdoms and amazing secrets of which the former and later peoples' intellects could not encompass even a drop from its ocean or a ray from its brilliance. So glory to the One Who creates and plans in perfect wisdom and ability without limit.

Enquiry 43
[External vs. Internal Speech]

It is evident from what we have said that speech upon the tongue is nothing but a convention between people to make these measured sounds and constructed letters stand for [meanings] within the self. If, hypothetically, they had agreed upon some other ways to express these internal

1 Evidently, the lungs have been left out of this anatomical account.

[meanings], those things would also be [considered] speech. It follows that [external] speech is not a true attribute along the lines of knowledge, ability and will; rather, it is a created and conventional matter.

To be precise: speech (*kalām*) is a specific action performed by a living and capable being in order to inform others of what he wills and believes within himself. Therefore, when a person is described as 'speaking' (*mutakallim*) with these letters it simply means that he is performing this action for that specific purpose; whereas speech as an attribute inherent in the self is a true attribute like knowledge, ability and volition.

Enquiry 44

Having established that words are guides to what is within the heart, and that their referents are beliefs, things willed and their like, [we say:] the Muʿtazilīs said that the [imperative] form *ifʿal* corresponds to an action willed, while the declarative (*khabar*) is to express that the speaker believes that such-and-such matter is as stated. Our [Ashʿarī] companions stated that an internal demand (*ṭalab nafsānī*) is distinct from volition (*irāda*), and that a mental proposition (*ḥukm dhihnī*) is distinct from belief (*iʿtiqād*):

1. The proof that an internal demand is distinct from volition is that the Almighty has ordered the disbeliever to believe—this being a matter of consensus—but He has not willed for him to believe. If He had so willed, it would have occurred. This is proven in the following two ways:
   a. If the disbeliever's ability (*qudra*) [i.e. free will] brings about his disbelief [necessarily], then the creator of that ability has willed that disbelief, because one who wills an efficient cause (*ʿilla*) has willed its effect. If his ability allows him to either believe or disbelieve, then one cannot be preponderant over the other except by a preponderator. If this latter emanates from the servant [i.e. the disbeliever], then the original disjunction applies; but if it is from God, then the combination of the ability and the motivation (*dāʿiya*) brings about the disbelief. Since the one who wills an efficient cause has willed its effect, it is shown that the Almighty has willed the disbelief of the disbeliever.
   b. Almighty God knows that the disbeliever will disbelieve; the fact of this [pre-eternal] knowledge is antithetical to the possibility of his belief, and two opposites cannot occur together. One who knows that something is impossible would not then will that thing. It is thus established that God has ordered the disbeliever to

believe, and that He does not will for him to believe; so it follows that the [internal state] indicated by a command from God must be something other than will—and this was the point to be proven.

2. The proof that a mental proposition is distinct from belief and knowledge is that if someone should say that 'the world is pre-eternal' then its referent is the speaker's judgment to that effect. However, someone may say this with his tongue while believing that the world is not pre-eternal, in which case the mental proposition is present, but not the belief. This shows that the two are distinct.

Enquiry 45
[Referents]

The referents of words may be things other than words; for example, 'sky' or 'earth'. The referents may also be words themselves; for example, 'noun', 'verb', 'particle', 'universal', 'particular', 'unclear' and 'clarified'[1]—these are named by words, and the referents, too, are words.

Enquiry 46
[Ways of Knowing Language]

[Conceptually,] the way to know languages is either through reason alone—which is impossible; or through transmission [alone], either mass-transmitted (*mutawātir*) or solitary (*āḥād*)—which is correct.

It may also be through a combination of the two. For example, transmission has established both that exception (*istithnā'*) may be applied to *man* (whoever) and that exception means to exclude that which would otherwise have been included; these two [premises] entail, by way of reason, that [*man*] has been coined to be universal. This is the way employed by the majority in order to establish [rules of] most languages, yet it is weak. This way of arguing would only be sound on the assumption that whoever established those two premises would accept that [the conclusion] follows from them, otherwise contradiction would result. If it were proven that languages were created by God, then one would have to declare Him above such contradiction. On the other hand, if they were made by human beings, that is not so.[2] Since this essential question is a matter of dispute,[3] so is this proof.

1 The latter four are textual categories discussed in jurisprudence (*uṣūl al-fiqh*) and Qur'ānic hermeneutics.

2 That is to say: there would be no difficulty in saying that there is a contradiction between various rules of language, rather than drawing conclusions on the assumption of non-contradiction.

3 See Enquiries 30–32 above.

Enquiry 47

Of the lexical items (*lughāt*)[1] which have been transmitted to us, some have been mass-transmitted while others have been transmitted singularly.

There has been critique of the claim of mass transmission, such that it was said: the most famous of all words is *Allāh*, yet some have said that it is of Hebrew [origin] rather than Arabic; some said it is a proper noun, while others that it is derived; then there are ten opinions regarding its derivation, and these matters have remained unresolved until now.[2] Likewise, there is sharp divergence over the terms *īmān* (belief) and *kufr* (disbelief), as well as forms pertaining to commands, prohibitions, universals and particulars, even though these are the most famous of words. If this is the case for the clearer and stronger [words], then what of the rest?

The truth is that the basic meanings of these words is known by mass transmission, but the differences have occurred over their precise details, which does not negate mass transmission altogether.

Enquiry 48

There are some who acknowledge the mass transmission of some of these words in the present time, but claim that the condition of previous eras is unknown and that the transmission may be have been singular at various points in the past. One cannot appeal to the idea that such [linguistic changes] would have become well known and reached the level of mass transmission, because this claim applies—at best—only to highly noteworthy events, whereas linguistic changes are trifling events.

The truth, to which necessary knowledge attests, is that for words like 'sky', 'earth', 'wall' and 'house', their condition has always been as it is today.

Enquiry 49

Without doubt, the majority of [items of] language have been transmitted through solitary (*āḥād*) reports, and such transmission delivers [no more than] speculation (*ẓann*) once the reliability or otherwise of the narrators is examined and taken into account. Indeed, people have [only] placed these conditions [of reliability] for the transmission of *ḥadīth* and not for language narrators, even though language is, as it were, a basis for *ḥadīth*.

This point is amplified when one considers that some men of letters have accused others of being, variously, unknown or impious. The

1 It appears that what is intended in this discussion are the words themselves, even within a single language (i.e. Arabic). An extended discussion is in Rāzī, *al-Maḥṣūl*, vol. 1, pp. 203–217.

2 Cf. Book II, Chapter Nine.

enmity between the Kūfan and Baṣran [schools] is well known, as is the fact that most *ḥadīth* scholars impugned most men of letters (*udabā'*). This being the case, [it may be argued that] their narrations ought to be considered unreliable, by which route most [items of] language would fall from acceptability [altogether].

However, the truth is that most of these are close to the level of mass transmission, so the [latter] contention does not stand.

Enquiry 50
[The Ten Dependencies]

Words' denotation of their meanings is speculative (*ẓannī*) because it is dependent on transmission of the [lexical items of] language along with grammatical and morphological [forms], even though the best case for these narrators is that they were solitary individuals [even if trustworthy]—and this type of transmission delivers nothing more than speculation.[1]

In addition, the denotations depend on the absence of homonymy (*ishtirāk*), metaphor (*majāz*), transference (*naql*), ellipsis (*ijmāl*) or particularisation (*takhṣīṣ*), as well as the absence of a rational impediment (*muʿāriḍ ʿaqlī*) which would necessitate the word being interpreted metaphorically.[2]

Undoubtedly, to assume all the above is pure speculation, and whatever depends upon speculation is speculation *a fortiori*. And God knows best.

1 The author acknowledges elsewhere that supporting factors (*qarā'in*) can raise the status of such reports to the degree of certainty. See Rāzī, *al-Maḥṣūl*, vol. 1, p. 408 (note 4). The last sentence of the preceding enquiry should also be kept in mind.

2 This latter point—that one cannot accept the textual indication until it has been shown that it is logically coherent—is original to the author. This is linked to his stance (along with other theologians) concerning resolution of conflicts between religious texts and reason, in which reason is taken as the basis on which scripture is recognised and interpreted. See Jaffer, *Rāzī*, pp. 86–94. Ibn Taymiyya composed his extensive work on scripture and rationality in response to this approach of 'Rāzī and his followers'; see Ibn Taymiyya, *Dar' taʿāruḍ al-naql wa'l-ʿaql*, ed. al-Sayyid al-Sayyid & Sayyid Ṣādiq, 6 vols., Cairo: Dār al-Ḥadīth, 2006, vol. 1, p. 4. Furthermore, it seems that he composed an earlier work specifically on the linguistic scepticism expressed here and elsewhere (see ibid., p. 22). See Yūsuf al-Qaraḍāwī, *Kayfa nataʿāmal maʿ al-Qur'ān*, Cairo: Dār al-Shurūq, 2000., pp. 45–46; and ʿAbd al-Qādir al-Ḥusayn, *Maʿāyīr al-qabūl wa'l-radd li-tafsīr al-naṣṣ al-Qur'ānī*, Damascus: Dār al-Ghawthānī, 2008, pp. 682–692.

Chapter Two
SOUNDS, LETTERS AND THEIR RULINGS

Enquiry 1
[Defining Sound]

The *Ra'īs*[1] Abū ʿAlī b. Sīnā defined sound as being 'a phenomenon emerging from waves of air pressure between something which strikes and something which is struck'.

I say: the quiddity of sound is perceived by the sense of hearing, and there is nothing which is more apparent than perceived things so as to be defined with reference to it. Therefore, the preceding words are, at best, a description of the cause of sound's production rather than a definition of its quiddity.

Enquiry 2

The theologian [Abū Isḥāq] al-Naẓẓām used to claim that sound is a body (*jism*). However, this has been refuted in numerous ways, among them: bodies share in corporeality (*jismiyya*), but not in sound; bodies are seen and felt, unlike sound; and bodies persist, unlike sound.

I say: al-Naẓẓām was an erudite [scholar] and it is unlikely that he would have believed that sound is, in itself, a body. [It may simply be that] when he said that sound is caused by waves in the air, the ignorant interpreted him as saying that the sound is the air itself.

Enquiry 3

It has been said that sound is 'the clashing of hard bodies', but this is false because clashing (*iṣṭikāk*) is a type of touching which would be visible, while sound is not. It was also said that sound is the [moment of] striking or separation itself; or that it is oscillating movement. All of these are false because the states described are visible, whereas sound is invisible. And God knows best.

1 Literally 'chief', this is a widespread epithet for Ibn Sīnā, or in full: *al-Shaykh al-Ra'īs* ('the Pre-eminent Teacher').

Enquiry 4

It has been said: its immediate cause is the oscillation of air. By this, we do not mean a movement transferring from one specific point to another, but rather a situation similar to waves in [water][1] which develop gradually from a sequence of impacts and rests. The cause of this oscillation is a violent impact (*qarʿ*) or violent separation (*qalʿ*). For elaboration, refer to my books on the rational sciences.

Enquiry 5
[Defining the Letter]

The Pre-eminent Teacher [Ibn Sīnā] said concerning the letter (*ḥarf*): it is a contingent state of a sound by which it is distinguished in the hearing from other sounds similar to it in terms of heaviness or lightness.

Enquiry 6

Letters are either voiced (*muṣawwat*)[2]—known in grammar as the letters of lengthening (*madd*) or gliding (*līn*) and cannot be pronounced at the beginning[3]—or silent (*ṣāmit*), which are the remaining letters.

The voiced letters are all contingent states of sound. As for the silent [i.e. consonants]:

1. Some cannot be stretched,[4] such as *bā'*, *tā'*, *dāl* and *ṭā'*. These only exist in the moment, i.e. the last moment of containment of breath and the first moment of its release. In relation to sound, these are like the point (*nuqṭa*) in relation to a line, or the moment (*ān*) in relation to time. These letters are not sounds or contingent [states] of sound; rather, they are occurrences at the onset of sounds. Naming them as *ḥurūf* (letters) is appropriate because this word means 'edge' (*ṭaraf*) and letters are the edges of sounds and their origins.
2. Some can be stretched[5] [at least] as is apparent, but these are of two categories. The first are letters which are most likely to be momentary despite sounding continuous; for example, *ḥā'* and *khā'*. It is

1 The printed editions have *hawā'*, but that would mean comparing air to air. A natural comparison is with water (*mā'*).

2 This and the subsequent 'silent' should not be confused with the meanings of these terms with reference to consonants in particular.

3 These are the vowelless *alif*, *wāw* and *yā'* which lengthen their respective vowels (and the latter two in diphthongs) as opposed to their consonantal usages.

4 In other words, they are plosives or stops.

5 These are fricatives and nasal letters.

probable that such letters come in a succession of instances, each momentary in itself, but the hearing does not perceive the distinction between them and therefore assumes it to be one continuous letter. The other category is letters which are, most likely, continuous in reality; for example, *sīn* and *shīn*. These are contingent states of sound which persist as long as [the sound].

Enquiry 7

A letter must be either vowelled (*mutaḥarrik*) or unvowelled (*sākin*). This does not mean the presence of motion (*ḥaraka*) or stillness (*sukūn*) in the letter, as these are properties of bodies. Rather, it is for a specific sound to occur immediately after the consonant.

Enquiry 8

[Short] vowels (*ḥarakāt*) are fractions of the voiced [long vowels], as evidenced by the fact that the latter are open to increase and decrease, and there is nothing on the side of decrease other than these vowels. Likewise, stretching the [short] vowels gives rise to those [long vowels], which also supports what we have said.[1]

Enquiry 9

Consonants are prior to these shortened voiced sounds known as vowels. This is because pronouncing the vowel depends upon pronouncing the consonant; so if the vowels were prior to the consonants, this would result in circularity and absurdity.

Enquiry 10
[Speech Between Eternality and Temporality]

It is self-evident that the speech which is made up of letters and sounds cannot be pre-eternal (*qadīm*), for the following reasons:

1. A word is, by definition, composed of letters in succession. As such, a preceding, completed letter is temporally originated (*muḥdath*) because anything which is affected by non-existence cannot be pre-eternal. Likewise, the following letter which comes into existence after the one preceding is obviously temporal.
2. If the letters making up a word were to occur in a single instant, the word could not be formed. This is because a three-letter word can be ordered in six different ways. If they appeared all at once, there

1 See Chapter Six, Enquiry 10 below.

would be no reason for one permutation to gain precedence over any other; if they came in succession, they would be temporal.

Those who argued for the pre-eternality of letters and sounds appealed to both reason and narration:

REASON: [they said:] each of these letters possesses a quiddity by which it is distinguished from others, and quiddities may not be non-existent or perish; therefore, they are pre-eternal.

NARRATIONS: the speech of God is pre-eternal, and this speech does not consist in anything but these letters, which entails that these letters are pre-eternal. [The proof] that God's speech is pre-eternal is that speech is an attribute of perfection and its absence is an attribute of imperfection. As such, if God's speech were not pre-eternal, one would have to conclude that God was imperfect in pre-eternity and became perfect subsequently—and this is false by the consensus of the Muslims. As for saying that the speech of God does not consist in anything but these letters, that is for the following reasons:

a. God said: 'If one amongst the polytheists asks you for asylum, grant it to him so that he may hear the word of God' (Q.IX.6), and it is known that the thing heard will be nothing except these letters. This shows that the letters are the speech of God.
b. Whoever makes an oath concerning 'hearing God's speech', his fulfillment or expiation will depend upon hearing these letters.
c. It has reached us through successive mass transmission (*tawātur*) that the Prophet (may God bless him and grant him peace) used to say that this Qur'ān, which is recited and heard, is 'the speech of God'. As such, one who rejects this has rejected a matter of successive mass transmission in the religion of Muḥammad (may God bless him and grant him peace), and is therefore charged with unbelief.

RESPONSE TO THE FIRST [CONTENTION]: what you have argued applies equally to all quiddities, so on that basis you would have to believe that everything is pre-eternal.

RESPONSE TO THE SECOND: the arguments you have presented are unconvincing when compared with the self-evident proofs [above], so they are negated.[1]

1 Further responses are in the next enquiry.

Enquiry 11

If we should describe these letters and sounds in succession as the speech of Almighty God, what is meant is that they are words which refer to the [unchanging] Attribute within God's Essence (*dhāt*); as such, the word 'speech' is used for them metaphorically.

Regarding fulfilment or expiation [of oaths],[1] that is because oaths are based upon custom. If we should say 'God's speech is pre-eternal,' we can only mean that pre-eternal Attribute which the words and expressions signify. If we should say 'God's speech is a miracle for Muḥammad (may God bless him and grant him peace),' we mean these letters and sounds which are temporal: since the pre-eternal was in existence before Muḥammad (may God bless him and grant him peace), how could it be a miracle for him? Likewise, if we should say 'God's speech consists of chapters and verses' or 'God's speech is eloquent,' or we embark on exegesis of His speech, then what we intend are these letters and words.

Enquiry 12

The Ḥashwīs[2] claimed that the sounds we hear emanating from a particular person [when reciting the Qur'ān] are themselves the speech of God Almighty. This is false, because we know *a priori* that these letters and sounds which we hear from a particular person are a property of his tongue and voice. If we were to say that they are the very speech of God, then that would entail that a specific attribute is simultaneously present in God's Essence and subsistent in the body of this person—and this is known by necessity to be unacceptable.

Moreover, this is the exact claim of the Christians, to the effect that the hypostasis (*uqnūm*) of the Word dwelt in explicit humanity (*nāsūt ṣarīḥ*)—specifically in the human person of Jesus (on whom be peace)—yet at the same time continued to be an Attribute of Almighty God. The Ḥashwīs said the same in their claim that God's speech subsists on the tongue of a particular person while remaining present in God's Essence. There is no difference between the two positions, except that the Christians made this claim regarding Jesus only, whereas these fools make their contemptible statement concerning every human being from the East to the West!

1 See point (b) in Enquiry 10 above.

2 This is a pejorative term referring to anthropomorphism (*tajsīm*) and naïve literalism in general.

Enquiry 13

The Karrāmīs[1] said: 'speech' describes the ability (*qudra*) to speak, as it is said concerning someone who is able to speak that he is a 'speaker' (*mutakallim*) even if he is not engaged in speech at that moment. Moreover, the opposite of speech is mutism (*kharas*), which means an inability to speak. Therefore, 'speech' must mean the ability to speak.

On this basis, they say that God's speech is pre-eternal in the sense that He is pre-eternally capable of speech. As for the words themselves, they are temporal. This is their stance in detail, which we have already refuted.

Enquiry 14

[OBJECTION:] the Ḥashwīs said to the Ashᶜarīs: if you mean by saying 'the Qur'ān is pre-eternal' that this Qur'ān signifies a pre-eternal Attribute [in God's Essence] connected to all commands and prohibitions, then this entails that every book compiled on this earth is pre-eternal! This is because each book has something signified and understood from it; and since the speech of God is universal in its connection to all things, it would also [contain] statements about the significations of that book. In this respect, there is no difference between the Qur'ān and all other books, [even] those containing profanity and vulgarity: all are pre-eternal upon this interpretation. However, if something else is meant by its pre-eternality, then this must be clarified.

RESPONSE: we do not accept the assumption that God's speech is connected to all statements; therefore, the contention falls. Our denial that His speech is connected to all statements is not due to their falsity (as falsehood is impossible in His speech); after all, when He states that certain people made various false or vulgar statements, that is not falsehood [on His part]. Rather, we avoid this for [another] reason based on declaring God's transcendence over all imperfections: as informing of these profanities and vulgarities would be a type of imperfection which is impossible for Him.

Know that enquiries concerning letters, sounds and their anatomical mechanisms, as well as the controversies over the pre-eternality of the Qur'ān, are thorny and subtle matters. It is, therefore, best to suffice with what we have mentioned. And God knows best where the truth resides.

1 This is another term linked to anthropomorphism, particularly corporealism (*tajsīm*).

Chapter Three
NOUNS, VERBS AND PARTICLES

Enquiry 1
[Types of Word]

The division of words into these three types [nouns, verbs and particles] can be presented in two ways. The first[1] is to say: a word is either such that it can be a subject (*mukhbar ʿanhā*) or predicate (*bihā*): this is a noun. If it can be a predicate but not a subject, it is a verb. If it can be neither, it is a particle.

Since this categorisation assumes that particles and verbs cannot be subjects, and that nouns can be subjects, let us consider both of these issues [in turn].

Enquiry 2

The grammarians agreed that verbs and particles may not be used as subjects, because one cannot say *ḍaraba qatala* ('struck killed').

One may point out that a single example is insufficient to prove a universal rule. After all, it is also incorrect to say *jidār samā'* ('wall sky') [both nouns], but that does not show that nouns are incapable of being subjects or predicates: this only shows that a single example is insufficient to prove a universal. Indeed, the following arguments have been advanced to the effect that verbs and particles *can* be subjects:

1. If we say '*Ḍaraba* (or *yaḍribu/iḍrib*) is a verb,' then the subject that is spoken of here must be either a noun, a verb or a particle. If the first [i.e. a noun], then the statement would be false; but that is not so. If the second [i.e. a verb], then it is a case of a verb *per se* being a subject. If one should reply that the subject here is these [verb] *forms* which are actually nouns, then we say: that is unconvincing, as it would entail that the subject being described as a verb is actually a noun. The matter then goes back to the first point which we have refuted.
2. If we state 'Verbs and particles are not nouns,' then the issue is as described above.

1 The second is under Enquiry 4 below.

3. [Indeed,] saying 'The verb may not be a subject' is to make it a subject to that effect, which is paradoxical. If one should reply that the subject here is simply the word itself, then we have already responded to that, saying: the subject concerning which you say that it 'may not be a subject' is either a noun—which is false because a noun may always be a subject, at least to say that *it is* a noun—or a verb, in which case the verb has managed to be a subject.
4. Verbs *qua* verbs, and particles *qua* particles are known quiddities by which they are distinguished from others. Any such thing may be a subject to the effect that it 'is distinct from others'. So if we say 'A verb (in itself) is a quiddity distinct from the noun' then we have made it a subject to this effect.
5. [We may say:] 'The *fiʿl* is either the [verb] form which denotes a specific meaning, or it is that [action] denoted by the form.' In the former statement, we have made it a subject to the effect that it denotes the meaning; in the latter, we have made it a subject to the effect that it is so denoted.

The aforementioned are difficult contentions in this connection.[1]

Enquiry 3

A group cast doubt on the claim that a noun is 'that which qualifies to be a subject', saying that *ayna*, *kayfa* and *idhā* are all nouns but cannot be subjects. ʿAbd al-Qāhir [al-Jurjānī] the grammarian responded to this, saying that if we say that a noun is that which qualifies to be a subject, we mean that its *meaning* may be a subject. [For example,] when you say 'I will come to you when (*idhā*) the sun rises' it is clear that *idhā* means 'time' (*waqt*), which can be a subject, as in 'The time is ripe'.

I say: this response is weak because *idhā* does not simply mean 'time', rather a time spoken of with respect to its containing [an occurrence], in which case it is certainly not possible to make it a subject. If they should say that because part of its reality [i.e. meaning of 'time'] is a noun then it should [in whole] be considered a noun, then I say: this is false because on that basis every verb should [also] be considered a noun, as part of the reality of a verb is the *maṣdar*, which is a [verbal] noun. Since this is false, so is their contention.

1 I am unsure why the author has described this as being so difficult. If a distinction is made between the word 'verb' and its meaning, the matter is simple. In the examples given, *al-fiʿl* would have to be a noun since it bears the definite article.

Enquiry 4
The Second Categorisation Scheme

This is to say: a word may either have an independently known meaning, or not. In the latter case, it is a particle. In the former case, the word either denotes a specific time for its meaning (in which case it is a verb), or not (in which case it is a noun).

This categorisation raises questions which we shall address via the definitions of noun and verb.

Enquiry 5
Defining the Noun

People have cited a number of definitions:

A. 'The noun is such that its meaning may be made a subject (*mukhbar ʿanhu*).' However, whether something may be made a subject can only be decided after it has been fully defined, so this is more like a description (*rasm*) than a definition (*ḥadd*). It faces two problems: first, that verbs and particles may also be made subjects; and second, that *idhā*, *kayfa* and *ayna* may not be made subjects. These have already been discussed.[1]

B. 'The noun is that which may be a subject (*fāʿil*) or an object (*mafʿūl*) [of a verb], or take an annexed genitive.' Effectively, this is the same as [the above].

C. 'The noun is a word which is originally deserving of inflection (*iʿrab*).' This, too, is [merely] a description, because the deservedness of inflection is a contingent matter external to its quiddity. [The proponents of this definition] have said 'originally' for two reasons:
   - Uninflected (*mabnī*) [nouns] are so because of the similarity between them and particles. Were it not for this similarity, they would accept inflection.
   - The imperfect [verb] is inflected, but not in its own right: it is due to its similarity to the noun.

   [I say:] this definition is also weak.

D. Zamakhsharī said in *al-Mufaṣṣal* that the noun is 'that which denotes a meaning in itself, with the denotation being free of any association (*iqtirān*)'. This definition is deficient for the following reasons:
   - He had defined the *kalima* as 'an utterance (*lafẓ*) which denotes a single meaning by convention'[2]—the supercommentaries state

1 Enquiries 2 and 3 above.

2 See Chapter One, Enquiry 21 above.

that the term *lafẓ* had to be included here because 'that which denotes' would fail to exclude lines, gestures and their like which are not [words].

- The pronoun of 'in itself' (*fī nafsihi*) might refer either to the denoting [noun] or the denoted [meaning], or to something else. In the FIRST case, this would mean 'the noun is that which denotes a meaning within the noun', which is to say 'the noun is that which denotes a meaning which it denotes'. Not only is this worthless, but it is contradicted by the fact that particles and verbs[1] also denote their denotations. In the SECOND case, it would mean 'the noun is that which denotes a meaning within that meaning', but a thing subsisting within its own self is absurd. If one should say that its subsistence within itself simply means that it does not subsist in something else, then we say: the definition is still negated by adjectival nouns (*asmā' al-ṣifāt*) and relations (*nisab*) in which the named [denotations] subsist elsewhere.

[THE PREFERRED DEFINITION][2]

The noun is a word which denotes an independently known meaning without denoting the time in which the meaning occurred. The 'word' (*kalima*) has been mentioned in order to exclude lines, gestures and so on. If one should ask why the term *lafẓa* was not used [instead of *kalima*], we reply that we have classed the *lafẓ* as the genus containing the *kalima*,[3] which in turn contains the *ism*; and definitions should mention the proximate genus rather than a distant one.

Regarding the clause of being 'independently known' (*mustaqill bi'l-maʿlūmiyya*), some have claimed that it is both insufficient and unnecessary.

INSUFFICIENT because:

a. Anything which is known is, necessarily, independently known: because as long as the quiddity of a thing has not been conceived, it cannot be conceived along with something else. If its conception by itself precedes its conception along with other things, then it is independently known.
b. The concept of 'particle' is independently known *not* to be independently known, which is [itself] independence.

1 Perhaps Zamakhsharī has already excluded verbs by saying 'without association', i.e. with a time.
2 The author has labelled this simply as 'the fifth opinion', which I have adjusted for clarity.
3 See Chapter One, Enquiry 24 above.

c. The grammarians agreed that [the particle] *bā'* entails attachment (*ilṣāq*)[1] and that *min* entails partitivity (*tabʿīḍ*).[2] Thus if the concept of 'attachment' is known independently, then the meaning of the *bā'* is known independently and it would become a noun [by this definition]. However, if [the meaning of the *bā'*] is not known independently, then [the noun] 'attachment' is not known independently, and the noun would become [upon the definition of] a particle.

As for its being UNNECESSARY, this is because *kam*, *kayfa*, *matā*, *idhā* and *mā* (interrogative and conditional) are all nouns despite their meanings not being independent; the same applies to relative pronouns.

[A FURTHER OBJECTION TO THE DEFINITION:] the clause 'without denoting the time of that meaning' is countered by the [nouns] *zamān* (time), *ghad* (morrow), *yawm* (day), *iṣṭibāḥ* (drink in the morning) and *ightibāq* (drink in the evening).

RESPONSE TO THE FORMER CONTENTION:[3] we comprehend the difference between the word 'attachment' and the particle *bā'* when we say *katabtu bi'l-qalam* ('I wrote by the pen'), and this much is what we mean by independence.

FURTHER RESPONSES: the referent of the words *zamān*, *yawm* and *ghad* is the time itself, and they contain no denotation of another time [in which that time occurred]. As for *iṣṭibāḥ* and *ightibāq*: the time is integral (*juz'*) to these, whereas verbs denote a time external to the referent, e.g. [the verbs] *ightabaqa/yaghtabiqu* in which the perfect and future tenses [respectively] have been applied to [the verbal nouns] *iṣṭibāḥ* and *ightibāq*.[4]

Enquiry 6
[Signs of Nouns]

Signs (*ʿalāmāt*) of a noun can either be verbal or semantic. Verbal signs can be before the noun, i.e. the definite article [*al-*] or a preposition. They can be in the middle, such as the *yā'* of diminution (*taṣghīr*) or letters for the broken [plural]; or at the end, such as the suffixes for the dual and [sound] plural.

1 That is, connecting the verb to a noun which is also an 'instrument' (*āla*). See Chapter Seven below.

2 These are *among* the denotations of each particle.

3 Namely point (c) above.

4 The example concerns the second of these verbal nouns, but the same can be said for *iṣṭabaḥa/yaṣṭabiḥu*, which means: he did drink by morning, and he does/will drink by morning.

As for semantic signs, they are for [the noun] to be described (*mawṣuf*) or adjectival (*ṣifa*), the subject (*fāʿil*) or object (*mafʿūl*) [of a verb], or to be an annexed genitive (*muḍāf ilayhi*),[1] or [general] subject (*mukhbar ʿanhu*), or originally deserving of inflection.[2]

Enquiry 7
Definitions of the Verb

The following have been mentioned in this regard:

A. Sībawayh said that they are forms (*amthila*) extracted from the verbal noun. This is negated by the forms *fāʿil* and *mafʿūl*.[3]
B. That it is attributed (*isnād*) to something but nothing is attributed to it. This is negated by the nouns *idhā* and *kayfa*, for they must be attributed to something else and nothing may be attributed to them.
C. Zamakhsharī said: 'The verb is that which denotes the association of an event with a time.' This is weak for two reasons:
    a. One ought to say 'a *word* which denotes…', for the following reasons:
        - Otherwise, the definition would be countered by our saying 'the association of an event with a time'—for this collection of words denotes the association of an event with a time despite not being a verb. If we specify 'a word', the problem would disappear because these are not a single word.
        - Otherwise, it would not exclude lines, gestures etc.
        - Since 'word' is the proximate genus containing these three [species], it is necessary to mention it in the definition (*ḥadd*).
    b. The other reason is what we shall mention below.[4]

[The Preferred Definition]

The verb is a word denoting that the verbal noun (*maṣdar*)[5] is established for something unspecified, in a specified time.

We have mentioned 'a word' because it is the proximate genus. We said 'the verbal noun' rather than merely 'something' because [the occurrence denoted by] the verbal noun may be something [positively] established

1 Or to take a genitive (i.e. be *muḍāf*), according to definition B in Enquiry 5 above (for the noun).

2 See definition C in Enquiry 5 above.

3 This is because the active and passive participles are also extracted from the verbal noun, yet are nouns themselves.

4 This would seem to refer to the author's reasons for supporting the fourth definition, which I have labelled as 'preferred' for clarity.

5 The Arabic term literally means 'source', which reflects the assumption that the verb is derived from it. The English terminology suggests the opposite.

(*thābit*), such as *ḍaraba* (to strike) and *qatala* (to kill); or something negative (*ʿadamī*), as is the case with *faniya* (to perish) and *ʿadima* (to be non-existent), of which the verbal nouns are *fanāʾ* and *ʿadam*, respectively. We said 'for something unspecified' because this much is considered, as we shall prove.[1] We said 'in a specified time' to distinguish [verbs] from nouns.

Know that there are issues related to these clauses (*quyūd*):

CLAUSE 1 ('denoting that the verbal noun is established for something') faces the following difficulties:

a. If we say 'God created (*khalaqa*) the world,' this [verb] either denotes that the [act] of creation is established for Almighty God, or it does not; if the latter, the clause is negated. If it does so denote, then the *khalq* (creation) must be distinct from the *makhlūq* (created). If [the latter] is temporally originated, then it is in need of another *khalq*, which leads to infinite regression; but if it is pre-eternal, this would entail a created thing being pre-eternal [which is absurd].
b. If we say 'Something exists (*wujida*),' does this [passive verb] denote that existence is established for that thing, or not? If not, the clause is negated. If so, it follows that existence has subsisted in something other [than existence] which must, in turn, subsist in itself: because anything which does not subsist in itself cannot have any other [attribute] subsist in it. Therefore, its existence must be preceded by another existence *ad infinitum*, which is absurd.
c. If we say 'Something perished, or was non-existent,' this implies that perishing and non-existence have *obtained* for that thing (quiddity), which is impossible because these are both pure negation and cannot conceivably obtain for anything external to them.
d. Assuming that existence (*wujūd*) is something external to quiddity (*māhiyya*), it would be true to say 'Existence obtained (*ḥaṣala*) for this quiddity,' which entails an additional existence which obtained for that existence, and so on *ad infinitum*, which is absurd. On the other hand, if we assume that existence is identical to quiddity, saying that 'Such-and-such thing took place (*ḥadatha*) and obtained' would not, in fact, entail that the existence of that thing has obtained. If it did, that would mean that existence is something distinct from quiddity, which is the opposite of what we have here assumed.

CLAUSE 2 ('in a specified time') faces the following objections:

a. If we say 'Time exists' or 'Time perishes,' these [verbs] entail

1 See Enquiry 9 below.

that time has taken place in another time, which leads to infinite regression. If one should suggest that the definition only requires for time to occur in another time by way of false supposition (*wahm kādhib*) [for the sake of argument], then we reply: there is consensus that the statement 'Time came into being after its non-existence' is entirely true, whereas your suggestion implies otherwise.

b. If we say 'The world was (*kāna*) non-existent in pre-eternity,' then this verb implies the existence of time in pre-eternity, which is impossible. If one should say that this is a hypothetical time, not real, we reply: if this mental hypothesis agrees with the external state of affairs then the objection stands; if it does not, then it is falsehood, and it follows that the definition is unfit.
c. If we say 'God was existent (*kāna mawjūdan*) in pre-eternity,' this implies that God is time-bound, which is impossible.
d. It is countered by deficient (*nāqiṣ*) verbs. When *kāna* is deficient,[1] it either denotes an event occurring in a time, or not. If so, it would be complete (*tāmm*) rather than deficient, because the denotation of a word to the effect that an event has occurred in a time is complete speech, not deficient. If it does not so denote, then it must not be a verb [at all].
e. It is countered by verb-nouns (*asmāʾ al-afʿāl*),[2] which denote words [i.e. verbs] which denote a specific time. Since to denote the denoter of something is [equivalent to] denoting that thing [directly], it follows that these nouns denote a specific time.
f. The active participle (*ism al-fāʿil*) expresses either the present or the future[3] but not the past; therefore, it denotes a specific time.

RESPONSE: the four contentions concerning Clause 1 and the [first] three concerning Clause 2 are responded to by saying: the linguist suffices, in terms of his knowledge, with conceiving the understood meaning, whether that be accurate or not.

As for the claim that [Clause 2] is countered by deficient verbs, let me say that the opinion I advance in this regard is that *kāna* is always a complete (*tāmm*) verb. The issue is that the noun to which *kāna* is attributed may be either a single and distinct quiddity; for example, *kāna al-shayʿu* ('the

1 That is, when it is copular and takes an accusative predicate.
2 Such as *mah* and *ṣah*, which are nouns performing the function of verbs, whether past, present/future or imperative. See Chapter One, Enquiry 21 for a previous mention.
3 I.e. when made to function grammatically and act upon an object.

thing was'), meaning that it occurred and obtained—or it may express the attribution of one thing to another. For example, *kāna Zaydun munṭaliqan* ('Zayd was departing') means that the property of departure (*inṭilāq*) has occurred in relation to Zayd. As such, *kāna* here means, likewise, to occur and obtain. The difference is that, in this case, the quiddity in question is a type of relationship; since relationships cannot be expressed without reference to both parties, they both had to be mentioned here. Just as saying *kāna Zaydun* means that he obtained and existed, saying *kāna Zaydun munṭaliqan* means that the property of departure occurred in relation to him. This is a profound, subtle and remarkable enquiry which the earlier [scholars] overlooked.[1]

As for their saying that it is countered by verb-nouns, we say: the defining factor for the verb is that it denotes a time directly, not via an intermediary. Regarding the sixth point, that the active participle is specific to the present or future, we do not concede this: for it is said that the [active participle] when referring to the past[2] does not act like a verb, but when referring to the present [or future], it does act like a verb.

Enquiry 8

A word either has a meaning which is independently known, or not. The latter is a particle; thus the particle is distinguished from the noun and verb by means of a negative clause. Then we say: the [word of] independently known [meaning] either denotes a specific time for its referent, or not. The latter is a noun, which is thus distinguished from the verb by means of a negative clause. As for the verb, its quiddity comprises positive clauses.

Enquiry 9
[The Unspecified Agent]

If we say *ḍaraba* ('he/it struck'), this denotes that the act of striking emanated from something or other, but that thing is not specified by the word.

[OBJECTION:] some may say that this is impossible, for two reasons:

a. If it were so, then the verb by itself could be categorised as true or false.
b. If it denotes that the act of striking is attributed to something which is *actually* unspecified, then it must be impossible to attribute [the

1 The author makes further reference to this contention in Book II, Chapter Four, under Section II, upon discussion of *al-Kā'in* as a description for God.

2 I.e. when annexing a genitive through *iḍāfa*.

verb] to something specified, or else there would be a contradiction. However, if it denotes the attribution of striking to something specified [but unstated], then this is untenable, because it is known by necessity that *ḍaraba* by itself was not coined to attribute striking to Zayd or ʿAmr[1] in particular.

RESPONSE: there is a single answer to both objections, namely that *ḍaraba* was not coined to attribute striking to something which is actually unspecified, but rather to a specified thing which the speaker will mention [subsequently]. Before the said mention, the speech is neither complete nor categorised as true or false; on this basis, the objection falls.

Enquiry 10
[A Problematic Definition]

It is said that the particle (*ḥarf*) is 'that which [was coined] for a meaning in other than itself'—but this is unclear. If they intend to say that the particle is anything whose meaning obtains and subsists in something other than it, then all names of attributes and accidents must be particles. However, if they intend that it is whatever denotes a meaning, but the denotation is other than the meaning, then this is obviously flawed. If they intend a third interpretation, then this must be explained.

Enquiry 11
[Word Combinations]

The possible combinations of these three [types] are six:[2] a noun with a noun, which is the [nominal] sentence comprising subject and predicate; a noun with a verb, which is the [verbal] sentence comprising verb and subject—these are both sound sentence types by consensus. As for the third—a noun with a particle—this is said to form a sound sentence in two situations:

FIRST [THE VOCATIVE]: to say *yā Zayd* ('O Zayd'). It has been said that this only forms a sentence on the basis of an implied [verb] *unādī* ('I address'), and that this is supported by the following:

a. The word *yā* can be affected by *imāla*,[3] and this only occurs in nouns and verbs.

1 These are generic names often employed by grammarians.

2 Three go unmentioned because they do not form sentences: a pair of verbs, a pair of particles and a verb with a particle.

3 A phenomenon of pronunciation in which the /ā/ sound 'swerves' towards /ī/, resulting in /ē/.

b. A [prepositional] *lām* can depend on it, such as to say *yā la-Zayd*. This *lām* is that of seeking succour (*istighātha*) and is a preposition. If *yā* were not standing in lieu of a verb, it would not be possible for the preposition to depend (*taʿalluq*) upon it, as a particle cannot enter upon another particle.

Others denied that *yā* has the meaning of 'I address,' on the following bases:

a. Saying 'I address' is a statement about addressing; since a statement about something is distinct from [that thing itself], saying 'I address Zayd' must be distinct from 'O Zayd'.
b. 'I address Zayd' is [declarative] speech which can be true or false, whereas 'O Zayd' is not.
c. 'O Zayd' is directed solely to the addressee, whereas 'I address Zayd' is not.
d. 'O Zayd' denotes addressing at the present time, whereas 'I address Zayd' is not specific to the present.[1]
e. It is acceptable to say *unādī Zaydan qā'iman* ('I address Zayd while standing'), but not *yā Zaydu qā'iman*.

So these five points demonstrate the distinction between these two.

SECOND [PREPOSITIONAL PREDICATE]: to say *Zaydun fī al-dār* ('Zayd is inside the home'). Here, *Zayd* is the subject, while the predicate is that which is denoted by [the preposition] *fī*. However, as this 'insideness' may pertain to the home or mosque [etc.], it is ascribed to the home to distinguish it from other possibilities.

If it is said that the sentence only works because of an implied [word], i.e. 'Zayd settled (*istaqarra*) in the home' or 'Zayd is settled (*mustaqirr*) in the home,' then we say: this is false, because [the verb] *istaqarra* is to say that settlement occurred for him (*ḥaṣala fīhi*), and saying this would entail another occurrence[2]—i.e. that the occurrence of settlement occurred for him—leading to infinite regression and absurdity. It is thus proven that 'Zayd is in the home' is complete speech which cannot be made dependent upon a hypothetical verb.[3]

Enquiry 12
[Compound Sentences]

A sentence may have either first-order or second-order construction. The former refers to [ordinary] nominal or verbal sentences. It is most appar-

1 The Arabic imperfect verb may refer to the future or to a habitual action.
2 This is because of the same preposition, namely *fī*, being present in this explanation.
3 This dependency is commonly known in grammar as *taʿalluq*.

ent that the nominal sentence is conceptually prior to the verbal sentence, because nouns are simple while verbs are complex, and the former has priority over the latter. It could also be said that the verbal sentence is prior because nouns are not attributed to others in an authentic sense.

As for second-order constructions, these refer to conditional sentences. For example, 'If (*in*) the sun is up, then (*fa-*) daytime is present'—where 'the sun is up' and 'daytime is present' are both sentences, and the particles of protasis [*in*] and apodosis [*fa-*] have entered their respective sentences and made them one sentence. And God—Perfect and Exalted—knows best.

Chapter Four
VARIOUS CATEGORISATIONS OF THE NOUN

The First Categorisation[1]

Either the mere conceptualisation of its meaning precludes it applying to multiple referents,[2] or it does not. In the former case, it may be either explicit, in which case it is a PROPER NOUN (*ʿalam*), or otherwise implicit, which is known [i.e. pronouns]. If multiple referents are not precluded, then: if the meaning is a specific quiddity, this is a GENERIC NOUN (*ism jins*). If it means that a certain thing is described by particular quality, then this is a DERIVED NOUN (*mushtaqq*); for example, saying *aswad* (black) means that something possesses blackness.

We have demonstrated that the noun is a genus encompassing three species: proper nouns, generic nouns and derived nouns; so let us discuss the rulings (*aḥkām*) of each.

First: Proper Nouns

Their rulings are numerous:

Ruling 1

The theologians (*mutakallimūn*) stated that the proper noun does not have any meaning (*fā'ida*). I say: it is true that it does not attribute anything to its referent, but it is not true that it does not denote anything: how could this be when, in fact, it specifies its particular referent?

Ruling 2

It is a matter of agreement that genera have [associated] proper names. For example, *asad* is a generic noun for this reality [lion], whereas Usāma is a proper noun for it. Likewise, *thaʿlab* is a generic noun for this reality [fox], while Thuʿāla is its proper noun.

There are two differences between the generic noun and its proper noun (*ʿalam al-jins*):

1 The author first divides nouns into proper nouns, generic nouns and derived nouns: the first of these is discussed in this chapter and the remaining two in Chapter Five. He then divides nouns into inflected and uninflected, which forms the topic of Chapter Six.

2 This is the logicians' definition of the *juz'ī* (particular).

a. The proper noun [in general] refers to a particular individual with respect to being that individual. If we were to give many individuals the name of Zayd, that is not because the word *Zayd* was coined to describe the shared characteristics of those individuals; rather, it is intended to identify each individual in and of himself, and the various individuals share it by way of homonymy (*ishtirāk*).

   Once this is clear, we say: if the person coining the name said 'I have coined the name Usāma to designate every individual lion in its own right, by way of homonymy,' then this is a proper noun. On the other hand, if he said 'I have coined the term *asad* to describe the quiddity (*māhiyya*) shared between these individuals, without specifying any individual,' then this is a generic noun. This clarifies the difference between the two.

b. The [linguists] observed that Usāma is a diptote, while knowing that two [factors] must obtain in the noun for it to become a diptote; since the word has a feminine [ending] but no other [relevant factor], they assumed it to be a proper noun on this basis.[1]

Ruling 3

Know that the wisdom behind the coinage of proper nouns is that a thing may have taken a particular ruling which needed to be expressed; since expressing the ruling is not possible without mentioning the thing to which it pertains, it was necessary to coin proper nouns.

Ruling 4

Due to the fact that the variety of needs exists more pronouncedly among human beings than other animals, it is natural that humans are recipients of proper names more than other beings.

Ruling 5
Categories of Proper Nouns

These are divided in a variety of ways:

THE FIRST DIVISION. A proper noun can be: a name (*ism*), like Ibrāhīm, Mūsā and ʿĪsā; a title (*laqab*), like Isrā'īl; or an agnomen (*kunya*),[2] like Abū Lahab. Then there are a number of rulings that follow from this:[3]

1. A thing may have a name only, or a title only, or an agnomen only;

1 Being a proper noun (*ʿalamiyya*) and femininity (*ta'nīth*) are two of the conditions involved in preventing a noun from *ṣarf*, i.e. *tanwīn*. See in Chapter Six, Enquiry 22 below.

2 My assignment of 'title' and 'agnomen' to these two terms is somewhat arbitrary.

3 The second ruling has been labelled as 'third', and so on, which may be a manuscript error. I have adjusted the numbers accordingly.

or a name with a title, a name with an agnomen, or a title with an agnomen. Sībawayh listed examples concerning the combination of agnomen and name, which number three:

a. Things with both a name and a title; for example, the hyena (*ḍabuʿ*), which has the [proper] name Ḥaḍājir and the agnomen Umm ʿĀmir. Likewise, a lion is Usāma and Abū al-Ḥārith; the fox is Thuʿāla and Abū al-Ḥuṣayn; and the scorpion (*ʿaqrab*) is Shabwa and Umm ʿIryaṭ.
b. Things with a name only; for example, Qutham for a male hyena, which has no agnomen.
c. Things with an agnomen but no name; for example, Abū Barāqish for that specific [bird].

2. An agnomen may involve ascription with 'father', 'mother', 'son' or 'daughter'. The first case is illustrated by a wolf (*dhi'b*) being known as Abū Jaʿda, and something white being called Abū al-Jūn.[1] As for mothers, this is illustrated by a calamity (*dāhiya*) being known as Umm Ḥabw Karā, and wine as Umm Laylā. As for sons, a crow (*ghurāb*) is called Ibn Da'ya, and a man whose condition is apparent is called Ibn Jalā. As for daughters, an echo is called Ibnat al-Jabal ('daughter of the mountain'), and pebbles are called Bint al-Arḍ ('daughter of the ground').
3. The attribution in the agnomen may be to an unknown relation, such as in Ibn ʿIrs (weasel: 'son of a mate') or Ḥimār Qabbān (woodlouse: 'donkey of domes'). Alternatively, it may be to a known relation, like Ibn/Bint Labūn[2] or Ibn/Bint al-Makhāḍ.[3] If a she-camel gives birth and is impregnated [soon] after, she does not become *makhāḍ*— i.e. pregnant and close to full-term—until a year has passed; and then her son is Ibn Makhāḍ and her daughter is Bint Makhāḍ. If she subsequently gives birth [again] and develops milk, she will be *labūn* (milk-bearing) and the offspring will be attributed to her in the same manner.
4. If a name and a title appear together, then the name is either annexed (*muḍāf*) [already] or not. If not, then the name is annexed to the title—for example, *Saʿīdu Karzin* or *Qaysu Baṭṭata*—such that they become as though a single name. However, if the name is [already] annexed, then the title is kept separate; for example, *ʿAbdu' Llāhi Baṭṭatu*.[4]

1 The printed edition has *li'l-abyaḍ wa-Abū al-Jūn*, with the conjunction in the wrong place. The Amīriyya edition is missing the conjunction altogether.

2 A two-year-old camel.

3 A one-year-old camel.

4 I have retained vocalisation in these examples to demonstrate the grammatical points.

5. A number of factors lead to an agnomen being coined:
    a. Expressing an actual relation; for example, Abū Ṭālib being named due to his son, Ṭālib.
    b. Hope and optimism; for example, to say Abū ʿAmr for one who longs for a child with lengthy life (*ʿumr*), or Abū al-Faḍl for one who longs for a child possessing many virtues (*faḍā'il*).
    c. Indicating an opposite; for example, Abū Yaḥyā (lit: father of 'he lives') as an agnomen for death.
    d. A man may be famous with a father who is also famous, so they exchange agnomens; for example, Yūsuf [Prophet Joseph] is known as Abū Yaʿqūb, and Yaʿqūb [Prophet Jacob] is known as Abū Yūsuf.
    e. A man may become famous for a certain quality so he is named by it: whether by his possessing that quality, or being ascribed to it in an obvious or obscure way.

THE SECOND DIVISION. A proper noun can be simple (*mufrad*), like Zayd; or constructed (*murakkab*) of two unrelated words, like Baʿla-bak. There may also be a relation between [the constructed parts], namely annexation (*iḍāfa*), as in ʿAbd Allāh and Abū Zayd; or attribution (*isnād*), i.e. nominal or verbal sentences. A pertinent detail in this regard is that, if you make a sentence into a proper name, you leave it completely unchanged; for example, Ta'abbaṭa Sharran[1] or Baraqa Naḥruh.[2]

THE THIRD DIVISION. A proper noun may be either transferred (*manqūl*) or improvised (*murtajal*). The transferred may come from a meaningful word or a meaningless [sound]. The former may be a noun, a verb, a particle or a combination of these. As for names transferred from nouns, these could be for a thing, such as Asad (lion) and Thawr (bull); or a concept, such as Faḍl (virtue) and Naṣr (succour); or a genuine attribute such as al-Ḥasan (good), or a relative attribute such as al-Madhkūr (mentioned) or al-Mardūd (rejected).

Names transferred from verbs may come from the perfect tense, such as Shammar (he rolled up); or the imperfect, such as Yaḥyā (he lives); or the imperative, such as Uṭruqā (knock). As for particles, this would occur if you named a man by one of those forms.

Regarding the transference of a name from a combination of these three, then if it is a meaningful [sentence], it has been mentioned under

1 A pre-Islamic poet. The title means 'he carried evil under his arm'.
2 A name from the pre-Islamic period, meaning 'his throat gleamed'.

the second division. If it is meaningless [originally], then it [becomes] meaningful. As for names transferred from a sound, this is like some ʿAlawīs[1] being known as Ṭabāṭabā.

As for the improvised [proper noun]: it may be based on analogy (*qiyās*); for example, ʿImrān and Ḥamdān, which are [on the form of] generic nouns such as *sirḥān* (wolf) and *nadmān* (regretful) [respectively]. Otherwise, it can be anomalous (*shādhdh*) with very few counterparts); for example, Muḥabbab and Mawhab.

THE FOURTH DIVISION. A proper noun may be either for essences (*dhawāt*) or attributes (*maʿānī*); in either case, it will be either a proper noun for the individual (*shakhṣ*) or genus (*jins*): this makes four categories. Before delving into their explanations, it is essential to know that the coinage of proper nouns for essences [i.e. things] is more frequent than for attributes, because individual essences are such that one is required to speak about them on a specific basis. As for attributes (*ṣifāt*), these do not generally [require this]. Let us return to consider the rulings of each of the four categories:

1. The proper name for [individual] essences: its prerequisite is that the referent is familiar (*ma'lūf*) to the coiner; this applies most originally to human beings, as it is humans who use names, and familiarity is most complete between members of the same species. After [fellow] humans come things which humans need and see frequently, which is why they have coined Aʿwaj and Lāḥiq as names for mares, Shadhqam and ʿAlī for stallions, and Ḍamrān and Kassāb for male and female dogs respectively. As for things which humans do not encounter frequently, their individual members would seldom be given proper names.
2. The proper name for a genus of essences, such as Usāma for the lion and Thuʿāla for the fox.[2]
3. Proper names for specific occurrences of attributes do not occur, as they would be of no benefit.
4. The proper name for an attribute genus: the guiding rule is that if we see [a word] in which [only] one factor—from the list of nine—for making it a diptote is present, yet it has indeed been made a diptote, then we know that it has been made a proper noun [as the second

1 Presumably, this means descendants of ʿAlī b. Abī Ṭālib. The name is still in use; for example, Muḥammad Ḥusayn Ṭabāṭabā'ī (d. 1981), author of *Tafsīr al-mīzān*.

2 See Ruling 2 under Proper Nouns, above.

factor]. This is because it would not become a diptote unless two factors are present. Ibn Jinnī mentioned a number of examples in this regard, including glorification (*tasbīḥ*) being called Subḥān and treachery (*ghadr*)[1] being called Kaysān; these are both diptotes, but the single cause—namely the [additional] *alif* and *nūn*—must be accompanied by being a proper noun as the second factor.

THE FIFTH DIVISION. Know that a generic noun may turn into a proper noun: a word may have a meaning which is universal and can apply to many [members], but then it is applied by custom to a particular individual. For example, *al-Najm* is originally a name for every star, but it refers customarily to the Pleiades (*al-Thurayyā*). Likewise, *al-Simāk* is a name derived from elevation, and then it is applied to a specific heavenly body.[2]

1 The printed edition mistakenly has *al-ghudū* (morning). In the Amīriyya edition, vol. I, p. 24, it is *al-ʿadū* (enemy). I have corrected it with reference to classical dictionaries.
2 There are two famous stars known by this name, *viz.* Spica and Arcturus.

Chapter Five
RULINGS CONCERNING GENERIC NOUNS AND DERIVED NOUNS

These are numerous:

[Second:][1] Generic Nouns

Ruling 1

The quiddity (*māhiyya*) is either complex (*murakkab*) or simple (*basīṭ*). It is established in the rational [sciences] that the complex is prior to the simple in terms of genus (*jins*), whereas the simple is prior to the complex in terms of differentia (*faṣl*). By means of examination, it is shown that the power and strength of the genus is greater than that of the differentia, so it follows that the names of complex quiddities are prior to those of simple ones.

Ruling 2

Generic nouns are conceptually prior to derived nouns, because a derived noun branches off from that noun from which it is derived. If that is itself derived, then this leads to infinite regression or circularity; since these are both impossible, it follows that there must be an endpoint consisting of coined, non-derived (*jāmid*) nouns.

The coined (*mawḍūʿ*) word is in no need of the derived, but the derived is in need of the coined; therefore, the coined noun must be conceptually prior to the derived. This underlines the futility of the linguists' and grammarians' frequent practice of striving to prove that every word is derived from something else.[2]

Ruling 3

Existent things are either necessary (*wājib*) or contingent (*mumkin*), and the contingent is either spatial (*mutaḥayyiz*), or [a property] subsistent in a spatial object (*ḥāll fī'l-mutaḥayyiz*). It may also be neither, but this is seldom perceptible, in contrast to the first two categories.

1 This is a continuation of 'The First Categorisation' of nouns from the previous chapter. The second categorisation is in the next chapter.

2 See a rejoinder in Rufayda, *al-Naḥw wa-kutub al-tafsīr*, vol. II, p. 807.

It has been proven [philosophically] that spatials are equal in terms of their essences, which entails that the distinction between them is by means of the properties subsistent in them. As such, the names used to refer to each species of body (*jism*) in fact refer to the combination of essence and the particular attributes subsistent therein. This is true in the majority of cases.

[Third:] Derived Nouns

Ruling 1

It is not necessarily the case that an essence described by a derived noun will possess the attribute described by the noun from which it was derived. For example, *maʿlūm* (known) is derived from *ʿilm* (knowledge), while knowledge does not [necessarily] subsist in the known. The same can be said of the *madhkūr* (mentioned), *mar'ī* (seen) and *masmūʿ* (heard), and also of *lā'iq* (appropriate) and *rāmī* (thrower).[1]

Ruling 2

The condition of a derived noun being true is that the [concept] from which it is derived holds true at the present time. For example, if someone who was an unbeliever (*kāfir*) embraced Islam, it would be true to say that he is *not* an unbeliever. This shows that the persistence of that from which the noun is derived (*mushtaqq minhu*) is a condition of the truth of the derived noun.

Ruling 3

If the noun from which another is derived [refers to] a complex quiddity, the parts of which cannot occur simultaneously—such as speech (*kalām*), statement (*qawl*) and prayer (*ṣalāh*)— then the derived noun will only be literally true when the last of these parts occurs.

Ruling 4

The meaning understood from [the active participle] *ḍārib* (striker) is that it is something to which *ḍarb* (striking) is attributed. Whether that thing is a body or otherwise is external to the meaning, and known only via concomitant signification.

1 The examples of the passive participle are clearer. *Lā'iq* is the active participle of *liyāqa* (propriety), which is a relative attribute and cannot subsist in any essence. *Rāmī* could refer to 'an archer', for whom *ramy* is a description of action and does not subsist in him. For an overview of types of attributes, see Book II, Chapter Three, Section ii, Enquiry 8.

Chapter Six

THE [SECOND] CATEGORISATION: INFLECTED AND UNINFLECTED NOUNS[1]

There are a number of enquiries in this connection:

Enquiry 1
[Understanding Inflection]

There are two explanations for the word *iʿrāb* (inflection).[2] The first is that it comes from the expression *aʿraba ʿan nafsihi*, meaning for one to express what is within one's self; so *iʿrāb* means 'to clarify the meaning'. The second is that it comes from *ʿaribat maʿidatu al-rajul*, i.e. for a man's stomach to turn bad (*fāsid*). As such, *iʿrāb* is the process of removing harm (*fasād*) and confusion. This is like describing dotting [letters] in a book as *iʿjām*, meaning 'to remove its ineloquence (*ʿujma*)'.[3]

Enquiry 2

When a word is coined for a quiddity (*māhiyya*) which is subject to various changes in state, then the word itself must be subject to changes in order to reflect the various semantic states. While the core of the word denotes the quiddity in itself, the changes in [word endings] reflect the changes in its states. These changes in the word which reflect changes in meaning are what we call 'inflection'.

Enquiry 3

Verbs and particles [represent] accidental states in the quiddity, and accidents are not—for the most part—such as can be subjected to further accidents. Rather, it is essences (*dhawāt*) which may be subject to various states. The words which refer to [essences] are nouns; therefore, it is nouns which are originally deserving of inflection.

1 Cf. the first categorisation which began in Chapter Four. Here, the usual system of 'enquiries' is resumed.

2 In the context of nouns, this is known as 'declension', and for verbs it is 'conjugation'. However, since the same word is used for both in Arabic, I have opted for the inclusive term 'inflection'.

3 The common feature is the use of the Form IV verb to entail 'removal'.

Enquiry 4

Inflection is specific to the ends of words for two reasons:

1. Accidental states do not affect an essence unless the essence first exists. A word does not exist until its final letter exists: therefore, the signs denoting the various semantic states must not occur until the word has been completed.
2. Changes in the [vowel] state of the first and second letter of a word are to signify the various forms (*awzān*) of the word; hence there is no letter left to accept inflection [vowels] but the last in the word.

Enquiry 5

The term 'inflection' does not refer to the vowels and silences found at the end of words, for these are also found on uninflected words. Rather, it refers to the words being *deserving* of certain vowels due to perceptible factors. Being deserving (*istiḥqāq*) is a conceptual rather than perceived matter, so inflection is [also] conceptual rather than perceived.

Enquiry 6
[Vowels]

Saying that a letter is *mutaḥarrik* [vowelled; lit. 'moving'] or *sākin* [unvowelled; lit. 'still'] is metaphorical, since movement and stillness are attributes of bodies, and letters are not bodies. Rather, what is meant by the *ḥaraka* (vowel) is a specific sound coming right after pronouncing the letter, while *sukūn* is when the letter is present without being followed by that sound, i.e. vowel.[1]

Enquiry 7

Vowels are either explicit (*ṣarīḥ*) or fleeting (*mukhtalas*). Explicit vowels are either pure (*mufrad*) or not. The pure vowels are three: *fatḥa*, *kasra* and *ḍamma*. The non-pure vowels are in-between, numbering six combinations, two for each vowel:[2] the *fatḥa* has a [sound] between it and the *kasra*, and another between it and the *ḍamma*; the *kasra* has a [sound] between it and the *ḍamma*, and another between it and the *fatḥa*; and the *ḍamma* is analogous to these, bringing the total to nine [vowels].

The above may be either long vowels (*mushbaʿ*) or otherwise, making the total eighteen. The nineteenth is the fleeting vowel which, although a vowel, has an origin obscure to the [ear] and is described as the 'unknown'

1 Cf. Chapter Two, Enquiry 7 above.

2 It is unclear to me why they are not only three, unless it is a matter of degree. The sound between /a/ and /i/ is known as *imāla*, and that between /u/ and /i/ is known as *ishmām*.

(*majhūl*) vowel. This is how Abū ʿAmr [al-Baṣrī] recited the [second *kasra*] vowel of *bāri'ikum* [in Q.ii.54], in a fleeting way rather than making it apparent.[1]

Enquiry 8

Since the vowels (and their absence) under discussion depend upon particular voices [and dialects], one cannot be certain in limiting them to the aforementioned number. Ibn Jinnī stated that a key is known in the Farsi tongue as *kelid*, in which it is unclear whether the first letter is vowelled or unvowelled. He further related from Abū ʿAlī [al-Fārisī] that he said: 'I entered a town in which I heard the people pronouncing a strange *fatḥa* I had never heard before. I was amazed by it, and spent some days there until I, too, could pronounce it. Once I left the town, I forgot it.'

Enquiry 9

Inflection vowels follow the [final] letters chronologically, as evidenced by the following:

1. Plosive (*ṣulb*) letters such as the *bā'*, *tā'* and *dāl* only come into being at the end of the time of the breath's containment and at the beginning of its release. This is an indivisible moment falling between the two times. The vowel is a sound which emerges upon the breath's release. It is evident that the [former] moment precedes this [latter] time, which shows that the letter precedes the vowel.
2. Plosive letters are not subject to lengthening, whereas vowels are; as such, they cannot occur simultaneously. Since the vowel is not before the letter, it remains that the letter is before the vowel.

Enquiry 10

Vowels are portions of the letters of lengthening (*madd*) and gliding (*līn*),[2] as evidenced by the following:

1. These letters are subject to increase and decrease, which means they have upper and lower limits: and the lower limits of these letters are none other than these vowels.

1 Works on recitations (*qirā'āt*) define *ikhtilās* as pronouncing a particular vowel (such as the *kasra* in the cited verse) with a shorter duration, described as two-thirds of the vowel. See ʿAbd al-ʿAlī al-Mas'ūl, *Muʿjam muṣṭalaḥāt ʿilm al-qirā'āt al-Qur'āniyya*, Cairo: Dār al-Salām, 2007, p. 41.

2 The letters of *madd* (*alif*, *wāw* and *yā'*) are used to lengthen their respective vowels, while the latter two, if preceded by *fatḥa*, form diphthongs described as *līn*.

2. If we stretch these vowels, the lengthening letters appear, showing that the vowels are simply the beginnings of those letters.
3. If the vowels were not portions of those letters, then it would not have been appropriate to suffice with the [vowels]. If they had been altogether different, they could not have stood in place of [the letters] and represented them, as found by reading through the Qur'ān, prose and poetry.[1] Even if we suppose that it is permissible to replace a thing with something similar to it, doing so with a portion of itself is more apt, so one must assume that to be the case here.

Enquiry 11

Beginning [a word] with an unvowelled letter is considered impossible by some. Others considered it possible, because the vowel occurs after the pronunciation of the letter and it is fallacious to make [the existence of] something dependent on that which occurs after it.

Enquiry 12

The heaviest of the vowels is the *ḍamma* because it is incomplete without pursing (*ḍamm*) the lips, which requires use of the firm muscles which link to the lips from both directions. As for the *kasra*, this only requires the use of one muscle, and the *fatḥa* uses the same but more lightly.

Just as the point may be thus proven via anatomy, experience testifies to it also. However, what we have said depends on the nature of each region, for the people of Azerbaijan tend to mix (*ishmām*) the *ḍamma* in all their words, while many places do so with the *kasra* in their dialects. And God knows best.

Enquiry 13
[Inflection Vowels]

The three vowels plus *sukūn* are known in the context of inflection as *rafᶜ*, *naṣb*, *jarr* (or *khafḍ*) and *jazm*.[2] In the context of uninflected [words], they are called *fatḥ*, *ḍamm*, *kasr* and *waqf*.

Enquiry 14

Quṭrub was of the opinion that end-vowels for uninflected words are like those for the inflected, while others refuted him. This is [merely]

1 For example, the *kasra* may indicate a *yā'* suffix which was removed (such as the end of Q.CIX.6).

2 Only verbs are inflected with *jazm* (the jussive mood), while *jarr* (the genitive case) is exclusive to nouns. *Rafᶜ* is both the nominative case (in nouns) and the indicative mood (in verbs), and *naṣb* is both the accusative and the subjunctive, respectively.

a semantic difference: if he means that they are the same in quiddity, then sense-perception testifies to that; but if he means they are similarly deserved due to various factors [acting upon the words], then the intellect rejects that.

Enquiry 15

Whoever wishes to pronounce the *ḍamma* must first purse (*ḍamm*) his lips and then lift them (*rafʿ*). To pronounce the *fatḥa*, he must open (*fatḥ*) the mouth such that the upper lip becomes established (*naṣb*). To pronounce the *kasra*, he must open the mouth strongly, which depends upon pulling (*jarr*) and lowering (*khafḍ*) the lower jaw: it is therefore natural for it to be termed *jarr* and *khafḍ*, and also *kasr* because strong pulling results in breaking (*kasr*). As for *jazm*, this means cutting (*qaṭʿ*); and the reason for it being named *waqf* (stopping) and *sukūn* (stillness) is obvious.

Enquiry 16

Some claimed that *fatḥ*, *ḍamm*, *kasr* and *waqf* are names for uninflected states, just as the other four[1] are names for inflected states. Some used the first four as names for both inflected and uninflected states, while making the second four specific to inflected states; thus the first four relate to the other four as a genus relates to its species.

Enquiry 17

Sībawayh called these [vowels] *majārī* (running routes) and counted them as eight. There are two issues in this regard:

a. Why did he term them as 'running routes' when vowels constitute the running (*jary*) itself? The [singular] *majrā* is 'the place of running', so this does not apply to vowels.

   RESPONSE: as we have explained, though [the vowel] is described as *ḥaraka*, it is not actually a movement. Rather, it is a sound which is pronounced after the preceding letter. When the speaker transitions from the consonant (*ṣāmit*) to this letter [i.e. vowel], then this voiced sound (*muṣawwat*) only occurred due to the running and extension of the breath. On this basis, it is proper to describe [the vowel] as a running route.

b. Māzinī said: 'Sībawayh was wrong to include the uninflected vowels in the category of running routes, because "running" only applies to that which comes and goes. Due to the fact that uninflected words

1 *Naṣb*, *rafʿ*, *jarr* and *jazm*, respectively.

remain in one state, it is not appropriate to describe [their vowels] as *majārī*. Rather, this term applies only to four [vowels], i.e. those of inflected [nouns].'

RESPONSE: [even] uninflected words may be vowelled in the flow of speech but unvowelled when stopping upon them, so they are not fixed upon one state absolutely.

Enquiry 18
[Definition of Inflection]

Iʿrāb means the variation of the end of a word due to various agents [acting upon it], with [the change] of a vowel or a letter, whether explicitly or implicitly. By 'variation', we mean the end of the word being described as [having] a particular vowel etc. after it has been described with another. Since this description (*mawṣūfiyya*) is a conceptual matter rather than a perceptible one, the grammarian ʿAbd al-Qāhir [al-Jurjānī] stated that inflection is conceptual rather than perceived.[1]

'Due to various agents': know that words which remain in one state are called 'uninflected' (*mabnī*), while those whose ending vary are of two types:

a. Those whose meaning is not affected by the various states; for example, saying *min Zayd* ('from Zayd') with *sukūn*, but *mina 'l-rajul* ('from the man') with a *fatḥa* [placed for liaison] on the *nūn*, and also *mini 'bnik* ('from your son') with a *kasra*. In this case, the end of the word has varied, but it is not inflection because the meaning of *min* is not subject to those variations.
b. Those whose endings vary due to their various states of meaning: this is inflection.

Enquiry 19
[Types]

Inflection is of three types:

1. That which is [manifest in] the vowel. This refers to three situations:
   a. A noun which does not end with one of the weak (*ʿilla*) letters,[2] regardless of whether such a letter appears at its beginning or middle. For example, *rajul* (man), *waʿd* (promise) and *thawb* (garment).
   b. The final letter is *wāw* or *yā'* and the preceding letter is

1 See Enquiry 5 above.

2 *Alif*, *wāw* or *yā'*. The second example has an initial *wāw*, and the third has a medial *wāw*.

unvowelled. Such a word acts like the sound (*ṣaḥīḥ*) words [mentioned above] in the way vowels appear on it; for example, *ẓaby* (deer) and *ghazw* (campaign). It applies similarly to those in which assimilation has occurred, such as *kursiyy* (chair) and *ʿaduww* (enemy),[1] as the [first] assimilated letter is unvowelled, so the *yā'* and *wāw* in these [latter] words are like the *bā'* and *zāy* in [the former].

c. The final letter is a *yā'* preceded by a *kasra*, in which case it will have one form for the nominative and genitive, i.e. with *sukūn*. In the accusative, the *yā'* takes a *fatḥa*, as in the verse *ajībū dāʿiya Allāh* ('Hearken to the caller to God') (Q.XLVI.31).

2. That which is by means of a letter. This also occurs in three situations:[2]
   a. In the 'six nouns' when they are annexed, i.e. *abūhu* (father), *akhūhu* (brother), *ḥamūhu* (in-law), *hanūhu* (thing), *fūhu* (mouth), *dhū māl* (possessor) [in the nominative], but *abāhu* [accusative] and *abīhi* [genitive], and thus for the rest.
   b. *Kilā* (both) when annexed to a pronoun, i.e. *kilāhumā* [nom.] and *kilayhimā* [acc./gen.].
   c. The dual and [sound masculine] plural: *muslimāni* and *muslimūna* [nom.], *muslimayni* and *muslimīna* [acc./gen.].
3. Implicit (*taqdīrī*) inflection, which occurs in words ending with an *alif* preceded by a *fatḥa*. These have the same form in all three cases; for example, *raḥā* (mill).

Enquiry 20

The original way (*aṣl*) of inflection is by vowel, because—as we have stated—inflection uses the accidental states of a word to signify the accidental states of the meaning. In the case of a letter, an accident means a vowel, not another letter. As for the scenarios in which inflection is by letter, this is due to the fact that these letters are of the same substance as those vowels.

Enquiry 21
[Triptotes and Diptotes]

The inflected (*muʿrab*) noun—which is also referred to as *mutamakkin* (established)[3]—is of two types:

1 I have used an alternative transliteration style to allow the point to be illustrated.

2 In the first, inflection is by means of *wāw*, *alif* and *yā'*; in the second, by *alif* and *yā'*; and in the third, by *alif* and *yā'* (dual) and *wāw* and *yā'* (plural).

3 That is, in its 'nounness'; c.f. the uninflected noun, which is considered weak in this regard.

1. That which uses all the inflection vowels, as well as nunation: this is called a 'triptote' (*munṣarif*)[1] and 'firmly established' (*amkan*).
2. That which, in contrast, is deprived of *jarr* [the /i/ vowel] and nunation, but given a *fatḥa* in the genitive case unless annexed or made definite by the article. This is called a 'diptote' (*ghayr munṣarif*). The factors preventing [a noun] from *ṣarf* are nine; whenever two occur in a noun, or one is repeated, it becomes a diptote. These are: being a proper noun (*ʿalamiyya*); femininity (*ta'nīth*) which adheres in form and meaning; taking a form (*wazn*) which is exclusive—or nearly—to verbs; being an adjective (*waṣfiyya*); alteration (*ʿadl*); a plural in whose form there are no singular words;[2] construction (*tarkīb*); foreignness (*ʿujma*) in proper names in particular; and the *alif-nūn* [in masculine] which is exchanged for the two [types of] *alif* in the feminine.

Enquiry 22

The reason for two factors from the nine being required to make [the noun] a diptote is that each one of them is a 'branch' (*farʿ*), and the verb is a branch from the noun. As such, if two of the factors are present for any noun, it becomes like the verb in being a branch, and this similarity entails being a diptote.

The aforementioned [argument] contains [three] premises:

1. Each of the nine is a branch. To explain: the PROPER NOUN is a branch because a name can only be coined for something once that thing is known; and a thing is unknown by default and then becomes known.

   That FEMININITY is a branch can be explained in terms of form and meaning. In terms of form, this is because any coined word without additions would refer to the male of that reality, while for the female it requires the addition of a feminine ending. In terms of meaning, it is because the male is more complete than the female[3]; the complete is sought in its own right, whereas the incomplete is sought indirectly.

1 The Arabic term is related to its right to bear nunation (*tanwīn*), in contradistinction to the diptotes which are 'forbidden from *ṣarf*', i.e. nunation.

2 The printed edition has an unclear expression here, which I have translated according to a subsequent occurrence.

3 This reflects the psyche of the language users, even if its attribution to the Creator could be disputed with reference to the Qur'ān. The author occasionally expresses views which may be judged discriminatory.

As for the FORM specific to the verb, or predominantly related to it, being a branch: this is because the form of a verb is a branch from the verb [itself], the verb is a branch from the noun,[1] and the branch of a branch is [itself] a branch.

The ADJECTIVE is a branch of the thing described. As for ALTERATION, that is a branch because changing from one thing to another requires the existence of that original thing.

The PLURAL in whose form there are no singular words is a branch because that form is a branch from the existence of plurals, given that it only exists in the plural. The plural is a branch from the singular because multitude is a branch from singularity, and the branch of a branch is [itself] a branch. By the same token, it becomes clear that CONSTRUCTION is a branch.

As for FOREIGNNESS, this is because for people to speak in their own tongue is the default, so speaking by other languages is a branch. As for the *ALIF-NŪN* in the likes of *sakrān* (intoxicated), these two entail being a branch because they are additional to the core of the word, and any addition is a branch. We have thus shown that these nine factors result in [nouns] being branches.

2. The verb is a branch. This is evidenced by the fact that verbs denote the occurrence of the [action denoted by] the verbal noun (*maṣdar*) in a specific time, so it is necessarily a branch from the verbal noun.
3. Based on what we have said, it follows that when a noun is affected by two of these nine factors, it becomes similar to a verb in the sense of being branch-like, while still distinct because it remains a noun. The default state of a verb is non-inflection, as we have mentioned. It therefore becomes necessary for two effects to occur in the noun due to these two factors. This is by allowing the noun to be inflected in most respects, but for this to be prevented in some respects, so that each of the two factors can have its appropriate effect.

Enquiry 23

The effect upon the noun of preventing nunation and *jarr* is because: nunation is a sign of the complete state of a noun, so when the noun becomes weaker due to being branch-like, the sign of its completeness is removed. As for *jarr*, this is because a verb may [also] have *rafʿ* and *naṣb*, but not *jarr*; therefore, when the noun becomes like a verb, it is deprived of *jarr* which is a unique feature of nouns.

1 As explained in the next premise.

Enquiry 24

Once these nouns have been deprived of *jarr*, they could either be left unvowelled while in the genitive, or given a vowel. It is more proper that they receive a vowel in order to show that they were only prevented from their [normal] vowel for a reason that is incidental, not inherent. The most appropriate vowel is *naṣb*, because we have seen that the accusative takes the form of the genitive in the case of the dual and [sound masculine] plural; it is only right for this to be mirrored by the genitive taking the form of the accusative here.

Enquiry 25

It is a matter of agreement that if the definite article enters upon a diptote, or if it is annexed [to a genitive], it regains *ṣarf*; for example, *marartu bi'l-aḥmari / bi'l-masājidi / bi-ʿUmarikum* ('I passed by the red one / by the mosques / by your ʿUmar').

It is said that this is because verbs are not treated in these two ways, so each of them restores the noun from its resemblance to the verb.

[OBJECTION:] ʿAbd al-Q̲āhir said: 'This [explanation] is weak, because these nouns became similar to verbs due to being adjectives, or having the form of verbs [etc.], and these factors remain even when the article or annexation affect them. Therefore, it is not true that the resemblance has been removed. Moreover: [following] prepositions, and being a subject or object [of a verb], are [also] unique to nouns—yet when they affect a diptote, it remains a diptote.'

RESPONSE TO HIS FIRST POINT: annexation and the definite article are unique features of nouns, and as such, they strengthen even those nouns which have become less noun-like due to a resemblance to verbs. [To understand why, consider that] the default state of nouns is to accept inflection fully, but resemblance to verbs presents an impediment to this. When this impediment is itself opposed by something, then that impediment weakens and the default is restored.

RESPONSE TO THE SECOND POINT: the article and annexation are stronger than being a subject or object, because the former two are contraries (*ḍidd*) to nunation, and contraries are equal to each other in force. Since nunation is a sign of complete power, so too must be annexation and the definite article.

Enquiry 26

If you named a man Aḥmar (Red), this would be a diptote by consensus due to the combination of being a proper name and having the form of a verb. If you [subsequently] made it indefinite, then Sībawayh said that he would still consider it to be a diptote, whereas al-Akhfash said that he would restore its *ṣarf*.

In support of Sībawayh's opinion, the majority cite the following from Māzinī, who said: 'I said to al-Akhfash: "Why is it that you say *marartu bi-niswatin arbaʿin* ('I passed by four women') and treat [the last word] as a triptote despite it being an adjective upon the form of a verb?" He replied: "Because it is originally a noun."[1] So I said: "Therefore, you [should] treat Aḥmar likewise when it is the name of a man made indefinite, because it is originally an adjective"—and al-Akhfash had no convincing answer.'

I say: Māzinī's explanation is weak, because the *ṣarf* [re-established] for the word *arbaʿ* (four) was according to its default state, and the least of factors can be used to return something to its default. On the other hand, preventing *ṣarf* means going against the default [of nouns], and this requires a strong reason.

Rather, the proof of the veracity of Sībawayh's opinion is that [Aḥmar] is affected by the form of a verb and its being an original adjective.[2] These necessitate it being a diptote.

[To explain:] the first premise depends on establishing three things:

a. [Aḥmar] is on the form of a verb, which is obvious.
b. It is an adjective, as proper nouns which are made indefinite become signifiers for anything described by that name. If one says *rubba Zaydin ra'aytuhu* ('Perhaps I saw a Zayd'), this means 'Perhaps I saw a person called Zayd,' and it is known that being called something is a description, not a matter of essence.
c. It is an adjective *originally*, as evidenced by the fact that when *aḥmar* was an adjective, it meant 'having redness'. When it is made a proper noun, then made indefinite, it means 'being called by this name', which is an accidental matter attributed to the person. The two meanings share in being descriptions, but the first is a true adjective, while the second is relative; the common aspect is that they are descriptions.

What we have stated shows that [Aḥmar] has been affected by having the form of a verb and being an original adjective, so it follows that it should be a diptote.

1 In most cases, numbers are mentioned first, followed by the counted thing as *tamyīz*.

2 In other words, it is still an adjective, which is the difference between the author's account and that of Māzinī. See the elaboration below.

OBJECTION: 'A counter to your explanation is the proper noun that was not previously an adjective: when made indefinite, it enjoys *ṣarf* even though—according to what you have said—it is [now] adjectival.'

RESPONSE: although it has become adjectival upon being made indefinite, that is not *original* because it was not previously an adjective. This is different from *aḥmar*, which was an adjective; and something which is an adjective both now *and* previously is stronger as an adjective than that which was not. This clarifies the difference.

AL-AKHFASH SUPPORTED HIS OPINION by saying that the cause of *ṣarf* remains, namely being a noun, and the opposing factor is not effective. This is because [Aḥmar] is an indefinite proper noun: such a proper noun is qualified by 'indefinite' yet it remains a proper noun, which precludes it being an adjective. Having eliminated its being an adjective, the only factor remaining is its having the form of the verb, and this is not sufficient to make it a diptote.

RESPONSE: we have proven through reason that when the proper noun is made indefinite, it becomes—in reality—an adjective, so this argument falls.[1]

Enquiry 27

Sībawayh said—contra the Kūfans—that a single factor cannot make a noun into a diptote. His reasoning is that the cause of *ṣarf* is still present, namely being a noun. While two factors would be stronger than one [i.e. its being a noun], when only one is present the noun must remain upon its original state.

The Kūfans' argument is as explained previously. The following [poetic verse] is also cited in this connection: *wa-mā kāna Ḥiṣnun wa-lā Ḥābisun yafūqāni Mirdāsa fī majmaʿī* [without nunation].[2]

RESPONSE: the authentic transmission of this verse has *yafūqāni* shaykhiya *fī majmaʿī*.

1 One might also point out that if the word remains a proper noun as al-Akhfash said, then, together with the form of the verb, there are two factors.

2 The line was spoken by ʿAbbās b. Mirdās: 'Neither Ḥiṣn nor Ḥābis [fathers of two men who were given a larger gift upon entering Islam than Abbās was initially] was superior to Mirdās [his own father] in any assembly.' The author's dismissal of this narration appears unfounded: see Yaḥyā b. Sharaf al-Nawawī, *al-Minhāj sharḥ Ṣaḥīḥ Muslim b. al-Ḥajjāj*, ed. Khalīl b. Ma'mūn Shīḥā, 10 vols., Beirut: Dār al-Maʿrifa, 2012, vol. IV, p. 156. As Nawawī mentions, a simple response is to attribute the diptote here to 'poetic necessity'.

Enquiry 28

Sībawayh said: 'Diptotes have *fatḥ* in place of *jarr*.' Some objected that *fatḥ* is a term related to uninflected [words], while diptotes are not [wholly] uninflected.

RESPONSE: *fatḥ* is a name for the vowel itself, whether it is for inflected or uninflected.

Enquiry 29
[Cases and Functions]

There are three cases for nouns: nominative (*rafʿ*), accusative (*naṣb*) and genitive (*jarr*). Each of these signifies a meaning. The nominative signifies being the subject (*fāʿil*); the accusative signifies being the object (*mafʿūl*); and the genitive signifies being annexed (*iḍāfa*). As for dependent nouns (*tawābiʿ*), these adopt the vowels of those which they follow.

Enquiry 30

There are several reasons for the subject being nominative, the object accusative and the [second] annexed noun genitive:

1. The subject [or agent] is one, whereas objects are many, as a verb may take one, two or three [direct] objects, and then may have an object of purpose (*mafʿūl lahu*), as well as [one or both of] the two *ẓarf*s [indicating place and time], the cognate accusative (*maṣdar*) and circumstance (*ḥāl*).[1] Since there are so many objects, the lightest vowel—namely *naṣb*—was assigned to them. On the other hand, the small number of subjects led to the heaviest vowel being assigned—namely *rafʿ*—so that the increase in quantity would be reflected by an increase in amount, resulting in balance.[2]
2. There are three grades of existent:
   a. That which affects but is not affected: this is the strongest, and applies to the subject.
   b. That which is affected but does not affect: this is the weakest, and applies to the object.
   c. That which affects in one respect, and is affected in another: this is a middle grade which applies to the [second] annexed noun.

   The vowels, too, are three: the strongest is *ḍamma*, the weakest is *fatḥa*, and *kasra* is in-between. Each was assigned to its appropriate

1 The *ẓarf* is also known as *mafʿūl fīhi*, and the *maṣdar* is also known as *mafʿūl muṭlaq*. The inclusion of the *ḥāl* as an object is strange; cf. Enquiry 32 below.

2 See Enquiry 12 above.

grade: the strongest, i.e. *rafᶜ*, went to the subject, being the strongest. *Fatḥa*, as the weakest, went to the weakest, i.e. the object. Then *jarr*, in the middle, went to the annexed noun in the middle.

3. The subject has priority over the object, because a verb cannot do without a subject whereas it might not have an object. As such, the subject is pronounced while the breath is strong,[1] which is why it was assigned the heaviest vowel; and then the lightest vowel was assigned to that which is pronounced subsequently.

Enquiry 31

The nominative nouns (*marfūᶜāt*) are seven: the [verb's] subject (*fāᶜil*); the nominal subject (*mubtada'*) and predicate (*khabar*); the subject of *kāna* ('to be'), as well as of [the negating] *mā* and *lā* when performing the grammatical function of *laysa*; the predicate of [emphatic] *inna*; and the predicate of the genus-negating *lā*.

Al-Khalīl [b. Aḥmad] said that the original nominative is the *fāᶜil*, and the rest are made to resemble it. Sībawayh said that the original is the *mubtada'* and the rest are made to resemble that. Al-Akhfash, on the other hand, stated that both are original.

Al-Khalīl argued that the *fāᶜil* is worthier of being assigned the nominative case than the *mubtada'*, and that being worthier (*awlawiyya*) entails that it came first (*awwaliyya*).

ELUCIDATION OF THE FIRST POINT: if you said *ḍaraba Zayd Bakr* ('Struck, Zayd, Bakr') without vowels [after the nouns], it would not be known which of them was the striker and which was struck. However, if you said *Zayd qā'im* ('Zayd, standing') without end vowels, you would know simply from the two words which is the subject and which the predicate. Therefore, the verbal subject is in greater need of inflection, and it must be the original.

ON THE SECOND POINT: being nominative is shared by the nominal subject and its predicate, so this feature does nothing to distinguish one from the other. On the other hand, [being nominative] does distinguish the verbal subject [from the object]. This proves that *rafᶜ* is the right of the *fāᶜil*; but since the nominal subject shares in being a subject (*musnad ilayhi*), it is also nominative in order to reflect this resemblance.

1 Reading *al-nafas qawī* for *al-nafs qawiyya*. The latter could still be interpreted with the same sense.

Sībawayh's argument is that the nominal sentence has precedence over the verbal sentence, so the *iʿrāb* of the former should take precedence over that of the latter.

RESPONSE: the verb is the original form of attribution (*isnād*) to other things, so it is the verbal sentence which takes precedence, in which case this argument supports al-Khalīl's opinion.

Enquiry 32

There are five [accusative] objects (*mafāʿīl*), because the agent must have an action, which is expressed by the cognate accusative (*maṣdar*); the action must occur in a time [the *mafʿūl fīhi*] and the agent must have an objective[1] [*mafʿūl lahu*]. The action might affect another thing which is the direct object (*mafʿūl bihi*), and may occur in a place [also *mafʿūl fīhi*] and with another thing [*mafʿūl maʿahu*]. This explains the various accusatives.

There are some rational enquiries in this connection:

a. The cognate accusative may be the same [entity] as the direct object. For example, in saying *khalaqa Allāhu al-ʿālama* ('God created the world'), if the 'creation' of the world is distinct from the world itself, then either it is pre-eternal—in which case the world, in turn, is pre-eternal and non-created—or temporal, in which case it requires another creation in order to be created, leading to infinite regression.
b. The actions of God are not bound by time: if that were the case, then the creation of that time would itself require another time, leading to infinite regression.
c. The actions of God are free from objectives (*gharaḍ*)[2] because such, if pre-eternal, would necessitate the pre-eternity of the action; and if temporal, would lead to infinite regression and absurdity.

Enquiry 33

There are four opinions concerning [the identity of] the agent acting upon the object to make it accusative:

A. The Baṣrans said that the verb alone makes its subject nominative and its object accusative.
B. The Kūfans said that the combination of verb and subject cause the object to be accusative.

1 The printed editions have *ʿaraḍ* (accident) here, but the context suggests that it should be *gharaḍ*.

2 Again, read in place of *ʿaraḍ*. For discussion of the issue of divine 'motivation' and the context in which the objective has here been denied, see Shihadeh, *Teleological Ethics*, p. 97.

C. Hishām b. Muʿāwiya, a Kūfan, said that it is the subject only.

D. Khalaf al-Aḥmar, also a Kūfan,[1] held that the agent in the case of the subject is the fact of its being a subject (*fāʿiliyya*), while for the object it is the fact of being an object (*mafʿūliyya*).

The Baṣrans' argument is that an agent must be connected to the thing acted upon; the two nouns [subject and object] have no connection to each other, so one cannot act upon the other. By elimination, the agent must be the verb.

The opponents of this view argued that a single agent cannot have two effects, as it is [rationally] proven that only one effect comes from one [agent].

RESPONSE: this only applies to effective causes (*mūjibāt*), not to signifiers (*muʿarrifāt*).[2]

Khalaf's argument is that 'being a subject' is an attribute of the subject, and 'being an object' is an attribute of the object, whereas the verb is separate from both: and explaining a ruling by means of something present in the place of that ruling is preferable to resorting to something external to it.

RESPONSE: the verb is something apparent, whereas 'being a subject/object' is obscure: and explaining the ruling by means of something apparent is preferable to doing so with the obscure. And God knows best.

1 Khalaf was a Baṣran.

2 See Enquiry 7 in the next chapter for this distinction again, but with *mu'aththirāt* in place of *mūjibāt*.

Chapter Seven
INFLECTION OF VERBS

The word *aʿūdhu* ('I seek refuge') entails the attribution of a verb to its subject, which leads us to the following enquiries:

Enquiry 1

In the context of grammar, we do not intend the meanings of *fiʿl* (verb) and *fāʿil* (subject) used by the scholars of theology (*uṣūl*). We say *māta Zayd* ('Zayd died'), even though he was not the agent of that action—grammatically, 'died' is a verb and 'Zayd' is its subject. Rather, the verb is a single word which denotes that the [action expressed by] the verbal noun (*maṣdar*) has obtained for something unspecified in a [specified][1] time. If we mention explicitly that thing for which the action has obtained, then that is the subject. Clearly, saying that it has obtained 'for him' is broader than saying either that it is by his creation and volition (like *qāma*, 'he stood') or that it is involuntary (like *māta*, 'he died').

OBJECTION: just as the action obtains in the subject, it may obtain in the object (*mafʿūl*).

RESPONSE: the very form of the verb entails that the action obtains for something, namely the subject. However, it does not so entail for the object, as there are intransitive verbs which do not take an object.

Enquiry 2

The verb must be placed before the subject, because the verb—whether affirmative or negated—entails the existence of something to which it is attributed. As such, the mental conception of the verb's quiddity leads to the [conception] of something to which the mind can attribute that verb. A thing which follows is conceptually secondary to that which it follows; hence, once it is [shown to be] necessary for the verb to precede the subject conceptually, it must be likewise in order of mention.

OBJECTION: there is no difference in our minds between *ḍaraba Zayd* and *Zaydun ḍaraba* [both 'Zayd struck'].

1 The printed editions have 'unspecified time'.

RESPONSE: the difference is clear. If you were to say *Zayd* alone, there would be no obligation, after conceptualising the meaning of this word, to consider any matter attributed to it. On the other hand, when we understand the meaning of *ḍaraba*, the mind necessarily judges that this meaning must be attributed to something.

Once this is known, then we say: upon [hearing] *ḍaraba Zayd*, the mind rules that striking must be attributed to something or other, and then it rules that this thing is Zayd who has just been mentioned. Thus Zayd is revealed to be that thing to which the mind had attributed the striking. Then the word *Zayd* becomes a subject (*mukhbar ʿanhu*) and *ḍaraba* is a verbal sentence coming as a predicate for that subject (*mubtada'*).[1]

Enquiry 3

It is said that the subject is, as it were, a part of the verb, whereas the object is not. This is demonstrated in several ways:

1. The [verb with subject pronoun suffix] is pronounced *ḍarabtu* ('I struck'), with the third radical [*bā'*] unvowelled in order to avoid having four vowelled letters in a single word, something generally avoided [by the Arabs]. They tolerated [the likes of] *baqaratun* (cow) because the [feminine ending] *tā'* is additional. They also tolerated [four vowels] in the case of the [suffix] object: for example, *ḍarabaka* ('He struck you'), which indicates that they considered the subject to be integral to the verb, whereas the object is separate.
2. When you say *al-Zaydāni qāmā* ('The two Zayds stood'), the subject pronoun is made explicit. For consistency, this entails the presence of an implied pronoun to which the verb is ascribed, when saying *Zaydun ḍaraba* ('Zayd struck').
3. A RATIONAL PROOF: saying *ḍaraba* means that striking has obtained for something or other in the past. As such, that thing is part of the meaning of *ḍaraba*, which shows that the subject is part of the verb.

Enquiry 4

There are several scenarios in which the pronoun precedes explicit mention [of the noun]:

1. Occurring in form and meaning; for example, *ḍaraba ghulāmuhu*

1 It is as though something has been missed out in this paragraph, as the latter part seems to describe the nominal sentence: *Zaydun ḍaraba*. Otherwise, it could be that the latter explanation is not intended in strictly grammatical terms.

Zaydan ('His servant struck Zayd'). The well-known position is that this is not allowed, as it involves making *ghulām* nominative by means of *ḍaraba* and fixing it in its place, after which it is not allowed to move it. In that case, the *hā'* is an example of a pronoun occurring before its explicit [noun].

As for the poetic line of al-Nābigha [in which this occurs]—*jazā* rabbuhu *ʿannī ʿAdiyya 'bna Ḥātimin* ('May his Lord, on my behalf, reward ʿAdī b. Ḥātim...')—the response is that the pronoun refers to a prior explicit referent. However, Ibn Jinnī said: 'Unlike the majority, I allow that the pronoun in *rabbuhu* should refer to ʿAdī,' and then he provided a very lengthy justification.

I would say that the best way to support this is to say: the verb in and of itself has no need for an object; however, a transitive (*mutaʿaddī*) verb is not free of this need. This is because the subject is the agent (*mu'aththir*) and the object is the recipient (*qābil*), and the [transitive] verb needs both of these. Neither has priority over the other, except in the sense that the subject, as agent, is nobler than the recipient and is given priority over the object accordingly. We have clarified that the transitive verb requires both agent and recipient; as such, it must be allowed for the object to precede the subject, just as it is allowed for the subject to precede the object.

2. The object precedes the subject[1] in form but not meaning; for example, *ḍaraba ghulāmahu Zaydun* ('Struck his slave, did Zayd'), in which *ghulāmahu* is the object and *Zayd* the subject. The object follows the subject in rank: therefore, even though it has preceded verbally, it comes later syntactically.
3. That it occurs in meaning, not in form: e.g. the verse, *wa idhi 'btalā Ibrāhīma Rabbuhu* ('When Abraham was tried by his Lord') (Q.II.124), in which the pronoun does not precede explicit mention verbally, but it does so syntactically in that the subject is syntactically prior. If it were brought forward verbally, that would result in a pronoun before explicit mention.

Enquiry 5

The subject may be an explicit [noun], as in *ḍaraba Zaydun*; or an apparent pronoun, as in *ḍarabtu* ('I struck') and *ḍarabnā* ('We struck'); or an implicit (*mustakinn*) pronoun, as in *Zaydun ḍaraba*, in which you intend

1 That is, resulting in the pronoun preceding the explicit mention likewise.

a subject [within the verb] and make the [resulting] sentence the predicate for *Zayd*. Another example of an implicit subject is to say *idhā kāna ghadan fa'tinī* ('When it is tomorrow, visit me'), i.e. 'When *what we are upon* is tomorrow.'

Enquiry 6

The verb may [also] be implied. If it is said *man faʿal* ('Who did it?'), you say *Zayd*, i.e. Zayd did it. Of this type is the verse: *wa-in aḥadun min al-mushrikīna istajāraka* ('If any one of the polytheists seeks your protection') (Q.ix.6), which, in terms of meaning, is: *in istajāraka aḥadun min al-mushrikīna*.[1]

Enquiry 7

If there are two verbs, one conjoined to the other, followed by a noun which could be acted upon by either of them, then there are two scenarios: either the two verbs denote a similar action, or two different actions. In each scenario, the following noun may be either singular or otherwise, and this amounts to four possibilities:

1. Two verbs denote a single action and are followed by a singular noun; for example, *qāma wa-qaʿada Zaydun* ('Zayd stood and sat'). Al-Farrā' claimed that both verbs act upon *Zayd* [to make it nominative]. The well-known opinion is that this is not allowed because it entails explaining a single ruling by two causes; rather, since the closest [i.e. the latter verb] is worthier due to its proximity, it must be designated [the agent]. Al-Farrā' responded to this, saying that, whereas explaining a single ruling by two causes is impermissible in the case of effective causes (*mu'aththirāt*), it is permitted for signifiers (*muʿarrifāt*).

   RESPONSE: a signifier effects knowledge (*maʿrifa*), so the matter returns to two effective causes for a single effect.
2. That the noun is non-singular; for example, *qāma wa-qaʿada akhawāka* ('Your two brothers stood and sat'). Here, you may make [the dual noun] nominative by the first or second verb. If the first, then you say: *qāma wa-*qaʿadā *akhawāka* [with the pronoun suffixed to the second], because it is as though you said: *qāma akhawāka wa-qaʿadā*. If you make the second verb the agent, you place the

1 Because the conditional particle *in* should be followed by a verb, the actual placing of the verb after the semantic subject is considered to indicate an implied verb occurring after the particle, i.e. *in istajāraka aḥadun istajāraka* (see Zamakhsharī's *Kashshāf* under Q.ix.6).

subject pronoun on the first, because a verb must have an explicit or implicit subject: qāmā *wa-qaʿadā akhawāka*.

The Baṣrans considered the second verb as the worthier agent, whereas the Kūfans said it should be the first. The Baṣrans argued that since both cannot be the agent, it can only be one, and proximity is a preponderator: so the nearest should be the agent. The Kūfans said that if the second is assumed to be the agent, then the first must be ascribed to a pronoun, resulting in a pronoun prior to explicit mention—and this is worthier of being avoided.

3. If the verbs denote two contradictory effects and the following noun is singular, then the Baṣrans said—contra the Kūfans—that the nearest is considered the agent, supporting this with the following arguments:
   a. In the verse *ātūnī ufrigh ʿalayhi qiṭran* ('Bring me, that I may pour over it molten lead') (Q.XVIII.96), there are two verbs, each requiring an object. The agent making *qiṭran* accusative is either *ātūnī* or *ufrigh*. It cannot be the former, as that would mean that after *ātūnī qiṭran* one would have to say *ufrigh*-hu *ʿalayhi* [with a pronoun]. Since that is not the case, we know that the agent is *ufrigh*.
   b. In the verse *hāʾumu iqraʾū kitābiyah* ('Take, read my book') (Q.LXIX.19), if the agent were the farther [i.e. former], it would have to read *iqraʾūhu* [with a pronoun].

      The Kūfans responded to these two arguments by saying that they [merely] show the permissibility of deeming the proximate verb to be the agent, which is not the point of contention. Rather, the dispute is over the permissibility of considering the farther verb as the agent, which [the Baṣrans] reject, while nothing in these verses supports this rejection.
   c. One says *mā jāʾanī min aḥadin* ('No one at all came to me'), in which the verb effects the nominative, whereas the preposition effects the genitive. However, the preposition is given precedence due to its proximity.
   d. Since there must be an agent and they cannot both be agents, there must be a way for one to be preponderant over the other. Proximity is a preponderator, so considering the proximate verb as the agent is worthier.

The KŪFANS argued [that the first is the agent] based on the following:

a. We have explained[1] that if the noun following the two verbs is in the dual or plural, then treating the second as the agent results in a pronoun for the first, which comes before explicit mention, which is not allowed. Therefore, it is necessary in that case to treat the first verb as the agent, and it follows that the same should be said concerning the singular noun, for consistency.

b. The first verb finds a [noun] to act upon without any impediment, as a [transitive] verb must take an object. As for the second verb, it finds that [noun] after the first verb has acted upon it, which prevents the action of the second. It is clear that an agent without any impediment is preferable to one which faces an impediment.

4. If the noun following the two verbs is dual or plural, then, taking the second verb as the agent, you would say *ḍarabtu wa-ḍarabanī al-Zaydān* and *ḍarabtu wa-ḍarabanī al-Zaydūn* ('I struck [the Zayds] and the Zayds struck me').[2] However, if you take the first as the agent, you would say *ḍarabtu wa-ḍarabānī al-Zaydayn* and *ḍarabtu wa-ḍarabūnī al-Zaydīn* ('I struck the Zayds and they struck me').[3]

Enquiry 8

Imru' al-Qays said:

> *fa-law anna mā asʿā li-adnā maʿīshatin;*
> *kafānī wa-lam aṭlub qalīlun min al-māli,*
> *wa lākinnamā asʿā li-majdin mu'aththalin;*
> *wa-qad yudriku 'l-majda 'l-mu'aththala amthālī*
>
> If I were to strive for the least of living,
> a little wealth would suffice me and I would not seek;
> But I only strive for opulent glory,
> and opulent glory can be attained by my like.

In these verses, the words *kafānī wa-lam aṭlub* are not directed to a single entity. Rather, *kafānī* is connected to *qalīlun min al-māl*, while *lam aṭlub* cannot be, otherwise it would mean: 'If I were to strive for the least of living, I would not seek a little wealth.' Since the particle *law* denotes one thing being negated due to another, it would follow that

1 See point 2 above.
2 The words for 'the Zayds' are nominative here.
3 The words for 'the Zayds' are accusative here.

he was not striving for the least of living and yet sought a little wealth, which is contradictory. Therefore, the meaning is: 'If I were to strive for the least of living, a little wealth would suffice me and I would not seek *dominion*.' As such, the two verbs are not directed to a single entity.

Let us suffice with this quantity of Arabic linguistics before delving into the exegesis.[1]

1 It is noteworthy that the author himself makes the distinction between what has preceded and *tafsīr* itself, although he has framed the linguistic discussion around *aʿūdhu bi'Llāh*. That is not to say that the following exegesis does not have lengthy considerations of theoretical aspects, including points of language. The core of the exegesis is in Book III, Chapter Five.

PART TWO: NARRATED AND RATIONAL EXEGESIS OF THE *ISTIᶜĀDHA*[1]

Chapter Eight
JURISTIC ISSUES CONNECTED TO THE *ISTIᶜĀDHA*[2]

Enquiry 1
[Time of Recitation]

The majority agree that the *istiᶜādha* is to be recited before the *Fātiḥa*, whereas it is related from [Ibrāhīm] al-Nakhaᶜī that it is after. This is also the opinion of Dāwūd al-Iṣfahānī [al-Ẓāhirī] and one of the two opinions transmitted from Ibn Sīrīn, i.e. that a person recites the whole of *Sūrat al-Fātiḥa*, followed by *āmīn* (amen), and then says the *istiᶜādha*.

THE FIRST GROUP supported their view with the *ḥadīth* from Jubayr b. Muṭᶜim that the Prophet (may God bless him and grant him peace) said, upon opening his prayer, *Allāhu akbaru kabīran* ('God is greater, greatly') three times, *wa'l-ḥamdu li'Llāhi kathīran* ('Praise belongs to God, profusely') and *subḥāna Allāhi bukratan wa-aṣīlan* ('Glory be to God, by morning and by evening') three times, followed by: 'I seek refuge in God from the accursed Satan: his incitement (*hamz*), blow (*nafkh*) and breath (*nafth*).'[3]

THE OTHER GROUP cited the verse 'When (*idhā*) you recite the Qur'ān, seek God's protection from Satan, the rejected one' (Q.XVI.98), which indicates that the recitation of the Qur'ān is a protasis [of a conditional] (*sharṭ*), and the seeking of refuge is an apodosis (*jazā'*). Since the apodosis should follow the protasis, the *istiᶜādha* should come after reciting [some] Qur'ān.

They further argued that this is appropriate to reason because one

1 The remaining four chapters in Book I originally begin again at 'Chapter One', but I have relabelled them to allow for more consistency in the volume as a whole.

2 Also to the rest of the *sūra* and the whole Qur'ān.

3 Recorded by Ibn Mājah and Abū Dāwūd. Some narrations have an explanation appended for these three afflictions, respectively: seizures, arrogance and [blameworthy] poetry.

who recites the Qur'ān has become deserving of tremendous reward, which would be nullified if any self-satisfaction (*ʿujb*) polluted the deed. This is according to the Prophetic description of three things which cause destruction (*thalāthun muhlikāt*), of which one is 'a person being impressed by himself'.[1] For this reason, Almighty God has instructed him to seek refuge from Satan, lest he cause him to commit an act after his recitation of the Qur'ān which nullifies the reward of that act of obedience.

It is incorrect, say this group, to suggest that the meaning of 'When you recite the Qur'ān' is 'When you *intend* to recite,' as in the other verse: 'When you stand for prayer, wash your faces…' (Q.v.6), which means 'When you *intend* to stand for prayer.' This cannot be so, they say, because: abandoning the apparent meaning in a case where there is evidence [obligating that] does not necessitate abandoning it in all other cases, without evidence.

THE MAJORITY OF THE JURISTS [i.e. the first group] said: certainly, the verse can mean 'When you intend to recite,' and once this possibility is established, it must be adopted in order to reconcile between the verse and the Prophetic narration we have cited. From a rational perspective, this is strengthened by saying that the purpose of seeking refuge is to avoid satanic whispers during recitation. God Almighty said: 'Never sent We a Messenger or a Prophet before you but when He recited (the message) Satan proposed (opposition) in respect of that which he recited thereof' (Q.xxii.52).[2] It is for this reason that God instructed [the servant] to begin by seeking refuge.

I say: there is a third position which can be performed in order to combine the two evidences as much as possible, namely to pronounce the *istiʿādha* before recitation—thereby acting on the Prophetic narration—and [again] afterwards—thereby acting upon the [verse of] Qur'ān.

Enquiry 2
[Ruling]

According to ʿAṭā' [b. Abī Rabāḥ], the *istiʿādha* is obligatory for every recitation, whether inside or outside of prayer (*ṣalāh*). Ibn Sīrīn said that

1 Recorded in the *Musnad* of al-Bazzār, *al-Awsaṭ* of Ṭabarānī and others—S.I.

2 I have selected Pickthall's translation here as an example of those who interpreted *tamannī* as recitation, which is assumed in the citation of the verse in this context. However, this interpretation—which is linked to the tale of the 'satanic verses'—is hotly contested on philological as well as theological grounds. See Ḥamīd al-Dīn al-Farāhī, *Taʿlīqāt fī tafsīr al-Qur'ān al-karīm*, ed. ʿUbayd Allāh al-Farāhī, 2 vols., Azamgarh: al-Dā'ira al-Ḥamīdiyya, 2010, vol. 1, p. 423.

if a man says it just once in his life, then that would be sufficient to discharge the obligation.

The majority of scholars said that it is not an obligation, basing this on the fact that the Prophet (may God bless him and grant him peace) did not teach it to the Bedouin[1] among the acts of prayer. However, it could be pointed out that the relevant *ḥadīth* does not clarify all the obligatory acts (*wājibāt*) of the prayer, so the lack of mention of the *isti*ʿ*ādha* does not entail it being non-obligatory.

ʿAṭā' supported his view that the *Isti*ʿ*ādha* is obligatory with the following:

a. The Prophet (may God bless him and grant him peace) recited it constantly, so it becomes obligatory with reference to God's saying 'Follow him' (Q.vii.158).
b. The word *ista*ʿ*idh* (seek refuge) [in Q.xvi.98] is a command, which entails obligation. Moreover, it must be considered obligatory upon every recitation, because in 'When you recite the Qur'ān, seek God's protection' the ruling [i.e. seeking refuge] has been mentioned after a compatible description (*waṣf munāsib*) [i.e. recitation], which indicates an explanation of cause. As such, the ruling reoccurs with the reoccurrence of the cause (ʿ*illa*).[2]
c. God prescribed the *isti*ʿ*ādha* for the purpose of deflecting the evil of the rejected Satan, as implied by the verse: 'Seek God's protection from Satan, the rejected one' (Q.xvi.98). Deflecting Satan's evil is obligatory, and anything that is necessary for discharging an obligation is itself obligatory. Therefore, it must be that the *isti*ʿ*ādha* is obligatory.
d. The way of caution necessitates *isti*ʿ*ādha*.

This completes our summary of this issue.

Enquiry 3

The majority consider seeking refuge before recitation to be recommended. Mālik [b. Anas] said that it is not [pronounced] in obligatory [prayers], but it is in the night prayers of Ramaḍān.

1 This is an allusion to the *ḥadīth* of the Bedouin man (*al-musī' ṣalātahu*) who was ordered to repeat his prayer several times until he admitted that he needed the Prophet to teach him all its steps. This *ḥadīth* is referred to at a number of points in the juristic discussions of this book; for example, Book III, Chapter Four, Enquiry 2.

2 See Rāzī, *al-Maḥṣūl*, vol. v, p. 157; Imran Nyazee, *Islamic Jurisprudence*, Petaling Jaya: The Other Press, 2003, p. 224.

Our view [of obligation] is supported by the verse and Prophetic narration previously cited, both of which indicate obligation. If not, then it is certainly no less than recommended.

Enquiry 4

Shāfiʿī (may God be pleased with him) said in *al-Umm*: 'It is narrated that when ʿAbd Allāh b. ʿUmar recited, he pronounced the *istiʿādha* inaudibly, whereas it is narrated from Abū Hurayra that he did so audibly,' concluding: 'It is therefore permissible both to say it aloud or silently.' In *al-Imlā'*,[1] he said: 'He should say the *istiʿādha* audibly, but if he does so inaudibly, there is no harm'—which shows that saying it audibly is preferable in his view.

I say: the *istiʿādha* is always recited between opening [the prayer] and the *Fātiḥa*. If we consider it as connected to the former, it should be pronounced inaudibly; but if to the latter, it should be said aloud. That being said, it is closer in similarity to the opening, given that both are optional (*nāfila*) in jurists' terms. Also, pronouncing audibly (*jahr*) is an existent quality, as opposed to inaudible pronunciation (*ikhfā'*) which is simply the absence of that quality, and absence is the default.

Enquiry 5

Shāfiʿī (may God be pleased with him) said in *al-Umm*: 'Some said that the *istiʿādha* is pronounced in every prayer cycle (*rakʿa*)...whereas I say that it is only in the first cycle.'

He could support this by the fact that absence is the default, and that we have only been instructed to seek refuge by the verse 'When (*idhā*) you recite the Qur'ān' (Q.xvi.98), in which [the conditional particle] *idhā* does not denote universality (*ʿumūm*).

Someone could reply: we have stated[2] that a ruling being made dependent on a compatible description indicates causality, so the ruling should reoccur with the reoccurrence of the cause. And God knows best.

Enquiry 6
[Wording]

Almighty God said in *Sūrat al-Naḥl*: 'When you recite the Qur'ān, seek God's protection from the rejected Satan' (Q.xvi.98). In another *sūra*, He said: 'Indeed, He is the Hearing (*al-Samīʿ*), the Knowing (*al-ʿAlīm*)'

1 This book has been lost; it is considered to belong to Shāfiʿī's later school.

2 See under Enquiry 2 above.

(Q.xli.36); and in a third: 'Indeed, He is hearing and knowing' (Q.vii.200).[1]

On this basis, the scholars differed. Shāfiʿī said that one must say *aʿūdhu bi'Llāh min al-shayṭān al-rajīm* ('I seek refuge in God from the rejected Satan'), and this is also the opinion of Abū Ḥanīfa. [Supporters of this view] say: this is because it accords with the wording of the verse [Q.xvi.98] as well as the text of the Prophetic narration from Jubayr b. Muṭʿim cited earlier. Aḥmad [b. Ḥanbal] said: it is best to say [the above, adding] *innahu huwa al-Samīʿ al-ʿAlīm* ('Indeed, He is the Hearing, the Knowing') in order to combine the two verses.

Some of our [Shāfiʿī] companions said that the ideal is to say *aʿūdhu bi'Llāh al-Samīʿ al-ʿAlīm min al-shayṭān al-rajīm* ('I seek refuge in God, the Hearing, the Knowing, from the rejected Satan'), because this, too, combines the two verses. Bayhaqī recorded in his *Sunan*, with his chain of narration to Abū Saʿīd al-Khudrī that he said: 'When the Messenger of God (may God bless him and grant him peace) arose [for prayer] at night, he made *takbīr*[2] three times, then said: "I seek refuge in God, the Hearing, the Knowing, from the rejected Satan."'

Thawrī and Awzāʿī stated that the best is to say *aʿūdhu bi'Llāh min al-shayṭān al-rajīm inna Allāh huwa al-Samīʿ al-ʿAlīm* ('I seek refuge in God from the rejected Satan. Indeed, God is the Hearing, the Knowing'). Al-Ḍaḥḥāk narrated from Ibn ʿAbbās that the first thing which [Archangel] Gabriel revealed to Muḥammad (may God bless him and grant him peace) was: 'Say, O Muḥammad: I seek refuge (*astaʿīdhu*) in God, the Hearing, the Knowing, from the rejected Satan,' followed by: 'Say: In the Name of God, the Compassionate, the Merciful. "Recite in the Name of your Lord, Who created..." (Q.xcvi.1).'[3]

In any case: the act of seeking refuge purifies the heart of all things which prevent being consumed in God; then mentioning His Name[4] directs the heart towards reverence of the Divine Majesty. And God is the Guide.

Enquiry 7

Is the *istiʿādha* in prayer for the sake of the [Qur'ān] recitation, or the prayer itself? Abū Ḥanīfa and Muḥammad [al-Shaybānī] held that it is for the recitation, whereas Abū Yūsuf considered it to be for the prayer.

1 These are cited in particular because they contain the same instruction to 'seek refuge'. See also Q.xl.56, which concludes: 'He is the Hearing, the Seeing'.

2 I.e. said *Allāhu akbar*.

3 This is recorded in Ṭabari's exegesis—S.I.

4 I.e. saying 'In the Name of God'.

There are two practical implications of this dispute:

1. Does a person being led in prayer say the *istiʿādha* behind his *imām* (leader), or not? According to the first opinion, he would not, as he does not recite; but according to the second, he would. [Abū Ḥanīfa's and Muḥammad's] opinion is supported by the verse 'When you recite the Qur'ān…' (Q.xvi.98), in which seeking refuge was made conditional on recitation. Since the follower does not recite, he does not seek refuge. Abū Yūsuf's argument is that if the *istiʿādha* were linked to recitation, it would have to be repeated upon every recitation, which is not the case. Since it actually reoccurs with the occurrence of every prayer, it is seen to be for the prayer, not the recitation.
2. When commencing the ʿĪd prayer, does the *imām* say the *istiʿādha* between saying *subḥānak Allāhumma wa-bi-ḥamdik* ('Glory and praise is for You, O God') [etc.] and saying [additional] *takbīrs*, or not? According to the former two, he says the *takbīrs* and then seeks refuge when he commences recitation. Abū Yūsuf would place the *istiʿādha* before the *takbīrs*.

There are a number of remaining enquiries in the *Fātiḥa* which we shall now address:

Enquiry 8
[Proper Recitation]

The Prophetic way (*sunna*) is for the Qur'ān to be recited with *tartīl*, as instructed in the verse: 'And recite the Qur'ān in measured rhythm (*tartīl*)' (Q.lxxiii.4). It means to pronounce the letters and words clearly and distinctly, and its benefit is that one who recites in this way will understand the words being recited, and the meanings will reach the listeners. As for swift recitation, neither the reciter nor the listener will comprehend it. Therefore, *tartīl* is preferred.

This is the purport of the narration of Abū Dāwūd with his chain from [ʿAbd Allāh] b. ʿUmar that he said: the Messenger of God (may God bless him and grant him peace) said: 'It will be said to the companion of the Qur'ān: "Recite and rise, and recite measuredly as you used to do in the [former] world."' Abū Sulaymān al-Khaṭṭābī said: 'It has been reported that the number of verses in the Qur'ān accords with the number of levels in Paradise. It will be said to the reciter: recite and rise through the levels in proportion to what you would recite of the Qur'ān. So whoever manages to recite the entire Qur'ān would attain the farthest reaches of Paradise.'

Enquiry 9

When a person recites the Qur'ān aloud, the *sunna* is to perfect the recitation. Abū Dāwūd narrated via al-Barā' b. ʿĀzib that the Messenger of God (may God bless him and grant him peace) said: 'Beautify the Qur'ān with your voices.'

Enquiry 10
[Difficult Letters]

The stance I adopt is that confusing between the letters *ḍād* and *ẓā'* does not nullify the prayer. This is because they are extremely similar and difficult to distinguish, which means that one should not be held accountable in this regard. The following points explain their similarity:

a. They are both [voiced] letters of *jahr*.[1]
b. They are both [fricative] letters of *rakhāwa*.[2]
c. They are both [strongly velarised] letters of *iṭbāq*.
d. Although *ẓā'* is articulated between the tip of the tongue and the upper incisors, and *ḍād* from the front of the tongue's edge together with the corresponding molars, the fact that *ḍād* is somewhat spread out—as a result of being fricative—means that its articulation point approaches that of *ẓā'*.
e. The pronunciation of the *ḍād* is unique to the Arabs. The Prophet (may God bless him and grant him peace) said: 'I am the most eloquent one to speak [the language of] *ḍād*.'[3]

These factors explain the similarity between the two letters and the difficulty in differentiating between them. On that basis, we say: if this difference were significant, it would have been asked about in the era of the Messenger of God (may God bless him and grant him peace) and his Companions, especially once the non-Arabs began to embrace Islam. Since there is no record of this query being raised at all, we know that distinguishing between these two letters is not a matter of accountability (*taklīf*).

Enquiry 11

[Authorities] differed over the velarised *lām* belonging to eloquent dia-

1 This term in *tajwīd*—the science concerned with pronunciation of the Qur'ān—is defined classically in terms of 'strong dependence on the articulation point'. However, modern Arabic phonetics uses this term for voiced letters. See Ghānim al-Ḥamad, *Abḥāth jadīda fī ʿilm al-aṣwāt wa'l-tajwīd*, Amman: Dār ʿAmmār, 2011, pp. 289–291.

2 Classical definitions pertain to 'flow of voice (or sound)'. It should also be noted that the *ḍād* among modern Qur'ān reciters is manifested more like a stop than a fricative.

3 Scholars have described this as a baseless narration, albeit with a true meaning.

lects. However, even assuming that it is eloquent, they agreed that it may not be velarised when vowelled with *kasra*. This is because the transition between *kasra* and the velarised *lām*[1] is difficult for the tongue, so it should not be counted as [eloquent].

Enquiry 12
[Multiple Readings]

There is consensus that it is forbidden to recite in prayer the non-canonical (*shādhdh*) readings (*qirā'āt*) of the Qur'ān, such as saying *al-ḥamdi li'Llāh* or *al-ḥamdu lu'Llāh*.[2] The evidence rules out reciting these ways at all, because if they were from the Qur'ān, they would have to be so famous as to reach the level of successive mass transmission (*tawātur*).[3] Since that is not the case, we know that they are not Qur'ān. Although we overlook this proof when it comes to recitation outside of the prayer, it is necessary to consider such recitation inside prayer prohibited, as per the default.

Enquiry 13

The majority agree that the well-known recitations[4] have been mass-transmitted. However, there is a problem in this regard: if they have indeed been mass-transmitted, then it would likewise be known by mass transmission that Almighty God has made them equivalent to each other and allowed people to choose between them. If that is the case, then preferring some over others would be against this ruling established by mass transmission; and those who did so would be guilty of wrongdoing (*fisq*), if not

1 When discussing in this order, this would explain the *lām* being light (non-velar) in the likes of *li'Llāh* and *bi'Llāh*. See Book II, Chapter Two, Enquiry 2 below.

2 These two are based on making one vowel match another, i.e. a matter of pronunciation only. See Khaṭīb, *Muʿjam al-qirā'āt*, vol. 1, p. 4.

3 This is the transmission by one large contingent to another from every generation, rather than chains of individuals or small groups. It is taken for granted that this applies to the Qur'ān and it is generally considered a prerequisite for any reading of a word to be accepted among the canonical *qirā'āt*. However, the definition of *tawātur* in relation to *qirā'āt* is not precisely that used in jurisprudence (*uṣūl al-fiqh*), nor is it necessarily applicable to every variation of every word within the ten canonical readings (known as *al-qirā'āt al-mutawātira*). With regards to canonisation and relegation to *shādhdh*, see Aḥmad ʿAlī al-Imām, *Variant Readings of the Qur'an*, Herndon, VA: IIIT, 1998; Shady Hekmat Nasser, *The Transmission of the Variant Readings of the Qur'ān*, Leiden: Brill, 2012.

4 This is apparently a reference to the Seven (from among the Ten) canonical readings; see Rufayda, *al-Naḥw wa-kutub al-tafsīr*, vol. II, pp. 820–1.

unbelief (*kufr*). However, we observe that each of these reciters[1] adopts a particular style of recitation, making it binding on people and forbidding them from others: this would mean they are guilty of what we have mentioned.

On the other hand, if we should say that these recitations have reached us by solitary reports (*āḥād*) rather than mass transmission, then the Qur'ān would fall from its level of decisiveness and certainty—and this is rejected by consensus.

RESPONSE:[2] some of the recitations are mass-transmitted, such that there is no dispute among the Muslims over the permissibility of reciting any of them, while some others have come through singular narrations. However, the latter fact does not remove the Qur'ān *in toto* from the sphere of certainty. And God knows best.

1 I.e. the Imāms of recitation. Each had a selection (*ikhtiyār*) from narrated readings which he preferred and taught his students, but this does not entail rejecting other authentic and authoritative readings. See Imām, *Variant Readings*, p. 144.

2 In this response (and in some of what precedes it), what is meant by individual 'recitations' is each way of pronouncing a particular word etc., as opposed to the meaning of 'recitation' as one of the compiled methods of reciting from cover to cover, via a particular authority.

Chapter Nine
RATIONAL ENQUIRIES CONCERNING THE *ISTIʿĀDHA*

The discussions in this chapter concern five pillars: the seeking of refuge (*istiʿādha*) itself; the seeker (*mustaʿīdh*); the giver of refuge (*mustaʿādh bihi*); the one from whom refuge is sought (*mustaʿādh minhu*); and the purpose of seeking refuge.[1]

The First Pillar: The *Istiʿādha*

Enquiry 1: Linguistic Derivation:

Aʿūdhu is derived from the [verbal noun] *ʿawdh*, which has two meanings: (a) seeking refuge and protection (*iltijāʾ*, *istijāra*); (b) attachment (*iltiṣāq*). It is said that 'the tastiest meat is the *ʿawdh*', i.e. that which is attached to the bone. Upon the first meaning, *aʿūdhu bi'Llāh* means: 'I seek refuge in God's mercy and protection (*ʿiṣma*),' and upon the second: 'I attach myself to the grace and mercy of God'.

Concerning *al-shayṭān* (Satan), there are two opinions:

A. It is derived from the noun *shaṭn*, meaning 'distance' (*buʿd*): one says *shaṭana dāruka*, i.e. 'Your home is distant.' On this basis, every rebellious jinn,[2] human or beast is called *shayṭān* due to its distance from guidance and propriety. Almighty God said: 'Likewise did We make for every Messenger an enemy, devils among men and jinns...' (Q.VI.112)—in which humans have been described as devils. ʿUmar once mounted a workhorse which began to sway with him, so he tried beating it. When this only made matters worse, he dismounted, saying: 'You have placed me on nothing but a *shayṭān*!'

B. It is derived from the verb *shāṭa/yashīṭu*, meaning 'to be false' (*baṭala*). Since every rebellious creature is, as it were, false in itself due to falsifying all things beneficial to it, it is known as *shayṭān*.

1 The order of the second and third pillars is reversed in the presentation below.

2 The concept of jinns is discussed under the 'Fourth Pillar' below.

As for *rajīm*, it means *marjūm* (lit. 'stoned'). This form is comparable to a 'coloured' hand (*khaḍīb*, i.e. *makhḍūb*), or a 'cursed' man (*laʿīn*, i.e. *malʿūn*). There are two senses in which [Satan] may be described as 'stoned':

a. He is cursed by Almighty God. God said: 'Then get out from here, for you are *rajīm*' (Q.xv.34), and cursing (*laʿn*) is also called *rajm*. He also quoted the father of Abraham (on whom be peace), saying: 'If you do not desist, I will indeed stone you' (Q.xix.46)—it is said that he meant 'verbal stoning' [i.e. abuse]. Also, quoting the people of Noah: 'If you desist not, O Noah! you shall be stoned (to death)' (Q.xxvi.116); and in [another story in] *Sūrat Yā-Sīn*: 'If you desist not, we will certainly stone you' (Q.xxxvi.18).[1]
b. Satan is described as 'stoned' because God commanded the angels to cast meteors and piercing bodies at the devils to repel them from the heavens; hence it became a name for any wicked and rebellious one.

The [relevance of adding] 'Indeed, He is the Hearing, the Knowing' can be explained in two ways:

a. The purpose of *istiʿādha* is to take refuge from the evil of [satanic] whispering, which resembles letters subtly [pronounced] in the heart of the human being such that none [outside] can hear. Thus it is as though the servant is saying: 'O You Who can hear all things and knows every concealed secret! You hear the whispering of Satan and You know his intent thereby. Moreover, You are capable of averting it from me, so do so by Your grace.' Therefore, the mention of hearing and knowledge was more appropriate in this context than any of the other Attributes.
b. This wording suits this context according to the wording of the Qur'ān: 'If a suggestion from Satan should assail you, seek refuge with God. Indeed, He is hearing and knowing' (Q.vii.200), and in *Sūrat Ḥā Mīm al-Sajda*: 'Indeed, He is the Hearing, the Knowing' (Q.xli.36).[2]

Enquiry 2:
Rational Consideration of its Quiddity

Istiʿādha consists of the following essentials: knowledge, a state (*ḥāl*) and an action.

The first is for the servant to know that he is unable to bring about religious and worldly benefits and to avert religious and worldly harms,

1 Clearly, most of these citations do not support the interpretation as 'cursed'.

2 See Enquiry 6 in the previous chapter for further details on wording and sources.

and that God is able to create all religious and worldly benefits and to avert all religious and worldly harms with His unstoppable power.

Once this knowledge is established in the heart, it gives rise to a state within it of brokenness and humility, expressed through submission and supplication to Almighty God. This state within the heart gives rise to another in the heart as well as one on the tongue: the former is that the servant wishes for God to protect him from all afflictions and pour upon him goodness and reward, and the latter is that he actually seeks this meaning with his tongue and entreats the Almighty, saying 'I seek refuge in God'.

Based on the above, you will realise that the greatest pillar of seeking refuge is a person's knowledge of God and knowledge of his own self.

The [relevant] knowledge of God is to know [first] that He has knowledge of all things. If that were not so, then it would be possible for God to know the person but not his condition, in which case seeking refuge in Him would be of no use. He must also know that God is capable of all possibilities, otherwise He might not be able to fulfil the need of the servant. He must also know that He is infinitely generous, for if miserliness were possible for Him, there would be no benefit in seeking refuge. He must also recognise that there is none besides God who can assist him in his purpose: if that were not the case, then the motivation to seek refuge in God would not be strong.

This [knowledge] must be based on absolute monotheism (*tawḥīd muṭlaq*), which means to know that the world has only one Controller (*mudabbir*), and that the servant is not autonomous in his actions. If it were the case that a servant possessed such autonomy, then there would be no sense in seeking refuge with another. We have thus shown that, unless a servant recognises the might of Lordship (*rubūbiyya*) and the lowliness of servanthood (*ʿubūdiyya*), he is not able to say [truly] 'I seek refuge in God from the rejected Satan.'

OBJECTION: some say that there is no need when stating these words of remembrance (*dhikr*) to be aware of all these premises; and even if we suppose that this is necessary, it would still be acceptable to say 'I seek refuge in God' with a general meaning.

RESPONSE: this is very weak, considering that Abraham (on whom be peace) blamed his father by saying: 'Why do you worship that which hears not, sees not, and can profit you nothing?' (Q.XIX.42). On the assumption that the deity is not knowledgeable and capable of all things, asking [anything] from it would be as asking one who hears not and sees not, and would be included in that for which Abraham criticised his father.

As for the servant's knowledge of his own self, he must realise his complete incapacity to take care of his own interests. Even if he were to know these interests in terms of their qualities and quantities, he would still be unable to create them when absent, or to preserve them when present. Once all this knowledge takes root in the servant's heart and he comes to witness it with certainty, such a heart will certainly develop a state of brokenness and humility, leading to a will to seek [refuge] in his heart, and words upon his tongue denoting that request, namely 'I seek refuge in God from the rejected Satan'.

[The Need for God in Knowledge and Action]

The servant's inability to secure his own worldly and otherworldly interests is proven by the fact that he is attributed with knowledge and action, yet he is, in reality, completely ineffective in both areas. As for KNOWLEDGE, then the need for seeking refuge in God is great indeed, both for attaining it and protecting one's self from its opposite. This is shown by the following proofs:

1. How many erudite thinkers have we observed lingering upon a single contention (*shubha*) for the whole of their lives, not discovering what counters it, but in fact believing and insisting that it was certain knowledge and clear proof; then, after they have passed from this life, someone comes and points out their error and the flaw in their ideas? If this is possible for some people, then it is possible for everyone; if it were not so, then there would have been no differences between religions and schools of thought. Therefore, [one is in abject need of] God's assistance, grace and guidance, for who is capable of steering the ship of his intellect safely through the waves of misguidance and the depths of darkness?
2. Every individual is seeking nothing other than true religion and correct belief; nobody would accept for himself to be upon ignorance and disbelief. If everyone received what he sought and strove for, then everyone would be truthful and correct, which is not the case. Rather, we find that the people of truth in comparison to the people of falsehood are like a white hair on the back of a black bull. This tells us that there is no salvation from the darknesses of misguidance without the aid of the God of heaven and earth!

3. When a person is uncertain concerning the verity or falsity of a proposition, there is no way for him to be certain unless [he finds] a medial position between [truth and falsehood]. If that medial position is already present in his mind then the matter is, in effect, already resolved: his intellect is in fact resolved to an opinion concerning that proposition, whereas we had posited the case where he is unsure—this is a contradiction.

   On the other hand, if we say that this medial position is not present in his mind, then can it be sought or not? [To say it can be sought] is negated, because if he does not know what it is, how can he seek it? Seeking a particular thing requires a perception of that thing. However, if he does know that particular thing, then there is no sense in seeking what is already present in his mind! As for [saying] that it cannot be sought, then this means that he is incapable of finding the path of freedom from his uncertainty and the darkness of confusion. This shows that the servant is in the utmost confusion and bewilderment.
4. Almighty God said to His Messenger (may God bless him and grant him peace): 'And say: "O my Lord! I seek refuge with You from the suggestions of the Evil Ones"' (Q.XXIII.97), and this seeking of refuge is not restricted to any specific context.

This shows the abject inability of the servant to attain [true] belief and knowledge. As for his inability in the field of external actions which bring about benefit for himself and drive off harm, then this is likewise. The following demonstrates this:[1]

1. It has become known to the people of spiritual insight (*arbāb al-baṣā'ir*) that this body bears resemblance to Hell, and that there are nineteen types of Tormentors (*zabāniya*).[2] These are: the five external (*ẓāhir*) senses; the five internal (*bāṭin*) senses; appetite (*shahwa*); anger (*ghaḍab*); and the seven natural [vegetative] faculties.[3] Each one of these is a singular genus, but encompasses an infinite number of members. Consider, for example, the sense of sight: it can perceive any number of objects, each one leaving a particular imprint on the

1 The printed edition is not clear in designating this section and numbering its proofs. I have opted to relabel the 'fifth' and 'sixth' proofs, respectively, as point 2 in the context of actions, and a separate proof related to all of the above. Part of what led me to this is the author's description of point 1 below as 'the first', although there is no obvious 'second' etc.

2 See Q.LXXIV.30 and Q.XCVI.18.

3 See Shihadeh, *Teleological Ethics*, p. 120; Ibn Sīnā, *al-Qānūn fī al-ṭibb*, Book 1, trans. O. Cameron Gruner as *The Canon of Medicine of Avicenna*, New York: AMS Press, 1973, p. 107.

heart and drawing the heart from the lofty spiritual world to the lowly corporeal world.

With this in mind, it is clear that the sheer number of obstacles and distractions entail that there is no escape for the heart from these darknesses unless by the support and succour of the Almighty. Since it is known that there is no end to the shortcomings of the servant, and no limit to the perfections of God in His ability and wisdom, it follows that seeking refuge in Him is a necessity at all times. Therefore, on commencing any statement and every moment, we must say 'I seek refuge in God from the accursed Satan.'

2. Pleasures (*ladhdhāt*) in this temporary life are of two types: physical and conceptual—the latter is the pleasure of leadership (*riyāsa*). In each type, if a person is not able to experience or pursue these pleasures, he cannot perceive them. If he has no perception of them, he has little desire for them. If he then experiences them, he derives pleasure and this increases his desire; and whenever a person strives to reach a new level of pleasures and good things, so does his desire and craving reach a higher level.

The outcome is that the more a person attains his goals, the more he craves an increase. Since the levels of perfection are endless, so too are the levels of desire; and just as it is impossible to attain to infinite levels of perfection, so it is impossible to remove the pain of longing and desire from the heart. This proves that this is an ailment which the servant has no power to cure, so he must turn back to the Merciful and Generous One Who aids His servants, by saying 'I seek refuge in God from the accursed Satan'.

[A FURTHER] PROOF[1] of what we have mentioned are the following verses: 'You do we worship, and Your aid we seek' (Q.I.5), 'Seek [God's] help with patient perseverance and prayer' (Q.II.45), and Moses' words to his people: 'Pray for help from God and (wait) in patience and constancy' (Q.VII.128).

It is narrated in the divine scriptures that God says: 'By My might and majesty, I shall cut the hope of anyone who hopes for other than Me with despair and dress him in the robe of humiliation in front of people. I shall dash his hopes of drawing close to Me and push him far from My approach. I shall make him full of worries and concerns. He hopes in others at the time of hardship, while hardships are in My hands. I am the

1 Originally the 'sixth proof', this is generally about the need to ask for God's help.

Living, the Self-Subsistent. He seeks others and his mind knocks at their doors, while in My hands are the keys to all locked doors. Yet My door is open to whoever calls upon Me.'

Enquiry 3
[Free Will and Preordainment]

How does the *istiʿādha* fit with the stances of the Jabrīs (fatalists)[1] and the Qadarīs (voluntarists)?[2] The Muʿtazilīs stated that saying 'I seek refuge in God' negates fatalism in a number of ways:

a. Saying 'I seek refuge in God' is an admission that the servant is the agent (*fāʿil*) [creating] that *istiʿādha*. If the creator of deeds were Almighty God, then the servant could not be the agent, as this would be a *fait accompli* and impossible. If God created it in the servant then it would be impossible to avoid, and if He did not, then it could not exist. This proves that saying 'I seek refuge in God' is an admission that the servant brings about his own actions.
b. Seeking refuge with God would only make sense if God is not the Creator of the things from which refuge is sought: if He is their agent, one cannot seek refuge in God from them, as that would effectively mean that the servant is seeking refuge in God from the very things that God is doing.
c. Seeking refuge in God from sins demonstrates that the servant is not pleased with them. If these sins occurred by the creation and decree of God, then the servant is obliged to be pleased with them because—by consensus—contentment with the divine decree is an obligation.
d. Seeking refuge in God from Satan is only appropriate and sensible if Satan is the agent of his whispers. If they were solely an act of God in which Satan has no role, then why seek refuge from the 'evil of Satan'? In that case, it would be necessary to seek refuge from the 'evil of God' since it emanates only from Him.

1 Rather than the putative extremists on this side of the debate, it seems that the author has used this term (often rendered 'determinist') for the Ashʿarī stance which he will defend in the ensuing discussion. His use of the term varies within this text and elsewhere. Shihadeh writes that 'al-Rāzī concludes that man, though a voluntary agent in the sense of acting with awareness, is ultimately compelled... It was almost unprecedented in Sunni theology that such an uncompromisingly bold and systematic determinism (*jabr*) be affirmed.' See Shihadeh, *Teleological Ethics*, pp. 37–38.

2 One should not be misled by the label 'Qadarī' and the description of the *qadar*-denying doctrine as *qadar*. This side of the debate is represented here by the Muʿtazilīs, who maintained that man has a God-given capacity to create his own actions, resulting in accountability.

e. [Imagine that] Satan says:

> If I have not, in fact, done anything, but You—God of creation—have known and ruled that whispering will come from me, whereas I have no ability to go against Your power and ruling; then You have said: 'On no soul does God place a burden greater than it can bear' (Q.II.286), 'God intends every facility for you; He does not want to put you to difficulties' (Q.II.185), and 'He has imposed no difficulties on you in religion' (Q.XXII.78)—then, bearing in mind these clear excuses and strong reasons, how could You—in Your wisdom and mercy—blame and curse me?

f. [Further:] 'Did You make me stoned and cursed due to a crime which emanated from me, or not? If so, then fatalism (*jabr*) is false; but if not, then this is complete injustice. Since You have said "God never wishes injustice to his servants" (Q.XL.31), how could that be worthy of You?'

[The Muʿtazilīs continue:] Someone might say: 'These problems are only applicable to those who advocate [absolute] fatalism, whereas I maintain a stance that is neither that nor its opposite. Rather, the truth is a medial position between fatalism and voluntarism, namely [the theory of] acquisition (*kasb*).[1]' We reply: that is weak, because either the servant's power has some independent effect upon the action, or not. If so, then this is exactly the position of Muʿtazilīs. If not, then it is pure fatalism and the above problems apply to this position. Therefore, how could a medial position obtain?

AHL AL-SUNNA WA'L-JAMĀʿA[2] **RESPOND**: the entirety of the problems you have levelled at us are in fact applicable to you [Muʿtazilīs], for the following two reasons:

a. The ability (*qudra*) of the servant is either designated to one of two options,[3] or it is applicable [potentially] to both options. According to the former hypothesis, fatalism follows. According to the second,[4] one option being preferred over the other would either depend on

1 This is the Ashʿarī concept of the servant 'acquiring' the action created by God. The author expressed reservations with this concept in some of his other late writings—see Shihadeh, *Teleological Ethics*, p. 39.

2 'The people of the Prophetic way and community': a term used here for the Ashʿarīs and those who agree with them.

3 That is to say: it cannot be used to do both a thing and its opposite, whichever is selected by will.

4 As held by both the Muʿtazilīs and the Ashʿarīs.

a preponderator (*murajjiḥ*), or not.[1] If it does [depend], then: if that comes from the servant, then the original [disjunction] applies here. If it is from God, then when He gives preponderance [to one action over the other], the action's occurrence becomes necessary.[2] If, on the other hand, He does not, the action's occurrence becomes impossible. As such, all you have mentioned applies to your stance.

As for saying that one option being preponderate over the other does not depend on a preponderator, then this is rejected for two reasons:

- If that were allowable, then one could not argue that one possible state of affairs occurring rather than another indicates the presence of a preponderator.[3]
- It would mean that one occurring rather than another is merely a matter of coincidence, not emanating from the servant. In that case, we have come back to pure fatalism. This has shown that the objections levelled at us in fact apply to you.

b. You have accepted that Almighty God knows all things. If something were to occur contrary to His [prior] knowledge, that would entail His knowledge being turned into ignorance; since that is impossible, what led to it is impossible. Therefore, everything pertaining to divine decree and preordainment works irrefutably against you as pertains to [divine] knowledge.

Then *Ahl al-Sunna wa'l-Jamāʿa* say [making a positive case]: saying 'I seek refuge in God from the rejected Satan' [actually] negates voluntarism, as follows:

1. One is either seeking for God to prevent Satan from his whispering by prohibiting and warning, or by compulsion and decree. If the former [as the Muʿtazilīs hold], then that has already occurred, so requesting it from God is meaningless. If the latter [as the absolute fatalists hold], this is not allowed because compulsion negates the accountability of the devils, whereas it is known that they are accountable.

THE MUʿTAZILĪS RESPOND: the *istiʿādha* is about requesting [God] to perform such kindnesses (*alṭāf*) as would encourage the [servant] to

1 For 'or not', i.e. a presumption of randomness, see the next paragraph.

2 Clarification of this point appears under the Ashʿarīs' 'point 1' below (first bullet-point).

3 This is an essential argument in numerous theistic proofs, etc.; see Shihadeh, *Teleological Ethics*, p. 20.

perform goodly deeds and abstain from the unseemly. It cannot be said that these kindnesses have already been performed in full, so there is no meaning to requesting them, because we say that there are some which only become appropriate upon this supplication; therefore, if they were to precede [the *istiʿādha*], they would be out of place.

AHL AL-SUNNA [ASHʿARĪS] RESPOND TO THAT: either [God's] performance of those kindnesses has an effect upon [the servant's] action being made preponderant over its non-performance, or it has no such effect:

- If it does have an effect, then upon this preponderance obtaining, the action's occurrence becomes necessary. The proof of this is that, if preponderance of existence obtained and non-existence were to follow, it would mean that preponderation of non-existence occurred concurrently with preponderation of existence—this is paradoxical. Therefore, when preponderation occurs, necessity follows. This refutes the Muʿtazilīs' position.
- If the performance of those kindnesses has no effect upon the existence [of the servant's action] being made preponderant [over non-existence], then there would be no effect at all in [God's] action, i.e. it is purposeless, which is impossible in the case of Almighty God.

2. Either God intends what is advantageous (*ṣalāḥ*) for the servant, or not. If it is true that He does, then: either Satan is expected to corrupt the servant, or not. If he is expected to corrupt the servant while God intends advantage for him, then why did He create him and give him power over the servant? On the other hand, if no corruption is expected from Satan, then what need is there to seek refuge from him? As for saying that God does not intend goodness for the servant: in that case, how could seeking refuge in Him protect from the evil of Satan?
3. Either Satan is compelled to perform evil, or he has the ability to perform both evil and good. In the first case, God has compelled him to perform evil, which creates a problem for the [Muʿtazilī] claim that God only intends the advantageous [for the servants]. As for the scenario in which Satan is capable of both evil and good, then

the preponderance of [evil over good][1] requires a preponderator, which must be from God. If that is so, then what benefit is there in seeking refuge?

4. Suppose that mankind only fell into sin due to satanic whispers, how did Satan fall into sin? If we suggest that it was by the whispering of another devil, this leads to infinite regression. If, on the other hand, he fell into sin without the influence of another devil, then why can the same not be said for mankind? In that case, there is no benefit in seeking refuge from Satan. As for saying that God gave Satan power over mankind but did not give another devil power over Satan, then this is injustice towards mankind, specifying them with greater burdens and harms. This would negate His being on the side of His servants.
5. If the action from which refuge is sought is known [by God] to occur, then its occurrence is necessary and there is no benefit in seeking refuge from it. However, if it is not known [by God] to occur, then its occurrence is impossible and [likewise] there is no benefit in seeking refuge from it.

The above debate demonstrates that there is no reality to the servant saying 'I seek refuge in God' unless he comes to realise that *everything is from God and through God*.[2] The conclusion in this regard is as the Messenger (may God bless him and grant him peace) said: 'I seek refuge in Your pleasure from Your displeasure; I seek refuge in Your pardon from Your anger; and I seek refuge in You from You! I cannot enumerate Your praises: You are as You have praised Yourself.'[3]

The Second Pillar: The Refuge (*mustaᶜādh bihi*)

The Qur'ān and Prophetic *ḥadīth*s contain two different expressions: 'I seek refuge in God,' and 'I seek refuge in God's perfect words (*kalimāt Allāh al-tāmmāt*).'[4]

The explanation of 'I seek refuge in God' depends upon our enquiry into the Name *Allāh*, which will come under our exegesis of the *basmala*.[5] As for 'God's perfect words', this is [what is referred to] in the verse: 'To

1 The printed edition has these the other way round.
2 Perhaps this succinct statement provides the basis to answer the contentions in the preceding few points, which the author has left as open questions.
3 Recorded by Muslim with slightly different wording. A fuller narration appears in Book II.
4 See also the fourth Prophetic narration under the third pillar below.
5 See Book II, Chapter Nine below.

anything which We have willed, We but say the word "Be!" (*kun*), and it is' (Q.XVI.40). What is intended by 'Be!' is the application of God's power (*qudra*) to possible things and the flow of His will into [the sphere of] existence such that no impediment can prevent it. Without doubt, seeking refuge in God is only appropriate because He possesses these Attributes of unstoppable power and effective will.

Physical bodies (*jismāniyyāt*) come into being by transferring and emerging from potentiality into actuality as a gradual process, whereas spiritual entities (*rūḥāniyyāt*) form and emerge all at once. As such, the formation of [the latter] is comparable to the emergence of a letter (*ḥarf*), which only exists at an indivisible moment—this is why the application of [God's] power is described as a 'word' (*kalima*).

[Another explanation:] the rational sciences indicate that the world of spirits dominates the world of bodies, and they [i.e. angels] are controllers (*mudabbirāt*) of affairs in this world, as in the verse: 'Then arrange to do the command (of their Lord)' (Q.LXXIX.5). As such, saying 'I seek refuge in God's perfect words' is for human spirits to seek refuge with the lofty spirits—pure, holy and goodly—to deflect the harms of the wicked, dark and shadowy spirits. In short, 'God's perfect words' denote those pure, lofty spirits [angels].

SPIRITUAL OBSERVATION: it is only appropriate [for the servant] to say 'I seek refuge in God's perfect words' while there remains in his vision some concern for something other than God. Once he becomes submerged in the sea of Oneness (*tawḥīd*) and delves deep to the floor of realities until he can see nothing in existence except Almighty God, then it is only God on Whom he depends, seeking His refuge and protection. No wonder, then, that he says: 'I seek refuge in God' and 'I seek refuge in God from God,' as in the Prophetic narration: 'I seek refuge in You from You.'

However, even at this station, the servant is still distracted by other-than-God, because the *istiʿādha* must necessarily be to seek something or escape something, and that is a distraction from Almighty God. If the servant rises beyond this station and becomes oblivious to himself, nay, oblivious to his oblivion, then he has risen beyond saying 'I seek refuge in God' and has become immersed in the light of 'In the Name of God.' Do you not see that once the Prophet (may God bless him and grant him peace) had said 'I seek refuge in You from You' he ascended beyond this and said: 'You are as You have praised Yourself'?

The Third Pillar: The Seeker (*mustaʿīdh*)

Know that His saying[1] 'I seek refuge' constitutes an instruction to His servants to say this. It is not directed at any particular individual, but universal. Indeed, God has quoted these words as uttered by Prophets and saints (*awliyā'*), which shows that every created being ought to seek refuge in God.

[Examples from the Qur'ān]

a. Noah (on whom be peace) is quoted as saying: 'O my Lord! I seek refuge with You, lest I ask You for that of which I have no knowledge' (Q.XI.47), upon which God gave him two gifts, i.e. peace and blessings: 'O Noah! Come down (from the Ark) with peace from Us, and blessing on you…' (Q.XI.48).
b. Joseph (on whom be peace) is quoted as saying, when the woman sought to seduce him: '(I seek) the refuge of Allah! Indeed, he is my master, who has made good my residence' (Q.XII.23). So Almighty God granted him two gifts by deflecting evil and shameful deeds from him: '…that We might turn away from him (all) evil and shameful deeds' (Q.XII.24).
c. When it was said to him 'Take one of us in his place' (Q.XII.78), he replied: '(I seek) the refuge of Allah from taking anyone other than him with whom we found our property' (Q.XII.79). So God honoured him, as He said: 'And he raised his parents high on the throne (of dignity), and they fell down in prostration, (all) before him' (Q.XII.100).
d. When Moses (on whom be peace) instructed his people to slaughter a heifer, 'They said: "Do you make a laughing-stock of us?" He said: "I seek God's refuge from being an ignorant (fool)!"' (Q.II.67). So God gave him two gifts: negation of the accusation, and bringing the dead to life: 'So We said: "Strike the (body) with a piece of the (heifer)." Thus God brings the dead to life and shows you His signs…' (Q.II.73).
e. When [Pharaoh's] people threatened to kill [Moses], he said: 'I have sought refuge with my Lord and your Lord against your injuring me' (Q.XLIV.20). And in another verse: 'I have indeed called upon my Lord and your Lord (for protection) from every arrogant one who

1 It is not clear where this is supposed to have been said, as such (cf. the *basmala* as a verse of Qur'ān). The actual instructions to say this have been discussed in Chapter One above.

believes not in the Day of Account!' (Q.xliv.27). Thus God granted him his wish by destroying his enemy and causing [his people] to inherit their land and homes.

f. The mother of Mary said: 'I commend her and her offspring to Your protection from the rejected Satan,' (Q.iii.36), so she received the gift of acceptance: 'Her Lord accepted her with gracious favour: He made her grow in purity and beauty' (Q.iii.37).

g. When Mary (on whom be peace) saw Archangel Gabriel approaching her solitude in human form, she said: 'I seek refuge from you with the Compassionate. Come not near if you do fear (God)!' (Q.xix.18). So she found two graces: a son without a father, and God's declaration of her blamelessness upon the tongue of that son, when he said: 'I am indeed the servant of God' (Q.xix.30).

h. Almighty God instructed Muḥammad (may God bless him and grant him peace) to seek refuge time after time: 'And say: "O my Lord! I seek refuge with You from the suggestions of the devils; and I seek refuge with You, O my Lord, lest they should come near me"' (Q.xxiii.97–98); 'Say: I seek refuge with the Lord of the dawn' (Q.cxiii.1); and 'Say: I seek refuge with the Lord of mankind' (Q.cxiv.1).

i. In *Sūrat al-Aʿrāf*: 'Hold to forgiveness; command what is right; but turn away from the ignorant. If a suggestion from Satan should assail you, seek refuge with God. Indeed, He is hearing and knowing' (Q.vii.200). And in *Ḥā Mīm al-Sajda*: 'Nor can goodness and evil be equal. Repel (evil) with what is better: then will he between whom and you was hatred become as it were your friend and intimate! [...] And if (at any time) an incitement to discord is made to you by Satan, seek refuge in God. Indeed, He is the Hearing, the Knowing' (Q.xli.34,36).

These verses demonstrate that the Prophets (peace be upon them) were constantly seeking refuge from the evil of human and spirit devils.

[Examples from *Ḥadīth*]

There are also many reports [in connection with the Final Messenger (may God bless him and grant him peace)]:

a. Muʿādh b. Jabal related that two men disputed angrily in front of the Prophet (may God bless him and grant him peace), who said of them: 'I know a word which, if he were to say it, would remove that [anger] from them: "I seek refuge in God from the rejected Satan."'[1] This is supported by reason in several respects:

- A person knows that his knowledge of the benefits and harms of this world is very limited and that he can only attain to that knowledge by means of his intellect. When he becomes angry, the intellect is depleted and his words and actions no longer follow the appropriate code. If he is aware of this [danger], then that should hold him back from uttering those words and performing those actions; rather, he should turn back to God in order to receive good and deflect harm. In this context, he naturally says: 'I seek refuge in God.'
- The person does not know with certainty whether the truth is with him or his opponent, so he should say: 'I relegate this dispute to Almighty God. If the truth is on my side, then God will extract my right from my opponent; but in case the truth is on his side, it is best that I do not wrong him.' As such, he relegates the judgment to God, saying: 'I seek refuge in God'.
- A person only becomes angry when he feels that he possesses the strength and severity to overpower his opponent. However, if he calls to mind: 'The God of the world is stronger and more capable than me; moreover, I have sinned against Him so many times, yet He has pardoned me in His grace: so it is better that I pardon this one who has angered me'—if he calls this to mind, he will abandon the conflict and disputation and say: 'I seek refuge in God.'

All these meanings can be derived from the following verse: 'Those who fear (God), when a thought of evil from Satan assaults them, bring (God) to remembrance, and immediately they see (aright)' (Q.vii.201). This means that when a person calls to mind these secrets and meanings, he sees the path of guidance and leaves off disputation and defence [of his ego], being satisfied with the decree of Almighty God.

b. Maᶜqil b. Yasār related that the Prophet (may God bless him and grant him peace) said: 'Whoever says three times upon waking: 'I seek refuge in God, the Hearing, the Knowing, from the rejected Satan', then recites three verses from the end of *Sūrat al-Ḥashr*, God will

1 Recorded by Abū Dāwūd and Tirmidhī. The sources indicate that one of the men was particularly angry, and the Prophet said this concerning him. The printed edition has *law qālāhā* ('if they both were to say it'), but I have reverted to the singular as in Amīriyya, vol. 1, p. 41.

appoint 70,000 angels to pray upon him until he enters the evening. If he dies that day, he dies as a martyr. Whoever recites likewise in the evening will have the equivalent station.'[1] The rational explanation for this is that saying 'I seek refuge in God' represents witnessing to the impotence and shortcomings of the self. The verses from *Sūrat al-Ḥashr* [Q.LIX.22–24] represent witnessing to divine perfection, greatness and grandeur. The station of servitude is not complete without these two aspects being fulfilled.

c. Anas [b. Mālik] related that the Prophet (may God bless him and grant him peace) said: 'Whoever seeks refuge in God from Satan ten times in a day, God will appoint for him thereby an angel to drive Satan off from him.'[2] The reason for this is that when he says 'I seek refuge in God' and comprehends its meaning, he realises the deficiency of his ability and knowledge. As such, he does not respond to what his [lower] self (*nafs*) commands him or perform those acts to which it invites. Since the greatest devil is the [lower] self, it is established that reciting these words drive off the devil from a person.

d. Khawla bint Ḥakīm related that the Prophet (may God bless him and grant him peace) said: 'Whoever dwells in a home and says: "I seek refuge in God's perfect words from the evil of what He created," nothing will harm him until he departs from that home.'[3]

To explain: it has been established in the rational sciences that spiritual beings are more numerous than corporeal beings and that the heavens are filled with pure spirits [angels], as the Prophet (may God bless him and grant him peace) said: 'The heaven has creaked, and that is to be expected: for there is not within it a single place for a footstep which is not occupied by an angel, standing or sitting.'[4] Likewise the ether and atmosphere are filled with spirits: some pure, radiant and virtuous; others shadowy, harmful and wicked. When a person says: 'I seek refuge in God's perfect words,' he has sought refuge in those pure spirits from the evil of the wicked ones. Also, the 'words of God' refers to His saying 'Be!' which represents His effective power. Whoever seeks refuge in God's power will be harmed by nothing.[5]

1 Recorded by Tirmidhī.
2 Recorded in Abū Yaʿla's *Musnad*, and considered 'very weak'—R.S.
3 Recorded by Muslim.
4 A similar wording is recorded by Tirmidhī.
5 See the Second Pillar above.

e. ʿAmr b. Shuʿayb narrated from his father, from his grandfather, that the Prophet (may God bless him and grant him peace) said: 'If one of you is [awakened by] fright from his sleep, let him say: "I seek refuge in God's perfect words from His anger, His retribution and the evil of His servants, and from the devils' incitements and that they should approach me." Then it will not harm him.' ʿAbd Allāh b. [ʿAmr] used to teach it to his mature servants; for the pre-pubescent, he would write it on a slip and hang it round their necks.[1]

f. Ibn ʿAbbās related that the Prophet (may God bless him and grant him peace) used to supplicate for refuge for al-Ḥasan and al-Ḥusayn (may God be pleased with them), saying: 'I seek refuge for you in God's perfect words from every poisonous devil and every harmful eye.' He would remark, 'My father Abraham used to say the same to seek refuge for Ishmael and Isaac (peace be upon them).'[2]

g. The Prophet (may God bless him and grant him peace) would consider the *istiʿādha* a tremendous matter, to the extent that when he married a woman and came to consummate with her, and she said to him 'I seek refuge in God from you,' he replied: 'You have taken a [true] refuge, so go back to your family.'[3] Know that the man who sees by the light of God does not concern himself with the speaker, but solely with the statement. Therefore, when the woman said 'I seek refuge in God,' the heart of the Messenger (may God bless him and grant him peace) became engaged with those words and not with whether they were intentional or not.

h. Al-Ḥasan [al-Baṣrī] narrated that a man was once beating one of his slaves when the slave began to say 'I seek refuge in God.' At that point the Prophet (may God bless him and grant him peace) passed by, so he said [instead]: 'I seek refuge in the Messenger of God.' The [master] then desisted, at which the Prophet (may God bless him and grant him peace) said: 'The seeker of refuge with God is most worthy of withholding [one's hand] from him.' He said, 'Then indeed, O Messenger of God, I bear witness that he is freed for the

1 This appears as a connected account in Tirmidhī. The grandfather of ʿAmr was the son of ʿAbd Allāh b. ʿAmr b. al-ʿĀṣ. Therefore, the reference is to that Companion, not to Ibn ʿUmar as in the printed editions.

2 Recorded by Bukhārī.

3 This alludes to a woman from the Jawn tribe, according to an account recorded by Bukhārī. The clause 'intentional or not' is explained by narrations which indicate that she was tricked by some co-wives into saying these words.

sake of God.' The Messenger (may God bless him and grant him peace) replied, 'By the One in Whose hand is my soul: if you had not said so, your face would have confronted the scorching Fire.'[1]

i. Suwayd[2] said: 'I heard Abū Bakr the Truthful (*al-Ṣiddīq*) saying from the pulpit: "I seek refuge in God from the rejected Satan," adding: "I heard the Messenger of God seeking refuge in God from the rejected Satan, so I would not wish to abandon that as long as I live."'
j. The Prophet (may God bless him and grant him peace) said: 'I seek refuge in Your pleasure from Your displeasure; I seek refuge in Your pardon from Your anger; and I seek refuge in You from You.'

The Fourth Pillar: From Whom Refuge is Sought (*mustaʿādh minhu*)

This refers to Satan, and the *istiʿādha* is intended to ward off his evil. This evil may be whispering (*waswasa*) or it may be otherwise, as indicated in the verse: '...except as stands one whom Satan by his touch has driven to madness' (Q.II.275).

This chapter contains a number of obscure and intricate enquiries from the perspectives of reason (*ʿaqliyyāt*) and spiritual unveilings (*mukāshafāt*).

Enquiry I

People have differed over the existence of jinns and devils, as there were some who denied their existence. It is necessary, in the first place, to investigate the nature (*māhiyya*) of jinns and devils. Everyone is agreed that they are not dense corporeal entities which come and go in the manner of humans and beasts. Rather, there are two opinions regarding them:

A. They are ethereal bodies (*ajsām hawā'iyya*) capable of taking various forms and possessing intellect, understanding and the ability to perform tremendous feats.
B. Many people have stated that they are neither spatial, nor subsistent within spatial objects; rather, they are incorporeal entities. These entities may be lofty and sanctified from [involvement in] the organisation of bodies altogether, and these are the angels brought near [to God]: 'Those who are in His (very) presence are not too

1 This *mursal* version appears in the *Muṣannaf* of ʿAbd al-Razzāq. A similar story, in which the master was Abū Masʿūd al-Badrī, appears in Muslim. Imām Nawawī suggests that the master did not hear the slave seeking refuge in God the first time, or he realised from his seeking refuge in the Prophet that he was present. See Nawawī, *al-Minhāj sharḥ Ṣaḥīḥ Muslim*, vol. VI, p. 133.

2 There are several people by this name who could have heard Abū Bakr. I could not source the narration or determine the narrator.

proud to serve Him, nor are they (ever) weary (of His service)' (Q.xxi.19). The next level comprises those which are involved in the organisation of bodies, of which the noblest are the bearers of the Throne (*ʿarsh*): 'And eight (angels) will, that day, bear the Throne of your Lord above them' (Q.lxix.17). The third level are the angels of the Footstool (*kursī*); the fourth are the angels of the heavens, [decreasing] level by level; the fifth are the angels of the ethereal sphere; the sixth are the angels of the sphere of air (*hawā'*) which is as the light breeze (*nasīm*); and the seventh are the angels of the sublunary sphere (*al-zamharīr*). The eighth level comprises spirits (*arwāḥ*)[1] connected to the seas; the ninth are the spirits of the mountains; and the tenth are the lower spirits which operate within bodies of this world, both plants and animals.

Following from either one of these opinions, those spirits consist of both the radiant, godly, good and felicitous ones known as the righteous jinns,[2] and the shadowy, lowly, evil and wretched ones known as the devils (*shayāṭīn*).

THOSE WHO DENIED THE EXISTENCE OF JINNS AND DEVILS argued as follows:[3]

1. If devils existed, they would have to be either dense (*kathīf*) or subtle (*laṭīf*) bodies. Since neither one may be true, Satan's existence is not possible. We say that they cannot be dense bodies because that would entail that anyone with sound eyesight could see them. If it were possible for there to be dense bodies in our presence yet hidden from our vision, then that would mean that there could likewise be tall mountains, radiant suns, thunder and lightning without our perceiving them; and whoever allows for that has departed from reason. On the other hand, they cannot be subtle bodies because that would necessitate that they be broken up by fierce and raging winds. Moreover, they would not have the strength and ability to perform tremendous feats, whereas that is attributed to them by affirmers of the jinns' existence. Since neither proposition is plausible, their existence is negated.
2. If these entities known as the Jinn were to live in this world and mix with human beings, it is highly probably that this prolonged

1 Here the author switches to another term, even though he has included angels (*malā'ika*) both in the genus of 'spirits' (see under the Second Pillar, above) and 'jinns'.

2 This would appear to include the angels.

3 These three contentions are refuted successively in this enquiry and the next.

mingling would result in either friendship or enmity. If the former, then beneficial effects of this friendship ought to be apparent; if the latter, then harmful effects should be apparent. However, we do not observe any effects indicating either. As for those who practise the art of conjuring spirits (*taʿzīm*), the repentant among them admit their dishonesty and that they have never seen the effects of jinns; this makes it highly likely that they do not exist. I heard[1] one of these who repented of this practice saying: 'I recited such-and-such charm continuously for a number of days, not leaving off for even a minute, yet I did not observe even a trace of the states which they mention.'

3. Things may be known via [three] routes: the senses, narrations [from authority] and [rational] proofs:
   a. Sense perception does not establish the existence of these beings, neither by form or sound. Since we do not see or hear them, how can it be claimed that we perceive them? Those who claim to have seen them or heard their voices are of two types: the deranged (*majnūn*) who hallucinate due to flaws in their disposition, and lying fraudsters.
   b. It is also not possible to establish their existence by means of statements of the Prophets and Messengers, because their very existence would negate the veracity of prophethood. It could be claimed that all the miracles performed by the Prophets occurred through the assistance of jinns and devils; and any branch which results in the negation of its origin is false.[2] If we should accept that jinns may penetrate the bodies of human beings, then why could it not likewise be said that the palm-trunk only moaned[3] due to a devil which entered it and created the sound? Or that the she-camel only spoke to the Messenger (may God bless him and grant him peace)[4] due to a devil which entered it? Or that the tree was uprooted[5] by a devil? It is thus shown that affirming

1 It is not clear who the speaker is here, as the author is citing arguments made by others.

2 In other words, it would negate the very thing being used to prove it, and is self-defeating.

3 The story recorded by Bukhārī and others is that the Prophet used to lean upon a palm-trunk while delivering his sermons; once his pulpit was constructed and he moved to it, the trunk moaned at the loss, so the Prophet comforted it.

4 The story is recorded by Abū Dāwūd: the Prophet entered a garden to find a camel crying in pain; he then addressed the owner, saying that the camel had complained to him of mistreatment.

5 The story is recorded by Ibn Ḥibbān: when asked to embrace the faith, a Bedouin demanded a witness to the Prophet's veracity. The Prophet called a tree to come and testify, and it came walking.

jinns and devils entails negation of the veracity of the Prophets (on whom be peace).[1]

c. As for proving these things by means of rational argument, then this [too] is unforthcoming, as there is nothing of this sort for establishing the existence of jinns and devils. Since there is no way of knowing that these things exist, the claim that they do so must be rejected.

The above represent the [faulty] arguments of those who deny jinns and devils.

THE RESPONSE TO THE FIRST: your argument suggests that a jinn cannot be corporeal, but why could one not say instead that it is a substance (*jawhar*) free of corporeality? Those who say this comprise [three] groups:

A. Those who said: the discursive (*nāṭiqa*) [i.e. rational] human souls which are separate (*mufāriq*) from bodies may be either righteous or wicked. The former are the angels of the earth, and the latter are its devils. If there came to be a body (*badan*) which strongly resembled the body of those transcendent souls, and which became associated with a soul closely resembling those souls, the result would be that the transcendent soul would become somewhat associated with that temporal (*ḥādith*) body. The transcendent soul would become a supporter of the soul [directly] associated with the body in performing tasks appropriate to it: if the two souls are of the pure, radiant and righteous ones, then this support is 'inspiration' (*ilhām*); but if they are wicked and evil then it is 'whispering' (*waswasa*).

   This is the nature of inspiration and whispering according to this group.

B. Those who said: jinns and devils are substances which are free of corporeality and its implications, but they are a different genus from the discursive human souls. This genus also contains various species: if they are pure and illuminated then they are the angels of the earth, also known as righteous jinns. If, on the other hand, they are wicked and evil, then these are the harmful devils. When this is known, then consider that homogeneity results in association:[2] so those pure and illuminated spirits join the pure and illuminated human souls and assist them in their tasks of virtue, righteousness and piety. On the other hand, the wicked and evil spirits join the wicked and shadowy

1 This is based on the *kalām* proposition that miracles are the basis of belief in the Prophets.

2 This is like the saying 'Birds of a feather flock together.'

human souls and assist them in their tasks of evil, sin and aggression.

C. Those who deny the existence of lower-order spirits but affirm the transcendent, celestial (*falakiyya*) spirits. They claim that these spirits are exalted, strong and powerful while having a variety of substances and quiddities.

[They explain:] just as every human spirit (*rūḥ*) is possessed of a specific body, so too does each heavenly spirit have a body, which is its specific celestial sphere (*falak*).[1] Just as the human spirit associates first with the heart and then, thereby, its effect spreads throughout the body, so does the heavenly spirit associate first with the planets (*kawākib*) before its effect spreads thereby throughout the sphere and to the entire world. Just as subtle spirits are generated in the heart and brain and spread via the arteries and nerves to the various body parts—thus allowing the powers of life, sense and motion to reach all these parts—so too do radiation lines emanate from the planets' bodies to the farthest reaches of the world, thereby spreading the power of those planets to all its parts.

Just as the spirits emanating from the heart and brain bring about various faculties responsible for nutrition, growth, reproduction and perception in each part of the body—such that the faculties are the products or derivatives of the substance of the soul controlling the entire body—likewise, by means of the radiation lines sent out from the planets and reaching the various parts of this world, specific souls are brought about in those parts, such as the souls of Zayd and ʿAmr.[2] These souls are derivatives of the heavenly souls; and since the heavenly souls are diverse in their substances and natures, the souls generated from the soul of Saturn's sphere, for example, are one group, whereas those generated from the soul of Jupiter's sphere are another. As such, the souls associated with the spirit of Saturn will be similar and there will be love and friendship between them, whereas they will be different by nature from those associated with the spirit of Jupiter.[3]

Following this, they said: the cause is stronger than the thing caused. Each group of human souls has a specific nature which is

1 See Setia, 'Fakhr Al-Din Al-Razi on Physics and the Nature of the Physical World', pp. 174–176, where it is argued that 'ultimately, al-Rāzī seems to be undecided as to which celestial models, concrete or abstract, most conform with external reality'.

2 As explained previously, these are generic names for individuals.

3 See Shihadeh, *Teleological Ethics*, p. 118.

caused by one of the heavenly spirits, so that nature will be much stronger and loftier in the heavenly spirit than in the human ones. The heavenly spirits are, to their corresponding human spirits, like a concerned father and compassionate ruler, so they assist their offspring with what benefits them and guide them—sometimes by dreams, or otherwise by waking inspiration. If it should happen that some human souls possess a strong faculty in this regard and develop a strong connection to the heavenly spirit which is its origin, then amazing feats and supernatural acts will appear at his hands.

These are details concerning the schools of thought which affirm jinns and devils and claim that they exist without corporeality. A group of philosophers criticised this stance by claiming that abstract (*mujarrad*)[1] entities cannot perceive particulars (*juz'iyyāt*) or perform particular actions. However, this is a false [objection] for the following reasons:

1. It is possible for us to judge that a particular individual is a human and not a horse. An entity which is to judge between two things must have the two things being judged [conceptually] present before it. As such, here we have a single entity—i.e. the [abstract] soul—perceiving the universal,[2] so it follows that the perceiver of the particular[3] is [also] the soul.
2. Even if we suppose that the abstract soul is unable by itself to perceive particulars, there is no dispute that it can do so by means of corporeal instruments.[4] Therefore, why could it not be said that those abstract substances known as jinns and devils have corporeal instruments in the ethereal or sublunary sphere by which it is able to perceive particulars and act upon these bodies?

This completes our discussion of this stance [denying corporeality].

[A fourth group] claimed that jinns are ethereal (*hawā'ī*) or infernal (*nārī*) bodies.[5] They said: bodies are equal in [having] proportionality and quantity, and these are both accidents. Since bodies are equal in being

1 Similar or identical in meaning to 'transcendent' above.
2 I.e. the definition or concept of 'human'.
3 I.e. the individual being identified.
4 Such as the eye or hand in the human body.
5 This is the first group mentioned at the outset of this Enquiry. Despite using the word *zaʿm* (claim) here, it is likely that the author supports this response to the first argument against the existence of jinns, rather than the three preceding versions of the non-corporeality thesis. See Enquiry 3 below.

receptive to these accidents, [it is seen that] there is no impediment to things with different quiddities sharing in certain concomitants. As such, it could be said that bodies are different in their respective essences and quiddities even though they share [the quality of] being receptive to proportionality and quantity.

Therefore, could it not [likewise] be said that there is one species of body which is subtle and penetrative, living and reasoning in its own right, capable of tremendous feats in its own right, while not being subject to fragmentation or dispersal? If that is so, then these bodies would be able to take on a variety of forms, and neither strong winds nor dense bodies would cause them to break up or disperse. Do the philosophers not say that the fire which separates from lightning bolts penetrates stone and iron in a mere instant, emerging from the other side? If so, is it inconceivable for similar to apply in this scenario? This would mean that jinns are able to penetrate human beings and act upon them, and that they remain alive, effective and safe from decay until their prescribed time.

All of these are clear possibilities which have not been disproven, so it is not reasonable to dismiss them.

THE RESPONSE TO THE SECOND ARGUMENT: the friendship or enmity is not necessarily experienced by every person, and each individual only knows his own situation. Since one cannot know the experiences of every other person, the matter remains in the domain of possibility.

THE RESPONSE TO THE THIRD: we do not concede that affirming jinns and angels constitutes an attack on the veracity of prophethood. The [full] response to your contentions will appear in due course, but this is all we shall say [here] in response to these doubts.[1]

Enquiry 2

The Qur'ān and [Prophetic] narrations (*akhbār*) prove the existence of jinns and devils:

THE QUR'ĀN: the first passage [to consider] is: 'Behold, We turned towards you a company of jinns (quietly) listening to the Qur'ān: when they stood in the presence thereof, they said: "Listen in silence!" When the (reading) was finished, they returned to their people, to warn (them of their sins). They said: "O our people! We have heard a Book revealed after Moses,

1 One part of the response is to provide authoritative texts, as follows. It is possible that the author has responded elsewhere in this exegesis and/or other works.

confirming what came before it: it guides to the Truth and to a Straight Path"' (Q.XLVI.29–30). This explicitly states that they exist and that they heard the Qur'ān and warned their people.

Secondly: 'They followed what the devils gave out (falsely) against the power of Solomon…' (Q.II.102).

Thirdly, [also] from the story of Solomon (on whom be peace): 'They worked for him as he desired, (making) arches, images, basins as large as reservoirs, and (cooking) cauldrons fixed (in their places)' (Q.XXXIV.13); 'As also the devils, (including) every kind of builder and diver, as also others bound together in fetters' (Q.XXXVIII.37–38); 'And to Solomon (We made) the wind (obedient): its early morning (stride) was a month's (journey), and its evening (stride) was a month's (journey); and We made a font of molten brass to flow for him; and there were jinns that worked in front of him, by the leave of his Lord' (Q.XXXIV.12).

Fourthly: 'O assembly of jinns and men! If it be that you can pass beyond the zones of the heavens and the earth…' (Q.LV.33), and fifthly: 'We have indeed decked the lower heaven with beauty (in) the stars: (for beauty) and for guard against all obstinate rebellious evil spirits' (Q.XXXVII.6–7).

PROPHETIC *ḤADĪTHS*: there are many:

a. Mālik recorded in *al-Muwaṭṭa'* from Ṣayfī b. Aflaḥ, via Abū al-Sā'ib (the freedman of Hishām b. Zahra), that [Abū al-Sā'ib] entered upon Abū Saʿīd al-Khudrī. He relates:

> I found him praying, so I sat and waited for him to finish. I heard a motion under his couch, which turned out to be a snake. I stood up in order to kill it, but Abū Saʿīd gestured to me to sit. Once he completed his prayer, he pointed to a [nearby] house, saying: 'You see that house?' I replied: 'Yes.' He said: 'There was a young man in it who had recently got married […][1] When he saw his wife standing [outside] among the people, he was overtaken with jealousy and pointed his spear at her, ready to attack. She said: "Do not be hasty, but go and see what is in your house [and has driven me out]!" When he entered, there was a snake coiled up on his bed, so he stabbed it with his spear. The snake

1 The author removed some details from the story for brevity. The young man had sought permission to return to his new bride from the Battle of the Trench.

> gyrated on the head of the spear and the boy fell dead. We do not know which of the two was first to die. When I recounted this to the Messenger of God (may God bless him and grant him peace), he said: "There are jinns in Medina who have become Muslim. If any of them appears before you, grant him three days [to leave]. If he appears to you after that, then kill him, for he is a devil."'

b. Mālik recorded in *al-Muwaṭṭa'* from Yaḥyā b. Saʿīd:

> When the Messenger of God (may God bless him and grant him peace) was taken on his Night Journey,[1] he saw a powerful (*ʿifrīt*) jinn aiming a flaming torch at him. Everywhere he turned, he would see him; so Gabriel (on whom be peace) said: 'Shall I not teach you words which, if you say them, would extinguish his torch and make it fall from him? Say: I seek refuge in God's noble Countenance and in His perfect words which neither righteous nor wicked escapes, from the evil of that which descends from the sky and that which ascends into it; and from the evil of that which enters the earth and that which emerges from it; and from the evil of the temptations of night and day; and from the evil of visitors by night and by day, except such as visit with goodness—O Compassionate!'

c. Also in the *Muwaṭṭa'* of Mālik, that Kaʿb al-Aḥbār used to say: 'I seek refuge in the Countenance of God the Great—there is nothing greater than Him; and by the perfect words of God which neither righteous nor wicked escapes; and by the Beautiful Names of God, those which I know and those which I know not, from the evil of what He created and made.'

d. Mālik also recorded that Khālid b. al-Walīd said: 'O Messenger of God! I see nightmares in my sleep.' The Messenger (may God bless him and grant him peace) said: 'Say: I seek refuge in the perfect words of God from His anger and retribution and the evil of His servants, and from the suggestions of the devils and that they should come near me.'

e. The *ḥadīth*s which have reached the level of mass transmission

1 This refers to the journey from the Sacred Mosque (in Mecca) to the Farthest Mosque (in Jerusalem)—see Q.XVII.1—and from there to the heavens—see Q.LIII.

(*tawātur*) concerning the Prophet (may God bless him and grant him peace) going out on the Night of the Jinns[1] and his reciting to them and inviting them to Islam.

f. The Qāḍī (judge) Abū Bakr [al-Bāqillānī] narrated in *al-Hidāya* that Jesus son of Mary (peace be upon them both) supplicated to God to show him the position of Satan in relation to the children of Adam. So He showed him, and [Satan's] head was like the head of a snake, which he placed upon [the person's] heart: whenever he mentioned God, [Satan] withdrew; but when he did not mention Him, he would replace his head upon his heart's core.[2]

g. The Prophet (may God bless him and grant him peace) said: 'Satan runs through the son of Adam like blood'[3] and 'There is not one of you who does not have an [appointed] devil.' It was said: 'Even you, O Messenger of God?' He replied: 'Even I, except that God has assisted me against him, so he accepted Islam.'[4]

There are many relevant narrations, but we shall suffice with this quantity.

Enquiry 3
Jinns Are Created From Fire

The proof of this is the verse: 'And the jinns, We had created before, from the fire of a scorching wind' (Q.xv.27). The Almighty also said, quoting Iblīs (may God curse him): 'You created me from fire, and him from clay' (Q.vii.12).

Know that for life to subsist in fire is not implausible. Physicians state that the first association of the soul is with the heart and spirit, which are extremely hot. Galen said: 'I once split open a monkey and inserted my hand into its belly. I inserted my finger into its heart and found it to be exceedingly hot.' We say: physicians are in consensus that life depends upon innate heat. Some have said that it is likely that the sphere of fire[5] is full of spirit [lives].

1 See Q.xlvi.30–32 and commentaries for associated *ḥadīths*.

2 See Ibn Ḥajar al-ʿAsqalānī, *Fatḥ al-Bārī sharḥ Ṣaḥīḥ al-Bukhārī*, 15 vols., Cairo: Dār al-Ghad al-Jadīd, 2012, vol. viii, p. 874.

3 Recorded by Bukhārī and Muslim.

4 Recorded by various authorities and in Muslim with the wording 'his own companion jinn'—S.I.

5 According to the nomenclature of astronomy (*falak*), this is a level above the atmosphere. See Ḥājī Khalīfa, *Kashf al-ẓunūn ʿan asāmī al-kutub wa'l-funūn*, ed. Muḥammad Yāltaqāyā, 2 vols., Beirut: Dār Iḥyā' al-Turāth al-ʿArabī, 1941, vol. ii, p. 1290.

Enquiry 4
[Origin of Name]

There are two opinions mentioned regarding why they are called *jinn*:

A. The word is derived from [the root's meaning] of concealment (*istitār*), from which also comes the word *janna* (garden) because the ground is concealed by trees; and *junna* (armour) because it covers [and protects] people; and likewise the jinns because they are concealed from sight. The *majnūn* (deranged) is so-called because his mind is covered over, and the *janīn* (foetus) is concealed in the belly. Almighty God said: 'They have made their oaths a *junna*' (Q.LVIII.16), i.e. a protective screen. Based on this opinion, the angels must also be *jinn* because they are invisible to the eyes, unless it is said that the unrestricted term is restricted by convention.[1]

B. They were so named because they were originally wardens of Paradise (*al-Janna*). However, the first opinion is stronger.

Enquiry 5

There are four groups among those charged with accountability (*mukallafūn*): angels,[2] humans, jinns and devils. Opinions diverged on the jinns and devils, with some saying that they are distinct genera, comparable to humans and horses. Others said that jinns consist of both righteous and wicked, and the latter are known as devils.

Enquiry 6
[Possession]

The famous opinion is that jinns have the ability to penetrate human bodies, while the majority of Muʿtazilīs denied that.

The affirmers depended on the following proofs:

1. If jinns are non-physical, incorporeal beings, then all that is meant by penetrating human bodies is the ability to affect them from the inside, and that is not implausible. If they are ethereal, subtle and

1 That is to say: although angels could technically be called *jinn*, common usage restricts it to the other class of unseen beings, i.e. those with free will.

2 The author states at numerous junctures that angels are prevented from sin (*maʿṣūm*), which need not negate volition and accountability; cf. Enquiry 7 below. In his commentary on Q.II.34 (Enquiry 3), Rāzī outlines the arguments for Iblīs being an angel versus the more common view (certainly in later scholarship) that he was from the distinct race of the Jinn. Although he does not make his preference explicit at that juncture, he sides more clearly with the latter view under Q.VII.12, Q.XVI.50 and Q.XVIII.50. He also rejects narrations portraying Hārūt and Mārūt as fallen angels: see under Q.II.102.

penetrative beings as we have described,[1] the penetration into the body of human beings is not impossible, by analogy with breath and its like.

2. Almighty God said: '[They] will not stand except as stands one whom Satan by his touch has driven to madness' (Q.II.275).
3. The Prophet (may God bless him and grant him peace) said: 'Satan runs through the son of Adam like blood.'

The deniers relied upon the following:

1. God said, quoting the accursed Iblīs: 'I had no authority over you except to call you, but you listened to me…' (Q.XIV.22). Here he is explicit in saying that he has no power over human beings except in one sense, namely to incite them with whispers and invite them to falsehood.
2. Certainly the Prophets (*anbiyā'*), scholars (*ʿulamā'*) and spiritual masters (*muḥaqqiqūn*) call people to curse and reject Satan, so the enmity of the devils towards these must be of the strongest type. If they were able to penetrate human beings and bring tribulations and evil to them, then it would follow that the Prophets and scholars would be the worst affected by this. Since that is not the case, we know that [the premise] is false.[2]

Enquiry 7

It is agreed that the angels do not eat, drink or marry; instead, they praise God throughout the night and day without ceasing. Jinns and devils, on the other hand, do eat and drink. The Prophet (may God bless him and grant him peace) said concerning dung and bones: 'They are the provision of your brothers among the jinns.'[3] They also procreate, as God said: 'Will you then take him and his progeny as protectors rather than Me?' (Q.XVIII.50).

Enquiry 8
Method of Whispering, Based on *Ḥadīths*

It has been said that [Satan] plunges inside the human being and places his head on the core of his heart, casting whispers upon him. This was supported by the narration from the Prophet (may God bless him and

1 Under Enquiry 1 above.

2 This argument overlooks the role of protection through spiritual training, let alone the special protection (*ʿiṣma*) of the Prophets.

3 Recorded by Ibn Ḥibbān.

grant him peace): 'Satan runs through the son of Adam like blood, so narrow its channels by hunger.'[1] He also said: 'Were it not that the devils encircle the hearts of the children of Adam, they would have gazed at the heavenly kingdom.'[2]

Some said that these reports must be subjected to interpretation (*ta'wīl*) because they cannot be taken at face value. They argued in the following ways:

1. It is impossible for Satan to penetrate the human body [as described], because it would require either the expansion of the [veins and arteries], or for the bodies to intersect.
2. We have mentioned the severe enmity between Satan and the religious folk, so if he had this ability then why does he not inflict increased harm upon them?
3. Satan is created from fire, so if he entered a body it would be as though fire has entered it: yet that is obviously not perceived.
4. The devils love sin and all types of unbelief and rebellion, so [some people][3] perform such as offerings before them, hoping to witness their varieties of wrongdoing, yet they find no effect or outcome from that. In short, there is no observable harm from their enmity, or benefit from their friendship.

The affirmers of the devils' [existence and effect] responded to the FIRST contention by saying that it is negated if they are abstract souls, and likewise if they are subtle bodies like light and air.[4] To the SECOND point, they said: it is plausible that God and His angels prevent [the devils] from harming the scholars among humanity. To the THIRD point, they said: since it was possible for Almighty God to say to the fire of Abraham: 'O fire! Be coolness and safety for Abraham!' (Q.XXI.69), why could the same not be possible in this case? And to the FOURTH: the devils have free will, so it could be that they perform some unseemly deeds and not others.

1 The first part is authentic, as mentioned previously. However, 'so narrow its channels' is an interpolation found in Sufi works including the *Iḥyā'* of Imām Ghazālī—S.I.

2 This is also in the *Iḥyā'*, which Rāzī cites explicitly under the following enquiry. A similar wording is recorded by Aḥmad.

3 In the text, this says 'we', as though on the tongue of the sorcerers cited above under Enquiry I in which arguments against the very existence of the jinns were presented. The author introduces the response to this section with reference to 'affirmers of the devils', even though that was not the point of contention here.

4 See Enquiry I above.

Enquiry 9

Shaykh Ghazālī provided the following explanation of whispering in the *Iḥyā'*:

> The heart is like a dome which has doors, and states (*aḥwāl*) flow into it through every door. Alternatively, it is like a target at which arrows are shot from every direction; or a standing mirror which people pass by, so image after image is displayed upon it; or a reservoir which is supplied by various waters from open rivers. Know that the entrances of these influences—which are renewed hour after hour—are either external (as the five senses) or internal, such as the imagination (*khayāl*), appetite (*shahwa*), anger (*ghaḍab*) and the character (*akhlāq*) constructed within the person. If he perceives something by his senses, that has an effect upon the heart. If his appetite or anger are inflamed, those states also leave traces upon the heart. Even if a person prevents his external perception, the imagination within his soul remains. As the imagination transfers from one thing to another, so does the heart transfer from one state to another. As such, the heart is constantly in a state of flux under these influences.
>
> The most particular type of impact upon the heart are the occurring thoughts (*khawāṭir*), by which I mean those thoughts and mentions which come about within it, i.e. perceptions and knowledge which are either fresh or renewed by memory. They are called *khawāṭir* because they occur (*takhṭuru*) to the imagination after the heart being oblivious to them. These thoughts are the motors of intentions, and intentions are the motors of the limbs. Moreover, these thoughts which drive intentions comprise both those which incite evil and cause harm eventually, and those which benefit, i.e. eventually. These are two types of occurring thoughts, and as such, they needed two different names. The praiseworthy thoughts are termed 'inspiration' (*ilhām*), while the blameworthy thoughts are called 'whisperings' (*wiswās*).
>
> Since you know that these thoughts all represent accidental states, they require a cause; and since infinite regression is impossible, they must all, ultimately, reach the Necessary Existent.

The above is a summary of Shaykh Ghazālī's words after removing lengthy [tangents].[1]

Enquiry 10
Further Examination of Ghazālī's Discussion

Know that this man has approached the core point, but the goal will not be reached except through further refinement. In order to delve into the main topic, we must begin with some premises:

FIRST PREMISE: There exist things which are sought after (*maṭlūb*), and others which are avoided (*mahrūb*). Anything which is sought is either sought for its own sake or due to another cause. Neither can everything be sought for another's sake, nor can everything be avoided due to another cause, as these would result in circularity or infinite regression, which are both absurd. This proves that there must exist something which is sought for its own sake, as well as something which is avoided for its own sake.

SECOND PREMISE: It is known inductively that that which is sought for its own sake is pleasure (*ladhdha*) and joy (*surūr*).[2] Things which are sought secondarily are those which lead to these. That which is avoided for its own sake is pain (*alam*) and grief (*ghamm*), whereas things which are avoided secondarily are those which lead to these.

THIRD PREMISE: The pleasurable varies with respect to each faculty of the self (*quwā al-nafs*): that which pleases the vision is one thing, whereas the pleasures of the hearing as well as the appetitive, irascible and rational faculties [respectively] are distinct things.[3]

FOURTH PREMISE: If the sense of sight perceives an external existent, that perception leads the mind to observe the nature of the viewed object. On this basis, it gains knowledge of whether that thing is pleasurable, painful, or neither of these. If it becomes known that it is pleasurable, this knowledge—or belief—leads to the development of attraction towards

1 This is extracted from the section entitled *Wonders of the Heart* (Book XXI of the *Iḥyā'*). See a synopsis in Abū Ḥāmid al-Ghazālī, *Iḥyā' ʿulūm al-dīn*, Books XXII and XXIII, trans. T.J. Winter as *Al-Ghazālī on Disciplining the Soul*, Cambridge: Islamic Texts Society, 2001, pp. 240–243.

2 *Ladhdha* is connected linguistically to 'taste' and is therefore more related to the physical, while *surūr* indicates spiritual pleasure. However, *ladhdha* is elsewhere used to represent both aspects. The same applies to 'pain and grief'; see Shihadeh, *Teleological Ethics*, p. 59. In other places, that which is sought for its own sake is 'perfection' (e.g. Book II, Chapter Nine, Enquiry 2), which amounts to the same; see ibid., p. 111.

3 For these latter three, see *Al-Ghazālī on Disciplining the Soul*, p. 19.

that thing; but knowledge or belief that it is painful will produce a tendency to distance one's self and flee from it. However, if it is neither known to be painful nor pleasurable, then the heart does not have a desire either to escape it or to attain it.

FIFTH PREMISE: Knowledge that a thing is pleasurable only necessitates a desire to attain it if that knowledge obtains in the absence of impediments and obstacles. If there is an impediment, then one does not follow from the other. For example, if we saw some food which we knew to be tasty, that knowledge would only persuade us to consume it if we did not believe that there would be excessive harm in so doing. If we did believe that, then the mind would weigh between competing [factors] and select [a course]: we act according to whichever seems most likely to be the correct [choice]. Another example in this regard is that a person might kill himself or throw himself from a high surface if he happens to believe that bearing that hardship would save him from greater pain, or deliver a greater benefit. What we have shown is that the belief that something is pleasurable or painful only necessitates desire or revulsion if that belief is free from impediment.

SIXTH PREMISE: What we have explained entails that animals' actions have levels according to an inherent, necessary and rational order. This is because the proximate cause of these actions are the powers contained in the muscles; however, since these powers can be either used or left unused, the powers alone cannot determine which option transpires unless they are joined by another factor, namely intentions. Those intentions, in turn, only come about due to the knowledge that something is pleasurable or painful. If that knowledge obtains due to the action of the person [etc.], then the original problem returns, leading to circularity or infinite regression. [Hence it must be due] to knowledge, perceptions and conceptions which obtain in the inner-self from external sources. These [sources or causes] are either communications from the heavenly spheres, as some believe, or—and this is the reality—Almighty God creates those beliefs or knowledge in the heart. This is a summary of how actions are produced in animals.

Once this is known: the DENIERS of [the existence of] devils and their whispering said that it is known that the proximate cause of animals' movements is the aforementioned power in their muscles and tendons, which does not become a cause for action or inaction unless it is accompanied by intention. This intention is concomitant to the perception that something is pleasurable or painful. This perception must be created by God, either directly or via intermediary stages, each of which leads to the next in the way we have described; they follow from each other according to an inherently necessary process.

As such, [they say,] if a person perceives a thing and knows it to be suitable [to his tastes], then his nature inclines towards it, and this inclination results in mobilising his power towards seeking it. Once these stages occur, the action follows necessarily. Therefore, if we suppose that there is an external devil and that this devil has the power to whisper, then that whispering would be devoid of effect. This is because the aforementioned stages result in the action necessarily, irrespective of the devil's existence; but without these stages, the action will necessarily not occur, irrespective of the devil's existence. Based on this, it is seen that belief in Satan and satanic whispering is false. Rather, the truth is that when these stages occur in a beneficial direction, we describe it as 'inspiration', whereas when they direct towards what is harmful, that is described as 'whispering'.

That completes our explanation of the objection.

RESPONSE: all that you have mentioned is truthful, but it is not implausible that a person should be unmindful of a thing, but when Satan reminds him of it, he recalls it. Upon this recollection, the inclination towards it follows, and then the action based on that inclination. As such, the external devil has only come with [the role of] reminding, and this is what is indicated by the following verse which quotes Iblīs: 'I had no authority over you except to call you, but you listened to me…' (Q.XIV.22).

However, it remains for a person to say: the human being only committed his sin due to the reminder from the devil; if that devil committed his sin due to the reminder of another devil, this leads to an infinite regression of devils. If his sin was not due to another devil, then the first devil must have committed his sin due to the belief forming in his heart. That accidental belief must have a cause, which can only be Almighty God. Therefore, it is seen that everything is from God.[1]

This is the limit of what can be stated concerning this deep and intricate enquiry. The conclusion is as stated by the Master of the Messengers (may God bless him and grant him peace): 'I seek refuge in You from You!' And God knows best.

1 This accords with Ashʿarī doctrine.

Enquiry II
[The Nature of Thoughts]

When a person sits in seclusion, many thoughts (*khawāṭir*) occur to his heart. It might seem as though he hears hushed sounds and letters within his heart and mind, as if someone is speaking and addressing him. This is an experiential matter which each person finds within himself.

People have differed over this phenomenon. THE PHILOSOPHERS stated that they are not letters and sounds, but rather the imagination (*takhayyul*) of letters and sounds, which means for the shape and form to appear in the mind. Compare this with imagining the image of the mountains, seas and people: the actual objects are not present in the mind or heart, but only their image and form. This can also be compared with the image which appears in the mirror: if we perceive in the mirror the images of heavenly bodies, sun and moon, then this is not because those entities have become present in the mirror—which is impossible— but what appears there are their forms and images. If you understand this with respect to visual imagination, then know that the matter is similar with respect to letters and words which are 'heard'. This is the view of the majority of philosophers.

Someone may say: this thing which you have described as the imagination of letters and words—is it equivalent in terms of quiddity to letters and words, or not? If they are equivalent, then we have returned to the issue of actual letters and sounds forming within the mind, and that the sea and sky actually obtain in the mind when they are imagined. Yet if the truth is the latter, and that which forms in the mind is something distinct from the objects seen or heard, then the question arises again: how do we find the images of these things within ourselves, and experience these words and expressions in a way which leaves us in no doubt that they are successive letters and sounds [presented] to the mind? This is the extent of the philosophers' discussions.

As for the VAST MAJORITY of the people of knowledge, they accept that these successive thoughts are letters and sounds, literally. According to them, the agent [producing] these letters and sounds is either that person or another person; it may also be a separate spiritual entity which is capable of casting those letters and sounds into [the mind of] that person: whether that speaker be a jinn/devil or angel. A [fourth] option is to say that the creator of those letters and sounds is God.

The first option—namely that the person himself produces those sounds—is false because whatever occurs by his choice, he is capable of abandoning. As such, if he were the agent producing those sounds, then he would be able to deflect or stop them if he so wished. The fact is that he is not able: whether he attempts to create them or deflect them, those thoughts present themselves to his mind, one after the other, regardless of his will. The second option—that they are from another person—is obviously false.

Since these two options fail, all that remains is the third [or fourth], i.e. that they are from jinns, angels or Almighty God. As for those people who say that 'It is not permitted for God to perform distasteful acts (*qabā'iḥ*),'[1] then their stance should lead them to say that unpleasant thoughts are not from God, so they must be from the jinns and devils. However, for those who say that 'Nothing from God is considered distasteful,'[2] there is nothing to preclude the attribution of these thoughts to the Almighty.

As for the DUALISTS (*al-thanawiyya*), they maintain that the universe has two gods: one is good and has the angels as his troops, while the other is evil and has the devils as his troops. These two are in constant conflict over everything in this world: each is connected to everything. The thoughts which invite to virtuous deeds originate in the troops of God, whereas the thoughts which incite to evil come from the troops of Satan.

However, know that belief in two gods is completely false, as established by [rational and textual] proofs. This is the most we shall say on the matter.

Enquiry 12
[Limits of Powers]

Some people have attributed to devils the power to give life and death, to create bodies, and to transform individuals from their original created forms. Others rule all of this out and deny their ability to do such things.

Our [Ashʿarī] companions have proven that the ability to create and bring things into existence belongs to none but God, so the other view is completely false [and no more need be said]. The Muʿtazilīs, however, accepted that humans are capable of creating certain things; as a result, they had to explain that the devils have no power to create bodies or life.

They said: 'The devil is a body (*jism*); a body is only able (*qādir*) due to ability (*qudra*); and ability is insufficient to create bodies.' These are three premises:

1. 'The devil is a body'—they have based this on [the supposition] that

1 Such as the Muʿtazilīs.
2 Such as the Ashʿarīs.

everything other than God is either spatial or subsistent within a spatial object. However, they have nothing even approaching a proof for this premise.[1]

2. 'A body is only able due to [an additional attribute of] ability'—they have based this on [the theory] that bodies are such as must be equivalent, so if any one of them were able in its own right,[2] then they would all be alike in that regard. This premise is based on the equivalence (*tamāthul*) of bodies.
3. 'The ability which we possess is insufficient to create bodies, so it must be that any temporally-originated (*ḥādith*) ability is insufficient to create bodies'—this is also weak, because it can be said: why could there not be an ability different from the one we possess, which is in fact sufficient to create bodies? Just because something does not exist presently [in our knowledge], that does not mean that it cannot exist.

This completes our discussion of this matter.

Enquiry 12

There is divergence of opinion over whether jinns have knowledge of the Unseen (*al-ghayb*). Almighty God made clear in His Book that they remained controlled and confined by Solomon (on whom be peace) even after his death, not realising for some time that he had died. This shows that they do not know the Unseen.[3]

Nonetheless, some people claimed that they do know the Unseen, and then they differed over the details. One view is that some jinns ascend to the heavens or approach them in order to be informed about matters of the Unseen from the speech of the angels. Others suggested that they have other methods of knowing the Unseen known only to God. However, know that opening the door to such enquiries leads to nowhere except speculation and guesswork, but it is God Who knows their realities.

The Fifth Pillar: Purpose (*mustaʿādh li-ajlihi*)

We have previously explained that the needs of the human being are

1 In Chapter Five above, the author says that contingent things may also belong to neither category, 'but this is seldom perceptible'.

2 They accept this for God only, denying the existence of a distinct Attribute called *qudra*, in contrast to the Ashʿarīs (see Book II, Chapter Seven below).

3 Q.xxxiv.14: '...the jinns saw plainly that if they had known the Unseen, they would not have tarried in the humiliating penalty'.

without end. There is no benefit except that he needs to attain it, and no harm except that he needs to deflect and remove it. Saying 'I seek refuge in God' relates to driving off all spiritual and physical evils, which are themselves without limit. Here we shall [merely] draw attention to their main categories.

Evils may occur in the context of BELIEFS residing in the heart, or in actions manifested by the limbs. The former encompasses all false beliefs. Things which may be known are infinite, and each thing may be believed either truly and correctly, or falsely and mistakenly. Within this category are the world's misguided sects, which number seventy-two within this [Muslim] nation (*umma*) and over 700 beyond this nation. Saying 'I seek refuge in God' means to seek refuge from all of these.

As for the physical ACTIONS, these are of two kinds: those which bring about religious harms, and those which bring about worldly harms. The former includes everything which God has prohibited in all spheres of accountability, and numbering these is next to impossible. Saying 'I seek refuge in God' applies to all of these [sins]. Worldly harms include all types of pain, ailments, burning, drowning, poverty, chronic illness and blindness —all these types would approach infinity. Saying 'I seek refuge in God' means to seek refuge from each one.

In other words, 'I seek refuge in God' encompasses three categories, each of which is, as it were, infinite:

1. IGNORANCE: since things which can be known are infinite, so too are types of ignorance. The servant, therefore, seeks refuge in God from these, including the numerous types of unbelief (*kufr*) and innovation (*bidʿa*).
2. SINFULNESS: since the areas of accountability are very numerous—as contained in the books of rulings[1]—saying 'I seek refuge in God' refers to all of these.
3. MISFORTUNES, AILMENTS AND SUFFERING: since these are without limit, saying 'I seek refuge in God' refers to them all. Whoever wishes to appreciate their breadth should consult the books of medicine to realise the types of pains and illnesses which can affect each organ.

The rational person must, when he says 'I seek refuge in God,' call to mind these three categories and their subcategories and so on, in as

1 Later editions have *aḥlām* in place of *aḥkām*, but the correct version is found in Amīriyya, vol. 1, p. 50.

much detail as possible. Once he has brought to mind all these things which cannot be defined or enumerated, then realised that the [collective] ability of all creation would be insufficient to deflect them all, his nature and intellect guide him to take refuge with the One Who is able to protect from the infinite number of things under [His] power. Therefore, he says: 'I seek refuge in God, Who has power over all types of ailments and feared things.'[1]

We will suffice with these enquiries in this chapter. And God is the Guide.

1 It is not clear that all these categories—such as illnesses—would be encompassed in saying 'from the rejected Satan'. This latter clause has been left out of the discussion under this 'pillar'.

Chapter Ten
SPIRITUAL ALLUSIONS OF THE *ISTIʿĀDHA*

First Point[1]

Saying 'I seek refuge in God' involves ascent from creation to the Creator and from the contingent to the Necessary.[2] This is the appropriate direction to begin with, as at first there is no way to know Him except to argue from the creation's need for the existence of the Real, the Self-sufficient, the Powerful. Saying 'I seek refuge' indicates this abject need, as without that need there would have been no benefit in seeking refuge; and saying 'in God' indicates His perfect self-sufficiency. Hence when the servant says 'I seek refuge,' he confesses the poverty and need within himself; and when he says 'in God', he admits two things: (a) He is able to fulfil all good things and deflect all harms; (b) no one else possesses this Attribute, so there is none who can deflect harm or deliver benefit except He.

Once he recognises this state of affairs, the servant flees from himself and from everything except the Real, witnessing the secret in God's saying: 'So flee to God…' (Q.LI.50). This state transpires upon saying 'I seek refuge.' Then, when he reaches the presence of the Real and becomes immersed in the light of His majesty, he witnesses God's saying: 'Say "God," then abandon them…' (Q.VI.91);[3] at this point, he says 'I seek refuge in God.'

Second Point

To say 'I seek refuge in God' is to admit the impotence of the self and the omnipotence of the Lord. This shows that there is no route to proximity to the divine presence except through helplessness and brokenness.

1 In contrast to most chapters, this one has 'subtle points' (*nukat*) in place of 'enquiries' (*masāʾil*). This term, as well as *laṭāʾif* in the chapter title, implies that these are points which depend upon, and nurture, spiritual and intellectual wisdom.

2 That is, by mentioning 'I' first and then 'God'.

3 The verse is here being used with a mystical interpretation in contrast to its actual exegesis, as the author acknowledges that the contextually-derived meaning is 'God [revealed the Torah].' It is cited in a similar way at the end of Book III.

Among the Prophetic words in this connection are: 'Whoever knows himself knows his Lord'[1]—meaning that one who recognises the weakness and shortcomings of his own self will realise that his Lord is capable of all things; whoever recognises his own ignorance will realise the grace and mercy of his Lord; and whoever recognises the lowliness of his own state will realise the perfection and majesty of his Lord.

Third Point

Performing acts of obedience is not possible until one has fled from Satan by pronouncing the *istiʿādha*. However, this is itself an act of obedience: so if every act of obedience depends on seeking refuge before it, then each *istiʿādha* is in need of a preceding *istiʿādha*, leading to infinite regression. If, on the other hand, obedience does not depend on seeking refuge, then there is no benefit in the *istiʿādha*. Thus it is as though it is said to [the servant by God]: 'Performing acts of obedience is not possible unless it is preceded by seeking refuge, but this would result in an infinite task which is beyond your capacity. However, if you recognise this fact, then you have witnessed your own helplessness and shortcomings, so I shall help you to perform those deeds and I shall teach you how to approach them. Say: "I seek refuge in God from the rejected Satan."'

Fourth Point

The wisdom behind seeking refuge is that it consists of turning to One Who is able to avert harms from you. Among the most significant contexts in which Satan casts his whispers is the recitation of the Qur'ān, because one who recites it with the intention of worshipping the Compassionate, and ponders upon its promises, warnings and clear signs—such a person will see his desire for good deeds increase along with his revulsion from forbidden things. For this reason, reciting the Qur'ān is considered among the greatest of deeds, so it is of little wonder that Satan is particularly keen to block people from it. This makes the servant's need for protection from Satan's evil more acute; this is the wisdom behind recitation being singled out for seeking refuge.

Fifth Point

Satan is the enemy of humanity: 'Indeed, Satan is an enemy to you: so treat him as an enemy' (Q.xxxv.6). The Compassionate is the Guardian of humanity, their Creator and Resolver of their affairs. When a person

1 This is a famous saying, but equally famous among *Ḥadīth* scholars as a fabrication.

goes to perform an act of obedience and worship, he fears his enemy and strives to attain the pleasure of his Master so that He preserves him from the approach of that enemy. Once he reaches the [divine] presence and witnesses all that beauty and honour, he forgets the enemy and turns fully to the service of his Beloved.

The first station is 'fleeing' (*firār*) by saying 'I seek refuge in God from the rejected Satan'; and the second is 'settling' (*istiqrār*) in the presence of the Overwhelming Sovereign, which is by saying: 'In the Name of God, the Compassionate, the Merciful.'

Sixth Point

Almighty God said: 'None shall touch [the Book] except for those who are purified' (Q.LVI.79). When the heart connects to other than God and the tongue mentions other than God, a certain type of impurity accrues upon them and purification becomes necessary. This is achieved by saying 'I seek refuge in God.' Then the person is ready to perform the true prayer (*ṣalāh*), which is the remembrance of God, saying: 'In the Name of God.'

Seventh Point

The people of allusions (*ishārāt*)[1] have said: you have two enemies: one outward (*ẓāhir*) and one inward (*bāṭin*); and you are commanded to fight them both. Concerning the former, God said: 'Fight those who believe not in God…' (Q.IX.29); and concerning the latter: 'Indeed, Satan is an enemy to you: so treat him as an enemy' (Q.XXXV.6).

It is as though God has said: 'When you fight your outward enemy, your support will be the angels (*malak*): "…your Lord would help you with 5,000 marked angels" (Q.III.125); but when you fight your inward enemy, your support will be the Sovereign (*al-Malik*): "Over My servants no authority shall you [Satan] have…" (Q.XV.42).'

Moreover, fighting the inward enemy is more important than fighting the outward. This is because the outward enemy, if given the opportunity, will attack the things of this world. The inward enemy, on the contrary, would attack religion and certainty. Also, if the outward enemy overcomes us, we are rewarded; but if the inward enemy overcomes us, we

1 The esoteric approach to Qur'ān commentary known as *tafsīr ishārī* has been criticised as flouting linguistic and exegetical principles. See Muḥammad al-Fāḍil Ibn ʿĀshūr, *al-Tafsīr wa-rijāluh*, Cairo: Majmaʿ al-Buḥūth al-Islāmiyya, 1997, pp. 168–9; his points echo criticism by Ghazālī of esoteric (*bāṭinī*) interpretations. Some scholars have discussed conditions under which such spiritual reflections may be accepted; see Dhahabī, *al-Tafsīr wa'l-mufassirūn*, vol. II, pp. 328–331.

are in tribulation. [Thirdly,] one who is killed by the outward enemy is a martyr, while one killed by the inward enemy is an outcast. Therefore, more precautions are needed against the inward enemy, and that is only by saying with one's heart and tongue: 'I seek refuge in God from the rejected Satan.'

Eighth Point

The heart of the believer is the noblest of places. You will not find any goodly mansion or green and tended garden except that the believer's heart is superior to it. The believer's heart is clean like a mirror, indeed more so: for a mirror displays nothing if a veil is placed in front of it, whereas the believer's heart is not veiled by the seven heavens, the Footstool or the Throne [from his Lord], as God said: 'To Him mount up (all) words of purity: it is He Who exalts each deed of righteousness' (Q.xxxv.10). Rather, despite all these veils, the heart reaches the majesty of Lordship and gains knowledge of the eternal Attributes.

The following points demonstrate that the heart is the noblest of places:

1. The Prophet (may God bless him and grant him peace) said: 'The grave is one of the gardens of Paradise'[1]—due only to its having become home to a righteous servant who has died. Since the heart is a couch for the knowledge of God, and a throne for His Divinity, it follows that it is the noblest of all places.
2. It is as though God says: 'O My servant! Your heart is your garden and Paradise is My Garden.[2] Since you were not miserly towards your garden—rather, you filled it with knowledge of Me—how could I be miserly towards you with My Garden and prevent you from it?'
3. God has described how the servant comes to dwell in the garden of Paradise, saying: 'In an assembly of truth, in the presence of an All-Powerful Sovereign' (Q.liv.55). He did not merely say 'the Sovereign' (*malīk*) [because] it is as if He said: 'That day, I shall be the All-Powerful Sovereign and My servants will be sovereigns, except that they are under My power.'

Once you have appreciated this introduction, then we say: it is as though Almighty God says: 'My servant, I have made My Garden for you, and you have made your garden for Me, but you have not done Me justice:

1 Recorded by Tirmidhī with the completion: 'or one of the pits of Hellfire'.
2 I have reversed the descriptions here as the printed version was inconsistent.

for have you seen My Garden and entered it?' The servant replies: 'No, my Lord.' The Almighty says: 'And have I entered your garden?' The servant must reply: 'Yes, my Lord.' The Almighty then says: 'Even though you have not yet entered My Garden, once the time of your arrival drew close,[1] I expelled Satan from it in preparation for you, saying to him: "Get you out, disgraced and rejected!" I expelled your enemy before your arrival; but as for you, how could it be that you do not cast out My enemy after I have dwelt in your garden for seventy years?' At this, the servant says: 'My God, You are capable of driving him out from Your Garden, whereas I am weak and helpless to drive him out.' So the Lord says: 'The helpless one, when he enters the protection of the powerful Sovereign, becomes strong. So enter into My protection and you will be able to cast the enemy from the garden of your heart. Say: "I seek refuge in God from the rejected Satan."'

One may ask: if the heart is God's garden, then why does He not cast Satan from it? The people of allusions reply that it is as though God says to the servant: 'You are the one who has given hospitality to the Sultan of [divine] knowledge[2] in the chamber of your heart. Whoever welcomes a sovereign in his room must accept the duty of sweeping and cleaning the room. This is not the duty of the Sultan: so you clean the chamber [which is] your heart from the impurities of [Satan's] whispers and say: "I seek refuge in God from the rejected Satan."'[3]

Ninth Point

It is as though God says: 'O My servant, you have not done Me justice. Do you know what spoiled the relationship between Me and Satan? He used to worship Me like the angels and recognised My Divinity; but then I ordered him to prostrate to your father Adam and he refused. Due to his arrogance, I banished him from My service. In reality, he did not have enmity towards your father [at first], but rather he refused to serve Me. Then he has waged war on you for seventy years, yet you love him! He opposes you in every good [you intend] while you follow him in all his intentions! Leave this blameworthy way and declare your enmity to him by saying: "I seek refuge in God from the rejected Satan."'

1 Presumably, this refers to the creation of Adam.

2 This gnosis is represented here as a majestic ruler. Here, as at various points in the preceding discussion, the symbolism is fluid between God and/or His knowledge dwelling in the heart.

3 However, it has already been explained in various ways that this does not constitute the action of the servant himself.

Tenth Point

If you look at the story of your father, [you find that Satan] swore to him that he was a sincere adviser,[1] but the outcome was that he strove to have them removed from Paradise. As for you, Satan has sworn that he will misguide and mislead you: 'Then, by Your might, I will surely mislead them all' (Q.xxxviii.82). If that is how he treated one whom he swore he was sincerely advising, then what of one whom he has sworn to misguide and mislead?

Eleventh Point

The Name *Allāh* has been used in this context ('I seek refuge in God') rather than another [Divine] Name because it has a greater effect in deterring one from sins than other Names and Attributes. This is because the *ilāh* (god)[2] is One deserving of worship, and this can only be if He is powerful, knowledgeable and wise. As such, 'I seek refuge in God' is like saying: 'I seek refuge in the Powerful, Knowledgeable and Wise One,' and these Attributes are the ultimate in deterrence.

This is so because a thief [for example] may know that the sultan is powerful, yet he steals from him anyway because he knows that, despite his power, the sultan lacks knowledge [i.e. of events around him]. This shows that power is not enough as a deterrent, but it requires knowledge alongside it. Even power and knowledge together are not enough, as the ruler might observe an evil but do nothing to discourage it, in which case his presence does nothing to prevent it. However, if power and knowledge are accompanied by the wisdom which prevents distasteful deeds, then full deterrence is achieved. Thus when the servant says 'I seek refuge in *Allāh*,' it is as though he has said: 'I seek refuge in the Powerful, Knowledgeable and Wise, Who does not accept any wrongdoing'—and this would certainly deter him completely.

Twelfth Point

When the servant says 'I seek refuge in God from the rejected Satan,' this indicates that he does not accept to be alongside Satan. He rejects this because Satan is a sinner, even though his sin does not, in reality, harm that Muslim. If the servant does not accept to be alongside a sinner, it is more fitting that he should refuse to be alongside [and commit] the sin itself.

1 See Q.vii.21.

2 This is on the frequently-occurring assumption that the name *Allāh* is derived from *ilāh*, but the author himself disputes that: see Book II, Chapter Nine below.

Thirteenth Point

'Satan' is a noun and 'rejected' is an adjective; God did not suffice with the noun but added the adjective as if to say: 'This Satan remained in [My] service for thousands of years, then do you suppose that [his rebellion] has harmed Me in any way? [That is impossible,] yet I stoned him and expelled him. As for you [O servant], if this devil sat with you for even a moment, he would cast you into eternal Fire: so how can you not busy yourself with repelling and cursing him? Say: "I seek refuge in God from the rejected Satan."'

Fourteenth Point

QUERY: why not say 'I seek refuge in the angels,' when it is known that the least of them would be sufficient to repel Satan? And what is the reason for this dog's name being mentioned in opposition to God's?

RESPONSE: it is as though God says: 'My servant, he sees you while you see him not'—as in the verse: 'He and his tribe watch you from a position where you cannot see them' (Q.VII.27)—'and this is the very reason he has been able to enact his plot against you. So hold fast to the One Who sees Satan, but Satan does not see Him, namely Almighty God, and say: "I seek refuge in God from the rejected Satan."'

Fifteenth Point

The [definite article] *al-* is attached to *al-shayṭān* in order to signify the genus (*jins*)—i.e 'the devils'—as the devils are numerous, both visible and invisible; indeed, the visible ones may be more dangerous.

It is narrated that a preacher declared in his gathering that when a man intends to give charity, seventy devils come and attach themselves to his hands, legs and heart in order to prevent him. Someone heard this and said: 'I will fight these seventy!' He left the mosque for his house and filled his garment with wheat, intending to give it in charity. His wife pounced on him and began to argue and forbid him until he removed the wheat from his garment. When he came back despondently to the mosque and the preacher asked him what had happened, he replied: 'I defeated the seventy but their mother overcame me!'[1]

It is also permitted to consider the article as making the word definite due to prior mention (*ʿahd*),[2] because all sins occur with the consent of this Satan and one who consents to an action is like the one who com-

1 Obviously, there are devilish men who obstruct the righteous deeds of women.

2 That is, to refer to a specific devil whose identity is known to the listener.

mits it. If you should think this fanciful, then consider an [analogous] legal issue: Abū Ḥanīfa counts the recitation of the *imām* as being also the recitation of the follower, in that [the latter] accepts it and remains silent behind him.[1]

Sixteenth Point

The word *shayṭān* is derived from [the verb] *shaṭana*, meaning 'to be distant'. This means that he has been sentenced with being distant, whereas the obedient one is near [to God]: 'Prostrate and draw near' (Q.xcvi.19), and God is near to you: 'When My servants ask you concerning Me, I am indeed near...' (Q.ii.186).

He is *rajīm* (stoned) in the sense of being pelted by arrows of accursedness and wretchedness. You, on the other hand, are connected by the rope of felicity. God said: '...and He made them stick close to the command of self-restraint' (Q.xlviii.26).

This shows that He made Satan distant and cursed, but made you close and connected. Then God has informed us that he will never make that distant Satan close, when He said: 'No divergence will you find in God's way' (Q.xxxv.43). Therefore, know that once He has made you close, he will never cast you out or isolate you from His grace and mercy.

Seventeenth Point

Jaʿfar al-Ṣādiq said, '*Istiʿādha* is required at the time of recitation but not for other acts of obedience. The wisdom behind this is that the servant's tongue may be polluted by lies, backbiting and slander, so God commanded him to seek refuge and make his tongue pure in order to recite the words revealed by the Pure and Goodly Lord.'

Eighteenth Point

It is as though God says: 'He is a rejected devil, and I am Compassionate, Merciful: so distance yourself from the rejected Satan in order to reach the Compassionate and Merciful.'

Nineteenth Point

Satan is your enemy, while you are heedless of him. The Almighty said: 'He and his tribe watch you from a position where you cannot see them' (Q.vii.27). Thus you have an enemy who is unseen (*ghā'ib*), and a Beloved

1 See Book III, Chapter Four, Enquiry 12.

Who is all-prevailing (*ghālib*): 'And God has full power and control over His affairs' (Q.xii.21). So when the unseen enemy approaches, flee to the all-prevailing Beloved.

And Almighty God knows best what He intends.

Chapter Eleven
FURTHER ENQUIRIES ASSOCIATED WITH THE *ISTIʿĀDHA*

[First Type of Enquiry]

Enquiry 1[1]

There is a difference between saying 'I seek refuge in God' and 'In God I seek refuge' (*bi'Llāhi aʿūdhu*), as the latter denotes exclusivity (*ḥaṣr*) in contrast to the former. If the latter is more emphatic, then why has only the former been commanded?

Also, there are [texts containing] both *al-ḥamdu li'Llāh* ('Praise is for God') and *li'Llāhi al-ḥamd* ('For God is all praise'), yet 'In God I seek refuge' has not appeared—so whence this difference?

Enquiry 2

'I seek refuge in God' is worded as a declarative (*khabar*), but its meaning is a supplication (*duʿā'*), i.e. 'O God! Give me refuge.' Do you not see that God said [quoting Mary's mother]: 'I commend her and her offspring to Your protection from the rejected Satan' (Q.III.36)? This is like saying 'I ask God's forgiveness' (*astaghfiru Allāh*), i.e. 'O God! Forgive me.' The proof of this is that 'I seek refuge in God' is a statement about [the servant's] action, which has no benefit unless God grants him that refuge.

Therefore, what is the reason for saying 'I seek refuge' rather than 'Give me refuge'? The reason is that there is a covenant between the Lord and the servant, as He said: 'Fulfil the covenant of God when you have entered into it...' (Q.XVI.91), 'And fulfil your covenant with Me so that I fulfil My Covenant with you' (Q.II.40). As such, it is as though the servant says: 'Despite my poor and wretched human state, I have fulfilled the

1 This chapter has the appearance of being unfinished, as a number of enquiries have been left as unanswered questions or like empty headings. The usual numbering system of enquiries has been replaced by, or subsumed within, a system of letters as well as a vaguely demarcated grouping of four 'types' of enquiry. I have taken some liberties in making the structure clearer in the translation of this chapter.

covenant of my servanthood by saying "I seek refuge in God," so You are worthier—in Your infinite bounty and unlimited beneficence and mercy—to fulfil the Covenant of Lordship by saying: "I give you refuge from the rejected Satan."'

Enquiry 3

Aʿūdhu ('I seek refuge') is an imperfect (*muḍāriʿ*) verb which is applicable to the present and future [tenses]—but is it literal (*ḥaqīqa*) [in expressing] both of these? The truth is that [the imperfect] is literally for the present and metaphorically (*majāz*) for the future. It is made specific to the latter by use of the letter *sīn* and [particle] *sawfa*.

Enquiry 4

Why does it share between present and future, and not present and past?

Enquiry 5

How is the imperfect verb similar to the noun?

Enquiry 6

What is the nature of the agent acting upon it, as it is—without doubt—acted upon?

Enquiry 7

'I seek refuge' denotes the servant seeking refuge in the present and the entire future: this is completeness. Therefore, does it entail that the *istiʿādha* remains in Paradise?

Enquiry 8

'I seek refuge' is a [first person] expression for the [singular] self, but necessarily the four [imperfect conjugation] letters must be used: *alif*, *tā'*, *yā'* and *nūn*.[1]

[Second Type of Enquiry: The Particle *Bā'*]

There are numerous rational enquiries connected to the [particle] *bā'* in *aʿūdhu bi'Llāh*. This is known as the *bā'* of attachment (*ilṣāq*). There are a number of enquiries in this regard:

Enquiry 1

The Baṣrans name this the *bā'* of attachment, whereas the Kūfans call it the *bā'* of instrument (*āla*), and some call it the *bā'* of inclusion (*taḍmīn*).

1 These give rise to the subjects 'I', 'you/she', 'he/they' and 'we', respectively.

The basic fact is that it must be connected to a verb.[1] Its benefit is that it is not possible to attach that verb by itself except with that [noun] upon which the *bā'* has entered: so it is called the *bā'* of attachment because it is the means of attachment.[2] It is [also called] the *bā'* of instrument because it is attached to the thing [functioning as] an instrument.

Enquiry 2

It is a matter of agreement that with [this *bā'*] there must a verb [even if] implicit. If you said *bi'l-qalam* ('by the pen'), that would not be meaningful unless you said *katabtu bi'l-qalam* ('I wrote by the pen'). This shows that the particle is connected to an implicit [verb].[3] A parallel case is 'By God (*bi'Llāh*), I shall do such-and-such,' which implies: 'I swear (*aḥlifu*) by God'—the ellipsis of the verb is [possible] due to contextual implication, and so it is here.[4]

Similarly, a man may say to someone who asks him permission to travel: *ʿalā 'smi 'Llāh* ('upon God's Name'), i.e. 'Proceed (*sir*) upon God's Name.'

Enquiry 3

Once it is known that a verb must be assumed, we [further] say: ellipsis [of that verb] is more eloquent in this context. This is because if the implicit [verb] were made explicit then that would limit [the meaning of] 'I seek refuge in God' to that specific matter. When it is removed, then the imagination goes in every direction and it comes to mind that every task depends for its completion upon seeking refuge in God, and upon commencing with the Name of God.[5]

The aforementioned is similar to the fact that we say *Allāhu akbar*

1 That is, it comes after a verb and performs a function on behalf of that verb.

2 This sentence is difficult to interpret and it seems to me that the words have been printed out of order. It could be: 'It is not possible to attach that verb to the [noun] upon which the *bā'* has entered except with that *bā'*.' For further explanations from grammarians, see Muḥammad ʿAbd al-Khāliq ʿUḍayma, *Dirāsāt li-uslūb al-Qur'ān*, 11 vols., Cairo: Dār al-Ḥadith, 2004, vol. II, p. 5.

3 That is, it must be so assumed if the verb is not explicitly stated: see the following example.

4 Enquiries 2 and 3 seem to assume that there is no verb in the formula 'I seek refuge in God,' even though *aʿūdhu* is present explicitly. Moreover, the author has not identified the 'implicit' or 'elliptical' verb to which he alludes. Cf. the implied verb with the *basmala*: Book II, Chapter One.

5 The difference between 'I seek refuge in God' and 'In the name of God' is that there is an explicit verb in the former, whereas the latter requires us to assume or supply one such as 'I begin'. One can understand from the author's comparison between the two that just as everything is to be done in God's Name and begun in God's Name, so everything is done 'in God' (*bi'Llāh*) and seeking His refuge.

('God is greater'), like so without specifying that He is 'greater than such-and-such thing'. This results in universality of meaning as we have said, and so it is here.[1]

Enquiry 4

Sībawayh said: this *bā'* has no role other than *kasr* [i.e. making things genitive], so it was given *kasr* [the /i/ vowel] for that reason. If it is pointed out that the *kāf* of similitude [also] has no role other than *kasr* and yet it has a *fatḥa* [the /a/ vowel], we reply: the [particle] *kāf* is interchangeable with a noun,[2] and [nouns] are weak as agents. As for the [pure] particle, it only exists to have its effect, so it is strong in that respect.

Enquiry 5

A *bā'* can be an original [part of the word], as in: 'Say: "I am not something novel (*bidᶜan*) among the Messengers"' (Q.XLVI.9); and it can be additional with the following [five][3] usages:

a. For attachment, such as *aᶜūdhu bi'Llāh* and *bi'smi 'Llāh*.
b. For partitivity (*tabᶜīḍ*), according to Shāfiᶜī (may God be pleased with him).[4]
c. To emphasise negation; for example, 'Nor is your Lord ever unjust (*bi-ẓallām*) to His servants' (Q.XLI.46).
d. For transitivity (*taᶜdiya*); for example, *dhahaba Allāhu bi-nūrihim* (Q.II.17), meaning 'God made their light depart (*adhhaba*).'
e. With the meaning of *fī* (in). This is found in the poetic line: *ḥalla bi-aᶜdā'ika mā ḥalla bī* ('What dwelt in [i.e. happened to] your enemies dwelt in me').

As for the *bā'* of oath—such as in *bi'Llāh* ('By God')—that falls within the *bā'* of attachment.[5]

Enquiry 6

Some said that the *bā'* in the verse '...and wipe your heads (*bi-ru'ūsikum*)' (Q.V.6) is otiose (*zā'ida*)[6] and the meaning is simply 'wipe your heads' (*wa'msaḥū ru'ūsakum*). Shāfiᶜī said that it has a partitive meaning [i.e. 'wipe (part of) your heads'], and his proofs are as follows:

1 See Book III, Chapter Six, Section IX.
2 I.e. *mithl*.
3 In the text: 'four purposes'.
4 See the following enquiry.
5 See Enquiry 2 above.
6 I.e. it does not have a clear semantic function, although it may have a rhetorical effect.

1. The *bā'* must either be meaningless or meaningful, and the former is false because that is completely unbefitting to the speech of the Lord of the worlds, the Most Wise. Indeed, the purpose of speech is to be informative, so claiming that [any speech] is meaningless is to go against the default. Therefore, it is known that [the particle] has an additional benefit, and the only benefit which has been identified [in this context] is partitivity.
2. The difference between *masaḥtu bi-yadī al-mindīl* ('I wiped, with my hand, the handkerchief')[1] and *masaḥtu yadī bi'l-mindīl* ('I wiped my hand with the handkerchief') is that [the latter] would hold true even if the person wiped his hand with merely a part of the handkerchief.
3. Some lexicologists said that the *bā'* may be used partitively, while others denied that. However, since the affirming narration takes precedence, it is established that it may be so used. Since the extent of that 'part' is not specified, it must apply to anything that can be termed 'part', i.e. the least part of the head must be sufficient.

The aforementioned is the position of Shāfiʿī, which faces a problem from another verse [concerning dry ablution (*tayammum*)]: '...then wipe your faces (*bi-wujūhikum*) and hands' (Q.iv.43). This would entail the sufficiency of wiping the least part of the face and hands in dry ablution, whereas Shāfiʿī considers it necessary to wipe them in full.

One could reply to this by saying: [true], this text implies that wiping the least part of the face and hands is sufficient in dry ablution, but in Shāfiʿī's view it is possible to add [a ruling] to a text without that constituting abrogation.[2] As such, we have made complete [wiping in dry ablution] obligatory due to all the other evidences, whereas in the case of wiping the head [in ordinary ablution] there is no evidence entailing the obligation of wiping it fully, so we suffice with the quantity indicated by this text.

Enquiry 7

The companions of Abū Ḥanīfa have derived a number of [juristic] issues concerning the *bā'* of attachment:

1. Muḥammad [al-Shaybānī] said in *al-Ziyādāt* that if a man says to his wife 'You are divorced by the will of God (*bi-mashī'at Allāh*),' then

1 The author quotes this under the relevant verse (Q.v.6, Enquiry 36) as: *masaḥtu al-mindīl* ('I wiped the handkerchief'), which—like this version—is to be understood as denoting that the entire handkerchief was wiped.

2 Contrary to Ḥanafī *uṣūl*.

divorce is not effected, as this is like saying: 'You are divorced if God wills.' However, if he says 'due to the will of God (*li-mashī'at Allāh*),' then divorce is effected, as that is like an explanation. It is the same if the [similar] term *irāda* is used [in place of *mashī'a*]. However, if he says 'You are divorced by God's knowledge (*ʿilm*)' or 'due to God's knowledge', then divorce is effected in both cases, so the difference should be [explained].

2. He said in the Book of Oaths (*aymān*) that if someone says to his wife 'If you exit this house—except with my permission (*bi-idhnī*)—then you are divorced', then she would require his permission on each occasion. However, if he said 'except if I permit you' and then gave her permission once, that would be sufficient—so the difference should be [explained].
3. If he says to his wife 'Divorce yourself three times for 1,000 (*bi-alf*) [*dīnārs*, etc.]' and she divorces herself once, then it would be effected [and he owes] a third of that sum. This is because the *bā'* here entails exchange (*badaliyya*), so the currency (*badal*) is distributed over the commodity (*mubdal*) such that each divorce is worth one third of 1,000. However, if he said 'Divorce yourself three times upon (*ʿalā*) 1,000' and she divorced herself once, then nothing would be effected according to Abū Ḥanīfa. This is because the [particle] *ʿalā* relates to a condition (*sharṭ*), which has not been fulfilled here. According to his two companions,[1] it would be effected for a third of the sum.

I say: there are numerous [other juristic] enquiries related to the *bā'*:

1. Abū Ḥanīfa said that the price (*thaman*) is only distinguished from the commodity (*muthman*) by the particle *bā'* entering the [former]; so if someone says 'I sell you this for that (*bi-kadhā*),' only the one with the *bā'* is the price. Upon this distinction, [Abū Ḥanīfa] based the issue of a vitiated (*fāsid*) transaction, saying: if someone says 'I sell you this garment for this wine,' the transaction is valid but vitiated.[2] However, if he says 'I sell you this wine for this garment,' it is invalid. The difference is that in the first scenario, the wine is [considered] the price, whereas in the second, it was the commodity; to treat wine as a price is permitted, whereas to treat it as a commodity is not.

1 I.e. Abū Yūsuf and Muḥammad.

2 In the Ḥanafī school, this implies that the transaction 'remains in a state of suspension' until the corrupting factor has been removed or resolved. See Ibn Rushd, *Bidāyat al-mujtahid*, trans. Imran Nyazee as *The Distinguished Jurist's Primer*, 2 vols., Reading: Garnet, 2004, vol. II, p. 153, note 120.

2. Shāfiʿī stated that if someone says 'I sell you this garment for this *dirham*,' it must be that specific *dirham*. According to Abū Ḥanīfa, it need not be.
3. Almighty God said: 'Indeed, God has purchased from the believers their souls and their wealth in exchange for Paradise being theirs' (Q.IX.111)—He made Paradise the price for their lives and wealth.

There are also enquiries arising in jurisprudence (*uṣūl al-fiqh*):

1. The *bā'* may denote causation; for example, 'That is because they (*bi-annahum*) contended against God and His Messenger' (Q.VIII.13). However, it was also said that this is not allowed, as one cannot say that a thing occurred *bi-hādhā al-sabab* ('for this reason') and attach the *bā'* to the cause.
2. If we say that the *bā'* can denote cause, then what is the difference between that and the *lām* of causation? This must be explained.
3. The *bā'* in *subḥānaka Allāhumma wa-bi-ḥamdika* ('Glory and praise is for You, O God!') must be researched, as it is not clear to what it is connected; likewise in '…while we celebrate your praises' (Q.II.30).[1]

It has been said: 'All fields of knowledge are contained within the four [major revealed] Books; all their knowledge is in the Qur'ān; all its knowledge is in the *Fātiḥa*; all its knowledge is in the *basmala*; and all its knowledge is in the *bā'* of *bi'smi 'Llāh*.' I say: this is because the goal of any knowledge is for the servant to reach the Lord: this *bā'* is for 'attachment' and attaches the servant to the Lord, and this is the complete purpose.

Third Type of Enquiry: The Preposition *Min*

This phrase comprises two such particles, namely the *bā'* and *min* (from). The latter contains a number of enquiries:

Enquiry 1

You say *akhadhtu al-māl mini 'bnik* ('I took the money from your son') with a *kasra* on the [final letter] *nūn*, but you say *mina 'l-rajul* ('from the man') with *fatḥa*.[2] The ending of the word has changed, and there are vowels specific to each situation. This means that the word-ending has changed due to varying agents (*ʿawāmil*), as an agent is nothing but that which

1 In his exegesis of this verse, the author quotes a grammatical explanation from Zamakhsharī and then provides two explanations of the intended meaning.

2 This is the phenomenon of *naql* (transference) of the following word's initial vowel to the *nūn* in order to resolve the concurrence of two unvowelled letters.

dictates that [the word] deserves particular vowels. [This implies that] the word must be inflected (*muʿrab*).[1]

Enquiry 2

The word *min* has four usages: for point of origin (*ibtidāʾ al-ghāya*); partitive (*tabʿīḍ*); clarifying (*tabyīn*); and otiose/emphatic (*ziyāda*).

Enquiry 3

Al-Mubarrad said that it is originally for point of origin and the other usages branch from that. Others said that it is originally partitive with the other usages branching from that.

Enquiry 4

Some denied that it can be otiose.[2] Concerning [for example] the verse '...He will forgive you [from] your sins (*min dhunūbikum*)' (Q.XLVI.31), they explained that [the particle] provides an additional meaning, as though to say that 'He will forgive [each] portion of your sins,' as whoever forgives every portion has indeed forgiven them all.

Enquiry 5

The difference between [particles] *min* and *ʿan* should be explained, as in Satan's saying [quoted in the Qurʾān]: 'Then will I assault them from (*min*) before them and from (*min*) behind them, from (*ʿan*) their right and from (*ʿan*) their left' (Q.VII.17). There are two questions in this connection: first, why was *min* used in the first two, and *ʿan* in the latter two?[3] Second, since Satan has expressed his point using both particles, why does the *istiʿādha* use *min* and not *ʿan*?

Fourth Type of Enquiry[4]

Enquiry 1

Al-shayṭān is an emphatic noun from *shayṭana* (rebelliousness) just as *al-Raḥmān* is an emphatic noun from *raḥma* (mercy). Satan being *rajīm*

1 It is not, but this is another of the unanswered queries raised in this chapter. See Chapter Six, Enquiry 18 above.

2 The word that is here used for 'otiose', *zāʾida*, is more generally a point of controversy theologically or from the viewpoint of etiquette in speaking of the Qurʾān.

3 Under the verse in question, the author provides two explanations. One is that Satan maintains a greater distance from the right and left sides (which the particle *ʿan* implies), due to the presence of recording angels on the right and left.

4 These have all been left unanswered, at least at this juncture.

is as the object [of stoning], whereas God's being *Raḥīm* is as the agent [of mercy]. As such, the [*istiʿādha*] implies that one is fleeing from the rejected Satan to the Compassionate and Merciful; this, in turn, implies an equivalence between the two. In this, the beliefs of the Dualists could find support, i.e. those who said that God and Iblīs are brothers, but that God is the noble, generous and merciful brother, while Iblīs is the lowly, wicked, and vicious one—so the sensible person flees from the evil to the virtuous.

Enquiry 2

Is God merciful and kind? If so, why did He create the rejected Satan and give him power over His servants? If not, then what benefit would there be in turning to Him and seeking His refuge from Satan's evil?

Enquiry 3

Do the angels in the heavens say 'I seek refuge in God from the rejected *shayṭān*'? If so, they are seeking refuge from the evil within themselves, not that of Satan.

Enquiry 4

Do the inhabitants of Paradise say 'I seek refuge in God'?

Enquiry 5

Why do the Prophets and saints say 'I seek refuge in God' even though Satan stated that he would have no influence on them: 'Then, by Your might, I will surely mislead them all—except Your servants amongst them, sincere and purified' (Q.xxxviii.82)?

Enquiry 6

Satan stated that he had no influence on [humans] except to incite them: 'I had no authority over you except to call you but you listened to me: then reproach not me, but reproach your own souls' (Q.xiv.22). It is the human being who has cast himself into tribulation, so it is more important and necessary for him to seek refuge from the evil of his own self: so why begin with the lesser priority and leave off the greater?

BOOK II

The *Basmala*

Chapter One
INTRODUCTORY ENQUIRIES

Enquiry 1

We have explained[1] that the [preposition] *bā'* in *bi'smi 'Llāh al-Raḥmān al-Raḥīm* ('In the Name of God, the Compassionate, the Merciful') is connected (*mutaʿalliq*) to something implicit (*muḍmar*). We now say: this could be either an implicit noun or verb; and in each case it may precede or follow [the explicit words].

This gives rise to the following four scenarios, whereby it is:

- a preceding verb—for example, 'I commence (*abda'u*) in the Name of God';
- a preceding noun—for example, 'The commencement of speech (*ibtidā' al-kalām*) is in the Name of God';
- a following verb—for example, 'In the Name of God I commence';
- a following noun—for example, 'In the Name of God is my commencement.'

As such, we must investigate two matters.[2] First, is it worthier for it to come before or after? Both of these occur in the Qur'ān. [The Name of God] comes first in: '…in the Name of God, whether it move or be at rest' (Q.XI.41), and after in: 'Read in the Name of your Lord' (Q.XCVI.1).[3]

I say that for [the Name of God] to precede is worthier for the following reasons:

1. Almighty God is pre-eternal and necessarily existent in His own right, so His existence is prior to any other existence. Precedence in essence makes one deserving of precedence in mention.
2. God said: 'He is the First and the Last' (Q.LVII.3) and 'To God belongs the command, before and after' (Q.XXX.4).[4]

1 See the previous chapter under the 'Second Type'.

2 The second of these is the subject of Enquiry 2.

3 In the former, the formula is followed by a noun; in the latter, it is preceded by a verb.

4 These do not seem to support either case against the other, unless it is said that the 'First' was mentioned first, and likewise 'before'.

3. Precedence in mention entails fuller magnification.
4. God said: *You we worship* (Q.1.5), in which the verb (*naʿbudu*) follows the [pro]noun (*iyyāka*). Therefore, it should be the same case with *In the Name of God*, i.e. it should be followed by 'I commence.'
5. I heard my father, Shaykh Ḍiyā' al-Dīn ʿUmar (may God be pleased with him), say that he heard Shaykh Abū al-Qāsim al-Anṣārī saying: Shaykh Abū Saʿīd b. Abī al-Khayr al-Mīhanī met with Ustādh Abū al-Qāsim al-Qushayrī, and the latter said: 'The spiritual masters have said: "We have not seen anything without seeing God after it."' Shaykh Abū Saʿīd b. Abī al-Khayr replied: 'That is the station of the disciples (*maqām al-murīdīn*). As for the spiritual masters (*muḥaqqiqūn*), they do not see anything without having seen God before it.'

I say: the resolution of the matter is that the transition [in speech] from creation to Creator is related to the 'Verily proof' (*burhān al-inna*), whereas the transition from Creator to creation is related to the 'Why proof' (*burhān al-lima*); and it is known that the latter is nobler.[1] Therefore, when a person expresses [implicitly] the verb first, it is as though he transitions from the vision of his own action to the vision of the necessity of seeking help through the Divine Name. However, if he says *In the Name of God* before the verb, it is as though he has begun by seeing the necessity of seeking God's help, then come down to his own personal state.

Enquiry 2
Is the Verb Worthier of Being Implied, or the Noun?

Shaykh Abū Bakr al-Rāzī said: 'The flow of the Qur'ān's recitation shows that it is a verb which is implied, specifically an imperative. God says: 'You we worship and from You we seek help' (Q.1.5), meaning '*Say*: You we worship…' Likewise, 'In the Name of God' means '*Say:* In the Name of God'.[2]

One may argue, on the contrary, that the noun is worthier of being implied, because if we say that the meaning is 'In the Name of God is the

1 This is to say that while he has known himself in order to know his Lord, it is the Lord Who is the cause of his existence, so mentioning himself first involves a certain reversal of the true direction. This reverse argument (*maʿlūl* to *ʿilla*) is called *innī*; and the argument following the causal order (*ʿilla* to *maʿlūl*) is called *limī*—see al-Sharīf al-Jurjānī, *al-Taʿrīfāt*, ed. Muḥammad al-Minshāwī, Cairo: Dār al-Faḍīla, 2004, p. 40. Shihadeh describes these, respectively, as 'demonstration of the fact' and 'demonstration turning on the question "why"'—see Shihadeh, *Teleological Ethics*, pp. 135–136. See also Ilai Alon & Shukri Abed, *Al-Fārābī's Philosophical Lexicon*, 2 vols., Cambridge: E. J. W. Gibb Memorial Trust, 2007, vol. 1, pp. 29–30.

2 The two cases are not comparable; moreover, the claim requires the verb to come first.

commencement of all things' [i.e. a nominal sentence], this is to say that He is the true Origin and Creator of all things, regardless of whether that is stated or mentioned by anyone—and this, without doubt, is worthier. The remainder of the argument would be to explain that saying *All praise is for God* is [worthier] than '*Say*: All praise is for God,' because [the former] is to say that He is deserving of that praise, whether it is declared by anyone or not.[1]

Enquiry 3

The genitive (*jarr*) occurs in two ways: by a preposition, as in *bi'smi*; or by annexation (*iḍāfa*), as in the [following] word *Allāhi*. As for the genitives *al-Raḥmāni* and *al-Raḥīmi*, those occurred because—as adjectives—they adopt the case of the described noun [*Allāh*].

There are a number of related queries:

1. Why do prepositions make [nouns] genitive?
2. Why does annexation make [the second noun] genitive?
3. Is the preposition [particle] stronger in this respect, or annexation?[2]
4. How many categories of annexation are there? It is said that annexing something to itself is impossible,[3] so all that remains are: annexation between a part and the whole, or between two distinct essences. Examples of the former are *bāb ḥadīd* ('a door of iron') and *khātam dhahab* ('a ring of gold'), in that the door is part of [the totality of] iron, and the ring is part of gold.[4] An example of the latter is *ghulām Zayd* ('the servant of Zayd'), in that the two annexed nouns are completely distinct. As for the [detailed] categories of annexations, these are apparently beyond enumeration, as [possible] relations are infinite.

Enquiry 4

For a noun to be the name of something means that there is a relation between the particular word which is the noun and the particular essence which is the referent. This relation comes into being when people agree by convention to make that word the means of defining that thing, as if by saying: 'Whenever you hear this word from us, you should understand that we intend this particular meaning.' Once this relation has been estab-

1 See Book III, Chapter Five, Verse 2: *All praise is for God*.

2 These three have been left unexplained.

3 This is said to occur for clarification (*bayān*); for example, *Sūrat al-Fātiḥa* (the chapter of the Opening) = the chapter which *is* the Opening.

4 That is, they are 'from' that substance, alongside many other iron and gold items.

lished between the name and the referent, it is certainly proper to attribute the name to that referent; and that is what is meant by attributing a Name to Almighty God [by saying *the Name of God*].

Enquiry 5

Abū ʿUbayd said that the mention of *ism* (name) in *bi'smi 'Llāh* is an addition without meaning (*ṣila zā'ida*), as the meaning is *bi'Llāh* ('In God' or 'By God'). He added that its inclusion is either for blessings (*tabarruk*), or to distinguish this from an oath.

I say: the meaning is actually 'Begin in the Name of God,' and Abū ʿUbayd's opinion is weak. This is because if we are commanded to 'begin', this must refer to one of our actions, namely our utterance [of the formula]. This entails that the meaning is 'I begin with the mention (*dhikr*) of God,' i.e. 'I begin with *In the Name of God*.'

Moreover, the benefit in [the mention of *Name*] is that, just as God's Essence (*dhāt*) is the noblest of all essences, so is His mention the noblest mention and His Name the noblest of names. Also, just as He precedes all things in existence, so should His mention precede all mentions, and His Name [must precede] all names. Thus there are lofty benefits to be found in the word *Name*.

Chapter Two
CONCERNING THE RECITATION AND WRITING OF THE *BASMALA*

Section 1: Enquiries Concerning Recitation

Enquiry 1
[Stopping Points]

It is a matter of consensus that stopping upon *bi'sm* is incomplete (*nāqiṣ*) and distasteful (*qabīḥ*), but it is sufficient (*kāfī*) and sound (*ṣaḥīḥ*) to stop upon *bi'smi 'Llāh* or *bi'smi 'Llāh al-Raḥmān*. However, the [sentence] is complete (*tāmm*) upon saying *bi'smi 'Llāh al-Raḥmān al-Raḥīm*.

Any stop must fall into one of these three categories: incomplete, sufficient or complete (*kāmil*).[1] Stopping upon speech which is not comprehensible by itself is deemed incomplete; a stop upon speech which is comprehensible, although what follows is connected to it, is deemed sufficient; and a stop upon speech which is complete, with what follows being separate from it, is deemed complete.

Someone may say: *All praise is for God, Lord of the worlds* (Q.1.2) is complete speech, even though [the following verses] *The Compassionate, the Merciful; Master...* (Q.1.3–4) are connected to it as adjectives following their described noun. If it is acceptable for a noun to be separated from its adjectives by making it a verse (*āya*) by itself, then why is it not said that *In the Name of God, the Compassionate* is a verse, with *the Merciful* being a second verse? If that is not allowed, then how was *The Compassionate, the Merciful* (Q.1.3) made an independent verse? This matter must be explained.[2]

1 The author has used two different terms for each of the three categories. Authorities in the science of Qur'ān recitation known as *tajwīd*, specifically the field of recitation breaks known as *al-waqf wa'l-ibtidā'*, have often divided stops into three or four categories (sometimes more), and modern books tend to describe them as *qabīḥ–ḥasan* (fair)–*kāfī–tāmm*. See Sayyid Baʿbūla, *al-Rawḥ wa'l-rayḥān fī kayfiyyat al-waqf wa'l-ibtidā fī al-Qur'ān*, n.p., 2009, pp. 29–31.

2 The author has not done so here.

Enquiry 2
[The Letter *Lām*]

The reciters are unanimous in not pronouncing the *lām* [of *Allāh*] with velarisation (*taghlīẓ*) in *bi'smi 'Llāh* and *al-ḥamdu li'Llāh*, because the transition from *kasra* to the velarised *lām*[1] is heavy [on the tongue]. This is due to the fact that the *kasra* requires the lowering (*tasafful*) [of the tongue] whereas the velarised *lām* is an elevated (*mustaʿlī*) letter, and transition from lowness to elevation is awkward.

They only considered it proper to velarise the *lām* of this word when it is *marfūʿ* or *manṣūb* [i.e. preceded by *ḍamma* or *fatḥa*]; for example,[2] 'God (*Allāhu*) is Gentle to His servants' (Q.XLII.19); 'Say: He is God (*huwa 'Llāhu*)' (Q.CXII.1); 'Indeed, God (*inna 'Llāha*) has purchased of the believers…' (Q.IX.111).

Enquiry 3

It is said that this velarisation is intended to distinguish it from the [ordinary] *lām* for two purposes:[3]

a. *Tafkhīm*[4] (velarisation) gives a sense of magnification (*taʿẓīm*), and this word is deserving of the utmost magnification.
b. The light (*raqīq*) *lām* is pronounced only with the tip of the tongue, whereas the velarised one is pronounced with the entire tongue. Since it requires more work, it deserves greater reward. Moreover, the Torah says: 'O Moses! Respond to your Lord with all your heart.'[5] In this case, the person mentions his Lord with his entire tongue, which signifies that he is remembering Him with his entire heart. This is certainly greater in reverence.

Enquiry 4

Someone may say: the relationship between the light *lām* and the velarised *lām* is like that between *dāl*[6] and *ṭā'*, or *sīn* and *ṣād*. *Dāl* is pronounced

1 When discussing in this order, this would explain the *lām* being light (non-velar) in the likes of *li'Llāh* and *bi'Llāh*.

2 The matter is unrelated to the grammatical case of the word *Allāh*, contrary to what the author's wording implies. In all three examples provided, the word is preceded by a *fatḥa* or commenced by itself with a *fatḥa*.

3 The printed edition has listed three purposes, the first of which I have incorporated into the introductory sentence.

4 The word itself conveys this sense, which is not apparent from the phonetic term used in translation.

5 This bears a similarity to Deuteronomy 6:5, in which the command is from Moses to his people.

6 Most (especially modern) phoneticians would cite the *tā'* for this comparison rather than *dāl*.

with the tip of the tongue, and *ṭā'* with the whole tongue. Likewise, *sīn* is pronounced with the tip of the tongue and *ṣād* with the whole tongue. This shows that the relationship between the light and velarised *lām*s is like *dāl* and *ṭā'*, or *sīn* and *ṣād*.

Nonetheless, we observe that the people have considered *dāl* and *ṭā'* to be two independent letters, and likewise for *sīn* and *ṣād*. Therefore, it should have been said that the light *lām* and the velarised *lām* are two independent letters; since that is not so,[1] the difference should be [explained].

Enquiry 5

The doubling (*tashdīd*) of the *lām* in the Name *Allāh* is due to assimilation (*idghām*), as two *lām*s have occurred here: the first is the unvowelled *lām* of the definite article,[2] and the second is original [to the word] and is vowelled [with a *fatḥa*]. When any two identical letters coincide, with the first being unvowelled and the second vowelled, the former is necessarily assimilated into the latter. This may occur between two words or within a single word. Examples between two words include: *rabiḥat tijāratuhum* (Q.II.16); *bikum min* (Q.XVI.53); and *lahum min* (Q.X.27). As for a single word, this [*Allāh*] is an example of it.

Know that it is not possible for two instances of unvowelled *alif*, *lām*, *wāw* or *yā'* [etc.] to coincide, so assimilation cannot occur [in this way]. However, if two identical letters coincide and [both] are vowelled, then assimilation is permissible.[3]

Enquiry 6

The people of spiritual allusions and striving have drawn attention to a subtlety here, namely that the *lām* of the definite article (*taʿrīf*) coincided with the original *lām* in *Allāh* and assimilated into it. The *lām* of *maʿrifa* [alternatively: 'gnosis'] disappeared, whereas the *lām* of the word *Allāh* remained. This is as though to demonstrate that when gnosis is acquired of the Known Presence, the gnosis itself dissolves and perishes, whereas the pre-eternal Known (*maʿrūf*) remains as He always was, with no increase or decrease.

1 Instead, they are treated as allophones of a single phoneme.

2 C.f. Chapter Nine below, in which the author denies that this Name is derived from anything. However, under Enquiry 3 in that chapter, he cites the Kūfans as saying it is from *al-ilāh*, and the Baṣrans as saying its origin is *al-lāh*.

3 The assimilation of two vowelled letters is known as *idghām kabīr* and is found in the canonical readings of Abū ʿAmr, Yaʿqūb and Ḥamza. All readings have this in Q.XII.11, in which the word *ta'mannā* is originally *ta'manunā*.

Enquiry 7
[Pronunciation of the Name *Allāh*]

It is not permitted to remove the [second] *alif* from *Allāh* during pronunciation, but this may be excused in poetry, as necessary, when one stops upon it. One poet said: *Aqbala saylun jā'a min ʿindi* 'Llah*; yaḥridu ḥarda 'l-jannati 'l-mughillah* (A torrent coming from God approached...).[1]

This leads to a number of juristic issues:

1. If a person made an oath by saying *bi'Llah* [with a short vowel], would that have the effect of an oath? Some said not, as *billa*[2] is merely a word for 'moisture' and it would have no effect as an oath. Others said that it would, as it is permitted linguistically and his intention necessitates that it be effected.
2. If he said [the Divine Name] in this way upon slaughtering an animal, would that be valid or not?
3. If he said *Allāhu akbar* in this way, would his prayer be valid or not?[3]

Enquiry 8

None recited *Allāh* with *imāla*[4] except Qutayba [b. Mihrān], according to some narrations. End quote.[5]

Enquiry 9
[Pronunciation of *al-Raḥmān*]

The doubling of the *rā'* in *al-Raḥmān al-Raḥīm*[6] is due to the assimilation of the definite article *lām* into it. The reciters agree that the article *lām* must be assimilated into a [following] *lām* as well as thirteen other letters,[7] namely: *ṣād, ḍād, sīn, shīn, dāl, dhāl, rā', zāy, ṭā', ẓā', tā', thā'* and *nūn*. For

1 The printed edition has the second line as *yajūdu jūda 'l-jannati*, which I have replaced with the words as found later in Rāzī's exegesis (Q.LXVIII.25) and in other *tafsīrs*. The phrase *ʿindi 'Llah* here is more commonly presented as *amri 'Llah*.

2 In pronunciation, this would be equivalent, though they appear different in Arabic script and transliteration.

3 The answer to the latter two is presumably upon the same divergence as the first. It should be noted that this pronunciation is fairly common among certain Arab and non-Arab populations.

4 As described previously, it is the 'swerving' of /ā/ towards /ī/. Qutayba, a narrator from Kisā'ī, did so with the word *li'Llāhi*—see ʿAlī b. Muḥammad al-Sakhāwī, *Jamāl al-qurrā'*, ed. Marwān al-ʿAṭiyya & Muḥsin Kharāba, Damascus: Dār al-Ma'mūn, 1997, vol. 1, p. 616.

5 This enquiry appears to have been a quote, but the name of the source is not mentioned.

6 The transliteration system I am applying does not reflect this. These would be pronounced *ar-Raḥmān* and *ar-Raḥīm*.

7 Known as the 'sun letters' because the initial letter of *shams* (sun) is among them.

example, 'Those that turn [pronounced: *at-tā'ibūn*] in repentance; that serve Him, and praise Him; that wander in devotion [*as-sā'iḥūn*]; that bow down [*ar-rākiᶜūn*] and prostrate themselves [*as-sājidūn*]; that enjoin good and forbid [*an-nāhūn*] evil' (Q.ix.112).

The cause behind this assimilation being permitted is proximity of articulation points (*makhraj*): the *lām* and these other letters are articulated from the tip of the tongue or nearby, so assimilation is appropriate.

They also agree that it is not permitted to assimilate the *lām* with other than these thirteen letters.[1] For example [in the same verse]: 'Those that turn in repentance; that serve Him [pronounced: *al-ᶜābidūn*], and praise Him [*al-ḥāmidūn*]; that wander in devotion; that bow down and prostrate themselves; that enjoin [*al-āmirūn*] good and forbid evil' (Q.ix.112) — these [definite articles] are pronounced distinctly.

Assimilation was not permitted here due to the distance between articulation points: whenever the first and second letters are articulated at points which are distant from each other, it becomes difficult to pronounce both concurrently. As such, they must be made distinct from each other. In contrast, those which are close in their articulation points are difficult to pronounce distinctly.

Enquiry 10

It is a matter of consensus that there is no *imāla* in the word *al-Raḥmān* [as recited], but there are two opinions among grammarians as to whether this would be permitted [in theory]. One is that it is permitted—and this is perhaps the view of Sībawayh—because of the *kasra* of the *nūn* following that *alif*. The other, held by the majority of grammarians, is that it is not permitted.

Enquiry 11

There is consensus that *al-Raḥmān* and *al-Raḥīm* are genitive because they are adjectives of the first genitive [*Allāh*]. However, being nominative or accusative are both possible from a [theoretical] grammar perspective.[2] The nominative: if it is understood as *bi'smi 'Llāhi* huwa *al-Raḥmānu al-Raḥīmu* ('In the Name of God; He is the Compassionate, the Merciful'); and the accusative: if it is understood as *bi'smi 'Llāhi* aᶜnī *al-Raḥmāna al-Raḥīma* ('In the Name of God; I mean the Compassionate, the Merciful').

1 Rather, fourteen including *lām*.

2 These are known in grammar as *qaṭᶜ* and *ikhtiṣāṣ*, respectively.

Section II: Enquiries Concerning Writing

Enquiry 1

The [scribes] heightened (*taṭwīl*) the *bā'* in *bi'smi 'Llāh* but not in any other words. There are two possible reasons for this differentiation:

a. Due to the fact that the following *alif* was removed, they heightened the *bā'* to indicate where it used to be. Compare this with *iqra' bi'smi Rabbik* (Q.XCVI.1) in which the *alif* is maintained and the *bā'* is in its original state.[1]
b. Qutaybī[2] said that they only heightened the *bā'* to ensure that the Book of God is opened with a magnified letter. ʿUmar b. ʿAbd al-ʿAzīz would say to his scribes: 'Heighten the *bā'* and make the *mīm* circular in order to aggrandise the Book of God.'

Enquiry 2

The people of spiritual allusion said: 'The *bā'* is a lowly letter in its written form, but through connection to the writing of the word *Allāh*, it became raised and lofty. Thus we hope that when the heart connects to the service of Almighty God, it is raised in state and status.'

Enquiry 3

The *alif* of *ism* was removed in *bi'smi 'Llāh* (Q.I.1), but it was retained in *iqra' bi'smi Rabbik* (Q.XCVI.1): the distinction between these [contexts] is in two respects:

a. *Bi'smi 'Llāh* ('In the Name of God') is uttered at the majority of times and with the majority of actions, so the *alif* was removed to lighten it. As for the other [expressions], their mention is [relatively] infrequent.
b. Al-Khalīl [b. Aḥmad] said: the *alif* was removed from *bi'smi 'Llāh* because it only entered [the word *ism*] due to the impossibility of commencing with an unvowelled *sīn*. Therefore, when the *bā'* connected to the word, it assumed the position of the *alif* and the latter was dropped from writing. This is different from *iqra' bi'smi Rabbik* because its *bā'* is not in place of the *alif*: after all, it is possible to remove the *bā'* with the meaning intact, i.e. to say *iqra' isma Rabbik* ('Read the Name of your Lord'). On the contrary, if you removed the *bā'* from *bi'smi 'Llāh*, the meaning would not be correct—so this clarifies the difference.

1 See Enquiry 3 below.
2 I assume this refers to Ibn Qutayba (see Appendix).

Enquiry 4

They wrote *Allāh* with two *lāms*, but [the relative pronoun] *alladhī* with a single *lām*, even though they are equal with respect to: pronunciation, frequency of mention and being definite. The differences between them are as follows:

a. The Name *Allāh* is a fully inflected noun, so it was written in its original state. *Alladhī*, on the other hand, is uninflected on account of its deficiency, i.e. that it has no meaning without its relative clause: as such, it is like a fragment of a word, and such a fragment must be uninflected. Therefore, they added [another type of] deficiency [by removing the *lām*]. Do you not see that [the dual] *alladhāni* was written with two *lāms*? That is because being in the dual [and being inflected accordingly] removed it from resembling particles, as particles do not occur in the dual.
b. If *Allāh* were written with a single *lām*, it could be confused for *ilāh* ('a deity'); but such confusion would not occur for *alladhī*.
c. Magnifying the mention of God is obligatory in writing as it is in pronunciation, and removing [the *lām*] would contradict this. Since there is nothing about the meaning of *alladhī* to be magnified, that was left out of its writing.

Enquiry 5

The *alif* before the [final] *hā'* of the word *Allāh* was left out of its writing in order to avoid a succession of similar-looking letters, which [the Arabs] disliked just as they disliked a succession of similar-sounding letters in recitation.

Enquiry 6
[Mystical Implications]

They say: the word *Allāh* was originally *al-ilāh*, which is composed of six letters. When it became *Allāh* only four letters remained in writing: *hamza*, two *lāms* and *hā'*. *Hamza* is [articulated] from the lowest part of the throat, *lām* from the tip of the tongue and *hā'* from the lowest part of the throat [again].

This alludes to a remarkable situation: the lowest part of the throat is the origin of the letters [of this word], then they ascend gradually until reaching the tip of the tongue, and then return with the *hā'* which is deep in the throat where the spirit (*ruḥ*) subsists. In this way, the servant starts off in a state of nothingness and anonymity, then ascends gradually through the stations of servitude until he attains the farthest reaches of his ability and power, entering into the world of lights and unveilings. Then he begins to retreat, little by little, until he ends up annihilated in the ocean of divine unity (*tawḥīd*). As such, it corresponds to the saying: 'The end is a return to the beginning.'

Enquiry 7

The *alif* before the [final] *nūn* in *al-Raḥmān* was only left out of its writing in order to lighten the word, so it would have been acceptable to write it with *alif*. However, it is not permitted to remove the *yā'* from *al-Raḥīm*, because it is not like the *alif* of *al-Raḥmān* which can be removed without damaging the word-form and creating confusion.

Chapter Three
CONCERNING THE NAME (*ISM*)[1]

Section 1: Enquiries Based on Transmission

Enquiry 1

There are two famous dialectal variations of this word among the Arabs: *ism* and *sim*. A poet said: *bi'smi 'lladhī fī kulli sūratin simuhū* ('In the name of the One Whose Name is in every *sūra*'). There are also said to be two other dialects: *usm* and *sum*.[2]

Kisā'ī said: 'The Arabs would sometimes say *ism* with a *kasra* on the *alif*, and at other times with a *ḍamma* [*usm*]. When they removed the *alif*, those who used to pronounce it with a *kasra* would say *sim*, while those who did so with a *ḍamma* would say *sum*.' Thaʿlab said: 'Whoever considered its origin to be *samā/yasmā* would say *ism* and *sim*, while whoever considered it to be from *samā/yasmū* would say *usm* and *sum*.' Al-Mubarrad said: 'I have heard the Arabs saying *ism*, *usm*, *sim*, *sum* and *simā*.'

Enquiry 2

It is a matter of agreement that its diminutive form is *sumayy* and its plurals are *asmā'* and *asāmī*.

Enquiry 3

There are two opinions concerning its derivation. The Baṣrans said that it is from *samā/yasmū*, meaning 'to be above (*ʿalā*) and appear (*ẓahara*) [on the surface]'. This is because the name of something is that which 'sits upon it' and by which it becomes apparent. I say: a word introduces its meaning, and is therefore prior in knowledge to the thing being introduced. As such, the name is 'above' the meaning in the sense of being prior.

1 The word *ism* means both 'noun' and 'name', and these terms are obviously intimately related. In this chapter as elsewhere, I have alternated between them as appropriate to context.

2 I have vocalised these after consulting a number of linguistic and exegetical sources as well as the following explanations. It appears that the printed editions are missing an *alif* in one of the versions of the word.

The Kūfans said that it is derived from *wasama/yasimu* [with verbal noun] *sima*, meaning 'a sign (*ʿalāma*)'. This is because the name is a sign by which the referent becomes known. [To this,] the Baṣrans said: if it had been derived from *sima*, its diminutive would have been *wusaym* and its plural *awsām*.

Enquiry 4

Those who said it is derived from *sima* said that its [verb] origin is *wasama/yasimu* but the [initial] *wāw* was removed and replaced by the liaising *alif*. This is like [the nouns] *ʿida*, *ṣifa* and *zina* which are originally from [nouns] *waʿd*, *waṣf* and *wazn*: in these, the *wāw* was removed and replaced by the *hā'* [i.e. *tā' marbūṭa*].[1]

As for those who said it is from [verbal noun] *sumū*, meaning 'elevation', there are two views:

A. Its origin is *samā/yasmū* or *samā/yasmī*. The imperative form is *usmu* upon the form of *udʿu* from [the verb] *daʿawta* ('you called').[2] Alternatively, it is *ismi* upon the form of *irmi* from [the verb] *ramayta* ('you threw'). Then they made this form [*usmu* or *ismi*] a noun and made it subject to declension, taking it out of the domain of verbs. It is said: this is comparable to how they named the camel *yaʿmal* [from the verb 'he works']. Al-Akhfash said that this is like *al-āna* ('now') which comes from *āna/ya'īnu* meaning 'to be present': they inserted the definite article upon its perfect tense verb but retained its /a/ vowel.

B. Its origin is *samw*, like *ḥamw*. The *wāw* was removed from its end due to the difficulty involved in pronouncing the various vowels upon it, as well as the frequency of the word's use. The *mīm* was made the letter of inflection once it became the final letter, so the vowel of the removed *wāw* was transferred to it. The *sīn* was made unvowelled because, after the removal of the *wāw*, there were two letters remaining: one vowelled, the other unvowelled [i.e. *sam*]. Then, when the *mīm* became vowelled, the other had to become unvowelled to restore balance. The [liaising] *hamza* [i.e. *alif*] entered at the beginning because it is not possible to begin with an unvowelled letter, so something was required to begin the word. The *hamza* was chosen because it is a letter of addition.

1 An alternative transliteration scheme would present these as *simah*, *ʿidah*, *ṣifah* and *zinah*.

2 The verb has been cited in this conjugation to reveal its third radical, the *wāw*. The same applies to *ramayta*.

Section II: Enquiries Based on Reason

The definition of the noun and its categories have been discussed previously,[1] but there are a number of enquiries remaining:

Enquiry 1
[Names and Referents]

The Ḥashwīs, Karrāmīs and Ashʿarīs[2] said that the name (*ism*) is equivalent to the referent (*musammā*), but distinct from the naming (*tasmiya*). The Muʿtazilīs said that the name is distinct from the referent and equivalent to the naming. My stance is that the name equals neither the referent nor the naming.

Before broaching the subject of the evidences, an introductory remark is required: the question of whether the name is equivalent to the referent should be preceded by an explanation of each, such that they can be compared.

On this basis, I say: if 'name' is intended to mean this utterance made up of ordered and composed letters and sounds, and 'referent' is intended to mean essences and realities in their own right, then it is known by necessity that the name is not the referent. As such, delving into this topic would be of no value. If, on the other hand, the 'name' is intended to mean the referent itself, and likewise the word 'referent', then that would mean that something is its own self, and that—while true—is a worthless tautology. What this shows is that this enquiry is—upon [both] hypotheses—not worthy of being explored.

Enquiry 2

I have formulated a subtle and effective way of interpreting their statement that 'The name equals the referent,' as follows. The 'noun' [or 'name'] is defined as 'a word that denotes a meaning without denoting a particular time', and the word *ism* is itself in this category. It follows that *ism* is a name for itself, and that word is the referent of the word itself. In this scenario, the name is equivalent to the referent.

However, there is a problem in this, as its being the 'name of the referent' would be a case of attributing (*iḍāfa*) something to itself, whereas the two parts of this construct must be distinct from each other.[3]

1 See Book One, Chapters Three to Six.

2 Although the author belongs to the latter school, he disagrees with them on this point.

3 Cf. Enquiry 3 of Chapter One above and Shihāb al-Dīn al-Khafājī, *ʿInāyat al-qāḍī wa-kifāyat al-rāḍī ʿalā Tafsīr al-Bayḍāwī* (*Ḥāshiyat al-Shihāb*), 8 vols., Beirut: Dār Ṣādir, n.d., vol. 1, p. 47.

Enquiry 3

1. Proofs that the name cannot be the referent:
2. It is possible for the name to exist while the referent is non-existent. For example, 'The non-existent is negated' is a completely negative statement with no affirmation, yet the word ['non-existent'] exists even though it refers to absolute nothingness. Also, the referent can exist without having a name, as there are realities for which no particular name has been coined. In short, each of these two is known to be possible in the absence of the other, so they are necessarily distinct.
3. Names can be numerous despite their referent being one, as in the case of synonyms (*tarāduf*). Moreover, there could be one name with numerous referents, as in the case of homonyms (*ishtirāk*). This, too, necessitates their distinction from each other.
4. For a name to be 'the name of' something, and for that thing to be 'named by' that name, is a case of annexation (*iḍāfa*) similar to possession; and the two sides [of this relationship] must be distinct from each other. However, one may say that this is countered by [the possibility of] a person knowing himself!
5. The name comprises sounds which have been coined to signify the referents: these sounds are fleeting accidents (*aʿrāḍ*), whereas the referent may be something which persists. Indeed, that referent may be necessarily existent in its own right [i.e. God].
6. If we utter 'fire' and 'ice', then these two words are present on our tongues; if the name were the same as the referent, it would mean that fire and ice are upon our tongues—and no sane person would suggest that!
7. The Almighty said: 'The most Beautiful Names belong to God: so call on Him by them' (Q.VII.180); and the Prophet said: 'Almighty God has ninety-nine Names'[1]—these are multiple Names for a single referent, namely Almighty God.
8. The verses *In the Name of God* (Q.I.1) and 'Blessed be the Name of your Lord' (Q.LV.78) contain the attribution (*iḍāfa*) of a Name to God, and it is impossible to attribute something to itself.
9. We recognise necessarily the difference between saying 'the Name of God', 'the name of the name', and 'God of God'—and this [substitution] shows that the name does not equal the referent.
10. We describe names as being [for example] Arabic or Persian: *Allāh*

1 Recorded by Bukhārī and Muslim—S.I.

is an Arabic name, whereas *Khudāy* is a Persian name.[1] As for the Essence of Almighty God, it is above being of this nature.

II. In the verse 'The most Beautiful Names belong to God: so call on Him by them' (Q.VII.180), we have been commanded to call upon God by His Names. As such, the Name is an instrument for supplication, whereas the One being called upon is God. The distinction between the object of supplication and the words used for the purpose is known by necessity.

On the other hand, those who said that the name equals the referent argued on the basis of a scriptural text and a juristic ruling:

THE SCRIPTURAL TEXT: 'Blessed be the Name of your Lord' (Q.LV.78), since it is God Who is blessed and exalted, not the sounds or letters.

THE RULING: it is that if a man said 'Zaynab is divorced' and that is the name of his wife, then this divorce takes effect. If the name were distinct from the referent, then he would have initiated divorce on something other than that woman, so it would not apply to her.

RESPONSE CONCERNING THE TEXT: given that we are required to believe that the Almighty is transcendent above all imperfections, why not stipulate likewise that words designated to describe His Essence are free from vanity, foulness and ill manners?

RESPONSE CONCERNING THE RULING: 'Zaynab is divorced' means that the essence described by means of this name is divorced, and that is why divorce is effected upon her.

Enquiry 4
[The Naming]

In our view, the naming (*tasmiya*) is distinct from the name. This is seen by the fact that naming means to designate a particular word to signify a particular essence. That designation refers to an act of choice and volition on the part of the coiner. The name (*ism*), on the other hand, is that particular word itself. The distinction between these two is known by necessity.

Enquiry 5
[Order of Coinage]

You are aware that the words denoting those meanings give rise to [the need for] words which denote the relations between those [referents]. For this obvious reason, coinage of nouns and verbs is prior to that of

1 See below Chapter Four, Section II, 'Name 10' for an explanation.

particles. But which is prior between verbs and nouns? It is more apparent that nouns would be prior, for the following reasons:

1. The noun is a word which denotes a quiddity, while the verb denotes the occurrence of the quiddity for an [unspecified] thing at a specified time. Therefore, the noun is simple and the verb is composite. Since the simple is prior to the composite in essence and status, it follows that it be prior to it in mention and word.
2. The verb cannot be uttered without ascribing it to an agent (*fāʿil*), whereas the word denoting that agent may be uttered without being attributed with an action. As such, the agent [noun] has no need for the verb, whereas the verb is in need of the agent. The self-sufficient is conceptually prior to the needy, so likewise should it be in mention.
3. Juxtaposing one noun with another results in a complete meaning, i.e. the [nominal] sentence comprising a subject and a predicate. A verb with another verb, on the other hand, does not result in a complete meaning; this will not be achieved until a noun appears in the sentence. This shows that the noun is conceptually prior to the verb, so it is most likely that it would be prior in terms of coinage.

Enquiry 6

You are aware that the noun may be a name for its quiddity in and of itself, or otherwise it could be derived, i.e. a noun denoting that the thing is described with a particular attribute, such as *ʿālim* ('knowledgeable') and *qādir* ('powerful'). It is more apparent that nouns of quiddity (*asmāʾ al-māhiyyāt*)[1] are conceptually prior to derived nouns, because the former are simple and the latter are composite, and the simple is prior to the composite.

Enquiry 7

It seems that the names of attributes are conceptually prior to those for self-subsistent essences. This is because we cannot know the essences except by means of the attributes subsisting in them. The signifier is known before the signified, and priority of mention is appropriate to this priority in knowledge.

Enquiry 8
Categories of Names Denoting Referents

There are nine categories:

1 These would generally be referred to as *jāmid* nouns.

1. The name which denotes an essence (*dhāt*).[1]
2. The name which denotes a thing in terms of a portion of its essence; for example, saying that a wall is a 'body' or a 'substance'.[2]
3. The name which denotes a thing in terms of an actual attribute (*ṣifa ḥaqīqiyya*) subsisting in its essence; for example, saying that something is 'black', 'white', 'hot' or 'cold'. This blackness, whiteness, heat and cold are actual attributes which subsist in the essence and have no connection to external things.[3]
4. The name which denotes a thing in terms of a relative attribute (*iḍāfiyya*) only; for example, saying that a thing is 'known', 'understood', 'mentioned', 'owner' or 'owned'.[4]
5. The name which denotes a thing in terms of an eliminative state (*ḥāla salbiyya*) ; for example, saying that someone is 'blind' or 'poor', or that one is 'free of ailments'.[5]
6. The name which denotes a thing in terms of a combination of an actual and relative attribute; for example, being 'knowledgeable' and 'able', as knowledge is considered by the majority of scholars to be an actual attribute which is connected to knowable things (*maʿlūmāt*), while ability is an actual attribute which is connected to possible things (*maqdūrāt*).[6]
7. The name which denotes a thing in terms of a combination of an actual and eliminative attribute; for example, what is understood from saying 'able and not prevented by anything', and 'knowledgeable and not ignorant of anything'.[7]
8. The name which denotes a thing in terms of a combination of a relative and eliminative attribute. One example is *awwal* ('first'), which means both to precede other things (which is relative) and not to be preceded by anything (which is eliminative). Another is *qayyūm* ('self-subsistent sustainer'), which means to be both self-subsistent (*qā'im*) and to sustain others (*muqawwim*). The former means that He is free of need of others (which is eliminative) and the latter means

1 See Enquiries 9–12 below.

2 That is to say: only a portion of its reality has been expressed, as many other things share in being a body or substance. See Enquiry 13 below.

3 See Chapter Four below for details.

4 These all involve a relation or connection with external things. See Chapter Five below for details.

5 See Chapter Six below for details.

6 See Chapter Seven below for details.

7 This combination has not been discussed in more detail below, perhaps because it is self-explanatory and there are no individual Divine Names which fall into this category.

that others need Him (which is relative).[1]

9. The name which denotes a thing in terms of a combination of an actual, relative and eliminative attribute.[2]

This is an explanation of the categories of names, whether they are the names of God (Exalted and High) or of created beings. There are no other categories [possible] besides what we have mentioned.[3]

Enquiry 9
Does God Have a Name Denoting His Very Essence (*Dhāt*)?

The answer to this question must be preceded by some lofty introductory points of theology:

1. The Almighty differs from His creation on the basis of His very Essence, not due to an Attribute. This is proven by considering that it could either be as we say, i.e. that His Essence in itself is distinct from creation regardless of all its Attributes, or not. If not, and His Essence is equivalent [in itself] to all other essences, then its distinction from the others must be due to an additional Attribute. Now, if His Essence [alone] possessed this distinguishing Attribute without there being a cause for that, then this is a case of one possible state of affairs obtaining without a preponderator (*murajjiḥ*). However, if it were brought about by something else, then this leads to infinite regression or circularity, which would be absurd. [This is because] it entails that [His Essence] being singular in possessing that Attribute is due to another Attribute, and this leads to infinite regression.
2. We say that Almighty God is 'not a body or a substance', and this negation of corporeality and substance is an eliminative (*salbī*) concept, whereas His very Essence is an affirmative (*thābit*) reality. The difference between negation and affirmation is known by necessity. Moreover, His Essence is not equivalent to His being able and knowledgeable, because being able (*qādiriyya*) and being knowledgeable (*ʿālimiyya*) are both relative concepts,[4] whereas His Essence subsists in its own right. The difference between a self-subsistent existent and these relative concepts is known by necessity.

1 See Chapter Seven, Section VI.

2 See Chapter Seven, Section VII.

3 For an overview of Divine Attributes and Rāzī's categorisations thereof, see Mohd. Farid Mohd. Shahran, *Fakhr al-Dīn al-Rāzī on Divine Transcendence and Anthropomorphism*, Putrajaya, Malaysia: Islamic and Strategic Studies Institute (ISSI), 2017, pp. 94–6. [A. Booso, ed.]

4 That is, related to things which are possible and knowable, respectively.

3. We do not, at this time,[1] know His very Essence. This is proven in the following ways:
   a. If we examine our minds and understandings, we find that their gnosis of God consists of only four types: knowledge of His existence; knowledge of His continuous existence; knowledge of the Attributes of Majesty (*jalāl*), which are the eliminative states; or knowledge of the Attributes of Beneficence (*ikrām*), which are the relative states.[2] Yet it has been proven that His very Essence is distinct from each one of these four: for it is proven that His reality (*ḥaqīqa*) is other than His existence (*wujūd*); and if that is so, then the same is true of the continuation (*dawām*) of His existence. It has likewise been proven that His reality is neither eliminative nor relative. Therefore, if the creation have no knowledge beyond these four matters which are shown to be distinct from His very Essence, then His very Essence is unknown to humankind.
   b. It is known inductively that we are unable to conceive of anything except through four means:
      - Things which are perceived by one of the five senses.
      - Experiential states of the body; for example, pain, pleasure, hunger, thirst, elation and sorrow.
      - Rational states; for example, knowing the realities of existence and non-existence, unity and plurality, necessity and contingency.
      - States which reason and imagination appreciate from the above three categories.[3]

      These are the things which we are able to conceive and perceive in themselves. If that is so, and it is known that God's

1 Although the evidences provided by the author are not bound by the limitations of time, this clause is perhaps understood in the light of his comments under points 4 and 5. For further reading on this topic, see Binyamin Abrahamov, 'Fakhr al-Dīn al-Rāzī on the knowability of God's essence', *Arabica*, vol. XLIX, 2002, pp. 204–230, in which it is argued that the denial of knowability was his later stance, and that Rāzī elaborated on this issue in his works more than any other thinker.

2 The latter two are further discussed in Chapter Seven, Section IX below, under the fourth benefit of saying 'O He.' See also the author's exegesis of Q.LV.27–28 (its Enquiry 6), in which they are said to signify 'eliminative' and 'affirmative' Attributes, respectively.

3 This last category may be distinct from the third as *a posteriori* is distinct from *a priori*. More generally, it could refer both to the results of the mind's processing of its essential states and sensory inputs, as well as those things which reach the mind through description and testimony of others.

reality (may He be exalted) is distinct from all these categories, then His reality is shown to be unknown to the creation.

c. His very Essence is the cause (*ʿilla*) of all its concomitant Attributes: actual, relative and eliminative. Knowledge of the cause is a cause for knowledge of the effect: so if His very reality were known, then His Attributes in their entirety would be known by necessity. Since that is not so, neither is [the protasis]; thus it is shown that His reality is unknown to the creation.

4. Although [His Essence] is not conceivable (*maʿqūl*) to creation, could it possibly become conceivable?
5. Even if human intellects cannot attain to knowledge of that Essential Reality, could this gnosis be possible for the angels, whether as a genus or for a particular individual?

   It is only fair to say that these are [both] difficult enquiries, and the intellect is in a state of inability to fulfil what they deserve. Some have said: the intellect and knowledge of created beings is finite whereas Almighty God is infinite, and the finite is unable to attain to the infinite. Moreover, the greatest of beings is God, and the greatest knowledge is His knowledge; since the greatest Being cannot be known except by the greatest knowledge, it is seen that 'none knows God except God'.[1]
6. Know that there are two types of gnosis (*maʿrifa*): indirect (*ʿaraḍī*) and direct (*dhātī*). The former is like seeing a building and knowing that it must have a builder; however, the builder's nature and reality is not denoted by the building. As for direct gnosis, it is like seeing a colour with our eyes, feeling heat by our touch and hearing a sound with our ears: there is no reality of heat or cold besides this modality of touch, nor of black or white besides the modality of vision. Once you have appreciated this, we say: recognising that created things depend on a Creator leads us to know Almighty God in this indirect way. What we have negated is only the *direct* gnosis of God, so bear this nuance in mind lest you fall into error.
7. Know that perceiving something in itself—which we have called 'direct gnosis'—occurs in the observed world in two ways: knowl-

1 Cf. Abū Ḥāmid al-Ghazālī, *al-Maqṣad al-asnā fī sharḥ maʿānī asmāʾ Allāh al-ḥusnā*, trans. David Burrell & Nazih Daher as *The Ninety-Nine Beautiful Names of God*, Cambridge: Islamic Texts Society, 1992, pp. 36–47.

edge (*ʿilm*) and vision (*ibṣār*). If we look at [something] black[1] and then close our eyes, we experience a self-evident difference between the two states. This shows us that knowledge and vision are two separate phenomena. Once you have appreciated this, we say: if it is supposed that it is possible for the creation to know [God] directly, then would that gnosis and perception be by one route only, or could it be two—knowledge and vision—as in the observed world? This, too, is a matter which cannot be settled definitively by the intellect. Supposing that there could be two routes—knowledge and vision—then is the matter limited to them, or could there be numerous routes and levels? All of these are questions concerning which the intellect can never be certain.

This concludes our introductory remarks.

Enquiry 10

Does God have a Name denoting His very Essence, or not? It is narrated that the early philosophers denied this, saying: 'The proof that this does not exist is that names are coined in order to denote a referent; so if God's Essence had a Name, that would have been coined in order to signify that referent alongside others. Since it is shown that no one at all in creation knows His very Essence, there would be no benefit in that coinage. As such, this kind of Name does not exist.' On this basis, they said that this reality does not have a Name, but only signifying concomitants, namely that He is pre-eternal and everlasting, and the Necessary Existent which does not accept non-existence.

On the other hand, some said that Almighty God is certainly able to honour some of His elect servants with the knowledge of that essential Reality. On that basis, they said that it is not impossible for a Name to be coined to denote that Essential Reality.[2]

Thus it is seen that this issue is based upon the preceding introductions.

Enquiry 11

Assuming that coining a Name for this Essential Reality is possible, it must be stated with certainty that this is the greatest Name and noblest

1 I understand this hue to be merely an example, in which case 'white' would have been clearer: the mind perceives or imagines the colour when the eyes are closed. The point extends to any external sense perception.

2 One could also argue that the fact we are even discussing this 'Essence' and 'Reality' allows for a name to be coined to denote it.

mention. This is because the nobility of knowledge depends on the nobility of what is known, and the nobility of a mention is proportional to the nobility of the mentioned. Since Almighty God's Essence is the noblest of things known and mentioned, the knowledge and mention of it are the noblest knowledge and mention. Furthermore, that Name must be the noblest of names, which is that one intended by the widely used expression: 'God's Greatest Name'. If it should happen that an elect angel or prophet should be made aware of that Name and its meaning manifests itself to him, it would not be implausible that the entire worlds of bodies and spirits would obey his will.[1]

Enquiry 12

Those who affirmed the existence of the Greatest Name differed concerning its identity:

A. Some said that it is *Dhū al-Jalāl wa'l-Ikrām* (the Possessor of Majesty and Beneficence) [see Q.LV.27]. The Prophet (may God bless him and grant him peace) said: 'Adhere to [saying] "O Possessor of Majesty and Beneficence."'[2] However, this [claim] is weak in my opinion, because Majesty signifies the eliminative Attributes (*al-ṣifāt al-salbiyya*), and Beneficence signifies the relative Attributes (*al-ṣifāt al-iḍāfiyya*);[3] and you have already come to know that God's Essential Reality is distinct from both the eliminative and relative [Attributes].

B. Some said that it is *al-Ḥayy al-Qayyūm* (the Living, the Self-subsistent Sustainer), due to the Prophet (may God bless him and grant him peace) saying to Ubayy b. Kaᶜb: 'What is the greatest verse in God's Book?' He replied: 'Allāh: there is no god but He, the Living, the Self-subsistent' (Q.II.255), to which the Prophet (may God bless him and grant him peace) said: 'May knowledge be pleasant for you, Abū Mundhir!'[4] This claim is also weak in my opinion, because *al-Ḥayy* is an expression for [being capable of] cognition (*darrāk*)

1 Naturally, this means by the permission of God. Cf. the 'Obeyed' in Book III, Chapter Six, Section 1.

2 Recorded by Tirmidhī and others—S.I.

3 In *Lawāmiᶜ al-bayyināt fī al-asmā' wa'l-ṣifāt*, Rāzī credits the 'metaphysical philosophers (*al-ilāhiyyūn min al-falāsifa*)' with the distinction between eliminative Attributes 'which signify God's transcendental qualities' and are Attributes of Majesty; and relative Attributes 'which signify God's qualities of involvement with the world' and are Attributes of Beneficence. See Robert Wisnovsky, 'One Aspect of the Akbarian Turn in Shīᶜī Theology', in Ayman Shihadeh, ed., *Sufism and Theology*, Edinburgh: Edinburgh University Press, 2007, p. 61. [A. Booso, ed.]

4 Recorded by Muslim.

and action (*faᶜᶜāl*)—and, being an attribute, this does not convey the utmost magnification.[1] Furthermore, *al-Qayyūm* is an emphatic term [derived from] *qiyām* (standing), which means that He subsists in His own right and causes the subsistence of others. The former is an eliminative Attribute to the effect that He is free of need of others, while the latter is a relative Attribute. As such *al-Qayyūm* is a combination of eliminative and relative Attributes and cannot represent the Greatest Name.

C. Some said that all of God's Names are great and holy, so it is not appropriate to describe one in particular as the greatest and thus imply that the others are deficient [in comparison]. However, I believe this is also weak, because I have explained that names are of nine categories[2] and that the Name which denotes God's very Essence must be considered the noblest and greatest of names. Once this is proven rationally, there is no room for rejection.

D. Some said that this Name is *Allāh*, and this is the most likely in my view, because—as I shall prove[3]—it is treated as a proper Name for the Almighty. If that is so, then it denotes His very Essence.

Enquiry 13[4]

A name which denotes its referent with respect to a portion of that referent's quiddity could not exist for Almighty God, as such is only possible for one whose quiddity is composed of parts, and that is impossible with respect to God. This is because every composite is in need of its parts, and since the part is other than [the whole], the composite is in need of other than itself. Then, since everything which has a need of others is contingent, this shows that every composite thing is contingent in its own right. Therefore, anything which is not contingent cannot be composite, and thus cannot have a name which refers to a portion of its quiddity.

1 See the end of the following chapter for further discussion, as well as the author's exegesis of Q.II.255, in which he explains that the essential meaning of *al-Ḥayy* is that of 'perfection' and it corresponds to the first of the two meanings of *al-Qayyūm*. What is presented here is a technical definition among the theologians. Cf. Jaffer's translation of *al-darrāk al-faᶜᶜāl* as 'Actively Perceiving' (Jaffer, *Rāzī*, p. 48).

2 Enquiry 8 above.

3 See Chapter Nine below. Throughout this translation, I have followed the convention of treating 'God' as an English equivalent for *Allāh*, but the limitations of that assumption should be clear and kept in mind. See Umar Faruq Abd-Allah, 'One God, Many Names', Nawawi Foundation paper, 2004 (www.nawawi.org).

4 This discusses the second category under Enquiry 8 above.

Enquiry 14

We have discussed whether God has a Name which denotes His Essence and the various opinions on this issue, then we proved decisively the impossibility of a Name for God which denotes a portion of the quiddity.

This leaves seven categories,[1] so we say regarding the name which denotes a thing with reference to an actual attribute subsisting in its essence: either that attribute is existence, a modality of existence, or something distinct from both existence and its modalities. We shall discuss the enquiries branching from each of these subcategories. And God is the Guide.

1 I.e. from those outlined in Enquiry 8 above. The remaining sentences of this chapter lead into the next chapter, which is concerned with the third category.

Chapter Four
NAMES DENOTING ACTUAL ATTRIBUTES

As just explained, these names are of three types.

Section 1: Names Denoting Existence

Enquiry 1
[*al-Shay'* (Thing)][1]

Most authorities agreed that it is permissible to refer to Almighty God as a 'thing', but it is narrated from Jahm b. Ṣafwān that it is impermissible. The majority position is supported by the following arguments:

1. The verse: 'Say: "What thing (*shay'*) is most weighty in evidence?" Say: "God..."' (Q.vi.19), as this demonstrates that it is permissible to describe God as *shay'*.

   OBJECTION: this argument would be fair if the speech concluded at 'Say: "God,"' but in fact the verse says: 'Say: "God is witness between me and you."' This is independent speech not bound to what precedes it, therefore it does not follow that God is named as *shay'*.

   RESPONSE: since the [question] came as 'What thing is most weighty in evidence?' followed by 'Say: "God is witness between me and you,"' the latter necessarily functions as a reply, and so our point stands.
2. The verse: 'Everything will perish except His Countenance' (Q.xxviii.88), in which 'countenance' means 'essence'. If His Essence were not a thing, it would not be proper to make it an exception to 'Everything will perish'. This shows that Almighty God is described as *shay'*.
3. ʿImrān b. al-Ḥuṣayn related that the Prophet (may God bless him and grant him peace) said: 'God was, while there was nothing other than Him'[2]—which shows that the name *shay'* can be used for God.

1 It should be noted that controversies over names and descriptions being appropriate in Arabic may become considerably more problematic in translation. All such glosses etc. here are approximations to facilitate understanding and readability.

2 Recorded by Bukhārī.

4. ʿAbd Allāh al-Anṣārī [al-Harawī] recorded in his book *al-Fārūq* that ʿĀ'isha (may God be pleased with her) heard the Messenger of God saying: 'There is nothing more protective (*aghyar*) than God, the Exalted.'[1]
5. A 'thing' [by definition] is that which can be known and spoken about; this applies to God's Essence, so He is a thing.

JAHM ARGUED [against this usage] with the following:

1. 'God is the Creator of all things' (Q.XXXIX.62) and 'It is He Who has power over all things' (Q.V.120)—these entail that every 'thing' is created and controlled, and since God is not so, He is not a 'thing'. If it is said that these verses are [originally] universal but have been affected by particularisation (*takhṣīṣ*),[2] we respond in two ways:
   - This particularisation would be contrary to the default, and that is sufficient in the context of linguistic evidences to [discount it].
   - The original justification for particularisation being possible is that people conventionally expressed the majority in terms of the entirety. As such, universal statements could be subjected to particularisation. However, speaking of the majority as though it were the entirety is only permitted wherever the exception to the rule is something negligible and insignificant, such that its existence is effectively like non-existence and the remainder can be treated as though it were the whole. Once that is known, then let us suppose that God may be described as a 'thing': in that case, He must be the greatest and most significant of all things, and such particularisation would not be permitted. It follows that the claim of particularisation is unfeasible.
2. In the verse '…there is nothing whatsoever like Him (*laysa ka-mithlihi shay'un*), and He is the Hearing, the Seeing' (Q.LXII.11), God decrees that the likeness of His likeness is not a thing.[3] Since it is clear that

1 Recorded by Bukhārī and Muslim. This term may otherwise be translated as 'jealous' or 'self-respecting', in the sense of guarding one's right. Based on the fuller narrations (see Enquiry 4 below), commentators explain that God protects his servants from falling into disgrace, by defining the boundaries of proper behaviour.

2 That is to say: other verses make clear that there is a singular exception to these rules, *viz.* God Himself.

3 A hyper-literal translation would be 'There is no thing like His likeness'. See Muḥammad ʿAbd Allāh Drāz, *al-Naba' al-ʿaẓīm*, trans. Adil Salahi as *The Qur'an: An Eternal Challenge*, Leicester: Islamic Foundation, 2001, pp. 116–119: the author dismisses all explanations which treat the 'double-preposition' *ka-mithli* as a problem to be explained away, including the claim of the *kāf* being otiose. Instead, he uses this construction to build two theological arguments from the verse. The first is that nothing resembles God in any way (hence does not even resemble a 'likeness'). The second argument is that incomparability is entailed by the very nature of Divinity.

everything must be deemed a likeness to its own likeness, it follows from this verse that God Almighty is not a 'thing'. If it is suggested that the *kāf* is otiose, we respond that this claim is tantamount to describing a letter from God's speech as useless vanity, and that is certain falsehood. Once we reject the idea that this letter is useless, the proof we have mentioned becomes remarkably strong and complete.

3. The word *shay'* does not denote an attribute of majesty, grandeur, praise and exaltation, whereas this must be the case for the Divine Names. This shows that *shay'* is not a Name for God. On the first premise: it is obvious that this name does not express praise and grandeur, considering that its meaning is shared between everything from a lowly speck to the noblest of things. If it applies to the most ignoble of things, then it cannot be a term of praise and grandeur.

   As for our saying that God's Names must denote praise and grandeur, its proof is: 'The most Beautiful Names belong to God: so call on him by them; but shun such as use profanity in his Names' (Q.vii.180). The description of the Names as 'beautiful' can only mean that they denote Attributes which are beautiful, lofty and majestic. Otherwise, they could not be described as 'beautiful' Names. Moreover, God has commanded us to call upon Him by these Names and instructed to 'shun such as use profanity in his Names'—this is as if to warn against calling Him by other than those Beautiful Names. As such, this verse indicates strongly that the servant is not permitted to call God by anything other than the most Beautiful Names which denote Attributes of majesty and praise. Once these two premises are established, the conclusion follows necessarily.

4. It has not been narrated from the Messenger of God (may God bless him and grant him peace) or any of his Companions that they addressed God by saying *yā shay'* ('O Thing'). And how could they when this word is as lowly as can be? How can the servant address God in this way? Rather, it was narrated that they used to say: 'O Creator of things (*munshi' al-ashyā'*), Creator of earth and heaven!'[1]

REMARK: there are people who claim that this disagreement pertains to [essential] meanings, but that is completely implausible. After all, there is no dispute concerning God being an existent, essence and reality, but only as to whether it is permitted to use this particular word for Him. This is

1 I could not source this.

a linguistic rather than [theological] dispute, so it should not be taken as a basis for declaring anyone as unbelievers or sinners. A person must be aware of this nuance, lest he fall into error.

Enquiry 2
al-Mawjūd (Existent)

The question of whether it is permissible to describe God with this word must be preceded by an introduction concerning the fact that the term *wujūd* has two distinct meanings. It may be used to refer to [subjective] perception and feeling ('finding')[1]: in that case, the term *mawjūd* means 'that which is perceived and felt'. Alternatively, it is for something to obtain and be real ('exist') objectively.

Know that there is a difference between these two, in that a thing being known to exist depends upon its being existent in itself. The opposite is not true, for a thing's actual existence is not dependent on its being known as such. It is not inconceivable[2] for a thing to obtain in and of itself without anyone being aware of it.

QUESTION: was the word originally coined for perception and feeling, and then extended to objective existence, or was it the opposite, or were the meanings defined simultaneously?

RESPONSE: I say: this difference is [purely] linguistic. The most likely is the first opinion because, were it not for the human's perception of the thing, he would not know of its objective existence. Hence the word is coined first for that feeling and perception, before the meaning of objective existence.

Once this introduction is known, we say: the use of the term *mawjūd* for God has two [possible] meanings: that He is known and perceived, and that He exists in and of Himself. The former meaning is present in the Qur'ān: 'They would have found God...' (Q.IV.64)—this refers to [the subjective aspect of] feeling (*wijdān*) and gnosis (*ʿirfān*). However, the latter meaning is not found in the Qur'ān.

CONTENTION: whenever *wujūd* as perception is present, its meaning as existence follows [necessarily], as something which is non-existent [cannot be perceived].

1 The verb *wajada* can simply be translated as 'to find'. By 'subjective', I mean that the presence and perspective of a 'finder' is assumed in describing the 'found'.

2 Most printed editions (including Istanbul) have 'it is inconceivable' (*yamtaniʿ fī al-ʿaql*), but Amīriyya (vol I, p. 65) has the expected negation.

RESPONSE: this is weak for two reasons:

a. The meaning of existence does not follow from the meaning of perception and knowledge, as a non-existent can also be known.[1]
b. We have clarified that this dispute is purely linguistic, so it does not follow that a name which is based on one meaning must also apply to another meaning.

Nevertheless, we say: this name is confirmed [for God] by the consensus of the Muslims, so [its permissibility] must be affirmed.

OBJECTION: did you not say[2] that the Divine Names must denote praise and exaltation? The word *mawjūd* does not convey such.

RESPONSE: we have overlooked that concern due to the force of consensus. Moreover, the word *mawjūd* conveys a greater sense of praise than *shay'*, as the following demonstrates:

a. Some people use the word *shay'* for both existents and non-existents, whereas *mawjūd* is specific to existents, which makes it worthier of being used as praise.
b. The meaning of *mawjūd* as 'known' denotes an attribute of praise, as though the sheer quantity of signifiers of His existence and Divinity has made Him known to every person and existent to everyone, such that it is incumbent on every intellect to recognise Him. Since this sense of the word conveys praise, the difference between it and the word *shay'* is clear.

Enquiry 3
al-Dhāt (Essence)

In his book entitled *al-Fārūq*, ʿAbd Allāh al-Anṣārī al-Harawī recorded a number of narrations pointing to this usage:

a. ʿĀ'isha related that the Messenger of God (may God bless him and grant him peace) said: 'Among the people who receive the greatest of reward is a righteous minister for a leader, who obeys him for the sake (*dhāt*) of God.'[3]
b. Abū Hurayra related that the Messenger of God (may God bless

1 This may apply to the conception of a thing known to be non-existent, as well the mistaken belief in a thing's existence.

2 The addressee and respondent is speaking, as it were, with what was previously the voice of Jahm b. Ṣafwān in Enquiry 1.

3 A similar narration is found in the *Muʿjam* of Ibn al-Aʿrābī and the *Musnad* of Qaḍāʿī with a 'very weak' chain—R.S. The wording there makes it more likely that it means that the leader 'obeys' the minister, who advises him sincerely.

him and grant him peace) said: 'Abraham did not lie except in three instances, two of which were for the sake of God.'[1]

c. [The son of] Kaᶜb b. ᶜUjra narrated from his father (may God be pleased with him) that the Messenger of God (may God bless him and grant him peace) said: 'Do not insult ᶜAlī, for he has been submissive (*makhshūsh*) for the sake of God.'[2]

d. Abū Dharr said: 'I asked the Messenger of God (may God bless him and grant him peace): which kind of struggle (*jihād*) is best? He replied: "To struggle against your ego and desires for the sake of God."'[3]

e. Al-Nuᶜmān b. Bashīr related that the Prophet (may God bless him and grant him peace) said: 'Satan has various traps and snares, which include [inciting] denial of God's favours, pride in God's bounty, arrogance towards God's servants, and following desires for other than the sake of God.'[4]

I say: whenever a thing has within it a certain matter, then if the word for that thing is masculine, it is described as *dhū* ('possessor of') such-and-such; in feminine, it is *dhāt* such-and-such. This [latter] word was thus coined to express this relationship [through annexation] and denote this attribution. Once this is known, then we say: it is impossible for an attribute to be possessed by a second attribute, and that one by a third, and so on *ad infinitum*. Rather, they must end at a single reality which subsists in itself and has an independent quiddity. That reality (*ḥaqīqa*) can be described as *dhāt* (possessor) of all these attributes. Saying '*dhāt* such-and-such' is literally true only for that independent quiddity (*māhiyya*), which is why they used this word separately to denote that reality.[5]

Since Almighty God is self-subsistent (*qayyūm*), the use of the word *dhāt* (essence) for Him is proper and true. However, the *ḥadīth*s which we have cited from Harawī do nothing to establish this, because the meaning

1 Recorded by Bukhārī and Muslim—S.I. As Imām Nawawī explains, all three were for God, but the third—in which he sought to save his wife Sarah from being seized by a tyrant ruler—included an aspect of personal interest; see Nawawī, *Sharḥ Ṣaḥīḥ Muslim*, vol. VIII, p. 123.

2 Versions of this appear in numerous sources but with the word *mamsūs* (i.e. harmed) in place of *makhshūsh* in the printed editions of Rāzī. Another account has: 'Do not complain about ᶜAlī, for he is *akhshan/ukhayshin* (rough in lifestyle, or tough in battle) for the sake of God'; other variants are *mukhshawshin*, *akhshā* and *aḥsan*.

3 Recorded by Abū Nuᶜaym in *Ḥilyat al-Awliyā'*—S.I.

4 Some narrations have this as a saying of al-Nuᶜmān himself (*mawqūf*), as in *al-Adab al-mufrad* of Bukhārī—S.I.

5 This explanation is helped by *ḥaqīqa* and *māhiyya* both being feminine words.

of *dhāt* in each of them is not this divine reality and Essence. Rather, they are about seeking the pleasure (*riḍwān*) of God. Do you not see that 'two of which were for the *dhāt* of God' means 'seeking His pleasure'? The same applies to the remainder.[1]

Enquiry 4
al-Nafs (Self)

This word occurs in the Qur'ān. God said [quoting Jesus (on whom be peace)]: 'You know what is within myself, and I do not know what is within Yourself' (Q.v.116); and He said: 'God cautions you (concerning) Himself' (Q.iii.28).

[Prophetic *ḥadīth*s in this connection:]

a. ʿĀ'isha said: 'I was sleeping beside the Messenger of God (may God bless him and grant him peace) when I noticed that he was missing, so I searched for him and my hand fell upon his feet while he was in prostration, saying: "O God! I seek refuge in Your pleasure from Your displeasure; I seek refuge in Your pardon from Your punishment; and I seek refuge in You from You! I cannot enumerate Your praises: You are as You have praised Yourself."'[2]

b. Abū Hurayra related that the Prophet (may God bless him and grant him peace) said: 'Almighty God says: "I am with My servant when he remembers Me. If he remembers Me to himself, I remember him to Myself; and if he remembers Me in a gathering, I remember him in a gathering better than his. If he seeks to draw nearer to Me by a hand span, I draw nearer to him by a forearm's length; and if he comes to Me by a forearm's length, I draw nearer to him by an arm's length. If he comes to Me walking, I come to him at speed."'[3]

c. Abū Ṣāliḥ narrated from Abū Hurayra that the Messenger of God (may God bless him and grant him peace) said: 'When God completed the creation, He wrote in the Book [in which He decreed] upon Himself, which was elevated above the Throne: "My mercy overcomes My wrath."'[4]

d. ʿAbd Allāh b. Masʿūd related that the Messenger of God (may God bless him and grant him peace) said: 'There is none who loves praise more than God, which is why He has praised Himself; and none

1 This is why I have translated them using the natural expression in English: 'for His sake'.
2 Recorded by Muslim—S.I.
3 Recorded by Bukhārī and Muslim—S.I.
4 Recorded by Bukhārī and Muslim—S.I.

is more protective than God, which is why He has prohibited abominable acts; and there is none who loves to excuse people more than God, which is why He revealed the Book and sent the Messengers.'[1]

e. ʿĀ'isha[2] related that the Prophet (may God bless him and grant him peace) taught her this formula of praise: 'Glory and praise is for You, O God, according to the number of Your creations, the ink of Your words, the pleasure of Your self, and the weight of Your Throne.'

f. Abū Dharr related that the Prophet (may God bless him and grant him peace) said that God said: 'I have forbidden oppression upon Myself and made it forbidden between you, so do not oppress one another'[3]—and the remainder of this *ḥadīth* is well known.

g. Ibn ʿUmar related: 'One day, the Prophet (may God bless him and grant him peace) recited from the pulpit: "No just estimate of God do they make..." (Q.vi.91), [and then he described the events of the Day of Judgment:] "Then God will praise Himself, saying: 'I am the Compeller, I am the Superior, I am the Mighty, I am the Noble.'" Then the pulpit began to shake under the Messenger of God (may God bless him and grant him peace) until we feared he would fall.'[4]

h. Abū Hurayra related that the Prophet (may God bless him and grant him peace) said: 'Adam and Moses met, and Moses said to Adam: "You are the one who put people in a miserable state and turned them out of Paradise!" Adam said to him: "You are the one whom God selected for His message and whom He selected for Himself[5] and upon whom He revealed the Torah." Moses said: "Yes." Adam said: "Did you find that it was written in my fate before He created me?" Moses said: "Yes." So Adam overcame Moses with this argument.'[6]

1 Recorded by Bukhārī and Muslim—S.I.

2 Recorded by Muslim and others; according to the sources, Juwayriya bint al-Ḥārith was the one taught these words, not ʿĀ'isha—S.I.

3 Recorded by Muslim—S.I.

4 Recorded by Ibn Khuzayma and Ibn Ḥibbān. The narration is clearer when more of the verse is quoted: the Prophet was demonstrating how God will grasp the creation and shake it, while declaring His perfect Names and superior Attributes. Apparently, the Prophet's action caused the pulpit to shake.

5 See also Q.xx.41.

6 Recorded by Bukhārī and Muslim—S.I.

i. Jābir related that the Messenger of God (may God bless him and grant him peace) said: 'God said: "This is a religion with which I am satisfied for Myself; nothing will make it right except generosity and good manners, so honour it by these two."'[1]
j. Anas b. Mālik related from the Prophet (may God bless him and grant him peace), who narrated from his Lord: 'Whoever dishonours a friend of Mine has openly declared war on Me, so I do not care in which valley of the world I destroy him and throw him into Hell. I do not hesitate in Myself concerning anything as much as I hesitate to take the soul of my believing servant. He dislikes death although there is no escape from it, and I dislike to harm him.'[2]
k. ʿAbd Allāh [b. Masʿūd] related that the Prophet (may God bless him and grant him peace) said: 'There is never a servant who is afflicted by grief and sadness, and says the following: "O God! I am Your servant, son of Your servant and son of Your maidservant. My forelock is in Your hand; Your ruling upon me is enacted, and Your decree upon me is just. I ask You by every Name You possess, by which You have named Yourself, or revealed in Your Book, or taught to any one of Your creation, or which You have kept hidden in the knowledge of the Unseen with You: that You make the Qur'ān the springtime of my heart, the light of my chest and the driving away of my sadness and grief"—but God drives away his grief and replaces his sadness with joy.'[3]
l. Abū Saʿīd al-Khudrī related: 'The Messenger of God (may God bless him and grant him peace) said: "Almighty God has sent me as a mercy to the worlds, and to destroy musical instruments and idols. My Lord has made an oath upon Himself that a servant will not drink wine without repenting thereafter to God, except that God will make him drink from the clay of corruption." I asked: "O Messenger of God! What is the clay of corruption?" He replied: "The pus of the inhabitants of Hell."'[4]

1 Recorded in Ṭabarānī's *Awsaṭ* and others, but considered 'very weak'—R.S.

2 I did not find a *ḥadīth* with the phrase 'hesitate in Myself', but the opening and ending of this narration resemble an authentic one in Bukhārī.

3 Recorded by Aḥmad, Ibn Ḥibbān and others.

4 I did not find a *ḥadīth* with the phrase 'made an oath upon Himself', but the latter part of this narration (concerning intoxicants) resembles an authentic one in Muslim. See also Maḥmūd al-Ālūsī, *Rūḥ al-maʿānī fī tafsīr al-Qur'ān al-ʿaẓīm wa'l-sabʿ al-mathānī*, ed. Māhir Ḥabbūsh et al., 30 vols., Beirut: Mu'assasat al-Risāla, 2010, vol. vii, p. 498.

Know that the 'self' (*nafs*) is an expression for the essence, reality and identity of a thing. It does not mean a body which is composed of parts, as [indeed] every body is composite, every composite is contingent, and every contingent is created—and this cannot be true for God. Therefore, the meaning of *nafs* [in His case] must be as we have said.

Enquiry 5
al-Shakhṣ (Individual)

Saʿd b. ʿUbāda related that the Prophet (may God bless him and grant him peace) said: 'There is no individual more self-respecting than God, which is why He has prohibited abominable acts, both open and secret. There is no individual who loves to excuse people more than God, which is why He sent the Messengers to bear glad tidings and as warners. And there is no individual who loves praise more than God.'[1]

Know that it is not possible for *shakhṣ* to mean a body which has individuation (*tashakhkhuṣ*) and proportionality. Rather, it is any essence and reality which is specified such as to be distinct from others.

Enquiry 6
al-Nūr (Light)

Is this name permitted to use for God? He has said: 'God is the light of the heavens and the earth' (Q.xxiv.35). In terms of Prophetic *ḥadīth*s, it is narrated that it was said to ʿAbd Allāh b. [ʿAmr]: 'It has been attributed to you that you have said that the wretched is wretched [from the time of being] in his mother's belly.' He said: 'I heard the Messenger of God (may God bless him and grant him peace) saying: "God created the creation in darkness, then cast upon it from His light. So whomsoever is touched by some of that light is guided, but whomever it misses has gone astray." This is why I say that the pen has dried upon the knowledge of Almighty God.'[2]

Know that the suggestion that this refers to the [familiar phenomenon of] light—or something of its genus—is false, as shown by the following:

1. Light is either a body or the quality of a body. Since bodies are temporally originated, so are their qualities—and God is far above being temporal.

1 Recorded by Muslim, and similar in Bukhārī (where the word *shakhṣ* is in the chapter heading, not the main text). The narrator is Mughīra b. Shuʿba, but Saʿd was involved in the story behind the *ḥadīth*.

2 Recorded by Ibn Ḥibbān. The printed editions have 'ʿUmar' without the final *wāw* to distinguish the two names.

2. Light has darkness as its opposite, whereas God is transcendent above having an opposite.
3. Light disappears and [illuminated bodies] set, whereas God is transcendent above the attribute of disappearance.[1]

Regarding the [apparent import of] the verse 'God is the light of the heavens and the earth' (Q.xxiv.35), our response is that it is one of the equivocal (*mutashābih*) verses, as evidenced by the rational proofs we have advanced.[2] Moreover, God said immediately thereafter: 'The parable of His light...' in which there is annexation (*iḍāfa*) of the owned [light] to its Owner. This shows that He is not—in Himself—light, but rather He is the Creator of light.

The question remains: what makes the use of this name [metaphorically] appropriate for Him? There are several responses to this:

a. Some recited this verse as *li'Llāhi nūr...* ('To God belongs the light...'),[3] in which case the issue disappears.
b. Since He is the Illuminator of lights and their Creator, it is appropriate to use the name *al-Nūr* for Him upon this interpretation (*ta'wīl*).
c. It is by His wisdom that the needs of the world are fulfilled and the affairs of this world and the next are organised. The one who organises such interests and strives to fulfil such benefits may be called *nūr*, as in the saying 'So-and-so is the light of this town' for someone who is as we have described [on a human scale].
d. He has graced His servants with faith, guidance and gnosis, and these are all attributes in the genus of lights.

[The last point] is demonstrated by the Qur'ān and *ḥadīth*s. As for the Qur'ān, there is: 'Light upon light! God guides whom He will to His light...' (Q.xxiv.35). As for *ḥadīth*s, there are many:

a. Abū Umāma al-Bāhilī related from the Prophet (may God bless him and grant him peace) that he said: 'Beware the insight (*firāsa*) of the believer, for he sees by God's light.'[4]
b. Anas b. Mālik related that the Prophet (may God bless him and grant him peace) said: 'Do you know which of the people is wisest?' They replied: 'God and His Messenger know best.' He said: 'The most frequent of them in remembering death and the best prepared

1 See Q.vi.76.
2 See the author's exegesis of the verse for detailed discussion. See also Jaffer, *Rāzī*, p. 148.
3 I found no reference to this reading in compilations of *qirā'āt*.
4 Recorded by Ṭabarāni (*al-Awsaṭ* and *al-Kabīr*).

for it.' They asked: 'Messenger of God, is there any sign of that?' He replied: 'Yes: forsaking the abode of deception and turning to the abode of eternity, for once light enters the heart, it becomes wide and spacious to prepare for the arrival of death.'[1]

c. Ibn Masᶜūd said: 'The Prophet (may God bless him and grant him peace) recited: "Is one whose heart God has opened to Islam, so that he has upon light from his Lord (no better than one hard-hearted)?" (Q.xxxix.22). Then I asked him: "O Messenger of God! How does God open his heart?" He replied: "When light enters the heart, it becomes wide and spacious." I asked: "And what is the sign of that, O Messenger of God?" He replied: "Turning to the abode of eternity and forsaking the abode of deception, and preparing for death before its arrival."'[2]

d. Anas said: 'While the Messenger of God (may God bless him and grant him peace) was walking, he was met by Ḥāritha [b. al-Nuᶜmān], so he said to him: "How are you upon rising, O Ḥāritha?" He replied: "I have risen as a true believer," upon which the Prophet said: "Pay attention to what you are saying, for everything has a reality! What is the reality of your faith?" He replied: "My soul has turned away from this world, so I have made my nights sleepless and my days thirsty. It is as though I am looking directly at the Throne of my Lord, and as though I am beholding the mutual visitations of the people of the Garden and the screams of the people of the Fire." The Prophet (may God bless him and grant him peace) said: "You have come to know, so stay steadfast." He then added: "Whomsoever it pleases to look at a man whose heart God has illuminated with faith, let him look to this man." [Ḥāritha] said: "O Messenger of God! Pray for me to attain martyrdom," so he prayed for him. The call was made thereafter: "Mount, O cavalry of God!" He was the first to mount and was martyred in God's path.'[3]

1 Although this is presented as one narration, it is more clearly represented as two. Similar to the first question and answer are found in Ibn Mājah and elsewhere. The second half appears to be based on the narration which follows.

2 Versions of this are reported in Ṭabarī's exegesis (*Jāmiᶜ al-bayān ᶜan ta'wīl āy al-Qur'ān*, ed. Maḥmūd Shākir & Aḥmad Shākir, 16 vols., Cairo: Dār al-Maᶜārif, 1961, vol. xii, pp. 98–102, under Q.vi.125) from Ibn Masᶜūd as well as ᶜAbd Allāh b. al-Miswar (Abū Jaᶜfar). Despite Ibn Kathīr's view that these chains support each other (see Ibn Kathīr, *Tafsīr al-Qur'ān al-ᶜaẓīm*, 7 vols., Cairo: Dār al-Āthār, 2009, vol. iii, p. 251), the modern scholar Maḥmūd Shākir argued that the former group of narrations is 'weak', and the latter 'fabricated' (see footnotes in his edition).

3 Recorded in *Shuᶜab al-īmān* of Bayhaqī—S.I.

e. Ibn ʿAbbās said: 'While I was sitting in the presence of the Messenger of God (may God bless him and grant him peace), he heard a sound from above so he raised his head towards the sky, saying: "This gate in the heaven has opened which has never opened before, and an angel descended from it, saying: 'O Muḥammad! Receive glad tidings of two lights which none was granted before you: the Opening (*Fātiḥa*) of the Book and the end of *Sūrat al-Baqara*.'"'[1]

f. Yaʿlā b. [Munya][2] related that the Messenger of God (may God bless him and grant him peace) said: 'The believer will pass over the [bridge] path on the Day of Judgment and the Fire will call out to him: "Pass by me, O believer, for your light has extinguished my flames."'[3]

g. Nāfiʿ narrated from ʿAbd Allāh b. ʿUmar that the Prophet (may God bless him and grant him peace) used to say: 'O God! By You we enter the morning and the evening; by You we live and die; and to You is the resurrection. O God! Make me of the most fortunate among your servants in receiving every good which You apportion this day: of light by which You guide, mercy which You spread, provision which You increase, harm which You lift, suffering which You remove, evil which You obliterate, or tribulation which You avert.'[4]

h. ʿAlī b. Abī Ṭālib related that the Prophet (may God bless him and grant him peace) was asked concerning the people of Paradise, so he said: 'The people of Paradise have unkempt hair and dirty clothes, yet if the light from one of them were distributed, it would suffice the inhabitants of earth.'[5]

i. Abū Hurayra related that the Prophet (may God bless him and grant him peace) said: 'The people of Paradise are the unkempt dusty ones

1 Recorded by Muslim—S.I.

2 The printed editions have 'Munabbih', whereas the correct name is an ascription to Yaʿlā's mother or paternal grandmother. He is also known as Yaʿlā b. Umayya after his father. The *ḥadīth* is recorded in Ṭabarānī's *Kabīr* and the chain has been criticised by numerous scholars.

3 There are many *ḥadīths*—some recorded by Bukhārī and Muslim—referring to the bridge (called *al-ṣirāṭ* or *al-jisr*) which all are made to cross in the Hereafter, with only the righteous being granted a swift safe passage in the first instance, to be followed in varying degrees by the other believers according to their piety, with some believers even slipping off the bridge for a temporary period in Hell. [A. Booso, ed.]

4 The first part until 'the resurrection' is a known Prophetic supplication in Abū Dāwūd, Tirmidhī, etc.; however, the second half is attributed not to the Prophet, but to Ibn ʿUmar himself in Ṭabarānī (*Kabīr*)—R.S.

5 This narration is only found in Rāzī's *Tafsīr*—S.I. Similar may be true of other junctures at which I 'could not source' the narration. The sources drawn upon by the author may be unpublished or no longer extant.

possessing two worn-out garments. If they asked to enter upon the rulers, they would be refused. If they came as suitors, they would not be married. If they should speak, they would not be heard. The need of each one turns over in his chest; yet if his light were distributed among the people of the earth, it would suffice them.'[1]

j. Anas b. Mālik related that the Messenger of God (may God bless him and grant him peace) said: 'Almighty God says: "My light is My guidance, and 'There is none worthy of worship but God' is My word, so I allow everyone who speaks it into My fortress. And whoever enters My fortress has attained security."'[2]

k. Hishām b. ʿUrwa narrated from his father that ʿĀ'isha said that the Prophet (may God bless him and grant him peace) used to supplicate: 'I seek refuge in God's perfect words and by His light through which the earth has become radiant and the darknesses have been illuminated, from Your grace turning away or from this well-being from You altering, from Your sudden punishment and from being caught by preordained misery and evil.'[3]

l. The Prophet (may God bless him and grant him peace) used to say: 'O God! Place light in my heart, light in my hearing and light in my vision'—this is a famous *ḥadīth*.[4]

Enquiry 7
al-Ṣūra (Image)

There are Prophetic *ḥadīth*s in this connection:

a. Abū Hurayra related that the Prophet (may God bless him and grant him peace) said: 'God created Adam upon his image.'[5] Ibn ʿUmar related that the Messenger of God said: 'Do not disfigure the face, for God created Adam upon the image of the Compassionate.'[6] Isḥāq b. Rāhawayh said that it has been authentically narrated that the Messenger of God (may God bless him and grant him peace) said: 'God created Adam upon the image of the Compassionate.'

b. Muʿādh b. Jabal said: 'The Messenger of God (may God bless him and

1 Recorded in *Shuʿab al-īmān* of Bayhaqī—S.I.
2 A 'very weak' chain recorded by ʿUqaylī in *al-Ḍuʿafā'*—S.I.
3 Recorded by Ṭabarānī in *al-Duʿā'*. Parts of this supplication (not including the mention of light) are in an authentic narration in Muslim, from Ibn ʿUmar.
4 Recorded by Bukhārī and Muslim—S.I.
5 Recorded by Bukhārī and Muslim.
6 Recorded by Ṭabarānī (*Kabīr*) and others, but most likely a *mursal* narration, hence weak. A similar narration in Muslim ends with 'upon his image' as above—R.S.

grant him peace) led us in prayer one morning, and someone said to him: "I have never seen you with such a bright face like the morning light." He replied: "Why not? Indeed, my Lord appeared to me in the best image and asked: 'Concerning what do the heavenly hosts dispute, O Muḥammad?' I replied: 'You know best, my Lord.' He placed His hand between my shoulders so I felt its coolness, then I came to know what is in the heavens and on earth.'"[1]

Know that the scholars have mentioned a number of interpretations of these *ḥadīth*s:

A. The pronoun in 'his image' refers to the one being hit,[2] i.e. that God created Adam in the [same] image as that person, so the latter's face must not be disfigured.
B. It means that God created Adam in his own final image; in other words, he did not develop from a sperm-drop through the stages of embryo, foetus and infant. Rather, God created him as a complete man all at once.
C. 'Image' here means 'description' (*ṣifa*), as one says 'The *ṣūra* of this issue is as follows,' i.e. its description. Therefore, 'upon the image of the Compassionate' means that he was created to be His trustee (*khalīfa*) upon His earth, having authority over earthly bodies while Almighty God enacts His power in the entire universe.

Enquiry 8
al-Jawhar (Substance)

The philosophers sometimes use this term for God's Essence, as do the Christians, whereas the theologians (*mutakallimūn*) refrain from it. The philosophers said that what is meant by substance is 'an essence which has no need of a locus-substrate (*maḥall*) or subject-substrate (*mawḍūʿ*)'; since God is like this, He must be a substance.

[They further explain:] the term *jawhar* is derived from *jahr* which means 'to be apparent', and the substance was so named because it is apparent due to its individuality (*shakhṣiyya*) and proportionality (*ḥajmiyya*). Being a substance means for its existence to be apparent; its proportionality is not the substance itself, but rather the reason it is a substance, i.e. for its existence being apparent. Almighty God is more apparent than anything due to the sheer quantity of signifiers of His

1 Recorded by Tirmidhī.

2 The statement was made in the context of forbidding a person from being excessive in hitting another human being of honoured form.

existence: as such, He is most deserving of being a *jawhar* [without proportionality].

As for the theologians, they stated that the Muslims have refrained from this word by consensus, so it is incumbent to do likewise.

Enquiry 9
al-Jism (Body)

Most of the Karrāmīs applied this word to God, while claiming: 'We do not mean by it that He is composite and made up of limbs etc., but rather that He is existent and self-subsistent, having no need for a substrate.' However, the remainder of the sects rejected this name unanimously.

We have two things to raise with the Karrāmīs:

1. We do not accept that they meant by 'body' anything other than length, width and depth. After all, they said that God is 'above the Throne' (*fawqa al-ʿarsh*). They do not say that He is infinitesimal like the atomic substance (*al-jawhar al-fard*) or the indivisible particle; rather, they say that He is greater [in magnitude] than the Throne. This necessitates being extended from one side of the Throne to the other, i.e. to be long, wide and deep. This, then, becomes the meaning of *jism*. As such, their claim to mean something other than this [implication] is a pure and utter lie.
2. The term *jism* implies something unacceptable and there is nothing in the Qur'ān or Prophetic narrations to support it, so one must refrain from its use. This is especially the case when the theologians have said that the word implies a multitude of parts extending in length, width and depth—so the word *jism* must necessarily convey the core of this meaning.

Enquiry 10
al-Inniyya (Being)[1]

This term is frequently used by the philosophers. Etymologically, it is from Arabic *inna* which conveys emphasis and strength of existence. Since Almighty God is necessarily existent in His own right, His existence is the most perfect, strong and emphatic: so it is natural that the philosophers used the term for God upon this meaning.

1 From Greek *ousia*, this Arabic term is contrasted with *ghayriyya*. See Rahim Acar, *Talking about God and Talking about Creation*, Leiden: Brill, 2005, p. 83; and Alon & Abed, *Al-Fārābī's Philosophical Lexicon*, vol. 1, p. 15.

Enquiry 11
al-Māhiyya (Quiddity)

The term *māhiyya* is not originally a single word. Rather, if a man wanted to ask about a certain reality, he would say *mā hiya?* ('What is it?'). The Prophet (may God bless him and grant him peace) used to say: '[O God!] Show us things as they are (*ka-mā hiya*).'[1] When this became used frequently to enquire about the realities of things, they made it as a single word equivalent to *ḥaqīqa* (reality), so the *māhiyya* of a thing is its particular reality and essence.

Enquiry 12
al-Ḥaqq (Reality)[2]

If this word is used concerning the ESSENCE of a thing, it means that it is truly existent in its own right. This is seen by the fact that the opposite of *ḥaqq* is *bāṭil*, which means 'non-existent (*maʿdūm*)'. Labīd said: *a-lā kullu shay'in mā khalā Allāha bāṭilun* ('Indeed, everything except God is falsehood'). Since the opposite of reality is non-existence, the Real must refer to the existent.

If it is used concerning a BELIEF, then it means that it is correct and corresponds to the [reality of] the thing [which it concerns]. The term *ḥaqq* is applied to correct beliefs in that they must be accepted and maintained. If it is used concerning STATEMENTS AND REPORTS, then it means that they are truthful and accurate, which entails that they be accepted and maintained.

Once this is known, then we say that Almighty God is most deserving of the name *al-Ḥaqq*. With regard to His Essence, He is that Existent which could never be absent or perish. In terms of belief, this is because belief in His existence and necessity is the correct and accurate one whose reality never alters. As for reports and being mentioned, then this report [of His existence] is the worthiest of being described as truthful and authoritative. Thus it is seen that He is the Truth in all these meanings and respects. And God grants success and guidance.

Section II: Names Denoting Modality of Existence

The contents of this section must be preceded by some rational introductions:

1. Know that God's being pre-eternal and everlasting does not necessitate

1 This is not known to be a *ḥadīth* of the Messenger (may God bless him and grant him peace).
2 Alternatively, this can be translated as 'truth'.

the existence of time without end. To explain: for something to exist eternally in itself either depends on the existence of time [in which to subsist], or not. We are proving that it is not, as this is what allows for Him to be pre-eternal and everlasting without need for (another) time to exist.[1]

If, on the other hand, [His being pre-eternal and everlasting] did depend [on a corresponding timeframe], then that time would itself either be pre-eternal, or not. If it should be pre-eternal, then—upon the initial assumption—that time would also depend upon another time [in which to subsist], and this dependence on another time would lead to infinite regression. If, on the other hand, we say that that time is not pre-eternal, then God existed pre-eternally before that time, and this only proves that being eternal does not depend upon the existence of (another) time—and that was our point. It is thus proven that God being pre-eternal does not force us to say that time itself is pre-eternal.

2. Anything which is pre-eternal (*azalī*) is also everlasting (*bāqī*), but it does not follow from something being everlasting that it is pre-eternal. The term *bāqī* occurs in the Qur'ān; for example, 'But will abide (forever) the Countenance of your Lord' (Q.LV.27). Also, 'Everything will perish except His Countenance' (Q.XXVIII.88)—and anything which does not perish is, necessarily, everlasting.

   God also said: 'He is the First and the Last' (Q.LVII.3). This means that He is 'first' in relation to all else, which entails that He does not have a 'first' [i.e. beginning]. If He did, then He would not be 'first' in relation to His own 'first'. Likewise, if He had a 'last' [i.e. end], then He would not be 'last' in relation to His own 'last'. Therefore, since He is 'first and last' to all things, it is impossible for Him to have a 'first' or 'last'. As such, these Names entail that He is pre-eternal without beginning, and everlasting without end.

3. If the Creator of the world were created (*muḥdath*), He would be in need of another creator, leading to infinite regression, which is absurd. Therefore, He is pre-eternal. Once this is proven, it follows necessarily that He can never cease to exist, for anything that is proven to be pre-eternal cannot conceivably be non-existent.

After these introductory remarks, let us turn to explain the names.

1 I am not sure why the author has referred to this time as 'other' twice in this discussion, as dependence on *any* time would be contrary to the perfection of Divinity. It may be because this infinite time is 'other' than the finite time of reality.

[Terms for 'Pre-eternal'][1]

Name 1: *al-Qadīm* (ancient)

Know that this word, in its original linguistic sense, denotes a lengthy period of time and does not negate [a thing having] a beginning. A house is said to be *qadīm* if it has existed for a long time. Almighty God said: '...until [the moon] returns like the old, lower part of a date-stalk' (Q.xxxvi.39), and [quoting the sons addressing Jacob]: 'Truly you are in your (same) old error!' (Q.xii.95).

Name 2: *al-Azalī* (pre-eternal)

This term denotes an ascription to the *azal* ('pre-eternity'), which gives the impression that the *azal* is something in which God's Essence has obtained [or subsisted]. This is false, as it would imply that God's Essence is in need of that thing, which is impossible. Rather, what is intended is an existence without any beginning.

Name 3: *Lā awwala lahu* (having no beginning)

This expression conveys the meaning explicitly. There are different opinions concerning whether it expresses an Attribute which is affirmative (*thubūtī*) or eliminative (*ʿadamī*).[2] Some said that it signifies the negation of a prior non-existence, which is negation of negation, hence affirmation. Thus, despite the apparent nature of the words, it is affirmative in reality.

Others said that it is an eliminative meaning, i.e. the negation of being preceded by non-existence. There is a difference between [the concepts of] being non-existent, on the one hand, and being preceded by non-existence, on the other. The latter is an affirmative modality, of which saying 'He has no beginning' is a negation. Therefore, 'having no beginning' is an eliminative concept.

THE FIRST GROUP REPLIED that if 'being preceded by non-existence' were an affirmative modality additional to the Essence, that additional modality would be temporally originated, meaning that it is preceded by non-existence. Then that would itself be an additional Attribute, leading to infinite regression, which is impossible.

1 I have added these subheadings partly to offset the difficulty of differentiating a number of these near-synonyms in translation.

2 Shahran writes that the 'most common' classification amongst the *mutakallimūn* of the Divine Attributes was into those which were 'necessary' (*al-wājiba* or *thubūtiyya*) and the 'negative' (*al-mumtaniʿa* or *salbiyya*). However, the complexity of the issue led to later refined classifications. See Shahran, *Fakhr al-Dīn al-Rāzī on Divine Transcendence and Anthropomophism*, pp. 94–5. [A. Booso, ed.]

[Terms for 'Everlasting']

Name 4: *al-Abadī*

It means to persist with reference to future time.

Name 5: *al-Sarmadī*

This is derived from *sard*, meaning 'to be continuous and consecutive'. The Prophet (may God bless him and grant him peace) said concerning the inviolable months: 'One single (*fard*) and three consecutive (*sard*),'[1] i.e. one after the other. Because time persists due to each of its parts following the other in sequence, and that sequence is known as *sard*, the [Arabs] inserted the letter *mīm* by way of making the meaning more emphatic.

Once this is known, we say: the original meaning of *sarmad* only applies to something which has parts that occur one after the other. Since this is impossible for Almighty God, the use of this word for Him must be metaphorical (*majāz*). If it appears in the Qur'ān or *Sunna* [as a Divine Name] we would use it, but otherwise not.

Name 6: *al-Mustamirr*

This is a [Form X] derivation from *murūr*, meaning 'to go and pass by'. Since the persistence of time is due to its parts passing by, one after the other, it is natural to call it *mustamirr*. However, this meaning is true for time but impossible for God, Who persists in His very Essence, not due to parts following one another.

Name 7: *al-Mumtadd*

A period of time was called *mudda* because it extends (*tamtaddu*) by means of its parts following one another. As such, describing the existence of a thing as being 'extended' is only appropriate with respect to time and its occurrences. As applied to Almighty God, it can only be metaphorical.

Name 8: *al-Bāqī*

God said: 'But will abide (forever) the Countenance of your Lord' (Q.LV.27). Know that everything which is pre-eternal must be abiding (*bāqī*), while the opposite is not true. Something may be abiding but not pre-eternal, and [indeed] not everlasting, as is the case with abiding bodies and accidents. Some people said that the word *bāqī* entails being everlasting, in which case it is not correct to describe bodies as *bāqī*. However, that is not the case, as it is accepted universally by custom to say to someone *abqāka Allāh* ('May God preserve you!').

1 I could not source this narration.

Name 9: *al-Dā'im*

God said: 'Perpetual is the enjoyment thereof and the shade therein' (Q.xiii.35). Since the worthiest thing of being perpetual is God, He is called *al-Dā'im*.

[Other Modalities]

Name 10: *Wājib al-wujūd li-dhātihi* (Necessary Existent)

This means that its quiddity and reality is what necessitates its existence, and as such it cannot accept non-existence or disappearance. Whatever is necessarily existent in itself must also be pre-eternal, though the converse is not true. It is not the case that everything pre-eternal must be necessary, as it is not inconceivable for a thing to be caused by a pre-eternal and everlasting cause (*ʿilla*). As such, this [effect] is also pre-eternal and everlasting along with its cause, despite not being necessarily existent in itself.

The Persian expression *Khudāy* [God] means that He is necessarily existent in Himself. It is composed of two Persian words, namely *khūd* (meaning the essence of a thing, its self and reality) and *āy* (which means 'he came'). Hence *Khudāy* means 'He came by Himself'. This is an allusion to His coming into existence by virtue of His own Self and Essence, not due to another. Thus the term *Khudāy* is explained as meaning that He has [always] existed in His own right.

Name 11: *al-Kā'in* (Entity)

This word appears frequently in the Qur'ān with reference to God's Attributes; for example, 'And God is ever (*kāna*) over all things perfect in ability' (Q.xviii.35) and 'Indeed, God is ever Knowing and Wise' (Q.iv.11).

As for its usage with reference to His Essence, that does not appear in the Qur'ān but does in some *ḥadīth*s. It is narrated in a supplication from the Prophet (may God bless him and grant him peace): 'O You Who is (*kā'in*) before every being (*kawn*), and You Who exists with every being, and You Who persists after every being perishes…'[1] or other wordings of similar meanings to what we have recounted.

Know also that there is a subtle grammatical enquiry which is relevant here.[2] The grammarians unanimously stated that the word *kāna* is of two types: the first is complete (*tāmm*), i.e. with the meaning of occurring and

1 I could not source this narration.

2 It was outlined previously in Book I, Chapter Three, Enquiry 7.

existing. God said: 'You are (*kuntum*) the best of peoples...' (Q.III.110), meaning that you came into being as the best of peoples. The second type is the deficient (*nāqiṣ*) [i.e. copular]. For example, *kāna Allāhu ʿalīman ḥakīman* ('God was all-knowing and wise'), in which case *kāna* must have a nominative [subject] and accusative [predicate]. They agreed that *kāna* is a verb in both cases, except that it is 'complete' as a verb in the former, but 'deficient' in the latter.

I said to [the scholars of Khwarezm]:[1] 'If this were a verb, it would denote the occurrence of an event in a particular time; and if we should attribute it to a single noun then it would denote the occurrence of an event for that thing. By that, the speech would be complete and there should be no need for an accusative: by this token, *kāna* would be a complete verb. Therefore, saying that this deficient word is a verb entails that it be complete, not deficient; whatever leads to its own negation is false, so it follows that the hypothesis that this word is deficient is false.' When I presented this contention to the grammarians, the astute among them remained in a state of confusion for a long time and were unsuccessful in coming up with an answer. Then, after a further reflection, I found the real answer which removes the confusion, and it is as follows.

The word *kāna* denotes nothing except occurrence and existence, but this is of two types: the occurrence of a thing in its own right; or for a thing to have another matter as a property. In the former case, *kāna* is complete when ascribed to that single thing, as it means that the thing occurred and obtained. In the latter, the meaning is not complete unless two nouns are mentioned: when that is done, the meaning is that [for example] the property (*mawṣūfiyya*) of Zayd having knowledge has obtained. This relation cannot be expressed without mentioning both elements, i.e. to say *kāna Zaydun ʿāliman* ('Zayd was knowledgeable')—that is to say, the property of being knowledgeable has obtained for Zayd.

What we have shown is that this word [with verbal noun] *kawn* only denotes occurrence and existence, except that in the first scenario, attribution to one noun suffices, and in the second, both nouns must be mentioned. This is a precious nuance in grammar. Once this is known, we say: on this basis, there is no distinction between *kā'in* and *mawjūd*, and therefore it must be permissible to use this word for Almighty God.

1 The author provides this detail under his exegesis of Q.II.280. Moreover, this point was noted by Naṣr al-Hūrīnī in the margin of the Amīriyya edition, vol. 1, p. 71.

Section III: Actual Attributes other than Existence and its Modalities

[Enquiry 1: Denial of Attributes][1]

This investigation depends upon the question of whether it is possible for these Attributes to subsist in God's Essence? The Muʿtazilīs and the philosophers denied this strongly, arguing as follows:

1. That Attribute must be in itself either necessary or contingent, but both possibilities are negated, so the belief in Attributes must be false. We say that they cannot be necessary for the following reasons:
   a. It has been proven rationally that the Necessary Existent can be only one.
   b. The Necessary Existent must be free of need of others, whereas the attribute is in need of the attributed thing. It is therefore impossible to combine between being necessary and being the attribute of something else.

   Yet we [Muʿtazilīs/philosophers] say also that they cannot be contingent, for the following reasons:
   a. A contingent thing must have a cause [which could either be the Divine Essence, or another cause]. It cannot be a cause other than the Divine Essence because, since that Essence cannot be without its Attribute, if that Attribute is in need of an external [cause], then the Essence itself depends on something external. This dependency entails contingency, and so the Necessary Existent would be described as contingent, which is a [contradiction]. On the other hand, the [cause] cannot be the Divine Essence itself, because it is the recipient of that Attribute. If it had an effect [in creating] that Attribute, then it would be, with respect to that Attribute, both agent (*fāʿil*) and recipient (*qābil*) at once, which is impossible because—as has been proven—a single thing cannot produce more than one effect, whereas acting and receiving are two distinct effects.
   b. An effect (*athar*) is in need of an agent (*mu'aththir*), and this need

1 The enquiry is not labelled in the printed edition. This position is known as *taʿṭīl* and can also be termed 'reductionism' with respect to God's Essence and Attributes, i.e. that the latter have no existence distinct from the Essence. See also Chapter Four of Ceylan, 'Theology and *Tafsīr* in the Major Works of Fakhr al-Dīn al-Rāzī', for discussion of the author's responses to these and other contentions in his other works.

either transpires after [the effect's] occurrence, at the time of the occurrence, or at the time of its non-existence. The first option is false, as it entails that the agent creates the effect [when it already exists] as a *fait accompli*, which is absurd. Only the latter two options remain, which implies that anything which is an effect of something else is also temporal (*ḥādith*). It follows that anything which is not created cannot be an effect of something else.

It is thus shown that belief in the Attributes is false.

2. Those Attributes must be either pre-eternal or temporal. The first option is impossible, because pre-eternality is an affirmative Attribute, as we have explained;[1] so if the Attributes were pre-eternal, they would be equal to the Essence in this respect. Then the two could only be distinguished by means of their individual quiddities, and they would have both common and distinct properties. This would entail that each of these pre-eternal realities would be composed of two parts:[2] and each of these parts would have to be pre-eternal also, as a portion of a pre-eternal quiddity must itself be pre-eternal. Then these parts would be equal [to each other and the other things] in being pre-eternal, distinguished by means of their quiddities, which means that they too are each composed of two parts. This is impossible because it leads to the Essence itself as well as all these Attributes being composed of an infinite number of parts.

   However, the Attributes cannot instead be temporal, for the following reasons:

   a. For temporal [Attributes] to subsist in the Divine Essence is impossible, because if that Essence is a sufficient [cause] for the existence of the Attribute or the continuation of its non-existence, it follows that the Attribute would continue to be existent or non-existent in accordance with the continuation of the Essence. If, however, the Essence is not a sufficient [cause], then it follows that the Essence is attributed necessarily with the existence or non-existence of that Attribute, and that existence or non-existence depends on an external factor. Now that which is dependent on an external factor, i.e. something other than itself, is contingent in itself. This would mean that the Necessary Existent is contingent, which is absurd.

1 See the previous section under 'Name 3'.
2 This is related to definitions according to genus and differentia.

b. If the Divine Essence could receive [to subsist within it] temporal things, this receptivity (*qābiliyya*) would be concomitant to its [existence]. This would mean that the receptivity is itself pre-eternal along with the Essence. However, receptivity of temporal things cannot be pre-eternal, because it is dependent on the possibility of temporal things existing. Since the existence of temporal things in pre-eternity is impossible, it follows that the existence of this receptivity of temporal [Attributes] is impossible too.

c. If those Attributes were temporal, then the Deity—possessing the [defining] properties of Divinity—must have existed before these Attributes. In that case, these Attributes are superfluous to the existence of Divinity, and should be rejected.

We have thus shown that since the Attributes cannot be either pre-eternal or temporal—and there is no third option—they cannot, then, exist.

3. Either those Attributes are such that Divinity obtains without them, or not. If the former, then they are superfluous and redundant and should be rejected. If the latter, then the Deity would be in need of something external in order to attain Divinity, and anything in need cannot be a deity.
4. The Divine Essence is either perfect in its possession of praiseworthy Attributes, or otherwise. If the former, then it has no need for these [additional] Attributes. If the latter, then the Essence itself would be deficient and in need of external factors to perfect it, and it could therefore not be described as divine.
5. If the Deity is a combination of Essence and Attributes, then He is composite and divided, which is implausible because composites are always contingent, not necessary.
6. Almighty God declared the Christians to be unbelievers due to their doctrine of Trinity (*tathlīth*).[1] Either this was because they affirmed the existence of three [Divine] Essences, or because they affirmed one Essence along with Attributes. The Christians do not say the former, so it cannot be that God declared them unbelievers due to something they do not say. Thus only the latter remains, and it follows that belief in the Attributes is unbelief (*kufr*).

These are the arguments advanced by the deniers of the Attributes.

1 See Q.v.73.

Upon their stance, it is not possible for God to possess any Name due to an actual Attribute subsisting in His [Essence].

Enquiry 2
Evidences of the Affirmers of Attributes

Know that it is proven that the Deity of the world must be knowledgeable, able and living. We say that it is impossible for His knowledge, power and life to be His Essence itself, as shown by the following:

1. We know by necessity that there is a difference between saying 'God's Essence is an essence' and 'God's Essence is knowledgeable and powerful.' This shows that the properties of being knowledgeable and powerful are not equivalent to that Essence.
2. It is possible to know that He exists without one having an awareness of His being powerful and knowledgeable. Likewise, one might know that He is powerful while being unaware that He is knowledgeable, and vice-versa. This shows that His properties of being knowledgeable and powerful are not equivalent to the Essence itself.
3. His being knowledgeable is universally applicable to necessary, possible and impossible things, whereas His being powerful is not so: rather, it is specific to the possible. If there were no difference between knowledge and power [as Attributes], this [distinction] would not be valid.
4. God's being powerful has an effect on the existence of possibilities, whereas His being knowledgeable [of that possibility] does not have this effect. If there were no difference, this would not be so.
5. Saying that something is 'existent' is contradicted by saying 'not existent', but not by saying 'not knowledgeable'. This shows that what is negated by 'not existent' is different from that negated by 'not knowledgeable'—and the same can be said for His being powerful.

The aforementioned are clear proofs demonstrating that the Attributes must be affirmed for Almighty God. It only remains to say:[1] why is it not possible for these Attributes to be relational and relative such that what is meant by His 'being powerful' is a state by which creation is possible, and that possibility (*ṣiḥḥa*) is explained in terms of His Essence? Likewise, 'being knowledgeable' means perception and cognition, which is a relative matter; and that relation is caused by His very Essence. This is the end of our discussion on this issue.

1 This appears to be a concession to the Muʿtazilī position.

Enquiry 3
[*al-Ḥayy* (Living)]

When we do affirm the actual Attributes, we say: the actual Attribute is either such as entails a relation [or it is free of relativity]. Examples of the first category are knowledge and ability: the existence of the former is concomitant with its connection to knowable things, and the latter is concomitant with being connected to the creation of possible things. As such, these attributes—while actual—have concomitants which are relational and relative.

As for the actual Divine Attribute which is free of all such relativity, that is none other than the Attribute of life (*ḥayāh*), so let us investigate it:

A. THE PHILOSOPHERS said that *ḥayy* means 'the cognisant (*darrāk*), the agent (*faʿʿāl*)'.

   OBJECTION: these are both relative attributes, so—upon this view—life is not a separate Attribute from knowledge (*ʿilm*) and ability (*qudra*).

B. THE THEOLOGIANS[1] said that it is an Attribute by which it is *possible* for one to be knowledgeable and able [to act]. They argued that essences are equal to each other in their essentiality but distinct from each other in terms of this potentiality. Therefore, the essences must vary with regards to possessing the Attribute of *ḥayāh*, which entails that it is an additional Attribute.

   OBJECTION: we have proven that the Divine Essence is distinct from all other essences by virtue of its own self, so your argument fails. Furthermore, [if] essences vary with regards to possessing the attribute of *ḥayāh*, then this potentiality must be itself dependent on another attribute, leading to infinite regression.

   RESPONSE: it may only be suggested that this potentiality is a concomitant of the Essence itself—and you may say the same for the potentiality of being knowledgeable [etc.].

C. A THIRD GROUP said that the meaning of being Living is that it is *not impossible* to be able and to know. As an expression negating impossibility, this is a double negative expressing affirmation.

   OBJECTION: this much is acknowledged, but why not say that this affirmation represents the Essence itself? They could reply: 'We

1 It seems that the author is siding with this group. However, in the following enquiry, he continues to engage the various opinions.

may conceive of the Essence despite being unsure of it being living, so it follows that being living is something distinct from the Essence [itself].' To this, it may be said: we have proven[1] that we cannot conceive of God's Essence in itself, but only indirectly, and this negates your argument. This is all we shall say on this issue.

Enquiry 4

The name *al-Ḥayy* occurs in the Qur'ān; for example, 'God: there is no god but He, the Living, the Self-subsistent' (Q.II.255); 'The faces will be humbled before the Living, the Self-subsistent' (Q.XX.111); and 'He is the Living; there is no god but He: call upon Him, giving Him sincere devotion' (Q.XL.65).

QUESTION: if *ḥayy* means one who cognises and acts, or one for whom it is not impossible to know and be able, then this does not contain tremendous praise: so why has Almighty God mentioned this Name in the context of tremendous praise?

RESPONSE: the praise was not merely for being living but for the combination of being *ḥayy* and *qayyūm*. This is because *al-Qayyūm* is the One Who rectifies the states of all others, which could not occur without complete knowledge and ability. *Al-Ḥayy* is the One Who cognises and acts. Therefore, *al-Ḥayy al-Qayyūm* means [first] that He cognises and acts, and [second] that He is aware of all possibilities and acts upon all created things and possibilities. Hence the expression conveys praise in this way.

1 See Chapter Three, Section II, Enquiry 9.

Chapter Five
NAMES DENOTING RELATIVE ATTRIBUTES

The contents of this chapter must be preceded by a rational introduction exploring whether existentiation (*takwīn*) is equivalent to the existentiated (*mukawwan*).[1] Contrary to some, the Muʿtazilīs and Ashʿarīs asserted that these two are equivalent.[2]

THE DENIERS [i.e. Muʿtazilīs and Ashʿarīs] argued as follows:

1. This Attribute described as *takwīn* is effective either potentially or necessarily. If the former, then it is nothing other than *qudra* (ability). If the latter, that would mean that God would be necessitated by Essence rather than acting by choice.
2. The attribute described as *takwīn*, if pre-eternal, would necessitate the pre-eternity of its effects. If temporal, then its existentiation would require another process of existentiation, leading to infinite regression.
3. The attribute called 'ability' (*qudra*) is either fit to bring about its effect when the other conditions are met—namely knowledge (*ʿilm*) and volition (*irāda*)—or it is not. If the former, then *qudra* is sufficient to bring its effect from non-existence into existence, in which case there is no need to affirm a separate attribute [*takwīn*]. If it is not fit to bring about its effect, then it cannot truly be described as ability, and that is a contradiction.

THOSE WHO AFFIRMED [existentiation] as a pre-eternal Attribute argued: 'One who is capable of an action may either bring it about, or not. Do you not see that God is able to create 1,000 suns and moons in this sky of ours, yet He has not done so? The possibility of affirming and negating such things signifies that the meaning of being the Creator is separate from that of being able.'

1 The term *takwīn* can be rendered simply as 'creation' or 'bringing into being', but I have opted for a term which differentiates it from the likes of *khalq* which is acknowledged as an Attribute of action.

2 The Māturīdī school affirms *takwīn* as a discrete and pre-eternal Attribute alongside ability and knowledge. Their position is explained below.

[They continued:]

> Either His being Creator means the entry of that effect into existence, or it is a discrete matter. The former hypothesis is false because in fact we explain (*taʿlīl*) the entry of that effect into existence by means of an agent which created it. You can see that if we are asked 'Why does the world exist?' we reply: 'Because God created it.' If being the Creator (*mūjid*) of that effect meant nothing more than the effect itself, then this explanation would amount to explaining something by its own self, in which case it would not be possible to attribute it to another. It is thus shown that explaining 'being Creator' in terms of the existence of the effect leads to the negation of being Creator. Whatever leads to its own negation is false, so explaining 'being Creator' in terms of the existence of the effect is rejected. This only leaves the possibility that the creator 'being Creator' is a separate matter from the agent being capable (*qādir*) of producing the effect. It is thus shown that existentiation (*takwīn*) is distinct from the existentiated (*mukawwan*).

Once you have appreciated the basis of the discussion, I say: those who stated that existentiation is equivalent to the existentiated said that God being the Creator, the Provider, the Bestower of life and death, the Controller of harm and benefit—all these are cases of particular relations, i.e. the effect of His ability upon the creation of these things. On the other hand, those who differentiated between the two said that His being the Creator, the Provider [etc.] is not merely a case of a relative Attribute, but it is an actual Attribute *described* by a relative Attribute.

Know that there are two categories of relative Attribute. The FIRST is God being known, mentioned, praised and glorified. It is said: 'O You Who are glorified by every tongue, You Who are praised by every human, and You to Whom [servants] return at every moment!' Since these types of relation are of an infinite number, so too are the possible Divine Names according to these Attributes. The SECOND is God being the agent of actions (*afʿāl*): this is a purely relative Attribute on the assumption that existentiation is not a discrete attribute.

Once this is known: the Attribute being described may be the simple fact of His being Creator, or it could describe His creation of a specific thing for a specific wisdom.

Type A

Names for the Simple Fact of Being Creator

There are a number of such Names which are close to being synonymous, but there are nuances between them. For example:

1. *Al-Mūjid*—the agent of existence.
2. *Al-Muḥdith*—the One Who made something existent after non-existence, which is therefore more specific than *al-Mūjid*.
3. *Al-Mukawwin*—this is almost synonymous with *al-Mūjid*.
4. *Al-Munshi'*—this is derived from the concept of development (*nushū'*) and growth, and refers to gradual [creation] in stages.
5. *Al-Mubdiʿ*—this refers to creation all at once. This and the previous are as two species under the genus of *al-Mūjid*.
6. *Al-Mukhtariʿ*—this is similar to the previous Name.
7. *Al-Ṣāniʿ*—this gives the impression of someone who performs an act which requires effort.[1]
8. *Al-Khāliq*—this refers to pre-planned creation (*taqdīr*), which is related to God's knowledge.
9. *Al-Fāṭir*—this is derived from splitting (*faṭr*), which would seem to refer to creation all at once.
10. *Al-Bāri'*—this means the One Who creates that which accords with the interests [of the creatures]. You say *barā* (*al-qalam*) meaning that you rectified [a writing reed] and made it fit for a specific purpose.

This is our explanation of these words indicating creation in general.

[Type B]

Names Pertaining to Specific Acts of Creation

These tend towards infinity, but what we shall mention here are examples:

a. When He creates something beneficial, He is called *Nāfiʿ*; and when He creates something painful, He is called *Ḍārr*.
b. When He creates life, He is called *Muḥyī*; and when He creates death, He is called *Mumīt*.
c. When He directs kind treatment towards a people, He is called *Barr* and *Laṭīf*; and when He directs pressure upon others, He is called *Qahhār* and *Jabbār*.
d. When He limits what He bestows, He is called *Qābiḍ*; and when He increases it, He is called *Bāsiṭ*.
e. If He recompenses the sinners with the [fitting] punishment, He is

1 That is, for the product to demonstrate the skill and perfection involved in its creation.

called *Muntaqim*; and if He leaves their retribution, He is called *ʿAfū*, *Ghafūr*, *Raḥīm* and *Raḥmān*.[1]

f. If the withholding and bestowing pertains to wealth, He is called *Qābiḍ* and *Bāsiṭ*; but if they pertain to status and supporters, He is called *Khāfiḍ* and *Rāfiʿ*.

Once you have known this, we say: since the types of things under God's power and ability are without limit, He may certainly have an unlimited quantity of Names in this respect.

There are some further subtleties to mention in this connection:

a. Something which is opposite to another may be either its contrary (*ḍidd*) or its negation (*ʿadam*).[2] The names *al-Muʿizz al-Mudhill* (the Ennobler and Disgracer), and likewise *al-Muḥyī al-Mumīt* (the Giver of life and death) are contraries.[3] However, *al-Qābiḍ al-Bāsiṭ* (the Withholder and Bestower) and *al-Khāfiḍ al-Rāfiʿ* (the Debaser and Promoter) are apparently mutually negating, because 'withholding' means 'not to grant a person abundant wealth', and 'debasing' means 'not to grant someone a lofty status'. In contrast, there is a difference between 'not ennobling' someone and 'disgracing' him.

b. There may be words which are almost synonymous, but deeper reflection brings out their nuances. For example, *al-Ra'ūf* and *al-Raḥīm*: the former is more closely related to the bestowal of benefits, whereas the latter is more related to averting harms. Other examples are *al-Fātiḥ/al-Fattāḥ*, *al-Nāfiʿ/al-Naffāʿ* and *al-Wāhib/al-Wahhāb*.[4] *Al-Fātiḥ* implies bringing about the cause of goodness; *al-Wāhib* implies making that goodness reach [the servant]; and *al-Nāfiʿ* implies having the goodness reach the individual in order that he derive benefit thereby. Once you appreciate the rule in this regard, you can discover the realities of this type of Name.

1 These Names have apparently been cited in ascending order of intensity and status.

2 There are four classes of opposites in Aristotelian logic: relative terms; contraries; privation and possession; and affirmation and negation.

3 It is a normal practice, observed here by the author, to mention these Name-pairs without an intervening conjunction, as though to say 'the Ennobler-Disgracer' (etc.). This has the effect of clarifying the sense of each individual Name, which is intended to complement another.

4 These pairs are alternative forms of the same Name, with the second of each being more intensive.

Chapter Six
NAMES DENOTING ELIMINATIVE ATTRIBUTES

The Qur'ān is full of this type. The way to recognise them is to say that the negation may be connected to the Essence, to Attributes or to actions.

Eliminatives for the Essence

This is to say that the Almighty is 'neither this, nor that'; for example, to say that He is neither substance (*jawhar*) nor body (*jism*); neither in place (*makān*) nor space (*ḥayyiz*); neither subsistent (*ḥāll*) [in another] nor substrate (*maḥall*).

We have already proven that His Essence is distinct from other essences and attributes in its own right as an essence,[1] but the types of essences and attributes which differ from Him are without limit. Therefore, there are infinite eliminatives. For example, 'But God is self-sufficient (*al-Ghanī*), and it is you that are needy' (Q.XLVII.38), and 'Your Lord is self-sufficient, full of mercy' (Q.VI.133). His being *ghanī* means that He has no need for anything, whether in His Essence or His actual or eliminative Attributes. Another example is: 'He begets not, nor is He begotten' (Q.CXII.3).

Eliminatives for the Attributes

It is necessary to declare God transcendent over any attribute which implies imperfection, such as those contrary to [perfect] knowledge, power, self-sufficiency or oneness.

The following are attributes eliminating matters contrary to KNOWLEDGE:

a. Negation of sleep: 'No slumber can seize Him nor sleep' (Q.II.255).
b. Negation of forgetfulness: 'And your Lord never forgets' (Q.XIX.64).
c. Negation of ignorance: 'From Him is not hidden the least little atom in the heavens or on earth' (Q.XXXIV.3).
d. His knowledge of some things does not prevent Him from having knowledge of others, as no matter keeps Him occupied from any other matter.

1 See above Chapter Three, Section II, Enquiry 9.

The following are attributes eliminating matters contrary to POWER AND ABILITY:

a. His actions do not result in fatigue or weariness: '…nor did any sense of weariness touch Us' (Q.L.38).
b. He is in no need of tools or instruments, nor even any existing material or time for His actions: 'For to anything which We have willed, We but say the word "Be!" and it is' (Q.XVI.40).
c. Great and small acts are no different for Him: 'And the decision of the Hour (of Judgment) is as the twinkling of an eye, or even quicker' (Q.XVI.77).
d. Negation of His power ceasing and neediness occurring: 'God has heard the taunt of those who say: "Indeed, God is indigent and we are rich!"' (Q.III.181).

There is negation of matters contrary to SELF-SUFFICIENCY (*istighnā'*); for example, 'And He it is that feeds but is not fed' (Q.VI.14) and 'He protects while none can protect against Him' (Q.XXIII.88).

As for negation of matters contrary to His ONENESS (*waḥda*)—such as having no partners, opposites or rivals—the Qur'ān is filled with this.

Eliminatives for the Actions

The Qur'ān is full of statements to the effect that God does not do such-and-such:

a. He does not create falsehood (*bāṭil*): 'Not without purpose did We create heaven and earth and all between: that were the thought of unbelievers' (Q.XXXVIII.27]; and God quotes the believers: 'They contemplate the creation in the heavens and the earth [saying:] "Our Lord, not for naught have You created (all) this!"' (Q.III.191).
b. He does not create play (*laʿib*): 'We created not the heavens, the earth, and all between them, merely in (idle) sport: We created them not except for just ends' (Q.XLIV.38–39).
c. He does not create vanity (*ʿabath*): 'Did you then think that We had created you in jest, and that you would not be brought back to Us? Therefore, exalted be God, the King, the Reality' (Q.XXIII.115–6).
d. He does not accept unbelief: 'And He does not approve for His servants unbelief' (Q.XXXIX.7).
e. He does not want injustice: 'But God never wishes injustice to His servants' (Q.XL.31).
f. He does not love corruption: 'And God does not like corruption' (Q.II.205).

g. He does not punish without a crime having occurred: 'What can God gain by your punishment, if you are grateful and believe?' (Q.IV.147).
h. He does not benefit from the obedience of the obedient, nor is He harmed by the sins of the sinners: 'If you did well, you did well for yourselves; if you did evil, (you did it) against yourselves' (Q.XVII.7).
i. None may object to His actions or decrees: 'He cannot be questioned for His acts, but they will be questioned' (Q.XXI.23) and 'Your Lord is the (sure) accomplisher of what He plans' (Q.XI.107).
j. He does not fail in His promises or threats:[1] 'The word changes not before Me, and I do not the least injustice to My servants' (Q.L.29).

[Related Names]

Once you have known this basic account, we say: the various types of negation in Essence, Attributes and actions are infinite, which means that there are infinite Names within this category. Let us mention some of the Names which correspond to these Attributes:

a. *Al-Quddūs* and *al-Salām*. The former would seem to express the fact of His Essence differing from all quiddities which are deficiencies in themselves. The latter expresses that this Essence is not attributed with any deficiencies. As such, *al-Quddūs* is an eliminative pertaining to the Essence, while *al-Salām* pertains to the Attributes.
b. *Al-ʿAzīz*—having no counterpart (*naẓīr*).
c. *Al-Ghaffār*—He who removes the sins from the sinners [by forgiveness].
d. *Al-Ḥalīm*—He does not hasten to punish, and indeed He does not hold back from bestowing mercy.
e. *Al-Wāḥid*—this means that none shares His unique reality, nor in the Attribute of Divinity, nor in creating spirits and bodies, nor in organising the world and the matters of the Throne.
f. *Al-Ghanī*—this means that He is transcendent above needs and necessities.
g. *Al-Ṣabūr*—[similar to] *al-Ḥalīm*, but different in that it means He does not punish the sinner despite His ability to do so. *Al-Ḥalīm* has this meaning with the addition that [the sin] does not prevent Him from bestowing His grace upon him.

You will know the rest by analogy And God is the Guide.

1 According to mainstream Ashʿarī doctrine, this does not negate the possibility of divine forgiveness of major sins, contra the Muʿtazilīs.

Chapter Seven
NAMES DENOTING COMBINATIONS OF ACTUAL AND RELATIVE ATTRIBUTES

This chapter is composed of sections.[1]

I: Names Connected to Power and Ability (*qudra*)

There are many Names denoting the Attribute of Power.

- *Al-Qādir*: 'Say: He is able to send calamities on you, from above and below' (Q.VI.65); and at the beginning of *Sūrat al-Qiyāma*: 'Does man think that We cannot assemble his bones? Nay, We are able to put together in perfect order the very tips of his fingers' (Q.LXXV.3–4), and at its end: 'Has not He, (the same), the power to give life to the dead?' (Q.LXXV.40).
- *Al-Qadīr*: 'Blessed be He in Whose hands is dominion; and He over all things has power' (Q.LXVII.1)—this is a more emphatic form of *al-Qādir*.
- *Al-Muqtadir*: 'And God is ever, over all things, perfect in ability' (Q.XVIII.45), and 'In an assembly of truth, in the presence of an Omnipotent King' (Q.LIV.55).
- He [sometimes] referred to Himself using the plural in connection with this Attribute: 'For We do determine (*qadarnā*); for We are the best to determine (*al-Qādirūn*)' (Q.LXXVII.23).

Know also that the word *milk/mulk*[2] also denotes power in a particular way. It has appeared in the Qur'ān in a variety of forms:

- *Al-Mālik*: 'Master of the Day of Judgment' (Q.I.4).[3]

1 I have formatted these headings like enquiries, because there are no enquiries falling under these sections. Based on the logic of the preceding chapters, it would have been expected for Section VI below to be the beginning of a new chapter, since it represents a new category—or rather, combination. Likewise, the sections which follow it represent distinct categories; as such, the title of this chapter does not reflect all its contents.

2 I have vocalised it in both ways (each a verbal noun, along with *malk*) to reflect the variety of forms below. The author did not explain the 'particular way (*sharṭ khāṣṣ*)'.

3 This is recited both as *mālik* and *malik* in the Ten Canonical Readings (*qirā'āt mutawātira*): the former is the reading of ʿĀṣim, Kisā'ī, Yaʿqūb and Khalaf, while the latter is the reading of Nāfiʿ, Ibn Kathīr, Abū ʿAmr, Ibn ʿĀmir, Ḥamza and Abū Jaʿfar. See Muḥammad Ḥabash, *al-Qirā'āt al-mutawātira wa-atharuhā fī al-rasm al-Qur'ānī wa'l-aḥkām al-sharʿiyya*, Beirut: Dār al-Fikr, 1999, p. 137.

- *Al-Malik*: 'High above all is God, the Sovereign, the Truth!' (Q.xx.114); 'He is God, other than Whom there is no god; the Sovereign, the Holy One...' (Q.LIX.23); and 'The Sovereign of Mankind' (Q.CXIV.2). Know that this word appears more frequently than *Mālik*, because the sovereign (*malik*) is of a higher status than the master (*mālik*).[1]
- *Mālik al-mulk*: 'Say: O God, Owner of dominion...' (Q.III.26).
- *Al-Malīk*: '...in the presence of an all-powerful Sovereign' (Q.LIV.55).
- The [verbal noun] *mulk* (dominion) itself: 'That day, the dominion as of right and truth, shall be (wholly) for the Compassionate' (Q.XXV.26), and 'To God belongs the dominion of the heavens and the earth' (Q.II.107).

Also, the word *quwwa* (strength) is closely related to *qudra*. This, too, has appeared in the Qur'ān in various forms:

- *Al-Qawī*: 'Indeed, God is full of strength, exalted in might' (Q.XXII.40).
- *Dhū al-quwwa*: 'Indeed, it is God who is the Provider, the firm Possessor of strength' (Q.LI.58).

II: Names Connected to Knowledge (*ʿilm*)

FIRSTLY: there are Names derived from the word *ʿilm*:

a. Affirmation of the Attribute itself: 'Nor shall they encompass aught of His knowledge...' (Q.II.255); 'And no female conceives, or lays down (her load), but with His knowledge' (Q.XXXV.11); 'God comprehends all things in (His) knowledge' (Q.LXV.12); and 'Indeed, the knowledge of the Hour is with God (alone)' (Q.XXXI.34).
b. *Al-ʿĀlim*: 'Knower of the unseen and the witnessed' (Q.VI.73).
c. *Al-ʿAlīm*—this is frequent in the Qur'ān.
d. *Al-ʿAllām*—God said, quoting Jesus (on whom be peace): 'For You know in full all that is hidden' (Q.V.116).
e. *Al-Aʿlam*: 'God knows best where to place His message' (Q.VI.124).
f. In the perfect tense: 'God has known that you used to deceive yourselves' (Q.II.187).
g. In the imperfect tense: 'And whatever good you do, God knows it' (Q.II.197); 'And God knows what you conceal and what you reveal' (Q.XVI.19).
h. The [Form II] verb to teach, *ʿallama*: 'And He taught Adam the names

1 Cf. discussion in Book III, Chapter Five, Verse 4.

of all things' (Q.II.31); and quoting the angels: 'Glory to You, of knowledge We have none, save what You have taught us' (Q.II.32); 'And He taught you what you knew not' (Q.IV.113).[1] However, it is not permitted to describe God as *muʿallim* (teacher) despite these many related citations, because the word itself is somewhat unbefitting.

i. It is also impermissible to use the word *ʿallāma* for God, for although it denotes possession of knowledge emphatically, it also implies that this level was attained through effort and struggle, which cannot be the case for God.[2]

SECONDLY: there are words derived from *khabar* (information)/*khibra* (expertise), which is like a synonym of *ʿilm* to the extent that some have defined *ʿilm* as *khabar*. This word has been used for God frequently in the Qur'ān.

THIRDLY: *shuhūd/mushāhada* (witnessing), from which comes the Divine Name *al-Shahīd*, if we explain it as meaning that He witnesses and knows all things. If we explain it in terms of testimony, it is an Attribute related to speech (*kalām*).

FOURTHLY: *ḥikma* (wisdom)—this may be used for knowledge, or for refraining from inappropriate acts and performing worthy deeds.

FIFTHLY: *al-Laṭīf* (subtle) means both that He is aware of minute details, and that He grants beneficial things to the servants in mysterious and remarkable ways.

III: Names Connected to Speech (*kalām*)

[FIRSTLY,] from the word *kalām*:

a. The noun itself: 'If one amongst the polytheists asks you for asylum, grant it to him, so that he may hear the word of God' (Q.IX.6).
b. The perfect tense verb: '...and to Moses, God spoke directly' (Q.IV.164); and 'When Moses came to the place appointed by Us, and his Lord spoke to him...' (Q.VII.143).
c. The imperfect tense: 'It is not fitting for a man that Allah should speak to him except by inspiration...' (Q.XLII.51).

SECONDLY, from the word *qawl*:

a. The perfect tense: 'Behold, your Lord said to the angels' (Q.II.30)—and there are many of this type in the Qur'ān.

1 There was an incongruous citation of the first two verses of *Sūrat al-Fātiḥa* here, which I have removed.

2 The word is used as an honorific for scholars.

b. The imperfect tense: 'Moses said: "He says: the heifer should be..."' (Q.II.68).

c. The nouns *qīl* and *qawl*: 'And whose word can be truer than God's?' (Q.IV.122); and 'The word changes not before Me' (Q.L.29).

THIRDLY,[1] from the word *amr*: 'To God belongs the command before and after' (Q.XXX.4); 'His is the creation and the command' (Q.VII.54); and quoting Moses (on whom be peace), God said: 'God commands that you sacrifice a heifer' (Q.II.67).

FOURTHLY, the word *waʿd*: 'A promise binding on Him in truth, through the Law, the Gospel, and the Qur'ān' (Q.IX.111); and 'The promise of God is true and sure. It is He Who begins the process of creation and repeats it' (Q.X.4).

FIFTHLY, *waḥy*: 'It is not fitting for a man that Allah should speak to him except by inspiration...' (Q.XLII.51); and 'So He revealed to His servant what He revealed' (Q.LIII.10).

SIXTHLY, that God is thankful (*shākir*) to His servants: 'It is those whose effort is ever appreciated' (Q.XVII.19); 'And ever is God appreciative and knowing' (Q.IV.147).

IV: Names Connected to Volition (*irāda*) and its Like

[FIRSTLY,] from the word *irāda* itself: 'God intends every facility for you; He does not want to put you to difficulties' (Q.II.185).

SECONDLY, *riḍā*: 'If you are grateful, He approves that for you,' but [before that]: 'He does not approve for His servants unbelief' (Q.XXXIX.7); and 'God's good pleasure was on the believers when they swore fealty to you under the tree' (Q.XLVIII.18). God also said, describing the [emigrant] vanguard: 'Well-pleased is God with them, as are they with Him' (Q.IX.100); and quoting Moses: 'I hastened to you, O my Lord, to please you' (Q.XX.84).

THIRDLY, *maḥabba*: 'He loves them and they love Him' (Q.V.54); and 'He loves those who keep themselves pure and clean' (Q.II.222).[2]

FOURTHLY, *karāha*: 'Of all such things the evil is hateful in the sight of your Lord' (Q.XVII.38); '...but Allah was averse to their being sent forth; so He made them lag behind' (Q.IX.46). The Ashʿarīs maintained that the

1 The remainder of this section pertains to specific types of speech, assuming that God's 'thankfulness' is also expressed in such a way.

2 The author has not selected an example which clearly reflects the sense of volition or will. An example (not related to God) is Q.XXVIII.56. There are discussions elsewhere concerning the distinction between God willing something, versus loving that thing.

word *karāha* ('dislike') expresses that [God] intends that [the person] does not do [the act], whereas the Muʿtazilīs[1] said that it is a distinct Attribute from volition. And God knows best.

v: Names Connected to Hearing (*samʿ*) and Vision (*baṣar*)

God said: 'There is nothing whatsoever like Him, and He is the Hearing, the Seeing' (Q.xlii.11); '…to show him of Our signs. Indeed, He is the Hearing, the Seeing' (Q.xvii.1); 'I am with you: I hear and see (everything)' (Q.xx.46); [and quoting Abraham:] 'Why worship that which hears not and sees not…?' (Q.xix.42); and 'No vision can grasp Him, but His grasp is over all vision' (Q.vi.103).

This is the completion of the discussion on actual and relative Attributes.

[Further Combinations and Categories][2]

vi: [Names Denoting] Combinations of Relative and Eliminative Attributes

Know that *al-Awwal* (the First) means He precedes all and is preceded by none: the former aspect is relative and the latter is eliminative, so the Name denotes a composite state of relative and eliminative. *Al-Ākhir* (the Last) is He Who outlasts all and is outlasted by none, and this is [the same combination] as the previous one.[3]

As for *al-Ẓāhir* (the Apparent), this is purely relative because it refers to His being apparent through evidence and signs. On the other hand, *al-Bāṭin* (the Hidden) is purely eliminative as it means that His Essence is concealed.

Another Name denoting a combination of relative and eliminative is *al-Qayyūm*, since it conveys an emphatic meaning comprised of two things:

1. He is in no need whatsoever of anything, and this is only the case for One Who exists necessarily in His Essence and all His Attributes.
2. All others depend upon Him in their essences and attributes, which

1 See Qāḍī ʿAbd al-Jabbār, *Mutashābih al-Qur'ān*, ed. ʿAdnān Zarzūr, 2 vols., Cairo: Maktabat Dār al-Turāth, 1969, pp. 332–4.

2 As mentioned at the start of the chapter, this would have been a natural place for a new chapter.

3 Compare these with the 'Names Denoting Modality of Existence' in Chapter Four, Section ii above. The following two are presumably mentioned here because they appear alongside 'the First and the Last' in Q.lvii.3, which was cited in the introductory remarks of the aforementioned section.

means that He is the origin of all besides Him. The first of these is eliminative, and the second is relative, combining to form the meaning of *al-Qayyūm*.

VII: Names for the Essence along with Actual, Relative and Eliminative Attributes

Among these is *al-Ilāh*, a Name which denotes all of this. It signifies His being existent along with the modalities of that existence—i.e. being pre-eternal, everlasting and necessary in Himself—as well as the eliminative Attributes of transcendence and the relative Attributes pertaining to creative action.

Authorities have differed as to whether this word can be used for other than Almighty God. The polytheists of Quraysh used it for their idols, but is that permitted in the religion of Islam? The widespread view is that it is impermissible. Some said that it is allowed because there is a narration saying: 'O God of gods (*ilāh al-āliha*)!'—but this is unpersuasive.

Concerning the Name *Allāh*, as we shall explain,[1] it is a proper Name for the Almighty. So does it denote all these Attributes? We say: no doubt, proper names have the effect of demonstratives, which is to say that if He were such as could be indicated [by gesture etc.], then this Name would stand in lieu of that indication. Then there is disagreement over whether the indication of a particular essence encompasses the attributes subsistent in that essence. If we accept that it does, then the Name *Allāh* denotes all His Attributes.

If one should object, saying that the indication cannot encompass eliminative attributes, so the Name *Allāh* likewise cannot, then we say: the indication we speak of concerning God is purely conceptual and free of any sensory considerations; and this sort of indication could encompass eliminatives.

VIII: Names Whose Denotation is Disputed

[There are] Names concerning which they differed: are they Names for the Essence, or for the Attributes? This enquiry has only arisen due to the dispute between the people of anthropomorphism (*tashbīh*) and the people of glorification (*tanzīh*). The former said that any existent must either be spatial subsistent in a spatial object; and anything which does not fit into one of these two categories is pure non-existence.

1 See Chapter Nine below.

As for [the glorifiers] who declare God's uniqueness and transcendence, they say: every spatial object is divisible (*munqasim*). Since everything divisible is needy, every spatial object is needy. Therefore, anything which is not needy cannot be a spatial object. As for that [property] which subsists in a spatial object, it is even more clearly needy. Therefore, the Necessary Existent cannot be either spatial or subsistent in a spatial.

Once this is known, we say: there are words which—on their apparent meanings—imply corporeality and existence in space and place. Among these is *al-ʿAẓīm*, which the anthropomorphists took to mean that the Divine Essence is greater in size and proportions than the Throne and everything below it. Another is *al-Kabīr* and its derivatives, namely *akbar*, *kibriyāʾ* and *al-Mutakabbir*.

Know that—as far as I have seen—the expert scholars have not clarified the difference between these two words,[1] even though—upon consideration—they are different in a number of ways:

a. In a *ḥadīth qudsī*,[2] God says: '*Kibriyāʾ* is My cloak and *ʿaẓama* is My lower garment.'[3] Here, the former attribute has been likened to the cloak (*ridāʾ*), which is known to be loftier than the lower garment (*izār*) that here represents the latter attribute, so it must be that *kibriyāʾ* is higher in status than *ʿaẓama*.
b. The Revealed Law (*Sharīʿa*) has differentiated between their usages, as the well-established Islamic practice is to open the formal prayer by saying *Allāhu akbar*, but nobody has ever said *Allāhu aʿẓam*. If there were no difference between the two, one would not have been specified in this way.
c. There are derivatives used from *al-Kabīr*—such as *al-Akbar* and *al-Mutakabbir*—contrary to *al-ʿAẓīm*, as the word *mutaʿaẓẓim* is not used for God.

However, God has used each of these words in the place of the other[4] by saying: 'He feels no fatigue in guarding and preserving them for He is the High, the Supreme (*al-ʿAẓīm*)' (Q.II.255); and 'When terror is removed from their hearts, they will say: "What is it that your Lord commanded?"

1 See also Book III, Chapter Six, Section VI.

2 These 'holy traditions' are teachings, generally spiritual in nature, in which the Prophet attributes the words directly to God. However, these are distinct from the Qurʾān 'in that they are not considered to be the *literal* word of God'. See Brown, *Hadith*, pp. 63–4.

3 Recorded by Abū Dāwūd and others—R.S.

4 Which is not to deny the specific reason for each being used in its respective verse.

They will say: "That which is true and just; and He is the High, the Most Great (*al-Kabīr*)"' (Q.xxxiv.23).

As you can see, the previous points imply a difference between *ʿAẓīm* and *Kabīr*, whereas the verses imply otherwise. This problem requires investigation, so I say, seeking God's guidance and instruction: it seems that *al-Kabīr* concerns [God's] greatness in His own right, regardless of whether anyone recognises that greatness or knows this Attribute. As for *al-ʿAẓīm*, this means being such that others extol His greatness. In this way, the former is an essential Attribute and the latter is incidental; and the essential is superior to the incidental. This is a possible explanation in this regard. And God knows best.

Further Names which give the impression of corporeality (*jismiyya*) and directionality (*jiha*) are those derived from *ʿulū* (elevation), such as *al-ʿAlī* (Q.ii.255), *al-Aʿlā* (Q.lxxxvii.1) and *al-Mutaʿālī* (Q.xiii.9). Also in this category is the word mentioned by all in conjunction with His every mention, and that is to follow His Name with [the verb] *taʿālā* ('exalted is He').[1] This is taken from the beginning of *Sūrat al-Naḥl*: 'Glory to Him, and exalted is He above having the partners they ascribe to Him!' (Q.xvi.1).

Those who ascribed direction and location (*makān*) to God said that all this means that He exists in the upward (*fawq*) direction. Among these, some said that He is sitting atop the Throne. Some said that He is set apart from the Throne by a finite distance, and still others opined that it is an infinite distance. However this may be, the anthropomorphists interpreted the words *al-ʿAẓīm* and *al-Kabīr* in terms of corporeality and size (*miqdār*), and *al-ʿAlī* in terms of location and direction.

As for the affirmers of PERFECTION AND TRANSCENDENCE, they interpreted *al-ʿAẓīm* and *al-Kabīr* in ways which do not entail corporeality and size:

a. He is Great in terms of duration of existence, being that He is pre-eternal and everlasting. This represents the utmost *ʿaẓama* and *kibriyā'* in existence and continuity.
b. He is Great in His knowledge and acts.
c. He is Great in mercy and wisdom.
d. He is Great in the completeness of His power.

Concerning God's 'elevation', the affirmers of perfection interpret this as His being transcendent above attributes of imperfection and need.

1 My convention throughout this volume is to render this as 'Almighty'—a term with a comparable ubiquity in the English language—or not at all.

Once you have known the aforementioned, [be aware that] *al-ʿAẓīm* and *al-Kabīr* are categorised by the anthropomorphists among the essential Names (*asmāʾ al-dhāt*), whereas the affirmers of God's uniqueness (*ahl al-tawḥīd*) consider them as attributive Names (*asmāʾ al-ṣifāt*). As for *al-ʿAlī*, this is agreed by all to be an attributive Name; however, whereas the former group consider it to mean subsistence in the highest possible space, the latter say that it denotes His transcendence above everything unbefitting of Divinity. This is the conclusion of this discussion.

IX: Pronominal Divine Names

There are three pronouns which are used in reference to Almighty God: *Ana* (I), *Anta* (You) and *Huwa* (He).[1]

The most definite of these is [the first person] 'I', because each person uses it to indicate himself, and there is nothing more definitively known to a person than his own self. This is followed by [the second person] 'you' because it is used to address someone else on the condition that he be present. Because it is addressed to the other, it comes after 'I', but the condition of being present raises it above [the third person] 'he'.

It is thus shown that the highest level is *Anā*, followed by *Anta*, then *Huwa*. The declaration of God's oneness has appeared with each one of these. The FIRST is at the beginning of *Sūrat al-Naḥl*: 'Warn (man) that there is no god but I' (Q.XVI.2), and in *Sūrat Ṭā-Hā*: 'Indeed, I am God: there is no god but I' (Q.XX.14).[2] The SECOND is in: 'He cried through the depths of darkness: "There is no god but You"' (Q.XXI.87). As for the THIRD, it first appears in *Sūrat al-Baqara*: 'And your god is One God: there is no god but He, the Compassionate, the Merciful' (Q.II.163); and its last occurrence is in *Sūrat al-Muzzammil*: 'Lord of the east and the west: there is no god but He: take Him therefore for (your) disposer of affairs' (Q.LXXIII.9).[3] As for this expression being connected to a noun other than these four,[4] there is the verse quoting Pharaoh when he said [with the relative noun *alladhī*]: 'I believe that there is no god except the One in Whom the Children of Israel believe' (Q.X.90)—then God made clear that this was not accepted from him.

1 The author has not mentioned *Naḥnu* (We) in this discussion, although it is frequently used as the first-person plural of majesty.

2 Also in Q.XXI.25.

3 There are twenty-nine such occurrences in total.

4 I can only surmise that the fourth is the explicit Name *Allāh*, which appears in Q.XXXVII.35 and Q.XLVII.19.

With that established, let us consider the rulings of each in turn.

1. 'There is no god but I' can only be said by God or by one quoting Him. Otherwise, it would be a claim of divinity on the part of the speaker, while that is the sole preserve of Almighty God. Know that knowledge of this expression depends upon knowledge of the 'I', which does not occur in fullness of perfection except for Him, the Real. This is because every individual knows himself better than others know him, and this is never more the case than for the Real (exalted is He). It is thus known that 'There is no god but I' is only perfectly known to Almighty God.
2. As for the second level, which is to say 'There is no god but You,' it is proper for the servant to utter this on the condition that he is present, not absent. Yet this state only transpired for Jonah (on whom be peace)[1] once he had made himself absent from all forms of self-interest. This signifies that as long as a person does not absent himself from his own interests, he will never attain to the station of witnessing (*mushāhada*). As for the third level, 'There is no god but He,' this is possible even for the absentees [from God].

   Know that levels of presence vary according to proximity and distance, as well as the perfection or deficiency of manifestation (*tajallī*). Every level of presence which is deficient is considered to be absence in comparison to the level of perfection. Since the levels of presence are infinite, the stages of perfection and deficiency are likewise infinite. This means that anyone who can be described as 'present' can be seen from another perspective as 'absent', and vice-versa.

   Upon this meaning, a poet said: *ayā ghā'iban ḥāḍiran fī 'l-fu'ādi; salāmun ʿalā 'l-ghā'ibi 'l-ḥāḍiri* ('O you who is absent but present in the heart: peace be on the absent-present one').

   It is related that when [Abū Bakr] al-Shiblī was close to death, some of the people who had gathered told him to pronounce 'There is no god but God.' Instead, he said:

   > A house in which You dwell is in no need of lanterns;
   > Your longed-for Countenance is our proof on the day
   > when folk bring their proofs.

3. Know that the word 'He' contains remarkable secrets and lofty states, some of which can be explained and detailed, while others

1 The author is alluding to the background story to Q.xxi.87.

cannot. The author of this book says:[1] by God's providence, I have written [many] subtle secrets, yet whenever I compare those written words with the joy and serenity I feel in my heart upon pronouncing *Huwa*, I find the written words to be insignificant next to those states of witnessing. Upon observing this, I realised that this word has a remarkable effect upon the heart which cannot possibly be expressed and explained. However, let us put down in writing whatever is possible to mention.

[SECRETS AND BENEFITS OF SAYING 'O HE' (*YĀ HUWA*)]

a. When a person says 'O He' it is as though he is saying: 'Who am I to know You? And who am I to address You? What has dust to do with the Lord of lords? What relation can there be between the product of sperm and blood, and He Who is pre-eternal and everlasting? You are transcendent above all likenesses and sanctified beyond the reaches of intellects and imaginations!' For this reason, the servant invokes Him with the word of absentees, saying 'O He.'

b. Just as this word denotes the servant's admission of his lowliness and nothingness, it also contains his acknowledgement that everything apart from God is pure non-existence. This is because, if he said 'O He' and there were two things in existence, then the pronoun would be fit for either one and neither would be specified by it. Therefore, when he says 'O He' it is a declaration that everything other than God is nothing at all, as God says: 'Everything will perish except His Countenance' (Q.xxviii.88).

These are two splendid stations of self-effacement from everything other than God, which cannot be attained except by frequent invocation by 'O He.'

c. When the servant mentions God with some of His Attributes, it means that he is not fully absorbed in gnosis of God. When he says *yā Raḥmān*, he recalls His mercy and his nature inclines towards seeking it, and this is the seeking of his own portion. Likewise, if he says 'O Generous, Benefactor, Forgiver, Bestower, Opener!' If he says 'O Sovereign!' he calls to mind God's kingdom and dominion and all the bounties contained therein, leading him to seek after some of that. The same is true of other Names by

1 This has been seen by some as indicative of the involvement of an author/editor other than Rāzī, but it is by no means explicit in that regard. See Michel Lagarde, *Index du Grand Commentaire de Fakhr al-dîn al-Rāzī*, Leiden: Brill, 1996, p. 60.

analogy.[1] However, when he says 'O He' he acknowledges that He is He, and does not refer to anything beyond that at all. This gives rise in his heart to the light of His remembrance, unpolluted by the murkiness of the mention of other-than-God. Thus his heart receives perfect light and complete uncovering.

d. All of the Divine Attributes known to creation are either Attributes of Majesty (*jalāl*) or of Beneficence (*ikrām*). The former are the likes of His being 'not body, substance or property, neither in locus nor substrate'. There is a subtle issue here, which is: if someone addressed the sultan by saying 'You are not blind or deaf, and neither this nor that...'—recounting every type of flaw and deficiency—he would bring about on himself only reprimand and chastisement! This is because addressing someone with the negation of these attributes is considered poor manners.

As for the Attributes of Beneficence, these refer to His being Creator and Organiser of all things in the most perfect way. There are also issues with this:

- Without doubt, the perfection of the Creator is far above the perfection of creation, indeed to an infinite extent. If we describe the perfection of God and His Attributes by saying that He created all these entities, then we have used created things as the explanation of the perfection and majesty of the Creator. This amounts to introducing the Transcendent and Exalted through a mean and lowly method, which constitutes poor manners.
- If a man began to praise the sultan by saying that he gave such-and-such indigent a scrap of bread or a drop of water, he would bring punishment upon himself. However, proportionally speaking, the entire world of creation—from the Throne to the farthest reaches of boundless space—is more insignificant next to the contents of the treasure-houses of divine power than that bread scrap and water drop compared to the storehouses of this world. If that is poor manners, then this is much worse.

It is thus seen that both ways of praising God are subject

1 The author has not here discussed the implications of saying *yā Allāh*. At the end of Chapter Nine, and based on the discussion in Section VII above, he notes that it encompasses all Attributes. Apparently, the speciality of 'He' is that it denotes no Attributes beyond pure existence.

to these objections. However, there is an excuse which can be presented for praising in these ways.[1] It is that the self (*nafs*) has become immersed in the world of senses and imagination, so when a person wishes to drag it to the threshold of the world of holiness (*ʿālam al-quds*), he must draw its focus upon the perfection of the Holy Presence (*al-ḥadra al-muqaddasa*). However, there is no route to knowledge of God's majesty and perfection besides these two, namely mentioning the Attributes of Majesty and the Attributes of Beneficence. Therefore, he continues to follow these methods until his self turns away from the world of senses and becomes accustomed to the threshold of holiness. Once he attains to this state, he becomes aware of the issues affecting each of these routes, so he leaves off those forms of remembrance and says: 'O He' It is as though the servant is saying:

> I revere Your Majesty too greatly to praise You by negating the flaws of creation from You or attributing the perfections of creation to You, for Your perfection is loftier and Your majesty is greater. Indeed, I do not praise You except by Your identity (*huwiyya*)[2] in and of itself. I do not even call upon You with the word 'You' because that would represent the pride and straying of my soul such that it says: 'I have reached the stage of being present, as it were, with the Necessary Existent.' No, I will not go beyond saying 'He' in order to confess that He is the One Who is praised for Himself, by Himself, and that His Majesty is too high and exalted for the creatures to be in His presence.

Thus this single word signifies all these secrets from the stations of manifestation and unveilings (*mukāshafāt*). It follows that this word is the noblest of remembrance on the condition that one is aware of these secrets.

e. Being constant upon this form of remembrance leads to longing (*shawq*) for God. Longing for God is the most pleasurable of stations and the one most filled with joy and felicity. I say that it leads to this longing because the word 'He' is a [third person] pronoun for one who is absent; therefore, when the servant utters it, he knows that

1 Apart from the obvious, which is the abundance of scriptural texts of these types.
2 The term may be rendered here as 'heity', reflecting its etymology.

he is absent from the Real. He further knows that this absence is not related to location or direction, but rather because he is characterised by the various deficiencies of createdness and contingency, and the flaws of one encompassed by space and time.

Once the intellect grasps this point and further appreciates that this is the condition of all contingents and created things, then he realises that all created things are absent from the threshold of the Exalted Truth, and that this absence is only due to the gap between deficiency and perfection, and between neediness and self-sufficiency. He thus has faith that God possesses aspects of perfection which are transcendent and far above any resemblance to created things, and that the conception of His [reality] is absent from reason, thought and mention. Thus those perfections are perceived only in part, and this partial perception creates a longing to experience all its levels. If those levels are without end, then likewise there is no end to the stages of longing. The easier it is for the servant to attain to a higher level, the greater his longing to ascend beyond it.

It is thus shown that the word 'He' leads to longing for Almighty God. We also said that this longing is the greatest of stations (*maqāmāt*), which is because longing entails a continuous alternation of pains and pleasures: insofar as [the seeker] attains, he experiences pleasure, but insofar as he falls short, he is pained. The feeling of pleasure together with the passing of pain itself creates increased pleasure, joy and delight, which goes to show that longing for the Almighty is the greatest of stations. We have thus shown that being constant upon invoking 'He' develops longing, which is the greatest and most delightful station. It follows, therefore, that being constant in this remembrance leads to the highest stations and loftiest levels.

f. [Our next] explanation of the greatness of this remembrance depends upon two premises: THE FIRST is that knowledge falls into two categories: conceptualisation (*taṣawwur*) and assent (*taṣdīq*).[1] The former is for [a thing's] image to obtain within one's self without making any judgment concerning it, whether positive or negative. The latter is for the particular image to obtain, and then one judges whether something exists or does not exist with respect to it. In this

1 These categories belong to Islamic *manṭiq* derived from Aristotelian logic. See H. A. Wolfson, 'The Terms *Taṣawwur* and *Taṣdīq* in Arabic Philosophy and their Greek, Latin and Hebrew Equivalents', *The Muslim World*, vol. XXXIII, 1943, pp. 1–15.

way, conceptualisation is the station of unity (*tawḥīd*), whereas assent is the station of multiplicity (*takthīr*).

THE SECOND premise is that conceptualisation is of two types: that over which the intellect has agency, and that with which it has none. The former concerns composite quiddities: these cannot be conceptualised without conceiving of the quiddities of the individual parts, which constitutes intellectual effort that is, to an extent, agency (*taṣarruf*). The latter refers to conceptualisation of simple quiddities which transcend all types of composition—the human being is unable to perform any process to conceive of such a quiddity.

Now that we have shown that conceptualisation represents unity, contrary to assent, and that conceptualisation of the simple quiddity represents the ultimate limit of unity and remoteness from multiplicity, we say: our saying concerning Almighty God 'O He' is pure conceptualisation with no trace of assent.[1] Moreover, it is a conceptualisation of a Reality transcendent above all manners of composition and multiplicity. As such, 'O He' is the utmost in [declaring] unity and being remote from multiplicity, and this is the greatest of stations.

g. A thing might be defined by its own self, by the parts integral to it, or by external matters. The first is impossible because the signified precedes the signifier, so defining a thing by itself would entail the knowledge of that thing preceding the knowledge of that thing, which is absurd. The second—i.e. defining by integral parts—is impossible for God, because this method can only apply to composite quiddities and that is unbefitting of Him. The third—i.e. defining by externals—is also impossible [for God], as there is nothing of the matters of creation which corresponds to any of the matters of the pre-eternal Necessary Existent. Rather, He is distinct from everything by His very Essence and particular identity; therefore, nothing in creation can be used to reveal God's own Essence and Reality.

If this is so, then all the potential doors of definition have been closed before the Divine Essence. The only route remaining to the human being is to direct the eye of his intellect and spirit to where light from that Essence emerges, in the faint hope that it might shine

1 That is to say: there is no declarative statement being made concerning the reality being conceptualised.

while he is facing the direction so that he is illuminated thereby. His saying 'O He' is like the turning of the eye of intellect and spirit towards the Holy Presence in the hope of being granted that felicity.

h. When a man enters upon a tremendous king or a powerful sultan and begins to reflect upon the completeness of that power and reverence, he may be overwhelmed by those feelings and become oblivious to all else, to the extent that he forgets—in that moment and state—the hunger or pain which he had been experiencing. He may even see his father or son and fail to recognise them, and all this because the sheer sense of awe overpowered him and took away all other feeling.

   This is the state of the servant who says 'O He' and for whom even a speck of light from that Majesty manifests to his intellect and spirit: that sense of wonderment and ineffability must overtake his heart and soul, clearing his mind and leaving him oblivious and unconcerned with all besides that Essence. There is nothing left for him in this state other than to say with his mind 'He', and to pronounce with his tongue 'He'. Therefore, when a servant is constant with remembrance by the word 'He', that is an emulation of that state in the hope of attaining it. And we ask Almighty God to make us felicitous thereby.

i. It is narrated that the Prophet (may God bless him and grant him peace) said: 'Whoever makes his concerns into a single concern, God will suffice him concerning all the concerns of this life and the Hereafter.'[1] Thus it is as though the servant is saying:

> My concerns in this life and the next are without limit, and none could take care of unlimited needs except One possessing infinite ability, mercy and wisdom. I am unable to fulfil my needs or achieve my goals, and indeed none can do either of these things except Almighty God. Therefore, I direct all my concern to His remembrance alone, keeping my tongue busy with His mention. When I do this, He will suffice me—by His mercy—all my concerns of this life and the next.

j. The mind is not capable of considering anything when it is submerged in the awareness of something else. Whenever one turns his thought to one thing, it must necessarily have turned away from

1 Similar is recorded by Ibn Mājah; it is considered 'very weak' but with attested meaning—R.S.

other things. Thus it is as though the servant is saying: 'Whenever I call the knowledge of one thing to mind, I miss out on some other knowledge for that duration. If this is inevitable, then it is only right to busy my heart and mind with the noblest of all knowledge, and busy my tongue with the noblest of mentions. This is why I remain constant on saying "O He"'[1]

k. Remembrance is the noblest of stations. The Prophet (may God bless him and grant him peace) said, conveying words from Almighty God: 'If he remembers Me to himself, I remember him to Myself; and if he remembers Me in a gathering, I remember him in a gathering better than his.'[2] Once this is established, we say: the best of remembrance is to praise God without asking for anything. The Prophet (may God bless him and grant him peace) said, conveying words from God: 'Whoever is kept busy by My remembrance from asking Me, I give him better than what I give to those who ask.'[3]

After this introduction, we say: the servant is indigent and needy, and when a needy indigent addresses the one he serves in a way that implies a request, then it is considered as such in reality. Thus when the needy one addresses the Self-Sufficient (*al-Ghanī*), saying 'O Generous One,' this is taken to mean: 'Be generous [to me].' If he says 'O Bestower of benefit,' that means he is seeking benefit; and if he says 'O Compassionate,' it means: 'Show compassion.' In this way, these words of remembrance are, in effect, requests—and we have explained that remembrance is greater when it is free from requests. However, when one says 'O He,' this gives no impression of asking for anything, which means it must be the greatest word of remembrance.

Let us conclude this section with noble words of remembrance which I found in a book: 'O He, O He other than Whom there is no He, O You other than Whom there is no god, O Pre-eternity, O Everlastingness, O Eternal Time,[4] O You Who is Living and never dies!'

A SUBTLE POINT IN THIS CONNECTION: Shaykh Ghazālī used to say that

1 This and the preceding point are not limited to this particular word of remembrance. The wording in the text implies that this is a received word of invocation: *uwāẓibu ʿalā qawlihi: yā Huwa*, whereas it is not known from the Qur'ān or the *Sunna*.

2 Cited previously.

3 Recorded by Tirmidhī—S.I.

4 The wording of this section is: *yā Dahr, yā Dayhār, yā Dayhūr*. While the former appears in some Prophetic traditions, the latter two are apparently derived forms conveying the same meaning.

'There is no god but God' is the monotheism of the common people (*tawḥīd al-ʿawāmm*), whereas 'There is no god but He' is the monotheism of the elite (*tawḥīd al-khawāṣṣ*).[1] I have approved of this statement and provided support for it from the Qur'ān and reasoning:

THE QUR'ĀN: God said: 'And call not, besides God, on another god. There is no god except He,' followed by: 'Everything will perish except His Countenance' (Q.XXVIII.88)—meaning 'except He'. The mention of 'except He' after 'no god' signifies that this word contains the utmost monotheism.

RATIONAL PROOF: some people have said that the effect of an agent (*fāʿil*) is not upon the creation of a quiddity, but only in granting it the attribute of existence. To this, I say: existence is itself a quiddity, so it follows [from your claim] that existence does not transpire as the effect [of that agent]. If they persist upon the claim that what transpires by the effect of the agent is the quiddity's property (*mawṣūfiyya*) of existence, then we say: if that property is not a distinct concept from the quiddity and its existence, then it would [upon your claim] be impossible to ascribe it to the agent. However, if it is a distinct concept, then it must have a quiddity—so [our] original point holds.

It is thus shown that the claim that the agent (*mu'aththir*) has no effect upon [creating] quiddities negates cause and effect, as well as Creator and creation, altogether. Since that is unacceptable, it is known that agents have effects upon quiddities. Anything which [subsists] in another disappears with the disappearance of that other; were it not for the agent, the quiddity would not be a quiddity or reality. It is by His power (*qudra*) that quiddities become quiddities and realities become realities. Before the effect of His power, there is no quiddity, no existence, no reality and no establishment. At this point, the truth of our statement 'There is no he but He'[2] becomes apparent. That is to say: no quiddities obtain and no realities are specified except by His will and specification; as such, there is no 'he' except He. And God knows best.

1 This could be a direct quote from Ghazālī's *Mishkāt al-anwār*, see ed. Abū al-ʿAlā ʿAfīfī, Cairo: al-Dār al-Qawmiyya, 1964, p. 60. Gairdner translates the phrase as 'There is no he but *HE*' (emphasis his); see *Al-Ghazzālī's Mishkāt al-anwār*, trans. W. H. T. Gairdner, London: Royal Asiatic Society, 1924, p. 64. I note that the expression *lā huwa illā huwa* occurs just prior to Ghazālī's contrast between two monotheisms, as it does at the end of Rāzī's discussion below. Concerning Rāzī's engagement with the *Mishkāt*, see Jaffer, *Rāzī*, pp. 145–159.

2 The meaning is better expressed as 'No *it* but He,' though the elegance of the expression would be lost.

Chapter Eight
REMAINING ISSUES PERTAINING TO DIVINE NAMES

Enquiry 1
[Are the Names Delimited by Revelation?]

The scholars have differed concerning the Names of Almighty God, as to whether they are delimited [by revelation] (*tawqīf*) or a matter of convention (*iṣṭilāḥ*). Some said that it is not permitted to describe God by any name or attribute unless it appears in the Qur'ān or authentic *ḥadīths*. [A second group] said that any word which denotes a meaning befitting of God's majesty and Attributes is permissible, but not if it fails to meet this condition.

Shaykh Ghazālī (may God have mercy on him) expressed [a third position], as follows: a distinction must be made between the name (*ism*) and the attribute (*ṣifa*). My name is Muḥammad and yours is Abū Bakr: these are names. As for attributes, this is to describe someone as tall, scholarly, and so on. Once you recognise this difference, it is said: it is not permissible to describe God with a name unless it occurs in the Qur'ān or *ḥadīths*, whereas attributes do not depend upon this rule.[1]

ON THE FIRST GROUP: they argued that there are numerous names for a knowledgeable person (*ʿālim*), yet for God we only use the word *ʿĀlim*—as opposed to *ṭabīb* (physician) or *faqīh* (scholar)—nor do we describe Him as having certainty (*mutayaqqin*) or clarity (*mutabayyin*). This shows that the limits are set by revelation.[2]

Some responded to this by saying that the word *ṭabīb* has indeed been narrated, as Abū Bakr was asked, when he fell ill: 'Shall we sum-

1 See Ghazālī, *The Ninety-Nine Beautiful Names of God*, pp. 177–181.

2 I.e. the other words are excluded from use despite the acceptability of their meanings; cf. the response below.

mon the physician?' He replied: 'The Physician made me ill.'[1] As for *faqīh*, this contains the meaning of understanding a speaker's intent after being unsure of it—and the latter clause is impossible for God. As for *mutayaqqin*, it is derived from *yaqana* for the gathering of water in a basin: this means that *yaqīn* is the knowledge that transpires due to a copious succession of evidences which gather to produce certainty—and this meaning is unbefitting for God. As for *tabyīn*, this is for something which becomes apparent after being hidden. It is derived from *baynūna* and *ibāna*, which express two connected things becoming distinct: so if two conceptions are confused within one's heart and then they become separate from each other, this is *baynūna*. From this, knowledge is termed *bayān* and *tabyīn*—and clearly this meaning is impossible for God.

ON THE SECOND GROUP: they said that there is no requirement of delimitation, and argued as follows:

1. The Names and Attributes of God are expressed also in the Persian, Turkish and Indian languages even though none of those words appeared in the Qur'ān or *ḥadīths*. Nevertheless, the Muslims have allowed this by consensus.
2. God has said: 'The most Beautiful Names belong to God: so call on Him by them' (Q.vii.180), and a name is only beautiful because it denotes attributes of praise and majesty. Therefore, any name which conveys such meanings is a beautiful name and its use must be permitted for Almighty God according to this verse.
3. There is no benefit in words except the meanings they convey. Therefore, if the meanings are correct, there is no sense in forbidding the use of any particular word.

ON SHAYKH GHAZĀLĪ: his reasoning is that coining a [new] name for any one among us would be considered contrary to good manners, and that should apply *a fortiori* in the case of God. However, expressing [known] attributes using a variety of words is acceptable among people, and the same applies to Almighty God.

Enquiry 2

There are words in the Qur'ān which [in their apparent meanings] imply

1 I could not source this, but similar is attributed to Ibn Masʿūd in Bayhaqī's *Shuʿab al-īmān*. A *ḥadīth* in the *Musnad* of Aḥmad relates that someone came to help the Prophet, saying 'I am a physician', to which the Prophet replied: 'God is the physician.' Rather than establishing an actual Name for God, this can be taken as mirroring and adjusting the visitor's statement, since God is responsible for the cure in reality.

attributes which cannot be affirmed for Almighty God. We shall mention here some examples:[1]

a. Mockery (*istihzā'*): 'God mocks them…' (Q.II.15). Mocking is ignorance (*jahl*),[2] as shown by Moses' response to his people: 'They said: "Do you make a mockery of us?" He said: "I seek refuge in God from being among the ignorant"' (Q.II.67).
b. Plotting (*makr*): 'They plotted, and God plotted…' (Q.III.54).
c. Anger (*ghaḍab*): 'God has become angry with them' (Q.XLVIII.6).
d. Wonderment (*taʿajjub*): 'I do wonder, while they ridicule' (Q.XXXVII.12).[3] When recited with a *ḍamma* [*ʿajibtu* rather than *ʿajibta*], the wonderment is ascribed to God. It is a state of the heart which occurs when one is unaware of the cause of something.
e. '…the Exalted in Might, the Compeller, the Superior (*al-Mutakabbir*)' (Q.LIX.23). *Takabbur* [if understood as 'arrogance'] is a blameworthy attribute.[4]
f. Shame (*ḥayā'*): 'God is not ashamed to strike any similitude…' (Q.II.26).[5] Shame refers to a change which occurs on the face and in the heart when one does something unseemly.

Know that the correct rule with regard to these words is to say: each of these states has circumstances occurring at the outset, and consequences which follow from it. For example, anger is a state which occurs in the heart when the blood 'boils' and the temperament becomes heated; but its outcome is causing harm to the object of that anger. Therefore, when you hear the term 'anger' in the case of Almighty God, you should apply it to the consequences, not the initial circumstances. So understand the rest by analogy with this.

1 I have opted, as far as practical, to keep these translations literal with respect to the point being problematised by the author, as translators often render the verses to convey the metaphorical import.

2 As Imām Rāzī explains in his exegesis of Q.II.67, the term *jahl* is considered by some as a term for mockery and foolishness, but if it is taken to mean 'ignorance', that represents a cause for mockery and foolishness.

3 This is according to the canonical reading of Ḥamza, Kisā'ī and Khalaf. The author explains in his exegesis of this verse that if *ʿajab* is ascribed to God, it means that He considers their action most serious and prepares a fitting punishment.

4 The author previously discussed the potential corporeal implications of this word. See Chapter Seven, Section VIII.

5 See the author's exegesis of this verse, in which he argues that the negation of one potential source of shame does not imply that the attribute is possible in itself. However, there are also Prophetic *ḥadīth*s alluding to this attribute without negation.

Enquiry 3

I have read in some books of admonitions (*kutub al-tadhkīr*) that Almighty God has 4,000 Names: 1,000 in the Qur'ān and authentic Prophetic *ḥadīths*; 1,000 in the Torah; 1,000 in the Gospel; and 1,000 in the Psalms (*Zabūr*). It is further said that there is another 1,000 in the Preserved Tablet (*al-lawḥ al-maḥfūẓ*), and these have not reached the world of mankind.

I say: this is not implausible, for we have proven and explained in great detail that the categories of Divine Names based upon eliminative and relative Attributes are infinite. Indeed, we can further say: the more a person is familiar with the effects of God's wisdom in planning and organising the upper and lower worlds, the more he is familiar with the Names of God and the Attributes which entail His praise and magnification.

As such, whoever consults the [books of] anatomy and comes across nearly 10,000 types of mercy and wisdom in the creation of the human body would thereby have 10,000 types of Divine Name formed in his mind, all of which denote His praise and magnification. Moreover, once his intellect has appreciated this vast number of wisdoms and mercies, it would become aware that the number of wisdoms and mercies which he has yet to discover in the creation of the body is even greater. This is because, once he knows that the neural spirits (*arwāḥ dimāghiyya*) proceeding through the nerves are seven, he would recognise the benefit and wisdom in each one. Then, upon realising that each spirit is divided into three or four parts, he would recognise instinctively how each one is full of wisdom. Thereafter the intellect realises that each part consists of minute splinters, each of which can be further divided: and each of these divisions connects with a specific limb in a particular way, reaching it via a particular pathway. However, the sheer multiplicity and subtlety [of these connections] takes them out of the scope of the intellect.

Thus it is shown that the 10,000 [wisdoms] only indicate to the intellect that the types of divine wisdom involved in the creation of this body are beyond enumeration and limitation, as God has said: 'But if you count the favours of God, never will you be able to number them' (Q.xiv.34). Hence whoever encounters another type of wisdom has come to know yet another Name of God; since there is no end to the levels of His wisdom and mercy, so too are His Beautiful Names and lofty Attributes without end.

Galen related in *The Usefulness of the Parts*[1] that when he composed it he left out the benefits of the optic chiasm (*majmaʿ al-anwār*). He said: 'I only left that out because I was jealously guarding that noble knowledge. Then, one night, I saw what appeared to be an angel descending from heaven, saying: "Galen, your God is asking: 'Why have you concealed My wisdom from My servants?'" So, upon completing the work, I compiled a separate book in which I explained that in great detail.'

Thus we have proven that there is no end to the most Beautiful Names of God.

Enquiry 4
[Concerning Mysterious Incantations]

In books of talismans (*ṭilasmāt*) and incantations (*ʿazā'im*), we find strange words of remembrance and unintelligible formulae. At times, not only the words but also the [forms of] writing are unknown.

I say: without doubt, writing denotes words, which—in turn—evoke mental images. Therefore, if those formulae do not denote anything at all, then they are of no benefit. If they do denote, then either they denote the Attributes of God and descriptions of His greatness, or they denote something else. If the latter, then again they are of no benefit, as the remembrance of other than God has no effect in encouraging or admonishing.[2]

It only remains, therefore, that these words denote remembrance and praise of God. On this basis, we say: since the types of remembrance are defined and cannot be extended, the best-case scenario for these words is that they are from the same genus as the [established and known] invocations. The differences caused by variation in language are of little significance. Therefore, the known words of remembrance must be considered as more effective than the recitation of unknown things.

OBJECTION: the souls of most of creation are full of shortcomings. If they recite these known words of remembrance with understanding of their apparent meanings, but they do not have strong and enlightened godly souls, then the divine effects will not be strong upon them, and their

1 This was previously cited in the introduction to this book: Section 1, under Verse 3. See May, *Galen on the Usefulness of the Parts of the Body*, pp. 490–1.

2 It seems that the discussion concerns driving off unwanted spirits etc., either by the direct effect of the words, or—as in the final paragraph of this enquiry—by strengthening the soul against them.

souls will not break free from corporeal things. Thus their souls will not obtain power and ability to have effect. On the other hand, if they recite these mysterious words without understanding them at all, yet they conceive in their minds that they are exalted words, then the sense of fear and apprehension will overcome their souls, resulting in their breaking free somewhat from the corporeal world and being directed to the world of holiness. This will give the souls an increased power and ability to have effect.

This is all I have to say regarding these mysterious incantations.[1]

Enquiry 5

There are wondrous connections between the creation and the Divine Names, and the intelligent person will certainly ponder on these in order to benefit from the remembrance.

This discussion depends on a rational introduction, which is that the discursive human souls differ from each other in substance and quiddity: some are godly, illuminated, free and noble, while others are lowly, dark, vile and wretched. Some are merciful and compassionate, while others are cruel and oppressive. Some have little inclination towards bodily and worldly pleasures, while others are full of love of leadership and power. Anyone who ponders upon creation will recognise the state of affairs which we have described.

Then we observe that these states are concomitant to the substance of the souls, as anyone who pays attention to his soul will find that it follows a particular approach and clear path in terms of inclinations and disinclinations, attractions and revulsions. [He further will find] that striving and self-discipline cannot turn the soul upon its head and change its natural condition. Rather, the effect of disciplining is to weaken the effect of [negative] character traits upon the person: not to transform the [soul] altogether, as that is impossible. This is the import of the Prophetic saying: 'People are substances (*maʿādin*) like gold and silver,' and also: 'The souls are mobilised troops.'[2]

Once you have known this, we say: homogeneity results in association, and each of God's Names denotes a particular meaning. Therefore, when that meaning is dominant in a soul, that soul is closely connected to that Name. This means that if the person mentions that Name constantly, he will benefit swiftly thereby.

1 Though he leaves it unanswered, it does not follow that the author accepts this objection.

2 These appear as a single narration in Muslim—R.S. See Shihadeh, *Teleological Ethics*, p. 119.

I heard that Shaykh Abū al-Najīb al-Suhrawardī of Baghdad used to instruct any disciple of his to [recite] *al-Arbaʿīn*[1] once or twice depending on what he considered appropriate, and then he would recite upon him the Ninety-Nine [Divine Names] while observing his face. If he saw no effect from this recital, he would say: 'Go out to the market and pursue worldly concerns, for you have not been created for this path.' However, if he noticed a strong effect from hearing a particular Name, he would instruct the disciple to remain constant upon that remembrance.

I say: this is to be expected. Since the souls differ from each other, each one accords with a particular state. Therefore, if the soul busies itself with that state, its transfer from potentiality to actuality will be smooth and easy.

Let this be the last of our general discussion on names. And God is the Guide.

1 This may refer to the 'Forty *Idrīsī* Names', a supplication consisting of Divine Names.

Chapter Nine
THE NAME *ALLĀH*

Enquiry 1
[Is it a Derived Name?]

My preferred opinion is that this word is a proper noun (*ʿalam*) for Almighty God which is not derived (*mushtaqq*) from anything.[1] This is the opinion of al-Khalīl and Sībawayh and the majority of the legal theorists and jurists, and is supported by a number of proofs:

1. If it were a derived word, its meaning would be universal and not, in itself, preclude its application to multiple referents. This is because a derived word denotes nothing more than that the meaning from which it was derived (*mushtaqq minhu*) has obtained for an unspecified thing; and this does not preclude the same obtaining for numerous others. If this were so [for the Name *Allāh*], then our saying 'There is no god but Allāh' would not constitute true monotheism which eliminates the possibility of others sharing in that designation, because—on that assumption—the word *Allāh* could indeed apply to numerous individuals. As a result, 'There is no god but Allāh' would be deprived of the absolute monotheism which all rational people have agreed it entails. Hence it is known that *Allāh* is a proper noun which was coined for that particular Essence, and is not a derived noun.
2. If one wished to mention a particular essence [along with] some attributes, one would mention the name first, followed by the attributes. For example, one may say: 'Zayd the jurist, grammarian and legal theorist.' Once this is known, we say: whoever wishes to mention God with His Holy Attributes will first say *Allāh*, followed by the Attributes of praise. For example, 'Allāh, the Knowing (*al-ʿĀlim*),

1 The fact that it is used as a proper noun cannot be disputed, but the meaning here is in opposition to being derived from a particular Arabic root (or of non-Arabic origin)—the expected opposite of that would be *murtajal* (coined). See the definition of 'derived' above, in Book I, Chapter Four (further discussion in Chapter Five).

the Powerful (*al-Qādir*), the Wise (*al-Ḥakīm*).' This is never reversed, so as to say *al-ʿĀlim al-Qādir Allāh*—which shows that it is a proper noun.

OBJECTION: is there not such an occurrence at the beginning of *Sūrat Ibrāhīm*: '...the Exalted in power, Worthy of all praise; Allāh, to Whom belongs...' (Q.XIV.1–2)?

RESPONSE: there are two ways of reciting this, as some pronounced *Allāh* here in the nominative,[1] which removes the objection: since its being a subject (*mubtada'*) precludes it being an adjective (*ṣifa*) to anything preceding. As for the [famous] genitive reading, this is comparable to saying: 'This home belongs to the noble and knowledgeable Zayd (*al-fāḍil al-ʿālim Zayd*).' It is not intended to make Zayd an adjective for what preceded; rather, it is that upon saying 'This home belongs to the noble and knowledgeable' there was some remaining confusion as to that person's identity. For this reason, 'Zayd' was added to remove that confusion. Since there is no need in this example to say that the proper noun became an adjective, the same applies to the verse.

3. God said: 'Do you know of any namesake (*samī*) for Him?' (Q.XIX.65). The 'name' in this verse does not refer to the attribute, otherwise the [implied negation] would be considered false.[2] Therefore, the meaning must be the proper noun, and those who affirm such for God say that it is none other than *Allāh*.

THOSE WHO DENIED that it is a proper noun argued on the following bases:

1. The verse: 'And He is Allāh in the heavens' (Q.VI.3); and 'He is Allāh, other than Whom there is no god' (Q.LIX.22).[3] The word *Allāh* here must be an adjective, not a proper noun, because it is not proper to say 'He is Zayd in the city' or 'He is Bakr [in some place].' However, one may say 'He is the pious scholar in the city.' In this way, an objection is raised against the grammarians' claim that a pronoun can neither be an adjective, nor be described by

1 This is the canonical reading of Nāfiʿ, Ibn ʿĀmir and Abū Jaʿfar. In this case, the second verse would be translated: 'God is He to Whom belongs...'

2 The point is unclear to me; it may be that the polytheists of Mecca did claim that their idols shared attributes with God, but acknowledged that there was one (supreme) Deity by this name, *Allāh*. Cf. the author's exegesis of Q.XIX.65, where his preferred interpretation is that the attribute of beneficence (*inʿām*) is intended.

3 The relevance of this second citation is not made explicit.

one.[1] If it is established that [the Name *Allāh*] is an adjective, then it cannot be a proper noun.

2. The proper noun stands in lieu of indication [for example, by gesture], and since that is impossible with respect to God, so too is the existence of a proper noun for Him.
3. Recourse to the proper noun is only made to distinguish an individual from another that bears resemblance in reality and quiddity. Since this is impossible for God, so too is the existence of a proper noun for Him.

RESPONSE TO THE FIRST POINT: why can this not be along the lines of saying 'This is Zayd who has no counterpart in knowledge and piety'?[2]

RESPONSE TO THE SECOND AND THIRD POINTS: the proper noun is that which is coined to denote a specific referent, regardless of whether that referent may be indicated physically or not.

Enquiry 2
[Possible Derivations]

[INTERPRETATION A: *ALAHA* (TO WORSHIP)][3]

Those who said that the Name is derived [from this] have discussed a number of issues (*furūʿ*):

FIRST: the *ilāh*[4] is the object of worship (*maʿbūd*), whether by right or in falsehood. Then religious convention made this refer predominantly to the One worshipped by right. On this interpretation, He was not *ilāh* [i.e. worshipped] in pre-eternity.

Know that God is [indeed] the One deserving of worship as the Bestower of all favours in root and branch. This is because an existent

1 It seems that this interpretation has *huwa* described by the adjective *Allāh*, with *fī al-samāwāt* in the place of the predicate. This would result in a translation something like this: 'And the Divine He is in the heavens'.

2 That is to say, the verse means: 'He is Allāh Who has no counterpart [in any Attribute] in the heavens.' However, the author may not accept the proper noun being used in this way: see his exegesis of Q.VI.3 where several interpretations are advanced after refuting the possibility of the verse attributing directionality to God.

3 The author discusses some 'points' (*furūʿ*) which are connected to the assumption that this Name is derived from *alaha* (to worship): this is frequently mentioned in other sources but not explicitly here. After these points, he discusses 'the second interpretation' and so on: which leads me to suppose either that a line of explanation went missing, or that the structure requires adjustment.

4 The implicit assumption is that *Allāh* is derived from *al-ilāh*, which in turn has a meaning known from its putative linguistic root. See Enquiry 3 below for this and an alternative hypothesis.

is either necessary or contingent: the necessary is only God, whereas all else is contingent. The contingent only comes into being by preponderance [of its existence over non-existence], so all contingents only exist by His creation, either from nothing or via an intermediary. Therefore, all types of favour which the servant experiences come, necessarily, from God. It is thus known that the utmost of favour comes from God. Furthermore, worship represents the utmost of magnification. Hence we say: the utmost of magnification is only deserved by One from Whom the utmost of favour has come; accordingly, the only One deserving of worship is Almighty God.

SECOND: there are those among mankind who worship God for the purpose of attaining reward, but this is ignorance and foolishness for the following reasons:

a. If one worships God in order for that worship to lead to some other thing, then that thing is, in reality, the object of his worship. Thus whoever worships God seeking [primarily] reward is actually worshipping the reward, whereas God is a means for him to reach that object of worship. This is great ignorance!
b. If one said [as an intention] 'I am praying to seek reward' or 'from fear of punishment', his prayer would be void.[1]
c. When a person does an action for a separate goal, then if that goal should be achievable through some other means, he would leave off that [original] means. Thus whoever worships God for recompense and reward would not, if that recompense and reward were available otherwise, worship God. Someone in this state is not a lover of God and has no desire to worship Him—and all of this is ignorance.

Yet there are people who worship God for a higher purpose, which is to be honoured to serve Him. This is because, when a person commences prayer, his intention forms in the heart; and this intention consists of knowledge of the exaltedness of Lordship and the lowliness of servitude. Furthermore, remembrance appears on his tongue and service manifests upon his limbs. Every part of the servant is thereby honoured by service to God, and this honour is the servant's goal.

THIRD: some have disputed the claim that *ilāh* means 'worshipped', citing the following:

a. Idols were worshipped even though they are not gods (*āliha*).[2]

1 Although intention resides in the heart, Shāfiʿīs recommend pronouncing it aloud before prayer.
2 Cf. above Chapter Seven, Section VII.

b. He is God of inanimate objects and [non-rational] beasts, even though it is impossible for them to worship.
c. He is God of insane people and children, even though they do not worship.
d. 'Being worshipped' does not represent an attribute, because it simply means that He is known and mentioned by that person who intends to serve Him. On this basis, Divinity (*ilāhiyya*) would not be an Attribute of God.
e. It would lead to the conclusion that He was not *ilāh* in pre-eternity.

FOURTH: some have said that *ilāh* does not mean 'worshipped', but in fact 'deserving of worship'. However, this too faces the objection that He would not be the *ilāh* of objects, beasts, children and the insane, nor would He have been *ilāh* in pre-eternity.[1] [A third opinion] is that it means 'capable of such acts which would make Him deserving of worship from such as can perform it'.

Know that the first two opinions mean that He was not *ilāh* in pre-eternity, whereas He was indeed *ilāh* in pre-eternity according to the third.

INTERPRETATION B

It is derived from the saying *alihta ilā fulān*, meaning that you found repose (*sakanta*) with someone. This is because the intellects do not find repose except in His remembrance, and the spirits do not ascend except by His gnosis. This is explained in the following ways:

a. Perfection (*kamāl*) is beloved in its own right, whereas all besides God is, in itself, deficient. This is because contingent things are essentially non-existent, and non-existence is the very source of deficiency. The deficient does not attain to perfection except by the agency of the Perfect in Himself. Since perfection is beloved in its own right and God is perfect in His own right, it follows that He is beloved in His own right.
b. Everything besides Him is contingent, and contingent things do not depend upon themselves but remain connected to another, in that they do not exist without the existence of another. Hence every contingent being depends for its existence upon connection to the Necessary Existent. If that is so for external existence, it applies likewise to rational existence: the intellects look with expectation

1 These objections would apply to the definition of *ilāh* as 'worshipped rightfully', but the wording here is: *alladhī yastaḥiqqu an yakūna maʿbūdan*—apparently an error. Note that Q.xvii.44 states that all created beings glorify God.

towards the threshold of His mercy and the thoughts grasp at the tails of His grace and bounty.

These are the two aspects upon which exegesis of the following verse is built: 'Without doubt, in the remembrance of God do hearts find satisfaction' (Q.xiii.28).[1]

INTERPRETATION C

It is derived from *walah*, meaning 'loss of mind'. Know that created beings are of two types: some have arrived (*wāṣilūn*) at the shore of the ocean of His gnosis, while others are prevented. The prevented ones remain in the darknesses of confusion, wandering in ignorance as though they have lost their minds and spirits. As for the finders (*wājidūn*), they have arrived at the court of light and the arena of grandeur and majesty; and thus become lost in the fields of eternity and perished in the court of singularity. It is thus seen that all the creation is lost in His gnosis, so the true God is certainly He.

Expressed in another way: the human spirits raced in the fields of monotheism and glorification: some lagged behind while others went forth. Those which lagged remained in dusky darkness, but those which proceeded reached the world of lights. The former perished in the valleys of darkness, while the latter were dazzled by the lights of the world of bounties.

INTERPRETATION D

It is derived from *lāha*, meaning 'to be elevated', as God is transcendent above resemblance to contingent and created things. This is because He is the only Necessary Existent, perfect in Himself, truly unique in His Essence, and the Creator of everything.

Moreover, He is elevated above it being said of Him that He is elevated in a place (*makān*). This is because any such spatial elevation belongs primarily (*bi'l-dhāt*) to the place itself, and only incidentally (*bi'l-ʿaraḍ*) to the object in that it is present in that place. Since primary matters are nobler than incidentals, it would be the case—if this elevation were spatial—that such a place is higher and nobler than the Divine Essence. Since that is false, we know that He is above being described as elevated in terms of being in a place, and too noble to be ascribed to things of the world of contingencies (*ʿālam al-imkān*).

INTERPRETATION E

It is from *aliha*, meaning 'to be confounded and fail to find one's way'. This is because when the servant reflects upon God [in His Essence],

1 The author's explanation in *Sūrat al-Raʿd* consists of three quite different points.

he is confounded due to God being distinct from anything which the human being can imagine or conceptualise. Even if his intellect rejects His existence, his soul belies [the intellect],[1] because all besides Him is needy and cannot occur without the existence of the Needed. If he points to something which is grasped by the senses and imagination and says 'That is He,' his soul belies him likewise, because anything which can be grasped by the senses and imagination necessarily displays the signs of createdness.

There is nothing left for the intellect, therefore, but to affirm His existence and perfection, and admit to its own inability to realise [His reality]. In this case, the inability to attain the reaches of realisation (*idrāk*) is [itself] realisation.[2] Without doubt, this is an astounding situation in which the intellects are confounded and perplexed at the very outskirts!

INTERPRETATION F

It is from *lāha/yalūhu*, meaning 'to be concealed'. This applies to Him in the following ways:

1. By His very sublimity (*ṣamadiyya*),[3] He conceals Himself[4] from the intellects.
2. Suppose the sun were fixed motionless in the middle of the sky: its rays would remain continuously upon all the surfaces. In that case, one would imagine that the light upon these surfaces is inherent to them. However, because we observe that the sun sets and this light disappears along with it, we realise that the light upon these surfaces originates in the disk of the sun. In a similar way, the [rays of] existence which land upon the entire world of creation from the divine power are like that light which emanates from the sun. If we imagine that it were possible for God to 'rise and set' and be absent as well as present, that 'setting' would extinguish the light of existence from all the contingent beings. This would reveal that the light of existence is from Him. However, since setting and rising are not befitting

1 That is, his human nature—including the essentials of rationality—would belie such a conscious attempt at rejecting God's existence.

2 This or similar wording is often attributed to Abū Bakr. It is to say that the realisation of one's utter inability is significant in itself, and can be said to represent—in a way particular to gnosis of God alone—the pinnacle of realisation.

3 See the exegesis of Q.cxii.2 for discussion of *al-Ṣamad*, which has been variously categorised as denoting a relative or eliminative Attribute.

4 My translation here follows the subtle distinction made by the author below.

of Him, it is little wonder that some deficient minds assumed that these things exist by themselves and for themselves.[1]

It is thus shown that there is no reason for His light being veiled other than the completeness of that light. Thus some spiritual masters said: 'Glory to the One Who veiled Himself from the intellects by being so strongly manifest, and concealed Himself from them by the completeness of His light!' If that is so, then the reality of His supremacy is 'self-veiling' (*muḥtajib*) from the intellects.

[Note:] one does not say 'veiled' (*maḥjūb*),[2] because that [passive form] implies one who is overcome (*maqhūr*), and that is the station of a servant. God, on the contrary, overcomes (*qāhir*)—and being self-veiling is an attribute of this type. The Divine Real is self-veiling, whereas the creation are veiled.[3]

INTERPRETATION G

It is from *aliha al-faṣīl*, meaning for a weaned camel to become devoted to its mother. This means that the servants are devoted and kept occupied by servitude to Him in every state. This is shown by the following:

a. When a great calamity befalls a person, he forgets everything except Almighty God and says from his heart and upon his tongue: 'O Lord, O Lord!' Once he escapes from that calamity and returns to the enjoyment of blessings and favours, however, he turns to attribute that escape to insufficient causes and lowly states.[4] This is a contradictory position, for if the saviour from these tribulations and the deliverer to all that is good were anyone other than God, one would have to turn at the time of calamity to that other. Yet if God is the one to resolve one's needs at such times, then this must be true of all times. It does not befit the people of guidance to flee to Him in times of need then turn away from Him at times of ease.
b. Goodness and ease are to be sought from God.
c. One's benefactor (*muḥsin*) may be, according to appearances, either God or someone else. If it is someone else, they do not do any good

1 Compare this with Ghazālī, *The Ninety-Nine Beautiful Names*, pp. 134–137, concerning the Names *al-Ẓāhir al-Bāṭin*.

2 The former is a Form VIII active participle, for which my translation is necessarily strained as there is no obvious corresponding word in English. The term 'veiled' is frequently used in this connection, even though it implies the latter word: a Form I passive participle.

3 The creation are veiled from God by their very createdness, as well as by their sins, etc.; this is the theme of the latter part of Ghazālī's *Mishkāt al-anwār*.

4 This is the import of verses such as Q.XXXIX.49.

unless God creates that motivation within their heart. Thus it is God Who is the Benefactor in reality, and therefore should be sought at all times. Created beings are devoted to returning to Him.

Once, some adepts complained of excessive satanic whispers, so their teacher said: 'I was a blacksmith for ten years, a cleaner for ten years, and a doorman for another ten.' They said: 'But we have not seen you do all this?' He replied:

> I did, but you saw not. Do you not know that the heart is like iron? I was the blacksmith who makes it soft by fire for ten years. Then I began to wash it of dirt and impurities for ten years, and thereafter I took a seat at the door of the heart for another ten years, brandishing the sword of 'No god but God.' I remained until the love of all but God departed, and the love of God entered.

Hence, when the court of the heart becomes void of other-than-God and the love for God becomes strong, a drop of light falls from the oceans of the world of majesty and the heart drowns in that droplet, oblivious to all things, leaving nothing within it but the secret of 'No god but God.'

INTERPRETATION H

It is from *aliha/ya'lahu* meaning 'to be terrified' by some event [and seek protection], and [likewise] 'to grant that protection'.[1] The Protector (*al-Mujīr*) of all creatures from every harm is Almighty God, as He said: 'He protects while none can protect against Him' (Q.XXIII.88). It is also because He is the Granter of favours (*al-Munʿim*): 'And whatever you have of favour, it is from God' (Q.XVI.53); and He is the One Who feeds (*al-Muṭʿim*): 'And He it is that feeds but is not fed' (Q.VI.14), and Who creates (*al-Mūjid*): 'Say: "All things are from God"' (Q.IV.78). Therefore, He overpowers non-existence to create existence and occurrence, overcoming it through potential, actualisation and perfection: in reality, this is all from God and none other.

There are some subtle and beneficial points in this connection:

a. Commonly, if a debtor sees his creditor from a distance, he will flee from him. However, [it is as though] God the Generous says: 'My servants, you are in debt to Me because of your many sins, but do not flee from Me. Rather, I say: "Flee to God" (Q.LI.50). Indeed, I am the One Who will settle your debts and forgive your

1 Both *aliha* and the explanatory term *faziʿa* are noted to have this bidirectional usage.

sins. Moreover, while the kings shut their doors upon the poor and admit only the rich, I do the opposite.'[1]

b. The Prophet (may God bless him and grant him peace) said: 'Almighty God has one hundred [portions of] mercy, of which He sends down one mercy shared between jinns, humans, birds, beasts and insects: it is by virtue of this that they show compassion and kindness. He has kept back ninety-nine mercies by which He will treat His servants on the Day of Judgment.'[2] I say: he only said this by way of illustration, as the oceans of mercy are infinite and cannot be limited to a particular number.

c. The Prophet (may God bless him and grant him peace) said: 'God will say to the believers on the Day of Judgment: "Did you love to meet Me?" They will respond: "Yes, our Lord." He will ask: "Why?" They will reply: "We longed for Your pardon and forgiveness." Then Almighty God will say: "My forgiveness has become incumbent for you."'[3]

d. ʿAbd Allāh b. ʿAmr related[4] that the Messenger of God (may God bless him and grant him peace) said:

> Indeed, God will lay ninety-nine scrolls before one of His servants [containing his deeds] on the Day of Judgment, each scroll as far as the eye can see. He will say: 'Do you deny any of this? Have the noble scribes wronged you?' He will reply: 'No, O Lord!' He will say: 'Did you have an excuse to perform these sins?' The servant will reply: 'No, O Lord!' placing his heart upon the fire.[5] Then God will say: 'You have a good deed [recorded] with Me, and there is no injustice this day.' He will bring out a slip on which it is written: 'I testify that there is no god but God, and I testify that Muḥammad is His Servant and Messenger.' The servant will say: 'O Lord! What good is this slip next to these scrolls?' So the scrolls will be put on one pan [of the scale], and the slip on the other. The scrolls will come up light and the slip will be heavy, for nothing outweighs the Name of God.

e. During a battle on a hot summer's day, a boy [from the captives] was

1 'Poor and rich' may be understood in spiritual terms, i.e. the humble versus the arrogant.
2 Recorded by Muslim—S.I.
3 Recorded by Aḥmad and others—S.I.
4 Recorded by Tirmidhī and others—S.I.
5 This appears to be an expression for fear and despair. It does not appear in Tirmidhī's narration.

standing to be sold off. A woman saw him, crossed over to the boy and clutched him to her belly. She then turned her back to the plain and placed him on her belly to guard him from the heat, saying 'My son, my son!' The people began to cry and stopped what they were doing. The Messenger of God (may God bless him and grant him peace) came to them and they informed him of what had occurred, on which he said: 'Are you amazed at the mercy of this woman upon her son? Indeed, God is more merciful to you all than this woman towards her son.' Then the Muslims parted with the greatest feelings of joy and glad tidings.[1]

Enquiry 3
Method of Linguistic Derivation

Some have said that this word is not Arabic [in origin], but in fact Hebrew or Syriac. They say *Ilāh*, *Raḥmān* and *Marḥiyān*, so when these were Arabised, they became *Allāh*, *Raḥmān* and *Raḥīm*.[2] However, this is implausible; the similarity between the words does not take away from the fact that this Name is authentically Arabic. The proof of that is: 'If you ask them who it is that created the heavens and the earth, they will certainly say "Allāh"' (Q.xxxi.25), and 'Do you know of any namesake for Him?' (Q.xix.65)—in which there is consensus that the reference is to the Name *Allāh*. Most authorities accepted that it is an Arabic word.

As for those who consider it to be a proper noun for Almighty God, they have no need of this particular enquiry, whereas those who deny it have two opinions:

A. The Kūfans said that it is derived from *ilāh*, upon which the [definite article] *al-* entered for glorification, becoming *al-ilāh*. Then the *hamza* was dropped due to the heaviness of this word along with its frequent use. This left two adjacent *lāms*, so the first was assimilated [into the second] to become *Allāh*.
B. The Baṣrans said that it is from *lāh*, to which *al-* was added. In support of this, they cited [this poetic line]: *ka-ḥalfatin min Abī Rabāḥin yasmaᶜuhā* lāhuhu *'l-kubbār* ('Like an oath by Abū Rabāḥ heard by his grand deity')—in which the word appeared in its original form.

Enquiry 4

Al-Khalīl said: the whole creation agrees that the Name *Allāh* is exclusive

1 This account appears at the end of Ghazālī's *Iḥyā'*. A short version of the *ḥadīth* is recorded by Bukhārī and Muslim.

2 Cf. Book III, Chapter Four, Enquiry 11, in which it is claimed that these words are at the opening of the Gospel.

to Almighty God, and likewise saying *al-Ilāh* is exclusive to Him. Those who used the word *ilāh* for other than God would do so in an annexed construct (*iḍāfa*), i.e. 'the *ilāh* of such-and-such'. Alternatively, they would make it indefinite; for example, the verse which quotes the statement of the people of Moses: '"Fashion for us a god like the gods they have." He said: "Indeed, you are a people without knowledge"' (Q.VII.138).

Enquiry 5
[Unique Features]

This Name has a number of features not found in the rest of God's Names. Let us point to some of these:

1. If you remove the [initial] *alif*, you are left with the form [which spells] *li'Llāh* ('to God'), which is specific to Him: 'To God belong the forces of the heavens and the earth' (Q.XLVIII.4), and 'To God belong the treasures of the heavens and the earth' (Q.LXIII.7). If you then remove the first *lām*, this leaves *lahu* ('to Him'), as in: 'To Him belong the keys of the heavens and the earth' (Q.XXXIX.63), and 'To Him belongs dominion, and to Him belongs praise' (Q.LXIV.1). If you then remove the remaining *lām*, this leaves *hu* (He), which also signifies the Almighty, as in: 'Say: He (*huwa*) is God, the One' (Q.CXII.1), and 'He is the Living: there is no god but He' (Q.XL.65). The *wāw* is additional, as can be seen by its being dropped from the dual and plural, as these are *humā* and *hum* [respectively].

   This is a feature unique to *Allāh*, not found in other Names. This uniqueness can be found in the meaning as well as the word: for if you invoke Him by the Name *al-Raḥmān*, you have described Him with compassion but not supremacy; and if you invoke Him by *al-ʿAlīm*, you have mentioned His knowledge, not His power. However, if you say *yā Allāh*, you have described Him with all His Attributes, because possessing all these Attributes is integral to being *ilāh*. It is thus seen that the Name *Allāh* possesses unique features as compared to other Divine Names.
2. The testimony of faith (*shahāda*) by which an unbeliever enters into Islam only contains this Name. Hence if an unbeliever said 'I testify that there is no god except *al-Raḥmān*' or 'except *al-Raḥīm*, *al-Malik*, *al-Quddūs*', he would neither leave his state of unbelief (*kufr*) nor enter Islam. If, on the other hand, he says 'I testify that there is no god except Allāh,' then he goes from unbelief to Islam. This demonstrates the uniqueness of this Name and its nobility. And God is the Guide to what is correct.

Chapter Ten
THE NAMES *AL-RAḤMĀN* AND *AL-RAḤĪM*[1]

Know that there are four types of things: those which are both beneficial and necessary; those which are beneficial but not necessary; those which are necessary but not beneficial; and those which are neither beneficial nor necessary.

THE FIRST—beneficial and necessary—may be so only in this life, such as breath: for if it is cut off even for a moment, death will result. Alternatively, it may be so in the Hereafter, such as gnosis of God: for if it disappears from the heart for even a moment, that heart will die, and it will become deserving of eternal punishment.

THE SECOND—beneficial only—includes wealth in this life, and the various types of knowledge and awareness in the Hereafter.

THE THIRD—necessary only—encompasses the unavoidable harms of this life; for example, illnesses, death, poverty and senility. There is no equivalent in the Hereafter, for the benefits there are not tainted by any harms.

THE FOURTH—neither beneficial nor necessary—includes poverty in this life[2] and punishment in the Hereafter.

Once you have known this, we say: we have mentioned that breath is beneficial and necessary in this life, such that if it were to be cut off, the person would die immediately. Similarly, gnosis of God is necessary in the Hereafter because even its momentary absence from the heart will lead unavoidably to its death. However, the first death is lighter than the second for its pain only lasts for [something like] an hour, whereas the pain of the second death lasts forever.

Also, just as breathing has two effects—(a) drawing in fresh air for the heart to maintain its balance and well-being, and (b) expelling corrupted, hot, scorched air from the heart—thinking (*fikr*) likewise has two effects:

1 Both of these Names denote the attribute of mercy, and the translation we have adopted (the Compassionate, the Merciful) is not necessarily more accurate than others. Rāzī himself does not explain the distinction at this juncture, but instead in Book III below: Chapter Five, Verse 3.

2 This was already included in the previous category.

(a) bringing the breath of evidence and proofs to the heart in order to maintain balanced faith and gnosis therein, and (b) expelling from the heart the corrupted air resulting from doubts (*shubuhāt*). This effect is only achieved by realising that these perceptible things are finite and will cease to exist in the Hereafter. Whoever appreciates these realities will remain safe from harms and will attain to the sources of goodness and pleasure.

These two matters[1] will be perfected once your intellect grasps the fact that everything you have attained and found is but a drop in the oceans of God's mercy, and an atom of the light of His kindness. Upon this realisation, the knowledge that God is *Raḥmān* and *Raḥīm* will be opened up to your heart.

[Manifestations of Mercy]

If you wish to understand this meaning in more detail, then you must know that you are a composite substance comprising soul (*nafs*) and body (*badan*), [or] spirit (*rūḥ*) and body (*jasad*).

As for your SOUL: without doubt, it was ignorant in its original state, as God said: 'It is God Who brought you forth from the wombs of your mothers when you knew nothing; and He gave you hearing, sight and intelligence, that you may give thanks' (Q.XVI.78). Then ponder upon the range of its faculties of sense (*ḥassāsa*), motion (*muḥarrika*), cognition (*mudrika*) and reason (*ʿāqila*), then upon the levels and types of conceivable things, which are absolutely without end. If a thinking person were to start gaining knowledge of all these things and continued to do so at the speed of lightning or gushing winds, remaining in this process for the rest of time, he would still only have gained a finite amount of knowledge. What remains would still be infinite, and the finite next to the infinite is [as nothing]. This underlines the truth and reality in what God said: 'Of knowledge it is only a little that is communicated to you' (Q.XVII.85).

As for your BODY: this is a composite substance made up by the four humours (*akhlāṭ*). Ponder upon its structure and anatomy, and familiarise yourself with the lofty benefits and noble effects present in each part and organ. This will display the truth of His saying: 'But if you count the favours of God, never will you be able to number them' (Q.XIV.34), and one of the effects of His mercy will have thus been manifested to you, in that He created and guided you. You will thereby understand something of His saying: 'The Compassionate, the Merciful.'

1 I.e. presenting proofs and eliminating doubts.

Does Anyone Besides God Have Mercy?

If someone asks this question, we say: the truth is that mercy only belongs to God. If we do say that another can be merciful, His mercy is certainly more perfect than any other. Hence these are two statements:

FIRST: 'Mercy only belongs to God,' which is shown by the following:

1. Generosity (*jūd*) is to give what is needed without receiving any return. Everyone besides God gives only to receive a return, although this return is of a variety of types. It may be physical, such as to give a *dīnār* in exchange for a garment. Other returns are spiritual, such as to give money in exchange for a service; for assistance; for goodly praise; for [heavenly] reward; to eradicate love of wealth from the heart; or to pacify the heart's generic sympathy.[1] All of the aforementioned are spiritual returns. In short, everyone who gives does so to attain thereby some form of perfection. As such, it is an exchange rather than generosity or a pure gift. On the other hand, since Almighty God is perfect in Himself, it is impossible that He would give in order to gain perfection: so the absolutely Generous and Merciful One is none but He.
2. Everything besides God is contingent, and every contingent depends for its existence upon creation by the Necessary Existent. Therefore, every mercy which appears from other-than-God only came into being by God creating it, so He is, in reality, the Mercy-giver.
3. A person has the potential to perform an action or not to perform it. Action will not take precedence over inaction until a strong motivation obtains in his heart: without that, mercy will not proceed from him. Once it takes root, the mercy necessarily follows. As such, the true Merciful One is He Who created that motivation in the heart, and that is none but God.
4. Suppose that someone gives a gift of wheat: the [recipient] will not derive any benefit unless he has a stomach which can digest it. Likewise, one cannot derive benefit from a gifted garden without the faculty of sight. The truth is that God alone is the Creator of that wheat and that garden, as well as the One Who makes it possible to benefit from them and preserves the beneficiary from every type of harm and defect so that he can continue to derive that benefit. Therefore, it must be said that the real Benefactor and Mercy-giver is Almighty God.

1 I.e. pity for one's fellow man. See Shihadeh, *Teleological Ethics*, pp. 52 and 78.

SECOND: 'Assuming that another can be merciful, God's mercy is greater and more perfect.' This is explained in the following ways:

1. The act of giving entails the superior status of the giver with respect to the recipient. If this lowly state transpires [for the recipient] in relation to his Lord God, that is preferable to the same occurring with respect to some of His creation.
2. When God bestows some blessing upon you, He asks that you do some act [of gratitude] which would make you deserving of the blessings of the Hereafter; it is as though He is instructing you to earn yourself eternal felicity. On the other hand, when someone other than God bestows something upon you, he expects you to busy yourself in his service to fulfil his own purpose. Without doubt, the first scenario is preferable.
3. The beneficiary becomes like a slave to the benefactor, and being a slave to God is worthier than any other servitude.
4. When the sultan bestows some favour upon you, he does so without knowing the details of your situation. He might give when you are in no need of receiving, or cut off his support when you are most in need. Moreover, he is incapable of bestowing upon you at all times and for every need. The Almighty, on the other hand, knows all things and is capable of all things. Therefore, if you experience any need, He knows it; and if you ask of Him, He is able to fulfil that request—and this situation is superior.
5. Giving brings about a sense of obligation, and accepting this from God is better than accepting it from any of His creatures.

What we have said has proven that God [alone] is *al-Raḥman* and *al-Raḥīm*; and even assuming that another merciful one could exist, His mercy is better, higher, more perfect and more desirable. And God knows best.

Chapter Eleven
SPIRITUAL ALLUSIONS OF THE *BASMALA*

Point 1

Moses fell ill and was experiencing severe pain in his stomach. He complained to God, Who directed him to a certain herb of the desert. Moses ate from it and became well again by God's permission. Later, the illness came back so he took the herb, yet his ailment only increased. He said: 'O Lord! I ate it the first time and benefited from it, but the second time I only felt worse!' God replied: 'The first time, you went from Me to the herbage and attained the cure. But the second time, you went from yourself to the herbage so the ailment increased. Do you not know that the whole world is a poison and the antidote is My Name?'

Point 2[1]

Rābiʿa spent a particular night in prayer and slept upon the breaking of dawn. A thief entered her home and took her clothes. As he headed for the door, he failed to find his way; so he put down the clothes and thereupon he found the door. This happened three times in succession, and then a voice came from the corner of the house: 'Put down the clothes and get out, for while the beloved sleeps, the Sultan is awake!'

Point 3

There was a mystic who used to tend sheep. One day, wolves came among his flock but did not harm them. A passing man saw this and called out: 'When did the wolves make peace with the sheep?' He replied: 'The day the shepherd made peace with God.'

Point 4

'In the Name of God' actually means 'I begin in the Name of God,' but that [verb] was removed in order to lighten it. Nevertheless, when you say 'In the Name of God,' it is as though you have said 'I begin in the

1 The relevance of this and the following anecdote is unclear.

Name of God.' The purpose of this is to demonstrate that the servant's path from its very outset is built upon ease, lightness and lenience. It is as though God has made the very first word [of His Book] a sign of His tolerance and kindness.

Point 5

It is narrated that before Pharaoh claimed divinity for himself, he built a palace and wrote upon its door: 'In the Name of God.' When he claimed divinity and Moses (on whom be peace) was sent to him, Moses invited him but saw no sign that he would be rightly guided, so he said: 'O God! I invite him so profusely yet I see no good in him.' The Almighty replied: 'O Moses! Perhaps you want to see him perish. You are looking at his unbelief, while I am looking at what he wrote above his door.'

LESSON: one who writes this word upon his external door becomes safe from destruction even though he be an unbeliever. So what of one who writes it upon his innermost heart from the start of his life until the end: what will be his outcome?

Point 6

He called Himself *Raḥmān* and *Raḥīm*, so how could He not show mercy? It is narrated that a beggar came to a grand, lofty door but was given very little. He came the next day with an axe and began to destroy the door. When he was asked why, he replied: 'Either the door must be made to match the donation, or the donation to match the door!'

O God of ours! The oceans of [human] mercy in comparison to Your mercy are less than an atom next to Your Throne. Therefore, as You have cast Your Attribute of mercy upon Your servants at the opening of Your Book, let us not be prevented from Your mercy and bounty!

Point 7

The Name *Allāh* signifies His power, dominance and transcendence. This mention is followed by [the two Names] *al-Raḥmān* and *al-Raḥīm*, showing that His mercy is more plentiful and complete than His dominance.

Point 8

It is often the case that servants of the sovereign, when they purchase some horses, mules or donkeys, brand upon them the name of the sovereign so that nobody will attempt any wrongdoing towards them. It is as though God says: 'Your obedience has an enemy in the form of Satan, so when you commence any action, brand My Name upon it by saying: "In the name of God, the Compassionate, the Merciful"—so that the enemy does not attempt anything.'

Point 9

Make yourself a companion to the remembrance of God so that you are never far from it in either abode. It is narrated[1] that the Prophet (may God bless him and grant him peace) passed a ring to Abū Bakr the Truthful and asked him to write upon it: 'There is no god but God.' So Abū Bakr gave it to an engraver and asked him to write: 'There is no god but God. Muḥammad is the Messenger of God.' When he collected the ring from the engraver and brought it back, the Prophet (may God bless him and grant him peace) saw within it: 'There is no god but God. Muḥammad is the Messenger of God. Abū Bakr is the Truthful.' So he asked him: 'What are these additions, Abū Bakr?'[2] He replied, 'O Messenger of God! I was not content to separate your name from the Name of God, but I did not say the rest!' Abū Bakr felt embarrassed, until Gabriel (on whom be peace) came and said: 'O Messenger of God! It was I who wrote the name of Abū Bakr. Since he was not content to separate your name from God's name, God was not content to separate his name from yours.'

LESSON: this miraculous occurrence was because Abū Bakr disliked separating the name of Muḥammad (may God bless him and grant him peace) from the Name of God. So what of a person who never separates from the remembrance of God?

Point 10

When Noah (on whom be peace) boarded the ship, he said: 'In the Name of God, whether it move or be at rest' (Q.xi.41). He attained salvation with half of this formula,[3] so how could one who adheres to these words throughout his life be prevented from salvation?

Furthermore, Solomon (on whom be peace) attained the kingdom of this world and the Hereafter by saying: 'It is from Solomon, and it is in

1 I could not source this story; rather, it is known from Bukhārī and Muslim that the Prophet's ring had only 'Muḥammad (is) the Messenger of God'—R.S.

2 As well as asking about the reason for the additions, this wording could also be because the Prophet (may God bless him and grant him peace) was not able to read them.

3 Either this means that he mentioned the *basmala* without 'the Compassionate, the Merciful', or that only the first half of the quoted statement—namely the shortened *basmala*—had the effect upon his salvation.

the Name of God, the Compassionate, the Merciful' (Q.xxvii.30). Thus it is hoped that the servant, by saying it, would triumph with the dominions of this world and the next.

Point 11

If one should ask why Solomon placed his own name before God's in the aforementioned verse, then we answer with the following [possibilities]:

a. When Bilqīs found the letter placed upon her pillow, knowing that none could have entered [her quarters] and seeing the hoopoe perched on the edge of the wall, she realised that it must be from Solomon. Thus when she picked it up, she said: 'It is from Solomon'; and when she opened it and found therein *In the Name of God, the Compassionate, the Merciful,* she said: 'And it is in the Name of God, the Compassionate, the Merciful.' As such, the words 'It is from Solomon' were uttered by Bilqīs, not Solomon.
b. Perhaps Solomon wrote 'It is from Solomon' on the title page, then at the top of the inner page he wrote *In the Name of God, the Compassionate, the Merciful*, as is customary with such letters. Thus when Bilqīs read the title page, she said: 'It is from Solomon,' then—upon opening it and reading the *basmala*—she said: 'And it is in the Name of God, the Compassionate, the Merciful.'
c. Bilqīs was an unbeliever, so Solomon may have feared that she would blaspheme against God when she looked at the letter. For that reason, he placed his own name before God's so that the cursing would be against himself and not God.

Point 12[1]

The letter *bā'* in *bi'sm* is derived from *birr* (kindness), for He is kind to His servants by bestowing all types of comfort in this life and the Hereafter. The greatest station of this kindness is that He honours them on the Day of Judgment with the vision of Him.

There was once someone whose Jewish neighbour fell ill. He related:

> I went to visit him and told him: 'Become Muslim.' He said: 'For what?' I replied: 'From fear of the Fire!' He said: 'I care not about it.' I said: 'Then to gain Paradise,' to which he replied: 'I do not want it.' So I asked him:

1 This point contains purely spiritual speculations, in contrast to the extensive discussions on linguistic meanings and derivations earlier in the book. It is based on the fact that 'In the Name (of)' is written with three letters: *b-s-m*.

> 'What do you want?' He replied: 'That He shows me His noble Countenance.' I said: 'Become Muslim and you shall have this.' He told me: 'Write down [a guarantee].' I did that, so he became a Muslim and died immediately. We prayed upon him and buried him. Then I saw him in my dream looking very satisfied, so I asked: 'Shimon, what did your Lord do for you?' He replied: 'He forgave me and said: "You submitted out of longing for Me!"'

As for the *sīn* [in *bi'sm*], that is derived from God's Name *al-Samī*ᶜ (the Hearing), as He hears the supplications of His creations from the Throne all the way to below the soil.

It is narrated[1] that Zayd b. Ḥāritha went from Mecca to Ṭā'if accompanied by one of the hypocrites. They came to a dilapidated building and the hypocrite said: 'Let us enter and take some rest here.' They did so, but when Zayd fell asleep, the hypocrite tied him up and intended to kill him. Zayd asked him: 'Why would you kill me?' He replied: 'Because Muḥammad loves you and I despise him.' Zayd called out: 'O Compassionate! Save me!' Upon this, the hypocrite heard a voice saying: 'Beware! Do not kill him.' He stepped outside and looked around, but saw no one. He came back and went again to kill Zayd, but was interrupted by a voice nearer than the first: 'Do not kill him.' Again, he looked but saw no one. On the third attempt, he heard the voice close by, saying: 'Do not kill him.' This time, when he went outside, he saw a horseman brandishing a spear. The horseman struck the hypocrite dead, and then went inside to release Zayd. He said: 'Do you not recognise me? I am Gabriel. When you called out, I was in the seventh heaven and God said: "Get to My servant." The second time, I was in the lowest heaven; and the third time, I had reached the hypocrite.'

As for the *mīm* [in *bi'sm*], it signifies that everything from the Throne to below the soil is His *mulk* (dominion) and *milk* (possession).

According to Suddī, the people were struck by a drought during the time of Solomon son of David (peace be upon them), so they came to him, saying: 'O Prophet of God! Please take the people out to pray for rain.' When they went out, there was an ant standing on its [hind] legs, stretching out its forearms, saying: 'O God! We are one of Your creations, and we cannot survive without Your bounty!' So God poured the rain down

1 I could not source this narration.

upon them, and Solomon said: 'Go back, for you have been answered by the supplication of another.'

As for [the Name] *Allāh*, then know, O people, that throughout my life I say *Allāh*. When I die, I shall say *Allāh*. When I am questioned in the grave, I shall say *Allāh*. When I arise on the Day of Judgment, I shall say *Allāh*. When I receive my book, I shall say *Allāh*. When my deeds are weighed, I shall say *Allāh*. When I pass over the path, I shall say *Allāh*. When I enter the Garden, I shall say *Allāh*. And when I see Him, I shall say *Allāh*!

Point 13

The wisdom in saying these three Names [*Allāh*, *al-Raḥmān* and *al-Raḥīm*] is that the addressees of the Qur'ān are three categories: 'There are among them some who wrong their own souls; some who follow a middle course; and some who are, by God's leave, foremost in good deeds' (Q.xxxv.32). [It is as though] God says: 'I am *Allāh* for the foremost, *al-Raḥmān* for the middling and *al-Raḥīm* for the wrongdoers.' Also, *Allāh* bestows the favours, *al-Raḥmān* pardons the mistakes of His friends, and *al-Raḥīm* overlooks disrespect [towards Him].

From His perfect mercy, it is as though He says: 'I know of you that which, if your parents knew, would cause them to abandon you. If your wife knew it, she would leave you; your maidservant would flee; and your neighbour would strive to demolish your house. I know all of that, yet I conceal it by My generosity so that you know that I am Generous.'

Point 14

The Name *Allāh* guarantees His patronage (*wilāya*): 'Allāh is the Protector of those who believe' (Q.ii.257); *al-Raḥmān* guarantees His love: 'On those who believe and work deeds of righteousness will the Compassionate bestow love' (Q.xix.96); and *al-Raḥīm* guarantees His mercy: 'And He is ever Merciful to the believers' (Q.xxxiii.43).[1]

Point 15

The Prophet (may God bless him and grant him peace) said: 'Whoever lifts a piece of paper from the ground on which is written *In the Name of God, the Compassionate, the Merciful* out of respect for Him, he will be written in the presence of God among the truthful ones (*siddīqūn*), and his parents'

1 The latter citation does not add anything to the meaning inherent to *al-Raḥīm*, contrary to the previous two.

[punishment] will be lightened, even if they were idolaters.'[1] The story of Bishr al-Ḥāfī in this connection is well known.[2]

> Abū Hurayra related that the Prophet (may God bless him and grant him peace) said: O Abū Hurayra! When you perform ablution, say 'In the Name of God' and your guardian angels will continue to write down your good deeds until you finish. When you have intercourse with your wife, say 'In the Name of God' and your guardians will write down your good deeds until you cleanse yourself of impurity. If that intercourse should result in a child, you will be rewarded for every breath it takes, and for all the breaths of its progeny if it has any, until there is none left. O Abū Hurayra! When you mount a beast, say 'In the Name of God, and all praise is for God' so you will be rewarded for every step. When you board a ship, say 'In the Name of God, and all praise is for God' so you will be rewarded until you alight.[3]

Anas b. Mālik related that the Messenger of God said: 'The screen between the eyes of the jinns and the private parts of the children of Adam when they remove their clothes is to say "In the name of God, the Compassionate, the Merciful."'[4]

LESSON: if this Name is a screen between you and your enemies among the jinns in this life, will it not also be a screen between you and the Tormenters (*zabāniya*) of the Hereafter?[5]

Point 16

Caesar wrote to ʿUmar saying: 'I have a chronic headache, so send me a remedy.' ʿUmar sent him a cap. Whenever [Caesar] put it on, the headache would be soothed, but when he removed it, the pain would return. He was amazed at this, so he inspected it and found inside a slip of paper on which was written: *In the name of God, the Compassionate, the Merciful.*

1 Recorded in minor sources, and considered 'very weak, if not fabricated'—R.S.

2 It is related that 'the beginning of his conversion' from being a drunkard was finding a piece of paper with God's Name upon it, which he picked up and anointed with perfume. A pious person was then instructed in a dream to go to Bishr and say: 'You anointed Our Name, so We anoint you.' See Farīd al-Dīn ʿAṭṭār, *Tadhkirat al-awliyā'*, trans. Paul Losensky as *Farid ad-Din 'Attar's Memorial of God's Friends*, New York: Paulist Press, 2009, pp. 154–5.

3 'Extremely weak or fabricated'—R.S.

4 Recorded in Ṭabarānī's *Awsaṭ*—S.I.

5 That is, the angels appointed over Hellfire (see Q.XCVI.18). See also Point 23 below.

Point 17

The Prophet (may God bless him and grant him peace) said: 'Whoever performs ablution without mentioning the Name of God, that purification is for those limbs [only]; but whoever performs ablution [after] mentioning the Name of God, the purification is for his entire body.'[1] If remembrance coupled with ablution purifies the entire body, then remembering Him from the core of the heart is more than worthy of being purification of the heart from unbelief and innovation.

Point 18

Some [Magians] sought a miracle from Khālid b. al-Walīd, saying to him: 'You claim that Islam [is true], so show us a sign so we may become Muslim!' He said: 'Bring me some deadly poison.' They brought a saucer of poison, which he took in his hand, saying: 'In the Name of God, the Compassionate, the Merciful.' He consumed it all, then stood up, unharmed by God's will. The Magians said: 'This is a religion of truth!'

Point 19

Jesus son of Mary (peace be upon him) passed by a grave and witnessed the Angels of Torment punishing its inhabitant. On his return journey, he passed that grave to find the Angels of Mercy bearing dishes of light. He was surprised at this, so he prayed and asked Almighty God [for the explanation], and God inspired him thus: 'O Jesus, this servant was a sinner and was confined to My punishment since his death. He had left behind him a pregnant wife who gave birth to a son. When he was old enough, she sent him to school (*kuttāb*) where the teacher taught him to say "In the Name of God, the Compassionate, the Merciful". Therefore, I was ashamed to punish My servant with My fire in the depths of the earth while his son mentions My Name upon the face of the earth.'

Point 20

ʿAmra al-Farghāniyya—one of the leading mystics—was asked: 'What is the wisdom behind the menstruating woman and the ritually impure man being forbidden from reciting the Qur'ān, but not from the *tasmiya* ["In the Name of God"]?' She replied: 'The *tasmiya* is mentioning the Name of the Beloved, and the lover is never prevented from mentioning the Beloved.'

1 Recorded in the *Sunan* of Dāraquṭnī and others, but considered 'very weak'—R.S.

Point 21

It was said concerning His being *al-Raḥīm* that He is merciful to [the people] at six junctures: in the graves with their insects; at the Resurrection in its darkness; at the Scale with its measures; upon reading the Book and its terrors; at [the crossing] of the Path with its horrors; and in the Fire with its levels.

Point 22

A mystic wrote down *In the Name of God, the Compassionate, the Merciful*, and ordered that [on his death] it be placed in his shroud. It was said to him: 'What is the benefit in that?' He replied: 'I will say on the Day of Judgment: "God, you sent a book and made its title *In the Name of God, the Compassionate, the Merciful*. So treat me according to the title of your book."'

Point 23

It is said that there are two benefits in the fact that *bi'smi 'Llāh al-Raḥmān al-Raḥīm* is made up of nineteen letters:

a. The Tormenters [over Hell] are nineteen,[1] so God drives off their aggression by means of these nineteen letters.
b. God has created the night and day as twenty-four hours, and made obligatory five prayers which correspond to five of the hours. These nineteen letters act as expiation for the sins which occur in the remaining nineteen hours.

Point 24

Due to the fact that *Sūrat al-Tawba* contains the order to fight, *In the name of God, the Compassionate, the Merciful* was not written at the beginning of that chapter. Also, it is the Prophetic practice to say at the time of slaughtering [an animal]: 'In the Name of God, God is greater (*Allāhu akbar*)'—and not 'In the Name of God, the Compassionate, the Merciful'.

This is because fighting and killing do not accord with the mention of the Merciful. Therefore, the fact that He guided you to recite this word seventeen times every day in the obligatory prayers[2] signifies that He did not create you to kill or torment. Rather, He created you for mercy, kindness and generosity.

And Almighty God is the Guide to what is correct.

1 See Q.LXXIV.30.
2 This is on the assumption that one recites it once in each cycle of the five obligatory prayers.

BOOK III

The *Fātiḥa*[1]

1 Book III contains four introductory chapters, the last of which discusses juristic issues including those pertaining specifically to the *basmala*. These were followed originally by a final chapter consisting of two parts, but I have divided this into two: Chapter Five discusses the remaining verses of the *Fātiḥa*, and Chapter Six (as redesignated) contains thematic reflections upon the whole *sūra*.

Chapter One
NAMES OF THIS *SŪRA*

Name 1: *Fātiḥat al-Kitāb* (The Opening of the Book)
It has been so named because it opens the written copies (*maṣāḥif*), [circles of] teaching and recitation in the prayer. It is also said that the name is due to praise (*ḥamd*) being the opening of any speech, as shall be explained in due course;[1] or because it was the first *sūra* to descend from heaven.

Name 2: *Sūrat al-Ḥamd* (The Chapter of Praise)
This is because its first word is *al-ḥamd*.[2]

Name 3: *Umm al-Qur'ān* (The Source of the Qur'ān)
This is explained in a number of ways.[3]

FIRST: the *umm* of something means its 'origin' (*aṣl*). The purpose of the Qur'ān as a whole is to expound on four matters: Divinity; the Hereafter; prophethood; and affirming God's decree and preordainment. *All praise is for God, Lord of the worlds; the Compassionate, the Merciful* pertains to Divinity. *Master of the Day of Judgment* pertains to the Hereafter. *You we worship and from You we seek help* denotes negation of fatalism (*jabr*) and voluntarism (*qadar*), affirming that everything occurs by God's decree and preordainment.[4] *Guide us upon the straight path; the path of those on whom You have bestowed favour, not of those who incur wrath, nor of those who are astray* also denotes divine decree, along with prophethood. These matters will be explained in full. Since the greatest purpose of the Qur'ān is [to expound on] these four issues and this *sūra* contains them all, it was described as the *umm* of the Qur'ān.

1 See Chapter Five, Verse 1: *All praise is for God*. As part of that discussion, there is a slightly different explanation given for this name (Benefit 11).

2 However, the author argues at length in Chapter Four below that this is the *second* verse.

3 Although this name is often translated as 'mother', its everyday sense, this does not accord with the explanations provided. However, a mother is a 'source' in an obvious way.

4 Imām Rāzi does not explain this point under his exegesis of the verse itself (Chapter Five). Evidently, he is supporting a moderate version of *jabr*.

SECOND: the [contents of] all revealed books can be expressed as three aspects: praise of God upon the tongue; acts of service and obedience; and seeking unveilings and witnessing. *All praise is for God, Lord of the worlds; the Compassionate, the Merciful; Master of the Day of Judgment* —all this is praise of God. *You we worship*[1] indicates effort and striving in servitude, followed by: *and from You we seek help*, which represents the servant's admission of his impotence, lowliness and poverty [necessitating] his turning back to God. As for *Guide us upon the straight path...*, this is a petition for unveiling, witnessing and [all] types of guidance.

THIRD: another reason for this *sūra* being named *Umm al-Kitāb*[2] is that the purpose of any field of knowledge is to recognise either the might of Lordship or the lowliness of servitude. *All praise is for God, Lord of the worlds; the Compassionate, the Merciful; Master of the Day of Judgment* denotes that He is the deity with complete control over the affairs of this life and the Hereafter. Then the remainder of the *sūra* from *You we worship and from You we seek help* denotes the lowliness of servitude, in that the servant cannot attain any outward deeds or inward unveilings except by the help and guidance of God.

FOURTH: human [religious] knowledge consists of [three aspects]:[3] knowledge of God's Essence, Attributes and actions, which is the science of fundamentals (*uṣūl*); knowledge of God's rulings and commandments, which is the science of branches (*furūʿ*); and knowledge of internal purification, spiritual illumination and divine unveilings. The purpose of the Qur'ān is to elucidate these three aspects, and this noble *sūra* encompasses their exposition in a most complete manner.

All praise is for God, Lord of the worlds; the Compassionate, the Merciful; Master of the Day of Judgment indicates the science of fundamentals, in that His existence is denoted by the existence of His creations. *Lord of the worlds* implies that there is no way to realise His existence except through His being Lord of the worlds. *All praise is for God* implies that He is deserving of this praise, which would only be true if He is capable of all possibilities and knowledgeable of all things. Then He is described with the utmost of mercy—*The Compassionate, the Merciful*—and with

1 The printed edition cites here the entirety of verses 1–5, which does not seem to fit the context.

2 This particular expression appears in Q.III.7 in a distinct sense, and in Q.XIII.39 and Q.XLIII.4 in yet another.

3 This three-fold scheme of religious knowledge consists of beliefs (also known as *ʿaqīda*, the domain of *kalām* scholarship); jurisprudence (*fiqh*, which is considered to be secondary to those belief principles); and spirituality (and mysticism) with which *taṣawwuf* is concerned.

perfect ability: *Master of the Day of Judgment*, in that He will not overlook the case of the oppressed, but instead will extract their full rights from the oppressors. This portion concerns the knowledge of God's Essence and Attributes, which is the science of fundamentals.

This is followed by reference to the science of branches [i.e. positive law], which is to engage in service and servitude: *You we worship*. This is then accompanied by another aspect of fundamentals [i.e. belief], to the effect that the roles of servanthood will never be completed without the aid of Lordship.

Thereafter is an exposition of the stages of unveiling, which—despite their abundance— are contained within three matters:

a. For the guidance of light to obtain in the heart. This is the meaning of *Guide us upon the straight path*.
b. For the stages of the pious and pure ones—such as God has favoured with holy manifestations and divine attractions—to become manifest to [the heart], until those purified spirits become like polished mirrors and the rays reflect off each of them towards the others. This is His saying: *The path of those on whom You have bestowed favour*.
c. For [the spirits] to remain safe and protected from the stains of desires: *not of those who incur wrath*, and from the burdens of doubts: *nor of those who are astray*.

It is thus shown that this *sūra* contains all these lofty wisdoms which are the noblest enquiries. Thus it was named the *umm* of the Book, just as the brain is called the *umm* of the head because it encompasses all the senses and benefits.[1]

FIFTH: Thaᶜlabī said: I heard Abū al-Qāsim b. Ḥabīb saying: I heard Abū Bakr al-Qaffāl saying: I heard Abū Bakr b. Durayd saying:

> *Umm* in the language of the Arabs refers to the banner held aloft by the troops. Qays b. al-Khaṭīm[2] said: *naṣabnā ummanā ḥattā 'bdhaᶜarrū; wa-ṣārū baᶜda ulfatihim shilālā* ('We raised our banner until they dispersed and became scattered after their solidarity'). This *sūra* has been named the banner of the Qur'ān because it is the safe haven of the faithful, just as the troops hasten to

1 See the author's second explanation of *umm* in Q.CI.9.

2 The printed edition has 'al-Ḥaṭīm'. There are several variations from the narration as it appears in Aḥmad al-Thaᶜlabī, *al-Kashf wa'l-bayān* (*Tafsīr al-Thaᶜlabī*), ed. Abū Muḥammad b. ᶜĀshūr, 10 vols., Beirut: Dār Iḥyā' al-Turāth al-ᶜArabī, 2002, vol. 1, p. 127.

> the banner at the time of fear. The Arabs call the earth *umm* because the creatures return to it in their lives and upon their deaths.

It is also because [the verb] *amma* is used for one person going towards another.[1]

Name 4: *al-Sab*ᶜ *al-Mathānī* (The Seven Oft-Repeated)

God said: 'We have bestowed upon you seven *mathānī*' (Q.xv.87). There are a number of explanations for this name for the *sūra*:[2]

a. It is dual (*muthannā*): half is praise of the Lord by the servant, and the other half is the favour of the Lord upon the servant.
b. Due to it being repeated in every cycle of the prayer.
c. Due to the fact that it is excluded (*mustathnāh*) from the other [revealed] books. The Prophet (may God bless him and grant him peace) said: 'By the One in Whose hand is my soul, the like of this chapter was not revealed in the Torah, the Gospel or the Psalms, nor [elsewhere] in the Criterion [i.e. Qur'ān]. It is the Seven *Mathānī* and the Glorious Recital.'[3]
d. Due to the fact that it consists of seven verses, each being equivalent to one seventh of the Qur'ān in its recitation.[4] Therefore, whoever recites the *Fātiḥa*, God will grant him the reward of reciting the entire Qur'ān.
e. It is seven verses, and the gates of Hellfire number seven. Whoever opens his tongue by reciting it, for him the seven gates will be closed. This is evidenced by the narration[5] in which Gabriel (on whom be peace) said to the Prophet (may God bless him and grant him peace): 'O Muḥammad! I used to fear for your nation the torment, but my fears were allayed by the revelation of the *Fātiḥa*.' He asked, 'Why, O Gabriel?' He replied: 'Because Almighty God said: "Indeed, Hell is the promised abode for them all. To it are seven gates: for each of those gates is a portion assigned" [Q.xv.43–44].[6] Its verses are seven,

1 The relevance of this is not explained, and it does not appear in the edition of Thaᶜlabī. On a separate note, this verb is cited in some explanations of the word *Āmīn* which is said at the end of the *Fātiḥa*, i.e. 'O God! Direct goodness towards us.'

2 Although the clearest sense is its being 'repeated', there are other senses derived from the root *th-n-y*.

3 Recorded by Tirmidhī.

4 The relevance here is that each verse is 'paired' with a portion of the Qur'ān.

5 I could not source this narration.

6 It is perhaps of interest that this appears earlier in the same *sūra* containing the name under discussion.

so whoever recites them, for him each verse will be a barrier upon one of the gates of Hell, so your nation will pass over it in safety.'

f. Due to the fact that it is recited in the prayer and then paired with another *sūra*.
g. Due to the fact that it consists of words of praise (*uthniya*) and exaltations of Almighty God.
h. Due to the fact that God revealed it twice.[1]

I have explained this name at length in [the exegesis of] *Sūrat al-Ḥijr*.[2]

Name 5: *al-Wāfiya* (The Complete)

Sufyān b. ᶜUyayna used to refer to it by this name. Thaᶜlabī said that this is explained by the fact that it does not accept division: while any other *sūra* may be split over two cycles of prayer, such is not permissible with this *sūra*.

Name 6: *al-Kāfiya* (The Sufficient)

It is so named because it is sufficient without other [*sūras*], whereas others are insufficient without it. Maḥmūd b. al-Rabīᶜ narrated that ᶜUbāda b. al-Ṣāmit said: the Messenger of God (may God bless him and grant him peace) said: 'The Source of the Qur'ān is a replacement for all else, but nothing else is a replacement for it.'[3]

Name 7: *al-Asās* (The Foundation)

This is explained in several ways:

a. It is the first *sūra* of the Qur'ān, so it is like its foundation.
b. As we have explained, it contains the noblest meanings, which form the foundation.
c. The noblest worship—after faith—is the prayer. This *sūra* contains everything upon which faith depends, and prayer cannot be performed without it.

Name 8: *al-Shifā'* (The Cure)

Abū Saᶜīd al-Khudrī related that the Messenger of God (may God bless him and grant him peace) said: 'The Opening of the Book is a cure from every poison.'

1 See Chapter Two, Enquiry 1 below.

2 See the author's exegesis of Q.xv.87. This statement implies that the exegesis of the *Fātiḥa* was composed later, and there is other evidence of this. However, it could also be the case that the author intended to expand his explanations there (understandably), or that he added this remark later.

3 Recorded by Dāraquṭnī and al-Ḥākim—R.S. The Dār al-Ḥadīth edition is missing the word *umm*.

On one occasion, a Companion passed by a man who was suffering a fit, so he recited this *sūra* in his ear and he became well. When they mentioned this to the Messenger of God, he said: 'It is the Source of the Qur'ān, and it is a cure from every ailment.'[1]

I say: ailments are either spiritual or physical. After all, God described unbelief as a disease: 'In their hearts is a disease' (Q.ii.10). This *sūra* contains knowledge of fundamentals, branches and unveilings, so it is actually a cause for healing in all these aspects.

Name 9: *al-Ṣalāh* (The Prayer)

The Prophet (may God bless him and grant him peace) said: 'Almighty God said: "I have divided the Prayer between Me and My servant into two halves..."'[2]—in reference to this *sūra*.

Name 10: *al-Su'āl* (The Request)

It is narrated that the Messenger of God (may God bless him and grant him peace) quoted the Lord of Majesty saying: 'Whoever is kept busy by My remembrance from asking Me, I give him better than what I give to those who ask.'[3] God's friend [Abraham] (on whom be peace) enacted this[4] when he said: 'He Who created me, and it is He Who guides me...O my Lord! Bestow wisdom on me, and join me with the righteous' (Q.xxvii.78–83).

In this *sūra*, too, praise of God is at the outset, i.e. *All praise is for God* until *Master of the Day of Judgment*. Then comes the mention of servitude: *You we worship and from You we seek help*, concluding with the request for guidance: *Guide us upon the straight path*, which shows that the greatest objective is guidance in religion. It further shows that the garden of gnosis is better than the garden of bounties, in that God concluded this speech with 'Guide us', rather than 'Grant us Paradise'.

Name 11: *Sūrat al-Shukr* (The Chapter of Gratitude)

This is because it is praise of God for His bounty, generosity and kindness.

Name 12: *Sūrat al-Duʿā'* (The Chapter of Supplication)

This is because it contains: *Guide us upon the straight path*.

Thus concludes our exposition of these names. And God knows best.

1 These narrations are 'very weak', but the meaning is supported by a *ḥadīth* in Bukhārī—R.S.

2 Recorded by Muslim—S.I. This will be discussed at a number of points below, and further in Chapter Six, Section iv.

3 This preceded in Book II.

4 I.e. to engage in remembrance and praise before asking anything of God.

Chapter Two
VIRTUES OF THIS *SŪRA*

Enquiry 1 [Time of Revelation]

There are three opinions mentioned concerning the revelation of this *sūra*:

A. IT IS MECCAN.

Thaʿlabī narrated with his chain to ʿAlī b. Abī Ṭālib that he said: 'The Opening of the Book descended in Mecca from a treasure beneath the Throne.'[1] Thaʿlabī added: this is the opinion of the majority of scholars.

He further narrated with his chain that ʿAmr b. Shuraḥbīl said:

> The first thing to be revealed of the Qur'ān was: *All praise is for God, Lord of the worlds*. This was when the Messenger of God (may God bless him and grant him peace) confided in Khadīja that he feared something had afflicted him. She asked: 'What is that?' He replied: 'Whenever I am alone, I hear a voice saying: "Read!"' Then he went to Waraqa b. Nawfal and asked him about this occurrence, so Waraqa told him: 'When this voice comes to you, remain firm toward it.' Then Gabriel came to him and instructed: 'Say: *In the Name of God, the Compassionate, the Merciful. All praise is for God, Lord of the worlds…*'[2]

Furthermore, he narrated with his chain via Abū Ṣāliḥ that Ibn ʿAbbās said: 'The Messenger of God (may God bless him and grant him peace) stood and recited *In the Name of God, the Compassionate, the Merciful*, and [the men of] Quraysh said: "May God smash your mouth!"'[3]

1 Thaʿlabī, *Kashf*, vol. 1, p. 89. Also recorded by Daylamī.

2 In ibid., in place of *bi-iqra'* is *fa-afirr* ('so I flee'), which is more consistent with the subsequent instruction to 'remain firm', as well as the claim that the *Fātiḥa* was revealed before *Sūrat al-ʿAlaq* (XCVI).

3 This chain contains Kalbī and is therefore assumed to be 'fabricated'—S.I.

B. IT WAS REVEALED IN MEDINA.

Thaᶜlabī narrated with his chain to Mujāhid that he said: 'The Opening of the Book was revealed in Medina.' [Thaᶜlabī added] that al-Husayn b. al-Faḍl said: 'Every scholar makes an error, and this is the error of Mujāhid, as the scholars maintain the contrary for two reasons: first, *Sūrat al-Ḥijr* is Meccan by consensus, and it includes God's saying: "We have bestowed upon you seven oft-repeated (verses)" (Q.xv.87), i.e. the *Fātiḥa*, showing that He had already bestowed this *sūra*. Second, it is implausible that [the Prophet] had resided at Mecca for more than ten years without the *Fātiḥa*.'

C. IT IS MECCAN-MEDINAN

Some scholars said that it was revealed first at Mecca, and then again at Medina. This repeated revelation is why it is known as *mathānī*,[1] and it only occurred in this way to underline its honoured status.

Enquiry 2: Explaining its Virtue

Abū Saᶜīd al-Khudrī related that the Prophet (may God bless him and grant him peace) said: 'The Opening of the Book is a cure from poison.'[2] Ḥudhayfa b. al-Yamān related that the Messenger of God (may God bless him and grant him peace) said: 'God will send an inevitable punishment upon a people, then one of their schoolboys will recite: *All praise is for God, Lord of the worlds*. God will hear this and lift the punishment from them for forty years because of that.'[3]

Al-Ḥusayn said:

> Almighty God revealed 104 scriptures from Heaven, and endowed the four with all the knowledge in the hundred: these are the Torah, Gospel, Psalms and the Criterion [*al-Furqān*, i.e. the Qur'ān].[4] Then He endowed the Criterion with the knowledge of the four, then the *mufaṣṣal*[5] with the knowledge of the

1 See the previous chapter under 'Name 4'.

2 See the previous chapter.

3 This is also in Thaᶜlabī's *Kashf* and also considered a 'fabrication'—R.S.

4 The most common understanding of the Qur'ān being described as *al-Furqān* is that it 'distinguishes' truth from falsehood, and lawful from prohibited. However, another view—which Rāzī seems to prefer (see his commentary on Q.xxv.1)—is that it refers to the verses being revealed 'distinctly' and gradually.

5 This refers to the shorter *sūras* of the Qur'ān located at its latter part, starting from *Sūrat Qāf* (L).

> Criterion, then the *Fātiḥa* with the knowledge of the *mufaṣṣal*. Therefore, whoever knows the explanation of the *Fātiḥa* is like one who knows the explanation of all God's revealed scriptures. Whoever recites it, it is as though he has recited the Torah, the Gospel, the Psalms and the Criterion.[1]

I say: the reason for this is that the purpose of all divine scriptures is [to expound on] the sciences of fundamentals, branches and unveilings. As we have explained, this *sūra* contains a complete account of these three sciences.[2] Since these lofty objectives are fulfilled therein, it can certainly be said to contain all divine objectives.

Enquiry 3

It has been pointed out that there are seven letters which have not appeared in this *sūra*, namely *thā'*, *jīm*, *khā'*, *zāy*, *shīn*, *ẓā'* and *fā'*. This is because these seven letters imply [various types of] punishment:

a. The *thā'* implies woe and destruction (*thubūr*): 'This day plead not for a single destruction: plead for destruction oft-repeated!' (Q.xxv.14).
b. *Jīm* is the first letter of *Jahannam* (Hell): 'Indeed, Hell is the promised abode for them all' (Q.xv.43), and 'Many are the jinns and men we have made for Hell' (Q.vii.179).
c. The *khā'* was left out because it implies disgrace (*khizy*): '...the day that Allah will not permit to be disgraced the Prophet and those who believe with him' (Q.lxvi.8); 'This day, indeed, are the unbelievers covered with disgrace and evil' (Q.xvi.27).
d. The *zāy* and *shīn* were left out because they are the initials of *zafīr* (exhaling) and *shahīq* (inhaling): 'For them therein is (violent) exhaling and inhaling' (Q.xi.106). Moreover, *zāy* stands for *Zaqqūm*: 'Indeed, the tree of Zaqqūm will be the food of the sinful' (Q.xliv.43–44); and *shīn* stands for wretchedness (*shaqāwa*): 'Those who are wretched shall be in the Fire' (Q.xi.106).
e. The *ẓā'* was left out because [it stands for the evil 'shade' (*ẓill*) in:] 'Depart to a shadow (of smoke ascending) in three columns, (which yields) no shade of coolness, and is of no use against the (fierce) flame' (Q.lxxvii.30–31). It also signifies the blaze (*laẓā*): 'But no! There is the blaze, plucking out (his being) right to the skull!' (Q.lxx.15–16].

1 Also in Thaʿlabī's *Kashf*—S.I.

2 See Chapter One above, 'Name 3'.

f. The *fā'* was left out because it signifies the parting (*firāq*): 'On the day that the Hour will be established, that day shall they be sorted out' (Q.xxx.14). Also, 'Moses said to them: "Woe to you! Forge not a lie against God, lest He destroy you utterly by chastisement: the forger must suffer frustration!"' (Q.xx.61).[1]

OBJECTION: there is no letter which does not feature in some [word or another] that indicates a type of punishment: thus the above is of no benefit!

RESPONSE: the benefit is that God has described Hell, saying: 'To it are seven gates: for each of those gates is a portion assigned' (Q.xv.44). God has removed seven letters from this *sūra*, the initials of words of punishment, to signify that whoever recites it—while believing in it and knowing its realities—will become safe from the seven levels of Hellfire. And God knows best.[2]

1 The latter citation is not explained and may have appeared in error. However, the root for 'forgery' is *f-r-y*, which could explain the relevance.

2 For a critique of this response, see Ālūsī, *Rūḥ al-maʿānī*, vol. 1, p. 178.

Chapter Three
RATIONAL WISDOMS DERIVED FROM THIS *SŪRA*

Know that when God says *All praise is for God*, it is as though an enquiring person will ask: 'Since this is based on two things—the existence of God and that He is deserving of praise—what is the proof of each [premise]?'

Once this dual question is raised, it makes sense that God mentioned [two things] which serve as answers to it. The answer concerning the first part is: *Lord of the worlds*, and to the second: *The Compassionate, the Merciful; Master of the Day of Judgment*.

[Section 1: Proving God's Existence][1]

The [expanded] response to the first question contains a number of enquiries:

Enquiry 1

Our knowledge of the existence of anything is either immediate (*ḍarūrī*)[2] or discursive (*naẓarī*). It cannot be said that knowledge of God's existence is immediate, because we know—immediately—that we do not know of God's existence immediately. Therefore, this knowledge is acquired discursively and depends upon evidence. The only evidence for God's existence is that this perceived world—with its skies, earths, mountains, seas, minerals, plants and vegetables—is in need of one to plan it, bring it into existence, nurture it and maintain it. As such, *Lord of the worlds* is an allusion to the proof of the existence of the powerful and wise Deity.

There are some subtleties in this connection:

1 I have shifted and re-designated this 'Enquiry 1' as a section heading, because the author has described both levels in this chapter as *masā'il*. I have also chosen section names to reflect that the subsequent sections provide various outlines of the *Fātiḥa* which bring to light its subtle structure and coherence.

2 I have elsewhere used a more literal rendering: 'necessary'.

1. *Al-ʿālamīn* signifies everything besides God,[1] so *Lord of the worlds* alludes to the fact that everything other than Him is impoverished towards Him, and needs Him in order to come into existence and remain in existence. This means that every indivisible particle and individual substance, along with every single property, is a blinding and binding proof of the existence of the wise, powerful and pre-eternal God. It is as He said: 'There is not a thing but glorifies His praise; and yet you understand not their glorification' (Q.xvii.44).
2. God said *All praise is for God, Lord of the worlds*, rather than 'Creator of the worlds'. This is because people are in agreement that every non-eternal being is in need of such as brings it into existence, but they disagree concerning its dependence on that entity for its continued existence. Some said that a persistent existent does not need a cause. The *murabbī*[2] is the one who causes the continued existence of a thing and maintains it as long as it exists, so *Lord of the worlds* is a statement to the effect that all existents besides God are dependent on Him as long as they persist. In short, the dependence [of created things] on the Creator at the time of creation is an agreed-upon matter, but their continuous dependence on the Maintainer and Nurturer is the point of dispute. As such, the Almighty specified this aspect for mention, in order to affirm that everything besides Him cannot do without Him: neither at the point of creation, nor thereafter.
3. Since this *sūra* is named *Umm al-Qur'ān*,[3] it must serve as an origin and source, with the rest [of the Qur'ān] being like streams branching off from it. His saying *Lord of the worlds* signifies that every existent besides Him is a proof of His Divinity. Then there are four other *sūras* which open with 'All praise is for God':
   a. *Sūrat al-Anʿām*: 'All praise is for God, Who created the heavens

1 As the author mentions in point 3 below, this meaning is fulfilled by the singular *ʿālam*—according to the usage of the theologians. See also below Chapter Five, Verse 2: *Lord of the worlds*; and Muḥammad al-Ṭāhir Ibn ʿĀshūr, *Tafsīr al-taḥrīr wa'l-tanwīr*, 30 vols., Tunis: Dār Suḥnūn, n.d., vol. 1, p. 168. In Rāzī's Introduction, he affirms the possibility of there being 'one million worlds external to [our] world', yet he does not appear to have attached much significance to this word appearing in the plural here. The form *al-ʿālamīn* has been argued recently to be a Quranic coinage; see Bassam Saeh, *The Miraculous Language of the Qur'an*, trans. Nancy Roberts, London: International Institute of Islamic Thought, 2015, p. 53; and the second volume of the author's fuller Arabic work, *al-Muʿjiza*.

2 The word *Rabb* is said to contain the meaning of this active participle. This is not reflected in the translation 'Lord', but some translators used 'Guardian Lord' or 'Lord and Cherisher'. I have used words including 'nurture' and 'cultivation' in this context.

3 See Chapter One above, 'Name 3'.

and the earth and made the darknesses and the light' (Q.VI.1). This meaning is a portion of *Lord of the worlds* because the word *ʿālam* refers to everything besides God, and the heavens, earth, light and darkness are categories within that. As such, what is mentioned at the beginning of *al-Anʿām* is like a category within that which is mentioned at the beginning of the *Fātiḥa*.

Moreover, the beginning of *al-Anʿām* states that He created the heavens and the earth, while the beginning of the *Fātiḥa* states that He is the Lord of the worlds. We have already explained that once it is proven that the world is dependent on God's maintenance in order to remain in existence, it must be said to depend upon His creative power—*a fortiori*—at the time of creation. On the other hand, dependence at the time of creation does not entail dependence for continued existence. Therefore, it is seen that what is mentioned at the beginning of *al-Anʿām* is like a category of that found at the beginning of the *Fātiḥa*.

b. *Sūrat al-Kahf*: 'All praise is for God, Who sent upon His servant the Book' (Q.XVIII.1). This is a reference to cultivation of the spirits through knowledge, for the Book which He sent down upon His servant is the means to attain unveilings and witnessing. As such, this signifies spiritual cultivation (*tarbiya*) only, whereas the beginning of the *Fātiḥa*—*Lord of the worlds*—pertains to general cultivation of all the worlds. This encompasses the spiritual cultivation of the angels, humans, jinns and devils, as well as physical cultivation within the heavens and the earths. As such, what is mentioned at the beginning of *al-Kahf* is one species of what is mentioned at the beginning of the *Fātiḥa*.
c. *Sūrat Saba'*: 'All praise is for God, to Whom belong all things in the heavens and on earth' (Q.XXXIV.1). As He made clear at the beginning of *Sūrat al-Anʿām* that the heavens and the earth belong to Him, here at the beginning of *Sūrat Saba'* it is stated that the things contained within the heavens and the earth are His. This, too, is a sub-category of *All praise is for God, Lord of the worlds*.[1]

1 As Rufayda points out, Rāzī refers back to the exegesis of the *Fātiḥa* at the beginning of both *al-Kahf* and *al-Anʿām*. However, the beginning of *Saba'* has a fresh account which differs somewhat from this, as though the author 'was encountering a *sūra* with this opening for the first time'. See Rufayda, *al-Naḥw wa-kutub al-tafsīr*, vol. II, p. 841. This supports his theory that *Saba'* and *Fāṭir* are among the additions by Rāzī's student(s)—see the Translator's Introduction above.

d. [*Sūrat Fāṭir*:] 'All praise is for God, Who created (out of nothing) the heavens and the earth' (Q.xxxv.1). The beginning of *Sūrat al-Anʿām* states that He is the Creator (*Khāliq*), which is in the sense of plan and decree (*taqdīr*). Here, He is said to be the *Fāṭir* who brings its essences into being, which is a distinct matter. In any case, it is also a sub-category of *All praise is for God, Lord of the worlds*.

Furthermore, He mentioned in *al-Anʿām*, after His being the Creator of the heavens and the earth, that He is the Maker (*Jāʿil*) of darkness and light. In *Sūrat al-Malāʾika* [i.e. *Fāṭir*], the Attribute of Creator is followed by the mention of His making the angels into 'Messengers' [Q.xxxv.1]. Thus the creation of heavens and earth was followed, in *al-Anʿām*, by the making of lights and darknesses, whereas in *Sūrat al-Malāʾika* the creation of heavens and earth is followed in mention by the making of spirits. While these are remarkable wisdoms and lofty subtleties, they are only like species under the greatest ocean of *All praise is for God, Lord of the worlds*.

This is our explanation of how *Lord of the worlds* is like a statement to prove the existence of the pre-eternal God.

Enquiry 2[1]

As well as proof of God's existence, this phrase also denotes the transcendence of His Essence above location, spatiality and direction. We have explained that *al-ʿālamīn* refers to all that exists other than God, and this includes place (*makān*) and time (*zamān*). 'Place' is an expression for space (*faḍāʾ*), dimensions (*ḥayyiz*) and extended void (*farāgh*), while 'time' is an expression for the extension (*mudda*) by which priority and posterity obtain.[2]

The phrase *Lord of the worlds* entails that He is *Rabb* also of space and time, and their Creator and Originator. Since it is known that the existence of the Creator must precede that of the creation, it must be that His Essence existed before space and dimensions, and is transcendent above direction and spatiality. If it were to be the case that His Essence obtained after the existence of space, and came into being within one part of space, the very reality of His Essence would be overturned—and this is impos-

1 The following four enquiries are related to the question of God being deserving of praise: this question is addressed directly in Section II below.

2 It seems that the author is describing time here as a dimension comparable to space dimensions.

sible. In this way, *Lord of the worlds* denotes transcendence of the Divine Essence over location and direction.

Enquiry 3

This wording denotes that He is transcendent above subsisting in a substrate (*maḥall*) as the Christians and incarnationists (*ḥulūliyya*) claim. Due to the fact that God is Lord of the worlds and Creator of all besides Him, and because the Creator is prior to the creation, it follows that His Essence existed before any substrate and was in no need of one. As such, He must remain free of need of the substrate once it exists.

Enquiry 4

This verse also denotes that the God of the world is not a necessitating cause by nature (*mūjib bi'l-dhāt*),[1] but instead He acts by His volition. The proof of this is that something which acts by its nature is not deserving of praise or exaltation for any of its actions. You do not see a man who benefits from the heat of fire or the coolness of ice praising the fire or the ice! This is because the heating effect of the fire and the cooling effect of the ice are not by their power or choice, but by their very nature. Therefore, the declaration that He deserves praise proves that He acts voluntarily.

[Moreover,] we know that He acts by His own volition because, otherwise, the resultant effects would remain in existence as long as the necessitating cause exists, and this would preclude changes occurring in [those effects]. However, since we observe such changes taking place, we know that their Cause acts by power and volition, and not by nature. It follows that He deserves praise.

Enquiry 5

Since God has created the world in accordance with the interests of the servants and meeting their needs, skill and perfection are manifest in the upper and lower worlds. One Who performs an act of skill and perfection must necessarily be knowledgeable.

We have thus shown that *All praise is for God, Lord of the worlds* denotes the existence of the Deity Who is transcendent above space and place and from being subsistent in a substrate. Moreover, He must possess the utmost power, knowledge and wisdom.

1 This is related to the concepts of *ʿilla* and *fayḍ*.

[Section II: On Deserving Praise][1]

SECOND QUESTION: assuming that the existence of the powerful Deity is established, why have you said that He is deserving of praise and exaltation?

THE RESPONSE IS: *The Compassionate, the Merciful; Master of the Day of Judgment*. To explain: the servant in this life is always between two states: either in well-being and felicity, or pain, poverty and misery. If he is well and honoured, then the causes of this well-being and honour only came about by the creative act of God, so He is the Compassionate, the Merciful.

If, on the other hand, he is suffering and unwell, then that suffering and those ailments may be either from other servants, or from God.[2] If they are from the servants, then Almighty God has promised to extract justice from the oppressors on behalf of the oppressed on the Day of Judgment. If they are from God, then He has promised tremendous bounty and generous reward in place of every hardship which He sent upon any of His servants in this life.[3] Therefore, it must be that God is deserving of unlimited praise.

[From the preceding discussion,] it has become clear that the verses *All praise is for God, Lord of the worlds; the Compassionate, the Merciful; Master of the Day of Judgment* (Q.1.2–4) are ordered in such a way that the intellect is incapable of conceiving of finer or more perfect speech!

After completing the discussion of the Attributes pertaining to Lordship, the Almighty followed this by words relevant to servanthood.[4]

Know that the human being is composed of body and spirit. The body's function is as a vehicle for the spirit to acquire things of benefit to it. Thus the best situation for the body is when it performs deeds which aid the spirit in attaining felicities and the remaining spirituality.[5] Those deeds are such as denote magnification of the Deity and service of Him, and these constitute acts of worship (*ʿibāda*). Therefore, the best situation

1 This section (not originally designated as such) contains one account of the structure of the *Fātiḥa* (incorporating the argument from Section I), which is followed by two more accounts in Sections III and IV. See also Chapter Six below.

2 Presumably, this means: either due to the actions of human beings, or beyond human control (including such as are commonly termed 'acts of God').

3 That is, if they are patient with their trials.

4 These are referred to at the conclusion of this discussion as 'the two covenants', or the two sides of the one covenant, and this describes the overall structure of the *Fātiḥa*.

5 This seems to mean: to attain to the ideals of the spirit rather than the baser functions of the body.

for a servant in this life is to be engaged continuously in worship; and this is the first level of a person's felicity which is referred to in His saying: *You we worship*.

If he continues upon this level for a time, something of the lights of the Unseen world[1] will become manifest to him, namely that he cannot produce these acts of worship and obedience autonomously. Rather, without the grace (*tawfīq*) of Almighty God and His assistance and protection, he cannot do any of that. This is the middle level in [attaining to] perfection, which is referred to in: *and from You we seek help*.

If he then passes this station, it will dawn on him that guidance is only obtained from God, and the lights of unveiling and manifestation only occur by the guidance of God. This is what is meant by: *Guide us upon the straight path*. There are some subtleties in this connection:

1. The true method in beliefs and actions is [known as] 'the straight path'.[2]

   CONCERNING BELIEFS, the explanation of this is as follows:

   a. Whoever goes to extremes in declaring transcendence (*tanzīh*) ends up in negation (*taʿṭīl*) of His Attributes,[3] whereas one who goes to extremes in affirming (*ithbāt*) will end up in anthropomorphism (*tashbīh*) and affirming corporeality and location. These are the deviant fringes. As for the straight path, that is acknowledgement (*iqrār*)[4] which is free from anthropomorphism and reductionism.
   b. Whoever says that 'The servant's actions are wholly from himself' has fallen into voluntarism (*qadar*), while one who says that 'The servant has no agency' has fallen into fatalism (*jabr*). These are the deviant fringes, whereas the straight path is to affirm the servant's agency while acknowledging that everything takes place by divine decree.[5]

   CONCERNING ACTIONS: one who goes to excesses in fulfilling his lusts has committed indecency (*fujūr*), while one who goes too far in absti-

1 I.e. a realisation of essential knowledge.

2 Here, the sense is of the middle course between extremes. See also the author's exegesis of Q.II.143.

3 This could also be expressed by saying: 'Extreme deanthropomorphism results in reductionism.' See Book II, Chapter Four, Section III concerning this stance.

4 Of course, the author's method very often involves interpretation (*ta'wīl*) with reference to metaphorical usages. See his discussion of various Divine Names and Attributes in Book II, Chapters Four to Eight.

5 As noted previously, the author sometimes speaks positively of *jabr*, albeit in its moderated form.

nence ends up in frigidity (*jumūd*). The straight path is in the middle, namely temperance (*ʿiffa*). Also, whoever goes to extremes in acting upon anger is guilty of recklessness (*tahawwur*), whereas one who restrains it too much is guilty of cowardice (*jubn*). The straight path is in the middle, namely courage (*shajāʿa*).[1]

2. God described that straight path with two attributes: one affirmative, the other eliminative. The former is that it is the path of those on whom God bestowed favour: the Prophets, the truthful ones, the martyrs and the righteous.[2] The latter is that it is neither the path of those whose *active* faculties were corrupted by acting upon their lusts until they brought God's anger upon themselves; nor of those whose *intellectual* faculties were corrupted until they strayed from true creed and certain knowledge.[3]
3. Some have said: God did not suffice with saying *Guide us upon the straight path*, but followed it with: *The path of those on whom You have bestowed favour*. This indicates that the seeker has no way to reach the stations of guidance and unveiling except by following a guide (*shaykh*) who can direct him to the upright path and divert him from sources of error and misguidance. This is because the majority of people are overwhelmed by deficiency and their intellects cannot fulfil the task of discerning truth and distinguishing right from wrong. Therefore, the deficient is in need of one who is [relatively] complete whom he may follow until his intellect is strengthened by the light of the intellect of the complete one. Then he will reach the steps to felicity and the ascent to perfection.

What we have discussed [thus far] makes apparent that this *sūra* provides an explanation of what must be known concerning the covenant of Lordship and the covenant of servanthood. This is as God says: 'And fulfil your covenant with Me so that I fulfil My covenant with you' (Q.II.40).

[Section III: Second] Approach to the Subtle [Structure] of this *Sūra*[4]

Know that all situations within this world are a mixture of good and evil, of pleasant and unpleasant. This is a reality beyond doubt; yet we assert

1 Cf. *Al-Ghazālī on Disciplining the Soul*, p. 20.

2 See Q.IV.69.

3 This is similar to the designation of the former group as 'sinners' and the latter as 'unbelievers' in Section III below. See also Chapter Five, Verse 7: *Not of those…*

4 In the original text, this is labelled as 'Enquiry 2', i.e. in the broader structure of Chapter Three.

that despite the proliferation of evil, the good is in fact more abundant. While there is much illness, health is more plentiful; and despite hunger being widespread, satiety is of greater measure. Moreover, every rational person who observes his own condition will find it in constant upheaval and change from state to state. Yet he will find, too, that the predominant state of affairs is well-being, dignity, comfort and happiness. As for the unpleasant states, these—even if numerous—are less than those of pleasure, happiness and comfort.

Once you have known this, we say: those changes, insofar as they entail a [state] coming into being after its non-existence, denote the existence of the powerful Deity. Insofar as the predominant aspect is comfort and goodness, they denote that this Deity is merciful, kind and generous.

The way that these changes denote God's EXISTENCE is that every [person with a] sound innate nature (*fiṭra*) recognises that a thing which came into existence after non-existence must have had a cause. Thus if we hear of a house which appeared after not being there, our intellects would assert that there must be someone who carried out the construction of that house. Even if someone were to argue against this, we would not admit any doubt in the matter. The One Who effects these changing states must be capable (*qādir*),[1] since if He were a necessitating cause by His very nature, the effects would remain [constant] as long as He exists. As such, the effect coming into being after non-existence denotes the existence of a capable [voluntary] cause.

As for how they denote that this cause is MERCIFUL AND KIND, this is because—as we explained—the predominant aspect of these changes is comfort, goodness, happiness and well-being. One whose actions are predominantly ones of comfort, goodness, happiness and well-being must be merciful and kind—as such, He is deserving of praise.

Since these conditions are known to every person and present in every rational mind, the motivation to praise and exalt God is also present in every mind. For this reason, He taught them the means to praise Him, saying: *All praise is for God.*

After drawing attention to this station, He described another station which is greater and loftier than its predecessor. It is as though it is said:

1 Above (Section 1, Enquiry 4), this point was made with explicit reference to volition (*ikhtiyār*). However, the point is the same: God has the power/ability (*qudra*) to perform or leave any action according to His will.

> You should not suppose that the God in Whose praise you are engaged is your God only; rather, He is the God of all the worlds. After all, you concluded that you are dependent on God based on the poverty, need, createdness and contingency within your own self: yet these things are found throughout all creation. This is known from the fact that they are subject to motion and stillness, and all types of change. Since the cause of your need for the Divine Controller is present in all the worlds, and sharing in cause entails sharing in effect, it follows that He is *Lord of the worlds*, God of the heavens and earths, Controller of each and every creation.

Once this meaning has been established, it further becomes clear that the One Who is able to create these worlds in all their magnitude, and to create the Throne, the Footstool, the heavens and the planets—must likewise be capable of destroying them, and He must be in no need of them. Thus the One Who is powerful, controlling and autonomous possesses the utmost magnificence and grandeur. [On pondering this,] it occurs to the servant's heart: 'In all my lowliness and insignificance, how can I draw near to Him, and by which means can I approach Him?' At this point, God mentions that which serves as a remedy for this ailment, as though He says:

> O My weak servant! Even though I am great in power, majesty and divinity, I am also great in mercy. I am *The Compassionate, the Merciful* and I am *Master of the Day of Judgment*: as long as you dwell in this earthly abode, I shall never deprive you of My mercies and bounties; and when you die, I am the Master of the Day of Judgment and will not allow any of your works to go to waste. If you come to Me with good, I shall meet your single good with infinite multiples of goodness. Yet if you come to Me with sin, I shall meet it with pardon, magnanimity and forgiveness.

Then, having elaborated on the matter of Lordship in this way, He commanded [the servant] with three things:

1. THE STATION OF *SHARĪʿA* (LAW), i.e. to be constant upon outward actions, expressed by: *You we worship*.
2. THE STATION OF *ṬARĪQA* (PATH), i.e. to attempt the journey from the observable world to the Unseen world, seeing the observed world as though it were a vehicle to reach the Unseen. Thus a person knows

that none of the outward acts will be possible for him except by support which reaches him from the Unseen world, and he says: *and from You we seek help*.

3. [THE STATION OF *ḤAQĪQA* (REALITY):][1] to see the observable world as completely cut-off, as the command belongs solely to God. At this point, he says: *Guide us upon the straight path*.

Then there is a subtlety in this connection, namely that a single spirit is weaker and less effective than a large collectivity of spirits seeking after a single goal.[2] In this way, the servant realises that his spirit alone is insufficient to obtain the desired effect: so he associates it with the community of pure and holy spirits which are devoted to seeking spiritual unveilings and godly lights. Once he has connected to these spirits and been subsumed into that community, the request [for guidance] becomes stronger and the potential [to receive] more complete, and so he achieves through that collectivity what he could never have achieved alone. This is why he says: *The path of those on whom You have bestowed favour.*

Then, having made clear that connection to purified spirits brings about increased power and potential, it is further explained that connection to wicked spirits brings about disappointment, loss, misery and deprivation. This is why he says: *Not of those who incur wrath*, alluding to the sinners (*fussāq*); and *nor of those who are astray*, alluding to the unbelievers (*kuffār*).[3]

Once these three levels and stations have been perfected—the *Sharīʿa* signified by *You we worship*, the *Ṭarīqa* signified by *And from You we seek help*, and the *Ḥaqīqa* signified by *Guide us upon the straight path*—and the person attains felicity by connecting with the people of purity, and attains perfection by shunning the people of alienation and misery, then the ascension and perfection of the human being has reached its goal.

[Section IV: Third] Approach to the Subtle [Structure] of this *Sūra*[4]

Know that the human being is created with the need to obtain various types of benefit and pleasure, and to avert unpleasant and harmful things

1 This name is given below, and is known as the third of these stations in Sufi discourse.

2 This point can also be made with reference to the plural pronouns in *You we worship* and *Guide us*. See below Chapter Five, Verse 5: *You we worship*, Benefit 4.

3 Cf. the range of opinions cited in Chapter Five below, including the standard explanation which accords with a well-known *ḥadīth*.

4 Originally called 'Enquiry 3'.

from himself. This world is the world of means (*asbāb*), so it is not possible for him to obtain this benefit and pleasure unless through specific means.[1] Neither can he avert the ailments and harms without specific means. Since obtaining benefit and averting harm are desirable (*maḥbūb*) in their own right; and it is known through an inductive study of the conditions of this world that both of these depend upon specific means; and it is established rationally, furthermore, that anything which is a necessary condition to obtain something desirable is itself desirable—it follows that this [reality] is a cause for extreme love for these outward means to take root.

Thus if a person knows that he cannot obtain benefit and pleasure except by serving the ruler or his vizier, courtiers and supporters, then his heart will remain attached to these matters and full of love and desire to do so. It has been proven in [ethical] philosophy that frequent repetition of an action brings about an established trait; and that love of imitation is predominant in human nature. [To demonstrate] the former point: if someone performs a certain trade or profession constantly for a long period, it will become a strong and established skill on his part; the more he continues, the stronger that trait becomes. On the latter point: if someone sits with sinful people, his nature inclines towards sin—this is only because spirits have been created in such a way as to love imitation.

We have already explained that studying this world inductively [reveals that] the heart is attached inevitably to the outward means by which one can obtain benefits and avert harms. We have further shown that the more a person continues [to be attached to these means], the stronger this inclination and desire become in his heart. Moreover, the majority of this world's inhabitants possess this description and are constantly in this condition. We have explained that the souls have an innate love of imitation, which further establishes this condition. On the basis of all this, it is clear that the factors which create love of this world—inviting people to become attached to its means—are extremely numerous and powerful.

Then we say: if a person is fortunate enough to receive divine guidance to the right path, it occurs to him to ponder deeply upon these means, such that he says: 'Such-and-such ruler has taken control in this world, but has he done so through the perfection of his own power and wisdom? That is impossible, because the ruler might be the weakest and

1 That is, through the created things within the world. What follows is an explanation of how people become attached to the trappings of the world.

least intelligent of all people.' Thus it becomes clear to him that the ruler did not attain his sovereignty by means of his power or wisdom, but only because it was apportioned to him by the unstoppable decree of One Who is all-knowing and wise.

When the aforementioned is accompanied by further reflection which supports this conclusion, the resultant unveiling causes his heart to become detached from these apparent means. Instead, it turns for all its needs and desires to the Cause of all effects and the Opener of all doors. As these reflections and unveilings continue to grow in number, the person reaches a state in which he says upon receiving any goodness or benefit: '[God] is the Giver of benefit'; and whenever some evil or harm reaches him, he says: 'He is the Giver of harm.'[1] As such, he does not praise anyone for any action except God, and his heart does not direct itself to seek anything except from God. Thus all praise and exaltation becomes for God, and the servant says: *All praise is for God.*

The inductive process we mentioned leads the servant to realise that the conditions of this world cannot be in order except by God's decree. Then he ascends from the micro-world to the macro-world and recognises that nothing of the affairs of the universe can be in order unless by God's decree, and this is reflected in: *Lord of the worlds.* Thereafter the servant ponders upon the conditions of the universe and observes that the affairs of the worlds are organised according to the most perfect order and upright method. He sees that the very atoms declare God's perfect mercy, beneficence and generosity. At this, he says: *The Compassionate, the Merciful.*

After appreciating that all his interests in this life have been prepared by the mercy, beneficence and generosity of God, his heart nevertheless remains concerned over what will happen to him in the Hereafter. Therefore, it is as though it is said: 'The *Master of the Day of Judgment* is none other than the One you have known to be the Compassionate, the Merciful.' At this, the servant becomes at ease and his heart relaxes in the knowledge that the One Who has taken responsibility for his affairs in this life and the Hereafter is none but God. As such, his attention is no longer diverted to anything other than God, and his heart is attached to none but God.

When the servant's heart was attached to the ruler and vizier, he was engaged in their service. After completing any service, he would seek

1 For the names *al-Nāfiᶜ* and *al-Ḍārr*, see Book II, Chapter Five.

their help to fulfil his needs and bestow goodness upon him. Once this attachment is broken, he knows that whereas he used to serve the ruler and vizier, now devoting himself to serving the Deity is worthier. At this, he says: *You we worship*. This is to say: 'I used to worship other than You; but now I worship none but You.'[1] Whereas he used to seek help from the ruler and vizier for his needs, seeking help from the True God to fulfil all needs is worthier, so he says: *And from You we seek help*, i.e. 'I used to seek help from other than You; but now I seek help from none but You.' Whereas he used to seek from the ruler and vizier wealth and status, both of which are ever on the verge of perishing, it is now more fitting to seek guidance and knowledge from the Lord of heaven and earth. Therefore, he says: *Guide us upon the straight path*.

Now the people of this world comprise two types: those who worship none but God and seek help and the fulfilment of their purposes from none but Him; and those who serve the creation, seeking help and goodness from them. Therefore, the servant is bound to say: 'My God, make me from the first group, those whom You have favoured with these divine lights and spiritual insights; and do not make me from the latter group who have incurred wrath and gone astray, for their path leads to nothing but loss and destruction.' This is as Abraham (on whom be peace) said: 'Why worship that which hears not and sees not, and can profit you nothing?' (Q.xix.34). And God knows best.

1 This can be taken as a constant renewal of the covenant, even between one prayer and the next.

Chapter Four
JURISTIC ISSUES CONNECTED TO THIS *SŪRA*[1]

[Is Recitation Obligatory in Prayer?]

Enquiry 1

The majority agree that recitation [of the Qur'ān generally] is obligatory in the prayer. However, the contrary is narrated from al-Aṣamm and al-Ḥasan b. Ṣāliḥ.

The evidence for our position is everything we shall mention subsequently in support of recitation of the *Fātiḥa* being obligatory: as that entails that recitation in itself is obligatory. Here we shall mention some additional points:

1. God said: 'Establish regular prayers at the sun's decline till the darkness of the night, and the *qur'ān* of dawn' (Q.XVII.78). Here, *qur'ān* means 'recitation' (*qirā'a*), so the meaning is 'Establish the recitation of dawn,' and the apparent sense of the imperative entails obligation.
2. Abū al-Dardā' related that a man asked the Prophet (may God bless him and grant him peace): 'Is there recitation in the prayer?' He replied: 'Yes,' to which the questioner said: 'It is obligated.' The Prophet (may God bless him and grant him peace) [tacitly] approved this man's statement that it was obligated.[2]
3. Ibn Masʿūd related that the Prophet (may God bless him and grant him peace) was asked: 'Does one recite in the prayer?' He replied: 'Would it be prayer without recitation?'[3]

I have cited these two *ḥadīths* from the *Taʿlīq* of Abū Ḥāmid al-Isfarā'īnī.

1 The original title had 'derived from this *sūra*', but the adjustment reflects the nature of the questions raised. Although the author did not divide this lengthy chapter into sections, I have added topic headings to facilitate navigation.

2 The author has stated his source below, namely the *Taʿlīq* of Isfarā'īnī, a Shāfiʿī work of comparative jurisprudence. It is also recorded by Nasā'ī and Aḥmad.

3 An alternative reference was not found—R.S.

Al-Aṣamm's evidence is the Prophetic *ḥadīth*: 'Pray as you have seen me praying,'[1] in that the prayer is here described as something visible. Since recitation cannot be seen, it must be external to the prayer.

RESPONSE: when the 'seeing' (*ru'ya*) takes two objects [as here], it has the sense of 'knowing'.[2]

Enquiry 2

Shāfiʿī (may God have mercy on him) said that reciting the *Fātiḥa* is obligatory (*wājib*) in the prayer, so if a person leaves off a single letter which he was able to recite, his prayer is invalid. This is the view of the majority [of jurists]. However, Abū Ḥanīfa said that recitation of the *Fātiḥa* is not obligatory.[3]

There are various arguments to support our position:

1. The Prophet (may God bless him and grant him peace) was consistent throughout his life in reciting the *Fātiḥa* in the prayer, so it must be obligatory upon us according to these verses: '...and follow him' (Q.VII.158); 'Let those beware who withstand the Messenger's order' (Q.XXIV.63); and '[Say:] Follow me: God will love you' (Q.III.31).

   How strange it is that Abū Ḥanīfa took the view that wiping [at least the amount of] the forelock [in ablution] is obligatory, based on a solitary report (*khabar al-wāḥid*) stating that Mughīra b. Shuʿba related that the Prophet (may God bless him and grant him peace) came to the dumping ground of a certain people and urinated, then he performed ablution and wiped his forelock and his leather socks.[4] As this indicates that the Prophet wiped his forelock, [Abu Ḥanīfa] made this amount of wiping a prerequisite for the validity of prayer. However, in this case, the people of knowledge have conveyed through successive (*mutawātir*) transmission that the Prophet (may God bless him and grant him peace) consistently recited the *Fātiḥa*

1 Recorded by Bukhārī—R.S.

2 The first object is 'me', the second 'praying'. Therefore, following the author's argument, the translation should be: 'Pray as you have known me to pray'.

3 In Ḥanafī terminology, recitation of the *Fātiḥa* is *wājib*, which is an obligation but a degree below that of the *farḍ*, whereas these terms are synonymous in other schools. However, it is true that prayer without the *Fātiḥa* is in some sense 'valid' in the Ḥanafī school. See Abū Bakr al-Kāsānī, *Badā'iʿ al-ṣanā'iʿ fī tartīb al-sharā'iʿ*, ed. Muḥammad Tāmir, 10 vols., Cairo: Dār al-Ḥadīth, 2005, vol. 1, p. 503; Ḥasan al-Shurunbulālī & Aḥmad al-Ṭaḥṭāwī, *Ḥāshiyat al-Ṭaḥṭāwī ʿalā Marāqī al-falāḥ*, ed. Muḥammad al-Khālidī, Beirut: Dār al-Kutub al-ʿIlmiyya, 2009, p. 247.

4 Recorded by Bukhārī and Muslim—S.I. The Shāfiʿī school considers the obligation to be less than that. See Book I, Chapter Four, Enquiry 6 above; and Kāsānī, *Badā'iʿ al-ṣanā'iʿ*, vol. 1, p. 23.

[in prayer] throughout his life, yet [Abū Ḥanīfa] said that the prayer's validity does not depend on it. This is indeed an astonishing thing!

2. God said: 'Establish the prayer' (Q.vi.72) and prayer (*al-ṣalāh*) is a singular word with the [definite article] *al-*, such that its sense is 'that which is already familiar'. The Muslims are not familiar with anything called prayer other than those actions which the Messenger of God (may God bless him and grant him peace) used to perform. Therefore, the effective meaning of 'Establish the prayer' is: 'Establish that prayer which the Messenger used to perform.' The prayer which the Messenger (may God bless him and grant him peace) used to perform contained the *Fātiḥa*, so 'Establish the prayer' is a command to recite the *Fātiḥa*, and the apparent sense of a command is obligation. As this word has appeared in the Qur'ān more than a hundred times,[1] this is a binding proof that the *Fātiḥa* must be recited in the prayer.
3. The Rightly-Guided Caliphs[2] recited it consistently throughout their lives. This is supported by the *ḥadīth* in the two *Ṣaḥīḥ* collections[3] that the Prophet (may God bless him and grant him peace) as well as Abū Bakr and ʿUmar used to begin their recitation [in prayer] with 'All praise is for God, Lord of the worlds.' If this is so, then it must be obligatory upon us based on the Prophet (may God bless him and grant him peace) saying: 'Hold to my example (*sunna*) and the example of the rightly-guided caliphs after me,'[4] as well as: 'Follow the two after me: Abū Bakr and ʿUmar.'[5]

It is strange that Abū Ḥanīfa (may God be pleased with him) adopted the report of ʿUthmān [b. ʿAffān] concerning divorce by a person who is evading [being inherited] (*ṭalāq al-fārr*):[6] this

1 By my reckoning, the expression 'establish prayer' in various forms (including the imperative) appears forty-one times in the Qur'ān. See Muḥammad Fu'ād ʿAbd al-Bāqī, *al-Muʿjam al-mufahras li-alfāẓ al-Qur'ān al-karīm*, Tehran: Avand Danesh, n.d.

2 I.e. Abū Bakr, ʿUmar, ʿUthmān and ʿAlī.

3 I.e. Bukhārī and Muslim. See below under Enquiry 9: the author would interpret 'All praise is for God' here as a reference to the *sūra*, not its first verse in particular.

4 Recorded by Aḥmad and Ibn Mājah—R.S. It is cited again later with the completion: 'bite onto it with your molars'.

5 Recorded by Tirmidhī—R.S.

6 ʿUthmān as caliph granted inheritance to the former wife of ʿAbd al-Raḥmān b. ʿAwf, who had divorced her on his deathbed. The lack of objection from the Companions in this case is taken by the Ḥanafīs and others as indicative of consensus. See Kāsānī, *Badā'iʿ al-ṣanā'iʿ*, vol. iv, p. 559; Ibn Rushd, *The Distinguished Jurist's Primer*, vol. ii, p. 98. The (later) Shāfiʿī position is that such a divorcée does not inherit, based on Q.iv.12 and similar.

despite the fact that ʿAbd al-Raḥmān [b. ʿAwf] and ʿAbd Allāh b. al-Zubayr[1] had the contrary view, as well as the fact that the text of the Qur'ān necessitates that [this divorcée] does not inherit. Therefore, why did [Abū Ḥanīfa] not adopt the practice of all the Companions with their consensus upon the obligation of reciting the *Fātiḥa*, considering also that it agrees with the Qur'ān, narrations and reason?

4. Even though the Muslim nation (*umma*) has differed over the [technical] obligation of reciting the *Fātiḥa*, they have agreed upon it in practice. You will not find any of the Muslims of the West or the East who do not recite the *Fātiḥa* in their prayers. If that is so, then we say: whoever should pray without the *Fātiḥa* would be abandoning the path of the believers and would fall under the verse: 'Whoever...follows a path other than that of the believers, We shall leave him in the path he has chosen, and land him in Hell: what an evil refuge!' (Q.IV.115).

   OBJECTION: those who believed that it is not obligatory still recited it in the belief that it is recommended: so there was never a consensus on its recitation being obligatory.

   RESPONSE: the acts of the limbs are distinct from the acts of the hearts.[2] We have shown that everyone has agreed on acting upon this recitation. Therefore, whoever does not recite [the *Fātiḥa*] would be acting contrary to the believers' path and the warning [in the verse] would apply to him. This is enough to establish this proof; we are in no need here to claim consensus of belief in its obligation.

5. The famous Prophetic *ḥadīth* in which God is [quoted as] saying: 'I have divided the Prayer between Me and My servant into two halves. So when the servant says *All praise is for God, Lord of the worlds*, God says: "My servant has praised Me"...' The relevance of this is that God has stated that every prayer is divided between Him and the servant into two halves, and that this division has only occurred due to the verses of this *sūra*. Therefore, as the prayer is always so divided, and the division is dependent upon this *sūra* [being recited therein]—and the concomitant of a concomitant is itself a concomi-

1 The latter expressed that he disagreed with ʿUthmān's ruling, as recorded by Bayhaqī.

2 That is, the argument here concerns the actual recitation, not anyone's opinion as to its obligation or otherwise.

tant[1]—it follows that this *sūra* must be a concomitant of the prayer. This is only the case if we say that reciting the *Fātiḥa* is a condition for the prayer to be valid.

6. The Prophet (may God bless him and grant him peace) said: 'There is no prayer except with the Opening of the Book.'[2]

   OBJECTION: [the Ḥanafīs] said that the negating particle (*lā*) has entered upon 'prayer', and that [absolute negation] is not possible, so it must be interpreted as pertaining to a particular ruling of the prayer. Interpreting it in terms of validity is not worthier than interpreting it in terms of perfection.[3]

   RESPONSES:

   a. Some narrations have it that 'There is no prayer *for one who* does not recite the Opening of the Book.' Here, the negation is not of the prayer itself, but of it transpiring with respect to that person. This refers to his deriving benefit from that prayer and discharging the obligation upon him thereby. On this basis, the negation can be applied in its apparent sense.
   b. For those who believe that the recitation of the *Fātiḥa* is an integral part of the prayer: if the *Fātiḥa* is not recited, the quiddity of prayer does not obtain. This is because the quiddity cannot obtain in the absence of any of its integrals. On this basis, their claim that the negating particle cannot enter upon the referent of the word 'prayer' would only hold true if they established that the *Fātiḥa* is not an integral of the prayer, which is the origin of the contention.[4] It is thus shown that—upon our view—the [negation] can be applied in its apparent sense.
   c. Suppose that the [negation] cannot be applied in its apparent sense (*ẓāhir*): nevertheless, there is consensus that when it is not possible to act upon the literal meaning (*ḥaqīqa*) and there are two metaphorical (*majāz*) usages—one of them closer to the literal meaning than the other—it is necessary to interpret the word in terms of the closer metaphorical meaning. If this is so, then the correspondence (*mushābaha*) between the non-existent and

1 *Lāzimu al-lāzimi lāzimun*, i.e. if A must have B, and B must have C, then A must have C.

2 Recorded by Bukhārī and Muslim with the wording cited subsequently by the author: 'There is no prayer *for one who* does not…' This first wording is weaker in attestation.

3 That is to say: it cannot mean that the prayer is not there at all (physically), but must mean either that it is not valid, or not perfect. The Ḥanafīs adopt the latter view.

4 That is, they are begging the question.

the invalid existent is more pronounced than that between the non-existent and the valid-but-imperfect existent. Therefore, interpreting the [negation] in terms of validity is more apt.

d. Interpreting it as negation of validity is more apt for several [other] reasons: first, the default is to maintain things upon their previous state.[1] Second, the aspect of prohibition is preponderant. Third, this is more cautious.

7. Abū Hurayra related that the Prophet (may God bless him and grant him peace) said: 'Any prayer in which the Opening of the Book is not recited is deficient (*khidāj*),[2] incomplete.'[3]

   OBJECTION: [the Ḥanafīs] said that *khidāj* signifies deficiency, so this does not denote negation of validity.

   RESPONSE: it does indeed denote negation of validity. This is because the obligation (*taklīf*) of the prayer exists, and—by default—it continues to exist until we go against that default by performing the prayer perfectly. In contrast, if the prayer is performed in a deficient manner, that obligation would not be discharged.

   This is supported by the fact that Abū Ḥanīfa considered a fast on the day of ʿĪd to be valid, but not if the person intended it to make up a missed fast of Ramaḍān. He explained [the latter] in that the obligation upon him [in Ramaḍān] was a perfect fast, whereas fasting on this day must be imperfect [due to its prohibition]. It follows that making up the fast in this way does not discharge the obligation. If this is so, then we ask: why did [Abū Ḥanīfa] not say the same in this scenario?

8. Shaykh Abū Ḥāmid [al-Isfarā'īnī] narrated in his *Taʿlīq* from Ibn al-Mundhir, that he narrated via his chain to Abū Hurayra that the Prophet (may God bless him and grant him peace) said: 'A prayer in which the Opening of the Book is not recited is not acceptable.'[4]

9. Rifāʿa [b. Rāfiʿ] b. Mālik related[5] that a man entered the mosque

1 This is a juristic maxim: *al-aṣl baqā' mā kān ʿalā mā kān*.

2 This root is used for a premature or miscarried foetus.

3 Recorded by Muslim—R.S.

4 In *al-Awsaṭ* of Ibn al-Mundhir, and others—S.I.

5 This famous *ḥadīth* is from Rifāʿa in various sources, and from Abū Hurayra in Bukhārī. This narration names the *Fātiḥa* explicitly, whereas the wording cited below under Enquiries 11 and 12 is 'whatever is easy': Rāzī takes this to refer to the *Fātiḥa* (see point 11 below).

and prayed; when he finished [...][1] the man then said: 'Teach me the prayer, Messenger of God.' The Messenger (may God bless him and grant him peace) said: 'When you turn to the *qibla*,[2] pronounce the *takbīr*[3] and recite the Opening of the Book.' Its relevance is that it contains an imperative, which denotes obligation. Moreover, the man said 'Teach me the prayer,' so everything described thereafter by the Messenger (may God bless him and grant him peace) must be integral to the prayer. Since he mentioned recitation of the *Fātiḥa*, it must be one of the integrals of the prayer.

10. It is narrated that the Prophet (may God bless him and grant him peace) said: 'Shall I not inform you of a *sūra* the like of which is not found in the Torah, the Gospel or the Psalms?' They said: 'Yes.' He said: 'What is it you recite in your prayers?' They replied: 'All praise is for God, Lord of the worlds'. He said: 'It is this.'[4] Its relevance is that they replied to the question about what they recite in their prayer by saying 'All praise is for God,' which shows that this was the widespread practice of the Companions, i.e. none of them would pray without this *sūra*. Hence it was a known consensus between them.

11. God said: 'So recite of the Qur'ān what is easy for you' (Q.LXXIII.20).[5] Its relevance is that it contains a command to 'recite', and this denotes obligation: so reciting what is easy from the Qur'ān is obligatory. The meaning of 'what is easy' may either be the *Fātiḥa* or something other than the *Fātiḥa*; or it may indicate a [person's] choice between the two. If it refers to the *Fātiḥa*, then it specifically is obligatory, which is our stance.

The second possibility entails that something other than the *Fātiḥa* is specifically obligatory upon us: but that is false by consensus. The third possibility entails that the person has the [free] choice to recite the *Fātiḥa* or something else, which is also false by consensus, as the Muslim nation is in agreement that the *Fātiḥa* is worthier [of being recited here] than anything else. Abū Ḥanīfa conceded that prayer without recitation of the *Fātiḥa* is deficient and incomplete—and it is not permissible to give [free] choice between deficient and perfect.

1 The details of the account have been omitted: the Bedouin man was sent by the Prophet to repeat his prayer several times, until he admitted that he needed to be taught.

2 The direction of the Kaʿba in Mecca.

3 To say *Allāhu akbar* ('God is greater').

4 This is the same *ḥadīth* as in Chapter One, 'Name 4'.

5 This is also a key evidence cited by the Ḥanafīs: see below.

Know that God has described the *Fātiḥa* as 'what is easy from the Qur'ān' because this *sūra* is memorised by all accountable Muslims, so it is readily available to them all. Every other *sūra* may be memorised or otherwise, so it is not readily available to everyone.[1]

12. The command [to establish] the prayer exists, and—by default—it continues to exist until we go against that default by performing the prayer complete with the *Fātiḥa*. This is because the Prophetic *ḥadīth*s denote that *Sūrat al-Fātiḥa* is superior to other *sūra*s, and because the Muslims are in consensus that prayer containing it is more complete than that without it. Therefore, if this *sūra* is not recited, [the command] would remain upon its default [i.e. undischarged].
13. Reciting the *Fātiḥa* results in discharging the obligation [of prayer] as a matter of certainty. It is therefore more cautious, and it must be deemed an obligation due to text and reason. The textual reference is that the Prophet (may God bless him and grant him peace) said: 'Leave what makes you doubt for that which does not make you doubt.'[2] As for reason, it is that [such caution] averts the harm of fear [and worry] from one's self, and averting harm from one's self is obligatory.

   OBJECTION: if we were to believe that [reciting the *Fātiḥa*] is obligatory, it would still be possible that we are mistaken, so the fear remains.

   RESPONSE: [granted,] belief in its obligation results in this hypothetical fear, but so does belief that it is not obligatory, so these two harms balance each other. However, in practice, reciting it does not result in fear, whereas not reciting it does. It is thus seen that the cautious approach is to act upon it.
14. If prayer were valid with or without the *Fātiḥa*, there would be no preference for prayer with the *Fātiḥa*, because being constant on such a prayer would mean—effectively – abandoning the rest of the *sūra*s, and such is not permissible. Yet there is consensus that prayer with this *sūra* is superior: so it follows that prayer without it is impermissible.
15. There is consensus that the bowing (*rukūʿ*) and prostration (*sujūd*) may not be replaced with alternatives. Therefore, it must be impermis-

1 I.e. in perfect ease without the need for a page from which to read. I have opted for this rendering of *mutayassira* to avoid a potential discord with God's declaration that He has made the Qur'ān easy for remembrance (Q.LIV.17, 22, 32, 40).

2 Recorded by Tirmidhī and others—R.S.

sible to replace the *Fātiḥa* with an alternative; the common factor being caution.

16. The default is for obligation to remain in force. Therefore, the claim that prayer without the *Fātiḥa* would discharge this obligation must be established either by text (*naṣṣ*) or analogy (*qiyās*). The former is negated, as the text that [Ḥanafīs] cite in this regard—'So recite of the Qur'ān what is easy for you' (Q.LXXIII.20)—is, as we have explained, a proof on our side. As for analogy, this too is negated because the prayer is predominantly in the domain of worship (*taʿabbud*), in which analogy is not appropriate.[1]
17. Since it is established that the Prophet (may God bless him and grant him peace) was constant in reciting [the *Fātiḥa* in prayer] throughout his life, reciting other than the *Fātiḥa* must be considered to be an innovation contrary to following [his way]. Such is forbidden by his saying: 'Follow and do not innovate'[2] and 'The best way (*hady*) is the way of Muḥammad, and the worst of affairs are invented matters.'[3]
18. It is either the case that prayer with or without the *Fātiḥa* is equivalent in virtue, or that prayer with the *Fātiḥa* is superior. The former is false by consensus, because the Prophet (may God bless him and grant him peace) was consistent in praying with the *Fātiḥa*. Therefore, the latter must be true. Thus we say: praying without the *Fātiḥa* amounts to foregoing the additional virtue without any replacement. It should thus be impermissible to do this, as it is distasteful by custom (*ʿurf*) and therefore distasteful according to religion (*sharʿ*).

ABŪ ḤANĪFA supported his view with Qur'ān and *ḥadīth*. The former is the verse: 'So recite of the Qur'ān what is easy for you' (Q.LXXIII.20). The latter is the narration of Abū ʿUthmān al-Nahdī via Abū Hurayra that he said: 'The Messenger of God (may God bless him and grant him peace) ordered me to go out and declare: "There is no prayer without recitation, even if it be the Opening of the Book."'[4]

THE RESPONSE concerning the verse is as we have already explained: it is among the strongest proofs for our position [...].[5] As for the *ḥadīth*,

1 The term *taʿabbud* is used for acts performed out of pure obedience to the Lawgiver, as their specifications are beyond the domain of reason.

2 This is a saying of Ibn Masʿūd, also attributed to other companions—R.S.

3 Recorded by Muslim—R.S.

4 This version (with slight variation) is in Abū Dāwūd—R.S.

5 Here, the printed edition reproduces the points from proof 11 above, verbatim; I have removed them for brevity.

there is a conflicting narration from Abū Hurayra in which he said: 'The Messenger of God (may God bless him and grant him peace) ordered me to go out and declare: "There is no prayer except with the Opening of the Book."'[1] (Moreover, why could it not be said that the meaning of 'even if it be the Opening of the Book' is that one may suffice by reciting it alone?)[2] Once it is shown that there is a conflict [of narrations], the preponderance must be for our stance because it is better and more cautious. And God knows best.

Enquiry 3

Given that Abū Ḥanīfa and his companions were of the opinion that recitation of the *Fātiḥa* [in prayer] is not obligatory,[3] it is natural that they had different opinions concerning the amount of recitation [which is obligatory]. Abū Ḥanīfa said that a single verse (*āya*) is sufficient, such as *alif-lām-mīm*,[4] *ḥā-mīm*[5] and *wa'l-ṭūr'* (Q.LII.1) or *mud-hāmmatān*[6] (Q.LV.64). On the other hand, Abū Yūsuf and Muḥammad [al-Shaybānī] said that the minimum is three short verses or one lengthy verse such as the Debt Verse [Q.II.282].

[Is the *Basmala* a Verse of Qur'ān?]

Enquiry 4

Shāfiʿī said that *In the Name of God, the Compassionate, the Merciful* is a verse at the beginning of *Sūrat al-Fātiḥa*, and must therefore be recited with the *Fātiḥa*.

Mālik and Awzāʿī (may God be pleased with them) said that it is not part of the Qur'ān except in *Sūrat al-Naml* [Q.XXVII.30], so it is not recited—neither audibly nor inaudibly—except in the night prayers during Ramaḍān, in which [one] does recite it.[7]

As for Abū Ḥanīfa, he did not discuss this explicitly. What he said

1 This version is also in Abū Dāwūd, as well as the *Musnad* of Aḥmad—R.S.

2 I have placed this in parenthesis because it interrupts the apparent connection between the sentences on either side. It is possible that it began life as a marginal comment from the author or a student.

3 As before, to say that it is 'not *wājib*' in the Ḥanafī view is imprecise, as they say that it is *wājib* but not *farḍ*.

4 These letters constitute the first verse of *sūras* II, III and XXIX–XXXII.

5 These letters constitute the first verse of *sūras* XL–XLVI.

6 We have adjusted the transliteration to avoid the letters 'd' and 'h' appearing to be the single letter 'dh'.

7 Cf. the later clarification that Mālik permitted its recitation in any optional prayer.

is that one is to recite it, but inaudibly.[1] He did not advance an opinion concerning its being a verse of the *sūra* or otherwise. Yaᶜlā[2] said: 'I asked Muḥammad b. al-Ḥasan concerning "In the Name of God, the Compassionate, the Merciful," and he said: "Everything between the two covers is Qur'ān." So I asked him: "Why do you read it inaudibly?" He did not reply.' Karkhī said: 'I have not encountered this issue being discussed by our early [Ḥanafī] companions, but their instruction to recite it inaudibly indicates that it is not part of the *sūra*.' Some Ḥanafī jurists said that Abū Ḥanīfa and his companions opted not to delve into this enquiry because the question of whether or not the *tasmiya*[3] is part of the Qur'ān is a tremendous issue, so it is better to remain silent in this regard [in the absence of decisive evidence].

In fact, this enquiry encompasses three issues:

1. Is it a matter open to scholarly opinion (*ijtihād*) such that it is permissible to use non-decisive texts (*ẓawāhir*) and solitary (*āḥād*) reports as evidence, or is it instead a definitive (*qaṭᶜī*) matter?
2. Assuming that it is open to opinion, what is the truth of the matter?[4]
3. Is it to be recited audibly or inaudibly?[5]

Let us discuss each of these in turn.

Enquiry 5

We shall explain that this is not a definitive matter. However, Qāḍī Abū Bakr [al-Bāqillānī] claimed that it is definitive, saying: 'As for committing error in this regard, if it is not as serious as to make someone an unbeliever (*takfīr*), then it is no less than to make someone a sinner (*tafsīq*).'[6]

His reasoning is that if the *tasmiya* were from the Qur'ān, it would be established by either mass transmission (*tawātur*) or solitary (*āḥād*) reports. The former is negated by the fact that if it had been so, we would know by necessity that it is part of the Qur'ān and there would not have been any dispute among the Muslim nation. The latter is negated because solitary

1 In the predominant view, this means a manner in which only the speaker can hear his own recitation.

2 Based on the time period, I suggest this refers to Yaᶜlā b. ᶜUbayd al-Ṭanāfisī.

3 As seen previously, this is an epithet for this formula/verse, along with *basmala*.

4 See Enquiry 6 below.

5 See Enquiry 9.

6 Cf. Abū Bakr al-Bāqillānī, *al-Intiṣār li'l-Qur'ān*, ed. ᶜUmar Ḥasan al-Qiyyām, 2 vols., Beirut: Mu'assasat al-Risāla, 2004, vol. I, pp. 185 and 196–7. Also cf. Ibn Rushd, *The Distinguished Jurist's Primer*, vol. 1, p. 138: the translator failed to identify the *Qāḍī* cited there.

reports deliver no more than speculation (*ẓann*):[1] therefore, if we took such as sufficient to prove [verses of] the Qur'ān, then the Qur'ān would fall from its status as a decisive proof and it would become speculative. If that were permitted, then so would be the claim of the Rāfiḍīs[2] that the Qur'ān has been subject to addition, deletion, change and distortion—and that would be the undoing of Islam.

Shaykh Ghazālī parallelled the Qāḍī's [argument] when he said: 'If *negation* of the *tasmiya* being from the Qur'ān were established by mass transmission, then there ought to be no dispute; but if it were established by solitary reports, the Qur'ān would become speculative.'[3] He then presented a potential objection to this effect: '[Saying] that it is *not* from the Qur'ān is a negation, so there is no need to establish this negation textually as that is the default. As for the claim that it *is* from the Qur'ān, that is affirmation, so it depends on textual proofs.'

[Ghazālī] responded to this, saying: 'Although [your stance] is negation, the fact that the *tasmiya* is written in the same script as the Qur'ān gives the impression that it is part of the Qur'ān. Therefore, we cannot rule that it is *not* Qur'ān without independent evidence, and the original contention remains intact: the way [to establish either stance] must be either mass or solitary transmission. Thus the argument made by the Qāḍī applies [equally] to him—and this is the last to be said in this connection.'

MY OPINION on the matter is that the fact of *In the Name of God, the Compassionate, the Merciful* being revealed by God to Muḥammad (may God bless him and grant him peace) is indeed established by mass transmission, as is the fact of it being written down in the codex (*muṣḥaf*) along with the Qur'ān. As such, there is no consequence of it being Qur'ān or not-Qur'ān other than some juristic rulings pertaining specifically to the Qur'ān. For example, is its recitation obligatory in the prayer? Is it permissible for a person in a state of major ritual impurity (*junub*) to recite it? May a person in a state of minor ritual impurity (*muḥdith*) touch its [writing]?

1 As opposed to certain knowledge (*yaqīn*) which is required for the Qur'ān.

2 I.e. Shiʿi extremists. See the introduction to Etan Kohlberg & Mohammad Ali Amir-Moezzi, eds., *Revelation and Falsification: The Kitāb al-qirā'āt of Aḥmad b. Muḥammad al-Sayyārī*, Leiden: Brill, 2009.

3 This may be from Ghazālī's *Mustaṣfā*, but I did not locate this exact quote. It should be noted that Bāqillānī was expressing a Mālikī view, whereas Ghazālī was defending the Shafiʿī stance. The 'parallel argument' (*muʿāraḍa*) was therefore intended to turn the argument on its head. See Ibn ʿĀshūr, *al-Taḥrīr wa'l-tanwīr*, vol. 1, p. 139.

It is known that these are all matters open to scholarly opinion. Therefore, since the effect of the question of it being Qur'ān or otherwise is limited to these juristic implications which are themselves open to opinion, the overall enquiry is seen to be open to opinion (*ijtihādī*) rather than definitive, the Qāḍī's hyperbole notwithstanding.

Enquiry 6

Is the *tasmiya* [in fact] part of the Qur'ān, and is it a verse of the *Fātiḥa*? The reciters of Medina and Baṣra, along with the jurists of Kūfa, said that it is not part of the *Fātiḥa*.

On the other hand, the reciters of Mecca and Kūfa, as well as most jurists of the Ḥijāz, said that it is a verse of the *Fātiḥa*. This is also the position of Ibn al-Mubārak and Thawrī, and is supported by the following evidences:

1. Shāfiʿī narrated via Muslim [b. Khālid], from Ibn Jurayj, from Ibn Abī Malīka that Umm Salama said: 'The Messenger of God recited the Opening of the Book and counted *In the Name of God, the Compassionate, the Merciful* as a verse; then *All praise is for God, Lord of the worlds* as a verse; then *The Compassionate, the Merciful* as a verse; then *Master of the Day of Judgment* as a verse; then *You we worship and from You we seek help* as a verse; *Guide us upon the straight path* as a verse; then *The path of those on whom You have bestowed favour, not of those who incur wrath, nor of those who are astray* as a verse.'[1] This is an explicit text [on the matter].
2. Saʿīd al-Maqbarī narrated via his father from Abū Hurayra that the Messenger of God (may God bless him and grant him peace) said: 'The Opening of the Book is seven verses: their first is *In the Name of God, the Compassionate, the Merciful.*'[2]
3. Thaʿlabī reported in his exegesis[3] via his chain to [Ibn] Burayda,[4] from his father, who said: 'The Messenger of God (may God bless

1 The wording 'recited the Opening of the Book' is specific to Rāzī, according to Ālūsī, *Rūḥ al-maʿānī*, vol. 1, p. 190; the *ḥadīth* is recorded by Dāraquṭnī and other sources with 'his recitation' and describes how the Prophet would stop after each of these verses.

2 Recorded in Bayhaqī's *Shuʿab al-īmān*; but it is more likely to be a saying of Abū Hurayra himself —R.S.

3 I.e. *al-Kashf wa'l-bayān*. The reports from this and the following proof are all from this source.

4 The printed editions have 'Abī Burayda' (also in Thaʿlabī, *al-Kashf*, vol. 1, p. 102), but I have corrected it with reference to ʿAbbās Ṣaqr & Aḥmad ʿAbd al-Jawwād, eds., *Jāmiʿ al-aḥādīth*, 21 vols., Beirut: Dār al-Fikr, 1994, vol. III, p. 347. The narrator from the Prophet is Burayda, and his son Sulaymān narrated from him. See also Ālūsī, *Rūḥ al-maʿānī*, vol. 1, p. 184.

him and grant him peace) said: "Shall I not tell you of a verse which did not descend upon anyone after Solomon son of David other than me?" I said: "Yes, do." He said: "What is the first of the Qur'ān when you commence the prayer?" I replied: "In the Name of God, the Compassionate, the Merciful," to which he said: "It is this."' This report denotes that the *tasmiya* is part of the Qur'ān.

4. Thaʿlabī reported via his chain to Jaʿfar b. Muḥammad, from his father, from Jābir b. ʿAbd Allāh that the Prophet (may God bless him and grant him peace) said to him: 'What do you say when you stand for prayer?' He replied: 'I say *All praise is for God, Lord of the worlds,*' to which he replied: 'Say: *In the Name of God, the Compassionate, the Merciful.*' He also reported via his chain to Umm Salama that the Prophet (may God bless him and grant him peace) used to recite: *In the Name of God, the Compassionate, the Merciful. All praise is for God, Lord of the worlds.*

   Also, via his chain to ʿAlī b. Abī Ṭālib (on whom be peace),[1] he reports that he used to commence the *sūra* in prayer with *In the Name of God, the Compassionate, the Merciful*, and used to say: 'Whoever leaves off its recitation has fallen short.'[2] Via his chain to Saʿīd b. Jubayr, he reported from Ibn ʿAbbās concerning 'We have bestowed upon you seven oft-repeated (verses)' (Q.xv.87) that it means the *Fātiḥa*. It was said to Ibn ʿAbbās: 'Then where is the seventh?' He replied: '*In the Name of God, the Compassionate, the Merciful.*'[3]

   He reported via his chain to Abū Hurayra that the Prophet (may God bless him and grant him peace) said: 'When you recite the Source of the Book, do not leave off *In the Name of God, the Compassionate, the Merciful*, for it is one of its verses.'[4] Also via his chain to Abū Hurayra, that the Prophet (may God bless him and grant him peace) said:

> Almighty God says: 'I have divided the Prayer between Me and My servant into two halves.' So when the servant says *In the Name of God, the Compassionate, the*

1 This formula is provided with the name of ʿAlī (as a member of the Prophetic household) at several junctures in the text, alternating with the more common Sunni convention of supplicating for a Companion with 'may God be pleased with him'.

2 Thaʿlabī, *al-Kashf*, vol. 1, p. 103.

3 Also recorded by Ḥākim—S.I. Ālūsī argued that this was the opinion of Ibn ʿAbbās, i.e. to designate this verse to the *Fātiḥa*; see Ālūsī, *Rūḥ al-maʿānī*, vol. 1, p. 193.

4 Like the earlier narration, this is more likely an opinion of Abū Hurayra—R.S.

> *Merciful*, God says: 'My servant has glorified Me.' When he says *All praise is for God, Lord of the worlds*, God says: 'My servant has praised Me.' When he says *The Compassionate, the Merciful*, God says: 'My servant has exalted me.' When he says *Master of the Day of Judgment*, God says: 'My servant has relegated to Me [his affairs].' When he says *You we worship and from You we seek help*, God says: 'This is [divided] between Me and My servant.' When he says *Guide us upon the straight path…*, God says: 'This is for My servant, and My servant shall have what he requests.'[1]

Also via his chain to Abū Hurayra, that he said:

> I was with the Messenger of God (may God bless him and grant him peace) in the Mosque as he was speaking to his companions when a man entered and began to pray. He opened his prayer and said the [formula of] seeking refuge, then he recited *All praise is for God, Lord of the worlds*. The Prophet (may God bless him and grant him peace) heard this, so he said to him: 'O man! You have chopped your own prayer. Do you not know that *In the Name of God, the Compassionate, the Merciful* is part of [the *Sūra* of] Praise? Whoever leaves it has left a verse from it, and whoever does that has chopped his prayer. There is no prayer without the Opening of the Book, and whoever leaves a verse from it, his prayer is void.'[2]

And via his chain to Ṭalḥa b. ʿUbayd Allāh, that the Messenger of God (may God bless him and grant him peace) said: 'Whoever leaves off *In the Name of God, the Compassionate, the Merciful* has omitted a verse from the Book of God.'

We have quoted this collection of reports from the exegesis of Shaykh Abū Isḥāq al-Thaʿlabī (may God have mercy upon him).[3]

5. Reciting *In the Name of God, the Compassionate, the Merciful* is obligatory at the start of the *Fātiḥa*; therefore, it must be a verse from it.

1 This version differs from earlier ones because it includes mention of the *basmala*, which is a 'very weak addition'—R.S.

2 See Thaʿlabī, *al-Kashf*, vol. 1, p. 104: there are gaps in the manuscript which leave the chain incomplete. The report is 'very weak'—R.S.

3 As Ālūsī notes, these are weak or spurious narrations which would have been sufficient to prove the Shāfiʿī stance, had they been reliable: *Rūḥ al-maʿānī*, vol. 1, p. 193.

Proof of the first statement is the verse: 'Recite in the Name of your Lord' (Q.xcvi.1). It cannot be said that the *bā'* [in *bi'smi*] is otiose, because the default is that every letter of God's speech is meaningful. If this [particle] delivers a meaning, it must be: 'Recite, commencing with the Name of your Lord.' The apparent sense of the imperative is obligation, and no such obligation is known except in the recitation of prayer. Therefore, it is necessary to include [the *tasmiya*] in the recitation during prayer in order not to void the text of meaning.

6. The *tasmiya* is written in the script of the Qur'ān, and anything which is not Qur'ān is not written in this way. Do you not see that [the Companions etc.] forbade from writing the *sūra* titles in the codex, as well as forbidding signs indicating groups of ten or five verses? The purpose of all that was to prevent the Qur'ān being infiltrated by anything external to it. As such, if the *tasmiya* were not from the Qur'ān, it would not have been written along with it. Since there was a consensus upon writing it in this way, we know that it is part of the Qur'ān.
7. The Muslims are in consensus that everything between the two covers [of the codex] is the speech of God. Since the *tasmiya* is found between the two covers, it must be considered as God's speech. This is why, as we cited previously, when Yaʿlā made this point to Muḥammad b. Ḥasan, [the latter] remained silent.

   Know that the opinion of Abū Bakr al-Rāzī [al-Jaṣṣāṣ] is that the *tasmiya* is part of the Qur'ān but not a verse of *Sūrat al-Fātiḥa*. Rather, it was revealed in order to identify the divisions between the *sūra*s. The two [preceding] proofs do not negate the view of Abū Bakr al-Rāzī.[1]
8. The majority agree that *Sūrat al-Fātiḥa* consists of seven verses. Shāfiʿī said that *In the Name of God, the Compassionate, the Merciful* is a verse, and that *The path of those on whom You have bestowed favour, not of those who incur wrath, nor of those who are astray* is one verse [7]. Abū Ḥanīfa, on the other hand, did not consider the former as a verse of the *Fātiḥa*, instead considering *The path of those on whom You have bestowed favour* as one verse [6] and *Not of those who incur wrath, nor of those who are astray* as a separate verse [7]. We shall show in a sub-

1 According to Ālūsī, this is the correct and preponderant view in the Ḥanafī school. He also argues concerning a number of the author's other arguments that they do not refute this position. See Ālūsī, *Rūḥ al-maʿānī*, vol. 1, p. 191.

sequent enquiry[1] that the latter view is weak and inferior; as such, the verses can only number seven if we take *In the Name of God, the Compassionate, the Merciful* as a complete verse in this *sūra*.

9. We argue that reciting the *tasmiya* before the *Fātiḥa* is obligatory,[2] and that it must therefore be a verse from it. To explain the first half: even Abū Ḥanīfa conceded that reciting it is preferable, which entails that the Prophet (may God bless him and grant him peace) must have practised this; therefore, it ought to be obligatory upon us based on the verse: '…and follow him' (Q.vii.158). [To explain the second half:] once it is shown that its recitation is obligatory, then it is known that it is part of the *sūra*, since no one has differentiated [between these points].[3]
10. The Prophet (may God bless him and grant him peace) said: 'Any matter of significance which is not commenced by "In the Name of God" is severed (*abtar/ajdham*).'[4] The greatest of all acts—after believing in God—is the prayer, so reciting the *Fātiḥa* therein without reciting 'In the Name of God' results in the prayer being deficient. The word *abtar* signifies the utmost deficiency, as God used this word in the context of dispraising the unbeliever who showed enmity to the Messenger (may God bless him and grant him peace): 'For he who hates you, he will be cut off' (Q.cviii.3). Therefore, it must be said that a prayer devoid of *In the Name of God, the Compassionate, the Merciful* is extremely deficient, and whoever admits this must concede that the prayer is invalid: which denotes that it is part of the *Fātiḥa* and must be recited.[5]
11. It is narrated that the Prophet (may God bless him and grant him peace) asked Ubayy b. Kaᶜb: 'What is the greatest verse in God's Book?' Ubayy replied with *In the Name of God, the Compassionate, the*

1 See Enquiry 7 below.

2 I.e. even assuming that it is not a part of the *Fātiḥa*. Compare with proof 5 above, in which only the first statement was explained.

3 *Lā qā'il bi'l-farq*: this is a frequently occurring phrase in this discussion, which I take to mean: none of the jurists has expressed a middle position, so if part of our case is proven, it should be deemed to be correct *in toto*.

4 This *ḥadīth* appears with various wordings in Abū Dāwūd, Ibn Mājah and Aḥmad; another variant is *aqṭaᶜ*—R.S. See also Ālūsī, *Rūḥ al-maᶜānī*, vol. 1, pp. 245–6.

5 Ālūsi remarks rather caustically that, based on this argument, one ought to pronounce the *basmala* before every bow or prostration, and even the opening *takbīr*! See Ālūsī, *Rūḥ al-maᶜānī*, vol. 1, p. 194.

Merciful, and the Prophet confirmed his statement.[1] The relevance of this is that it shows that [what Ubayy uttered] is a verse, whereas it is not a complete verse when it appears in 'It is from Solomon, and it is in the Name of God, the Compassionate, the Merciful' (Q.xxvii.30)—rather, here is only part of a verse. Therefore, it must be a complete verse elsewhere, and anyone who says so identifies it as a complete verse at the beginning of *Sūrat al-Fātiḥa*.[2]

12. [Anas related that][3] Muʿāwiya arrived at Medina and led the people in a prayer in which the Qur'ān is recited audibly. He recited the Source of the Book without *In the Name of God, the Compassionate, the Merciful*. When he completed the prayer, the Emigrants and Helpers called out to him from all around: 'Did you forget? Where was *In the Name of God, the Compassionate, the Merciful* when you commenced the recitation?' So Muʿāwiya repeated the prayer and recited *In the Name of God, the Compassionate, the Merciful*.[4] This report indicates that the Companions were in consensus that this is part of the Qur'ān and the *Fātiḥa*, and that it is better to recite it audibly.

13. The rest of the Prophets (peace and blessings be upon them) used to begin any good works by saying 'In the Name of God,' so it follows that this was obligatory upon our Messenger (may God bless him and grant him peace). If it was obligatory upon the Messenger, then it must also be obligatory for us. If that is so, then it must be a verse from *Sūrat al-Fātiḥa*.

    PROOF OF THE FIRST PREMISE: when Noah intended to board the ship, he said: 'In the Name of God, whether it move or be at rest' (Q.xi.41). When Solomon wrote to Bilqīs, he wrote: 'In the Name of God, the Compassionate, the Merciful.' If it is said that the verse 'It is from Solomon, and it is in the Name of God, the Compassionate, the Merciful' (Q.xxvii.30) indicates that Solomon placed his own name before God's, we reply: God forbid that it should be so. Rather, when the [hoopoe] bird came with Solomon's letter and placed it upon the chest of Bilqīs—while none could have entered

1 I could not source this, and it conflicts with the *ḥadīth* of Muslim (cited in Book II) in which Ubayy points to *Āyat al-Kursī* and this is confirmed by the Prophet—R.S.

2 Cf. the opinion of al-Jaṣṣāṣ cited under proof 7 above.

3 This phrase is not in the printed editions, but it is in Ālūsī, *Rūḥ al-maʿānī*, vol. 1, p. 187, and the author does refer back to this narration with Anas' name. See Enquiry 9 below.

4 Recorded in the *Musnad* of Shāfiʿī, but without 'repeated the prayer' being explicit—R.S. See Ālūsī, *Rūḥ al-maʿānī*, vol. 1, p. 194.

her home due to the large number of guards surrounding it—she knew that it could only have been brought by that bird. She had already heard of Solomon, so when she took hold of the letter, she herself said: 'It is from Solomon.' Then, upon opening the letter and seeing the *tasmiya* therein, she said: 'And it is in the Name of God, the Compassionate, the Merciful.'[1] It is thus shown that whenever the Prophets would commence any goodly task, they would start by saying 'In the name of God, the Compassionate, the Merciful'.

ON THE SECOND PREMISE: once it has been established for the other Prophets, it must be obligatory on our Messenger too, due to God saying: 'Those were the (Prophets) who received God's guidance, so copy the guidance they received' (Q.VI.90).[2] So once it has been established for him, it must be obligatory on us: '…and follow him' (Q.VII.158). Then, once it is shown to be obligatory to recite, it is known to be a verse of the *Fātiḥa*, as no one has differentiated [between these points].

14. The existence of God is prior to that of all other existents: He is the pre-eternal Creator whereas all else is created, and the pre-eternal is necessarily prior to the created. Once it is known that He is prior to all else, then—by rational relation—His mention ought to be prior to all other mentions. This, in turn, will only be the case if the recitation of *In the Name of God, the Compassionate, the Merciful* precedes any other mention or recitation. Once it is shown that the opinion stipulating the obligation of this priority seems good to the intellect, it must therefore be given consideration in the Law, as the Prophet (may God bless him and grant him peace) said: 'What the Muslims consider good is good in the sight of God.'[3] Then, once it shown to be obligatory to recite, it is known to be a verse of the *Fātiḥa*, as no one has differentiated [between these points].
15. Certainly 'In the Name of God, the Compassionate, the Merciful' is in the Qur'ān in *Sūrat al-Naml* [Q.XXVII.30]. Then we see it repeated in the Qur'ānic script, which means that it is Qur'ān [in those other places], just as we see 'Then which of the favours of your Lord will you deny?' (Q.LV.13, etc.) and 'Ah woe, that day, to the Rejecters of

1 See for more explanations: Book II, Chapter Eleven, Point 11.

2 Ālūsī is very scathing about this argument and use of this verse. See Ālūsī, *Rūḥ al-maʿānī*, vol. 1, p. 195. Although he did not elaborate, the concept of abrogation of earlier prophetic legal codes would be relevant here.

3 This is attributed, rather, to Ibn Masʿūd (in Aḥmad and Dāraquṭnī)—R.S.

Truth!' (Q.LXXVII.15 etc.) repeated in the same script and form[1] and say that all of this is Qur'ān.

16. It is narrated that the Prophet (may God bless him and grant him peace) used at first to write in the way of Quraysh: *bi'smika Allāhumma* ('In Your Name, O God'), until the revelation came with: 'Embark upon it in the Name of God, whether it move or be at rest' (Q.XI.41), so he wrote *bi'smi 'Llāh* ('In the Name of God'). Then came: 'Say: Call upon Allāh, or call upon al-Raḥmān…' (Q.XVII.110), so he wrote: *bi'smi 'Llāh al-Raḥmān*. Subsequently, when 'It is from Solomon, and it is in the Name of God, the Compassionate, the Merciful' (Q.XXVII.30) was revealed, he wrote its like [in full].[2] The relevance of this is that all the portions of this formula are found in the Qur'ān, as is the combined form. As it is seen to be in the Qur'ān, it must be decisively stated as being part of it. Otherwise, if we allow for it to be excluded from the Qur'ān despite all these factors and how well known it is, it would be possible for all the other verses to be excluded, and this would result in doubt being cast upon the [whole] Qur'ān.
17. We have explained that it is proven through mass transmission that Almighty God would reveal this formula upon Muḥammad (may God bless him and grant him peace) and instruct that it be written in the script of the codex. We further explained[3] that the consequences of this dispute over it being part of the Qur'ān are limited to certain rulings: for example, whether it must be recited, whether one may recite it in a state of major impurity, or touch it in a state of minor impurity. Therefore, we say: to affirm these rulings[4] is more cautious, so that approach must be adopted. This is because the Prophet (may God bless him and grant him peace) said: 'Leave what makes you doubt for that which does not make you doubt.'

PROPONENTS OF THE OPPOSITE VIEW argued as follows:

1. They cited the *ḥadīth* of Abū Hurayra that the Prophet (may God bless him and grant him peace) said:

1 Also, in these two cases, numerous times in the same *sūra*.

2 A concise version of this account (without mention of Q.XI.41 and Q.XVII.110) is in the *Muṣannaf* of ʿAbd al-Razzāq, and Abū Dāwūd's *Marāsīl*. If this narration were accepted, it would imply that the *basmala* was not already present at the beginning of *sūras*—including the *Fātiḥa*—which were revealed before *al-Naml*.

3 Enquiry 5 above.

4 That is, to believe that there is obligation or prohibition in these scenarios.

> Almighty God says: 'I have divided the Prayer between Me and My servant into two halves, and My servant shall have that which he requests.' So when the servant says *All praise is for God, Lord of the worlds*, God says: 'My servant has praised Me.' When he says *The Compassionate, the Merciful*, God says: 'My servant has exalted me.' When he says *Master of the Day of Judgment*, God says: 'My servant has glorified Me.' When he says *You we worship and from You we seek help*, God says: 'This is [divided] between Me and My servant.'[1]

The relevance of this is twofold: first, the Prophet (may God bless him and grant him peace) did not mention the *tasmiya*, whereas if it were a verse of the *Fātiḥa*, he would have done so. Second, God said 'I have made the prayer (*ṣalāh*) between Me and My servant into two halves,' by which is meant the *Fātiḥa*. This halving can only occur if the *tasmiya* is not a verse of the *Fātiḥa*, because it is composed of seven verses. Hence there must be three-and-a-half verses for God, i.e. from *All praise is for God* until *You we worship*. Then the [remaining] three-and-a-half verses are for the servant, i.e. from *And from You we seek help* until the end. On the other hand, if *In the Name of God, the Compassionate, the Merciful* is deemed to be a verse of the *Fātiḥa*, there would be four-and-a-half verses for God, and two-and-a-half for the servant: this would nullify the halving mentioned [in this *ḥadīth*].

2. ʿĀ'isha (may God be pleased with her) related that the Prophet (may God bless him and grant him peace) used to commence his prayer with the *takbīr* and his recitation with *All praise is for God, Lord of the worlds*.[2] This denotes that the *tasmiya* is not a verse of the *Fātiḥa*.
3. If *In the Name of God, the Compassionate, the Merciful* were a verse from this *sūra*, there would be repetition in [the third verse,] *The Compassionate, the Merciful*, and that would be contrary to evidence.[3]

RESPONSE TO THE FIRST POINT:

a. We have cited from Shaykh Abū Isḥāq al-Thaʿlabī via his chain that when the Prophet (may God bless him and grant him peace) taught this *ḥadīth*, he counted *In the Name of God, the Compassionate, the Merciful*

1 This is the authentic version recorded by Muslim.

2 Recorded by Muslim—S.I.

3 That is, it would be contrary to the lofty discourse of the Qur'ān in which no word is without specific purpose.

as a complete verse of *Sūrat al-Fātiḥa*.[1] As the two narrations conflict, preponderance is for our [opinion] because the narration containing affirmation is given precedence over that containing negation.[2]

b. Abū Dāwūd [al-Sijistānī][3] reported via Nakhaʿī, from Mālik, from al-ʿAlā' b. ʿAbd al-Raḥmān, from his father, from Abū Hurayra that the Prophet (may God bless him and grant him peace) said: 'When the servant says *Master of the Day of Judgment*, God says: "My servant has glorified Me, and this is between Me and My servant."' That is to say that this [fourth] verse is divided between [God and the servant], so there are indeed three before and three after. This, in turn, only holds if the *tasmiya* is counted as a verse of the *Fātiḥa*—hence this *ḥadīth* is actually a proof for us.

c. The word 'half' (*niṣf*) can be applied not only to the number of verses, but also to a conceptual half.[4] The Prophet (may God bless him and grant him peace) said: 'Inheritance (*farā'iḍ*) is half of knowledge.'[5] This is because these rules are concerned with the affairs of the deceased, and death and life are two parts of a pair. [Qāḍī] Shurayḥ said: 'I woke up with half of the people angry with me,' meaning that some were happy with him and others angry.

d. Our evidences are explicit in saying that *In the Name of God, the Compassionate, the Merciful* is a verse of the *Fātiḥa*, whereas this *ḥadīth* which they have clung to was not intended to clarify whether or not it is part of the *sūra*; rather, its purpose is something else.[6] Therefore, our evidences are stronger and clearer.

e. As we have explained, our opinion is more on the side of caution.

1 See Enquiry 6 above, proof 4.

2 This is a principle in resolving such conflicts: the narration containing the additional evidence is given consideration, as the absence of mention (in the other) does not prove actual absence. Moreover, there is a general difficulty in proving the non-existence of something. However, Ālūsī argues that this principle is not applicable here; see Ālūsī, *Rūḥ al-maʿānī*, vol. 1, p. 195.

3 The printed editions have 'al-Sakhtiyānī'. Disappointly, both Sayyid ʿImrān and Rashā Sulaymān sufficed by saying that this is the same *ḥadīth* as above. According to the editor of *Rūḥ al-maʿānī*, this is not in Abū Dāwūd's *Sunan* at all. Moreover, the manner of the division of this verse is less clear here than in the authentic narration. See Ālūsī, *Rūḥ al-maʿānī*, vol. 1, p. 195 (note 2).

4 Ālūsī comments that this non-literal interpretation is unjustified; see Ālūsī, *Rūḥ al-maʿānī*, vol. 1, p. 196.

5 Recorded by Ibn Mājah, and considered 'very weak'—R.S.

6 Namely the spiritual significance of the *Fātiḥa* and the dynamic relationship between Lord and servant.

RESPONSE TO THE SECOND POINT: it is as Shāfiʿī said: 'Perhaps ʿĀ'isha was treating *All praise is for God, Lord of the worlds* as the name of the *sūra*, just as one may say that a person recited "All praise is for God, Who created the heavens" and mean that he recited that *sūra* [namely *al-Anʿām*, VI].' The remainder of the response concerning the *ḥadīth* of Anas will come later.[1]

RESPONSE TO THE THIRD POINT: repetition for the purpose of emphasis is frequent in the Qur'ān. Indeed, emphasising that God is Compassionate and Merciful is among the greatest of purposes. And God knows best.

Enquiry 7
The Number of Verses of this *Sūra*

I have seen in some anomalous (*shādhdh*) narrations that al-Ḥasan al-Baṣrī said that this *sūra* comprises eight verses. However, the famous narration upon which the majority agree is that it comprises seven verses, and their exegesis of: 'We have bestowed upon you seven oft-repeated (verses)' (Q.xv.87) accords with this.

Thus the people [including Shāfiʿī] who held that *In the Name of God, the Compassionate, the Merciful* is a verse of the *Fātiḥa* said that *The path of those on whom You have bestowed favour, not of those who incur wrath, nor of those who are astray* is a complete verse [7]. However, since Abū Ḥanīfa did not count the *tasmiya* within the *sūra*, he had to consider *The path of those on whom You have bestowed favour* as one verse [6], and *Not of those who incur wrath, nor of those who are astray* as another [7].

Once you have known this, we say: what Shāfiʿī said is worthier for the following reasons:

1. The [end] syllable[2] in *The path of those on whom You have bestowed favour* [i.e. *anʿamta ʿalayhim*] is not in agreement with those of the preceding

1 The report of Anas is cited and discussed in detail under Enquiry 9 below. It seems that it was supposed to be mentioned alongside that of ʿĀ'isha above.

2 The term *maqāṭiʿ* is generally used to describe syllables, but Rāzī is making a point about the verse endings. These are generally described as *fawāṣil* and contrasted with the *qāfiya* of Arabic poetry in which *sajʿ*—not quite like rhyme, this involves the agreement of the final letter of the line—is the norm. In the Qur'ān, generally there is agreement within a *sūra* or a smaller collection of verses upon a final letter: if this is complete agreement, it is like *sajʿ*, whereas it is common (as in *Sūrat Qāf* and indeed the *Fātiḥa* itself) to have approximate agreement, i.e. letters with similar attributes. See Muḥammad al-Ḥasnāwi, *al-Fāṣila fī al-Qur'ān*, Amman: Dār ʿAmmār, 2000, p. 139.

verses [*ʿālamīn*, *raḥīm*, *al-dīn* etc.].[1] It is essential to observe agreement in the endings, as the Qur'ān contains two types: approximate agreement (*mutaqārib*) and complete agreement (*mutashākil*). The first is as in *Sūrat Qāf* [L], while the second is as in *Sūrat al-Qamar* [LIV]. *Anʿamta ʿalayhim* is in neither of these categories, so it may not be considered a verse ending.

2. If we were to make *Not of those who incur wrath*... a [new] verse, then the word *ghayr* would be at the start of the verse. However, this word can be one of two things: an adjective (*ṣifa*) for what preceded, or an exception (*istithnā'*) from what preceded.[2] An adjective and its described [noun] are like a single unit, as are the exception and that from which it is excepted: so separating them is contrary to the evidence. However, if we consider *The path of those on whom You have bestowed favour* until the end of the *sūra* as a single verse, we have kept the adjective and its noun—or the exception and that from which it is excepted—together as one utterance in a single verse. This is more appropriate to the evidence.
3. [In a grammatical substitution,] the original (*mubdal minhu*) is as though it has been removed (*maḥdhūf*).[3] Thus the meaning of the verse is: 'Guide us upon the path of those on whom You have bestowed favour.' However, the request to be guided on the path of those on whom God bestowed favour is qualified by two conditions: that those who received that favour be not [subsequently] objects of [divine] anger; and that they go not astray. Without these stipulations, it would not be permissible to follow in their way. This [interpretation] is evidenced by His saying: 'Have you not turned your vision to those who have changed the favour of God into blasphemy...?' (Q.XIV.28), which shows that He did bestow His favour upon them. However, once they became objects of wrath and strayers from the path, it is no longer permissible to follow them. This

1 The word *ʿalayhim* ends in a short syllable, whereas the other verses end a long syllable. Otherwise, it does share a final letter with some of the verses (and approximate agreement with the others).

2 The translation 'Not of those who incur wrath' is based on interpreting it as a disconnected exception, while a connected exception would be: 'Except those who incur wrath' (i.e. after receiving God's favours: see point 3 below). A translation based on the adjectival interpretation would be: 'Who do not incur wrath'—this follows, likewise, from substitution (see point 3, where I have, nevertheless, retained the standard translation).

3 This is in reference to the grammatical function of *ṣirāṭ* at the beginning of the last verse (upon the author's opinion). In a sense, it substitutes for 'the straight path' in the preceding verse.

shows that it is not permissible to separate *The path of those on whom You have bestowed favour* from *Not of those who incur wrath, nor of those who are astray*—rather, this is a single utterance and must therefore be accepted as a single verse.

OBJECTION: is it not the case that *All praise is for God, Lord of the worlds* is one verse, followed by *The Compassionate, the Merciful* as another verse, even though the latter is dependent upon the former?

RESPONSE: the difference is that *All praise is for God, Lord of the worlds* is a complete utterance even without *The Compassionate, the Merciful*, so it is acceptable for the former to be an independent verse. The case under discussion is different, in that—as we explained—*Guide us upon the straight path; the path of those on whom You have bestowed favour* is not a complete utterance. Rather, this [request] would not be proper until it is followed by *Not of those who incur wrath, nor of those who are astray*—so the difference is clear.[1]

Enquiry 8

On the question of *In the Name of God, the Compassionate, the Merciful* being a verse at the beginning of the rest of the *sūra*s, some of our companions have ascribed two opinions to Shāfiʿī. However, the most erudite (*muḥaqqiqūn*) among them have agreed that it is part of the Qur'ān in all the *sūras*,[2] stating that the 'two opinions' concern whether it is an independent verse at the beginning of each *sūra*, or whether it forms a verse together with whatever follows it. However, some of the Ḥanafīs stated that Shāfiʿī violated consensus (*ijmāʿ*) on this issue, as none before him claimed that the *basmala* is a verse at the beginning of the other *sūras*.

OUR EVIDENCE: the *basmala* is written at the beginning of each *sūra* in the Qur'ānic script, so it must be Qur'ān.

[OBJECTION:] proponents of the other view cite the narration of Abū Hurayra in which the Prophet (may God bless him and grant him peace) said that *Sūrat al-Mulk* [LXVII] is thirty verses and *Sūrat al-Kawthar* [CVIII] is three verses.[3] Since it is agreed that these *sūras* contain these numbers of verses without counting the *tasmiya*, it follows that it is not a verse in these *sūras*.

1 The author has not addressed here the existence of other such cases in the Qur'ān. For example, it is agreed that 'So woe to the worshippers' (Q.CVII.4) is an independent verse despite its semantic dependence on the following verse.

2 The famous exception is *Sūrat al-Tawba* (IX).

3 The narrations concerning *al-Mulk* are recorded by Abū Dāwud and others—R.S. I could not locate the exact narration concerning *al-Kawthar*.

RESPONSE: if we say that *In the Name of God, the Compassionate, the Merciful* forms a verse together with that follows it, then their contention falls.

FURTHER OBJECTION: you have counted it as a complete verse at the beginning of the *Fātiḥa*, so how can you then say that it is part of a verse in the rest?

RESPONSE: we say that this is not implausible. Do you not see that *All praise is for God, Lord of the worlds* is a complete verse, but then it also appears as part of a verse in: '...and the close of their cry will be "All praise is for God, Lord of the worlds"' (Q.x.10)?[1] Such is the case here.

[FURTHER RESPONSE:] the Prophet's saying that *Sūrat al-Kawthar* is three verses is in reference to that which is unique to this *sūra*. As for the *tasmiya*, it is something common to all *sūra*s [and thus went unmentioned]. On this basis, their contention falls.

[Is the *Basmala* Recited Audibly in Prayer?]

Enquiry 9

It is narrated that Aḥmad b. Ḥanbal said that although the *tasmiya* is a verse of the *Fātiḥa*, it is to be recited inaudibly in every cycle (*rakʿa*) of prayer. Shāfiʿī said that it is a verse of the *Fātiḥa* and is to be recited audibly. Abū Ḥanīfa said that it is not a verse of the *Fātiḥa*,[2] but he also said that it is recited inaudibly in every cycle.

[EVIDENCES FOR AUDIBLE RECITATION:] we say that reciting it audibly is a Prophetic practice (*sunna*), as shown by the following proofs:

1. We have shown that the *tasmiya* is a verse of the *Fātiḥa*. It is known inductively that a single *sūra* is recited either inaudibly *in toto* or audibly *in toto*; the possibility of reciting one part inaudibly and another part audibly is not acted upon in any *sūra*. Therefore, reciting the *tasmiya* audibly is legislated for audible recitation [of the *Fātiḥa* etc.].
2. Without doubt, *In the Name of God, the Compassionate, the Merciful* is praise and exalting mention of God. Therefore, it ought to be legislated for this to be recited audibly, as God has said: 'Celebrate the praises of God, as you (used to) celebrate the praises of your fathers; indeed, with far more (heart and soul)' (Q.II.200). It is known that a person [in Arab society] would take great pride in his father [and

1 The printed edition has cited the beginning of this verse, obscuring the point being made. Regarding this analogy, Ālūsī argues that it is unsatisfactory because of the clear semantic reason for it being part of the verse in that case; see Ālūsī, *Rūḥ al-maʿānī*, vol. 1, p. 196.

2 Cf. Enquiry 4 above, in which it is said that he did not address this question explicitly.

ancestry] and announce this pride with great fanfare. If one were to mention his father quietly, this would signify that he is embarrassed. Therefore, if a person expressing pride in his father would do so loudly and clearly, it is all the more proper to do so with the remembrance of God, acting upon the verse cited.

3. Pronouncing God's remembrance audibly signifies that the person is proud of that [honour] and cares not for anyone's blame. Without doubt, this is considered good according to the intellect: it must, therefore, be so in the Law, as the Prophet (may God bless him and grant him peace) said: 'What the Muslims consider good is good in the sight of God.' After all, being quiet and clandestine is only appropriate for something which is shameful or flawed, so a person hides it lest it be revealed. Therefore, how could it be reasonable to hide that which represents the greatest source of pride, virtue and achievement?

   There is no achievement greater or more complete than for a servant to be in the remembrance and glorification of God. For this reason, the Prophet (may God bless him and grant him peace) said: 'Successful is he who dies while his tongue is moist with God's mention.'[1] ᶜAlī b. Abī Ṭālib used to say: 'O You Whose mention is an honour for the mentioners.' How, then, could a rational person strive to conceal this? On this basis, it is narrated that the way of ᶜAlī was to recite *In the Name of God, the Compassionate, the Merciful* audibly in all prayers. I say: this proof is strong and convincing to my soul and intellect, and will never fade in the face of the opponents' words.

4. Shāfiᶜī narrated via his chain that Muᶜāwiya arrived at Medina and led the people in prayer. He did not recite *In the Name of God, the Compassionate, the Merciful*, nor did he make the *takbīr* on moving to bowing and prostration. When he completed the prayer, the Emigrants and Helpers called out: 'O Muᶜāwiya! You have stolen the prayer from us! Where was *In the Name of God, the Compassionate, the Merciful*, and where was the *takbīr* for bowing and prostration?' So Muᶜāwiya repeated the prayer with the *tasmiya* and the *takbīrs*. Shāfiᶜī commented: 'Muᶜāwiya was a great ruler with tremendous power; were it not that pronouncing the *tasmiya* audibly was an established matter among all the Emigrants and Helpers, they would not have managed to rebuke him for leaving off the *tasmiya*.'

1 Similar is recorded in *Khalq afᶜāl al-ᶜibād* by Bukhārī.

5. Bayhaqī reported in *al-Sunan al-kabīr* that Abū Hurayra said: 'The Messenger of God (may God bless him and grant him peace) used to recite *In the Name of God, the Compassionate, the Merciful* audibly in the prayer.' Shaykh Bayhaqī then attributed this loud recitation also to ʿUmar b. al-Khaṭṭāb, Ibn ʿAbbās, Ibn ʿUmar and Ibn al-Zubayr. As for ʿAlī b. Abī Ṭālib, the fact that he used to recite it audibly is established through mass transmission (*tawātur*), and whoever takes ʿAlī b. Abī Ṭālib as his guide in religion has indeed been rightly guided. The Prophet (may God bless him and grant him peace) said: 'O God! Make the truth go with ʿAlī wherever he goes.'[1]
6. *In the Name of God, the Compassionate, the Merciful* is connected to a verb which must be left implicit.[2] The meaning is: 'With the help of God's Name begin your acts of obedience,' or something of this nature. No doubt, hearing these words makes the intellect aware that one has no ability to avoid disobedience of God except through the protection of God, and no power to obey Him except through His grace. It further makes one aware that no goodness or blessing occurs [in one's actions] without commencing with the remembrance of God. It is known that the purpose of all acts of worship and obedience is for these meanings to take root in the intellect; therefore, since hearing this formula brings about such lofty goodness and blessings, the speaker would be included in the verse: 'You are the best of peoples, evolved for mankind: enjoining what is right, forbidding what is wrong…' (Q.III.110). This is because, by pronouncing it aloud, he has enjoined the right in the best of ways, i.e. [inviting others] to return to God completely, seeking His help in all good actions. If this is so, then how could a rational person claim that [reciting it audibly] is an innovation (*bidʿa*)?

PROPONENTS OF THE OPPOSITE VIEW cited the following:

1. Bukhārī reported via his chain to Anas [b. Mālik] that he said: 'I prayed behind the Messenger of God (may God bless him and grant him peace), and behind Abū Bakr, ʿUmar and ʿUthmān, and they used to commence their recitation with *All praise is for God, Lord of the worlds*.' Muslim [b. al-Ḥajjāj] also reported this in his *Ṣaḥīḥ* collection, [with the addition] that they used not to mention *In the Name of God, the Compassionate, the Merciful*. In another narration, it says: 'I did not hear any of them saying *In the Name of God, the Compassionate,*

1 Recorded by Tirmidhī, and considered 'very weak'—R.S.

2 See the beginning of Book II.

the Merciful'; and in a fourth: 'None of them recited *In the Name of God, the Compassionate, the Merciful* audibly.'

2. [The son of][1] ʿAbd Allāh b. al-Mughaffal said: 'My father heard me reciting *In the Name of God, the Compassionate, the Merciful*, so he said to me: "My son, beware of innovation in Islam. I prayed behind the Messenger of God (may God bless him and grant him peace), and behind Abū Bakr, ʿUmar and ʿUthmān, and they commenced their recitation with *All praise is for God, Lord of the worlds*. Therefore, when you pray, say *All praise is for God, Lord of the worlds*."'[2]

   Note that Anas and Ibn al-Mughaffal specified the [first] three Caliphs as not having recited *In the Name of God, the Compassionate, the Merciful*. The fact that they did not mention ʿAlī indicates that there was unanimous agreement that ʿAlī used to recite this audibly.

3. Almighty God said: 'Call on your Lord with humility and in private' (Q.VII.55), and 'Bring your Lord to remembrance in your (very) soul, with humility and in reverence, without loudness in words' (Q.VII.205).[3] Since *In the Name of God, the Compassionate, the Merciful* is remembrance of God, it must be kept quiet. The jurists deduced this proof based on the preceding two reports.[4]

THE RESPONSE CONCERNING THE *ḤADĪTH* OF ANAS [i.e. points 1 and 2] is as follows:

To begin with, Shaykh Abū Ḥāmid al-Isfarā'īnī said that there are six different narrations from Anas in this regard. The Ḥanafīs narrated three of these:

a. 'I prayed behind the Messenger of God (may God bless him and grant him peace), and behind Abū Bakr, ʿUmar and ʿUthmān, and they used to commence their recitation with *All praise is for God, Lord of the worlds*.'
b. [The variant:] 'They used not to mention *In the Name of God, the Compassionate, the Merciful*.'
c. 'I did not hear any of them saying *In the Name of God, the Compassionate, the Merciful*.'

1 This detail fell from the printed editions but it is found in the source and accords with the author's subsequent mentions of this report.

2 Recorded by Tirmidhī—R.S.

3 I added the latter clause from the verse to this citation in order to make its relevance clearer. However, the expression *fī nafsika* ('in yourself') may be interpreted in this way.

4 This is a very subtle criticism of interpreting the Qur'ān based on prior judgments and opinions—something which is not limited to any particular school.

The above support the Ḥanafīs' position. However, another three work against them:

a. We have mentioned how Anas related that, when Muʿāwiya omitted *In the Name of God, the Compassionate, the Merciful* in prayer, the Emigrants and Helpers rebuked him; and how this denotes that reciting it audibly was something widespread and well known among them.
b. Abū Qilāba narrated from Anas that the Messenger of God (may God bless him and grant him peace), Abū Bakr and ʿUmar used to recite *In the Name of God, the Compassionate, the Merciful* audibly.[1]
c. [Anas] was asked concerning loud or quiet recitation of *In the Name of God, the Compassionate, the Merciful*, and he replied: 'I have no knowledge of this issue.'[2]

It is thus seen that the narration from Anas in this regard is full of confusion and contradiction; therefore, recourse must be made to the other types of proof [either way].

Moreover, there is another problem [with citing these reports]. ʿAlī used to be very particular about reciting the *tasmiya* audibly. So when the Umayyads came to power, they made a point of forbidding it from being read audibly, as they sought to abolish the effects of ʿAli's [rule]. It is possible that Anas was afraid of them, hence his contradictory statements on the issue. Whatever doubt might affect us, we would never be in doubt if a conflict arises between the statements of Anas and Ibn al-Mughaffal [on one hand] and the view of ʿAlī b. Abī Ṭālib on which he acted throughout his life [on the other], then the view of ʿAlī is worthier of adoption. This is the decisive reply on this issue.

Then we say [to them]: assuming that there is [parity and] conflict between your proofs and ours, then preponderance must belong to our view, for the following reasons:

a. The narrators of your reports are Anas and Ibn al-Mughaffal, whereas the narrators of our opinion are ʿAlī b. Abī Ṭālib, Ibn ʿAbbās, Ibn ʿUmar and Abū Hurayra.[3] The [latter] group were greater in knowledge and proximity to the Messenger of God (may God bless him and grant him peace) than Anas and Ibn al-Mughaffal.

1 This narration claims the opposite to that recorded by Bukhārī. However, the narrations via Abū Qilāba found in Ibn Ḥibbān and al-Bazzār confirm that these three would *not* recite the *basmala* audibly—R.S.

2 I could not source this—R.S.

3 See comments in Sulaymān, *Riwāyāt*, pp. 183–5.

b. The position (*madhhab*) of Abū Ḥanīfa is that if a solitary report (*khabar al-wāḥid*) conflicts with analogy (*qiyās*),[1] then such a report is not adopted. For this reason, he did not accept the *ḥadīth* concerning the *muṣarrāh*[2] even though it was uttered by the Messenger of God (may God bless him and grant him peace). He said that this is because it conflicts with analogy. Once this is known, we say: we have explained that clear reason dictates that reciting this formula aloud is preferable to concealing it. Therefore, what reason could he have for preferring the statement of Anas and Ibn al-Mughaffal over this clear and commonsense explanation?

c. Something which is known by necessity is that the Prophet (may God bless him and grant him peace) used to advance the senior figures over their lesser counterparts, the scholars over the laymen, and the refined over the uncouth. Without doubt, ʿAlī, Ibn ʿAbbās and Ibn ʿUmar were more advanced in knowledge, honour and status than Anas and Ibn al-Mughaffal. Thus it is probable that ʿAlī, Ibn ʿAbbās and Ibn ʿUmar would have stood close to the Messenger of God (may God bless him and grant him peace) [in the prayers], whereas Anas and Ibn al-Mughaffal would have been farther away. Also [take into account] that the Prophet (may God bless him and grant him peace) would not have been extremely loud, as God said: 'Neither recite your prayer aloud, nor recite it in a low tone' (Q.XVII.110). Moreover, when a person begins to recite, his voice will begin at a weak level and become gradually stronger. These are all manifest reasons to explain how ʿAlī, Ibn ʿAbbās, Ibn ʿUmar and Abū Hurayra could have heard the Messenger of God (may God bless him and grant him peace) reciting the *tasmiya* audibly while Anas and Ibn al-Mughaffal did not.

d. Shāfiʿī said: 'Perhaps what Anas meant by saying that the Messenger of God (may God bless him and grant him peace) would commence his prayer with *All praise is for God, Lord of the worlds* is that he would recite this *sūra* before any other. Thus by *All praise is for God, Lord of the worlds* he meant that and the rest, i.e. he used it as a name for the *sūra*.'

1 In this context, *qiyās* refers to the norms established by other traditions along with reason.

2 This refers to a report in which the Prophet forbade people from leaving their livestock unmilked for several days in order to give buyers the impression that their yield is more plentiful. See Ibn Rushd, *The Distinguished Jurist's Primer*, vol. II, p. 210.

e. Perhaps what is meant by 'not reciting aloud' in the *ḥadīth* of Ibn al-Mughaffal[1] is to avoid raising the voice too much, as God has said: 'Neither recite your prayer aloud, nor recite it in a low tone' (Q.xvii.110).
f. Reciting audibly is an affirmative modality, whereas doing so inaudibly is a negative one. Therefore, the affirmative narration is given precedence over the negation.
g. The rational evidences are on our side, as is the practice of ʿAlī b. Abī Ṭālib. Now whoever takes ʿAlī as a leader (*imām*) in his religion has indeed grasped 'the most trustworthy handhold'[2] for his religion and his self.

RESPONSE TO THEIR CITATION OF THE VERSE 'Bring your Lord to remembrance in your (very) soul, with humility and in reverence' (Q.vii.205): this is interpreted as referring to remembrance in and of itself. On the other hand, what is intended by *In the Name of God, the Compassionate, the Merciful* is recitation of God's speech in worship and humility, and reciting audibly is more suitable in this context.

Enquiry 10
Assorted Issues (*Furūʿ*) Concerning the *Basmala*

Issue 1

The Shiʿa said that the Prophetic way (*sunna*) is to recite the *tasmiya* audibly, whether in a loud or silent prayer. However, the majority of jurists differed with them on this point.

Issue 2

Those who said that the *tasmiya* is not a verse at the beginning of the [other] *sūra*s had various explanations for it being written in the codex before each *sūra*. There are two [main] opinions:

A. The *tasmiya* is not part of the Qur'ān [at all]. Those who say this consist, in turn, of two groups. The first said that it was written to separate between the *sūra*s,[3] but now that the divisions are known [by all], there is no need for the *tasmiya* and it would be permissible for it not to be written [any longer]. The second group said that it must be maintained in the codex and it will never be permissible to omit it.
B. It is part of the Qur'ān and was revealed by God, but it is an

1 This is not present in the wording cited above. It could apply to one of the narrations from Anas.
2 See Q.ii.256 for this expression.
3 Both groups agree up to here.

independent verse and not part of these *sūras*. These, too, consist of two groups. The first said that God would reveal it [repeatedly] with the start of each *sūra*. The others said that He only revealed it once and instructed that it be placed at the beginning of each *sūra*.

The evidence for it being a divinely-revealed part of the Qur'ān is the narration of Umm Salama that the Prophet (may God bless him and grant him peace) used to count *In the Name of God, the Compassionate, the Merciful* as a verse upon which to stop (*āya fāṣila*).[1]

Ibrāhīm b. Yazīd [al-Khawzī] said: 'I said to ʿAmr b. Dīnār: "Al-Faḍl al-Raqqāshī claims that *In the Name of God, the Compassionate, the Merciful* is not from the Qur'ān." [ʿAmr] replied: "Glory be to God! How brazen this man is! I heard Saʿīd b. Jubayr say that he heard Ibn ʿAbbās say that whenever *In the Name of God, the Compassionate, the Merciful* was revealed upon the Prophet (may God bless him and grant him peace), he would know that that *sūra* had been completed and another one had commenced."'[2]

It was narrated from ʿAbd Allāh b. al-Mubārak: 'Whoever omits *In the Name of God, the Compassionate, the Merciful* has omitted 113 verses'[3]—its like was narrated from Ibn ʿUmar and Abū Hurayra.

Issue 3

Whoever affirms that the *tasmiya* is a verse of the *Fātiḥa* and that the *Fātiḥa* must be recited in the prayer necessarily considers the recitation of the *tasmiya* to be obligatory [in prayer]. As for those who hold another opinion, they differ concerning this [latter ruling].

Abū Ḥanīfa and his followers, along with al-Ḥasan b. Ṣāliḥ b. [Ḥayy][4], Sufyān al-Thawrī and Ibn Abī Laylā, stated that it is recited inaudibly. Mālik said that it is not to be recited in obligatory prayers, neither audibly or inaudibly; but in optional prayers, a person may choose to recite it or not.[5]

Issue 4

The position of Shāfiʿī entails that it is obligatory to recite [the *tasmiya*] in every prayer cycle (*rakʿa*).

As for Abū Ḥanīfa, there are two narrations from him: Yaʿlā narrated

1 This alludes to the report from Umm Salama mentioned earlier: the Prophet would recite and stop at the end of the *basmala* before proceeding to the next verse. In some narrations, this was described as reciting '*āya* by *āya*'.

2 The main part of this narration is found in Ṭabarānī's *Kabīr*—S.I.

3 One for each of the *sūras* of the Qur'ān, minus one (*al-Tawba*, ix).

4 The printed editions have 'Jinnī' in place of 'Ḥayy'.

5 See Ibn Rushd, *The Distinguished Jurist's Primer*, vol. 1, p. 136.

via Abū Yūsuf that Abū Ḥanīfa said it is to be recited in every cycle before the *Fātiḥa*. [On the other hand,] Abū Yūsuf, Muḥammad [b. al-Ḥasan] and al-Ḥasan b. Ziyād all narrated that Abū Ḥanīfa said that if one recites it in the first cycle upon commencing the recitation, he does not need to recite it again in the rest of that prayer. However, if he recites it with every *sūra*, that is good.

Issue 5

The apparent [consequence] of Abū Ḥanīfa's position is that once a person has recited the *tasmiya* at the beginning of the *Fātiḥa*, he does not repeat it at the start of the other *sūras*. According to Shāfiʿī, it is preferable to repeat it with every *sūra*, based on the Prophet (may God bless him and grant him peace) saying: 'Any matter of significance which is not commenced by "In the Name of God" is severed.'

Issue 6

[Authorities] differed concerning whether a menstruating woman or a person in a state of major ritual impurity may recite *In the Name of God, the Compassionate, the Merciful*. The correct view according to our [Shāfiʿī school] is that it is not permitted.

Issue 7

The scholars are in consensus that mentioning God's Name with the *tasmiya* is recommended when performing ablution (*wuḍū'*). The vast majority do not consider it obligatory, as the Prophet (may God bless him and grant him peace) said: 'Perform ablution as God commanded,'[1] and the *tasmiya* is not mentioned in the verse of ablution (Q.v.6).

However, the literalists (*ahl al-ẓāhir*) said that it is obligatory, such that the prayer of one who misses it—deliberately or forgetfully—is not valid. As for Isḥāq [b. Rāhawayh], he said that if one misses it deliberately, it is not permitted; but if it is missed due to forgetfulness, that is excused.

Issue 8

Is [an animal] which is slaughtered without the *tasmiya* being pronounced permitted to eat, or not? This is an extremely well-known issue.[2] Almighty God said: 'Then pronounce the Name of God over them as they line up (for sacrifice)' (Q.xxii.36), and 'Eat not of (meats) on which God's Name has not been pronounced' (Q.vii.121).

1 Recorded by Nasā'ī and Ibn Mājah—R.S.

2 See Ibn Rushd, *The Distinguished Jurist's Primer*, vol. 1, p. 541.

Issue 9

The scholars are in consensus that it is recommended that one does perform any action without saying 'In the Name of God.' When he sleeps, he says 'In the Name of God.' When he rises, he says 'In the Name of God.' When he intends to worship, he says 'In the Name of God.' When he enters the home, he says 'In the Name of God'; and when he exits, he says 'In the Name of God.' When he eats or drinks, takes or gives, he says 'In the Name of God.'

It is recommended for the midwife, upon taking hold of the child from the mother, to say 'In the Name of God' in order that it be his first state in this world. When he dies and is placed in the grave, it is said: 'In the Name of God'—and this is his last state in this world. When he rises from the grave, he also says 'In the Name of God'; and when he attends the standing [before God], he says 'In the Name of God.' Indeed, Hellfire retreats from him by the blessings of saying 'In the Name of God.'

[Reciting the Qur'ān in Translation]

Enquiry 11

Shāfiʿī said that the translation of the Qur'ān is not sufficient for the validity of prayer, regardless of whether the person is capable of reciting [in Arabic] or not.

Abū Ḥanīfa said that it is sufficient both for the capable and the incapable. Abū Yūsuf and Muḥammad said that it is sufficient for one who is incapable, but not for one who is capable [of reciting in Arabic]. Know that the position of Abū Ḥanīfa is extremely dubious, which is why the jurist (*faqīh*) Abū al-Layth al-Samarqandī and Qāḍī Abū Zayd al-Dabūsī expressly rejected it.[1]

THE FOLLOWING ARE OUR PROOFS [of its invalidity]:

1. The Prophet (may God bless him and grant him peace) only ever recited the Qur'ān as it was revealed to him from Almighty God in the Arabic tongue, and this was so for the entirety of his life. It follows that this is obligatory upon us, due to His saying: '...and follow him' (Q.VII.158).

   It is astonishing that [Abū Ḥanīfa] took the fact of the Prophet (may God bless him and grant him peace) wiping his forelock on one occasion as proof of [this amount] being a condition of the

1 See Kāsānī, *Badā'iʿ al-ṣanā'iʿ*, vol. 1, pp. 363–5.

validity of ablution, yet he has not taken into account the fact that he continuously recited the Qur'ān in Arabic throughout his life!

2. The Rightly-Guided Caliphs prayed with the Arabic Qur'ān, so that must be obligatory upon us, as the Prophet (may God bless him and grant him peace) said: 'Follow the two after me: Abū Bakr and ʿUmar.' He also said: 'Hold to my example (*sunna*) and the example of the rightly-guided caliphs after me: bite onto it with your molars.'
3. Neither the Prophet (may God bless him and grant him peace) nor any of his companions recited anything in their prayers other than this Arabic Qur'ān, so that must be obligatory upon us as the Prophet (may God bless him and grant him peace) said: 'My nation will divide into seventy-odd sects, all of them in the Fire except one.' It was said: 'Who are they, O Messenger of God?' He replied: 'What I and my companions are upon.'[1] The relevance of this is that he and all the companions were agreed upon reciting the Arabic Qur'ān in their prayers; this entails that one who recites in Persian[2] is among the people of Hellfire.
4. The people of the Islamic lands are in complete agreement on reciting the Qur'ān in prayer just as God revealed it. Anyone who swerves from this path is indeed one who 'follows a path other than that of the believers' (Q.IV.115).
5. People are commanded to recite 'the Qur'ān' in prayer. One who recites in Persian has not [in fact] recited the Qur'ān, so he has not discharged the obligation. We have said that we are ordered to recite the Qur'ān based on the verse: 'So recite of the Qur'ān what is easy for you' (Q.LXXIII.20), and on the Prophet (may God bless him and grant him peace) saying to the Bedouin: 'Then recite whatever is easy for you of the Qur'ān.'[3]

As for composed speech in Persian not being Qur'ān, this is shown by the following:

a. God said: 'Indeed, this is a revelation from the Lord of the worlds...In a perspicuous Arabic tongue' (Q.XXVI.192–195).

1 This is a version of the first *ḥadīth* cited in Book I.

2 This is the example which is frequently used in the discussions. The author himself was born and raised in a Persian environment, although his lineage was Arab. Some of his books are in Persian, and he has provided small translations below.

3 This is the same account of the Bedouin who was taught to pray, cited in Book I and earlier in this chapter. This portion was not quoted previously.

b. God said: 'We sent not a Messenger except (to teach) in the language of his (own) people' (Q.xiv.4).

c. God said: 'Had We sent this as a non-Arabic Qur'ān...' (Q.xli.44) in which the [conditional particle] *law* signifies the negation of one thing [apodosis] due to the negation of another [protasis]. This means that He did not make it a non-Arabic (*aʿjamī*) Qur'ān, and it follows that anything which is non-Arabic is not Qur'ān.

d. God said: 'Say: If the whole of mankind and the jinns were to gather together to produce the like of this Qur'ān, they could not produce the like thereof, even if they reinforced each other with help and support' (Q.xvii.88). Regarding the composed speech in Persian, it must either be that very Arabic speech or its like (*mithl*), or else neither identical nor similar. The first option is necessarily false. As for the second, that too is false: for if the Persian composition were the like of the Arabic speech, the one who produced it would have produced the like of the Qur'ān, which would be to belie God's declaration that they 'could not produce the like thereof'. Therefore, since the Persian composition is neither the Qur'ān itself nor its like, it is proven that one who recites it is not reciting the Qur'ān—and this is what we sought to prove. It is thus shown that such a person was commanded to recite [the Qur'ān] and did not discharge that, so the burden remains upon him.

6. Ibn al-Mundhir reported via Abū Hurayra that the Prophet (may God bless him and grant him peace) said: 'A prayer in which the Opening of the Book is not recited is not acceptable.' Abū Ḥanīfa would have to say concerning these words in Persian either that they are Qur'ān or not-Qur'ān. The first would be tremendous ignorance and a departure from consensus, as shown by the following:

   a. It could never be allowed rationally or religiously for a person to claim that *dūstān dar behesht*[1] is Qur'ān.

1 As found in the printed editions, this phrase reads as 'friends in heaven'. As used by the author here and the following point, it seems to be an extract from a Persian Qur'ān translation; however, it does not correspond to anything I could locate. For a broader context, see Travis Zadeh, *The Vernacular Qur'an: Translation and the Rise of Persian Exegesis*, Oxford: Oxford University Press, 2012.

b. It would follow that one who is capable of translating the Qur'ān is able to produce a Qur'ān like the original, and that is false.

7. ʿAbd Allāh b. Abī Awfā related that a man said: 'O Messenger of God! I am unable to memorise the Qur'ān as is needed for the prayer!' He replied: 'Say "Glory be to God, praise is for God..."'[1] The relevance of this is that when the man asked how to fulfil his prayer while unable to recite the Arabic Qur'ān, the Messenger (may God bless him and grant him peace) instructed him to say words of glorification (*tasbīḥ*). This refutes the claim that it would be sufficient to say *dūstān dar behesht*.
8. It is said that the beginning of the Gospel is *bi'smi ilāhan raḥmānan wa-marḥiyānan*,[2] which is an exact translation of [the Arabic] *bi'smi 'Llāh al-Raḥmān al-Raḥīm*. Therefore, if the translation of the Qur'ān were itself Qur'ān, the Christians would say: 'This Qur'ān has merely been taken from the Gospel itself.' Since this has not been said, we know that the translation of the Qur'ān is not Qur'ān.
9. If we were to translate the verse 'Now send then one of you with this money of yours to the town: let him find out which is the best food and bring some to you as sustenance...' (Q.XVIII.19), it would be as follows: *bifarastīd yakī az shumā bā nuqrah bishehr, pas bingar digar kodām behtar'st bārah azān biyāward*. Clearly, this [latter composition] is from the genus of human speech in both form and meaning. As such, it could not be used in prayer, as the Prophet (may God bless him and grant him peace) said: 'In this prayer of ours, nothing of people's speech is appropriate.'[3] If prayer would not be valid with the translation of this verse, the same would apply to all other verses, since no one has differentiated [between these types].

   The same proof applies to the translation of 'A slanderer, going about with calumnies; hindering good, transgressing beyond bounds, deep in sin; violent, and with all that, base-born' (Q.LXVIII.11–13)—it would constitute cursing in human speech, both in form and meaning.[4] The same applies to 'So beseech your Lord for us to produce

1 Recorded by Abū Dāwūd—R.S.

2 This would seem to be on the presumption of an Aramaic original (or Hebrew or Syriac). Cf. Book II, Chapter Nine, Enquiry 3. The remainder of this argument presumes that the Christians know this to be the opening of the Gospel, which makes it even more problematic.

3 Recorded by Muslim—R.S.

4 Of course, the same applies to the English translations provided in the midst of this translation of the author's argument! NB: a negating particle was wrongly included in some editions (*lā takūnu shatman*), but it is correct in Amīriyya, vol. 1, p. 115.

for us of what the earth grows: its pot-herbs, its cucumbers...' (Q.II.61)—its translation would be from the genus of human speech in form and meaning. On the other hand, when we recite the verses themselves in their [Arabic] words, then—by their inimitable composition and remarkable arrangement—they are distinct from the speech of men. It is astonishing that our opponents argued that if a person includes, at the end of the sitting (*tashahhud*) in prayer, a supplication which is from the genus of human speech, his prayer becomes invalid; yet they accept that prayer is valid using the translation of these verses, even though that translation is itself human speech in form and meaning!

10. The Prophet (may God bless him and grant him peace) said: 'The Qur'ān was revealed upon seven modes (*aḥruf*), each of them valid and sufficient.'[1] If the translations of the Qur'ān in each language (*lugha*) were also Qur'ān, this would mean that the Qur'ān was revealed upon more than seven modes, as—according to their claim—every language would have its own Qur'ān. In that case, it would not be correct to limit the modes of the Qur'ān to seven.
11. According to Abū Ḥanīfa, prayer is valid with any verses. Without doubt, there are many verses in the Torah which agree with the contents of the Qur'ān in terms of praise of God, magnification of the Hereafter and dispraise of this world. Therefore, it follows from the position of our opponent that prayer is valid with recitation of the Gospel and the Torah, and by the recitation of 'Zayd and *insān*'.[2] Indeed, [according to them] if he were to enter this world and live for a hundred years without ever reciting a letter of the Qur'ān, but instead continued to recite according to 'Zayd and *insān*', he would then meet God in a state of obedience! It is known by necessity that this claim is not befitting of the religion of the Muslims.

1 Versions of this *ḥadīth* are in Bukhāri and Muslim. This particular wording is recorded by Ṭabarī in his exegesis (cf. Scott Lucas' translation, *Selections from The Comprehensive Exposition of the Interpretation of the Verses of the Qur'ān*, 2 vols., Cambridge: Islamic Texts Society, 2017, vol. 1, p. 26). The argument here is based on the interpretation that the seven 'letters' or 'modes' represent seven dialects (also referred to as *lughāt*) upon which the Qur'ān was revealed and recited. For an overview of opinions, see Imām, *Variant Readings*, pp. 3–20.

2 This expression is unclear to me, but appears to mean that if any particular person or even unknown person were to express the meanings of the Qur'ān in their own tongues, that reciting that would be sufficient for prayer, according to the author's claimed implication of Abū Ḥanīfa's position.

12. Any translation of the *Fātiḥa* will read [something like this:][1] 'Exalted be God, Lord of the worlds, Merciful to the needy and Powerful over Judgment Day. You are the object of worship and the One asked for help. Guide us to the path of the people of gnosis, not the path of the wretched.' If the translation of the *Fātiḥa* is only this or similar, then it is known that every sermon (*khuṭba*) contains this amount: so it would follow that prayer is valid by reciting any sermon [therein]. Since that is false, the falsity of their claim is known.
13. If it were allowed, then the Messenger of God (may God bless him and grant him peace) would have permitted Salmān the Persian to recite the Qur'ān in Persian and pray in that way. Likewise, he would have permitted Ṣuhayb to recite in the Byzantine [tongue], and Bilāl in the Abyssinian. If that were legislated, its permissibility would have been widely known among the people, as speakers of the various languages would have greeted this with enthusiasm, in that it alleviates them of the difficulties of learning Arabic. [If it should be permitted,] then each community would take great pride in having a Qur'ān in their own language. Clearly, this would lead to the complete obliteration of the Qur'ān, and no Muslim could accept this!
14. If it were permissible to recite in Persian in the prayer, then it would [no longer] be permissible to recite it in Arabic: whereas [in reality, the latter] is permissible and [the former] is not. To explain this entailment: the Persian man who understands nothing of Arabic does not, as a result, understand anything of the Qur'ān. However, if he were to recite in Persian, he would understand its meaning and grasp its purpose, appreciating what it contains of praise of God, invitation to the Hereafter and deprecation of the worldly life. It is known that the highest purpose of establishing the prayer is to inculcate these meanings, as God said: 'Establish regular prayer for My remembrance' (Q.xx.14), and 'Do they not reflect upon the Qur'ān, or are there locks upon (their) hearts?' (Q.xlvii.24). Thus reciting the translation achieves these great benefits [for him] while reciting it in the Arabic prevents them. Therefore, if we were to accept that reciting in Persian is equivalent in validity to reciting in Arabic, then, since the Persian achieves great

1 The preceding sentence in the printed edition is unclear, but I have translated according to the context. What follows in quotation marks was originally an Arabic paraphrase of the *Fātiḥa*, so I have translated it in this manner to reflect this intention. In a similar vein, see Muḥammad Rashīd Riḍā, *Tafsīr al-manār* (*Tafsīr al-Qur'ān al-ḥakīm*), ed. Fu'ād ʿAbd al-Ghaffār, 12 vols., Cairo: al-Maktaba al-Tawfīqiyya, n.d., vol. 1, pp. 93–6.

benefits [for such people] and the Arabic precludes them, it follows that reciting in Arabic ought to be prohibited. Since that is not the case, we know that reciting in Persian is not permitted.

15. The cause (*muqtaḍī*) for the command to pray remains in effect, and the difference (*fāriq*) is apparent.[1] On the first point: the obligation was established, and remains in effect by default. On the second point: just as one is instructed to recite the Arabic Qur'ān for its meaning, it is also for the sake of its words, for two reasons:
    a. Its inimitability (*iʿjāz*) is in its eloquence (*faṣāḥa*), which is contained in its words.
    b. Making the validity of the prayer conditional upon reciting its words makes it necessary to memorise those words. When there is copious memorisation done by a great many people, this results in [the Qur'ān] being preserved from distortion until the end of time, which fulfils God's promise: 'We have, without doubt, sent down the Message; and We will assuredly guard it (from corruption)' (Q.xv.9). On the other hand, if we were to say that the validity of the prayer is not conditional upon reciting these Arabic words, then this purpose would not be achieved.

THE PROPONENT OF THE OPPOSITE VIEW ARGUES: the command is to recite the Qur'ān, and reciting the translation is indeed recitation of the Qur'ān. This is supported by the following:

1. It is narrated that ʿAbd Allāh b. Masʿūd was teaching a man the Qur'ān, and came to 'Indeed, the tree of Zaqqūm will be the food of the sinful (*ṭaʿām al-athīm*)' (Q.xliv.43–44). The man was non-Arab and kept saying *ṭaʿām al-yatīm* ('food of the orphan'). Ibn Masʿūd told him: 'Say: *ṭaʿām al-fājir* ("food of the sinner").' He added: 'It is not an error in Qur'ān to say *al-Ḥakīm* (the Wise) in place of *al-ʿAlīm* (the Knowing), but rather error is to recite a verse of mercy in place of a verse of torment.'[2]

1 The point here is that the obligation is not fulfilled by reciting the *meanings* of the Qur'ān, because there is a significant difference between this (in translation) and the *words* of the Qur'ān together with their meanings.

2 This is recorded by Abū ʿUbayd in *Faḍā'il al-Qur'ān*. See Ālūsī, *Rūḥ al-maʿānī*, vol. xxiv, pp. 487–8 for comments on these narrations. At most, this was a temporary dispensation for the learner. For further discussion of such instances that suggest an early textual 'multiformity' abrogated by Caliph ʿUthmān's establishment of a single 'textual skeleton (*rasm*)', see Yasin Dutton, 'Orality, Literary and the "Seven *Aḥruf*" *Ḥadīth*', *Journal of Islamic Studies*, vol. xxiii, no. 1, 2012, pp. 1–49.

2. God said: 'Without doubt it is in the scriptures (*zubur*) of former people' (Q.xxvi.196), i.e. the Qur'ān is [present] in the former scriptures. He also said: 'And this is in the earlier books (*ṣuḥuf*); the books of Abraham and Moses' (Q.lxxxvii.18–19]. There is consensus that these [Arabic] words of the Qur'ān were not present in previous scriptures, as those were in Hebrew and Syriac.
3. God said: '[Say:] "This Qur'ān has been revealed to me by inspiration, that I may warn you thereby and all whom it reaches"' (Q.vi.19);[1] however, the non-Arabs do not understand the Arabic words unless the meanings are conveyed to them in their own language. Nevertheless, it was described as 'Qur'ān', which shows that the [translation] composed in Persian is also Qur'ān.

RESPONSE TO THE FIRST POINT: these people's condition is indeed astonishing! For it is narrated that Ibn Masʿūd used to say 'I am a believer, if God wills,'[2] and none of the Companions was said to insist on this statement as he did. Yet the Ḥanafīs pay no attention to this [narration], instead saying[3] that one who makes this statement has doubted concerning his religion, and such a person cannot be considered a believer! If the opinion of Ibn Masʿūd is a proof [in religion], then why did they not accept it in that issue? If it is not a proof, then why did they adopt it here? Indeed, these are quite remarkable contradictions. Moreover, it has been narrated that Ibn Masʿūd removed the two protection-seeking *sūras* (*muʿawwidhatān*) [cxiii and cxiv] as well as the *Fātiḥa* from the Qur'ān.[4] However, we must assume the best of him, i.e. that he retracted [all] these views.

RESPONSE [CONCERNING THE VERSES:] 'Without doubt it is in the scriptures of former people' (Q.xxvi.196) means that its stories are present in previous scriptures [in general meaning]. Regarding '…that I may warn you…' (Q.vi.19), this means to warn 'with its meaning'. This small amount of metaphorical [interpretation] is acceptable due to the sheer weight of the decisive evidences we have presented.

1 I have expanded this citation in order to make the explanation clearer.

2 The author is alluding to a dispute between the Ḥanafīs and Shāfiʿīs (or more related to the theological schools dominant among each group, respectively the Māturīdī and Ashʿarī) over whether it is acceptable to say 'I am a believer, if God wills,' in the sense that one does not know whether his fate has been so written. The Ḥanafī-Māturīdīs considered this to express doubt in faith: see ʿUmar al-Ashqar, *al-Madkhal ilā al-sharīʿa wa'l-fiqh al-Islāmī*, Amman: Dār al-Nafā'is, 2005, p. 316.

3 The printed edition has *bal naqūl*, but the correct word—as in Amīriyya, vol. 1, p. 116—*is taqūl*.

4 See also the end of this chapter, and Muḥammad Muṣṭafā al-Aʿẓamī, *The History of the Qur'ānic Text*, Leicester: UK Islamic Academy, 2003, pp. 195–202.

[Does the Follower in Prayer Recite?]

Enquiry 12

Shāfiʿī said in his new school[1] that it is obligatory for the follower [in prayer] to recite [the *Fātiḥa*], whether the *imām* is reciting audibly or inaudibly. In his old school, he said that it is obligatory if the *imām* recites inaudibly, but not if he recites audibly—and this was the position of Mālik and Ibn al-Mubārak. Abū Ḥanīfa said that reciting behind the *imām* is [prohibitively] disliked in every case.[2]

The following are our evidences [for the later Shāfiʿī position]:

1. God said: 'So recite of the Qur'ān what is easy for you' (Q.LXXIII.20), and this command encompasses both the person praying individually and the follower.[3]
2. The Prophet (may God bless him and grant him peace) used to recite in his prayers, so that is obligatory upon us as God said: '...and follow him' (Q.VII.158). It could be claimed that [his practice] would be otherwise if he were to be a follower, but this is a [speculative] contention.[4]
3. We have explained[5] that the command 'Establish the prayer' (Q.VI.72) refers to the collection of actions which the Messenger of God (may God bless him and grant him peace) used to perform. Among these was to recite the *Fātiḥa*, so this command includes recitation of the *Fātiḥa*.
4. The Prophet (may God bless him and grant him peace) said: 'There is no prayer except with the Opening of the Book'—its evidential relevance has already been explained.[6]

OBJECTION: The [Ḥanafīs] might argue that this is specific to the case

1 Famously, Shāfiʿī has an earlier school developed in Iraq, and a later one developed in Egypt. The author argues here for the later position; and this is considered the authoritative one in general for Shāfiʿīs.

2 The *imām* recites audibly in the *fajr*, *maghrib* and *ʿishā'* prayers, and inaudibly in *ẓuhr* and *ʿaṣr*. See Ibn Rushd, *The Distinguished Jurist's Primer*, vol. 1, p. 171.

3 The author previously argued (see Enquiry 2 above, point 11) that 'what is easy' refers to the *Fātiḥa*.

4 Naturally, the Prophet was usually the leader of his community in prayer. The writing here is terse; an alternative reading of the contention is that one cannot know how to 'follow' the Prophet when he is in the position of follower in prayer. The response (if the last word of the sentence is read as *muʿāraḍ*) can be taken as a concession to the point, with the rejoinder that other evidences confirm that the Prophet recited even while in the position of follower.

5 See Enquiry 2, point 2 above.

6 See Enquiry 2, point 6 above.

of praying individually, as Jābir related that the Prophet (may God bless him and grant him peace) said: 'Whoever performs a prayer without reciting the Source of the Book, he has not [in fact] prayed, unless that was behind the *imām*.'[1]

RESPONSE: the authenticity of this report has been questioned.

5. The Prophet (may God bless him and grant him peace) said to the Bedouin: 'Then recite whatever is easy for you of the Qur'ān.' This encompasses both the individual worshipper and the follower.
6. Abū ʿĪsā al-Tirmidhī reported in his *Jāmiʿ* collection via his chain to Maḥmūd b. al-Rabīʿ, from ʿUbāda b. al-Ṣāmit: 'The Prophet (may God bless him and grant him peace) was reciting in the dawn prayer (*ṣubḥ*), but found the recitation difficult [due to a disturbance]. When he finished, he said: "Why does it seem to me that you recite behind your *imām*?" They said: "Indeed, by God [we do]." He said: "Do not do that, except with the Source of the Book, for there is no prayer for one who does not recite it."' Abū ʿĪsā al-Tirmidhī said: 'This is a fair (*ḥasan*) *ḥadīth*.'
7. Mālik reported in *al-Muwaṭṭa'* from ʿAlā b. ʿAbd al-Raḥmān that he heard Abū al-Sā'ib (the freedman of Hishām) saying: 'I heard Abū Hurayra say that the Messenger of God (may God bless him and grant him peace) said: "Whoever performs a prayer without reciting the Source of the Qur'ān, that [prayer] is deficient and incomplete." So I said: "O Abū Hurayra! But sometimes I am behind the *imām*." He replied: "Recite it within yourself, O Persian!"' This is relevant in two ways: first, our opponents claim that the follower's prayer is free of deficiency if he does not recite, which is contrary to this text. Second, the questioner [Abū al-Sā'ib] raised the issue of prayer behind an *imām* with Abū Hurayra, who [gave the ruling (*fatwā*)][2] that it is obligatory for him to recite in this situation, which is the point we are proving.
8. Abū Hurayra related that the Prophet (may God bless him and grant him peace) said: 'Almighty God said: "I have divided the Prayer between Me and My servant into two halves..."'—in which it is made clear that the division has only taken place due to the recitation. Therefore, recitation must be a concomitant of the prayer, and this division occurs both in an individual's prayer and that of a follower.

1 This is attributed more correctly to Jābir himself—S.I.

2 This phrase is missing from some editions, but present in Amīriyya, vol. 1, p. 117.

9. Dāraquṭnī recorded via his chain to ʿUbāda b. al-Ṣāmit: 'The Messenger of God (may God bless him and grant him peace) led us in one of the prayers in which recitation is audible, then, upon finishing, he turned to us with his noble face and asked: "Do you recite while I recite aloud?" Some of us replied: "We do indeed." He said: "I say: how is it that I compete [with you] in the Qur'ān? Do not recite anything of the Qur'ān while I am reciting aloud, except the Source of the Book, for there is no prayer for one who does not recite it."'
10. There are numerous Prophetic *ḥadīth*s describing the great reward associated with reciting the Qur'ān, and these encompass both the individual worshipper and the follower. It follows that reciting behind the *imām* in prayer makes one deserving of great reward, and anyone who says this [also] says it is obligatory.
11. Abū Ḥanīfa conceded that reciting behind the *imām* does not nullify the prayer. On the contrary, leaving off recitation nullifies the prayer according to our school. Therefore, to recite is more cautious, hence it is obligatory according to the Prophetic saying: 'Leave what makes you doubt for that which does not make you doubt.'
12. If the follower stays silent and does not recite even though he cannot hear the *imām*'s recitation, he will remain unoccupied [for that duration]. As such, one who recites is in a superior state, as the Prophet (may God bless him and grant him peace) said: 'The best of deeds is the recitation of the Qur'ān.'[1] Since it is proven that recitation is superior to silence in this situation, it follows that it is obligatory, since no one has differentiated [between these points].
13. If following [an *imām*] precluded one's own recitation, then being a follower would be prohibited. This is because recitation is a great act of worship; and anything which prevents one from a noble worship is prohibited, so it follows that being a follower [in prayer] is prohibited. Since this is not the case, we know that being a follower does not preclude one's recitation.

ABŪ ḤANĪFA'S EVIDENCE: he cited the Qur'ān and *ḥadīth*s. The former is God's saying: 'When the Qur'ān is recited, listen to it with attention and hold your peace, that you may receive mercy' (Q.VII.204). However, we have explained at great length in the exegesis of this

1 A similar narration is found in Bayhaqī's *Shuʿab al-īmān*—R.S.

verse that it does not support their position: so consult that juncture in this work.[1]

As for the latter, they cited numerous *ḥadīth*s, but Shaykh Aḥmad al-Bayhaqī has clarified the weakness of these. Supposing, nevertheless, that they are authentic, the presence of numerous contradictory reports still requires us to prefer [some over others], and this should be done in our favour, for the following reasons:

a. Our position entails that a person be busy with the recitation of the Qur'ān, which is one of the greatest acts of obedience. Their position entails being inactive and silent instead of mentioning God: so ours is preferable without doubt.
b. Our position is more cautious.
c. Our position entails that all parts of the prayer are filled with obedience and beautiful remembrance, whereas theirs entails spending time doing nothing in place of obedience and remembrance.

[Is the *Fātiḥa* Recited in Every Cycle?]

Enquiry 13

Shāfiʿī said that reciting the *Fātiḥa* is obligatory in every prayer cycle (*rakʿa*): so if he misses it in any cycle, his prayer would be void. Shaykh Abū Ḥāmid al-Isfarā'īnī said: 'This opinion had the consensus of the Companions. It was expressed by Abū Bakr, ʿUmar, ʿAli and Ibn Masʿūd.'

Know that there are six opinions on the matter:

A. That of al-Aṣamm and Ibn ʿUlayya: that recitation is not obligatory at all.
B. That of al-Ḥasan al-Baṣrī and al-Ḥasan b. Ṣāliḥ b. [Ḥayy][2]: that recitation is only obligatory in one cycle. This is because the Prophet (may God bless him and grant him peace) said: 'There is no prayer except with the Opening of the Book'—since an exception from a negation is [equivalent to] affirmation, reciting the *Fātiḥa* [even] once necessitates that prayer be considered valid according to that exception.

1 The author has argued based on context that this verse was addressed to the unbelievers, contrary to the various deductions of the jurists. This cross-reference implies (more strongly than that to *Sūrat al-Ḥijr* earlier) that the exegesis of the *Fātiḥa* was written later than *al-Aʿrāf*.

2 The printed editions again have 'Jinnī'. At the start of the chapter, the author attributed to al-Ḥasan b. Ṣāliḥ the same opinion as al-Aṣamm.

C. That of Abū Ḥanīfa: that recitation is obligatory in the first two cycles, but a person has the choice in the remaining cycles[1] between recitation, glorification (*tasbīḥ*) and silence. In the book of *al-Istiḥbāb*, he said that recitation is obligatory in two cycles, without specifying.

D. Ibn al-Ṣabbāgh narrated in his book *al-Shāmil* that Sufyān [al-Thawrī] said that recitation is obligatory in the first two cycles, and disliked in the remainder.

E. Mālik said that recitation is obligatory in the majority of cycles, not all of them. Thus, for a prayer consisting of four cycles, it is sufficient to recite in three. In the sunset prayer (*maghrib*) [of three cycles], it is sufficient to recite in two. Yet in the dawn prayer (*ṣubḥ*) [of two cycles], it is necessary to recite in both.

F. Shāfiʿī said that recitation is obligatory in all cycles.

THE VERACITY OF SHĀFIʿĪ'S POSITION is shown by the following:

1. The Prophet (may God bless him and grant him peace) used to recite in every cycle of prayer, so the same is obligatory upon us, as God said: '…and follow him' (Q.VII.158).
2. When he taught the Bedouin how to pray, the Prophet (may God bless him and grant him peace) instructed him to recite the Source of the Book, then said: 'And do the same in every cycle'—and the imperative signifies obligation.

   OBJECTION: 'do the same' refers to the actions rather than the words.

   RESPONSE: [reciting] words is an action of the tongue and must therefore be included.
3. Shaykh Abū al-Naṣr b. al-Ṣabbāgh narrated in *al-Shāmil* from Abū Saʿīd al-Khudrī: 'The Messenger of God (may God bless him and grant him peace) instructed us to recite the Opening of the Book in every cycle, whether [the prayer] be obligatory or optional.'[2]
4. Reciting in all cycles is more cautious, so it must be deemed obligatory.
5. [God] commanded us to pray, and this remains in effect by default; we judge that the obligation is discharged when one recites in all cycles, because this prayer is more complete. However, when recitation is not done in all cycles, the obligation must remain.

PROPONENTS OF THE OTHER VIEW cite the *ḥadīth* of ʿĀ'isha, who said: 'The

1 Here and below, this word is in the dual, although the remaining cycle may be just one, or none at all.

2 Recorded also by Tirmidhī and Ibn Mājah—S.I.

prayer was originally obligated as two cycles, then that was confirmed in [the case of] travel, but increased for [times of] residence.'[1] [They say:] based on this, the first two cycles are original and the remainder are derivative (*tabaʿ*). Derivative matters are generally treated as lighter: that is why one does not recite an additional *sūra* therein, nor is recitation done audibly.

RESPONSE: our evidences are stronger and more numerous, and our position is safer, so this is preferable.

Enquiry 14
Assorted Issues (*Furūʿ*) Concerning the *Fātiḥa*

The following are issues which follow from considering the *Fātiḥa* to be one of the requirements of the prayer:

Issue 1

We have explained that if a person deliberately misses the *Fātiḥa* or even one letter thereof, his prayer is void. However, what if he does so *forgetfully*? Shāfiʿī said in his old school that it does not vitiate the prayer, citing the report of Abū Salama b. ʿAbd al-Raḥmān, who said: "ʿUmar b. al-Khaṭṭāb led us in the sunset prayer and omitted the recitation. When the prayer was over, it was said to him: "You missed the recitation!" He asked: "How were the bowing and prostration?" They replied: "Fine," so he said: "Then there is no problem.""[2] Shāfiʿī said: 'Since this incident occurred in front of [numerous] Companions, it is considered a consensus.'

However, he recanted this opinion in his new school, saying that [missing recitation] does vitiate the prayer, because the aforementioned evidences encompass both the deliberate and the forgetful. His response concerning the story of ʿUmar is twofold: first, [ʿĀmir] al-Shaʿbī narrated that ʿUmar repeated that prayer.[3] Second, he may simply have recited inaudibly, and not missed the recitation altogether. Shāfiʿī said: 'This is what we must assume of ʿUmar.'

Issue 2

The order of recitation must be observed. Hence if a person recited the second half [of the *Fātiḥa*] followed by the first half, only the first [half] would be counted [towards his prayer].

Issue 3

A man who is not skilled at [reciting from memory] the whole of the

1 Recorded by Bukhārī and Muslim—S.I.

2 This is recorded in some transmissions of Mālik's *Muwaṭṭāʾ*—R.S.

3 This is in Bayhaqī's *Kubrā*—R.S.

Fātiḥa may have memorised part of it, or none at all. In the former case, he should recite that verse together with six [other] verses, according to the strongest opinion.[1] In the latter case, i.e. one who has not memorised any of the *Fātiḥa*, then if he has memorised anything else of the Qur'ān, he must recite from what he has memorised, as God said: 'So recite of the Qur'ān what is easy for you' (Q.lxxiii.20).

If he has memorised nothing of the Qur'ān, then [according to Shāfiʿī] he must pronounce words of remembrance (*dhikr*), namely the *takbīr* and *taḥmīd* ['Praise is for God']. According to Abū Ḥanīfa, in such a case there is no obligation upon the person. Shāfiʿī's proof is the narration of Rifāʿa [b. Rāfiʿ] b. Mālik, that the Messenger of God said: 'When one of you stands to pray, let him make ablution as God commanded, then pronounce the *takbīr*. Thereafter, if he has [memorised] anything of the Qur'ān, he should recite. If he has nothing of the Qur'ān with him, then let him praise God and pronounce the *takbīr*.'[2]

One scenario remains, namely that a person has not memorised the *Fātiḥa* or anything of the Qur'ān, nor even any Arabic words of remembrance. My opinion is that he should be instructed to remember Almighty God in any language he can manage, according to the Prophet's saying: 'When I command you with something, do of it what you are able.'[3]

Enquiry 15
[Ibn Masʿūd's Stance on Particular *Sūras*]

It is recorded in early sources that Ibn Masʿūd denied that *Sūrat al-Fātiḥa* is part of the Qur'ān, and the same for the two protection-seeking *sūras* [cxiii and cxiv]. Know that this is extremely problematic, for if we say that there was widespread (*mutawātir*)[4] communication at the time of the Companions of the fact that the *Fātiḥa* is part of the Qur'ān, then Ibn Masʿūd must have known that; as such, denying it would entail either unbelief or loss of mind.

If, on the other hand, we say that there was no widespread communication to this effect during that period, then it follows that the Qur'ān

1 Alternatively, *ʿalā al-wajh al-aqrab* may mean that he should recite verses which correspond as closely as possible to the verses of the *Fātiḥa* in length.

2 This is a variation on the earlier *ḥadīth* via Rifāʿa, recorded in the *Musnad* of Shāfiʿī.

3 Recorded by Bukhārī and Muslim—R.S.

4 I have opted for 'widespread' here rather than the usual 'mass transmission' because the reference is to the first stage of that mass transmission, by which is meant a succession of multiples.

was not subject to mass transmission (*tawātur*) at its origin, which in turn would preclude its status as a decisive proof.

Most likely, these narrations concerning Ibn Masʿūd are deceitful and false; this allows us to escape the thorny problem.

With that, we conclude our discussion of the juristic enquiries arising from *Sūrat al-Fātiḥa*. And God is the Guide to what is correct.

Chapter Five
EXEGESIS OF *SŪRAT AL-FĀTIḤA*[1]

Exegesis of *All praise is for God* (Verse 2)[2]

[Benefit 1: Lexical Subtleties]

There are three [related] words: *ḥamd*, *madḥ* and *shukr*.[3] There are several distinctions between *ḥamd* and *madḥ*:

a. *Madḥ* may be [expressed for both] living and non-living entities. One who sees an incredibly beautiful pearl or gem might express *madḥ* for them, but it is impossible that he would give *ḥamd*. The former is more encompassing than the latter.
b. *Madḥ* may be given before [or without] an act of kindness (*iḥsān*) [from the one praised], whereas *ḥamd* is only after kindness.
c. Some *madḥ* is forbidden, as the Prophet (may God bless him and grant him peace) said: 'Cast dust in the faces of the praisers (*maddāḥīn*).'[4] On the other hand, *ḥamd* is always commanded, as the Prophet (may God bless him and grant him peace) said: 'One who does not do *ḥamd* to people has not done so to God.'[5]

1 The structure of the remainder of the volume is counter-intuitive. As acknowledged by its title, this chapter contains the content most closely pertaining to the exegesis of the *Fātiḥa*. As such, it is surprising that it is relatively brief and occupies only the first Part (*qism*) within the fifth Chapter (*bāb*) of the third Book (*kitāb*). Although Part One is not labelled explicitly, there is a Part Two with general themes of the *sūra*, which I have relabelled as Chapter Six. Each of the verses (or phrases) is discussed in a section (*faṣl*), which I have labelled with verse numbers. Each section is comprised of 'benefits' (*fawā'id*) which are the equivalent of 'enquiries' elsewhere in the work.

2 The discussion begins here with what the author deemed to be the second verse of the *sūra*, due to the extensive discussion of the first verse (i.e. the *basmala*) in Book II.

3 These may all be translated as praise, thanks, etc. but I have left them untranslated here in order not to obscure the distinctions being made between the Arabic words. The purpose is to demonstrate the implications of the word *ḥamd* being used in this verse. Another word used in the author's explanations could have been included in this account: *thanā'*.

4 Recorded by Muslim. As Imām Nawawī explains in his chapter heading to this *ḥadīth*, this pertains to exaggerated praise which could mislead the praised one. See Nawawī, *Sharḥ Ṣaḥīḥ Muslim*, vol. IX, p. 326.

5 The wording in the sources pertains to *shukr*, not *ḥamd*—S.I.

d. *Madḥ* is to express that someone possesses some virtuous attribute or another, while *ḥamd* pertains to one particular virtue, namely kindness and generosity. Thus we have shown that *madḥ* is a broader term than *ḥamd*.

As for *ḥamd* and *shukr*, the difference is that *ḥamd* encompasses all [praise for kindness], whether that kindness reaches you or others, whereas *shukr* is specific to kindness which reaches you [personally].

Once the above is known, we say: since *madḥ* encompasses the animate and the inanimate, as well as beings with and without volition, saying *al-madḥu li'Llāh* would not denote that God possesses agency and volition. *Al-ḥamdu li'Llāh*, on the other hand, denotes this volition, and one who utters these words is acknowledging that the God of the universe is not a necessitating cause by His very nature (*mūjib bi'l-dhāt*) as the philosophers say; rather, He is a voluntary agent (*fāʿil mukhtār*).

Al-ḥamdu li'Llāh is also more appropriate than *al-shukru li'Llāh*, in that the former constitutes praise of all types of kindness emanating from Him and reaching [any of the creation], whereas the latter is specific to kindness which reached the speaker. Without doubt, the former is worthier, as it is as though the servant says: 'Whether You bestow upon me or not, Your kindness extends to all the worlds, and You are deserving of tremendous praise.'

It is also said that *ḥamd* pertains to tribulations which God averts [from the servant], while *shukr* is for goodness which He bestows.

OBJECTION: to bestow [goodness] is a greater favour than to avert tribulations, so why would the lesser be mentioned in place of the greater?

RESPONSES:

a. It is as though one is saying: 'I am grateful for the lower of the two favours, so [I must be more so] for the higher.'
b. Prevention is infinite, whereas bestowal is finite.[1] As such, it is more appropriate to begin with thanks for the infinite tribulations being averted.
c. Preventing harm takes precedence over achieving benefit,[2] so it was expressed first.

1 That is to say: for each good thing bestowed upon a person, there are unlimited harmful things which have been kept at bay.

2 A famous legal maxim.

Benefit 2

Almighty God did not say: 'I praise God (*aḥmadu Allāha*),' but instead 'All praise is for God.' The latter is superior for the following reasons:

1. Saying 'I praise God' implies that the speaker is capable of celebrating His praise. On the other hand, *All praise is for God* entails that He was ever Praiseworthy prior to anyone's praise or thanks. Therefore, whether they praise and thank Him or not, the Almighty is undeniably Praised from pre-eternity and forever, due to His pre-eternal praise and speech.
2. *All praise is for God* means that praise is His right and possession. Almighty God is deserving of praise due to His abundant and diverse bounties upon the servants. It means that praise belongs to God and is His by right. 'I praise God,' on the other hand, does not denote that He is deserving of praise in His own right: therefore, the former is superior in that it conveys this meaning, rather than the mere fact of one person praising Him.
3. If He had said 'I praise God,' that would be praise, but of a grade unworthy of Him. However, when one says *All praise is for God*, it is like saying: 'Who am I to praise Him? Rather, He is praised by all the praisers.' This is similar to a situation where you are asked: 'Has so-and-so done good for you?' If you reply 'Yes,' then you have praised him, but weakly; whereas perfect praise is to say: 'Not only that: He does good for all the creatures.'
4. Praise expresses an attribute of the heart, namely the belief that the praised one is kind, beneficent and worthy of being magnified and exalted. As such, if a person were to utter 'I praise God' while his heart is inattentive to the magnification due to God's majesty, he would be [in effect] a liar, in that he claimed to have praised [God] without genuinely doing so. If, on the other hand, he says *All praise is for God*, then—whether he is attentive or inattentive to the meaning of magnification—he is truthful, for its meaning is that praise is God's right and possession. This meaning holds irrespective of the servant being attentive to God's magnification and exaltation.

It is thus shown that *All praise is for God* is superior to saying 'I praise God.' This [latter argument] is comparable to the fact that 'There is no god but God' is a statement which cannot be belied, unlike 'I bear witness (*ashhadu*) that there is no god but God.' A person may be false in his claim to witness [to God's oneness], which is why God belied the claims of the hypocrites: '...and God bears witness that the hypocrites are indeed liars'

(Q.LXIII.1).[1] Also for this reason, though we are instructed to say in the call to prayer (*adhān*) 'I bear witness,' its conclusion is to say: 'There is no god but God.'

Benefit 3

The [preposition] *lām* in *al-ḥamdu li'Llāh*' can be interpreted in numerous ways:

a. Specification (*ikhtiṣāṣ*) of being appropriate (*lā'iq*), like saying 'Reins are for horses.'
b. Possession (*milk*), like saying 'The house is for Zayd' [or 'is Zayd's'].
c. Power (*qudra*) and control (*istīlā'*), like saying 'The land is for the sultan.'

In *All praise is for God*, all three meanings are possible. As for the first: it is known that praise is not appropriate except for the Almighty, due to His great majesty and countless favours and bounties. As for the second: it is known that He is the Owner of all, which entails His possession of their acts of praise. As for the third: by virtue of being the Necessary Existent while all else is contingent, He has power and control over all.

Therefore, *All praise is for God* in that it is only appropriate for Him; that it is His possession and dominion; and that He is superior to and in control of all.

Benefit 4

Al-ḥamdu li'Llāh consists of eight letters, and the gates of Paradise are eight. Thus whoever utters these letters from his very heart will become deserving of the eight gates of Paradise.

Benefit 5

Al-ḥamd is a singular word which has been preceded by the definite article [*al-*]. There are two opinions concerning this:

a. If it is preceded by a prior mention (*maʿhūd*), it is taken to refer to that. If not, then it is taken to be universal (*istighrāq*)—this is preferable to considering the words unclear (*ijmāl*).
b. It does not have a universal meaning, but refers to the quiddity and reality only.

Once this is known, we say: if we take the first opinion, *All praise is for God* denotes that everything which constitutes praise belongs to God as His right and possession, which implies that anything other than God

1 See above in Book I, Chapter One, Enquiry 18.

does not deserve praise at all. If we take the second opinion, this means that the quiddity of praise is God's right and possession, which negates that any individual instance of this quiddity should be for other than God. Therefore, based on both opinions, *All praise is for God* negates praise for other-than-God.

OBJECTION: does not every benefactor deserve the praise of the beneficiary, as does the teacher from the pupil, and the just ruler from the populace? After all, the Prophet (may God bless him and grant him peace) said: 'One who does not praise people has not praised God.'[1]

RESPONSE: we say: in all cases, the true benefactor is God, for if He did not create that motivation in the heart of the kind [human], he would not have given anything. Moreover, if He had not created that blessing, and given the benefactor the ability [to deliver] it and the beneficiary the ability to benefit [from it], then the blessing would not have taken effect. Therefore, the Benefactor in reality is Almighty God.[2]

Benefit 6

Just as the words *All praise is for God* denote that there is none to be praised but God, so does the intellect denote this meaning. The explanation of this is as follows:

1. Were it not for God creating the relevant motivation in the heart of the benefactor, he would never give, so the true Benefactor is God Who creates the motivation.
2. Anyone who gives to another does so seeking some kind of return, whether that be [divine] reward, [human] praise, fulfilling a right, or freeing the soul from the trait of miserliness. One who seeks a return is not truly a benefactor, and is therefore not deserving of praise. Almighty God, on the other hand, is perfect in His own right and does not seek after any perfection, as that would be an impossible *fait accompli*. As such, His giving is pure beneficence and generosity, and He is deserving of praise. This shows that none deserves praise but God.
3. Every favour is a contingent existent, and every contingent only exists by divine creation, whether *ex nihilo* or via an intermediary. Therefore, every favour is from God—and this meaning is sup-

1 As noted previously, the correct wording is 'thanked' (from *shukr*).

2 On this and the following points, compare with the discussion in Book II, Chapter Ten: 'Does Anyone Besides God Have Mercy?'

ported by the verse: 'Whatever you have of favour, it is from God' (Q.xvi.53). Since praise (*ḥamd*) is related to the bestowal of favours, and there is no favour except that it comes from God, one must be certain that none is deserving of praise but God.

4. A favour is not complete unless three factors obtain:
    a. It is beneficial, which depends on [the beneficiary] being alive and cognisant. His being so, in turn, depends on God's creative act.
    b. A benefit is only complete when there is no trace of harm or misfortune contained therein. Yet only God can remove all traces of harm from beneficial things.
    c. Likewise, it is only complete when there is no fear of it coming to an end—and this can only be bestowed by God.

Therefore, a perfect favour can only come from Almighty God, so He must be the only One deserving of perfect praise.

By these proofs, the truth of *All praise is for God* has been shown.

Benefit 7

You have come to know that *ḥamd* is the praise of someone for being a generous benefactor. As long as a person lacks appreciation of the favours reaching him, he cannot be expected to praise or give thanks. Once this is known, we say: the human being is surely incapable of praising and thanking God. This is seen in the following ways:

1. The favours of God are so numerous as to be beyond the scope of the human intellect to grasp; it is as God said: 'But if you count the favours of God, never will you be able to number them' (Q.xiv.34). If a person cannot realise the full extent of God's favours, he cannot praise and thank Him as befits them.
2. A person can only praise and thank God if God grants him the ability to praise and thank Him, as well as creating the motivation to do so within his heart and removing impediments which may prevent him. All of that is favour from Almighty God. Therefore, one is not able to show gratitude to God except by means of tremendous favours from God, and those—in turn—necessitate gratitude. As such, the servant is not able to give praise and thanks without having to do that over and over *ad infinitum*, which is impossible. Now that which depends on something impossible is itself impossible; therefore, man is incapable of praising and thanking God as He deserves.
3. Praising and thanking God is not merely to utter *All praise is for God* with one's tongue. Rather, it is for the beneficiary to recognise that

the Benefactor possesses the Attributes of perfection and majesty. However, whatever a person may conceive of God's perfection and majesty, the truth is that God is greater and higher than that conception. If that is so, then the person is not capable of fulfilling [the true meaning of] praise and thanks for God.

4. When a beneficiary engages in praise and thanksgiving, this implies that he [supposes himself] to be repaying the favours which were bestowed by the benefactor by means of the thanks and praise from his side. However, this is unfeasible [with respect to God] for several reasons:
   a. The favours of God are abundant and without limit, so being able to match them with this one belief and this single utterance is extremely implausible.
   b. Anyone who believes that his praise and thanks are equal to God's favours has blasphemed. This is the meaning of the saying of [Abū Bakr] al-Wāsiṭī: 'Thanksgiving (*shukr*) is blasphemy (*shirk*).'[1]
   c. The human being is dependent on God's beneficence in his essence, attributes and conditions, while God has no need of anyone's praise and thanks. How, then, could God's favours be matched by this praise and these thanks?

We have thus established that the servant is incapable of truly praising and thanking God. This is why He did not say: *iḥmadū Allāha* ('Praise God') [in the imperative], but instead: *All praise is for God.* If He had instructed the servants to praise God, it would have been an impossible burden.[2] On the other hand, *All praise is for God* means that perfect praise is His rightful possession, regardless of the creation's ability or inability to express it.

It was narrated that David (on whom be peace) said: 'O Lord! How can I thank You when my thanks depend upon Your favours upon me, such that You guide me to thank You?' He replied: 'O David! By acknowledging your inability to thank Me, you have thanked Me as much as you are able.'

Benefit 8

It is narrated that the Prophet (may God bless him and grant him peace) said: 'When God bestows a favour upon His servant and the servant

1 Although the term *shirk* is often used for polytheism or idolatry, the sense of the sin here is to blaspheme against God by attributing an equal to Him, even in one aspect or Attribute.

2 Unlike the case with *shukr*, the imperative for *ḥamd* does not appear in the Qur'ān. However, 'the praisers' (*al-ḥāmidūn*) are lauded in Q.IX.112. See also Benefit 14 below.

says "All praise is for God," Almighty God says: "Look at My servant! I gave him something of no [substantial] quantity so he gave me something without limit."'[1] The explanation of this is that [the reference is to] one of God's everyday favours, such as feeding him when he is hungry, quenching his thirst or clothing his nakedness. When the servant says *All praise is for God*, this entails that all praise ever expressed by anyone belongs to God, alongside any praise which is conceivable but has never been expressed.

Now included in these [categories] are the words of praise uttered by the angels of the Throne and the Footstool and the dwellers of the various heavens, as well as by the Prophets from Adam to Muḥammad (peace be upon them all), and by the saints and scholars and the entire creation, continuously until the time that: 'Their cry therein will be: "Glory to You, O God!" and Peace will be their greeting therein. And the close of their cry will be: "All praise is for God, Lord of the worlds!"' (Q.x.10). Yet all of the aforementioned words of praise are finite; the infinite quantity of praise is that which they shall declare into the ends of eternity. All these categories are encompassed by saying *All praise is for God, Lord of the worlds*, which is why God said, 'Look at My servant! I gave him a single favour of no [substantial] quantity, so he gave me thanks without limit or end.'

There is another subtlety here, in that God's favours upon the servant are finite, while saying *All praise is for God* entails infinite praise. It is known that when the finite is subtracted from infinity, the remainder is [still] infinite. Thus it is as though God says: 'My servant, when you say *All praise is for God* in response to that favour, you have infinite surplus good deeds within that utterance, so those must be met with infinite favours.' This is how the servant becomes deserving of eternal reward and goodness. It is thus shown that *All praise is for God*, when said by the servant, leads to boundless felicity and infinite goodness.

Benefit 9

Without doubt, existence is superior to non-existence, as demonstrated by the fact that every living existent hates to become non-existent—and were it not that existence is superior to non-existence, that would not be so.

Once this is known, we say: the existence of everything other than Almighty God has only transpired by His creative act in kindness and generosity. Since existence is a favour, every existent being in the spiritual

1 I could not source this. Here it is translated according to the explanation provided, although the interpretations of *lā qadra lahu* and *lā qīmata lahu* seem counter-intuitive.

and corporeal worlds, or the lofty and lowly worlds, is indebted to God's favour, mercy and kindness: and these favours and mercies necessitate praise and thanks. Therefore, when the servant says *All praise is for God*, this is not praise merely for the favours which have reached him personally. Rather, it is praise for all favours which emanate from Him.

We have explained that God's favour reaches all that exists besides Him, so it is as though the servant says: 'All praise is for God for His favours upon every being He created and originated: from light and darkness, stillness and motion, Throne and Footstool, jinns and humans—to every essence, body and property until the ends of eternity. I bear witness that all of this is Your due right and possession, and there is none to share or compete with You in that.'

Benefit 10

[QUESTION:] someone may point out that glorification (*tasbīḥ*) takes precedence over praise (*taḥmīd*), such as in [the formula of remembrance] *subḥāna Allāhi wa'l-ḥamdu li'Llāh*. So what is the reason for praise coming first here?

[PHILOSOPHICAL] RESPONSE: praise denotes glorification by implication (*taḍammun*). This is because 'glorification' is [to declare that God] is pure and free in His Essence and Attributes of any defect or flaw, and then 'praise' assumes that Attribute and adds that He is kind, generous and merciful to the creation. Thus glorification declares that God is perfect, while praise denotes something above perfection. Therefore, it is more appropriate to begin with praise. This answer is based on philosophical (*ḥikma*) principles.

THEOLOGICAL (*UṢŪL*) RESPONSE: God could not be a benefactor to His servants without being knowledgeable of all things, such that He is aware of their needs. He must also be capable of all things, such that He can fulfil their needs. [Thirdly,] He must be self-sufficient, as otherwise His own need would preoccupy Him from fulfilling the needs of the servants. This shows that being a [praiseworthy] benefactor depends upon being perfectly free from flaws and defects, so it is more appropriate to begin with *All praise is for God* than 'Glory be to God.'

Benefit 11

All praise is for God is connected both with the past and the future. Its connection to the past is that it is expressed in thanks for favours which have preceded. As for its connection to the future, it is that [saying it] brings about renewed favours in the future, as God said: 'If you are grateful, I will certainly give you more' (Q.xiv.7). This is supported by reason, in that preceding favours motivate a person to perform acts of servitude and obedience; then, when he is engaged in this thanksgiving, the doors of God's favours open to his heart and mind, as well as the doors to knowing and loving Him—and this is among the greatest of favours.

In this way, praise closes off from you the gates of Hellfire through its connection to the past, and it opens the gates of Paradise for you through its connection to the future. The past effect closes off the ways to being veiled from God, and the future effect opens the ways to gnosis of God. Then, just as there is no limit to the levels of God's majesty, there is no end to the ascent of the servant in this gnosis. There is no key (*miftāḥ*) to all this except *All praise is for God*—and this is why the *sūra* was named as the Opener (*al-Fātiḥa*).

Benefit 12

All praise is for God is a lofty and noble word, yet it must be uttered in its proper place, lest its purpose be misdirected. Al-Sarī al-Saqaṭī was asked: 'How should obedience be fulfilled?' He said: 'For the past thirty years, I have been seeking God's forgiveness for one occasion when I said "All praise is for God."' They asked: 'How could that be?' He replied: 'A fire broke out in Baghdad, destroying its shops and homes. When I was informed that my shop had been spared, I said "All praise is for God." This implied that I was relieved at the survival of my property even though the people's had been destroyed, whereas the right of religion and honour [upon me] demanded that I not be pleased in this situation. Therefore, I have been seeking forgiveness for thirty years for that one utterance.' What this shows is that the words —despite their nobility—must be put in their proper place.

Furthermore, God's favours upon His servant are abundant, yet they may be divided in the first order into two categories: worldly and religious. Favours pertaining to religion are superior for many reasons. Therefore, since *All praise is for God* is such a noble expression, the rational person should preserve it from being used in relation to worldly favours; rather, it should be reserved for religious favours.[1]

Religious favours, in turn, are of two types: acts of the limbs and acts of the heart—the latter are superior. Worldly favours are also of two

1 In the exegesis of *Lord of the worlds* below (Benefit 2), it is explained that one ought to ask God for the most trivial of worldly needs. In that case, it seems strange to be prevented from thanking Him for the same, unless the idea is to use some wording of lesser status!

types: those which are received as favours *per se*, and those which are received with the consciousness that they are gifts from the Benefactor. Of these, the latter [consideration] is superior. These are matters which ought to be borne in mind so that saying *All praise is for God* will be in its proper place and appropriate context.

Benefit 13

The first thing uttered by our father Adam was 'All praise is for God,' and the last word to be pronounced by the people of Paradise is 'All praise is for God.' The former was when the spirit reached [Adam's] navel and he sneezed, so he said: 'All praise is for God, Lord of the worlds.'[1] The latter is described in the verse: '...and the close of their cry will be "All praise is for God, Lord of the worlds"' (Q.x.10).[2] As such, the beginning of the world is built upon praise, and so is its conclusion. Therefore, strive to begin and conclude your own actions with these words, for the human being is a microcosm and his condition ought to be in synergy with that of the greater universe.

Benefit 14

Some people have claimed that the implied meaning here is '*Say* (you all): "All praise is for God"'; however, in my opinion, this is weak because one should only resort to [hypothesising] implied words when the speech would not be meaningful otherwise.[3] On the contrary, in this case that implied [imperative verb] would vitiate the meaning, for the following reasons:

a. *All praise is for God* is a [declarative] statement to the effect that praise is His right and possession. As such, it is complete speech without need for any implied [verb].
b. *All praise is for God* denotes that He is deserving of praise due to His Essence and actions, irrespective of anyone praising Him or not. [This is superior] because what obtains in itself is worthier and nobler than that which depends on others.
c. It is said in practical [ethics][4] that a father ought not to say to his child 'Do such-and-such,' lest he ignore that command and earn sin as a result. Rather, he should say: 'Such-and-such ought to done,' and a

1 Recorded by Tirmidhī.

2 As previously, the citation in the printed edition was of the first part of the verse, missing the relevant portion. NB: the exegesis of this verse clarifies that this formula is 'last' in a relative sense, as there is no end to the life of the Hereafter.

3 Cf. the beginning of Book II concerning 'In the Name of God'.

4 This is what I understood from *al-wāqiʿāt*.

respectful child will respond to that and obey. If the child disobeys [in that case] he would not have rejected the command directly, so his sin is lighter. In a comparable way, God said *All praise is for God* so that the obedient ones will praise Him, while the sin of the disobedient will be less severe.

Benefit 15

The Jabrīs (fatalists) and the Qadarīs (voluntarists) both cited this verse [for their respective purposes].[1]

THE JABRĪS argued the following with reference to *All praise is for God*:

1. The more noble and perfect someone is, the greater and loftier the favours emanating from him become, and the more he is deserving of praise. Certainly the noblest of creations is faith (*īmān*): therefore, if faith were an act of the servant, he would be more deserving of praise than God! Since that is not so, we know that faith is created by God, not by the servant.
2. The Muslim nation is in consensus [that one may say]: 'All praise is for God, for the blessing of faith.' If faith were an act of the servant and not from God, then this saying would be rejected. This is because praising someone for an act for which he is not responsible is false and distasteful, as God said: '… and they love to be praised for what they have not done' (Q.III.188).
3. As we have shown, *All praise is for God* has the apparent denotation that praise is exclusively God's and no one else deserves it at all. This would only be true if all favours come from God, and since faith is the greatest of all favours, it must be from God.
4. *All praise is for God* is God praising Himself, which would be a distasteful action for any of the creation. Therefore, the fact that He opened His Book with this self-praise denotes that He is not like His creation, and there are acts which are appropriate for Him but inappropriate for others. This, in turn, implies that it is contrary to His transcendence to compare His actions to those of the creation. There are some actions which are distasteful when performed by people, whereas the [related] actions from Almighty God are not so. This completely destroys [one of] the principles of the Muʿtazilīs.

1 See also Book I, Chapter Nine, Enquiry 3 (under the 'first pillar'). The interpretations of these two groups are mentioned at the end of several sections (verses or fragments) below. At this juncture and various others, it seems that the author supports a moderate version of *jabr*, and the voluntarists are represented by the Muʿtazilīs.

5. The Muᶜtazilīs believe that all divine actions must be 'good', then they must possess an additional attribute [of purpose], otherwise they would be in vain, which is impossible for God. This additional attribute may either be obligatory or from extra [generosity]. An example of the obligatory is to give reward and recompense to the servants [for obedience]. An example of the extra is to give more than the obligated [reward] out of kindness.

   [ASHᶜARĪ CRITIQUE:] this actually undermines the fact of Almighty God being deserving of praise, and negates the meaning of *All praise is for God*. This is because, in the first place, carrying out an obligation does not make one deserving of praise. After all, we do not praise someone for repaying a *dīnār* which he borrowed. As for extra acts, our opponents consider these to deserve increased praise, such that if He did not perform them, He would not be deserving of that [extra] praise. This implies that He is deficient in His own right and seeks perfection in external [actions], which, in turn, would entail that He is not deserving of praise.
6. *All praise is for God* denotes that He is praised [and praiseworthy]. We say: His being deserving of praise and exaltation must either be inherent to His Essence, or otherwise. If it is inherent, then it cannot be that any of His actions brings about His right to be praised: because what is established in itself cannot [then] be established due to another. This also implies that nothing of His actions could cause Him to deserve blame, since what is established in itself cannot be removed due to another. If this is so, then no obligation can be established upon Him, which means that He cannot be obliged to reward and recompense the servants. This, too, refutes the principles of the Muᶜtazilīs. The second possibility—that God's right to praise is not inherent to His Essence—entails that He is deficient in Himself and seeks perfection in others, which is impossible for God.

AS FOR THE MUᶜTAZILĪS, they claimed that *All praise is for God* is only [meaningful] according to their theories. They said:

> This is because He could only deserve praise in an absolute sense if there is nothing distasteful in His actions, no injustice in His decrees and no oppression in His rulings. We say that God is described thus, so He is deserving of the loftiest of praise. However, according to the Jabrīs, there is no distasteful act,

injustice or vanity which He has not performed! This is because [the Jabrīs say that] He creates unbelief in the unbeliever then punishes him for it, and gives pain to animals without recompensing them—so how could He be deserving of praise upon this belief? Moreover, that praise which Almighty God deserves by virtue of His Divinity is either binding upon the servant or upon Himself. If the former, the servant must possess the ability to enact [that praise] (*fiʿl*), which negates the claims of the Jabrīs. If the latter, then it would mean that God is obliged to praise Himself, which is false. Therefore, *All praise is for God* only holds true according to our beliefs.

Benefit 16

There are different opinions concerning the obligation of thanksgiving: has that obligation been established by reason, or by revelation (*samʿ*)?

Some argued that it is established by revelation,[1] as God said: 'Nor would We punish until We had sent a Messenger' (Q.XVII.15), and 'Messengers who gave good news as well as warning, that mankind, after (the coming) of the Messengers, should have no plea against God' (Q.IV.165).

Others said that it was established [by reason] before the coming of [revealed] legislation (*sharʿ*) as well as after, as proven by this verse: *All praise is for God*. The explanation [of this proof] is as follows:

a. *All praise is for God* denotes that this praise is His rightful property absolutely, which entails that this right existed before revelation.
b. God said: *All praise is for God, Lord of the worlds*, and it is known in jurisprudence that linking a ruling to a compatible description (*waṣf munāsib*) denotes that the description forms the underlying cause (*ʿilla*) for that ruling. Here, God affirmed that praise is for Him, then described Himself as Lord of all creatures, Compassionate and Merciful to them, Master of their fate in the Hereafter. All this shows that His right to [their] praise is specifically due to being their Merciful Lord. If that is so, then He possesses this right at all times, both before and after the sending of Prophets.[2]

1 The point here is that all religious obligations, including that of expressing praise and thanks, depend upon the guidance of revelation in order to become binding.

2 Cf. Ālūsī, *Rūḥ al-maʿānī*, vol. 1, p. 288; he contends that this argument works against the author's point in that it is a textual proof in revelation.

Benefit 17

We must investigate the reality and quiddity of *ḥamd*. To praise Almighty God is not reducible to saying 'All praise is for God,' for this is merely to declare that praise has occurred. Since the declaration (*ikhbār*) must be distinct from that which is declared (*mukhbar ʿanhu*), it follows that praise is not equivalent to pronouncing this formula.

Rather, praise is defined as any act which expresses magnification of the Benefactor due to His being the Benefactor. That act may be within the heart, upon the tongue or through the limbs. The act of the HEART is to believe that He possesses the Attributes of perfection and majesty. The act of the TONGUE is to utter such words as denote His possession of Attributes of perfection. The acts of the LIMBS are such as denote that He possesses the Attributes of perfection and majesty. This is the meaning of *ḥamd*.

Know that the people of knowledge have divided here into two groups:[1]

THE FIRST GROUP said that it is not possible that God would command His servants to praise Him, for the following reasons:

1. That praise is either [obligatory] due to favours which reached them, or otherwise. The first option is negated because it entails that God requested a return or payment for His kindness, and this is contrary to perfect generosity as the generous one gives without seeking anything in return. The second [i.e. obligation not due to the favours] entails putting [the servant] to difficulty with no preceding [cause], and that is oppression.
2. Engaging in praise is tiring for the praiser while being of no benefit to the Praised, in that He is perfect in His own right and cannot be perfected by anything external. Therefore, this praise is both useless and harmful, so it could not possibly be legislated [in religion].[2]
3. Obligation entails that one who leaves the action becomes deserving of punishment. Therefore, if praise were made obligatory, it would be as though God has said: 'If you do not engage in this praise, I shall punish you.' Since this praise does not benefit God or anyone else, it would be unbefitting of the Wise and Generous One to punish those who neglect it.

1 The categorisation here is clearly not comprehensive, as both are quite counter-intuitive contentions (following from related points within this section) and could have been expressed by a single group. A response from the author to these contentions was desirable.

2 See Shihadeh, *Teleological Ethics*, p. 102.

THE SECOND GROUP said that engaging in praise of God is bad manners,[1] for the following reasons:

1. It gives the impression that God's kindness is being repaid by that small quantity of thanks.[2]
2. To give thanks requires that one be conscious of those favours; yet when the heart is busy conceptualising the favours, it is prevented from being submersed in gnosis of the Benefactor.
3. When one praises God upon finding one of His favours, it implies that one would not have praised Him had it not been for that favour. This, in turn, implies that his purpose in engaging in worship and praise is to attain such favours, and such a person must be said to have taken those favours and personal gains as his object of worship. That is indeed a lowly station.

And God knows best.

Exegesis of *Lord of the worlds* (Verse 2)

Benefit 1

Know that every existent is either necessary or contingent. The only Existent necessary in His own right is Almighty God. As for contingents, these are all existents other-than-God and are known [collectively] as the 'world' (*ʿālam*), as the theologians defined the world as 'every existent besides God'. It has been named *ʿālam* [derived from *ʿalāma* (sign)] because everything apart from God signifies His existence. Therefore, every existent apart from God is described as *ʿālam*.[3]

Once this is known, we say: everything other than God is either a spatial object (*mutaḥayyiz*), a property (*ṣifa*) of a spatial object, or neither of these two. This gives three categories:

1. The spatial object is either divisible or indivisible: the former is a body (*jism*) and the latter is the atomic substance (*jawhar fard*). Bodies are divided into lofty and lowly: the former are the celestial spheres (*aflāk*) and heavenly bodies (*kawākib*). Further [lofty bodies] are

1 See also Benefit 7 above.

2 Cf. Benefit 8 above.

3 The expressions here seem to alternate between all non-divine existence being collectively *al-ʿālam*, and this describing individual existents; for the latter, the translation 'world' is unsuitable. If both the individuals and their collective are called *ʿālam*, then the significance of the plural form *al-ʿālamīn* is not clear. If singular *al-ʿālam* is used for the universe, the possibility of the plural relating to 'multi-verse' theories becomes apparent. See Rāzī's Introduction re: the conceivability of 'one million worlds (*ʿawālim*) external to [our] world'.

known through revelation, such as the Throne, the Footstool, the Farthest Lote Tree, the Tablet, the Pen and the Garden. As for lowly bodies, these are divided into simple (*basīṭ*) and composite (*murakkab*). The former are the four elements: first, the sphere of the earth with its deserts, mountains and inhabited lands; second, the sphere of water, meaning the encompassing ocean as well as these large seas [or lakes] within this inhabited quarter in which only God knows the number of great reservoirs; third, the sphere of air; and fourth, the sphere of fire. As for composite bodies, these are plants, minerals and animals with all their species and varieties.

2. Contingent properties [subsistent in] spatials: these are accidents (*aʿrāḍ*), of which the theologians have listed nearly forty genera.
3. There are contingents which are neither spatial nor properties of spatials: these are spirits (*arwāḥ*), which are either lowly or lofty. The lowly spirits may be righteous, i.e. the goodly jinns; or they may be wicked and evil, i.e. the rebellious devils. Lofty spirits are either connected to bodies, i.e. the spirits of the spheres; or they are not connected to bodies, i.e. the pure and sanctified spirits [angels].

This is an overview of things which exist in this world, yet if a person were to write a million volumes explaining these categories, he would barely scratch the surface. However, since there is only one Necessary Existent, all else is contingent and thus dependent upon His creative act. Moreover, the contingent cannot continue to exist without a Maintainer (*mubqī*). Almighty God is 'God (*ilāh*) of the worlds' in that He brought them from non-existence into existence, and 'Lord (*rabb*) of the worlds' in that He causes them to stay in existence and stability.

Once you have known this, a little understanding of *All praise is for God, Lord of the worlds* has become manifest to you. The more a person comes to know of these three categories [of existents], the more he has grasped the explanation of *Lord of the worlds*.

Benefit 2

The *murabbī*[1] is of two types: one either trains or cultivates something [such as an animal] in order to profit from it, or in order for that thing to profit. The care (*tarbiya*) [performed] by any of the creation falls into the first category, as they only do so in order to gain either reward or praise.

1 It is taken as unstated that the word *rabb* is derived from this word which denotes care and cultivation. See Chapter Three above: Section 1, Enquiry 1.

The second category only applies to Almighty God, as He said: 'I created you in order that you should profit, not that I should profit from you.'[1] The Almighty cares and gives in kindness in a way distinct from all other carers or givers.

The difference between divine care and that of people is as follows:

1. He cares for His servants not for His own sake, but for theirs. Others do so [in reality] for their own sake.
2. For others, caring [and spending] results in depletion of their resources and wealth. God, on the contrary, is not affected by decrease or harm; for it is as He said: 'There is not a thing but its (sources and) treasures (inexhaustible) are with Us; but We only send down thereof in due and ascertainable measures' (Q.xv.21).
3. [Human] philanthropists hate for a needy person to ask repeatedly and insistently, and would turn such a person away. God is the opposite of this, as the Prophet (may God bless him and grant him peace) said: 'Indeed, God loves those who are insistent in their supplications.'[2]
4. Others do not give until their support is sought, whereas God gives before anyone asks. Do you not see that He developed you while you were a foetus in the womb, and when you were ignorant and lacked the intellect by which to ask Him? He protected you and bestowed upon you even though you had not requested that and had not been guided [to do so].
5. The philanthropy of human beings ceases due to poverty, absence or death, whereas God's benefaction is never interrupted.
6. People direct their kindness to particular recipients and cannot possibly make it universal, whereas the care and benefaction of Almighty God extends to all. God said: '...but My mercy extends to all things' (Q.vii.156).

It is thus shown that He is Lord of the worlds, Benefactor of the entire creation. This is why He said of Himself: *All praise is for God, Lord of the worlds.*

Benefit 3

[When people] in this world praise and exalt someone, this is for one of four reasons: for being perfect in Essence and Attributes, transcendent

1 I could not trace this narration, but the meaning may be derived from the likes of Q.xlvii.36 and Q.li.56.

2 Recorded in Bayhaqī's *Shuʿab al-īmān*, and considered 'very weak'—R.S.

above all flaws and defects, even if they received no favours from Him[1]; or due to the fact that [the praised person] has been kind and generous to them; or in the hope that his generosity will be extended to them in the future; or from fear of his power, authority and dominance.

These are the factors resulting in [praise and] exaltation. Thus it is as though God says: 'If you are such as do exalt inherent perfection, then praise Me, for I am God of the worlds'—this is signified by *All praise is for God*—'and if you are such as exalt generosity, then I am *Lord of the worlds*. If you exalt seeking something in return, then I am *the Compassionate, the Merciful*; and if you exalt out of fear, then I am *Master of the Day of Judgment*.'

Benefit 4

The ways in which God cares (*tarbiya*) for His servant are without limit. Let us mention some examples:

FIRST EXAMPLE: when the sperm-drop reached the womb of the mother from the loins of the father, see how it became first a clinging form (*ʿalaqa*), then a lump (*muḍgha*), then the various organs and members developed from it, including bones and cartilage, nerves and sinews, veins and arteries. Then these things became connected together and the various faculties developed within them: vision in the eye, hearing in the ear and speech upon the tongue. Glory be to the One Who gave vision by bone, hearing by fat, and speech by flesh![2] The books of human anatomy are well known, and [their contents] demonstrate God's care for His servants.

SECOND EXAMPLE: if a single seed falls into the earth and moisture from the earth reaches it, it will swell. Even though it swells in all directions, splitting of the seed only occurs in two: above and below. From the upper split emerges the ascending portion of the tree, and from the bottom comes the portion which delves into the earth, namely the roots. Once the rising portion passes [the surface], it develops [into] a trunk, from which emerge numerous branches. Upon those branches appear blossoms at first, then fruits. Those fruits develop parts of various densities and textures, namely skins, cores and oils.

As for the descending portion of the tree, the roots have ends which are so subtle as to be like solid water, yet they are able to penetrate

1 The capitalisation reflects that, unlike the subsequent categories, this only holds for the Divine.

2 This may be read as describing the basic content of each of the organs (in which case 'bone' for the eye is surprising), or as related to the process of development just described, i.e. that these elements came to form the sophisticated organs of perception and expression.

the hard and rough earth. Moreover, God has bestowed them with the power to draw particles of clay towards them. The wisdom behind all these designs is for the servant to find what he needs of nutrition, condiments, fruits, drinks and remedies. Almighty God said: 'For that We pour forth water in abundance; then We split the earth in fragments…' (Q.LXXXI.25–26)—and the following verses.

THIRD EXAMPLE: He placed the heavenly spheres and their bodies in such a way that they became causes for the interests of the servants [to be achieved]. He created the night in order to provide rest and tranquillity, and the day in order to provide for livelihood and activity: 'It is He Who made the sun to be a shining glory and the moon to be a light (of beauty), and measured out stages for her; that you might know the number of years and the count (of time). God did not create this but in truth and righteousness' (Q.X.5); 'It is He Who makes the stars (as beacons) for you that you may guide yourselves, with their help, through the dark spaces of land and sea' (Q.VI.97); and read these verses: 'Have We not made the earth as a wide expanse, and the mountains as pegs?' (Q.LXXVIII.6–7)—and those which follow them.

Know that if you should ponder upon the wonders of the mineral, plant and animal [kingdoms], as well as the effects of divine wisdom in the creation of mankind, you will judge by plain reason that God has numerous methods of nurturing and caring [for creation], and that the proofs of His mercy are present in clear sight. At this point, you will have encountered one drop from the oceans of secrets within *All praise is for God, Lord of the worlds*.

Benefit 5

God attributed praise to Himself [with a preposition] by saying *All praise is for God*, then attributed Himself [in grammatical annexation] to the worlds, saying *Lord of the worlds*. The implied meaning is thus: 'I love praise, so I attributed it to Myself as My possession. Then, when I mentioned Myself, I introduced Myself as Lord of the worlds.'

When introducing one's self through a particular attribute, one chooses the best and most perfect attribute. This shows that 'Lord of the worlds' is the most perfect attribute, and this is indeed the case: for the best of levels is to be perfect and above perfection. The Name *Allāh* [in *All praise is for God*] signifies that He is the Necessary Existent in and of Himself, and this represents perfection (*tamām*). Then *Lord of the worlds* means that every other existence emerges from His care and generosity, which is what we mean by 'above perfection'.

Benefit 6

God has servants other than you: '...and none can know the forces of your Lord, except He' (Q.LXXIV.31), but you have no Lord but Him. However, He nurtures you as though He had no other servant, yet you serve Him as though you had another Lord! So how wonderful is His nurturing!

Is it not the case that He preserves you by day from ailments, and by night from what you fear, without seeking any recompense? Although the guards surround the king every night, can they protect him from the sting of insects, or that he should be afflicted with misfortune? As for Almighty God, He protects from all defects and afflictions, even when a person has begun his night engaging in sin and immorality. So how great and beautiful is His nurturing!

Is it not from His care that, as the Prophet (may God bless him and grant him peace) said, 'The human being is the construction of the Lord: so cursed is he who destroys the Lord's construction'?[1] In the same vein, God said: 'Say: "Who can keep you safe by night and by day from the Compassionate?"'[2] (Q.XXI.42). That is none other than the Irresistible Sovereign, the Unique and Overwhelming, the Turner of hearts and visions Who is aware of the inner conscience and secrets.

Benefit 7

The Qadarīs said: 'God could only be the Lord of the worlds if He shows them kindness and averts harms from them. However, if He created the unbelief of the unbeliever then punished him for it, and commanded people to have faith yet prevented them from it, He would not be a Lord at all: rather, a harmer.'

The Jabrīs said: 'He could only be the Lord if [all] favours and kindnesses flow from His mercy. Since faith is the greatest and noblest of favours, it must come from God for Him to be Lord of the worlds, i.e. showing them kindness by creating faith within them.'[3]

Benefit 8

The Name *Allāh* is nobler than *Rabb*, as we have shown in a number of ways in *The Explanation of God's Names*.[4] However, a supplicant usually

1 I could not source this.

2 That is, from the various types of affliction and punishment which He may decree. The mention of the Name *al-Raḥmān* here is 'to signify the response'—see the author's exegesis of the verse.

3 As before, these two groups correspond to Muʿtazilī voluntarism and Ashʿarī fatalism, respectively.

4 Apparently, this is the book known as *Sharḥ asmā' Allāh al-ḥusnā* and *Lawāmiʿ al-bayyināt* (ed. Muḥammad Badr al-Dīn Abū Firās, Cairo: Maktabat al-Khānjī, 1905).

calls out *yā Rabb, yā Rabb*. There are various explanations for this listed in *The Explanation of God's Names*, so we shall not repeat them here.

Exegesis of *The Compassionate, the Merciful* (Verse 3)

Benefit 1

Al-Raḥmān [describes] One Who bestows favours of a genus not attainable by benefactors among the servants, while *al-Raḥīm* is One Who bestows favours of a type which the servants can conceivably [give].[1]

[Tales of Divine Mercy]

It is narrated that Ibrāhīm b. Adham said: 'While I was visiting someone, he offered me a spread of food. A crow descended and snatched a loaf. I followed it in wonderment, until it landed upon a hill upon which there was a man bound up, his hands tied. The crow cast the loaf upon his face.'

It was narrated from Dhū al-Nūn [al-Miṣrī][2] that he said:

> I was at home when I experienced a pang in my heart and lost, as it were, my self-control. So I went out and ended up at the bank of the Nile and saw a powerful scorpion making its way. I followed it to the water's edge. There, I saw a frog standing. The scorpion hopped upon its back and it began to swim across. I took a boat and followed them, until the frog reached the opposite bank of the Nile. The scorpion alighted and departed, so I followed it. I then saw a young man asleep under a tree, and a [venomous] snake approaching it. Just as the snake got close to the man, the scorpion leapt onto it and stung it. The snake also bit the scorpion, and both of them died, while the man remained secure from both.

It is said that the offspring of the crow emerges from the egg without any feathers, so it resembles a lump of red meat. The [mother] crow is repulsed by this and refuses to care for the young. Then mosquitoes gather upon it due to its resemblance to carrion meat, and the young crow seizes them [in its beak] and is nourished by them. It continues to grow stronger in this way until its feathers emerge and cover over its

1 These meanings are not reflected in the translations as 'Compassionate, Merciful', but the distinction between the Names (derived from same root *raḥma*, denoting 'mercy') is subject to numerous opinions. As such, the chosen translation is very much an approximation.

2 Lagarde in his *Index* mistakenly identified him with Prophet Jonah.

flesh, at which point the mother returns to it. This is why the Arabs have a supplication: 'O You Who provides for the one that caws in its nest!'

These examples demonstrate that God's beneficence is universal, His kindness is all-encompassing and His mercy is vast.

Know that occurrences [include] two types: some have the appearance of mercies while they are not so: rather, they are punishment and tribulation. Others have the appearance of punishment and tribulation, while they are—in reality—beneficence, kindness and mercy:

[EXAMPLE OF] THE FIRST TYPE: if a father allows his son to do whatever he wishes and does not discipline him and push him to study, this has the appearance of mercy but its reality is tribulation.

THE SECOND TYPE: if a father confines his son to the classroom and forces him to study, this appears to be a tribulation while in fact being a mercy. Likewise, if gangrene afflicts a person's hand and he has it amputated, this seems like a punishment but its reality is relief and mercy.

The simpleton is fooled by outward appearances, while the rational person looks to inner wisdoms. Based on this: every type of tribulation, pain or difficulty in this world—though it appears outwardly to be torment and suffering—is, in reality, wisdom and mercy. The explanation of this is as expressed in philosophy: 'Abandoning abundant good due to a little evil is a great evil.'

Now the purpose of [being burdened with] religious duties is to purify the spirits of their corporeal accretions, as God said: 'If you do well, you do well for your own selves' (Q.XVII.7). The wisdom in creating Hellfire is to drive the wicked to perform the deeds of the righteous, drawing them from the fleeting abode to the everlasting home: 'So flee to God' (Q.LI.50).

In this regard, the most appropriate illustration is the story of Moses and al-Khaḍir[1] (peace be upon them). Because Moses was basing his judgments upon outward appearances, he condemned the scuttling of the boat, the killing of the child and the fixing of the decrepit wall. Al-Khaḍir, on the other hand, based his judgments upon realities and inner secrets:

> As for the boat, it belonged to certain men in dire need who work upon the sea, and I but wished to render it unserviceable, for there was after them a certain king who seized on every [sound] boat by force. As for the youth, his

1 This (also vocalised as al-Khiḍr) is the name given by tradition to the 'servant of God' in Q.XVIII.65. The author states in the exegesis of *al-Kahf* that he must have been a Prophet.

> parents were people of faith, and we feared that he would grieve them by obstinate rebellion and ingratitude. So we desired that their Lord would give them in exchange (a son) better in purity (of conduct) and closer in affection. As for the wall, it belonged to two youths, orphans, in the town; there was, beneath it, a buried treasure to which they were entitled, and their father had been a righteous man. So your Lord desired that they should attain their age of full strength and get out their treasure—a mercy from your Lord... (Q.XVIII.79–82).

The above story illustrates that the wise and astute person builds his judgments upon realities rather than appearances. Therefore, if you should observe [in divine decree] that which your nature dislikes and your intellect rejects, know that beneath it are hidden secrets and great wisdoms, and that it has been decreed by His wisdom and mercy. Upon this, an effect will have become apparent to you from the oceans of the verse *The Compassionate, the Merciful*.

Benefit 2

Al-Raḥmān is a Name exclusive to God, whereas *al-Raḥīm* can be applied to others as well as God. On this basis, one may ask: the greater Name is *al-Raḥmān*, so why was the lesser Name mentioned after it?[1]

RESPONSE: this is because [ordinarily] one does not request small and trivial needs from the great and mighty. It was narrated that somebody went to a nobleman and said: 'I have come to you with a simple request.' The nobleman replied: 'Take your simple request to a simple man.'

Thus it is as though God says: 'If I had only mentioned *al-Raḥmān*, you would have felt ashamed and reluctant to ask Me for simple needs. However, just as you have known Me as *al-Raḥmān* from Whom great things are sought, I am also *al-Raḥīm*, so request from Me the lace for your sandal and the salt for your pot.' This is like what He said to Moses [according to tradition]: 'O Moses! Seek from Me the salt for your pot and the fodder for your sheep.'

Benefit 3

God described Himself as *al-Raḥmān* and *al-Raḥīm*, and He granted Mary (on whom be peace) a single mercy, as described in the verse: '...and a

1 This question arises because the norm in Arabic speech is to mention multiple attributes in ascending importance and praise.

mercy from Us: it is a matter so decreed' (Q.XIX.21). By this mercy, she was saved from the censure of the unbelievers and sinners.[1]

As for us, we describe Him as *al-Raḥmān* and *al-Raḥīm* thirty-four times each day: this is because the [obligatory] prayers consist of seventeen cycles, and these Names are recited twice in each: in the *basmala* and in this verse. If one mention of mercy was sufficient to save Mary from all those harms, is it not the case that mentioning it so many times throughout our lives is enough to save the Muslims from Hellfire, disgrace and destruction?

Benefit 4

He is *al-Raḥmān* in that He creates what man cannot, and *al-Raḥīm* in that He does what man cannot come close to duplicating. It is as though He says: 'I am *Raḥmān* in that you present Me with a putrid sperm-drop and I return it to you in a beautiful form'—as God said: 'He has given you shape, and made your shapes beautiful' (Q.XL.64)—'And I am *Raḥīm* in that you present Me with deficient obedience and I grant you a perfect Garden.'

Benefit 5

It was narrated[2] that a young man on his deathbed found himself unable to utter the testimony of faith, 'There is no god but God.' The people went to inform the Prophet (may God bless him and grant him peace) of this situation, so he came to him and began to dictate the testimony to him, but the man only shook and shifted while his tongue failed to work. The Prophet (may God bless him and grant him peace) asked: 'Did he not observe his prayers, fasting and alms-giving?' They said: 'Yes, indeed.' He then asked: 'Did he disobey his parents?' They said: 'Yes.' The Prophet (may God bless him and grant him peace) said: 'Bring his mother.' His mother—who was elderly and blind in one eye—arrived, and the Prophet said: 'Will you not pardon him?' She replied: 'I will not pardon him for punching me and ruining my eye!' He said [to those around]: 'Bring me firewood and a torch.' She asked: 'What will you do with the fire?' He said: 'I shall burn him in front of you in retribution for what he did to you.' She cried: 'I pardon him, I pardon him! Did I carry him for nine

1 This does not accord in an obvious manner with the interpretations provided in the author's exegesis of that verse.

2 The story of this man—known as ʿAlqama—is recorded in Bayhaqī's *Shuʿab* but has been identified by various scholars as a fabrication.

months and suckle him [only to be burned] in the fire? Where is the maternal mercy in that?' At this point, the man's tongue became freed and he testified that 'There is no god but God.'

The lesson here is that [the mother] was *raḥīma* but not *raḥmāna*, yet—thanks to that small quantity of mercy—she could not permit [her son] to be burnt with fire. As for *al-Raḥmān* and *al-Raḥīm*, Who is not harmed by the servants' crimes but is concerned for their welfare, how could He accept for the believer who has been constant in testifying that 'There is no god but God' for seventy years to be burnt by the Fire?

Benefit 6

It is well known that when the lateral incisor of the Prophet (may God bless him and grant him peace) was broken [at the battle of Uḥud], he said: 'O God! Guide my people, for they know not.'[1] On the Day of Judgment, he will be [the only one] saying: 'My nation, my nation!'[2] These are great manifestations of kindness on his part in this life and the Hereafter, and this quality is only a result of his being a mercy, as God said: 'We sent you not but as a mercy for the worlds' (Q.xxi.107). If this is the effect of a single mercy, then what magnanimity is expected of One Who is *the Compassionate, the Merciful*?

Also, it is narrated that the Prophet (may God bless him and grant him peace) said: 'O God! Allow me to be the judge of my nation.'[3] Yet he refused to pray upon someone who died with an unpaid debt of two *dirhams*,[4] and he sent ʿĀ'isha out of the house due to the slander [against her].[5] Therefore, it is as though God [replied to his request] saying:

> You have one mercy—i.e. that in "We sent you not but as a mercy for the worlds" (Q.xxi.107)—and that is not sufficient to set right the world of creation. So leave Me and My servants: leave Me [to judge] your nation, for I am *the Compassionate, the Merciful*. My mercy is

1 Recorded by Bukhārī and Muslim with 'Forgive my people'. Ibn Masʿūd said that it was as though the Prophet (may God bless him and grant him peace) was quoting the words of a previous Prophet who had been hurt similarly. Ibn Ḥajar suggests that this refers to Prophet Noah; see Ibn Ḥajar, *Fatḥ al-Bārī*, vol. vi, p. 765. It resembles Luke 23:34, quoting Prophet Jesus.

2 Recorded by Bukhārī and Muslim—S.I.

3 This 'very weak' narration is connected with accounts of the Prophet's Night Journey—R.S.

4 The narrations I consulted refer to 'two *dīnārs*' (Abū Dāwūd) or 'three *dīnārs*' (Bukhārī).

5 The *ḥadīth* in Bukhārī has ʿĀ'isha's own explanation that she sought permission to stay with her parents, which the Prophet granted to her. More generally, it is quite surprising to find a scholar clutching at reports to belittle the mercy of the Messenger (may God bless him and grant him peace), even though no mercy is comparable to that of the Creator.

infinite, while their sins are finite: and the finite next to the infinite becomes nothing at all. Thus the sins of the entire creation will perish in the seas of My mercy: I am *the Compassionate, the Merciful.*

Benefit 7

The Qadarīs said: 'How would He be Compassionate and Merciful if He made some of His creation destined for Hellfire and eternal torment? How could the Merciful create unbelief in the unbeliever and then punish him for it? How could the Merciful command people to believe and then prevent them from doing so?'

The Jabrīs said: 'The greatest favour and mercy is faith, so if it were not from God but by the servant's doing, the servant would be worthier of the names *al-Raḥmān* and *al-Raḥīm*.' And God knows best.

Exegesis of *Master of the Day of Judgment* (Verse 4)

Benefit 1

Yawm al-dīn refers to the Day of Resurrection and Recompense (*al-baʿth wa'l-jazā'*). To explain [its necessity]: the righteous must be distinguished from the wicked, the obedient from the sinful and the follower [of divine guidance] from the rejecter. This does not become manifest except on the Day of Judgment, as God said: '...that He rewards those who do evil according to their deeds, and He rewards those who do good with what is best.' (Q.LIII.31); 'Shall We treat those who believe and work deeds of righteousness as those who do mischief on earth? Shall We treat those who guard against evil as those who turn aside from the right?' (Q.XXXVIII.28); and 'Indeed, the Hour is coming—My design is to keep it hidden—for every soul to receive its reward by the measure of its endeavour' (Q.XX.15).

Know that if someone gave authority to an oppressor over his victims and did not then exact revenge upon him, that must be due to his inability, ignorance, or being pleased with that oppression. These three attributes are unbefitting of Almighty God, so it must be that He avenges the oppressed. Since this does not [always] happen in the worldly abode, it has to occur in the next life. This is what is meant by *Master of the Day of Judgment* as well as: 'Then shall anyone who has done an atom's weight of good, see it; and anyone who has done an atom's weight of evil shall see it' (Q.XCIX.7–8).

It is narrated that a man will be brought on the Day of Judgment who will look at his own state and believe that he has not a single good deed in his account. Then a call will be sounded: 'O so-and-so, enter Paradise by your works.' He will ask, 'My God, what have I ever done?' God will say: 'Is it not the case that on such-and-such a night you turned in your sleep from one side to the other and said "*Allāh*," then you were overtaken with sleep and forgot about that? As for Me, drowsiness and sleep do not overcome Me, so I have not forgotten!'

Another man will be brought and his good and evil deeds weighed, but his good deeds will come up short. Then a slip will be brought, on which is written the testimony of 'There is no god but God,' and nothing will outweigh the mention of God.[1]

KNOW THAT DUTIES ARE OF TWO CATEGORIES: the rights of God and the rights of the servants. As for the rights of God, these are based upon pardon and ease (*musāmaḥa*), because the Almighty is free of any need from created beings. The rights of the servants, however, are those which must be strictly observed.[2]

It is narrated that Abū Ḥanīfa had a loan due to be repaid by a Magian, so he went to the latter's home to request it. When he reached the door, some impurity became attached to his sandal, so he shook his sandal in such a way that the impurity came off his sandal and stuck to the wall of the Magian's home. Abū Ḥanīfa started to worry: if he left it there, it would make the wall unsightly; but if he scratched it off, it may cause part of the wall to crumble. So he knocked the door and asked the maidservant to tell her master that Abū Ḥanīfa is at the door. When the Magian came to the door, he assumed that he had come to request his money and began to apologise. Abū Ḥanīfa said: 'There is something more important here!' and told him what had happened to the wall, asking how it would be possible to purify it. The Magian said: 'Let me begin by purifying my own self!' and embraced Islam on the spot.

The lesson here is that when Abū Ḥanīfa took care not to wrong the Magian in that minor way, the Magian took the step from unbelief to faith [in Islam]. Therefore, what will be the condition in the sight of God of one who avoids wrongdoing?

1 This *ḥadīth* was cited previously in Book II, Chapter Nine.

2 This is to say that God may choose to forgive whatever He pleases of sins against Him, but to pardon someone for a wrong committed against another person (without that person's forgiveness) would amount to injustice.

Benefit 2

The reciters diverged in their pronunciation of this word: some read it as *Mālik* (Master) and others as *Malik* (Sovereign).[1]

The justification (*ḥujja*) of those who read it as *Mālik* is as follows:

a. It contains an extra letter [*alif*], so its recitation is worthy of greater reward.
b. There will be many sovereigns (*mulūk*) on the Day of Judgment, but the Master [or Owner] of that day is none but God.
c. A master may also be a king, or not. Likewise, a king may be a master, or not: therefore, mastery and sovereignty may obtain independently of each other. However, mastery is a cause for absolute freedom of action, whereas sovereignty is not. In this way, mastery is superior.
d. The sovereign has that role with respect to his subjects (*raʿiyya*),[2] whereas the people's relation to the master is as servants. A servant [or slave] is of a lower status than a subject, so it follows that the dominance of mastery must be greater than that of sovereignty. This means that the master is superior in status to the sovereign.
e. The subjects may release themselves from being subjects of a particular sovereign by their own volition. As for the servant (*mamlūk*), he cannot escape being owned by his master through his own volition, and this, too, shows that the dominance of mastery is more complete than that of sovereignty.
f. The sovereign must pay attention to the condition of his subjects, as the Prophet (may God bless him and grant him peace) said: 'Each of you is a shepherd, and each of you is responsible for his flock'[3]—and the subjects are not obliged to serve the sovereign. The slave, on the other hand, must serve his master and may not perform any action without his approval. This is to the extent that he is not permitted to be a judge, leader (*imām*) or witness; if the master makes the intention

1 As noted at the beginning of Book II, Chapter Seven, the former is the reading of ʿĀṣim, Kisāʾī, Yaʿqūb and Khalaf, while the latter belongs to the remainder of the Ten Reciter-Imāms (including Abū ʿAmr, who is referenced below—he and Kisāʾī were also leading grammarians). The concept of *ḥujja/iḥtijāj* stems from the era before seven (then three more) readings became canonical and recognised as equally authoritative, at which point the more fitting term is *tawjīh*, i.e. explaining the soundness and import of each, as well as *tafsīr* (exegesis) which takes multiple readings into account. In this case, some of the justifications are irrelevant because God is described elsewhere in the Qurʾān (by consensus) both as *Mālik* and *Malik*, as Imām Rāzī notes below concerning the latter (and see Q.III.26 for *Mālik*).

2 This term may also be translated as 'flock', as I have rendered the Prophetic saying in point (f) below.

3 Recorded by Bukhārī and Muslim—R.S.

to be a traveller, he becomes a traveller as well, and if the master intends to be a resident, he becomes a resident along with him. This shows that obedience and submission are more pronounced for the servant than the subject.

Those are the arguments for reciting it as *Mālik*.

What follows are the arguments of those who said that *Malik* is the preferred reading:

a. Every person in the land may be a master [or owner], but the sovereign is the highest and greatest of the people, so a sovereign is nobler than a master.
b. There is consensus [among the reciters] that the word is *Malik* in 'Say: I seek refuge with the Lord of mankind; the Sovereign of mankind…' (Q.cxiv.1–2). Were it not that the sovereign is superior to the master, this would not have been specified.
c. *Malik* is preferable because it is shorter and the opportunity to recite it fully in the available time is more likely. Since *Mālik* is longer, there is [more of] a possibility that the time will not be sufficient. This was narrated from Abū ʿAmr.

Kisāʾī responded [to this last point], saying: 'I commence the recitation of this word, so if I do not reach its end, the firm intention [is what counts].' A comparable case in the juristic context is that if someone makes the intention before sunset to fast the following day of Ramaḍān, that is not sufficient for him, as he is still engaged in the fast of the current day, so intending another day would be considered [excessive] extension of hope [i.e. to live longer]. However, if he makes this intention after sunset, that is sufficient because—although it is also an extension of hope—he has now completed the preceding fast. Now he might die that very night, so he says 'If I do not reach the morrow, at least I shall be upon the intention to fast.' Such is the case here, i.e. a person begins to recite *Mālik*, and if he completes it, that is well and good; otherwise, he certainly had that intention, and this is our point.

[Implications of Each Reading]

There are rulings which follow from the *Malik* reading and also from the *Mālik* reading.

As for the implications of *Malik*, they are as follows:[1]

1. Authority (*siyāsa*) exists on four levels: the authority of masters (*mullāk*), that of sovereigns (*mulūk*), that of angels (*malāʾika*) and

1 Note that the names are now being discussed in reversed order.

that of the Sovereign of sovereigns. The authority of sovereigns is stronger than that of masters, for if a worldful of masters were to gather, they could not overrule a single sovereign. An illustration of this is that—according to Abū Ḥanīfa—a master cannot enact *ḥadd* penalties[1] upon his servant, but there is consensus that the sovereign has the authority to enforce the penalties. As for the angels, their authority surpasses that of the sovereigns, because a worldful of the greatest [human] sovereigns could not overrule a single angel.

As for the Sovereign of sovereigns, His authority surpasses that of the angels, as God says: 'The day that the Spirit and the angels will stand forth in ranks, none shall speak except he who is permitted by the Compassionate, and he will say what is right' (Q.LXXVIII.38); 'Who is there who can intercede in His presence except as He permits?' (Q.II.255); and in reference to the angels: 'They offer no intercession except for those whom He approves' (Q.XXI.28).

Therefore, O you sovereigns [of this earth]! Do not be fooled by the wealth and dominion in your hands, for you are but captives in the mighty grip of the Sovereign of the Day of Judgment. And O you subjects! If you fear the authority of the sovereign, then should you not fear the authority of Sovereign of sovereigns—the Sovereign of the Day of Judgment?[2]

2. He is a Sovereign unlike other sovereigns: for if they should spend anything, it would decrease their kingdoms and their treasures. However, God's dominion is not decreased by His generous benefaction; on the contrary, it increases! To explain: if God bestowed upon you a single child, His rule would be applicable to that one child. However, if He gave you ten children, His rule and law would apply to them all, so the more that God bestows, the vaster His kingdom.
3. The third implication is the perfection of His mercy. This is proven by the following verses:
   a. This *sūra* states that He is a Lord most Compassionate and Merciful.
   b. 'He is God, other than Whom there is no god; Who knows (all things) both secret and open; He is the Compassionate, the Merciful' (Q.LIX.22), which is followed by: 'He is God, other than Whom there is no god; the Sovereign…' (Q.LIX.23)—then

1 I.e. those for theft, adultery, murder etc.

2 Both occurrences in this paragraph are provided in the printed editions as *Mālik yawm al-dīn*, which conflicts with the context.

He mentions that He is Transcendent (*Quddūs*) above tyranny and oppression; and that He is Peace (*Salām*), i.e. He Whose servants are safe from His [ever engaging in] tyranny and oppression; then that He is the Protector (*Mu'min*), i.e. of His servants from His tyranny and oppression. It is thus seen that being the Sovereign is not possible without perfect mercy.

c. 'That day, the dominion, as of right and truth, shall be for the Compassionate' (Q.xxv.26). After affirming dominion for Himself, He described Himself as *al-Raḥmān*. Therefore, whereas His dominion on that day denotes His complete dominance, the fact that He is *Raḥmān* implies that fear will vanish [from the believers] and mercy will obtain.

d. 'Say: I seek refuge with the Lord of mankind; the Sovereign of mankind…' (Q.cxiv.1–2)—He mentioned that He is their Lord (*Rabb*) [which implies mercy], followed by His being their Sovereign.

These verses denote that dominion is not complete or perfect without kindness and mercy. Therefore, O you sovereigns! Listen to these verses and show mercy to these poor people, and do not seek after a higher sovereignty than that of Almighty God.

4. The fourth ruling is that the subjects are obliged to obey [any] sovereign, as their disobedience would result in chaos and anarchy in the world, leading to destruction and loss of lives. If that is the outcome of disobeying a metaphorical [i.e. human] sovereign, to what extent, then, must disobeying the Sovereign of sovereigns result in the destruction of interests and the creation of harms?

To explain more fully: God has made clear that unbelief is a cause for destruction in the world: 'At it the skies are ready to burst, the earth to split asunder, and the mountains to fall down in utter ruin: that they should invoke a son for the Compassionate' (Q.xix.90–91), and that obedience of Him is a cause for benefits obtaining: 'Enjoin prayer on your folk, and be constant therein. We ask you not to provide sustenance: We provide it for you. But the (fruit of) the Hereafter is for righteousness' (Q.xx.132).

Therefore, O you subjects! Be obedient to your sovereigns. And O you sovereigns! Be obedient to the Sovereign of sovereigns—in this way, the affairs of the world will be in goodly order.

5. Having described Himself as Sovereign of the Day of Judgment, God made clear to the worlds how perfect is His justice: 'Nor is your

Lord ever unjust (in the least) to His Servants' (Q.xli.46). Then He explained the nature of this justice: 'We shall set up scales of justice for the Day of Judgment, so that not a soul will be dealt with unjustly in the least' (Q.xxi.47). This demonstrates that being the True Sovereign of the Day of Judgment is manifested in His justice. Therefore, a metaphorical [earthly] sovereign is considered a true sovereign if he is just; otherwise, he is a false sovereign. Through the blessings of justice of a true sovereign, goodness and peace obtain in the world; but the false sovereign is a cause for goodness being lost from the world.

It is narrated that Anushirwan[1] went out one day to hunt, but he hastened so much that he became separated from his troops. Feeling extreme thirst, he came to a garden full of pomegranate trees and asked a boy who was present there to pass him one fruit. Upon splitting it open, extracting the seeds and pressing them, he found the juice plentiful and drank it. Having so enjoyed this pomegranate, he decided to seize this garden from its owner. He asked the boy to pass him another fruit, but this time he found its juice to be very scarce and marred by a putrid and unpleasant taste. He asked the boy: 'Why has this pomegranate turned so?' The boy replied: 'Perhaps the sovereign of the land has intended to commit injustice, and the evil of that injustice had an effect on this pomegranate.' At this, Anushirawan repented within his heart and requested a third fruit. This time, he found it better and sweeter than the first. He asked the boy: 'How has its condition changed?' The boy replied: 'Perhaps the sovereign of the land has repented from his injustice.' When Anushirawan heard this explanation from the boy in precise accordance with his inner states, he repented altogether from injustice, and it is little wonder that his name became immortalised throughout the world [as an emblem of] justice. Indeed, some people narrate that the Messenger of God (may God bless him and grant him peace) said: 'I was born in the era of the just sovereign.'[2]

As for the rulings which follow from God being *Mālik*, they are as follows:[3]

1. Reciting it as *Mālik* entails a greater level of hope than *Malik*, because

1 The Persian ruler, also known as Khosrau I, who died in 579 CE, soon after the birth of the Final Prophet (may God bless him and grant him peace).

2 This is a 'baseless' narration—S.I.

3 The points here appear to be an extension to the earlier section arguing for this reading over the other.

the most that can be hoped for on the part of a sovereign is for him to be just and fair, such that a person remains safe from him. As for the master, the servant depends on him for his clothing and food as well as mercy and nurturing. Thus it is as though God says: 'I am your Master, so your food, your clothes, your reward and your Paradise are My responsibility.'

2. Although the sovereign is richer than the master, the former seeks something from you, whereas you seek from the latter. We do not [truly] possess our goodly acts, so [the Master] does not wish to seek these from us on the Day of Judgment. Rather, He wishes that, on that day, we seek from Him to pardon and forgive, and to grant us Paradise purely from His generosity. For this reason, Kisā'ī said: 'Recite it as *Mālik*, for this reading denotes great generosity and vast mercy.'
3. When the troops are presented before the sovereign, he will only accept those who are physically strong and emotionally sound. If he finds one who is ill, he will send him back and not assign him any duty. The master, on the other hand, takes care of his servant if he falls ill, assists him if he becomes weak, and saves him if he finds himself in trouble. Therefore, the *Mālik* reading is more suited to the sinful and needy.
4. The sovereign possesses reverence and authority, while the master possesses kindness and mercy. Our need for the latter is more pronounced than our need for the former.

Benefit 3

Dominion (*mulk*) is an expression for power, so God being *Mālik* and *Malik* refers to His power [over things].

PROBLEM: is God's dominion [effected] upon existent things or non-existents? The first possibility is negated because bringing existents into existence is impossible, so God's power would be limited to removing things from existence. On that basis, there is no Master except for effacement. The second possibility is also negated, in that it implies that His power and dominion are over non-existence, and that God does not have mastery or sovereignty over existent things, which is unacceptable.

RESPONSE: Almighty God is the Master and Sovereign of existent things. This entails that He can take them from existence to non-existence, as well as from one state to another. This power is possessed solely by God, so He is the True Sovereign. Once you have known this, we say:

God is Sovereign of the Day of Judgment because the power to resurrect the creation belongs to none but Him, and knowledge of the scattered parts of people's bodies is possessed only by Him. If the gathering, resurrection and judgment are dependent upon knowledge of all things and power over all possibilities, it is clear that there is no Master of the Day of Judgment except God. Further details of this discussion are connected with the issue of Gathering and Resurrection.

OBJECTION: a Master is only such if the thing possessed actually exists, whereas the Day of Judgment is not yet in existence. Therefore, God cannot be Master *of* the Day of Judgment [in grammatical annexation]; rather, it ought to be expressed as *Mālikun yawma al-dīn* [indicating a future act]. This is evidenced by the fact that saying *ana qātilu Zaydin* [annexed] is a confession ('I am Zayd's killer'), whereas *ana qātilun Zaydan* is a threat ('I shall kill Zayd').

RESPONSE: the truth is as you described. However, because the establishment of Judgment is such a [pronounced] reality which wisdom dictates as a necessity, its existence was treated as something established at the present time. Moreover, when a person dies, the Day of Judgment has begun [from his perspective], which means that it exists in the present—so the contention disappears.

Benefit 4

God has mentioned in this *sūra* five of His Names: *Allāh*, *al-Rabb*, *al-Raḥmān*, *al-Raḥīm* and *al-Mālik* [or *al-Malik*]. The reason behind this is as though to say: 'First I created you, so I was *God*. Then I nurtured you with all types of favour, so I was the *Lord*. Then you sinned and I covered that for you, so I was *the Compassionate*. Then you repented and I forgave you, so I was *the Merciful*. Then I must deliver the recompense to you, so I am *Master of the Day of Judgment*.'

QUESTION: *al-Raḥmān al-Raḥīm* was mentioned first in the *tasmiya*, then [again] in the *sūra*: as such, these Names are repeated while the others are not, so what is the wisdom behind this?

RESPONSE: it is as though [God] says: 'I mention once that I am God and Lord,[1] but I mention twice that I am Compassionate and Merciful so that you know that mercy is more important [to Me] than anything else.' Then, after this repetition of the Names of mercy, it is as though He says: 'But do not become complacent in this regard, for I am Master of

1 The Name *Allāh* was also repeated, as noted by Ālūsī, *Rūḥ al-maʿānī*, vol. 1, p. 278.

the Day of Judgment.' This is comparable to the verse: 'He Who forgives sin, accepts repentance, is strict in punishment, and has a long reach (in all things)' (Q.xxxv.3).

Benefit 5

The Qadarīs said: 'If God were the Creator of people's actions, then there could not be any reward or punishment, because to reward a man for what he did not do is vanity, and to punish him for what he did not do is oppression. In that case, God could not be Master of the Day of Judgment.'

The Jabrīs said: 'If it were not that the actions of the servants are by God's decree and decision, He would not be the Master [of those actions]. Since the Muslims are in consensus that God is Master of the servants and their actions, we know that He is their Creator and Decider.' And God knows best.

Exegesis of *You we worship...* (Verse 5)

Benefit 1

Worship (*ʿibāda*) refers to any action which is performed with the purpose of exalting its object. It is derived from a path being *muʿabbad*, i.e. trodden [and subdued].

Know that *You we worship* means 'I worship none but You.' The evidence for this meaning of exclusivity (*ḥaṣr*) and specification (*taʿyīn*) is as follows:[1]

1. Worship represents the uppermost limit of magnification, and is therefore not appropriate to any but such as has bestowed the greatest of favours. The greatest type of favour is to bestow life by which one is able to derive benefit [from all favours], as well as to create the things from which benefit is derived. Thus the first stage is the creation of life by which deriving benefit is made possible, and this is indicated by: 'I did indeed create you before, when you had been nothing' (Q.xix.9) and 'How can you reject the faith in God, seeing that you were without life, and He gave you life? Thereafter He will cause you to die, and will again bring you to life; and again to Him will you return' (Q.ii.28). The second stage is the creation of the things of benefit, which is indicated by: 'It is He Who has cre-

1 The author has here provided theological and philosophical reasons for worship being solely for God. As for the linguistic reasons for interpreting (and translating) the phrase in this way, reference is usually made to the pronoun *iyyāka* being used and brought to the front. See Benefit 3 below.

ated for you all things that are on earth…' (Q.II.29).[1] Then, since the interests [of humans and others] in this lower world depend for their structure upon the regular movements of the heavenly spheres, it is understandable that He said next: 'Moreover, His design comprehended the heavens, for He gave order and perfection to the seven firmaments; and of all things He has perfect knowledge' (Q.II.29). It is thus shown that all favours occur by the creation of Almighty God, so it follows that worship is only appropriate for Him. This is why He said: *You we worship*, which denotes limitation.

2. God has described Himself in this [*sūra*] with five Names: *Allāh*, *al-Rabb*, *al-Raḥmān*, *al-Raḥīm* and *Mālik yawm al-dīn*. The servant has three situations: the past, the present and the future.
   a. In the past, he was completely non-existent, as God said: 'I did indeed create you before, when you had been nothing' (Q.XIX.9). He was dead and God gave him life: 'How can you reject the faith in God, seeing that you were without life, and He gave you life?' (Q.II.28). He was ignorant and God taught him: 'It is God Who brought you forth from the wombs of your mothers when you knew nothing; and He gave you hearing, sight and intelligence' (Q.XVI.78). The servant only went from non-existence into existence, from death to life, from impotence to ability and from ignorance to knowledge because Almighty God created him and took him from one state to the other by virtue of His pre-eternal power and knowledge. In this sense, He is God (*ilāh*).[2]
   b. As for the present time, the servant is in pressing need. Back when he did not exist, he was [not][3] in need of a Compassionate and Merciful Lord. However, upon coming into existence, the doors of neediness opened upon him so he is faced by various necessities. Thus [it is as though] God says: 'I am *Ilāh* in that I brought you from non-existence into existence. Now that you exist, your need for Me has become great indeed, so I am *Rabb Raḥmān Raḥīm*.'

1 This verse immediately follows the one previously cited.

2 As usual, the assumption is that *Allāh* is derived from *ilāh*. Cf. Book II, Chapter Nine.

3 This negating particle is required by context, but missing from the printed editions. I found it preserved in the manuscript at the University of Michigan, digitised and provided online by the Hathi Trust Digital Library, under the title *Tafsīr Sūrat al-Fātiḥah nuqila min Tafsīr al-kabīr* (copied in 1823 by Muḥammad ʿAlī), p. 124. The manuscript only contains Book III.

c. As for the servant's future, this refers to his state after death. The Attribute connected to that is *Mālik yawm al-dīn*.

In this way, these five Divine Attributes are connected to the three states of the servant. This shows that none of his past, present or future needs and interests could be fulfilled or achieved without God's grace and benefaction. Since that is so, the servant should not devote himself to any worship except of Almighty God, hence *You we worship* and its entailment of exclusivity.

3. The fact that God must be powerful, knowledgeable, kind, generous and forbearing is established via decisive proofs. As for others possessing these qualities, such is open to doubt. This is because any effect which could be attributed to nature—to heavenly spheres and bodies, to the intellect or the soul—could equally be attributed to the power of God, such that the first attribution becomes uncertain. It follows that Almighty God being the object of the creation's worship is a matter of certainty, whereas anything else being [worthy of] their worship is subject to doubt. It is more proper to act upon certainty than doubt, so the doubtful matter should be cast aside for that which is known. Therefore, there is none to be worshipped but God, and this is meant by *You we worship*.
4. Servitude is a lowly and humiliating state, but the higher the status and nobility of the master, the more that servitude is agreeable and dignified. Since Almighty God is the noblest and loftiest of all beings, servitude to Him is preferable to any other. Moreover, His power, knowledge and generosity surpass those of any other, so it must be stated with certainty that servitude to Him is superior to any other servitude. For this reason, He said: *You we worship*.
5. Everything other than the Necessary Existent is contingent, and consequently in a state of need. A needy being is preoccupied with meeting that need, and so cannot fulfil the needs of others. Anything which is not self-sufficient can be of no help to others. The only Self-sufficient Being is Almighty God, so He it is Who fulfils all needs. Therefore, He [alone] is deserving of worship: *You we worship and from You we seek help*.
6. The fact that God is deserving of worship follows from His power to hold in place the sky without any attachment, and the earth without supports; to cause the sun and moon to run, and keep the two

poles still;[1] to bring out from the clouds at one time fire in the form of lightning, sometimes air in the form of wind, and at other times water in the form of rain. Upon the earth, sometimes He brings water from rocks, which is known; and sometimes rocks from water, i.e. ice. He made some bodies fixed and never moving, namely the mountains; and others travelling and never stopping, i.e. the rivers.

He caused Qārūn to be swallowed so that the earth was above him (Q.xxviii.81), and raised Muḥammad (may God bless him and grant him peace) until there were two bow-lengths beneath Him.[2] He made water like fire for the people of Pharaoh who were drowned and entered a fire (Q.lxxi.25); and he made fire coolness and peace for Abraham (Q.xxi.69). He raised Moses above the mountain and told him to remove his sandals,[3] and he raised the mountain above Moses and his people: 'And (remember) We took your covenant and We raised above you the mount (Sinai)' (Q.ii.63). He drowned the world from a dry oven[4] '…and the oven overflowed' (Q.xi.40); and He made the sea dry for Moses (on whom be peace)!

Therefore, how could worship of such a Powerful God be considered equivalent to worship of inanimate objects, plants, animals, humans, heavenly spheres or angels? To equate the deficient to the perfect and the meagre to the precious is only indicative of ignorance and foolishness.

Benefit 2

You we worship denotes that there is none to be worshipped (*maʿbūd*) except God. It follows that there is no deity (*ilāh*) except God, so this verse denotes pure monotheism.

Know that polytheists (*mushrikūn*) are of various kinds, because any partner (*sharīk*) which a person associates with God must either be a body or not a body. The corporeal 'partner' is either from the lowly bodies or lofty bodies. Of the lowly bodies, some are composite and others simple. Composite bodies may belong to the mineral, plant or animal [kingdoms] or the human race. 'Partners' from the minerals are the idols which people take for worship, such as from stone, gold or silver. Of plants, some

1 If this refers to the north and south poles, the expression may mean that stability is experienced upon the earth.

2 This is a reference to the Ascension (*miʿrāj*), and the expression from Q.liii.9, but the wording here is ambiguous. See Chapter Six, Section v below.

3 In Q.xx.12, the instruction to remove the sandals was in the valley of Ṭuwā.

4 This is the interpretation chosen by the author for *al-tannūr*. See his exegesis of Q.xi.40.

worshipped a particular tree. Of animals, some worshipped the heifer. Of mankind, there were some who claimed that Ezra or the Messiah were 'the son of God' [Q.IX.30]. From simple bodies [i.e. elements], some—the Magians—worship fire. Among lofty bodies, some people worship the sun and the moon and other heavenly bodies, and attribute felicity and calamity to them: these are the Sabians and the majority of the astrologers (*munajjimūn*).

As for those who associated non-corporeal partners with God, these are also of various groups:

A. Some said that the world is controlled by Light and Darkness: these are the Manicheans and dualists.
B. Others said that the angels are heavenly spirits, and each region and every type [of thing] has a particular spirit which controls it. These are the angel-worshippers who construct images and statues of these spirits and worship them.
C. Some said that the world has two gods: one good, the other evil. They said that the world is controlled by God and Iblīs, and that they are brothers; and that everything good in the world is from God, and everything evil is from Iblīs.

Once these details are known to you, we say: anyone who sets up a partner with God must worship that 'partner' in some way, whether seeking benefit from it or evading its harm. As for those who insist upon monotheism and reject the claims of partners or rivals to God, they worship only God and look to none but God. Their hope is in Him and their fear is of Him; He is their desire and their source of awe. Therefore, they worship none but God and seek help from no other, which is why they say: *You we worship and from You we seek help*, which is equivalent to saying, 'There is no god but God'.

[Further Parallels]

The well-known words of remembrance are to say: *subḥāna Allāh* ('Glory be to God'), *wa'l-ḥamdu li'Llāh* ('All praise is for God'), *wa-lā ilāha illa Allāh* ('There is no god but God') *wa'Llāhu akbar* ('God is greater'), and *wa-lā ḥawla wa-lā quwwata illā bi'Llāh al-ʿAlī al-ʿAẓīm* ('There is no effect or power except by God, the High, the Great').

We have already shown[1] that *All praise is for God* encompasses the meaning of 'Glory be to God' in that the latter denotes His being perfect and complete in His own right, while the former denotes that He perfects

1 See Section 1 above.

and completes others; that, in turn, is predicated upon being perfect and complete in His own right. Therefore, *All praise is for God* encompasses the meaning of 'Glory be to God' and [further] affirms all forms of praise for Him. That which follows it comprises the reasons for His being deserving of all praise: the Five Attributes through which all the interests of the servant are fulfilled in his three time periods—as we have explained.[1] Therefore, it is seen that [these verses correspond to the formula] 'Glory be to God, and all praise is for God'.

After that, God said: *You we worship*, and we have shown that it is equivalent to 'There is no god but God.' Then comes *And from You we seek help*, which means God is so high and great that no purpose could ever be achieved without His help, grace and kindness. This is what is intended by '[God is greater, and] there is no effect or power except by God, the High, the Great.'

Thus it is seen that *Sūrat al-Fātiḥa* is, from beginning to end,[2] in agreement with that word of remembrance, as though its verses serve as elucidation and elaboration on the five stations mentioned in that formula.

Benefit 3

God said *You we worship* (*iyyāka naʿbudu*) and brought this [pronoun] to the front, rather than saying 'We worship You' (*naʿbuduka*). This is explained in a number of ways:

1. God placed His own mention first so that the worshipper pays full attention to Him as the true object of worship, and so he is not distracted from his [duty of] exaltation, looking instead right and left. It is narrated that a master wrestler competed against an uncouth villager, who repeatedly overpowered the master. Someone said to the villager: 'That is the Master so-and-so!' Immediately, the villager was defeated, only due to awe of his [status]. The case is similar here, i.e. that God introduced Himself first so that worship would be characterised by that awe and reverence, lest inattention affect it.
2. [It is as though God says:] 'If obedience and worship—such as standing, bowing and prostrating—should become difficult and tiresome for you, then first remember *You we worship* so that you remember Me and call to mind My gnosis. Then, when you remember My majesty, greatness and might, knowing that I am your Master and you are My servant, those acts of worship will be easy for you.'

1 See Benefit 1 above, point 2.

2 Or from verses 2–5, according to this explanation.

This is comparable to one who wishes to lift a heavy object: he will prepare by ingesting that which boosts his strength. Thus the servant who intends to carry out weighty duties first consumes the 'paste' of divine gnosis from the 'vessel' of *iyyāka* so that he is able to bear the burden of servitude. Another example is when a lover is beaten up because of his beloved: the beating is made easier when he is in the beloved's presence. Thus it is here: when the servant witnesses the beauty of *iyyāka*, it becomes easy for him to endure the hardships of servitude.

3. God said: 'Those who fear (God), when a thought of evil from Satan assaults them, bring (God) to remembrance, and immediately they see (aright)' (Q.vii.201). When one of these souls is afflicted by a Satanic suggestion to be lazy or inattentive, it calls to mind the presence of divine majesty, [taking light] from the rising-point which is *iyyāka*, such that its vision is returned and it becomes ready to perform acts of worship and obedience.
4. If you were to say 'We worship You,' you would have begun by mentioning your own worship before specifying to whom it is directed. Thus Iblīs could suggest that this worship is for the idols or the [heavenly] bodies, the sun or the moon. However, when the order is reversed and you say *iyyāka* (You) first, then *naʿbudu* (we worship), the first word is explicit in directing the worship to Almighty God. This is more emphatic in declaring monotheism and farther removed from the suggestion of polytheism.
5. The pre-eternal and necessary Being exists prior to that which is contingent and created, so His mention must precede all other mentions. This is why God's mention—*iyyāka*—was placed before that of the creation: *naʿbudu*.
6. Some of the spiritual masters said: whoever, at the time of receiving a favour, directs his vision towards the Benefactor instead of the favour, [he will find that] in times of trial his vision is directed to the One testing him rather than that trial. Such a person is submersed at all times in the gnosis of Almighty God, and is constantly in the highest state of felicity. As for one who directs his vision to the favour rather than the Benefactor, his vision will be directed in times of trial to the trial instead of the One testing him. Such a person is drowned in concern with other-than-God and lives in constant misery. This is because, when he encounters a favour, he fears that it will pass from him and this [feeling] is torture. When it happens that he

loses a favour, he experiences disgrace and despair. Thus he is bound up in chains and fetters. For this subtle reason, God said to the nation of Moses: 'Remember My favour' (Q.II.40), but He said to the nation of Muḥammad: 'Remember Me; I will remember you' (Q.II.152).

Once this is known, we say: God ordered the words thus, so that the servant will be submersed in witnessing the light of the majesty of *iyyāka*. In such a state, [he will feel that] he is dwelling in Paradise itself when he worships. This is as God said [in a *ḥadīth qudsī*]: 'My servant continues to draw closer to Me through optional acts until I love him. When I love him, I am his hearing and sight.'[1]

7. If it had been 'We worship You' it would not have negated the worship of others beside Him, as there is nothing impossible about worshipping God alongside others as the polytheists do. *You we worship*, on the other hand, denotes that they worship none but Him.

[QUESTION: why not 'I worship'?][2]

8. This *nūn* [indicating plural] signifies grandeur, so it is as though it is said [by God to the servant]: 'When you are outside of the prayer, do not say "We" even if you are among a million servants. But when you stand in prayer and manifest your servitude to Me, then say *we worship* to show the world that anyone who is a slave to Me is a king in this life and the next.'
9. If it had been 'You I worship,' it would have implied arrogance on the servant's part, as if to say 'I am the [true] worshipper.' However, *You we worship* means 'I am one of Your servants.' The former is arrogance, the latter humility. Whoever lowers himself for God's sake, God raises him. But whoever considers himself high is cast down by God![3]

OBJECTION: all that you have mentioned could be directed at *All praise is for God*, but there the mention of praise (*ḥamd*) preceded the mention of God!

RESPONSE: 'praise' could be understood as being for God or other-than-God. When you say 'for God' it specifies that the praise belongs solely to Him. Similarly, if you began with 'We worship' it could be understood as worshipping God or other-than-God, but the latter is unbelief (*kufr*). The subtlety is that since praise is—on the surface—permissible for others

1 Recorded by Bukhārī—S.I.

2 Although labelled in the same list, the remaining two points pertain to a different aspect of *iyyāka naʿbudu* from that which preceded. See also Benefit 4 below.

3 This alludes to a *ḥadīth* recorded by Ibn Mājah and others.

as well as God, to mention *ḥamd* first was appropriate. On the contrary, worship may not be directed to anyone but God, so *iyyāka* had to be mentioned before *naʿbudu*. This removes the possibility that the worship could be for anyone but God.

Benefit 4

[PROBLEM:] someone may say: the *nūn* in *naʿbudu* (*we worship*) must either denote a [literal] plural or else signify grandeur. The first is negated because one individual cannot be a plural. The second is negated because the appropriate state during worship is to mention one's lowliness and impotence, not to use lofty terms of grandeur.

RESPONSE: this can be solved in various ways, each of which points to a lofty wisdom:

1. It does denote the plural, which is to allude to the fact that prayer is best performed in congregation. The superiority of congregational prayer is [elaborated] in the relevant places, and it is indicated by this *ḥadīth*: 'The opening *takbīr* of the prayer performed in congregation is better than the world and all it contains.'[1] We add: a person who has [just] eaten garlic or onion may not attend the congregation, lest any person be offended by that [odour].[2] It is as though God says: 'This act of obedience is so full of reward that it is not befitting that any individual Muslim should be harmed by the odour of garlic and onion. If such impairs that reward, then what of harming a Muslim through slander and backbiting?'
2. When someone is praying in congregation, then *we worship* is in reference to that. When he prays individually, he means 'I worship and the angels worship alongside me,' so the plural refers to the person and all the angels devoted to worship.
3. The believers are brothers; if he were to say 'You I worship,' he would have mentioned only his own worship and neglected the others. With *You we worship*, he mentions the worship of all the believers in the East and West, and it is as though he is petitioning for the needs of all to be fulfilled. Hence God fulfils his needs, as the Prophet (may God bless him and grant him peace) said: 'Whoever meets the need of a Muslim, God will meet all his needs.'[3]

1 I could not source this narration—R.S.

2 This ruling is taken from a *ḥadīth* in Bukhārī and Muslim.

3 I could not locate this exact wording, but a *ḥadīth* in Muslim (cited below) states that 'God remains at the aid of the servant as long as the servant is at the aid of his brother.'

4. It is as though Almighty God says to the servant: 'Since you have praised Me by saying *All praise is for God, Lord of the worlds; the Compassionate, the Merciful; Master of the Day of Judgment*, and thereby ascribed to Me all praise in this life and the next, your status has been raised in My presence. Therefore, do not limit yourself to seeking your own needs, but ask for the needs of all the Muslims and say: *You we worship and from You we seek help*.'
5. It is as though the servant says: 'My worship has not reached such a state to make it worthy of being mentioned alone: it is polluted with all types of shortcoming. However, I combine it with the worship of all the worshippers and mention them all with one expression, saying *You we worship*.'

   RELATED JURISTIC ISSUE: if a man buys ten slaves [on behalf of someone], then the purchaser has the choice between accepting them all or none at all. He does not have the option of being selective within that transaction. So it is that when the servant says *You we worship*, he has presented all the worshippers' acts before God; therefore, it does not befit His generosity to discriminate by accepting some and rejecting others. It cannot be that He rejects them all, for among them is the worship of the angels, Prophets and saints. Thus if He accepts them all, the speaker's worship became acceptable by the blessings of the worship of others. It is as though he says: 'My God, if my own worship is not acceptable then do not reject me, for I am not alone in this worship: rather, we are many. If am not deserving of response and acceptance, then I seek the intercession of the worship of all other worshippers, so accept me.'

Benefit 5

Anyone who comes to know the benefits of worship will find delight in performing it, and find it difficult to be away from it. This is explained as follows:

1. Perfection is desirable in its own right. The most perfect and fortunate state for a person is to be engaged in the worship of God, as his heart is illuminated thereby with divine light, his tongue is honoured with remembrance and recitation, and his limbs are beautified with service to God. These states represent the zenith of humanity. If it is the case that these states bring about the greatest possible joy in the present moment, and that they bring about the most perfect bliss in the future, then whoever experiences them will find the burdens

involved in worship vanish, and it will be great sweetness in his heart.

2. Worship is a trust (*amāna*)—as God said: 'We did indeed offer the Trust to the heavens, the earth and the mountains...' (Q.xxxiii.72)—and fulfilling trusts is obligatory according to religion and reason. God said: 'God commands you to render back your trusts to those to whom they are due' (Q.iv.58). Fulfilment of trusts is an attribute of perfection which is desirable in its own right, and also because fulfilment from one side is a cause for it being fulfilled from the other.

   One of the Companions said:

   > I saw a Bedouin approach the door of the mosque, dismount his camel and leave it [aside]. He entered the mosque and prayed in peace and tranquillity, supplicating as much he wished, such that we were amazed [at his serenity]. When he came out, he could not find his camel, so he said: 'My God, I have fulfilled Your trust, so where is my trust?' We were astonished even more. After a few moments, a man arrived upon his camel, his hand having been cut [for theft], and he handed the camel back.[1]

   The lesson is that when this man preserved God's right, God preserved his right. This is what was meant by the Prophet (may God bless him and grant him peace) saying to Ibn ʿAbbās: 'O boy! Preserve God in seclusion and He will preserve you in the open.'[2]

3. To engage in worship is to travel from the world of deception (*ghurūr*) to the world of bliss (*surūr*), and from contact with creation to the presence of the Real. This creates the utmost pleasure and joy.

   It is narrated that while Abū Ḥanīfa was praying, a snake fell from the ceiling; the people scattered [in fright], but Abū Ḥanīfa did not notice. ʿUrwa b. al-Zubayr was afflicted by gangrene in one of his limbs, which had to be cut off. They performed the amputation while he stood in prayer and he did not feel it. When the Messenger of God (may God bless him and grant him peace) would commence his prayer, the people would hear a humming sound from his chest, as though from a [boiling] kettle.[3]

1 I could not source this narration.

2 I could not find this exact wording, but this must allude to the well-known *ḥadīth* in Tirmidhī.

3 Recorded by Abū Dāwūd and others—R.S.

Anyone who finds [these events] implausible should read the verse: 'When they saw him, they did extol him, and (in their amazement) cut their hands' (Q.XII.31). When the women's hearts were overcome by the beauty of Joseph (on whom be peace), they ended up cutting their hands without feeling anything. If this is possible on a human level, then God's majesty is even more likely to take control of one's heart. Moreover, if someone enters upon an awe-inspiring sovereign, his own parents and children could pass in front of his gaze without him recognising them due to the effect of that king's presence upon his heart. If that is possible for a created and metaphorical king, then it is much more so for the Creator of the universe!

THREE LEVELS OF WORSHIP ACCORDING TO THE SPIRITUAL MASTERS:[1]

The first: to worship God hoping for reward or fearing punishment. Although this is known as worship (*ʿibāda*), it is of a very low status because such a person's object of worship is, in reality, that reward. He has [in effect] made God a means to attain that object: and anyone who seeks after created things—with God being the means to attain them—is pitiful indeed.

The second: to worship God for the honour of worshipping Him, or the honour of receiving His commandments and being connected to Him. This is a higher level than the previous, but it is still not perfect in that the thing being sought is not God Himself.

The third: to worship God because He is Lord and Creator, and due to being His servant. Divinity obligates reverence and servitude obligates submission and humility. This is the highest of levels and the noblest of stations. It is called 'servitude' (*ʿubūdiyya*) and is indicated by a worshipper saying [prior to] prayer: 'I pray for [the sake of] God.' If he were to say 'I pray for God's reward' or 'fleeing His punishment', the prayer would be void.

Know that worship and servitude represent a lofty and noble station, as shown by a number of VERSES:

a. God said at the end of *Sūrat al-Ḥijr*: 'We do indeed know how your heart is distressed at what they say. But glorify the praises of your Lord, and be of those who prostrate themselves in adoration; and worship your Lord until Certainty (death) comes to you' (Q.XV.97–99). This is relevant in two ways: first, He said: 'Serve your Lord until Certainty comes to you,' which means to remain constant upon worship until death. This entails that it is not permissible to abandon

1 Cf. the critique of worshipping for reward in Book II, Chapter Nine, Enquiry 2.

worship at any time, which indicates its great importance. Second, He said: 'We do indeed know how your heart is distressed at what they say,' then commanded the Prophet (may God bless him and grant him peace) to do four things: glorification, praise, prostration and worship. This shows that worship alleviates the heart's distress and causes relief in the chest. This is only because worship means to return from the creation to the Real.

b. God said: 'Glory to the One Who did take His servant for a journey by night...' (Q.xvii.1). Were it not that worship is the noblest of stations, He would not have described [the Prophet] this way at the highest point of his Ascension. Some said that servitude is nobler than prophethood, because the former is movement from the creation to God, whereas the latter is movement from God to creation. Also, servitude is to give up agency [to God], whereas prophethood involves a level of agency; and it is more fitting for a servant to abandon agency. [Thirdly,] the master takes care of the needs of the servant, while the Prophet must take care of his nation, and these are starkly different situations.

c. The first thing uttered by Jesus (on whom be peace) was: 'I am indeed a servant of God' (Q.xix.30), and these words caused his mother's purity [to be proven] and his own existence to be vindicated. It became the key to all good and the preventer of all harms. Then, because Jesus' first words affirmed his servitude, his end was to be raised up: '...and raise you to Myself' (Q.iii.55). The lesson here is that one who declared his servitude through speech was raised up to Paradise. What, then, of one who declares it through his actions for seventy years: how could such be deprived of Paradise?

d. God said to Moses (on whom be peace): 'Indeed, I am God: there is no god but I, so worship Me...' (Q.xx.14). He commanded him first with monotheism, then with servitude, because monotheism is primary and servitude is secondary. If monotheism is a tree, servitude is its fruit: neither of them is complete without the other.

The aforementioned are verses which demonstrate the nobility of servitude.

As for RATIONAL PROOF, this is obvious. The servant is created and contingent; were it not for the effect of God's power upon him, he would have remained in the darkness of non-existence and absolute oblivion. He would not have come into existence at all, let alone with such perfection. Thus when the divine power turned to him and the effects of God's generosity and creative will poured out upon him, he attained existence and its perfections.

There is no meaning to him being the object of God's power—and the effect of God's creative act—other than servitude: for every honour, perfection, virtue, pleasure and achievement which occurs for the servant has come about through servitude. It is thus seen that servitude is the key to every good and felicity, and the means of ascent to the ranks of honour. This is why the servant says: *You we worship and from You we seek help*.

ʿAlī (may God ennoble his face) used to say: 'It is sufficient pride for me that I am a servant of Yours, and it is sufficient honour for me that You are my Lord. O God! I have found You to be the God that I want, so make me into the servant that You want.'

Benefit 6

Know that the stations are reducible to two: knowledge of Lordship and knowledge of servanthood. When these are combined, they represent the Covenant mentioned in the verse: 'And fulfil your covenant with Me so that I fulfil My covenant with you' (Q.II.40).

Knowledge of Lordship is fully represented in: *All praise is for God, Lord of the worlds; the Compassionate, the Merciful; Master of the Day of Judgment*. The servant's transfer from prior non-existence into existence denotes that He is God (*Ilāh*). His attainment of goodness and felicity after coming into existence denotes that He is a Compassionate and Merciful Lord. The servant's state in the Hereafter denotes that God is Master of the Day of Judgment. Once these attributes are comprehended in full, knowledge of Lordship will have reached its pinnacle.

After this comes knowledge of servanthood, which has a starting point and perfection, or a beginning and an end. As for the beginning, it is to engage in servitude, and this is indicated by: *You we worship*. Its perfection is for the servant to know that he is helpless against [the temptation of] sin without God's protection, and he is powerless to obey God without His grace.[1] At this point, he seeks God's help in attaining all his needs, and this is indicated by: *and from You we seek help*.

Once the covenants of Lordship and servanthood have been fulfilled, the [natural] conclusion is the request for the return and the fruit, as in:

1 See the following section on this point.

Guide us upon the straight path.... This is a noble and lofty [*sūra*] structure which the intellects could never surpass.

Benefit 7

QUESTION: *All praise is for God, Lord of the worlds; the Compassionate, the Merciful; Master of the Day of Judgment* is all in the third person (*ghayba*), then *You we worship and from You we seek help* involves a switch to the second person (*khiṭāb*). Why is this?

RESPONSE: there are several explanations:

a. At the beginning of the prayer, the worshipper was like a stranger, so he praised God with the appropriate form until *Master of the Day of Judgment*. Then [it is as though] God says to him: 'You have praised Me and acknowledged that I am God, Lord, Compassionate, Merciful and Master of the Day of Judgment. What a good servant you are! We have raised the veil and replaced distance with closeness: so address Me [directly] and say *You we worship*.'
b. The best kind of request is that made directly. After all, when the Prophets asked something of their Lord, they directed their speech to Him. For example, 'Our Lord, we have wronged our own souls' (Q.VII.23); 'Our Lord, forgive us our sins' (Q.III.147); 'O my Lord! Grant to me...' (Q.III.38); and 'My Lord, show me...' (Q.II.260). The reason is that it is unlikely that one who is generous would reject a request made directly and in person. Moreover, worship is service, and that is best done in the presence [of the one served].
c. From the beginning of the *sūra* until [before] *You we worship* is praise, and that is more appropriate in one's absence. From *You we worship and from You we seek help* until the end is supplication, and that is best done in person.
d. When the servant commences his prayer and says [beforehand]: 'I have intended to pray to draw closer to God,' he intends to attain closeness. Then he proceeds to praise God with various words, so God's generosity dictates that He grant him that closeness and take him from the station of distance to the station of presence, such that he says: *You we worship and from You we seek help*.

Exegesis of *And from You we seek help* (Verse 5)

Know that it is proven rationally that one is helpless against [the temptation of] sin without God's protection, and powerless to obey God without His grace. This is denoted both by reason and scripture:

RATIONAL EVIDENCES:

1. A capable person is equally able to perform an action or leave it. Therefore, without a preponderator (*murajjiḥ*), neither would take precedence over the other. Such a preponderator cannot emanate from the servant, or else that too would be subject to the same problem; hence it must be from Almighty God. Thus it is seen that the servant is unable to perform any action without the help of God.
2. All people seek after correct religion and true belief, and they are equal [on average] with respect to ability, intellect, seriousness and effort. Therefore, those who obtain the truth must owe their success to a Helper; and this can be none other than God, since a human or angel would be subject to the same problem.
3. A person may be asked over a long period to do something yet he refrains, until one day he carries out the requested action. This does not occur except by means of a strong motivation which forms in his heart to perform the action. The act of placing this motivation in the heart and removing the opposing motivations is due to Almighty God, and this is the very meaning of 'help' (*iʿāna*).

TEXTUAL PROOFS: in addition to this verse *And from You we seek help*, a second verse is: 'Seek help from God' (Q.VII.128).

The Jabrīs and the Qadarīs disputed over this verse. The former said: 'If the servant were capable of autonomous action, there would be no benefit in seeking help to perform it.' The latter said: 'Seeking help is only appropriate if the servant is basically capable of doing the action, but seeks the help of others [due to difficulty].[1] If he were not capable of acting at all, then there would be no benefit in seeking help.' In my view, ability does not impact upon action except when coupled with the strong motivation. Therefore, the seeking of help pertains to creation of this strong motivation and the removal of its opposite.

Subtleties of this Verse[2]

QUESTION: seeking help for an action is only appropriate before commencing that action. Therefore, what is the wisdom behind *You we worship* coming before *from You we seek help*?

1 I have read *fa-yaṭlub* in place of the printed editions' *fa-tabṭul*. I found this confirmed by the Michigan manuscript, p. 145.

2 The author has used the plural and labelled what follows as 'Benefit 1,' but there are no further *laṭā'if* or *fawā'id* labelled in the section. However, points c and d do not appear to answer the question posed, so they may be considered more broadly as subtle points concerning the verse.

RESPONSES:

a. It is as though the worshipper says: 'I have commenced my worship, so I seek Your help in completing it. Let me not be so deprived through death, illness or a change in motivations.'
b. It is as though he says: 'My God, I have brought myself, but I have a heart which flees from me. Therefore, I seek Your help in making it present.' After all, the Prophet (may God bless him and grant him peace) said: 'The heart of the believer is between two of the fingers of the Compassionate.'[1] This shows that the human being is incapable of making his heart present without divine assistance.
c. [The worshipper says:]

> I do not want help from anyone but You: not Gabriel or Michael, only You. In this, I adopt the way of Your Friend [*Khalīl*, namely Abraham] (on whom be peace): when Nimrod shackled his hands and feet and threw him into the fire, Gabriel came and asked him: 'Do you have any need?' [Abraham] replied: 'None from you.' Gabriel said: 'Ask Him,' to which he replied: 'His knowledge of my condition suffices me from asking.' Indeed, I may exceed the Friend in this respect, in that only his hands and feet were bound. As for me, my feet are restrained so I cannot walk; as are my hands, so I cannot move them; my eyes, so I cannot see; my ears, so I cannot hear; and my tongue so I cannot speak. The Friend was about to be cast into the fire of Nimrod, while I am about to be cast into the fire of Hell. Therefore, just as he refused anyone but You as Helper, so do I refuse. *You we worship and from You we seek help*.

Then it is as though God says:

> You followed the action of the Friend and increased; therefore, I shall increase the reward. At that time, I said: 'O fire! Be cool and (a means of) safety for Abraham' (Q.xxi.69). As for you, I have saved you from the Fire and delivered you to Paradise, and increased you by allowing you to hear the pre-eternal Speech and see the

1 Recorded by Muslim—R.S.

> pre-eternal Existent.[1] Just as We commanded Nimrod's fire to be coolness and safety for Abraham, the Fire of Hell will tell you: 'Pass over, O believer, as your light has extinguished my flame.'

d. *From You we seek help*, that is, 'I ask of no other but You, for any other is not able to help me unless You help him to help me. Therefore, if the help of others is dependent upon Your help, I shall reject this intermediary and seek Your help alone.'

e. *You we worship* leads to the soul achieving a great status through devotion to the worship of God, but this can produce self-satisfaction. This is why it was followed immediately by words signifying that this status achieved through worship was not by the servant's power, but rather by the help of God. Thus the purpose of mentioning *from You we seek help* is to remove any trace of pride and conceit.

Exegesis of *Guide us upon the straight path* (Verse 6)

Benefit 1

PROBLEM: a worshipper must surely be a believer, and every believer is guided, so every worshipper is guided. Therefore, when he says *Guide us*, effectively this is for someone guided to seek guidance, and creating what already exists is impossible.

RESPONSE: the scholars answered this in a number of ways:

1. What is meant is the path of the former peoples who withstood great burdens for the sake of God's pleasure. It was narrated that Noah (on whom be peace) used to be beaten a certain number of times every day, and upon each beating would say: 'O God! Guide my people, for they know not.' One might suggest that this implies that Noah was better than our Messenger (may God bless him and grant him peace), in that the latter said this only once whereas Noah did so many times each day. The response is that *Guide us upon the straight path* is a supplication to God for those virtuous traits, and the Messenger (may God bless him and grant him peace) would recite the *Fātiḥa* numerous times each day. Therefore, his utterance of this formula exceeded Noah's.
2. The scholars have explained that for every character trait there are two extremes: laxity (*tafrīṭ*) and excess (*ifrāṭ*)—and both are blameworthy. The true [path] is in the middle, as confirmed by God's

1 There could be an allusion here to Q.x.26 and Q.l.35.

saying: 'And thus have We made of you a nation justly balanced (*wasaṭ*)' (Q.II.143), and that *wasaṭ* means justice and correctness.[1] Therefore, once a believer comes to know God through evidence, he becomes a guided believer.[2] Upon attaining this state, he needs to know the way of justice, which is the medial line between the extremes of excess and laxity, with respect to acts of the appetitive and irascible faculties as well as his spending of wealth. Thus the believer asks God to guide him to that straight path which runs between excess and laxity in all character traits as well as actions. On this basis, the objection falls.

3. [Even] when the believer has come to know God through one proof, [it is still the case that] every single thing in existence contains proofs of God's existence, knowledge, power, generosity, mercy and wisdom. A person's religion may be correct based on one proof, while he remains unaware of all the rest. Thus *Guide us upon the straight path* means: 'Inform us, O our God, how every object indicates Your Essence, Attributes, power and knowledge.' On this basis, the objection falls.
4. Almighty God said: 'And indeed, you (Prophet) guide to a straight path: the path of God, to Whom belongs whatever is in the heavens and whatever is on the earth' (Q.XLII.52–53), and also: 'Indeed, this is My path, leading straight: so follow it' (Q.VI.153). That straight path is for the servant to turn away from other-than-God and direct all his heart, thought and remembrance to God. Thus what is intended by saying *Guide us upon the straight path* is for God to guide him to the straight path which has this description.

   [The aim] is to reach a state whereby, if he were ordered to slaughter his son, he would obey as did Abraham (on whom be peace); if he were ordered to be led to the slaughter, he would obey as did Ishmael (on whom be peace); if he were ordered to throw himself into the sea, he would obey as did Jonah (on whom be peace); if he were ordered to be a pupil to one more knowledgeable, despite having [himself] reached the highest possible position,

1 See also Chapter 3, Section II above.

2 This alludes to the Ashʿarī insistence upon rational evidence in order for true faith to obtain. The author seems to have presented a less stringent account here, in which the believer requires evidence in order to be 'guided', and then (see next point) he increases in guidance by appreciating more proofs. However, he then implies that at least one proof was required for correctness of faith.

he would obey as did Moses with al-Khaḍir (upon them be peace); and if he were ordered to be steadfast upon enjoining the right and forbidding the wrong while being killed and cut into two, he would obey as did John and Zechariah (upon them be peace).

Thus what is meant by *Guide us upon the straight path* is to adopt the way of God's Prophets in being patient upon hardship and steadfast at times of tribulation. Without doubt, this is a tremendously difficult station which the majority of the creation would be unable to reach. Yet we can say: O people! Do not fear or be grieved, for there is nothing constricted in God's religion except that it contains expanse. Within this verse there is an indication of ease and facilitation, for God did not mention 'the path of those who were beaten and killed', but rather *The path of those on whom You have bestowed favour*. Therefore, let your intention when reciting this verse be: 'My God, I saw my father committing major sins, and I have done the same. Then I saw him repenting on his deathbed, and You saved him from Hellfire and delivered him to Paradise: thus he is among those whom You favoured by guiding him to repentance, and then by accepting his repentance. Therefore, I say: guide us to that same straight path so we may attain the rank of the repenters.' Then, if you achieve this, ask for the ranks of the Prophets. This is the explanation of *Guide us upon the straight path*.

5. It is as though the person says while on his journey:

> My many friends are pulling me towards one path, my enemies to another, and Satan to a third. The same applies to [the further paths of] desire, anger, hatred and envy, as well as [the extremes of] negation (*taʿṭīl*) and anthropomorphism (*tashbīh*),[1] fatalism (*jabr*) and voluntarism (*qadar*),[2] postponement (*irjā'*) and threat (*waʿīd*),[3] rejection (*rafḍ*) and secession (*khurūj*).[4] The

1 These are two extremes with respect to the Divine Attributes. See Chapter 3, Section II above.

2 This refers to the two main positions regarding free will, of which the author and other Ashʿarīs are closer to the former.

3 'Postponement' refers to the beliefs of the Murji'ī sect who maintained that every believer would be saved by faith alone, irrespective of actions and sins. The opposing doctrine in its Muʿtazilī form was called *al-waʿd wa'l-waʿīd*, in which it was held that God was obliged to punish anyone who became deserving of that punishment, because His threats as well as His promises must be fulfilled.

4 The Shiʿa are sometimes described pejoratively as Rāfiḍīs. Their split from the Sunnis originated in disputes over governance of the early Muslim community; the same applies to the historical sect of the Khārijīs.

> intellect is weak, life is short, the road is long, the task is fraught with danger and fate is hard to bear. I am at a loss concerning all of this, so guide me to the path which takes me safely past it, all the way to Paradise.

The word *mustaqīm* means 'smooth and even, having no roughness'.[1]

It is narrated that Ibrāhīm b. Adham was walking [from a great distance] towards the House of God [in Mecca] when a Bedouin riding upon a camel said: 'O *shaykh*! Where are you headed?' He replied: 'To the House of God.' The Bedouin said: 'Are you mad? I do not see with you any mount or provision, and the journey is long!' Ibrāhīm said: 'I have many mounts which you cannot see.' He asked: 'And what are those?' Ibrāhīm replied: 'When a tribulation afflicts me, I ride the mount of patience; when a favour descends upon me, I ride the mount of gratitude; when [hardship] is decreed for me, I ride the mount of contentment; and when my soul incites me to some [sin], I have certainty that what remains of my life is less than what has passed.' The Bedouin said: 'Carry on, for you are the rider, and I am the walker!'

6. Some [exegetes] said that *the straight path* is 'Islam' or 'the Qur'ān'. However, that is incorrect, as [the following verse:] *The path of those on whom You have bestowed favour* is a [grammatical] substitute for *the straight path*. Thus the meaning is 'Guide us upon the path of the preceding people on whom You bestowed favour,' and none of the preceding nations had the Qur'ān or Islam.[2] Once that is ruled out, the meaning must be: 'Guide us upon the path of those who walked rightly and were deserving of Paradise.'

   The word *ṣirāṭ* was used [for 'path']—rather than *sabīl* or *ṭarīq* which share its meaning—in order to bring to mind the bridge over Hellfire, so that a person increases in fear and awe.

7. The second interpretation for *Guide us* is 'Make us firm upon the guidance which You have granted us.'[3] This is like the verse: 'Our Lord! Let not our hearts deviate now after You have guided us'

1 This is along with the meaning of 'straight' which is assumed elsewhere in the discussion and used in the translation.

2 It can certainly be said that they had Islam in its broader sense, as the Qur'ān affirms in numerous verses. Furthermore, Ālūsī points out that the author's earlier explanation in terms of the 'middle path' (point 2 above) could be said not to have been available to preceding nations (according to exegeses of Q.II.143); see Ālūsī, *Rūḥ al-maʿānī*, vol. 1, p. 303.

3 This point was not originally labelled as point 7, but it does serve to answer the same question.

(Q.III.8), i.e. establish us firmly upon guidance. After all, many a scholar has been affected by a weak doubt which took root in his mind, and by which he deviated and went astray from the straight and true path of religion.

Benefit 2

QUESTION: why did He say *Guide us* and not 'Guide me'?

RESPONSES:

1. The more encompassing the supplication, the more likely it is to be accepted. One of the scholars used to say to his students:

    > When you recite in *Khuṭbat al-sabq*[1] 'May God be pleased with you [singular] and with the Muslim community!' then if you intend me when you say 'with you' that is good, but otherwise is fine. But by no means forget me when you say 'and with the Muslim community', for the former is specification of the supplication [to one person] and might not be accepted, but as for the latter: there must be someone among the Muslims who deserves that acceptance, so if God accepts the supplication for some of them, He is too generous to reject the rest.

    This is why it is from the *Sunna* to begin one's supplication by sending salutations upon the Prophet (may God bless him and grant him peace), followed by one's supplication, concluding again with salutations upon the Prophet. This is because God will certainly accept the supplicant's salutations upon the Prophet (may God bless him and grant him peace), so if the two ends of his supplication are accepted, the central part will not be rejected.
2. The Prophet (may God bless him and grant him peace) said: 'Call upon God using tongues with which you have not disobeyed Him.' The [Companions] asked: 'O Messenger of God! Who among us has such a tongue?' He replied: 'You should supplicate on behalf of one another, for you did not sin with [your brother's] tongue, and he did not sin with yours.'[2]
3. It is as though [God] says: 'O servant! Did you not say at the beginning of the *sūra*: *All praise is for God* rather than "I praise God"? In

1 I could not ascertain this reference, which may be to a particular book. I have rendered the word according to Amīriyya, vol. 1, p. 140, whereas some editions have *al-sābiq*.

2 I could not source this narration—R.S.

that way, you mentioned the praise of all the praisers. Therefore, when you come to supplicate, include them and say *Guide us*.'

4. It is as though the servant says:

> I heard Your Messenger saying: 'Collectivity is mercy and division is torment.'[1] Therefore, when I intended to praise You, I mentioned everyone's praise and said *All praise is for God*. When I mentioned worship, I mentioned everyone's worship and said *You we worship*. When I mentioned seeking help, I mentioned everyone's seeking of help and said *Your help we seek*. Thus when I come to seek guidance, I seek it on behalf of everyone, saying: *Guide us upon the straight path*. When I seek to follow the righteous, I seek to follow them all: *The path of those on whom You have bestowed favour*. And when I ask to be averted from the rejected ones, I flee from them all: *Not of those who incur wrath, nor of those who are astray*. Since I have not parted from the Prophets and righteous in this life, I hope that I will not be parted from them on the Day of Judgment, as God said: 'Whoever obeys God and the Messenger is in the company of those on whom is God's favour: of the Prophets, the truthful ones, the witnesses and the righteous. Ah, what a beautiful fellowship!' (Q.IV.69).

Benefit 3

Know that the people of geometry (*handasa*) have said: the straight line is the shortest line between two points. This means that the straight line is shorter than all the crooked ones. Thus the servant says *Guide us upon the straight path* for a number of reasons:

a. 'It is the shortest and most direct line; I am weak and can only manage this straight path.'
b. 'There is only one straight path and all the others are crooked. Since they resemble each other in their crookedness, I cannot tell them apart and find my way. The straight path, on the other hand, is distinct from any other so it is the safest way and farthest from danger.'
c. The straight path directs to the goal, unlike the crooked.
d. The straight path never alters, unlike the crooked.

1 Recorded in Mundhirī's *al-Targhīb wa'l-tarhīb*.

These are the reasons for asking for the straight path. And God knows best.

Exegesis of *The path of those on whom You have bestowed favour...* (Verse 7)

Benefit 1

There are various opinions on the definition of 'favour' (*niʿma*). Some said that it is any beneficial act (*manfaʿa*) performed out of kindness. Others said that it must be a good and beneficial act, because a favour must be worthy of gratitude, and anything distasteful [i.e. prohibited] is not. However, in truth, this qualification is unnecessary because one may deserve thanks for his kindness even if what he did was prohibited, as the thanks due [from the beneficiary] are one thing, while the sin and punishment accrued are another. Why could these not co-occur? A sinner deserves gratitude for his acts of kindness, but also blame for his disobedience to God: so why not the same in this case?

Let us return to the above definition. We have said 'benefit' because a pure harm cannot be a favour. We have said 'performed out of kindness' because if it is truly a beneficial thing but done for the doer's own benefit rather than the beneficiary's, then it would not be considered a favour. An example would be for someone to be kind to one's slave-girl in order to profit from her.

Once this definition is known, there are several issues following from it:

Issue 1

Know that any benefit which reaches the creation, and any aversion of harm, comes from Almighty God: 'And whatever you have of favour, it is from God' (Q.xvi.53). Then favours are of three categories:

a. That which God alone can bring into being; for example, to create and provide.
b. That which comes from other-than-God according to appearances, but depends upon God in reality. This is because God is the Creator of that favour and of the benefactor, as well as the motivation of kindness in his heart. When God delivered that favour upon that servant's hands, the servant received gratitude; yet the real One deserving of gratitude is Almighty God. This is why He said: 'Show gratitude to Me and to your parents: to Me is (your final) goal' (Q.xxxi.14)—beginning with Himself in order to draw attention to the fact that the kindness of created beings depends upon His kindness.

c. That which comes to us from God due to our obedience. These are also from Him [completely], for if He had not guided us to worship Him, and graced us with support and the removal of impediments, we would not have achieved any of this.

This shows that all favours, in reality, come from God.

Issue 2

Know that the first of God's favours upon the servants is that He created them alive, and this is indicated by reason and scripture:

RATIONAL PROOF: a thing is not a favour unless it is possible to derive benefit from it, and this depends upon being alive. Dead or inanimate things cannot benefit from anything, so it is clear that the origin of all favours is life.

SCRIPTURAL PROOF: God said: 'How can you reject the faith in God, seeing that you were without life, and He gave you life?' (Q.II.28). Then He said in the next [verse]: 'It is He Who has created for you all things that are on earth…' (Q.II.29). He began by mentioning life and then mentioned the things of benefit, which shows that the origin of all favours is life.

Issue 3

[Scholars] differed over the question: 'Does God bestow favours upon the unbelievers?' Some of our [Ashʿarī] companions said that God does not bestow favours upon the unbelievers. The Muʿtazilīs said: God bestows religious and worldly favours upon the unbelievers.

OUR COMPANIONS argued for their position with reference to the Qur'ān and reason. From the Qur'ān, they cited: *The path of those on whom You have bestowed favour*, in that if God bestowed favours upon the unbelievers, they would be included in this supplication, which would then mean asking God to guide to the path of the unbelievers, which is absurd. Therefore, according to this verse, God does not bestow favours upon the unbelievers. If one should object that *the straight path* [in the preceding verse] resolves this, the response is that the *The path of those…* is a grammatical substitute for that, such that the meaning is 'Guide us upon the path of those on whom You have bestowed favour,' in which case the aforementioned problem remains.

They also cited: 'Let not the unbelievers think that our respite to them is good for themselves: We only grant them respite so that they may grow in their iniquity' (Q.III.178).

As for reason, [the Ashᶜarīs argued]: the favours of this world are like mere drops in the ocean compared to eternal punishment in the Hereafter. In this case, they cannot be [called] 'favours'. If you were to add poison to a sweet dish, the [enjoyment] derived from that dish would not be a favour, in that the benefit was meager indeed compared to the great harm caused. Such is the case here.

As for [THE MUᶜTAZILĪS] who argued that God bestows many favours upon the unbelievers, they cited various verses:

a. 'O people! Adore your Guardian-Lord, Who created you and those who came before you, that you may learn righteousness; (He) Who has made the earth your couch, and the heavens your canopy...' (Q.II.21–22). These verses say that all must obey God due to these tremendous favours.
b. 'How can you reject the faith in God, seeing that you were without life, and He gave you life?' (Q.II.28). This was mentioned in the context of recounting God's favours.
c. 'O Children of Israel! Call to mind the (special) favour which I bestowed upon you' (Q.II.40).
d. God said: '...but few of My servants are grateful' (Q.XXXIV.13), and [quoting] Iblīs: 'Nor will you find, in most of them, gratitude' (Q.VII.17). If there were no favours, there would be no cause for gratitude, and they would not have done wrong by not giving thanks. This is because thanks are only possible once a favour has been received.

Benefit 2

In these verses is [a proof for] the leadership (*imāma*) of Abū Bakr (may God be pleased with him). As we have mentioned, the meaning is 'Guide us upon the path of those on whom You have bestowed favour,' and God has explained in another verse who these are: '...those on whom is God's favour: of the Prophets, the truthful (*ṣiddīqīn*)...' (Q.IV.69)—and without doubt, the chief and leader of the truthful is Abū Bakr the Truthful (*al-Ṣiddīq*).[1] Thus the verse is a divine instruction to seek that guidance which Abū Bakr and the other truthful ones were upon. If Abū Bakr had been an oppressor,[2] it would not have been permissible to

1 As the author explains in his exegesis of Q.IV.69, this term refers to one for whom truth is a defining quality. Abū Bakr earned this title for preceding others in believing (*taṣdīq*) in the Prophet (may God bless him and grant him peace) and for being an example to others in this respect.

2 I.e. by wrongfully claiming the role as the first Caliph, as the Shiᶜa maintain.

follow his way. Hence it is seen how this verse denotes the [rightful] leadership of Abū Bakr.

Benefit 3

Those on whom You have bestowed favour encompasses all upon whom God has bestowed favour. The 'favour' mentioned must be either of the worldly or religious kind: since the former is [obviously] false, it must be the latter. In that case, we say: every religious favour other than faith is conditional upon faith being present, whereas it is possible to have the favour of faith without any other religious favours. This shows that what is intended by this verse is the favour which is faith, and that is what is sought by: *Guide us upon the straight path; the path of those on whom You have bestowed favour*.

Having established this principle, there are a number of [theological] rulings which follow:[1]

1. Since what is intended by this 'favour' is faith, and the verse is explicit in that God is the Bestower of this favour, it follows that the Creator and Bestower of faith is Almighty God, and this denotes the falsity of the Muʿtazilī position. Moreover, because faith is the greatest of all favours, if it were by the act of the servant then his benefaction would be greater than God's; and in that case, it would not be apt for God to mention His benefaction in the context of praise.
2. It cannot be that the believer remains eternally in Hell, because *Those on whom You have bestowed favour* is mentioned in a context of magnification of this favour [i.e. faith]. If this did not have any effect in averting eternal punishment, it would be of little benefit and would not be fitting to mention in the context of praise.
3. The verse denotes that God is not obliged to perform what is advantageous (*ṣalāḥ*) and most advantageous (*aṣlaḥ*) in the matter of religion, for if guidance were obligatory upon Him, that would not be benefaction on His part: to discharge an obligation is not considered a favour. Since God has named it so, it must not be an obligation.
4. It cannot be that what is intended by this favour is [merely] that God gave the person the ability to achieve it, directed him to it and removed impediments from his way: for this is equally true

1 These are intended as refutations of Muʿtazilī doctrines.

of the unbelievers. Since God specified certain people with this favour [of faith], whereas the ability and removal of impediments applies to all, we know that what is intended here is other than granting ability and removing impediments.

Exegesis of *Not of those who incur wrath, nor of those who are astray* (Verse 7)

Benefit 1

The well-known opinion [among exegetes] is that *those who incur wrath*[1] are the Jews, based on: '...those who incurred the curse of God and His wrath' (Q.v.60), and that *those who are astray* are the Christians, based on: '...who went wrong in times gone by, who misled many, and strayed (themselves) from the even way' (Q.v.77).[2]

Some argued that this is weak, because disbelievers in the Creator and polytheists are worse in religion than the Jews and Christians, so avoiding their path would have been worthier [of mention].[3] Rather, [they argue,] it is better to interpret the former as all those who err with respect to outward actions, i.e. sinners (*fussāq*), and the latter as all those who err with respect to belief. This is because the wording is universal, so particularising it is contrary to the default.

It is also possible to say that the former are the unbelievers (*kuffār*), and the latter the hypocrites (*munāfiqūn*). This is because God began with the mention and praise of the believers in the first five verses of *Sūrat al-Baqara* (Q.II.1–5), followed by mention of the unbelievers from 'As to those who reject faith...' (Q.II.6), and then discussion of the hypocrites from 'Of the people there are some who say: "We believe..."' (Q.II.8). Likewise, here the mention is first of the believ-

1 This part of the verse is particularly difficult to translate. *Al-maghḍūb ʿalayhim* is the equivalent of a passive participle for an indirect object that is also plural, i.e. 'the angered-upon', which is rather inelegant. *Al-ḍāllīn* is a straightforward plural meaning 'strayers'. Both of these translations are further complicated by the grammatical relation of this fragment to the sentence preceding. See also Chapter Four, Enquiry 7 (with footnotes).

2 Ālūsī argued that it is better to prove this via the Prophetic reports bearing this explanation, and criticised Rāzī for contradicting those via rational considerations; see Ālūsī, *Rūḥ al-maʿānī*, vol. 1, p. 313. This famous explanation does not entail the descriptions being exclusive to these two groups. See Ibn ʿĀshūr, *al-Taḥrīr wa'l-tanwīr*, vol. 1, p. 199, where it is taken as an 'illustration' based on the communities known to the Arabs at the time of revelation. It may also be expressed as: 'Not like the *worst* members of former communities,' a sentiment well attested in the Qur'ān.

3 Ālūsī responds: 'One who follows no religion is not worthy of mention.' See Ālūsī, *Rūḥ al-maʿānī*, vol. 1, p. 312.

ers on whom favour was bestowed, followed by the unbelievers who receive anger, and then the hypocrites who go astray.

Benefit 2

Since God has ruled that they are astray, it is impossible for them to become believers. Otherwise, the true statement of God would become false, which is absurd—so the premise leading to it must be rejected.

Benefit 3

This verse indicates that none of the angels or Prophets (on whom be peace) ever acted contrary to the actions or beliefs of those whom God favoured, because in that case they would have strayed from the truth, as God said: 'What can be beyond truth except error?' (Q.x.32). If they were in error, it would not be permissible to follow their way or derive guidance from their example; indeed, they would be outside the scope of those whom God favoured. Since all that is false, this verse proves the infallibility (*ʿiṣma*) of the Prophets and angels.

Benefit 4

Anger (*ghaḍab*) is a change of state in which the blood of the heart 'boils' in desire for revenge. Know that this [literal meaning] is impossible for God. However, the general principle connected to such 'emotional' properties—i.e. mercy (*raḥma*), elation (*faraḥ*), joy (*surūr*), anger, shyness (*ḥayā'*), jealousy (*ghīra*), plotting (*makr*), trickery (*khidāʿ*), haughtiness (*takabbur*) and mockery (*istihzā'*)[1]—is that they consist of an initial state and a consequence. For example, anger begins with this 'boiling' of the heart's blood, and ends with intending to cause harm to the object of that anger. Therefore, in the case of God it is not understood in terms of an initial circumstance, but instead in terms of the consequence: intention to harm.

Also, shyness has an initial state which is 'brokenness' of the soul, and its consequence is to abandon performing an action. Therefore, when used

1 These are all terms which are used in the Qur'ān or *Sunna* to describe some state or action of God, often referred to as *al-ṣifāt al-khabariyya*. Together with descriptions implying corporeality and direction, these are the subject of lengthy debates between various factions of theologians. Our author is famous for the extent to which he advocated *ta'wīl*, i.e. interpretation with reference to metaphorical uses of the language. It is also possible to refer to context in order to understand each expression: one would thus differentiate between various items on the list, contrary to the 'universal principle' advocated here. See Yūsuf al-Qaraḍāwī, *Fuṣūl fī al-ʿaqīda bayna al-salaf wa'l-khalaf*, Cairo: Maktabat Wahba, 2005, pp. 118–132; cf. above Book II, Chapter Eight, Enquiry 2.

for God[1] it is understood only to mean that He abandons an action, and not in terms of brokenness. This is the overarching principle in such cases.

Benefit 5

The Muʿtazilīs said: 'The fact that God is angry with them shows that they performed sinful acts by their own volition, or else His anger upon them would be unjust.'

Our [Ashʿarī] companions said: 'God mentioned His anger upon them and followed this by saying they are astray, which indicates that God's anger was the cause for their straying. As such, God's Attribute takes effect upon the attribute of the servant. If we were to say that their being astray caused God's anger upon them, then that would entail the servant's attribute taking effect upon God's, which is impossible.'

Benefit 6

The beginning of the *sūra* contains praise and exaltation of God, and its end contains dispraise of those who turn away from faith in Him and obedience to Him. This signifies that the starting point of all goodness and felicity is in directing one's self to Almighty God, and that the source of all misery is to turn away from God and decline to obey and serve Him.

Benefit 7

This verse denotes that accountable people (*mukallafūn*) are of three categories: the people of obedience on whom God *bestowed favour*; the people of sin *who incur wrath*; and the people of ignorance concerning God's religion, and unbelief, *who are astray*.

QUESTION: why were the sinners mentioned before the unbelievers?

RESPONSE: this is because every [rational] person seeks to avoid unbelief. However, since some people do not avoid sins, this was more important to emphasise and was therefore mentioned first.

Benefit 8

PROBLEM: an issue arises from this verse: God's anger only came about as a result of His knowledge of the sin on the part of [the servant],

1 In his commentary on Q.II.26, the author cites a *ḥadīth* recorded by Abū Dāwūd and others, which describes God as *ḥayī karīm* ('shy and generous') because He does not send a supplicant back empty-handed. Rāzī also refutes the claim that the verse implies that *ḥayā'* is possible for God; by the same token, refutations of the belief that He has begotten a son do not imply the possibility of such.

and that knowledge must be said either to be pre-eternal, or temporal. If that knowledge is pre-eternal (*qadīm*), then why did He create [that servant], knowing that he will not gain anything from being in existence except [to earn] eternal punishment? How can one who is angered by something actually create that thing? If, on the other hand, that knowledge were temporally originated (*ḥādith*), then God would be a substrate (*maḥall*) for temporal [Attributes]. Moreover, it would follow that the creation of that knowledge is dependent on a prior knowledge, which leads to infinite regression and absurdity.

RESPONSE: God does what He wills and judges as He pleases.[1]

Benefit 9

QUESTION: whoever receives God's favour could not be the object of His wrath or among those who stray, so why, after *those on whom You have bestowed favour*, did He mention the two other categories?

RESPONSE: faith is only complete when it consists of [both] hope and fear, as the Prophet (may God bless him and grant him peace) said: 'If the fear of the believer and his hope were placed in the scales, they would be equal.'[2] The mention of God's favour inspires complete hope, but the mention of divine anger and those who go astray inspires complete fear, so faith is strengthened by means of these two pillars and thus approaches perfection.

Benefit 10

QUESTION: what is the wisdom behind God describing the accepted people as one group whom God favoured, whereas the rejected ones are two groups?

RESPONSE: the people upon whom God's favour was perfected were those who combined knowledge of the truth in its own right, and [knowledge of] good in order to act upon it. Those are the ones referred to as *those on whom You have bestowed favour*.

However, if the clause pertaining to action is neglected, then those are the sinners who earn divine wrath, as God said: 'Whoever kills a

1 The Ashʿarī position is that knowledge is a pre-eternal Attribute which may be connected to created things. Thus the statement of response can be seen as directed particularly to the part saying: 'If that knowledge is pre-eternal'. The response has been interpreted as a denial of moral realism, making it 'futile' to articulate a 'working theodicy' on the part of Rāzī; see Shihadeh, *Teleological Ethics*, p. 168. Further reflections relevant to theodicy can be found below in Chapter Six, Section IV, Benefit 3.

2 Recorded in Abu Nuʿaym's *Ḥilya* and Bayhaqī's *Shuʿab*—R.S.

believer intentionally, his recompense is Hell to abide therein (forever), and the wrath and the curse of God are upon him' (Q.iv.93). If the clause pertaining to knowledge [of truth] is neglected, then those are the strayers, as God said: 'What can be beyond truth except error?' (Q.x.32).

This is the last of our detailed exegesis of each of the verses of this *sūra* in turn. And God knows best.

Chapter Six
EXEGESIS OF THE *SŪRA* AS A WHOLE[1]

Section 1: Rational Subtleties Derived from this *Sūra*

Know that this world (*dunyā*) is the world of taintedness, whereas the Hereafter (*ākhira*) is the world of purity. The Hereafter in relation to this world is like the origin in relation to its branch, and like a body in relation to its shadow.[2] Therefore, everything in this world must have an original [form] (*aṣl*) in the Hereafter; otherwise it would be a mere illusion and mirage. Conversely, everything in the Hereafter must have a similitude (*mithāl*) in this world, or else it would be like a tree with no fruit, or a referent with no signifier.

The world of spirituality is the realm of illumination, beauty, joy and pleasure. Certainly there must be variation between these spirits in terms of perfection and deficiency, which entails that there is one which is the most perfect, noble and lofty. The others must be under his authority, obeying his command and prohibition, as God said: 'Endued with power, with rank before the Lord of the Throne; obeyed there, faithful to his trust' (Q.LXXXI.20–21). Likewise, there must be in this world an individual who is its most perfect, noble and lofty, with all others under his authority and command.

The first 'Obeyed one' (*muṭāʿ*)[3] is of the spiritual world, while the second is of the corporeal world: the former has authority in the upper world, while the latter has authority in the lower world. Since we have said that the corporeal world is like the shadow or effect of the spiritual world, it follows that there must be a relation and similarity between

1 As explained at the beginning of Chapter Five, this is originally the second part of Chapter Five; however, it is more logically presented as a separate chapter.

2 The evocation of Plato's theory of Forms is evident. In this discussion, the contrast between *dunyā* and *ākhira* is not made in temporal terms, but in terms of physical and spiritual realms.

3 The term appears in Q.LXXXI.21 just cited, and the concept features in Ghazālī; see Gairdner's introduction to *Al-Ghazzālī's Mishkāt al-anwār*, pp. 7–25. See also Shihadeh, *Teleological Ethics*, p. 138.

these two Obeyed ones. The Obeyed in the spiritual world is like the source (*maṣdar*), while that in the corporeal world is like the manifestation (*maẓhar*): the source is the angelic Messenger, and the manifestation is the human Messenger. By these two, the felicity of the Hereafter and this world is realised.

[STUDY OF THE END OF *SŪRAT AL-BAQARA*][1]

Once you have known this, we say: the perfection of the human Messenger's state is manifested in calling to God, and this call depends upon seven matters which God mentioned at the end of *Sūrat al-Baqara* [Q.II.285, starting from]: '…as do the believers. Each one (of them) believes in God, His angels, His books and His Messengers'. Still among the rulings pertaining to the Messengers is: 'We make no distinction (they say) between one and another of His Messengers.' These four points are concerned with knowledge of the starting point (*mabda'*), which is to know Lordship.

Then He mentioned that which pertains to knowledge of servitude, which is based on two things: a starting point and its perfection. The starting point is to say: 'We hear, and we obey…' as this is essential to anyone intending to journey to God. The perfection [of servitude] is in complete dependence upon God, turning fully to Him: '(We seek) Your forgiveness, our Lord…' This means to turn one's vision completely away from [one's own] human works and acts of obedience, turning instead completely to God and seeking His mercy and forgiveness.

Then, once Lordship is known through those four principles [of creed], and servitude is known through these two principles [of the journey], there is nothing left but to travel to the presence of the Beneficent Sovereign and prepare for the next life. This is what is referred to in: '…and to You is the destination'.

As you can see, there are three stages: start, middle and destination. The start is only made complete by four types of knowledge: of God, the angels, the scriptures and the Messengers. The middle depends on knowledge of two matters: 'We hear, and we obey' is the portion of the corporeal world, and 'Your forgiveness, our Lord' is the portion of the spiritual world. As for the ending, this is completed with one thing only: 'To You is the destination.' Thus the start is four, the middle is two and the end is just one.

1 These verses are used to develop a theory which is then applied more directly to the *Fātiḥa*. See also Section III below. There is a tradition linking the revelation of these two passages, cited above in Book II, Chapter Four, Section I (Enquiry 6); cf. the discussion of the *Fātiḥa*'s revelation in Chapter Two above.

Then these seven stations of knowledge give rise to seven stations in supplication:[1]

1. 'Our Lord! Condemn us not if we forget or fall into error' (Q.II.286). The opposite of forgetting is remembrance (*dhikr*), as God said: 'O you who believe! Remember God much' (Q.XXXIII.41), 'And remember your Lord when you forget' (Q.XVIII.24), '...they bring (God) to remembrance, and immediately they see (aright)' (Q.VII.201), and 'But keep in remembrance the Name of your Lord' (Q.LXXIII.8). This remembrance is only realised by saying: *In the Name of God, the Compassionate, the Merciful* (Q.I.1).
2. 'Our Lord! Lay not on us a burden like that which You did lay on those before us' (Q.II.286). The removal of the burden is a cause for praise, which is realised in: *All praise is for God, Lord of the worlds* (Q.I.2).
3. 'Our Lord! Lay not on us a burden greater than we have strength to bear' (Q.II.286). This is an indication of His perfect mercy, which corresponds to: *The Compassionate, the Merciful* (Q.I.3).
4. 'Pardon us' (Q.II.286), because You are the Sovereign with complete authority on the Day of Judgment: *Master of the Day of Judgment* (Q.I.4).
5. 'And grant us forgiveness' (Q.II.286), because we worshipped You in our worldly lives and sought Your help for our needs: *You we worship and from You we seek help* (Q.I.5).
6. 'Have mercy on us' (Q.II.286), because we sought Your guidance: *Guide us upon the straight path* (Q.I.6).
7. 'You are our Protector; help us against those who (stand) against faith' (Q.II.286) corresponds to: *Not of those who incur wrath, nor of those who are astray* (Q.I.7).

Thus the seven stations which were mentioned at the end of *Sūrat al-Baqara* were described by Muḥammad (may God bless him and grant him peace) in the world of spirituality when he made his Ascension. When he returned, the effect of the 'source' emanated upon the 'manifestation' and was expressed in the form of *Sūrat al-Fātiḥa*.[2] Therefore, whenever it is

1 These are drawn from the following verse (the last of *Sūrat al-Baqara*), and compared with verses of the *Fātiḥa* in turn.

2 These terms were previously used for Gabriel (angelic messenger) and Muḥammad (human messenger) respectively. The wording is rather ambiguous, but an interpretation that the seven verses came from the Prophet (may God bless him and grant him peace) himself must be ruled out. The assumption here is that the *Fātiḥa* was revealed just prior to the Emigration to Medina, before any of *Sūrat al-Baqara* was revealed.

recited in the prayer, the lights of the manifestation ascend to the source, just as they had descended in the time of Muḥammad (may God bless him and grant him peace) from source to manifestation. For this reason, the Prophet said: 'Prayer is the ascension of the believer.'[1]

Section II: The Approaches of Satan

Know that Satan has three primary means by which he makes his approach: appetite (*shahwa*), anger (*ghaḍab*) and desire (*hawā*). Appetite belongs to the beasts, anger to the predators, and desire to the Devil.

Appetite is a defect, but anger is worse than it, and desire worse still. When God said: ['...and He forbids all shameful deeds, evil and oppression' (Q.XVI.90)],[2] 'shameful deeds' (*faḥshā'*) refers to the effects of [sexual] appetite, 'evil' (*munkar*) to the effects of anger, and 'oppression' (*baghy*) to the effects of desire. Appetite causes a human being to wrong himself, anger to wrong others, and desire to extend his wrongdoing to the Divine Majesty.

This is why the Prophet (may God bless him and grant him peace) said: 'Wrongdoing (*ẓulm*) is of three kinds: that which is not forgiven, that which is not overlooked, and that which God may overlook. The wrongdoing which is not forgiven is associating partners with God. That which is not overlooked is when the servants wrong one another, and that which may be overlooked is a person wronging his own self.'[3] The origin of the first is desire, that of the second is anger, and that of the third is the appetite.

Then these [chief defects] have outcomes: appetite gives rise to covetousness and miserliness; anger gives rise to self-satisfaction and arrogance; and desire gives rise to unbelief and innovation. If these six traits emerge among the children of Adam, they give rise to a seventh, namely envy, which is the pinnacle of blameworthy traits just as Satan is the pinnacle of blameworthy persons. This is why God concluded the exposition of human evils with envy, saying: 'And from the mischief of the envious one as he practises envy' (Q.CXIII.5), just as He concluded the exposition of satanic evils with whispering: 'Who whispers into the hearts of mankind; among jinns and men' (Q.CXIV.5–6). Thus there is nothing more evil among humans than envy, and nothing more evil among the devils than whispering.

1 I could not source this narration—R.S. See Section v below for an expansion of this concept.

2 The printed editions cite part of Q.XXIX.45, but the author must have intended this other verse, which gathers all three terms under discussion (including *baghy*).

3 Recorded in Ṭayālisī's *Musnad*—S.I.

Indeed, it has been argued that the envier is worse than Iblīs, because it is narrated that Iblīs came to the door of Pharaoh and knocked it; when Pharaoh asked who was there, Iblīs said: 'If you were truly a god, you would not fail to recognise me.' As he entered upon him, Pharaoh asked: 'Do you know anyone on earth more wicked than you and me?' He replied: 'Yes, the envier: for it was through envy that I fell into this tribulation.'

[Role of the *Fātiḥa*]

Once you have known this, we say: the origins of all blameworthy traits are those three [above], then the seven mentioned [after] are their derivatives and outcomes. Therefore, God revealed *Sūrat al-Fātiḥa* with its seven verses to counteract these seven defects. Moreover, the origin of *Sūrat al-Fātiḥa* is the *tasmiya*, which contains the three Names [*Allāh, al-Raḥmān, al-Raḥīm*] which are in opposition to the three chief blameworthy traits. Thus the three Names counteract the three chief defects; the seven verses of the *Fātiḥa* counteract the seven [derivative] defects, then—since the Qur'ān as a whole branches off from the *Fātiḥa*, and all other defects are like branches and derivatives of those seven—the entire Qur'ān works as a cure for all blameworthy character traits.

Explanation of the three primary [Names] counteracting the three primary [defects]: when a person knows God and that there is no god but He, Satan and desire are repelled from him, for desire is a god which is worshipped besides God: 'Do you see such a one as takes as his god his own desire?' (Q.xlv.23). God said to Moses: 'O Moses! Act contrary to your desire, for I have not created anything which competes with Me for dominion except desire.' When a person knows that He is the Compassionate, he does not become angry, for anger stems from seeking authority, which is the preserve of the Compassionate: 'That day, the dominion, as of right and truth, shall be for the Compassionate' (Q.xxv.26). When he knows that God is the Merciful, he must strive to imbibe that characteristic in himself; being merciful, he will not wrong his own self and sully it with beastly behaviour.

The seven derivatives are counteracted by the seven verses. Before we explain this, let us mention another subtle point, namely that God mentioned those three Names in the *tasmiya* also in the *sūra* itself along with two other Names: *Rabb* and *Malik* [or *Mālik*]. The former is closely related to *al-Raḥīm*, as seen in the verse: '"Peace!"—a word (of salutation) from a Merciful Lord' (Q.xxxvi.58). The latter is closely related to *al-Raḥmān*, as God said: 'That day, the dominion, as of right and truth, shall be for the Compassionate' (Q.xxv.26). As a result, there are three Names: *Rabb* [=*Raḥīm*], *Malik* [=*Raḥmān*] and *Allāh*. This is why God sealed the Qur'ān with these Names in its final *sūra*. It is as though He said: 'If Satan comes at you from the direction of appetite, say: "I seek refuge with the Lord of mankind" (Q.cxiv.1). If he comes at you from the direction of anger, say: "The Sovereign of mankind" (Q.cxiv.2). And if he comes at you from the direction of desire, say: "The God of mankind" (Q.cxiv.3).'

Coming back to the seven counteracting seven, we say: one who says *All praise is for God* has thanked the Almighty and shown contentment for his lot, so his appetite vanishes. One who knows that He is *Lord of the worlds* does not covet what he does not have, nor is he miserly over what he has. This counteracts the defect of appetite and its [derivatives].[1] When a person knows that He is *Master of the Day of Judgment* after knowing that He is *The Compassionate, the Merciful*, his anger will vanish. When he says *You we worship and from You we seek help*, his arrogance is removed by the first and his self-satisfaction by the second: thus the defect of anger and both its derivatives are counteracted. When he says *Guide us upon the straight path*, the Devil and his desire are driven off; with *The path of those on whom You have bestowed favour*, unbelief and its doubts are defeated; and with *Not of those who incur wrath, nor of those who are astray*, his innovation is extinguished. Thus it is seen that the seven verses [of the *Fātiḥa*] counteract the seven dispraised traits.[2]

Section III: How the *Fātiḥa* Contains All the Requisite Knowledge of the Beginning, the Middle and the End[3]

Know that *All praise is for God* alludes to proof of the existence of the Voluntary Creator.

EXPLANATION: the norm in the Qur'ān is to prove the Creator's existence with reference to the creation of mankind. Abraham (on whom be peace) is [quoted] as saying: 'My Lord is He Who gives life and death' (Q.ii.258), and in another place: '...Who created me, and it is He Who guides me' (Q.xxvi.78). Moses (on whom be peace) said: 'Our Lord is He Who gave to each (created) thing its form and nature, and further, gave (it) guidance' (Q.xx.50), and elsewhere: 'Your Lord and the Lord of your fathers from the beginning' (Q.xxvi.26). God said [near] the beginning of *Sūrat al-Baqara*:

1 The printed editions have 'and its pleasures' (*wa-ladhdhātihā*), but I believe the correct reading in context is *wa-waladāhā*, the author's term for the derivatives (literally 'two children').

2 The seventh, envy, was not included in this explanation; however, it was previously described as arising from the other six derivatives, so it would likewise be defeated upon their defeat.

3 This section contains elaboration on points made in Section i.

'O people! Adore your Lord, Who created you and those who came before you, that you may learn righteousness' (Q.II.21), and in the first revelation upon Muḥammad (may God bless him and grant him peace): 'Read! In the Name of your Lord, Who created; created man, out of a (mere) clinging form' (Q.XCVI.1–2). These six verses demonstrate that Almighty God used the creation of mankind as proof of His existence; and if you study the Qur'ān with care, you will find this type of argument very frequent.

Know also that [man's creation] is not only a proof, but also a great favour. It is a proof in that it directs us to know of God's existence, and a favour in that it is a great benefit and kindness from God to the servant: a proof in one aspect, and a favour in another. Without doubt, whenever someone does a kind act intending it as a favour, he is deserving of praise. The creation of the human body is an example of this, as the generation of various kinds of organs and limbs from a uniform sperm-drop is not possible unless the Creator intended for those various forms and natures to develop. Therefore, their existence denotes the existence of an omniscient and omnipotent Creator Who intended—by His mercy and kindness—to create our body parts in the way which would meet our best interests. On this basis, He is deserving of praise and exaltation. Thus *All praise is for God* denotes the existence of the Creator and His knowledge, power, mercy and wisdom, and that He is deserving of praise, exaltation and magnification—this phrase conveys all these meanings.

As for *Lord of the worlds*, it denotes that this Creator is One God, and that the entire creation is His property and dominion: there is no deity and none to be worshipped but He. *The Compassionate, the Merciful* then denotes that this One and Only God possesses the Attributes of perfect mercy, generosity and kindness before [a person's] death, at the time of death and after death. *Master of the Day of Judgment* denotes that His wisdom and mercy necessitate that after today there is a day in which the righteous will be differentiated from the wicked and the oppressed will exact revenge upon their oppressors. If the resurrection and gathering did not take place, His mercy and compassion would be in question.

Thus it becomes clear that *All praise is for God* denotes the existence of the Voluntary Creator; *Lord of the worlds* denotes His oneness; *The Compassionate, the Merciful* denotes His mercy in this life and the next; and *Master of the Day of Judgment* denotes His wisdom and mercy in creating the abode of the Hereafter. Up to this point, the required knowledge concerning Lordship has been completed.

Then, *You we worship*… until the end of the *sūra* indicates what is required in terms of knowledge of servitude, which is reducible to two categories: the acts performed by the servant, and the effects which follow from those acts.

As for the servant's acts, these have two pillars: his performance of the worship, which is indicated by *You we worship*; and his knowledge that he is incapable of doing so without the help of God, as indicated by *And from You we seek help*. Here open the floodgates [to discussion of] free will and preordainment.[1] As for the effects from those acts, these are the attainment of guidance, unveiling and manifestation, and this is indicated by *Guide us upon the straight path*.

Then [know] that the people of this world are of three types:

a. Those who are complete, correct and sincere, who have combined knowledge of the truth with knowledge of goodness in order to act upon it. These are the ones on whom God *bestowed favour*.
b. Those who failed to do good works: they are the sinners, referred to as those *who incur wrath*.
c. Those who failed to believe correctly: they are the people of innovation and unbelief, *who are astray*.

Once this is known, there are two ways for the human soul to attain to completion and perfection through knowledge: first, the attempt to attain it through reflection and rational proofs. Second, imbibing the accumulated [knowledge] of the former peoples in order to perfect one's self. *Guide us upon the straight path* signifies the first of these, while the second is signified by: *The path of those on whom You have bestowed favour, not of those who incur wrath, nor of those who are astray*. This latter category contains a plea to be led by the lights of that rightly-guided party who combined true beliefs with virtuous actions, together with a disavowal of those who failed in actions and earned [divine] anger, and those who failed in terms of belief and went astray.

This is the end of the *sūra*, and a study of what we have summarised here demonstrates that it encompasses all the relevant stations of knowledge of Lordship and servitude.

Section IV: God's Division of the Prayer into Two Halves

The Prophet (may God bless him and grant him peace) said:

> Almighty God says: 'I have divided the Prayer between Me and My servant into two halves.'[2] So when the

1 See above, Chapter Five, Verse 5; and below, Section IV, Benefit 3.

2 As noted previously, this version is problematised by the addition of the *basmala*.

> servant says *In the Name of God, the Compassionate, the Merciful*, God says: 'My servant has remembered Me.' When he says *All praise is for God, Lord of the worlds*, God says: 'My servant has praised Me.' When he says *The Compassionate, the Merciful*, God says: 'My servant has exalted Me.' When he says *Master of the Day of Judgment*, God says: 'My servant has glorified Me. (In another narration: 'My servant has relegated to Me [his affairs].') When he says *You we worship*, God says: 'My servant has worshipped Me'; and when he says *...and from You we seek help*, He says: 'My servant has depended upon Me.' (In another narration: When he says *You we worship and from You we seek help*, God says: 'This is [divided] between Me and My servant.') When he says *Guide us upon the straight path...*, God says: 'This is for My servant, and My servant shall have what he requests.'

Benefit 1

His saying 'I have divided the Prayer between Me and My servant into two halves' signifies that divine legislation is based around the interests of the creation, as God said: 'If you do well, you do well for your own selves; if you do evil, it is to yourselves' (Q.XVII.7). This is because the most important need of the servant is to illuminate his heart with knowledge of Lordship, then with knowledge of servitude, because he was only created to observe this Covenant. God said: 'I have only created jinns and men so that they may serve Me' (Q.LI.56); 'Indeed, We created man from a drop of mingled sperm, in order to try him: so We made him hearing and seeing' (Q.LXXVI.2); and 'O Children of Israel! Call to mind the (special) favour which I bestowed upon you; and fulfil your covenant with Me so that I fulfil My covenant with you' (Q.II.40).

Because of these realities, God sent this *sūra* down upon Muḥammad (may God bless him and grant him peace) and made its first half an exposition of Lordship, and its second half an exposition of servitude, such that it encompasses all that is required to observe that Covenant.

Benefit 2

God named the *Fātiḥa* as 'the Prayer' (*ṣalāh*), which denotes a number of rulings. First, that omitting the recital of the *Fātiḥa* entails that the prayer has not occurred, which demonstrates that the *Fātiḥa* is an integral (*rukn*) of the prayer as our [Shāfiʿī] companions maintain.[1] This is supported by other evidences:

1. The Prophet (may God bless him and grant him peace) was constant throughout his life in reciting it, so it must be obligatory upon us according to the verse: '...and follow him' (Q.vii.158), and the Prophetic *ḥadīth*: 'Pray as you have seen me praying.'
2. The Rightly-Guided Caliphs recited it consistently, so it must be obligatory upon us based on the *ḥadīth*: 'Hold to my example (*sunna*) and the example of the rightly-guided caliphs after me.'
3. None of the Muslims of the East or the West pray without reciting the *Fātiḥa*. Following their way must be obligatory, as God said: 'Whoever...follows a path other than that of the believers, We shall leave him in the path he has chosen, and land him in Hell: what an evil refuge!' (Q.iv.115).
4. The Prophetic saying: 'There is no prayer except with the Opening of the Book.'
5. God said: 'So recite of the Qur'ān what is easy for you' (Q.lxxiii.20). The word 'recite' is an imperative, the apparent sense of which is obligation: so reciting what is easy from the Qur'ān is obligatory. [Certainly] nothing other than the *Fātiḥa* is obligatory, so reciting the *Fātiḥa* must be obligatory according to the apparent sense of the command.
6. Reciting the *Fātiḥa* is more cautious, so this approach must be adopted, as the Prophet (may God bless him and grant him peace) said: 'Leave what makes you doubt for that which does not make you doubt.'
7. The Prophet (may God bless him and grant him peace) was consistent in this action, so abandoning it must be deemed impermissible: 'Let those beware who withstand the Messenger's order' (Q.xxiv.63).
8. There is no dispute among the Muslims over the fact that recitation of the *Fātiḥa* in prayer is more complete and superior to recitation of anything else. Once this is known, we say: the servant was commanded to establish the prayer, and—by default—this duty continues to exist until it is discharged by the performance of

1 This is the only ruling provided here, but elaborated through its evidences. These evidences were provided in greater detail in Chapter Four, Enquiry 2. However, point 9 below was not mentioned there.

prayer complete with the *Fātiḥa*. We have shown that this prayer is superior to a prayer without the *Fātiḥa*: and it does not follow from the complete action discharging the obligation that a deficient action does likewise. As such, when the prayer is performed without the *Fātiḥa*, the obligation would remain in force.

9. The purpose of prayer is for remembrance to take hold in the heart: 'And establish regular prayer for My remembrance' (Q.xx.14). Despite the brevity of this *sūra*, it encompasses the stations of Lordship and servitude, which are the goal of all acts of obedience. This is why God made this *sūra* equivalent to the entire Qur'ān, when He said: 'And We have bestowed upon you seven oft-repeated (verses) and the Glorious Qur'ān' (Q.xv.87). Therefore, it must be that nothing whatsoever can stand in its place.
10. The narration which we have provided [in this chapter] denotes that without the *Fātiḥa*, there is no prayer.

Benefit 3

He said: 'When the servant says *In the Name of God, the Compassionate, the Merciful*, God says: "My servant has remembered Me."' There are some issues connected to this:

1. Almighty God said: 'Remember Me; I will remember you' (Q.II.152). Therefore, when the servant mentions God, God certainly mentions him in a superior gathering.
2. This denotes that remembrance (*dhikr*) is a noble and lofty station of servitude, in that it was mentioned first. Its significance is seen by the fact that God commanded it, saying: 'Remember Me; I will remember you' (Q.II.152); 'O you who believe! Remember God much' (Q.XXXIII.41); 'Those who celebrate the praises of Allah, standing, sitting and lying down on their sides' (Q.III.191); and 'Those who fear (God), when a thought of evil from Satan assaults them, bring (God) to remembrance, and immediately they see (aright)' (Q.VII.201). There is no station of servitude which God emphasised more frequently than that of remembrance.
3. His saying 'My servant has remembered Me' indicates that the Name *Allāh* is a proper Name for His very Essence.[1] If it were a derived Name, its meaning would be universal,[2] and thus His specific Essence

1 See Book II, Chapter Nine.

2 That is, it could apply to more than one referent. The meanings of *al-Raḥmān* and *al-Raḥīm* could have other referents, even though they are used as proper nouns for God.

could not be named by it. It is clear that *al-Raḥmān* and *al-Raḥīm* are universal words [and cannot be intended here], so it is known that *Allāh* is a proper name.

AS FOR HIS SAYING 'When he says *All praise is for God, Lord of the worlds,* God says: "My servant has praised Me,"' this indicates that the station of praise is above that of remembrance. This is seen by the fact that the first word to be mentioned upon the creation of the world was of praise, as the angels said upon Adam's creation: '...whilst we do celebrate Your praises and glorify Your Holy (Name)' (Q.II.30). Then the final word to be spoken after the world has perished will be that of praise, as God said concerning the people of Paradise: '...and the close of their cry will be "All praise is for God, Lord of the worlds"' (Q.X.10).

This is further supported by reason, in that pondering upon the Essence of God is impossible, as the Prophet (may God bless him and grant him peace) said: 'Ponder upon the creation, but do not ponder upon the Creator.'[1] Being able to ponder upon something depends upon first conceptualising it, whereas conceptualisation of the very Essence and reality of God is impossible. Therefore, pondering upon God's Essence is impossible, so it must instead be directed to His acts and creations.

Then it is known through evidence that goodness is sought in its own right, whereas evil [occurs] secondarily. Thus whoever ponders upon God's creations will encounter far more in terms of mercy, kindness and beneficence. As such, he will be more frequently engaged in praise and thanks, and will say *All praise is for God, Lord of the worlds.* At this, God says: 'My servant has praised Me,' bearing witness thereby that the servant has realised through his intellect how divine grace and bounty are manifested in the structure of the upper and lower worlds, and that his tongue has testified to what his mind has realised. If he should become submersed in the ocean of faith in God and recognition of His generosity—[engaged] with his heart and tongue, mind and expression—then how noble is this state!

AS FOR HIS SAYING 'When he says *The Compassionate, the Merciful,* God says: "My servant has exalted Me (*ʿaẓẓamanī*),"' someone may ask: the servant had already mentioned these two Names when saying *In the Name of God, the Compassionate, the Merciful,* but God did not say at that point: 'My servant has exalted Me' as He did here, so what is the difference?

1 Recorded in *al-ʿAẓama* by Abū al-Shaykh—S.I.

RESPONSE: the [preceding] statement, *All praise is for God*, denotes the servant's acknowledgement of God's perfection in Himself, as well as His perfecting of others. Then he says: *Lord of the worlds*, which denotes that this God Who is perfect in Himself and perfects others must be One and without partner. Thus when he follows this with *The Compassionate, the Merciful*, it means that this perfect and perfecting God Who is free of any partner, likeness, equal or rival is, moreover, full of mercy, beneficence and generosity upon His servants. Without doubt, this station is the farthest that [human] intellect, comprehension and imagination can reach in conceptualising His perfection and majesty; so for this reason, God says at this point: 'My servant has exalted me.'

AS FOR HIS SAYING 'When he says *Master of the Day of Judgment*, God says: "My servant has glorified Me (*majjadanī*),"' this means that he has declared God holy and transcendent above all unbefitting things. To explain: we observe in this worldly abode that oppressors have authority over the oppressed, and the strong exploit the weak. We see a perfect and saintly scholar living in the most straitened circumstances, while the sinful unbeliever enjoys the utmost ease and pleasure. This situation [by itself] is not befitting of the mercy of the Merciful and Most Wise. If it were not that the resurrection and gathering is to take place, upon which God will enact justice upon the oppressors on behalf of the oppressed, reward the obedient and punish the rejecters, this would be considered remiss on the part of God and would constitute injustice upon His servants.

However, with the existence of the Day of Reckoning and Recompense, this imputation of injustice vanishes; thus God said: '...that He rewards those who do evil according to their deeds, and He rewards those who do good with what is best' (Q.LIII.31). This is the meaning of God saying 'My servant has glorified Me,' i.e. declared Me above any suggestion of injustice.

AS FOR HIS SAYING 'When he says *You we worship and from You we seek help*, God says: "This is [divided] between Me and My servant,"' this [contains] an allusion to the secrets of free will and preordainment. *You we worship* involves the servant declaring that he is undertaking these acts of worship and obedience. The issue of free will and preordainment arises due to the question: does the servant perform these acts autonomously, or not? The truth is that he is not autonomous, because: the ability of the servant is either [equally] suitable for performance and non-performance of the action, or not. If it is the former, then that ability could not serve as the source of the action except with a preponderator (*murajjiḥ*). If that comes from the servant, then the original disjunction applies to it. Otherwise, it is from Almighty God.

This creation of the motivation—and removal of its opposite—is the divine help referred to in *From You we seek help*. This is also the meaning of: 'Our Lord! Let not our hearts deviate now after You have guided us' (Q.III.8), i.e. 'Do not create in our hearts the motivation towards false beliefs and corrupt actions, but grant us mercy in the form of the motivation to do righteous deeds and hold true beliefs.' This is what is intended by seeking help, and anyone who does not acknowledge this will never understand *You we worship and from You we seek help*.

Thus the truth of God's saying 'This is [divided] between Me and My servant' becomes clear. The portion from Him is to create that firm motivation; as for the servant, when his ability and that motivation combine, the effect follows from them. This is a subtle discussion which requires careful reflection.

AS FOR HIS SAYING 'When he says *Guide us upon the straight path*, God says: "This is for My servant, and My servant shall have what he requests,"' its explanation is that we observe the people of the world differing over all enquiries pertaining to Divinity, as well as every issue concerning prophethood and the Hereafter.[1] Doubts and false beliefs are predominant, and only a tiny minority among the great masses of humanity have reached objective truth. This is despite the fact that all share in possessing intellects and the ability to think, ponder and investigate deeply. Therefore, were it not that God guides and helps, making the truth attractive to the mind of the seeker and making falsehood ugly—as He said: 'But God has endeared the faith to you and has made it beautiful in your hearts; and He has made hateful to you unbelief, wickedness and rebellion' (Q.XLIX.7)—then not a single person would attain to truth. As such, *Guide us upon the straight path* alludes to this situation.

This is supported by the fact that one who is upon falsehood is not satisfied to be upon falsehood. Rather, he had sought after true belief and sound religion; if the matter were in [people's] hands, then nobody would fall into error. However, since we observe that most people have drowned in the seas of misguidance, we know that reaching the truth is

1 These are the three classical chapters of *kalām* works: Divinity (*ilāhiyyāt*), Prophethood (*nubuwwāt*) and Eschatology or Hereafter (*samʿiyyāt* or *al-maʿād*). The science of Divinity is a central concern in the metaphysics of classical Arabic philosophy.

only by the guidance of God. Indeed, all the angels and Prophets agreed on this point. The angels said: 'Glory to You! Of knowledge We have none, save what You have taught us: in truth it is You Who are perfect in knowledge and wisdom' (Q.II.32). Adam (on whom be peace) [and his wife] said: 'Our Lord! We have wronged our own souls: if You forgive us not and bestow not upon us Your mercy, we shall certainly be losers' (Q.VII.23); Abraham (on whom be peace) said: 'Unless my Lord guides me, I shall surely be among those who go astray' (Q.VI.77); Joseph (on whom be peace) said: 'Take my soul (at death) as one submitting to Your will (as a Muslim), and unite me with the righteous' (Q.XII.101); Moses (on whom be peace) said: 'O my Lord! Expand for me my breast' (Q.XX.25); and Muḥammad (may God bless him and grant him peace) said: 'Our Lord! Let not our hearts deviate now after You have guided us, but grant us mercy from Your own presence; for You are the granter of bounties without measure' (Q.III.8).

This concludes our discussion of the subtleties of this Prophetic *ḥadīth*, although what we have left unsaid is more plentiful.

Benefit 4
[Actions of the Prayer][1]

The verses of the *Fātiḥa* are seven, as are the physical actions of the prayer: standing, bowing, straightening up, the first prostration, arising [briefly], the second prostration and sitting. Since the number of verses matches these actions, the actions are like the [body of the] person, and the *Fātiḥa* like the spirit: one is only complete when the spirit joins the body:

1. *In the Name of God, the Compassionate, the Merciful* corresponds to the standing (*qiyām*). Do you not see that when the *bā'* in *bi'smi 'Llāh* became attached to the Name of God, it became upright?[2] The *tasmiya* is for the beginning of things, as the Prophet (may God bless him and grant him peace) said: 'Any matter of significance which is not commenced by "In the Name of God" is severed,' and God said: 'He has succeeded who purifies himself, and mentions the Name of his Lord, and prays' (Q.LXXXVII.14–15). Likewise, the standing is the first of the actions, so there is correspondence between the *tasmiya* and the standing in these ways.

1 See Sections V and VI below for more accounts of the prayer and its correspondence to the *Fātiḥa*.
2 See Book II, Chapter Two, Section II.

2. *All praise is for God, Lord of the worlds* corresponds to the bowing (*rukūʿ*). This is because, when he is engaged in praise, the servant is looking both to God and to the creation, because praise means to exalt God due to a favour which has come from Him. Thus the servant is looking both to the Benefactor and that benefaction, and this is a middle state between turning away [from Him] and being submersed. Likewise, bowing is a middle state between standing and prostration. Moreover, praise implies a multitude of favours, and such would be weighty upon the back, causing one to bend into the bowing position.
3. *The Compassionate, the Merciful* corresponds to straightening up (*intiṣāb*). This is because, after the servant has humbled himself before God by bowing, His mercy dictates that the servant be brought back upright. This is why the Prophet (may God bless him and grant him peace) said: 'When the servant says "May God hear [and answer] the one who praises Him!" God looks to him with mercy.'[1]
4. *Master of the Day of Judgment* corresponds to the first prostration (*sajda*), in that it denotes His complete dominance, majesty and magnificence. The resultant fear and awe lead to the expression of humility and submission as manifested in the prostration.
5. *You we worship and from You we seek help* corresponds to the sitting between prostrations. This is because *You we worship* refers to the prostration just performed, then *From You we seek help* is to seek His aid in performing the next.
6. *Guide us upon the straight path* is to ask for the most important of things, so it corresponds to the second prostration, which denotes the utmost submission.
7. *The path of those on whom You have bestowed favour*...corresponds to the sitting (*qaʿda*). This is because, when the servant displays the utmost humility, God meets that with generosity by instructing him to sit before Him. This is a tremendous favour from God to the servant, so it corresponds to the verse.

Moreover, when Muḥammad (may God bless him and grant him peace) received divine favour by being raised up to two bow-lengths,[2] he said:

1 I could not source this narration—R.S. The phrase is said upon arising from the bowing position.

2 See Section v below.

'Blessed salutations, prayers and goodly [remembrance] are for God.'[1] The prayer is the believer's ascension, so when the believer reaches within that ascension to the apex of [divine] generosity by being seated before God, he must recite those same words uttered by Muḥammad (may God bless him and grant him peace). Thus he recites the *taḥiyyāt*, which signifies that this ascension of his is a reflected ray from that of Muḥammad (may God bless him and grant him peace), and a drop in that ocean. This fulfils the verse: '...they are in the company of those on whom is God's favour: of the Prophets, the truthful, the witnesses and the righteous. Ah, what a beautiful fellowship!' (Q.IV.69)

Know that [just as] the seven verses of the *Fātiḥa* become like the spirit of these seven postures, these seven postures [in turn] are like the spirit of the seven stages of man's creation described in these verses: 'Man We did create from a quintessence (of clay); then We placed him as a (sperm) drop in a place of rest, firmly fixed. Then We made the drop into a clinging form; then of that clinging form We made a (foetus) lump; then we made out of that lump bones and clothed the bones with flesh; then we developed out of it another creature. So blessed be God, the best to create!' (Q.XXIII.12–14).

Thus it is discovered that there are numerous stages of the body as well as of the spirit. The Spirit of spirits and the Light of lights[2] is Almighty God, as He said: 'That to your Lord is the final goal' (Q.LIII.42).

Section V: The Prayer is the Ascension of the Gnostics

Know that the Messenger of God (may God bless him and grant him peace) had two ascensions: one from the Sacred Mosque [in Mecca] to the Farthest Mosque [in Jerusalem],[3] and the second from there to the highest reaches of God's kingdom. That is the description of outward realities.

As far as the spiritual world is concerned, there were [also] two ascensions: one from the observed world (*shahāda*) to the world of the Unseen (*ghayb*), and the second from there to the Utmost Unseen (*ghayb al-ghayb*). These two [journeys] were like two connected bow-

1 This formula with what follows it is known as the *taḥiyyāt* and is recited in the seated position. I have translated it with reference to the author's own explanation in the following section, as well as Nawawī, *Sharḥ Ṣaḥīḥ Muslim*, vol. II, p. 337. The common meaning of 'salutations' is retained because the author appears to interpret it that way.

2 For discussion of the Name *Nūr* for God, see Book II, Chapter Nine, Enquiry 6. However, the author has not explained the use of the description *Rūḥ*.

3 'The Farthest Mosque' is *al-Masjid al-Aqṣā*. This first journey is usually referred to as the *Isrā'*; see Q.XVII.1.

lengths which Muḥammad (may God bless him and grant him peace) crossed; and this is what is intended by: 'It was a distance of but two bow-lengths or (even) nearer' (Q.LIII.9)—where 'or nearer' signifies his self-annihilation.[1]

As for the journey from the observed world to the Unseen, know that all things related to the body and corporeality are described as observables, in that one can perceive them with the eyes [etc.]. Thus the transfer of the spirit from the corporeal world to the spiritual world is described as the journey from the observed to the Unseen world.

The spiritual world is without end: at its lowest level are the human spirits, then at a level higher in perfection and felicity there are the spirits associated with the lowest heaven. Higher still are the spirits of the second heaven, and so on until we reach the inhabitants of the levels of the Footstool, which themselves are of various levels. Above them are the angels described in the verse: 'And you will see the angels surrounding the Throne on all sides' (Q.XXXIX.75). Loftier and more magnificent still are those described in: 'And there will bear the Throne of your Lord above them, that day, eight (angels)' (Q.LXIX.17)—and there are secrets in the number eight which cannot be discussed here.

Beyond even them are the spirits transcendent above connection to bodies, whose food is remembrance of God, whose drink is love of God, whose company is the praise of God and whose pleasure is the service of God. These are mentioned in: 'Those who are in His (very) Presence are not too proud to serve Him, nor are they (ever) weary. They celebrate His praises night and day, nor do they ever flag or intermit' (Q.XXI.19–20). Even they are of various levels and ranks, in such a way as the human intellect is incapable of encompassing and describing; yet it is as God says: 'Over every possessor of knowledge is one (more) knowing' (Q.XII.76).

This ascension continues until it reaches the Light of lights and the Cause of causes, the Origin of all and the Wellspring of good and mercy: Almighty God. It is thus seen that the world of spirits is the Unseen world, and the presence of Divine Majesty is the Utmost Unseen. On this, the Prophet (may God bless him and grant him peace) said: 'God has seventy veils of light: were He to lift them, the splendours of His Countenance would consume everything in sight.' This number seventy

1 Cf. the interpretations provided under the exegesis of Q.LIII.9. The disparity could give support to the theory of alternative authors for particular *sūras* in the exegesis, including *al-Najm*. See Rufayda, *al-Naḥw wa-kutub al-tafsīr*, vol. II, p. 828.

is such as could not be known except through the light of prophethood.[1]

We have explained that the ascension is of two types: from the observed world to the Unseen, and from the Unseen world to the Utmost Unseen. These are words of certain proof and reality. Once that is known, we return to our main topic.

[The Gift of Prayer]

When Muḥammad (may God bless him and grant him peace) accomplished his Ascension and Night Journey and intended to return, he said: 'O Lord of Majesty! A traveller who intends to return to his homeland needs to take gifts for his companions and loved ones.' Thus it was said to him: 'The gift of your nation is the prayer.'[2] This is because it combines the physical ascension with the spiritual ascension: the former through its actions, and the latter through the remembrance therein.[3]

Therefore, O servant of God, when you wish to begin your ascension, first purify yourself, for this is a holy pursuit. So let your clothes and body be pure, for you are in the sacred valley of Ṭuwā.[4] Also, you have an angel and a devil, so decide which of them to grant your company. You have religious and worldly [concerns], so decide which of them to grant your company [and attention]. You have intellect and desire, so decide which of them to accompany. Do likewise for good and evil, honesty and lies, truth and falsehood, discretion and rashness, contentment and covetousness.

For all such opposite pairs of character traits, consider which you take for company, for once companionship has taken hold, parting is [near] impossible. Do you not see that [Abū Bakr] the Truthful chose the companionship of Muḥammad (may God bless him and grant him peace) and stayed at his side in this life and in the grave, [and it will continue] on the Day of Judgment and in Paradise? Also, a dog accompanied the People of the Cave[5] and remained with them in this life and [it will be so] in the Hereafter. Due to this reality, God said: 'O you who believe! Fear God and be with the truthful' (Q.ix.119).

1 The *ḥadīth* is recorded by Muslim, but without the number 'seventy'. This narration forms the basis for the latter part of Ghazālī's *Mishkāt*.

2 I did not find a source for these particular words, but the *ḥadīth*s of the Ascension indicate that the five daily prayers were legislated while the Prophet was making his return.

3 The first account here focuses on the words of the Prayer, followed by an account of the actions in the next 'benefit'.

4 An allusion to Q.xx.12 (also Q.lxxix.16).

5 See Q.xviii.18.

Once you have purified yourself, raise your hands to signify bidding farewell to this world and the Hereafter, averting your vision from both completely. Rather, direct your heart, spirit, inner soul, intellect, understanding, remembrance and thought to God [alone], and say 'God is greater' (*Allāhu akbar*). This means that He is greater than everything in existence; loftier and more magnificent than anything which can be known. Indeed, He is too great for anything to be compared to Him such that He would be called greater [than that thing].[1]

Then say: 'Glory and praise is for You, O God' (*subḥānaka Allāhumma wa-bi-ḥamdika*). At this station, the light of divine splendour will become manifest to you. Thereafter you ascend from glorification to praise, saying 'Blessed is Your Name' (*wa-tabāraka ismuka*). At this station, the lights of pre-eternity and everlastingness are unveiled to you, as the [verb] *tabāraka* signifies 'existence without end', and [comprehending] that is connected to the realities of pre-eternity before existence, and eternity after existence. Then say 'Exalted is Your majesty' (*wa-taʿālā jadduka*), which implies that He is too lofty and great for His Attributes of perfection and majesty to be confined to those which are mentioned. Then say: 'And there is no god but You' (*wa-lā ilāha ghayruka*), which means that all Attributes of glory and perfection belong to Him alone. He is the Perfect other than Whom there is no perfection, the only Holy and Transcendent. Nay, in reality there is 'no he but He'[2] and no god but He. At this, reason fails; the tongue falters; the imagination is confounded and the intellect becomes like a cripple. Therefore, turn back to yourself and your own state, and say: 'I have set my face, firmly and truly, towards Him Who created the heavens and the earth, and I am not of the polytheists' (Q.vi.79).[3]

The formula [beginning] 'Glory and praise is for You, O God' is the ascension of the elite angels, as expressed in: 'We celebrate Your praises and glorify Your Holy (Name)' (Q.ii.30). It is also the ascension of Muḥammad (may God bless him and grant him peace), as his ascension began with 'Glory and praise is for You, O God.'[4] As for [the other formula] 'I have set my face…' that is the ascension of Abraham the Friend of God; and [to add] 'Indeed, my prayer and my service of sacrifice, my life and my death, are for God, Lord of the worlds' (Q.vi.162) is the ascen-

1 See Section v below.

2 See Book II, at the end of Chapter Seven.

3 This is to be followed by Q.vi.162, as described in the explanation following.

4 I am unsure of the reference. The description of the Prophet's journey begins with the word *subḥāna*, i.e. Q.xvii.1—this point is made below in Section vii, Point ii.

sion of Muḥammad the Beloved (may God bless him and grant him peace). Therefore, if you recite these two formulas, you have brought together the ascensions of the senior angels of lofty status and the greatest of the Prophets and Messengers.

When you have done this, you are to say 'I seek refuge in God from the rejected Satan' in order to avert the evil of conceit from your soul. Know that Paradise has eight gates, and by the [preceding] station one of these has been opened for you, namely the gate of gnosis. The second is the gate of remembrance [which is opened by] *In the Name of God, the Compassionate, the Merciful*. The third is the gate of gratitude: *All praise is for God, Lord of the worlds*. The fourth is the gate of hope: *The Compassionate, the Merciful*. The fifth is the gate of fear: *Master of the Day of Judgment*. The sixth is the gate of sincerity, which flows from knowledge of Lordship and servitude: *You we worship and from You we seek help*. The seventh is the gate of humble supplication, as God said: 'Or, Who listens to the (soul) distressed when it calls on Him' (Q.xxvii.62) and 'Call on Me, I will answer your (prayer)' (Q.xl.60)—here it is [opened by]: *Guide us upon the straight path*. The eighth is the path of following the pure and goodly spirits and walking in their light: *The path of those on whom You have bestowed favour, not of those who incur wrath, nor of those who are astray*.

Thus when you recite this *sūra* and encounter its secrets, the eight gates of Paradise open for you, which is indicated by God's saying: 'Gardens of Eternity, whose doors will be open to them' (Q.xxxviii.50). The gates of the gardens of divine knowledge were opened by these spiritual keys.

[Journey of the Body]

The above is an explication of the spiritual ascension within the prayer. As for the bodily ascension, this begins when you stand before God as the People of the Cave stood: 'Behold, they stood up and said: "Our Lord is the Lord of the heavens and of the earth"' (Q.xviii.14). Indeed, you should stand as the people do on the Day of Judgment: 'The day when mankind will stand before the Lord of the worlds' (Q.lxxxiii.6). Then recite 'Glory and praise is for You…' and 'I have set my face…' followed by the *Fātiḥa*, together with anything from the Qur'ān which is easy for you. Strive to look from God to your worship so that you see it as trifling; but do not look from your worship towards God, lest you perish. This is the secret of *You we worship and from You we seek help*.[1]

At this point, the soul is like a plank that is presented to the fire that

1 See above Chapter Five, Verse 5: *You we worship*, Benefit 3.

is the fear of the Divine Majesty, so it bends. Thus you should bow and [thereafter] say 'May God hear the one who praises Him,' and allow it to return upright, for [as the Prophet (may God bless him and grant him peace) said]: 'This religion is tough, so traverse through it gently and do not make God's worship hateful for your own selves: for the hasty one neither covers the distance nor spares his ride.'[1] After returning to uprightness, fall down to the earth with the utmost humility and mention your Lord in terms of utmost ascendancy, saying 'Glory be to my Lord, Most High.'

Once you have prostrated a second time [within the cycle], you will have performed three types of obedience: one bow and two prostrations, by which three destructive impediments are removed from your path. By bowing, you are saved from the impediment of appetite; by the second, from the impediment of anger, which is the chief of harmful things; and by the third, from the impediment of desire, which calls to all forms of destruction and misguidance.[2] Once you are freed from these impediments, then you reach the lofty levels and take hold of the goodly and lasting [rewards]. Now that you have reached the threshold of the majesty of the Controller of the heavens and the earth, say [while seated]: 'Blessed salutations, prayers and goodly [remembrance] are for God.' The blessed salutations (*taḥiyyāt*) are with the tongue, the prayers (*ṣalawāt*) with the limbs and the goodly [remembrance] (*ṭayyibāt*) with the heart and the strength of faith.

At this station, the light of your spirit ascends and the light of Muḥammad's (may God bless him and grant him peace) spirit descends, so the two spirits meet, resulting in relief, comfort and bounty. Thus one must extend praise and salutations to the spirit of Muḥammad, saying: 'Peace be on you, O Prophet, and God's mercy and blessings.' In turn, Muḥammad (may God bless him and grant him peace) says: 'Peace be on us and on God's righteous servants.' Then it is as though you are asked: by what means did you attain all this goodness and blessing? So reply: it was by my saying: 'I bear witness that there is no god but God, and I bear witness that Muḥammad is the Messenger of God.'

Following that, it is said to you: Muḥammad directed you to this, so what is your gift to him? Therefore say: 'O God! Send blessings upon Muḥammad and the folk of Muḥammad...' Then it is said: Abraham is the one who asked God to send such a Messenger to you when he said:

1 Recorded in Bayhaqī's *Kubrā*.

2 These are explained in Section II above.

'Our Lord! Send amongst them a Messenger of their own...' (Q.II.129), so how do you thank him? Therefore say: '...as you send blessings upon Abraham and the folk of Abraham'. Then it is said: is all this good from Muḥammad, or from Abraham—or from God? Therefore say: 'You [God] are Praiseworthy and Magnificent.'[1]

When the servant mentions God with all these words of praise, Almighty God mentions him in the congregations of the angels, as in the Prophetic *ḥadīth* quoting the Almighty: 'If he remembers Me in a gathering, I remember him in a gathering better than his.' When the angels hear this, they long to meet that servant, so [it is as though] God says: 'The angels of the heavens longed to visit you and be close to you, and now they have come to you; therefore, salute them first so that you may attain the rank of the foremost in good deeds (*sābiqūn*).' The servant thus turns to his right and left, saying: 'Peace be on you, and God's mercy and blessings.' It is little wonder, therefore, that when he enters Paradise, the angels come to him from every direction, saying: 'Peace be upon you for persevering in patience! Now how excellent is the final home!' (Q.XIII.24).

Section VI: On Divine Superiority and Greatness[2]

The greatest and most tremendous of all creations are place (*makān*) and time (*zamān*). 'Place' refers to endless space and unlimited void. As for 'time', this is the perceived extension which proceeds from the dark hollow of the mountain of pre-eternity to the darkness of the world of eternity. It is like a river which emerges from the hollow of one mountain (pre-eternity) and continues until it enters the other (eternity), but its sheer profusion makes its precise origin and final destination unidentifiable.

Thus the attributes of being 'first' and 'last' pertain to time, while 'apparent' and 'hidden' pertain to place. The perfection of these four belongs to the Compassionate and Merciful One, for He has encompassed place as *al-Ẓāhir* (the Apparent) and *al-Bāṭin* (the Hidden), and encompassed time as *al-Awwal* (the First) and *al-Ākhir* (the Last).[3] Since the Almighty is the Controller of space and time, He must be transcendent beyond space and time.

1 Together these words constitute the formula of blessings upon the Prophet (may God bless him and grant him peace) that are to be recited in the prayers (termed the *ṣalawāt Ibrāhīmiyya*), which are then repeated with the word *Allāhumma bārik* in place of *Allāhumma ṣalli*.

2 The relevance of this section within the chapter is that one declares repeatedly in the prayer: *Allāhu akbar*.

3 For these, see Book II, Chapter Seven, Section VI. See also Section II in the same chapter for elaboration on *al-Awwal*, *al-Ākhir* and related Names.

Once that is known, we say: Almighty God possesses a Throne (*ʿarsh*) and Footstool (*kursī*). He associated the Footstool with place by saying: 'His Footstool extends over the heavens and the earth' (Q.ii.255), and the Throne with time by saying: 'And His Throne was over the water' (Q.xi.7), because the flow of time resembles that of water.[1] Thus there is no space beyond the Footstool and no time beyond the Throne. Elevation (*ʿulū*) is an attribute of the Footstool as in the [aforementioned] verse, and greatness (*ʿaẓama*) is an attribute of the Throne: 'Say: "God suffices me: there is no god but He. On Him is my trust; He is the Lord of the Great Throne!"' (Q.ix.129). Supreme elevation and greatness belong to God, as He said: 'For He is the High, the Great' (Q.ii.255).

Know that elevation and greatness are two levels of perfection, but the level of greatness surpasses that of elevation—and above them both is that of superiority (*kibriyāʾ*). God said [in a Prophetic *ḥadīth*]: '*Kibriyāʾ* is My cloak and *ʿaẓama* is My lower garment'—without doubt, the cloak is greater than the lower garment.[2] Above all of these Attributes in rank and nobility is majesty (*jalāl*), which means the transcendence of His Essence and unique reality above resemblance to anything contingent: by this uniqueness He is deserving of the Attribute of Divinity (*ilāhiyya*). Upon this meaning is the Prophetic saying: 'Adhere to [saying] "O Possessor of Majesty and Beneficence."' God said: 'But will abide (forever) the Countenance of your Lord, full of majesty and beneficence' (Q.lv.27); and 'Blessed be the Name of your Lord, full of majesty and beneficence' (Q.lv.78).[3]

[Approaching the Prayer]

Once you have understood this principle, know that when the worshipper turns to pray, he becomes one of those whom God described as 'seeking His Countenance' (Q.vi.52). Anyone who wishes to enter upon a great sultan must first cleanse himself of filth and impurities. This purification [before prayer] has stages: the first is to remove the filth of sins through repentance: 'O you who believe! Turn to Allah with sincere repentance' (Q.lxvi.8). He who is at the station of asceticism (*zuhd*) purifies himself of [the things of] this world, both lawful and prohibited. He who is at the station of sincerity (*ikhlāṣ*) purifies himself of regarding his own deeds. He who is at the station of the people of excellence (*muḥsinūn*) purifies

1 This interpretation is not mentioned by the author in the exegesis of Q.xi.7.

2 See Book II, Chapter Seven, Section viii.

3 For discussion of *jalāl* and *ikrām*, see Book II, Chapter Seven, Section ix: under the fourth benefit of saying 'O He.'

himself of looking towards reward. He who is at the station of the truthful (*ṣiddīqūn*) purifies himself of everything other than God. In short, there are many levels and varying stations which seem to be without limit, as God said: 'So set your face steadily and truly to the faith: (establish) God's handiwork according to the pattern on which He has made mankind: no change (let there be) in the work (wrought) by God' (Q.xxx.30).

Therefore, if you wish to be among those who are 'seeking His Countenance', then stand up straight and bring to mind all of God's creations in the worlds of bodies and spirits. Begin with yourself, pondering on all your simple or complex parts and all your natural, animal and human faculties. Next, call to mind all that the world contains of minerals, plants and animals—humans and others—and add to this the seas, mountains, hills, deserts and all the wonders they contain of plants, animals and [even] specks of dust. Then raise your vision to the lowest heaven and its scale and grandeur, and continue to progress from heaven to heaven until you reach the Farthest Lote, the *Rafraf*,[1] the Tablet, the Pen, Paradise, Hellfire, the Footstool and the Great Throne. Then from the world of bodies, proceed to the world of spirits and call to mind all the lower spirits of the earth, both human and non-human; the spirits of the mountains and the oceans as the Prophet (may God bless him and grant him peace) described. Then the angels of the lowest heaven and all the seven heavens, as the Prophet said: 'There is not within the heavens a single handspan which is not occupied by an angel, standing or sitting.' Call to mind all the angels surrounding the Throne and the bearers of the Throne and Footstool. Then take your mind beyond this universe, as God said: 'And none can know the forces of your Lord, except He' (Q.lxxiv.31).

Once you have brought to mind all these spiritual and corporeal categories, then say 'God is greater' (*Allāhu akbar*). By 'God', you mean that Essence by which all things came into existence and attained their perfection in attributes and actions. By 'greater', you mean:

a. God is transcendent beyond resemblance to any of those things, and indeed beyond the mind even deeming it feasible to compare Him with these things. This is the [first] explanation of saying 'God is greater' at the outset of prayer.
b. The second explanation is as the Prophet (may God bless him and

1 This may describe a covering of the Lote Tree, as described in some exegeses of Q.liii.16. The word also appears in the description of the garment of Archangel Gabriel, or a 'cushion' on which he was seated when the Prophet (may God bless him and grant him peace) witnessed him filling the horizon. See Ibn Ḥajar, *Fatḥ al-Bārī*, vol. vi, p. 679.

grant him peace) said: 'Excellence (*iḥsān*) is to worship God as though you see Him; if you do not see Him, indeed He sees you.'[1] You are thus saying: 'God is too great[2] not to see me and hear my speech.'

c. God is too great for the creation to reach Him with their intellects, imaginations or comprehension. ʿAlī b. Abī Ṭālib said: 'Monotheism (*tawḥīd*) is that you do not imagine Him.'
d. God is too great for the creation to fulfil His due right of servitude, as their obedience will always fall short in His service; their praise will not reach His superiority; and their knowledge will never encompass His supremacy.

Therefore, O servant [of God], even if your intellect were to encompass all the wonders of the corporeal and spiritual worlds, do not be deceived into thinking that you have reached even the beginning of the fields of Divine Majesty, let alone their utmost limit! The poet spoke rightly when he said: 'They are but Names which have not made Him any more known; we mention them only to experience their delight.' Among the supplications and invocations of praise used by the Prophet (may God bless him and grant him peace) were: 'The delving mind does not penetrate Your depths, and searching sight does not rest upon You. The Attributes of Your power transcend the attributes of created things, and the sublimity of Your greatness surpasses all.'[3]

Once you have said 'God is greater,' turn the vision of your intellect to the horizons of Divine Majesty, and say [the formulas] 'Glory and praise is for You, O God' and 'I have set my face...' (Q.VI.79).[4] Thereafter, move to the world of commands and obligations, making *Sūrat al-Fātiḥa* the mirror by which you observe the wonders of this life and the next and encounter the illuminations of God's Names and Attributes, as well as past religions and communities and the secrets of heavenly scriptures and prophetic guidance. You thereby reach the Law (*sharīʿa*), and from there the Path (*ṭarīqa*), then the Reality (*ḥaqīqa*) and encounter the stations of the Prophets and Messengers in contrast to the levels of the accursed, rejected strayers.

When you say *In the Name of God, the Compassionate, the Merciful*, you see this world: for it was by His Name that the heavens and earths took

1 Recorded by Bukhārī and Muslim—S.I.

2 When used with a verbal noun or a verb in the subjunctive mood (acting like an infinitive), the comparative form *akbar* can mean 'too great'.

3 I could not source this as a Prophetic supplication, but I found it attributed to ʿAlī as part of *Duʿāʾ al-Yamānī*.

4 See the previous section for details.

form. When you say *All praise is for God, Lord of the worlds*, you see the Hereafter, as it is established by the word of praise: 'And the close of their cry will be "All praise is for God, Lord of the worlds"' (Q.x.10).

When you say *The Compassionate, the Merciful*, you see the world of beauty as manifested in mercy, beneficence and generosity. When you say *Master of the Day of Judgment*, you see the world of majesty, and the tremendous events of that day.

When you say *You we worship*, you see the world of Law. Then, when you say *From You we seek help*, you see the Path. When you say *Guide us upon the straight path*, you see the Reality.[1]

When you say *The path of those on whom You have bestowed favour*, you see the ranks of the people of felicity and honour: the Prophets, the truthful, the martyrs and the righteous. When you say *Not of those who incur wrath*, you see the lowly levels of the sinners and possessors of flaws.[2] And when you say *Nor of those who are astray*, you see the people of unbelief, division, disgrace and hypocrisy in all their various levels and types.

Once these lofty states and exalted stations have been unveiled to you, think not that you have reached the end and destination. Rather, return to confess once again God's superiority and your own lowliness and poverty, and say 'God is greater.' Then descend from the attribute of superiority to that of greatness[3] and say [in the bowing posture]: 'Glory be to my Lord, the Great' (*subḥāna Rabbī al-ʿAẓīm*). If you wish to appreciate one atom of the Attribute of greatness, then know—as we have explained—that it is also an attribute of the Throne, and no creation may grasp the enormity of that Throne, even if he strove to do so until the end of the world. Yet the greatness of the Throne is but a drop in the ocean of God's greatness, so how could you comprehend that?

There is a remarkable secret here in that [upon bowing] one says 'Glory be to my Lord, the Great (*al-ʿAẓīm*),' rather than saying 'the Greatest' (*al-Aʿẓam*); but [in prostration] it is 'Glory be to my Lord, the Most High (*al-Aʿlā*),' rather than 'the High' (*al-ʿĀlī*). The differentiation between these states conceals remarkable secrets which cannot be mentioned here.[4]

After you have bowed and declared God's greatness, straighten up and supplicate for all those who stand as you do and praise as you do, saying:

1 See above Chapter Three, Section III.
2 The printed editions have *ahl al-āfāq*, which I have read as *āfāt*.
3 See the hierarchy presented at the beginning of this section.
4 One explanation is provided below.

'May God hear the one who praises Him.' Whatever you seek on behalf of others, you find for yourself: this is the import of the Prophet's (may God bless him and grant him peace) teaching: 'God remains at the aid of the servant as long as the servant is at the aid of his Muslim brother.'[1]

QUESTION: why is there no *takbīr* at this stage [in the prayer]?

RESPONSE: *takbīr* is derived from *kibriyā'* which entails reverence and fear. However, this stage is one of intercession (*shafāʿa*), and these two cannot coincide.[2]

Then, once you have completed this intercession, return to the *takbīr* and lower yourself [further] to the attribute of elevation,[3] saying: 'Glory be to my Lord, the Most High.' This is because prostration is a humbler posture than bowing, so the remembrance therein—*al-Aʿlā*—has the more intensive form [i.e. the comparative] than that in the bowing position, namely *al-ʿAẓīm*. It is narrated that Almighty God has an angel below the Throne, named Ezekiel. God inspired him, saying: 'O angel! Fly!' He took flight and continued for 30,000 years, then another 30,000, then another, yet he did not reach from one side of the Throne to the other. God said to him: 'Even if you were to fly until the Trumpet is blown, you would never reach the other side of the Throne.' At this, the angel said: 'Glory be to my Lord, the Most High.'

QUESTION: what is the wisdom in there being two prostrations?

RESPONSE: there are various explanations:

a. The first prostration represents pre-eternity, and the second represents eternity. The rising between the two signifies the [fleeting] existence of this world between pre-eternity and eternity. This is because you know from His pre-eternal existence that He is the First with none before Him, so you prostrate to Him; and you know from His everlastingness that He is the Last with none beyond Him, so you prostrate to Him again.
b. It was said: 'Know with the first prostration that this world vanishes into the next; and with the second, that the world of the Hereafter vanishes upon the manifestation of the light of Divine Majesty.'
c. The first prostration alludes to everything perishing in its own right,

1 Recorded by Muslim, with the wording 'his brother'—R.S.

2 If the servant were made to say 'God is greater' at this point, bearing in mind the meanings previously expounded, he could not be so bold as to supplicate on behalf of his brothers and himself.

3 This is according to the same hierarchy from the beginning of this section.

and the second alludes to everything remaining in existence by God's power: 'Everything will perish except His Countenance' (Q.xxviii.88).

d. The first prostration denotes the submission of this observed world to God's power, and the second denotes the submission of the world of spirits, as God said: 'Indeed, His is the creation and the command' (Q.vii.54).
e. The first is a prostration of gratitude for all that He has granted us of gnosis of His Essence and Attributes; the second is a prostration of weakness and fear concerning that which we have not fulfilled of the rights of His majesty and supremacy.

[Refuting Anthropomorphism]

Know that people [commonly] understand *ʿaẓama* to denote 'greatness in body size'; by *ʿulū*, they understand 'elevated direction'; and by *kibar*[1] they understand a 'lengthy duration'. Almighty God is free of all such false conceptions, for He is *ʿAẓīm* without body, *ʿĀlī* without direction, and *Kabīr* without duration. How could these things be attributed to Him when He is the One and Only, and therefore transcendent above proportionality and direction? Moreover, duration is something which changes hour after hour, and is therefore a created entity and its Creator must have preceded it. Thus God is above place, but not in spatial terms. He precedes time, but not in a temporal sense. His *kibriyāʾ* is understood in terms of *ʿaẓama*, which is understood in terms of *ʿulū*, which is understood in terms of *jalāl* (majesty).[2]

Therefore, He is too majestic to be compared to things which can be perceived or imagined, greater than anything which people conceptualise or describe, and beyond even the [praise] of the exalters. If your senses present you with any example, say to it: 'God is greater!' If your imagination designates an image, say: 'Glory and praise is for You, O God.' If you should find yourself falling into the [contrary] error of negating His attributes, say: 'I have set my face, firmly and truly, towards Him Who created the heavens and the earth...' (Q.vi.79).

When your spirit has explored the fields of Might and Majesty and ascended to [witness] the lofty Attributes and most Beautiful Names, and that which the Pen has inscribed upon the face of the Tablet, and when it hears the glorifications of the angelic spirits brought near [to God]—then

1 This is the verbal noun at the root of Names such as *al-Kabīr* and al-*Mutakabbir* and in the terms *akbar* and *kibriyāʾ*. As the author says, one of its denotations is 'old', when applied to a person.
2 In other words, they all point to transcendence, far from notions of corporeality etc.

if any image [should form from these words], you should say at all stages: 'Glory to your Lord, the Lord of Honour and Power: (He is free) from what they ascribe (to Him). Peace be on the Messengers. And all praise is for God, Lord of the worlds!' (Q.xxxvii.180–182].

Section vii: Subtleties Concerning *All praise is for God* and the Five Divine Names

There are four subtle [spiritual] points to mention in relation to *All praise is for God* (Q.1.2):

Point 1

It was narrated that the Prophet (may God bless him and grant him peace) said that Abraham, the Friend [of God], asked his Lord concerning the reward of one who says 'All praise is for God.' The Lord replied: '"All praise is for God" is the opening of gratitude and its conclusion.'[1] The spiritual masters said that it is due to its being the opening of gratitude that God made it the opening of His Book, and due to its being the conclusion [of gratitude] that He made it the conclusion of the speech of the people of Paradise: '...and the close of their cry will be "All praise is for God, Lord of the worlds"' (Q.x.10).

It was narrated that ʿAlī said:

> God created the Intellect from a hidden and stored light from His pre-eternal knowledge. He made knowledge its soul, understanding its spirit, asceticism its head, modesty its eye, wisdom its tongue, goodness its hearing, compassion its heart, mercy its concern and patience its belly. It was then said to it 'Speak!' so it said: 'All praise is for God Who has no rival, no opposite, no likeness and no counterpart, and before Whose might all things are brought low!' At this, the Lord said: 'By My might and majesty, I have not created anything more precious to Me than you.'[2]

1 I could not source this.

2 I could not source this, but it contains fragments of other narrations which themselves have been critiqued extensively. See Ismāʿīl b. Muḥammad al-ʿAjlūnī, *Kashf al-khafā' wa-muzīl al-ilbās ʿammā ishtahar min al-āḥādīth ʿalā alsinat al-nās*, ed. ʿAbd al-Ḥamīd Hindāwī, 2 vols., Beirut: al-Maktaba al-ʿAṣriyya, 2012, vol. 1, pp. 269 and 300. The doctrine of the First Intellect is found among the philosophers, with an alternative approach among the Ismāʿīlīs; see Daniel de Smet, 'Ismāʿīlī Theology', in Sabine Schmidtke, ed., *The Oxford Handbook of Islamic Theology*, New York: Oxford University Press, 2016, p. 315.

It was also narrated that when Adam (on whom be peace) sneezed, he said 'All praise is for God,' so this was the first of his speech.

Once this is known, we say: the first stage in creation was the Intellect and its final stage was Adam. As we have mentioned, the first words of the Intellect were 'All praise is for God,' which were also the first words of Adam. Thus they were the first words of the beginning of all created things, as well as of the seal of all creations: so it is natural that God made them the opening of His Book: *All praise is for God, Lord of the worlds*.

Furthermore, since it is known that the first of God's words are 'All praise is for God'[1] and the last of His Prophets and Messengers was Muḥammad (may God bless him and grant him peace), the correspondence between the first and the last made it appropriate for *All praise is for God* to be the first verse[2] of the Book revealed to His Messenger Muḥammad (may God bless him and grant him peace). Since that is so, he was given two names derived from praise: *Aḥmad* (most praising) and *Muḥammad* (praiseworthy, much praised); and he [elaborated], 'I am Aḥmad in heaven, and Muḥammad on earth.'[3] The inhabitants of the heavens praise God, and His Messenger (may God bless him and grant him peace) praises Him more than any of them. Almighty God praises and thanks the people of the earth—as He said: 'They are the ones whose striving is appreciated (by God)' (Q.xvii.19)—and His Messenger (may God bless him and grant him peace) is the most praised of them all.

Point 2

Praise (*ḥamd*) only occurs when one has attained a favour and mercy. Since the first words were praise, this means that favour and mercy must have been the first act and ruling. This is why God said: 'My mercy has preceded My wrath.'[4]

1 No evidence has been provided for this: clearly what is meant in this premise is something distinct from its meaning in the conclusion, i.e. that it appears at the opening of the Qur'ān.

2 The author makes explicit here that this is the first verse (as has been implicit at numerous other junctures), despite the lengthy arguments in Chapter Four above to establish—in defence of the Shāfiʿī school—that it is the second verse after the *basmala*.

3 I could not source this. However, a *ḥadīth* in Bukhārī and Muslim mentions these two names—without specifying their locus—along with *al-Māḥī* (the Obliterator), *al-Ḥāshir* (the Gatherer) and *al-ʿĀqib* (the Last in Succession)—S.I.

4 Recorded by Bukhārī and Muslim.

Point 3

The Messenger (may God bless him and grant him peace) is called *Aḥmad*, which means that he is the most praising of all the praisers: as such, God's favours upon him must be more abundant, since we have explained that praise is proportional to favours and mercies. This entails that God's mercy must be greater upon Muḥammad (may God bless him and grant him peace) than upon the rest of the worlds, which is why He said: 'We sent you not but as a mercy for the worlds' (Q.xxi.107).

Point 4

The Sender [of the Messenger] has two Names derived from mercy, namely *al-Raḥmān* and *al-Raḥīm*, which convey emphatic meanings. The Messenger, too, has two names derived from mercy, namely *Muḥammad* and *Aḥmad*. This is because—as we have explained—mercy is a prerequisite of praise, so these two names are equivalent to *Marḥūm* (object of mercy) and *Arḥam* (most merciful).[1] There are some narrations which say that the Messenger (may God bless him and grant him peace) also has the names *al-Ḥamd* (Praise), *al-Ḥāmid* (the Praiser) and *al-Maḥmūd* (the Praised).[2] Thus these are five Prophetic names denoting mercy.

Once that is known, Almighty God said: 'Tell My servants that I am indeed the Oft-forgiving, the Merciful' (Q.xv.49). The [imperative verb] 'Tell' is directed to Muḥammad (may God bless him and grant him peace), who is thus mentioned before the servants. The first-person pronouns in *ʿibādī* ('My servants') and *annī* ('that I') refer to God, as does *ana* ('I'),[3] and these are followed by two divine Attributes: *al-Ghafūr* and *al-Raḥīm*—making five words in reference to God, the Merciful and Generous.

Hence the servant will proceed on the Day of Judgment with the Messenger (may God bless him and grant him peace) before him, bearing his five names denoting mercy; and behind him will be five divine Names denoting mercy. The mercy of the Messenger (may God bless him and grant him peace) is plentiful, as God said: 'We sent you not but as a mercy for the worlds' (Q.xxi.107); and the mercy of God is infinite, as He said: 'My mercy extends to all things' (Q.vii.156). Therefore, how

1 Apparently these should be the other way round, since the direction of mercy is the opposite of the direction of praise. The obvious sense of the Prophet (may God bless him and grant him peace) being 'most merciful' is to the creation, for which he earns the praise of the Creator.

2 I could not source these.

3 This succession of pronouns creates emphasis and particularisation, but is difficult to represent in English.

could the sinner perish amongst these ten abundant oceans overflowing with mercy?

AS FOR THE FIVE [DIVINE] NAMES mentioned in this *sūra*, there are also some points to mention:[1]

Point 5

Sūrat al-Fātiḥa contains ten things: five of them are Attributes of Lordship, namely *Allāh*, *al-Rabb*, *al-Raḥmān*, *al-Raḥīm* and *al-Mālik*. The other five are attributes of the servant, i.e. servitude,[2] seeking help,[3] seeking guidance,[4] seeking steadfastness[5] and seeking favour: *The path of those on whom You have bestowed favour*.

Those five Names correspond to these five states [of the servant], as though to say: 'You we worship because You are God (*Allāh*), and from You we seek help because You are the Lord. Guide us upon the straight path because You are the Compassionate, and grant us steadfastness [upon that path] because You are the Merciful. And pour upon us Your abundant favours and bounties, for You are the Master of the Day of Judgment.'

Point 6

The human being is composed of five things: his body, his satanic ego (*nafs shayṭāniyya*), his appetitive ego (*nafs shahwāniyya*), his irascible ego (*nafs ghaḍabiyya*),[6] and his angelic-rational essence (*jawhar malakī ʿaqlī*). The Almighty manifests Himself to these five aspects via the five Names:

a. The Name *Allāh* is manifested to the angelic, rational, heavenly, purified spirit; hence it submits and obeys, as God said: 'Without doubt, in the remembrance of God do hearts find satisfaction' (Q.xiii.28).
b. He manifests to the satanic ego through kindness, as represented in the Name *al-Rabb*, so it abandons disobedience and follows the way of God.
c. To the predatory irascible ego, He manifests the name *al-Raḥmān*, which refers both to authority and compassion, as God said: 'That day,

1 The author numbered these from 'Point 1' again, but I have renumbered them to fit better with the section structure. See previous discussions of these Names in Chapter Five, under Verse 4 (Benefit 4) and Verse 5: *You we worship*.

2 I.e. *You we worship*.

3 I.e. *and from You we seek help*.

4 I.e. *Guide us*.

5 I.e. *upon the straight path*, as the noun from being 'straight' (*istiqāma*) may also be translated as 'uprightness' or 'steadfastness'.

6 These three aspects of the baser self relate, respectively, to desire, appetite and anger—as described in Section ii above.

the dominion, as of right and truth, shall be for the Compassionate' (Q.xxv.26). Thus the ego abandons its disputation.

d. He manifests to the beastly appetitive ego with the name *al-Raḥīm*, by providing the servant with goodly and permissible things: 'Lawful to you are (all) things good and pure' (Q.v.4). Thus it yields and abandons disobedience.
e. To the physical bodies, He manifests the authority in the Name *Mālik yawm al-dīn*, for the body is dense and tough and requires the powerful force created by fear of the Day of Judgment.

Thus, when God has manifested Himself by these five Names to the various aspects [of the human being], the gates of Hellfire are closed and the gates of Paradise are opened. Then these aspects begin to reflect back in reverse order: the bodies submit and say *You we worship*; the appetitive egos submit and say *From You we seek help*, i.e. to turn away from pleasures; the irascible egos submit and say *Guide us* to Your way and keep us firm; the satanic egos submit and ask God for steadfastness and protection from deviation, saying *Guide us upon the straight path*. The pure angelic spirits humbly request that God connect them to the holy, elevated, exalted spirits, saying: *The path of those on whom You have bestowed favour, not of those who incur wrath, nor of those who are astray*.

Point 7

The Prophet (may God bless him and grant him peace) said: 'Islam is built on five [pillars]: to bear witness that there is no god but God and that Muḥammad is the Messenger of God; to establish the prayer; to give the poor-due; to fast in Ramaḍān; and to make pilgrimage to the House [in Mecca].'[1]

a. The testimony that 'There is no god but God' obtains from the manifestation of the Name *Allāh*.
b. The establishment of prayer is from the manifestation of the Name *al-Rabb*, because it is derived from *tarbiya* (to nurture), and the servant nurtures his faith by means of the prayer.
c. Paying the poor-due is from the manifestation of the Name *al-Raḥmān*, because it is an intensive Name derived from *raḥma* (mercy), and the poor-due is given out of mercy for the needy.
d. The obligation to fast Ramaḍān is from the manifestation of the Name *al-Raḥīm*, because when the fasting person feels the pangs

1 Recorded by Bukhārī and Muslim—R.S.

of hunger, he remembers the hunger of the poor and gives them what they need. Also, his experience of hunger weans him from his attachment to worldly pleasures, so it is easier for him to part from them at death.[1]

e. The obligation to make pilgrimage is from the manifestation of the Name *Mālik yawm al-dīn*, because the pilgrim must depart his homeland and part from his family, and this evokes the journey to the Hereafter. Moreover, he becomes barefoot and unclothed in a way reminiscent of the Day of Judgment. Indeed, there are a great many comparisons to be made between the pilgrimage and the events of the Hereafter.

Point 8

There are five types of prayer-direction (*qibla*): Jerusalem, the Kaᶜba [in Mecca], the Frequented House [see Q.LII.4], the Throne and the Divine Presence. Hence you can allocate each of the five Names to one of these directions.[2]

Point 9

There are five senses. God disciplined the sight by saying: 'Take warning, then, O you with eyes (to see)!' (Q.LIX.2); also hearing: 'Those who listen to the word, and follow the best (meaning) in it' (Q.XXXIX.18); and taste: 'O Messengers! Eat things good and pure, and work righteousness' (Q.XXIII.51); and smell: 'I do indeed scent the presence of Joseph: nay, think me not a dotard' (Q.XII.94); and touch: 'And who guard their private parts' (Q.XXIII.5). Therefore, make use of the lights of the five Names in order to avert the harms of these five [potential] enemies.

Point 10

Know that the first half of the *Fātiḥa* contains the five Names, emanating lights upon the hearts. The second half contains the five attributes of the servant,[3] such that the hearts ascend towards those lights. Due to these two realities, the servant experiences ascension in the prayer. The first is the descent [of lights], and the second is the ascent [of hearts], and the meeting point is the dividing line between *Master of the Day of Judgment* and *You we worship*.

1 This is a mercy from God upon the servant.

2 The author does not explain how this is so. Keeping in mind the preceding discussions, the concept of 'direction' is not intended to be applied literally to God.

3 See Point 1 above.

To explain further: the servant's needs pertain either to this life or the next. The former consists of two things: averting [worldly] harm or attaining benefit. The latter also consists of two things: averting harm by fleeing from Hellfire, or seeking good, i.e. Paradise. These make a total of four categories, and the fifth—the noblest category—is to seek only to serve and obey God for His own sake, not due to the love or fear [of anything else].

Thus if you witness the light of the Name *Allāh*, you would not seek anything from God except God. If you observe the light of *al-Rabb*, you will seek from Him the blessings of Paradise. If you observe the light of *al-Raḥmān*, you will seek from Him the good things of this life. If you observe the light of *al-Raḥīm*, you will ask Him to protect you from the harms of the next life. If you observe the light of *Mālik yawm al-dīn*, you will ask that He preserve you from the harms of this world, as well as distasteful actions that would make you deserving of punishment in the Hereafter.

Point 11

These five Names may also be applied to the five stations in the well-known words of remembrance: *subḥāna Allāh* ('Glory be to God'), *wa'l-ḥamdu li'Llāh* ('All praise is for God'), *wa-lā ilāha illā Allāh* ('There is no god but God') *wa'Llāhu akbar* ('God is greater'), *wa-lā ḥawla wa-lā quwwata illā bi'Llāh al-ʿAlī al-ʿAẓīm* ('There is no effect or power except by God, the High, the Great'):[1]

a. 'Glory be to God' is the opening of one *sūra*, namely: 'Glory to the One Who did take His servant for a journey by night…' (Q.xvii.1).
b. 'All praise is for God' is the opening of five *sūras*.[2]
c. 'There is no god but God' is the opening of one *sūra*, namely: '*Alif-lām-mīm*. God! There is no god but He, the Living, the Self-Subsisting' (Q.iii.1–2).
d. 'God is greater' is mentioned in the Qur'ān—albeit not explicitly—in two places: once in connection with remembrance, and the other time in connection with approval: 'And remembrance of God is the greater' (Q.xxix.45) and 'But approval from God is greater' (Q.ix.72).
e. 'There is no effect or power except by God…' is not mentioned explicitly in the Qur'ān because it is one of the treasures of Paradise,[3] and it is in the nature of a treasure to be concealed, not displayed.

1 See also Chapter Five, Verse 5: *You we worship*, Benefit 2.
2 See Chapter Three, Section 1, Enquiry 1 (point 3).
3 This is the import of a *ḥadīth* recorded by Bukhārī and Muslim.

The five Names in *Sūrat al-Fātiḥa* correspond to these five phrases of remembrance. *Allāh* is the basis of 'Glory be to God,' and *Rabb* is the basis of 'All praise is for God.' *Al-Raḥmān* is the basis of 'There is no god but God,' because the One Who possesses the exclusive right to be worshipped must possess both perfect power and perfect mercy, and that is *al-Raḥmān*. *Al-Raḥīm* is the basis of 'God is greater,' i.e. too great not to have mercy upon His weak servants. *Mālik yawm al-dīn* is the basis for 'There is no effect or power except by God...' because the Sovereign or the Master is such that His servants cannot do anything contrary to His will. And God knows best.

Section VIII: The Reason for the *Basmala* Containing the Three Names[1]

God manifests [His greatness] to the intellects of creation, but this manifestation is on three levels: first, through His acts and signs; then, on the middle level, through His Attributes; and at the ultimate level, with His Essence.

It is said that the Almighty manifests to the common people among His servants through His acts and signs: 'And among His signs are the ships, smooth-running through the ocean, (tall) as mountains' (Q.XLII.32); 'Behold! In the creation of the heavens and the earth, and the alternation of night and day, there are indeed signs for people of understanding' (Q.III.190). Then, to His select friends, He does so through His Attributes: '...and they contemplate the (wonders of) creation in the heavens and the earth, (with the thought): "Our Lord, not for nothing have You created (all) this!"' (Q.III.191).[2] But to the senior Prophets and elect angels, He manifests His Essence: 'Say "God", then leave them to plunge in vain discourse and trifling' (Q.VI.91).

Once this is known, we say:

a. The Name *Allāh* is the strongest in manifesting His essence, because it is the most direct as a word, but its meaning is the least comprehensible to the intellect. As such, it is apparent (*ẓāhir*) and hidden (*bāṭin*): it cannot be denied, but its secrets cannot be grasped. Al-Ḥusayn b. Manṣūr al-Ḥallāj said [in a poem]:

    A Name which has confounded the creation who
    sought to know of its meanings.
    By God, they will never gain a way to it until the One
    Who revealed it reveals it!

1 The text says that there are several reasons and labels this as the 'first', but there are no more provided.

2 This verse is connected to the previous citation.

He also said:

> O Secret of secrets, hidden from the conceptions
> of every living thing;
> Apparent and Hidden, manifested to everything
> through everything!

b. The name *al-Raḥmān* denotes His being manifest through His lofty Attributes, which is why He said: 'Say: Call upon *Allāh*, or call upon *al-Raḥmān*. By whatever Name you call upon Him, (it is well): for to Him belong the most Beautiful Names' (Q.xvii.110).
c. The name *al-Raḥīm* denotes His being manifest through His actions and signs: 'Our Lord, You have encompassed all things in mercy and knowledge!' (Q.xl.7).

Section IX: The Reason for the *Fātiḥa* Containing the Five Names

The reason for this relates to the five stages of creation:

a. Creation itself.
b. Nurturing with respect to worldly interests.
c. Nurturing through the explanation of origin.
d. Nurturing through the explanation of destination.
e. Transferring the spirits from the corporeal world to the abode of the Hereafter.

The Name *Allāh* represents the Source of creation, formation and initiation; the Name *al-Rabb* represents His kind and generous nurturing; the Name *al-Raḥmān* denotes nurturing through making [one's] origin known; the name *al-Raḥīm* is concerned with knowledge of the destination, such that a person may do what is required and avoid that which is unbefitting; and the name *al-Malik* signifies that He transports them from the present world to the abode of recompense.

Once the servant has traversed these stations, the discourse switches from the third person to the second person: *You we worship*. It is as though he says [to himself]: 'Now that you have benefited from these five Names with respect to these five stages and transferred to the abode of recompense, you are now able, as it were, to behold God: therefore, speak to Him with words of presence, not absence.'

So it is as though he now says: '*You we worship* because You are *Allāh* the Creator; *and from You we seek help* because You are the Providing Lord (*Rabb*). *You we worship* because You are the Compassionate (*al-Raḥmān*);

and from You we seek help because You are the Merciful (*al-Raḥīm*). *You we worship* because You are the Sovereign (*al-Malik*); *and from You we seek help* because You are the *Master* (*al-Mālik*).'

Know that *Master of the Day of Judgment* signifies that the servant has transferred from this world to the next, and from the abode of evil to the realm of happiness. He says: 'One must prepare and take provision for that day, and that is none other than worship: *You we worship*.' He goes on to say: 'Whatever I have gained through my own power and ability is only a little and cannot suffice me on that lengthy day. Therefore, [O Lord,] grant me from the treasure houses of Your mercy that which will suffice me that day: *from You we seek help*.'

Once he has attained the provision for the Day of Resurrection, he says: 'This is a long and strenuous journey and there are many routes. I see that the people have wandered and strayed in that wilderness, so the only solution is that I seek direction from One Who can guide aright: *Guide us upon the straight path*.'

Then, as any traveller requires a companion, guards and a guide, he says: *The path of those on whom You have bestowed favour*. This refers to the Prophets, the truthful, the martyrs and the righteous [Q.IV.96]. Thus the Prophets are the guides, the truthful (*ṣiddīqūn*) are the guards, and the martyrs and the righteous are the companions. He adds: *Not of those who incur wrath, nor of those who are astray*, because the veils from God are of two types: veils of fire, i.e. this world; and veils of light, i.e. the world of spirits. Therefore, seek Almighty God's protection from both these matters lest your innermost heart (*sirr*) be diverted either by the veils of light or the veils of fire.

Section X: [Concluding Observation]

In this *sūra*, there are two words annexed to the Name *Allāh*, and two other annexations (*muḍāfān*).[1] The two words annexed to the Name *Allāh* are in: *bi'smi 'Llāh* ('In the Name of God') and *al-ḥamdu li'Llāh* ('All praise is for God'). The former is for the beginning of things, and the latter is for endings. Furthermore, the former is remembrance and the latter is gratitude. Therefore, when the [servant] says *In the Name of God*, he becomes deserving of mercy. When he says *All praise is for God*, he deserves another mercy. By the first, he earned mercy from the Name *al-Raḥmān*; by the

1 The author may be referring to *Rabb al-ʿālamīn*, or *Mālik yawm al-dīn* (which itself contains two annexations), or *ṣirāt alladhīna*. Alternatively, he may mean something different by *iḍāfa*, as his second example suggests.

second, from the Name *al-Raḥīm*. This is why it is said: 'O *Raḥmān* of this world, and *Raḥīm* of the next!'

As for *Lord of the worlds; the Compassionate, the Merciful; Master of the Day of Judgment*—the Lordship (*rubūbiyya*) refers to the first state of [the servants], as seen in: '"Am I not your Lord?" They said: "Yes, indeed"' (Q.VII.172). The Attribute of mercy pertains to their middle state [i.e. their lifetime], and the Attributes of mastery and sovereignty to their final state: 'Whose will be the dominion that day? It belongs to God, the One, the Irresistible!' (Q.XL.16).

God knows best, and He is the Guide to what is right and true. The exegesis of *Sūrat al-Fātiḥa* has now been completed, with praise of God for His aid.

APPENDIX: PERSONS CITED IN THE TEXT

Brief information is given here concerning scholars and other personages cited in this volume of *The Great Exegesis*. Data has been drawn from a multitude of sources and is tailored to the purpose of elucidating the text and the context of citations.

Companions of the Prophet are presented alphabetically according to transliteration. Others are listed in order of their date of death, provided according to the Hijrī calendar before the name. The two entries whose dates of death were not found have been placed at a logical point within the chronology. Anyone who is credited with an opinion is included here, together with *ḥadīth* compilers and the highest link in any chain of narration, but I opted to leave out only a few names which had no role except being links in a chain.

Companions

ʿABD ALLĀH B. ʿABBĀS. A cousin of the Prophet who accompanied him for several years in Medina. Ibn ʿAbbās was thirteen years of age upon the Prophet's passing, and learned from senior Companions. He established the Meccan 'school' of Qur'ānic exegesis and is cited frequently in the works of transmitted *tafsīr* as well as books of *Ḥadīth*. He died in 68 AH in Ṭā'if.

ʿABD ALLĀH B. ABĪ AWFĀ. He participated in Ḥudaybiyya and subsequent campaigns, later settling in the Iraqi town of Kufa, where he died around 68 AH.

ʿABD ALLĀH B. ʿAMR B. AL-ʿĀṢ. Son of another famous Companion, with whom he settled in Egypt after its conquest during the caliphate of ʿUmar. ʿAbd-Allāh was given express permission by the Prophet to keep a written record of *ḥadīths*. He died around 65 AH.

ʿABD ALLĀH B. MASʿŪD. One of the first converts, he participated in the emigrations and the Prophet's military campaigns. Noted for his expertise in the Qur'ān, the second Caliph ʿUmar appointed him as judge and teacher in Kufa. His non-canonical readings are often cited in works of *tafsīr* and sometimes have bearing on legal questions. Ibn Masʿūd died in 32 AH in Medina.

ʿABD ALLĀH B. AL-MUGHAFFAL. He pledged allegiance to the Prophet under the tree at Ḥudaybiyya and remained in Medina until being sent by Caliph ʿUmar as a teacher to the people of Basra, Iraq, where he died around 60 AH.

ʿABD ALLĀH B. ʿUMAR B. AL-KHAṬṬĀB. He converted along with his father before the Emigration to Medina and became known for his close adherence to the Prophet's practice. Ibn ʿUmar was a prolific teacher and *ḥadīth* narrator. He lived through much of the civil strife after the Prophet's passing, until his own death in Mecca in 73 AH.

ʿABD ALLĀH B. AL-ZUBAYR. The son of the Companions al-Zubayr b. al-ʿAwwām and Asmā', daughter of Abū Bakr, he was the first child born in Medina after the arrival of the Prophet. He was inactive during the initial civil strife after the passing of ʿUthmān, the third caliph, but later opposed the accession of Yazīd and established a rival caliphate in Mecca. This was eventually quashed by al-Ḥajjāj b. Yūsuf, a governor under the Umayyad caliph ʿAbd al-Malik, and Ibn al-Zubayr was killed in 73 AH.

ʿABD AL-RAḤMĀN B. ʿAWF. One of the earliest converts to Islam, he was among the emigrants to Abyssinia and was renowned for his generosity and wealth. He fought alongside the Prophet with special distinction at Badr and Uḥud. Later, ʿUmar appointed him to the committee who chose his successor as caliph. He died in 33 AH and is buried in Amman, Jordan.

ABŪ BAKR AL-ṢIDDĪQ (ʿABD-ALLĀH B. ABĪ QUḤĀFA). The first adult male to embrace Islam, he remained close to the Prophet throughout his life and was the first caliph after his passing. He died in 13 AH and is buried next to the Prophet in Medina.

ABŪ AL-DARDĀ' (ʿUWAYMIR B. ʿĀMIR). He participated in all the Prophet's campaigns after Uḥud, and later settled in Syria. He served as a judge during the caliphate of ʿUthmān, and died soon after 31 AH.

ABŪ DHARR AL-GHIFĀRĪ (JUNDAB B. JUNĀDA). An early convert who returned to his own tribe and only joined the Prophet in Medina after the Battle of the Trench. He later settled in Syria and died in the Ḥijāzī town of Rabadha in 32 AH.

ABŪ HURAYRA (ʿABD AL-RAḤMĀN B. ṢAKHR). Prolific narrator of *ḥadīth* who accompanied the Prophet from the seventh year of the Hijra. Hailing from the tribe of Daws, he remained in Medina most of his life and died there in 59 AH.

ABŪ AL-SĀ'IB (ʿABD ALLĀH B. AL-SĀ'IB). Medinan, freedman of Hishām b. Zahra.

ABŪ SAʿĪD AL-KHUDRĪ (SAʿD B. MĀLIK B. SINĀN). He was among the Helpers of Medina and participated in the Prophet's battles from the Trench onwards. He remained in Medina after the Prophet's death and narrated many *ḥadīth*s until his death around the year 64 AH.

ABŪ UMĀMA AL-BĀHILĪ (ṢUDAYY B. ʿAJLĀN). He converted late in the Prophet's life and came to settle in Homs. He was among the last Companions to pass away in Syria (in 81 or 86 AH).

ʿĀ'ISHA BINT ABĪ BAKR. The beloved wife of the Prophet who stayed with him from the second year of the Hijra. She remained in Medina teaching the religion and Prophetic practices until her death in 56 AH. ʿĀ'isha briefly played a role in the civil strife between the Companions, supporting Ṭalḥa and al-Zubayr at the Battle of the Camel.

ʿALĪ B. ABĪ ṬĀLIB. The cousin of the Prophet who was among the first to believe in him, and married his daughter Fāṭima soon after the Hijra. He became caliph after Abū Bakr, ʿUmar and ʿUthmān and established himself in Kufa, but faced hostilities from both Muʿāwiya's forces and the Khārijīs. Though revered by both Sunnis and Shiʿis, the latter count him as the first *Imām* to inherit Prophetic authority. He was assassinated in 40 AH and is buried in Najaf, Iraq.

ANAS B. MĀLIK. He was around ten years old when the Prophet arrived in Medina, and Anas took the role of his servant. He later settled near Basra and narrated many *ḥadīths* until he died around 93 AH.

AL-BARĀ' B. ʿĀZIB. He converted at a young age and accompanied the Prophet in numerous battles. He was made governor of al-Rayy (where Imām Rāzī was later born) during the caliphate of ʿUthmān, and died in Kūfa in 71 AH.

BILĀL B. RABĀḤ. An Abyssinian born into slavery in Mecca, Bilāl was an early convert who was freed by Abū Bakr and became the first caller to prayer (*mu'adhdhin*) in Islam. He died in Damascus in 17 AH or slightly later.

BURAYDA B. AL-ḤUṢAYB. A leader of the Aslam tribe who embraced Islam during the Prophet's Emigration to Medina and fought in all the battles. He died in Khorasan around 63 AH.

ḤĀRITHA B. AL-NUʿMĀN. A Khazrajī Helper who participated in all the Prophet's campaigns. He died during the caliphate of Muʿāwiya.

AL-ḤASAN B. ʿALĪ B. ABĪ ṬĀLIB. A grandson of the Prophet through his daughter Fāṭima. He was born in the third year after Hijra and, along with his younger brother al-Ḥusayn, was extremely beloved to the Prophet. He would later receive allegiance as caliph after the death of his father ʿAlī, until abdicating four months later after signing a treaty with Muʿāwiya. He died between 49 and 51 AH in Medina.

ḤUDHAYFA B. AL-YAMĀN. Son of another Companion, he was born in Mecca, participated in the Prophet's campaigns after the Hijra, and died in 36 AH in al-Madā'in. He is known as the 'Keeper of the Prophet's secrets'.

AL-ḤUSAYN B. ʿALĪ B. ABĪ ṬĀLIB. The younger brother of al-Ḥasan by one year. After the death of al-Ḥasan and then Muʿāwiya, he objected to the succession of the latter's son, Yazīd, to the caliphate. He moved from Medina to Mecca, then heeded a call in 61 AH from the residents of Kufa. En route, he was intercepted and killed in the tragic events at Karbala, Iraq, which remains a defining event for Shiʿi Muslims in particular.

ʿIMRĀN B. AL-ḤUṢAYN. He converted in the seventh year after Hijra and carried the banner of the Khuzāʿa tribe at the Conquest of Mecca. He was sent as a teacher and appointed judge in Basra during the caliphate of ʿUmar, where he died in 52 AH.

JĀBIR B. ʿABD-ALLĀH B. ʿAMR. The son of another Companion, Jābir gave allegiance to the Prophet at the Second ʿAqaba meeting, carried water as a youth at Badr, and participated fully in subsequent battles. He died in Medina around 78 AH.

JUBAYR B. MUṬʿIM. A nobleman from Quraysh, son of al-Muṭʿim b. ʿAdī who gave protection to the Prophet though not a believer. Jubayr embraced Islam at Ḥudaybiyya or the Conquest of Mecca, and died around 58 AH.

KAʿB B. ʿUJRA AL-BALAWĪ. Confederate of the Anṣār. He died around 52 AH.

KHADĪJA BINT KHUWAYLID. The beloved first wife of the Prophet, a successful businesswoman who was also the first to believe in him when he was visited by the Archangel Gabriel. She was mother of his four daughters and two sons, and passed away in the tenth year of Prophethood (two years before the Emigration), which became known as the Year of Sorrow.

KHĀLID B. AL-WALĪD. Son of the Qurayshī leader al-Walīd b. al-Mughīra, he was a military leader against the Muslims in several battles until his conversion after the Treaty of Ḥudaybiyya. He became known as 'the Sword of God' and went on to achieve great victories under the caliphates of Abū Bakr and ʿUmar before his death in 21 AH.

KHAWLA BINT ḤAKĪM AL-SULAMIYYA. An early convert to Islam who was an adviser to the Prophet and friend of his wife Khadīja, and married to ʿUthmān b. Maẓʿūn.

LABĪD B. RABĪʿA. A poet from the Banū ʿĀmir tribe, author of one of the seven 'Hanging Odes' (*al-Muʿallaqāt*), who embraced Islam and apparently ceased composing poetry thereafter. He died around 41 AH.

MAʿQIL B. YASĀR. He converted before Ḥudaybiyya, and was appointed by Caliph ʿUmar as governor of Basra, where he died around 50 AH.

MUʿĀDH B. JABAL. A Helper who participated in the Second ʿAqaba pledge and all subsequent campaigns. The Prophet stationed him in Mecca as a teacher before sending him to Yemen. He later participated in the conquest of the Levant, and died in Jordan from the plague in 18 AH.

MUʿĀWIYA B. ABĪ SUFYĀN. Along with his father Abū Sufyān b. Ḥarb and his mother Hind, Muʿāwiya became Muslim after the Conquest of Mecca. He served the Prophet as a scribe. He was appointed as governor of Syria during ʿUmar's caliphate. After the assassination of the third Caliph ʿUthmān, Muʿāwiya's kinsman, he faced ʿAli in battle until a resolution was negotiated. Following the assassination of ʿAlī and a treaty with his son al-Ḥasan, Muʿāwiya became caliph for twenty years. Before his death in 60 AH, he appointed his son Yazīd as his successor.

MUGHĪRA B. SHUʿBA. He converted before the Treaty of Ḥudaybiya and lost an eye at the battle of Yarmouk or the battle of Qādisiyya. He later governed Basra for three years, leading the conquests of Azerbaijan and Hamadhān. He was governor of Kufa at the end of his life, passing away in 50 AH.

AL-NUʿMĀN B. BASHĪR. He was the first child born to the Helpers in Medina after the Prophet's arrival. He fought at Ṣiffīn with Muʿāwiya, who appointed him as governor of Kufa, then Homs. He was killed in 65 AH after pledging allegiance to ʿAbd Allāh b. al-Zubayr.

RIFĀʿA B. RĀFIʿ B. MĀLIK. He participated along with his father in the Second ʿAqaba pledge and subsequent campaigns, then supported ʿAlī at the Battles of the Camel and Ṣiffīn. He died in 41 AH.

SAʿD B. ʿUBĀDA. He was leader of the Khazraj before the arrival of the Prophet to Medina. He participated in the ʿAqaba pledges and subsequent military campaigns. He was killed in the Levant in 13 or 14 AH.

SALMĀN THE PERSIAN. Salmān came to Medina as a slave after spending years in search of the true religion. Upon the arrival of the Prophet, he embraced Islam. He later participated in the Conquest of Persia and was appointed governor of al-Madā'in. He died around 33 AH.

ṢUHAYB B. SINĀN B. MĀLIK. Commonly known as Ṣuhayb al-Rūmī (the Byzantine), he was born to Arab parents but kidnapped and enslaved in the Byzantine provinces before coming to Mecca as a slave. He became free and embraced Islam in its early days, facing persecution along with the underprivileged Companions. Nevertheless, he gathered some wealth which he then abandoned for the sake of migrating to the Prophet in Medina, where he died in 38 AH.

ṬALḤA B. ʿUBAYD ALLĀH. One of the earliest Muslims in Mecca, he migrated to Medina and participated in the Prophet's battles from Uḥud onwards. After the assassination of ʿUthmān, he was among those calling for justice to be served. He was killed at the Battle of the Camel in 36 AH.

ʿUBĀDA B. AL-ṢĀMIT. A leader of the Khazrajī Helpers who witnessed both ʿAqaba pledges and fought alongside the Prophet in subsequent campaigns. ʿUmar later sent him to Syria as a teacher and judge. He died in 34 AH and his tomb is in Jerusalem.

UBAYY B. KAʿB. A Helper who participated in the Second ʿAqaba pledge and all subsequent campaigns. He is best known for his knowledge of the Qur'ān and was among the scribes of revelation. He died in Medina sometime between 19 and 32 AH.

ʿUMAR B. AL-KHAṬṬĀB. An Emigrant Companion who played a pivotal role in the defence of the early Muslim community and was the second to take the role of caliph, after Abū Bakr. Under his rule, the conquests of Syria, Palestine, Egypt, Iraq and Persia occurred. He was assassinated in 23 AH and is buried next to the Prophet in Medina.

UMM SALAMA (HIND BINT ABĪ UMAYYA). A beloved wife and advisor of the Prophet, who married him after the death of her husband Abū Salama. Both were among the early converts. Umm Salama died around 64 AH.

ʿUTHMĀN B. ʿAFFĀN. One of the earliest converts, he was known for his modesty and generosity and had the honour of marrying two of the Prophet's daughters in succession. ʿUthmān was to become the third caliph after the death of ʿUmar and oversaw further expansion of Muslim-governed territories. One of his significant edicts was to standardise the Qur'ānic codex to put an end to disagreements concomitant with this expansion. His assassination in 35 AH, following a siege of his home, precipitated the first conflict between groups of the Companions.

WARAQA B. NAWFAL. The first cousin of the Prophet's wife Khadīja, to whom she took him for consultation after the first visitation of Angel Gabriel. Waraqa was a scholar of the Jewish and Christian scriptures, and expressed his belief in the genuineness of the Prophet Muḥammad's experience of revelation. He died soon after.

YAʿLĀ B. MUNYA (or B. UMAYYA). He converted upon the Conquest of Mecca and participated in subsequent battles under the Prophet, Abū Bakr and ʿUmar. In the civil war following ʿUthmān's assassination, he sided with ʿĀ'isha then ʿAlī. Note: his name is often printed as Ibn Munabbih, as in previous editions of this text.

ZAYD B. ḤĀRITHA. He was a slave and then freedman and adoptive son of the Prophet. He was married to Zaynab bint Jaḥsh, who subsequently married the Prophet; Zayd's name and these circumstances are mentioned in Q.xxxiii.37. Zayd was martyred at the Battle of Mu'ta in 8 AH.

Appendix: Persons Cited in the Text

Scholars, Poets, etc.

< 100 BH	IMRU' AL-QAYS B. ḤUJR AL-KINDĪ. Pre-Islamic poet, composer of one of the seven 'Hanging Odes'.
19 BH	AL-NĀBIGHA AL-DHUBYĀNĪ (ZIYĀD B. MUʿĀWIYA). Pre-Islamic poet.
2 BH	QAYS B. AL-KHAṬĪM. Pre-Islamic poet.
32 AH	KAʿB AL-AḤBĀR. A Yemeni former rabbi who converted after the death of the Prophet and came to Medina during ʿUmar's caliphate. He is known for narrating from pre-Islamic scriptures and traditions.
63 AH	ʿAMR B. SHURAḤBĪL. A senior Kufan Successor.
90 AH	AL-AKHṬAL (GHIYĀTH B. GHAWTH AL-TAGHLIBĪ). A Christian Arab poet of the Umayyad period.
94 AH	ʿURWA B. ZUBAYR B. AL-ʿAWWĀM. The son of a famous Companion, he is counted among the seven prominent jurists of Medina and a key figure in the composition of the Prophetic biography (*sīra*).
94 AH	ABŪ SALAMA B. ʿABD AL-RAḤMĀN B. ʿAWF. The son of a famous Companion, he is counted among the seven prominent jurists of Medina.
95 AH	SAʿĪD B. JUBAYR. Kufan Successor and major student of Ibn ʿAbbās. His narrations are found in the books of exegesis and *Ḥadīth*.
96 AH	IBRĀHĪM B. YAZĪD AL-NAKHAʿĪ. Kufan Successor, jurist, *ḥadīth* transmitter and reciter.
< 99 AH	SHURAYḤ AL-QĀḌĪ. He accepted Islam in Yemen during the Prophet's lifetime, though he never met him. He served as judge in Kufa during ʿUmar's caliphate and Damascus under Muʿāwiya.
100 AH	ʿĀMIR AL-SHAʿBĪ. A Successor and leading scholar born in the caliphate of ʿUmar.
UNKNOWN	ABŪ AL-NAJM AL-ʿIJLĪ (AL-FAḌL B. QUDĀMA). Umayyad poet of the early second/eighth century.
101 AH	ʿUMAR B. ʿABD AL-ʿAZĪZ. A Successor, grandson of ʿUmar b. al-Khaṭṭāb, and Umayyad caliph. He is often described as the fifth of the 'Rightly-Guided Caliphs' after Abū Bakr, ʿUmar, ʿUthmān and ʿAlī. He died near Homs, Syria.
102 AH	AL-ḌAḤḤĀK B. MUZĀḤIM. A successor from Balkh who settled in Kufa. He is best known for his narrations in Qur'ānic exegesis.

104 AH MUJĀHID B. JABR. A Meccan Successor and major student of Ibn ʿAbbās. His narrations are found in the books of exegesis and *Ḥadīth*.

107 AH ABŪ QILĀBA (ʿABD-ALLĀH B. ʿAMR). A senior Basran Successor.

110 AH MUḤAMMAD B. SĪRĪN. Basran scholar and ascetic, and freedman of the Companion Anas b. Mālik. A famous book of dream interpretations is attributed to him.

110 AH AL-ḤASAN AL-BAṢRĪ. A Successor famed for his knowledge and piety. He was born in Medina and served as a judge in Basra.

110 AH NĀFIʿ, the freedman of ʿAbd Allāh b. ʿUmar. A leading Successor in Medina. Imām Mālik was among his students.

110 AH AL-KHALĪL B. AḤMAD AL-FARĀHĪDĪ. Basran linguist born in Oman, and compiler of the first Arabic dictionary, *al-ʿAyn*.

UNKNOWN AL-FAḌL B. ʿĪSĀ AL-RAQQĀSHĪ. Basran preacher associated with the Muʿtazila.

114 AH ʿAṬĀ' B. ABĪ RABĀḤ. A Successor of Nubian descent, born in Yemen and raised in Mecca, where he was a major legal authority.

126 AH ʿAMR B. DĪNĀR. Meccan Successor, jurist and *ḥadīth* transmitter.

127 AH ISMĀʿĪL B. ʿABD AL-RAḤMĀN AL-SUDDĪ. Kufan Successor famous for Qur'ānic exegesis.

128 AH JAHM B. ṢAFWĀN. A theologian who was born in Kufa and settled in Tirmidh. His doctrines on Divine Attributes were the subject of extensive critique from *Ḥadīth* scholars.

144 AH YAḤYĀ B. SAʿĪD AL-ANṢĀRĪ. A major Medinan scholar.

148 AH IBN ABĪ LAYLĀ (MUḤAMMAD B. ʿABD AL-RAḤMĀN). His father was a Successor who fought with ʿAlī and collected his traditions. He was born in Kufa and came to serve as its chief judge

148 AH JAʿFAR AL-ṢĀDIQ. A descendent of ʿAlī b. Abī Ṭālib who is counted by the Shiʿa as the 'Sixth Imām'. He is revered by Sunnis as a jurist, mystic and transmitter of *ḥadīth*s.

150 AH ABŪ ḤANĪFA (AL-NUʿMĀN B. THĀBIT). Kufan jurist and theologian. He is the eponymous founder of the Ḥanafī school of jurisprudence, hence one of the 'Four Imāms' of Sunni Islam.

154 AH ABŪ ʿAMR B. AL-ʿALĀ' AL-BAṢRĪ. One of the Seven Readers in canonical transmission of the Qur'ān, and considered the founder of the Basran school of grammar.

158 AH — ZUFAR B. AL-HUDHAYL. A major disciple of Abū Ḥanīfa, ranked after or alongside Abū Yūsuf and Muḥammad al-Shaybānī.

158 AH — ʿABD AL-RAḤMĀN B. ʿAMR AL-AWZĀʿĪ. A major scholar who lived in Damascus then Beirut. He was an authority in *Ḥadīth* and law.

161 AH — SUFYĀN B. SAʿĪD AL-THAWRĪ. A major scholar from Kufa who spent time in Yemen, Mecca and Basra. He was an authority in *Ḥadīth*, law and Qur'ānic exegesis.

165 AH — IBRĀHĪM B. ADHAM. A prominent ascetic from Balkh, modern-day Afghanistan.

169 AH — AL-ḤASAN B. ṢĀLIḤ B. ḤAYY. A Zaydī theologian and jurist from Kufa.

179 AH — MĀLIK B. ANAS. Leading jurist of Medina and *Ḥadīth* scholar, who compiled *al-Muwaṭṭa'*. He is the eponymous founder of the Mālikī school of jurisprudence, hence one of the 'Four Imāms' of Sunni Islam.

180 AH — SĪBAWAYH (ʿAMR B. ʿUTHMĀN). Persian linguist and author of *al-Kitāb*, the first written account of Arabic grammar.

180 AH — KHALAF AL-AḤMAR. Poet and grammarian from Basra; and a freedman of the Basran leader Bilāl b. Abī Barada.

181 AH — ʿABD ALLĀH B. AL-MUBĀRAK. A *ḥadīth* transmitter and ascetic of Khorasan whose teachers included Sufyān al-Thawrī and Abū Ḥanīfa.

181 AH — ABŪ YŪSUF (YAʿQŪB B. IBRĀHĪM). A major student of Abū Ḥanīfa and independent jurist in his own right, he served as chief justice of the Abbasid caliphate under Hārūn al-Rashīd. Along with Muḥammad b. al-Ḥasan, he is one of the 'Two Companions' with significant status in the Ḥanafī school.

185 AH — RĀBIʿA AL-ʿADAWIYYA. Hailing from Basra, she is considered the first and most important female Sufi saint.

UNKNOWN — ʿAMRA AL-FARGHĀNIYYA. An early female mystic included in Abū ʿAbd al-Raḥmān al-Sulamī's (d. 412 AH) *Ṭabaqāt al-Ṣūfiyya*. I could not locate biographical details.

189 AH — ʿALĪ B. ḤAMZA AL-KISĀ'Ī. Founder of the Kufan school of Arabic grammar and one of the Seven Readers to whom the various canonical recitations of the Qur'ān are ascribed.

189 AH — MUḤAMMAD B. AL-ḤASAN AL-SHAYBĀNĪ. A major transmitter of the Ḥanafī school. He studied only two years with Abū Ḥanīfa

until his death, when Muḥammad was eighteen years of age; he continued his studies with Abū Yūsuf and others. A number of his works are known collectively as *ẓāhir al-riwāya* and are considered authoritative by Ḥanafīs. He also transmitted from Imām Mālik and taught Imām Shāfiʿī, thus representing a confluence between the major Sunni schools.

193 AH IBN ʿULAYYA (ISMĀʿĪL B. IBRĀHĪM). *Ḥadīth* scholar and jurist from Basra.

198 AH SUFYĀN B. ʿUYAYNA. Meccan authority in Qur'ānic exegesis and *Ḥadīth*.

200 AH AL-AṢAMM (ʿABD AL-RAḤMĀN B. KAYSĀN). Basran theologian and exegete associated with the Muʿtazila.

201 AH QUTAYBA B. MIHRĀN. Qur'ān reciter from Isfahan, and a lesser-known narrator from Kisā'ī.

204 AH AL-ḤASAN B. ZIYĀD AL-LU'LU'Ī. A Kufan judge and lesser-known disciple of Abū Ḥanīfa.

204 AH MUḤAMMAD B. IDRĪS AL-SHĀFIʿĪ. Student of Imām Mālik who went on to become the eponymous founder of the Shāfiʿī school of jurisprudence to which Imām Rāzī belonged. Hence he is one of the 'Four Imāms' of Sunni Islam. Shāfiʿī was born in Gaza, travelled through various lands and settled in Egypt. He also studied with Muḥammad al-Shaybānī, the disciple of Imām Abū Ḥanifa. He authored *al-Umm* in positive law, and *al-Risāla*, considered the first systematic work of Islamic legal methodology.

206 AH QUṬRUB (MUḤAMMAD B. AL-MUSTANĪR). Basran philologist who left behind numerous works, including a grammatical exegesis, *Maʿānī al-Qur'ān*.

207 AH AL-FARRĀ' (YAḤYĀ B. ZIYĀD). A famous Kufan grammarian and author of *Maʿānī al-Qur'ān*.

209 AH HISHĀM B. MUʿĀWIYA. Kufan grammarian and student of Kisā'ī.

215 AH AL-AKHFASH AL-AWSAṬ (ABŪ AL-ḤASAN SAʿĪD B. MASʿADA). Arab philologist and disciple of Sībawayh. He was born in Balkh but lived mostly in Basra.

224 AH ABŪ ʿUBAYD AL-QĀSIM B. SALLĀM. A jurist and *Ḥadīth* scholar from Herat, and author of numerous works including *Faḍā'il al-Qur'ān*.

230 AH AL-NAẒẒĀM (IBRĀHĪM B. SAYĀR). Muʿtazilī theologian and poet.

238 AH ISḤĀQ B. RĀHAWAYH. A prominent *Ḥadīth* scholar and jurist of Khorasan, and teacher of Imām Bukhārī.

241 AH AḤMAD B. MUḤAMMAD B. ḤANBAL. Born in Baghdad, he studied under Imām Shāfiʿī as well as Abū Yūsuf, the disciple of Abū Ḥanifa, and is the eponymous founder of the Ḥanbalī school of jurisprudence. Hence he is considered one of the 'Four Imāms' of Sunni Islam. Imām Aḥmad is known for his traditionalist approach to theology and as author of his *Musnad* collection of *ḥadīth*s.

247 AH ABŪ ʿUTHMĀN BAKR B. MUḤAMMAD AL-MĀZINĪ. Basran grammarian and theologian.

248 AH DHŪ AL-NŪN AL-MIṢRĪ. A prominent ascetic, mystic and scholar from Upper Egypt.

250 AH ʿABBĀD B. SULAYMĀN. A Muʿtazilī theologian of Basra.

251 AH AL-SARĪ AL-SAQAṬĪ. An important early figure of Baghdadi Sufism, the uncle and teacher of al-Junayd.

256 AH MUḤAMMAD B. ISMĀʿĪL AL-BUKHĀRĪ. Persian *Ḥadīth* scholar whose compilation *al-Jāmiʿ al-musnad al-ṣaḥīḥ al-mukhtaṣar* came to be considered by Sunni Muslims as the most authentic book after the Qur'ān. He was born in Bukhara and settled in Nishapur before moving near Samarqand due to political pressure.

261 AH MUSLIM B. AL-ḤAJJĀJ. Persian scholar and student of Bukhārī whose *Ṣaḥīḥ* ranks alongside his teacher's among the most authentic and renowned *Ḥadīth* collections.

270 AH DĀWŪD B. ʿALĪ AL-IṢFAHĀNĪ. Considered the founder of the Ẓāhirī (literalist) school of law. He may have had ancestry from Isfahan but was most likely born in Kufa and lived mostly in Baghdad.

275 AH ABŪ DĀWŪD AL-SIJISTĀNĪ (SULAYMĀN B. AL-ASHʿATH). Persian *Ḥadīth* scholar and compiler of *al-Sunan*.

276 AH ʿABD ALLĀH B. MUSLIM B. QUTAYBA (AL-QUTAYBĪ). A jurist and belletrist from Baghdad who settled in Kufa and composed significant works concerning *ḥadīth* and exegesis, including *Ta'wīl mushkil al-Qur'ān*.

279 AH ABŪ ʿĪSĀ AL-TIRMIDHĪ (MUḤAMMAD B. ʿĪSĀ). Persian *Ḥadīth* scholar, compiler of *al-Jāmiʿ al-mukhtaṣar*. Bukhārī and Muslim were among his teachers.

282 AH AL-HUSAYN B. AL-FAḌL. A Kufan exegete who settled in Nishapur.

286 AH ABŪ AL-ʿABBĀS AL-MUBARRAD (MUḤAMMAD B. YAZĪD). Leading proponent of the Basran school of grammar, he spent most of his life in Baghdad.

291 AH THAʿLAB (AḤMAD B. YAḤYĀ AL-SHAYBĀNĪ). Though born in Baghdad, he was a founder of the Kufan school of grammar.

309 AH AL-ḤUSAYN B. MANṢŪR AL-ḤALLĀJ. Persian mystic and poet who became notorious for his ecstatic pronouncements, for which he was put to death by the Abbasid authorities.

318 AH IBN AL-MUNDHIR (MUḤAMMAD B. IBRĀHĪM). A jurist and *Ḥadīth* scholar from Nishapur who later settled in Mecca. He is associated with the Shāfiʿī school. His authored works include *al-Mabsūṭ*, a major work in comparative jurisprudence no longer extant, of which *al-Awsaṭ* is the author's abridgement.

320 AH ABŪ BAKR AL-WĀSIṬĪ (IBN AL-FARGHĀNĪ). A major Sufi figure from Khorasan.

321 AH ABŪ BAKR B. DURAYD. Poet and philologist from Basra.

334 AH ABŪ BAKR AL-SHIBLĪ. A major Sufi of Persia, and disciple of al-Junayd al-Baghdādī.

340 AH ABŪ AL-ḤASAN AL-KARKHĪ (ʿUBAYD ALLĀH B. AL-ḤUSAYN). Ḥanafī jurist and author of *al-Uṣūl*.

370 AH ABŪ BAKR AL-RĀZĪ AL-JAṢṢĀṢ (AḤMAD B. ʿALĪ). Ḥanafī jurist, author of *Aḥkām al-Qurʾān* and other important works. He was born in Rayy and eventually settled in Baghdad.

373 AH ABŪ AL-LAYTH AL-SAMARQANDĪ (NAṢR B. MUḤAMMAD). Ḥanafī jurist and ascetic of Transoxania.

377 AH ABŪ ʿALĪ AL-FĀRISĪ (AL-ḤASAN B. AḤMAD). Prolific Arabic grammarian born in the Persian town of Fasā. He spent most of his life in Baghdad, with periods in Aleppo and Damascus.

385 AH ʿALĪ B. ʿUMAR AL-DĀRAQUṬNĪ. *Ḥadīth* scholar from Baghdad and compiler of *al-Sunan*.

388 AH ABŪ SULAYMĀN AL-KHAṬṬĀBĪ. Major Shāfiʿī jurist born in Bost (modern-day Lashkargah, Afghanistan).

392 AH ʿUTHMĀN B. JINNĪ. Iraqi grammarian who left behind influential works including *al-Khaṣāʾiṣ* in Arabic linguistics.

403 AH ABŪ BAKR AL-BĀQILLĀNĪ (MUḤAMMAD B. AL-ṬAYYIB).

Ashʿarī theologian and Mālikī jurist. Born in Basra, he became the chief judge in Baghdad. His most extensive theological work entitled *Hidāyat al-mustarshidīn* is cited by Imām Rāzī but only partially extant today.

406 AH ABŪ ḤĀMID AL-ISFARĀʾĪNĪ (AḤMAD B. MUḤAMMAD). A Shāfiʿī scholar of law, *Ḥadīth* and Sufism. He spent most of his life in Baghdad and is the author of *al-Taʿlīq* on comparative jurisprudence.

427 AH ABŪ ISḤĀQ AL-THAʿLABĪ (AḤMAD B. MUḤAMMAD). Exegete from Nishapur, and author of *al-Kashf wa'l-bayān*.

428 AH ABŪ ʿALĪ B. SĪNĀ (AL-ḤUSAYN B. ʿABD ALLĀH). A Persian polymath and major commentator on Aristotle, known in the West as Avicenna. He authored numerous works including *The Canon of Medicine*, and *al-Mukhtaṣar al-awsaṭ* in logic.

430 AH ABŪ ZAYD AL-DABŪSĪ (ʿUBAYD ALLĀH B. ʿUMAR). Ḥanafī jurist from Bukhara who was a founder of the method of comparative jurisprudence.

440 AH ABŪ SAʿĪD B. ABĪ AL-KHAYR AL-MĪHANĪ. A major figure in Persian Sufism.

449 AH ABŪ AL-ʿALĀʾ AL-MAʿARRĪ (AḤMAD B. ʿABD ALLĀH). Levantine poet-philosopher who was blind from a young age. He became known for his irreligious views.

458 AH AḤMAD B. HUSAYN AL-BAYHAQĪ. Shāfiʿī jurist and *Ḥadīth* scholar, compiler of *al-Sunan al-kubrā* and an Ashʿarī creedal treatise *al-Asmāʾ wa'l-ṣifāt*.

465 AH ABŪ AL-QĀSIM AL-QUSHAYRĪ. Author of *The Epistle on Sufism* (*al-Risāla al-Qushayriyya*) and an exegesis entitled *Subtle Allusions* (*Laṭāʾif al-ishārāt*).

471 AH ʿABD AL-QĀHIR AL-JURJĀNĪ. Influential linguist and literary theorist from Gorgan, modern-day Iran.

477 AH ABŪ AL-NAṢR B. AL-ṢABBĀGH (ʿABD AL-SAYYID B. MUḤAMMAD). Shāfiʿī jurist from Baghdad, and author of *al-Shāmil* in positive law.

481 AH ʿABD ALLĀH AL-ANṢĀRĪ AL-HARAWĪ. A Ḥanbalī polymath from Herat, known as *Shaykh al-Islām* and famed for works including *Manāzil al-sāʾirīn*, a Sufi treatise. His book on Divine Attributes, *al-Fārūq fī al-ṣifāt*, is not extant.

505 AH ABŪ ḤĀMID AL-GHAZĀLĪ (MUḤAMMAD B. MUḤAMMAD).

Major Ashʿarī theologian and Shāfiʿī jurist, credited with synthesising law and Sufism in his magnum opus *Iḥyā' ʿulūm al-dīn*. He was born and died in Ṭūs, Khorasan, spending periods of his life in Baghdad and Jerusalem.

512 AH ABŪ AL-Q̲ĀSIM SALMĀN AL-ANṢĀRĪ. Major Ashʿarī theologian born near Nishapur, and teacher of Imām Rāzī's father, Ḍiyā' al-Dīn ʿUmar. His teachers include Abū al-Q̲āsim al-Q̲ushayrī and Abū al-Maʿālī al-Juwaynī.

538 AH MAḤMŪD B. ʿUMAR AL-ZAMAKHSHARĪ. Exegete and linguist belonging to the Muʿtazilī school. He was born in Khwarezm and lived mostly in Bukhara, Samarqand and Baghdad. His works include *al-Mufaṣṣal* in Arabic grammar, and his seminal exegesis *al-Kashshāf*.

559 AH ḌIYĀ' AL-DĪN ʿUMAR AL-MAKKĪ. Ashʿarī theologian, Shāfiʿī jurist and father of Fakhr al-Dīn al-Rāzī. He was the preacher at the main mosque in Rayy.

563 AH ABŪ AL-NAJĪB AL-SUHRAWARDĪ. Shāfiʿī jurist and founder of the Suhrawardī Sufi order. He was born in Persia and settled in Baghdad.

BIBLIOGRAPHY

Abd-Allah, Umar Faruq, 'One God, Many Names', Nawawi Foundation paper, 2004 (www.nawawi.org).

ʿAbd al-Bāqī, Muḥammad Fu'ād, *al-Muʿjam al-mufahras li-alfāẓ al-Qur'ān al-karīm*, Tehran: Avand Danesh, n.d.

Abrahamov, Binyamin, 'Fakhr al-Dīn al-Rāzī on the knowability of God's essence', *Arabica*, vol. XLIX, 2002, pp. 204–230.

Acar, Rahim, *Talking about God and Talking about Creation*, Leiden: Brill, 2005.

ʿAjlūnī, Ismāʿīl b. Muḥammad al-, *Kashf al-khafā' wa-muzīl al-ilbās ʿammā ishtahar min al-āḥādīth ʿalā alsinat al-nās*, ed. ʿAbd al-Ḥamīd Hindāwī, 2 vols., Beirut: al-Maktaba al-ʿAṣriyya, 2012.

Alon, Ilai & Shukri Abed, *Al-Fārābī's Philosophical Lexicon*, 2 vols., Cambridge: E. J. W. Gibb Memorial Trust, 2007.

Ālūsī, Maḥmūd b. ʿAbd Allāh al-, *Rūḥ al-maʿānī fī tafsīr al-Qur'ān al-ʿaẓīm wa'l-sabʿ al-mathānī*, ed. Māhir Ḥabbūsh et al., 30 vols., Beirut: Mu'assasat al-Risāla, 2010.

ʿAlwāni, Ṭāhā Jābir al-, *al-Imām Fakhr al-Dīn al-Rāzī wa-muṣannafātuhu*, Cairo: Dār al-Salām, 2010.

Ashqar, ʿUmar Sulaymān al-, *al-Madkhal ilā al-sharīʿa wa'l-fiqh al-Islāmī*, Amman: Dār al-Nafā'is, 2005.

ʿAṭṭār, Farīd al-Dīn, *Tadhkirat al-awliyā'*, trans. Paul Losensky as *Farid ad-Din 'Attar's Memorial of God's Friends*, New York: Paulist Press, 2009.

Aʿẓamī, Muḥammad Muṣṭafā al-, *The History of the Qur'ānic Text*, Leicester: UK Islamic Academy, 2003.

Baʿbūla, Sayyid, *al-Rawḥ wa'l-rayḥān fī kayfiyyat al-waqf wa'l-ibtidā fī al-Qur'ān*, n.p., 2009.

Bāqillānī, Abū Bakr Muḥammad al-, *al-Intiṣār li'l-Qur'ān*, ed. ʿUmar Ḥasan al-Qiyyām, 2 vols., Beirut: Mu'assasat al-Risāla, 2004.

Brown, Jonathan A. C., *Hadith: Muhammad's Legacy in the Medieval and Modern World*, 2nd ed., London: Oneworld Academic, 2018.

Calverley, Edwin & James Pollock, eds., *Nature, Man and God in Medieval Islam* (Bayḍāwī's *Tawāliʿ* with Iṣfahānī's *Matāliʿ*), 2 vols., Leiden: Brill, 2002.

Ceylan, Yasin, 'Theology and *Tafsīr* in the Major Works of Fakhr al-Dīn al-Rāzī', PhD thesis, University of Edinburgh, 1980.

Dhahabī, Muḥammad Ḥusayn al-, *al-Tafsīr wa'l-mufassirūn*, 3 vols., Cairo: Dār al-Ḥadīth 2005.

Drāz, Muḥammad ʿAbd Allāh, *al-Naba' al-ʿaẓīm*, trans. Adil Salahi as *The Qur'an: An Eternal Challenge*, Leicester: Islamic Foundation, 2001.

Dutton, Yasin, 'Orality, Literary and the "Seven *Aḥruf*" *Ḥadīth*', *Journal of Islamic Studies*, vol. xxiii, no. 1, 2012, pp. 1–49.

Farāhī, Ḥamīd al-Dīn al-, *Taʿlīqāt fī tafsīr al-Qur'ān al-karīm*, ed. ʿUbayd Allāh al-Farāhī, 2 vols., Azamgarh: al-Dā'ira al-Ḥamīdiyya, 2010.

Galen, *Peri Chreias Morion*, trans. M. T. May as *Galen on the Usefulness of the Parts of the Body*, 2 vols., Ithaca: Cornell University Press, 1968.

Ghazālī, Abū Ḥāmid Muḥammad al-, *Iḥyā' ʿulūm al-dīn*, Books xxii and xxiii, trans. T. J. Winter as *Al-Ghazālī on Disciplining the Soul*, Cambridge: Islamic Texts Society, 2001.

——, *al-Maqṣad al-asnā fī sharḥ maʿānī asmā' Allāh al-ḥusnā*, Cairo: Dār al-Salām, 2008. And trans. David Burrell & Nazih Daher as *The Ninety-Nine Beautiful Names of God*, Cambridge: Islamic Texts Society, 1992.

——, *Mishkāt al-anwār*, ed. Abū al-ʿAlā ʿAfīfī, Cairo: al-Dār al-Qawmiyya, 1964. And trans. W. H. T. Gairdner as *Al-Ghazzālī's Mishkāt al-anwār*, London: Royal Asiatic Society, 1924.

——, *Tahāfut al-falāsifa*, trans. Michael E. Marmura as *The Incoherence of the Philosophers*, Provo: Brigham Young University Press, 2000.

Groff, Peter S., *Islamic Philosophy A–Z*, Edinburgh: Edinburgh University Press, 2007.

Ḥabash, Muḥammad, *al-Qirā'āt al-mutawātira wa-atharuhā fī al-rasm al-Qur'ānī wa'l-aḥkām al-sharʿiyya*, Beirut: Dār al-Fikr, 1999.

Ḥājī Khalīfa, Muṣṭafā b. ʿAbd Allāh, *Kashf al- ẓunūn ʿan asāmī al-kutub wa'l-funūn*, ed. Muḥammad Yāltaqāyā, 2 vols., Beirut: Dār Iḥyā' al-Turāth al-ʿArabī, 1941.

Ḥamad, Ghānim Qadūrī al-, *Abḥāth jadīda fī ʿilm al-aṣwāt wa'l-tajwīd*, Amman: Dār ʿAmmār, 2011.

Hamadhānī, ʿAbd al-Jabbār b. Ahmad al-, *Mutashābih al-Qur'ān*, ed. ʿAdnān Zarzūr, 2 vols., Cairo: Maktabat Dār al-Turāth, 1969.

Ḥasnāwī, Muḥammad al-, *al-Fāṣila fī al-Qur'ān*, Amman: Dār ʿAmmār, 2000.

Ḥusayn, ʿAbd al-Qādir al-, *Maʿāyīr al-qabūl wa'l-radd li-tafsīr al-naṣṣ al-Qur'ānī*, Damascus: Dār al-Ghawthānī, 2008.

Ibn ʿĀshūr, Muḥammad al-Fāḍil, *al-Tafsīr wa-rijāluhu*, Cairo: Majmaʿ al-Buḥūth al-Islāmiyya, 1997.

Ibn ʿĀshūr, Muḥammad al-Ṭāhir, *Tafsīr al-taḥrīr wa'l-tanwīr*, 30 vols., Tunis: Dār Saḥnūn, n.d.

Ibn Ḥajar al-ʿAsqalānī, *Fatḥ al-Bārī sharḥ Ṣaḥīḥ al-Bukhārī*, 15 vols., Cairo: Dār al-Ghad al-Jadīd, 2012.

Ibn Jinnī, ʿUthmān, *al-Khaṣāʾiṣ*, ed. Muḥammad ʿAlī al-Najjār, 3 vols., Cairo: al-Maktaba al-ʿIlmiyya, 1952.

Ibn Kathīr, Ismāʿīl, *Tafsīr al-Qurʾān al-ʿaẓīm*, 7 vols., Cairo: Dār al-Āthār, 2009.

Ibn Rushd, Muḥammad b. Aḥmad, *Bidāyat al-mujtahid*, trans. Imran Nyazee as *The Distinguished Jurist's Primer*, 2 vols., Reading: Garnet, 2004.

Ibn Sīdah al-Mursī, *al-Muḥkam wa'l-muḥīṭ al-aʿẓam*, ed. ʿAbd al-Ḥamīd Hindāwī, Beirut: Dār al-Kutub al-ʿIlmiyya, 2000.

Ibn Sīnā, *al-Qānūn fī al-ṭibb* Book 1, trans. O. Cameron Gruner as *The Canon of Medicine of Avicenna*, New York: AMS Press, 1973.

Ibn Taymiyya, Aḥmad b. ʿAbd al-Ḥalīm, *Darʾ taʿāruḍ al-naql wa'l-ʿaql,* ed. al-Sayyid al-Sayyid & Sayyid Ṣādiq, 6 vols., Cairo: Dār al-Ḥadīth, 2006.

Ibrahim, Bilal, 'Freeing Philosophy from Metaphysics: Fakhr al-Dīn al-Rāzī's Philosophical Approach to the Study of Natural Phenomena', PhD thesis, McGill University, 2013.

Imām, Aḥmad ʿAlī al-, *Variant Readings of the Qur'an*, Herndon, VA: IIIT, 1998.

Jabal, Muḥammad Ḥasan, *ʿIlm al-ishtiqāq naẓariyyan wa-taṭbīqan*, Cairo: Maktabat al-Ādāb, 2012.

Jaffer, Tariq, *Rāzī: Master of Qurʾānic Interpretation and Theological Reasoning*, New York: Oxford University Press, 2015.

Jurjānī, al-Sharīf al-, *al-Taʿrīfāt*, ed. Muḥammad al-Minshāwī, Cairo: Dār al-Faḍīla, 2004.

Juwaynī, ʿAbd al-Malik b. Muḥammad al-, *Kitāb al-irshād ilā qawāṭiʿ al-adilla fī uṣūl al-iʿtiqād*, trans. Paul E. Walker as *A Guide to Conclusive Proofs for the Principles of Belief*, Reading: Garnet, 2000.

Kafrawi, Shalahudin, 'Fakhr al-Dīn al-Rāzī's Methodology in Interpreting the Qurʾān', PhD thesis, McGill University, 1998.

Kāsānī, Abū Bakr b. Masʿūd al-, *Badāʾiʿ al-ṣanāʾiʿ fī tartīb al-sharāʾiʿ*, ed. Muḥammad Tāmir, 10 vols., Cairo: Dār al-Ḥadīth, 2005.

Khaṭīb, ʿAbd al-Laṭīf al-, *Muʿjam al-qirāʾāt*, 10 vols., Damascus: Dār Saʿd al-Dīn, 2009.

Kohlberg, Etan & Mohammad Ali Amir-Moezzi, eds., *Revelation and Falsification: The Kitāb al-qirāʾāt of Aḥmad b. Muḥammad al-Sayyārī*, Leiden: Brill, 2009.

Lagarde, Michel, *Index du Grand Commentaire de Fakhr al-dîn al-Rāzī*, Leiden: Brill, 1996.

Mas'ūl, ʿAbd al-ʿAlī al-, *Muʿjam muṣṭalaḥāt ʿilm al-qirāʾāt al-Qurʾāniyya*, Cairo: Dār al-Salām, 2007.

Muʿallimī, ʿAbd al-Raḥmān al-, *al-Majmūʿ*, ed. Mājid al-Ziyadī, Mecca: al-Maktaba al-Makkiyya, 1996.

Nasr, Seyyed H., Dagli, C. et al., eds., *The Study Quran*, New York: HarperOne, 2015.

Nasser, Shady Hekmat, *The Transmission of the Variant Readings of the Qurʾān: The Problem of Tawātur and the Emergence of Shawādhdh*, Leiden: Brill, 2012.

Nawawī, Yaḥyā b. Sharaf al-, *al-Minhāj sharḥ Ṣaḥīḥ Muslim b. al-Ḥajjāj*, ed. Khalīl b. Ma'mūn Shīḥā, 10 vols., Beirut: Dār al-Maʿrifa, 2012.

Nyazee, Imran, *Islamic Jurisprudence*, Petaling Jaya: The Other Press, 2003.

Qaraḍāwī, Yūsuf al-, *Fuṣūl fī al-ʿaqīda bayna al-salaf wa'l-khalaf*, Cairo: Maktabat Wahba, 2005.

——, *Kayfa nataʿāmal maʿ al-Qurʾān*, Cairo: Dār al-Shurūq, 2000.

Rāzī, Muḥammad b. ʿUmar al-, *Lawāmiʿ al-bayyināt sharḥ asmāʾ Allāh al-ḥusnā wa'l-ṣifāt*, ed. Muḥammad Badr al-Dīn Abū Firās, Cairo: Maktabat al-Khānjī, 1905.

——, *al-Maḥṣūl fī ʿilm uṣūl al-fiqh*, ed. Ṭāhā al-ʿAlwānī, 6 vols., Beirut: Mu'assasat al-Risāla, 1992.

——, *al-Tafsīr al-kabīr* (*Mafātīḥ al-ghayb*), ed. Sayyid ʿImrān, 16 vols., Cairo: Dār al-Ḥadīth, 2012. Also: ed. Naṣr al-Hūrīnī, 6 vols., Būlāq: al-Maṭbaʿa al-Amīriyya, 1862. Also: digitised manuscript (Book III only) at the Hathi Trust Digital Library: *Tafsīr Sūrat al-Fātiḥah nuqila min Tafsīr al-kabīr* (copied in 1823 by Muḥammad ʿAlī). Also: translated by Alphousseyni Cissé (Vol. I only) as *Le Commentaire de Faẖr d-Din r-Rāzī sur la Fātiha*, Paris: L'Harmattan, 2017.

Riḍā, Muḥammad Rashīd, *Tafsīr al-manār* (*Tafsīr al-Qurʾān al-ḥakīm*), ed. Fu'ād ʿAbd al-Ghaffār, 12 vols., Cairo: al-Maktaba al-Tawfīqiyya, n.d.

Riddell, Peter G. & Tony Street, eds., *Islam: Essays on Scripture, Thought and Society: A Festschrift in Honour of Anthony H. Johns*, Leiden: Brill, 1997.

Rufayda, Ibrāhīm, *al-Naḥw wa-kutub al-tafsīr*, 2 vols., Misrata: al-Dār al-Jamāhīriyya, 1990.

Saeh, Ahmad Bassam, *The Miraculous Language of the Qur'an*, trans. Nancy Roberts, London: International Institute of Islamic Thought, 2015.

Sakhāwī, ʿAlī b. Muḥammad al-, *Jamāl al-qurrāʾ*, ed. Marwān al-ʿAṭiyya & Muḥsin Kharāba, Damascus: Dār al-Ma'mūn, 1997.

Ṣaqr, ʿAbbās & Aḥmad ʿAbd al-Jawwād, eds., *Jāmiʿ al-aḥādīth* (*al-Jāmiʿ al-ṣaghīr*, *Zawāʾid* and *al-Jāmiʿ al-kabīr* by Suyūṭī), 21 vols., Beirut: Dār al-Fikr, 1994.

Schimmel, Annemarie, *The Mystical Dimensions of Islam*, Chapel Hill: University of North Carolina Press, 1975.

Schmidtke, Sabine, ed., *The Oxford Handbook of Islamic Theology*, New York: Oxford University Press, 2016.

Setia, Adi, 'Fakhr Al-Din Al-Razi on Physics and the Nature of the Physical World: A Preliminary Survey', *Islam & Science*, vol. 11, no. 2, 2004, pp. 161–180.

Shāfiʿī, Ḥasan Maḥmūd al-, *al-Madkhal ilā dirāsat ʿilm al-kalām*, Cairo: Maktabat Wahba, 1991.

Shahran, Mohd. Farid Mohd., *Fakhr al-Dīn al-Rāzī on Divine Transcendence and Anthropomorphism*, Putrajaya, Malaysia: Islamic and Strategic Studies Institute (ISSI), 2017.

Shihāb al-Dīn al-Khafājī, Aḥmad b. Muḥammad, *ʿInāyat al-qāḍī wa-kifāyat al-rāḍī ʿalā Tafsīr al-Bayḍāwī* (*Ḥāshiyat al-Shihāb*), 8 vols., Beirut: Dār Ṣādir, n.d.

Shihadeh, Ayman, *The Teleological Ethics of Fakhr al-Dīn al-Rāzī*, Leiden: Brill, 2006.

Shurunbulālī, Ḥasan al- & Aḥmad al-Ṭaḥṭāwī, *Ḥāshiyat al-Ṭaḥṭāwī ʿalā Marāqī al-falāḥ*, ed. Muḥammad al-Khālidī, Beirut: Dār al-Kutub al-ʿIlmiyya, 2009.

Sulaymān, Rashā Ṭāriq Shafīq, *al-Riwāyāt al-wārida fī tafsīr Sūrat al-Fātiḥa min Tafsīr al-Rāzī*, Master's thesis, An-Najah National University (Nablus), 2016.

Ṭabarī, Muḥammad b. Jarīr al-, *Jāmiʿ al-bayān ʿan ta'wīl āy al-Qur'ān*, ed. Maḥmūd Shākir & Aḥmad Shākir, 16 vols. (incomplete edition), Cairo: Dār al-Maʿārif, 1961. And trans. Scott Lucas as *Selections from The Comprehensive Exposition of the Interpretation of the Verses of the Qur'ān*, 2 vols., Cambridge: Islamic Texts Society, 2017.

Thaʿlabī, Aḥmad al-, *al-Kashf wa'l-bayān* (*Tafsīr al-Thaʿlabī*), ed. Abū Muḥammad b. ʿĀshūr, 10 vols., Beirut: Dār Iḥyā' al-Turāth al-ʿArabī, 2002.

ʿUḍayma, Muḥammad ʿAbd al-Khāliq, *Dirāsāt li-uslūb al-Qur'ān*, 11 vols., Cairo: Dār al-Ḥadith, 2004.

ʿUmar, Aḥmad & Makram, ʿAbd al-ʿĀl, *Muʿjam al-qirā'āt*, 6 vols., Riyadh: ʿĀlam al-Kutub, 1997.

Versteegh, Kees, 'The linguistic introduction to Rāzī's *Tafsīr*', in Petr Zemánek, ed., *Studies in Near Eastern Languages and Literatures: Memorial Volume of Karel Petráček*, Prague: Academy of Sciences of the Czech Republic, 1996, pp. 589–603.

Wahba, Murād, *al-Muʿjam al-falsafī*, Cairo: Dār Qubā', 1998.

Wāṣil, Muḥammad Aḥmad, *Aḥkām al-tarjama fī al-fiqh al-Islāmī*, Riyadh: Dār Ṭayba, 2012.

Wisnovsky, Robert, 'One Aspect of the Akbarian Turn in Shīʿī Theology', in Ayman Shihadeh, ed., *Sufism and Theology*, Edinburgh: Edinburgh University Press, 2007, pp. 49–62.

Wolfson, H. A., 'The Terms *Taṣawwur* and *Taṣdīq* in Arabic Philosophy and their Greek, Latin and Hebrew Equivalents', *The Muslim World*, vol. XXXIII, 1943, pp. 1–15.
Zadeh, Travis, *The Vernacular Qur'an: Translation and the Rise of Persian Exegesis*, Oxford: Oxford University Press, 2012.
Zamakhsharī, Maḥmūd b. ʿUmar al-, *al-Kashshāf ʿan ḥaqā'iq al-tanzīl wa-ʿuyūn al-ghawāmiḍ fī wujūh al-ta'wīl*, 1 vol., Beirut: Dār Maʿrifa, 2009.
Zarkān, Muḥammad Ṣāliḥ al-, *Fakhr al-Dīn al-Rāzī wa-ārā'uhu al-kalāmiyya wa'l-falsafiyya*, Beirut: Dār al-Fikr, 1963.

INDEX

ᶜAbbād b. Sulaymān, 30
ᶜAbd Allāh b. Abī Awfā, 332
ᶜAbd Allāh b. ᶜAmr b. al-ᶜĀṣ, 114, 192, 252
ᶜAbd al-Raḥmān b. ᶜAwf, 298
ablution, 90, 296, 329–30; *Basmala* and, 265, 266, 328; dry ablution/*tayammum*, 150
Abraham, 84, 99, 100–101, 114, 127, 188, 222, 276, 294, 336, 398, 417, 426, 431, 433–4, 441; fire of Nimrod, 383, 396–7
Abū al-ᶜAtāhiya, 8
Abū Bakr b. Durayd, 273–4
Abū Bakr al-Qaffāl, 273
Abū Bakr al-Ṣiddīq, 26, 115, 236–7, 261, 297, 322–3, 324, 330, 340, 430; leadership of, 405–406; see also Rightly-Guided Caliphs
Abū al-Dardā', 295
Abū Dāwūd al-Sijistānī, 94, 95, 316
Abū Dharr al-Ghifārī, 188, 190
Abū Ḥanīfa, 23–4, 25, 93–4, 144, 150–2, 296–8, 300, 301, 303, 304–305, 310–11, 317, 320, 325, 327–8, 329, 331, 333, 337, 339, 341, 343, 372, 375, 390
Abū Hurayra, 92, 187–8, 189, 190, 195–6, 265, 300, 303–304, 307, 308–309, 314–15, 316, 319, 322, 324, 325, 327, 331, 338
Abū al-Najm, al-ᶜIjlī, 26
Abū al-Qāsim b. Ḥabīb, 273
Abū Qilāba, 324
Abū al-Sā'ib, 122, 338
Abū Saᶜīd b. Abī al-Khayr al-Mīhanī, 158
Abū Saᶜīd al-Khudrī, 93, 122, 191, 275, 278, 341
Abū Salama b. ᶜAbd al-Raḥmān b. ᶜAwf, 342
Abū Ṣāliḥ, 189, 277
Abū Sulaymān al-Khaṭṭābī, 94
Abū ᶜUbayd al-Qāsim b. Sallām, 160
Abū Umāma al-Bāhilī, 193
Abū ᶜUthmān al-Nahdī, 303
Abū Yūsuf, 93–4, 151, 304, 328, 329
accusative case, see *naṣb*
Adam, 30–1, 124, 126, 127, 265, 352, 355, 415, 423, 426; 'All praise is for God', 352, 355, 442; 'God created Adam upon his image', 196–7; Q.II.31: 'He taught Adam the names of all things', 30, 219–20; Moses and, 190; Satan and, 141, 142
adjective, 27, 73, 74, 76–7, 143, 244, 245, 318
ᶜĀ'isha b. Abī Bakr, 184, 187, 189, 190, 196, 315, 317, 341–2, 370
al-Akhfash al-Awsaṭ, 76, 77, 79, 170
ākhira, see Hereafter
akhlāq, see character
al-Akhṭal, 26

al-ᶜAlā' b. ᶜAbd al-Raḥmān, 316, 338
ᶜ*alam*, see proper noun
ᶜAlī b. Abī Ṭālib, 188, 195, 277, 308, 321, 322, 323, 324, 325, 326, 340, 393, 441; see also Rightly-Guided Caliphs
'All praise is for God', 4–5, 159, 161, 271, 272, 281, 293, 319, 320, 401–402, 414, 438; action of prayer: bowing/*rukū*ᶜ, 427; *Allāh*, annexation in, 450; angels, Prophets, saints and scholars, 352; Arabic language, linguistic/grammatical issues, 345–9, 355–6, 450; Ashᶜarīs on, 357; beginning and concluding all actions with, 355; connected with the past and the future, 353–4; definite article *al-*, 348–9; engaging in praise of God is bad manners, 360; exegesis of, 345–60; as first verse of the Qur'ān, 442; glorification and praise, 353; 'Glory be to God', 384–5, 447; God as Benefactor, 349–51, 353, 355, 359, 360; God praising Himself, 356, 364; *ḥadīth*, 345, 351–2, 441; *ḥamd/madḥ* distinction, 345–6; *ḥamd/shukr* distinction, 346; *al-ḥamdu li'Llāh*, 346; *al-ḥamdu li'Llāh* consists of eight letters, 348; 'I praise God'/*aḥmadu Allāha*, 347; imperative verb in, 355–6; as infinite praise, 352; Intellect and, 441, 442; Jabrīs on, 356, 357–8; *lām* in *al-ḥamdu li'Llāh*, 348; Muᶜtazilīs on, 356–8; none is deserving of praise but God, 349–50, 356; obligation to engage in praise, 359; as the opening of gratitude and its conclusion, 441; praise/*ḥamd*, 4, 272, 276, 285, 286, 289, 350–1, 357, 358–9, 387, 423, 442; as praise for all favours emanated from God, 353; as proof of the Creator's existence, 417–18; proper use and appropriate context, 354–5; revelation of, 277; servant's incapability of truly praising and thanking God, 350, 351; superiority of the expression, 347; *sūra*s which open with 'All praise is for God', 282–4, 447; *Sūrat al-Baqara* and, 414; thanksgiving, 351, 354, 358
Allāh, 28, 38, 108, 142, 172–3, 243–54, 260, 264, 364; Arabic language, linguistic/grammatical issues, 163, 164, 167, 244, 245–54, 450; an Arabic word, 253; assimilated *lām*s, 163, 253; *Basmala* and,108, 159, 450; denoting all Divine Attributes, 223, 254; denoting God's Essence/*Dhāt*, 181, 422, 448; five Divine Names in the *Fātiḥa*, 379, 381, 416, 444–8, 449–50; *iḍāfa*/annexation, 450; *Istiᶜādha*, 142; mystical implications of the word, 167–8; pronunciation of the word, 163, 164, 167, 244; as proper Name for the Almighty, 10, 223, 243–5, 253–4, 422–3; Q.XVII.110: 'Say: Call upon *Allāh*, or call upon

al-Raḥmān…', 314, 449; shahāda/ testimony of faith, 254; three Divine Names in the Basmala, 416, 448–9; unique features of, 254; writing of the word, 167; see also Allāh, possible derivations; Divine Names
Allāh, possible derivations, 245–54; aliha, 248–9; aliha al-faṣīl, 250–1; aliha/ya'lahu, 251–2; alihta ilā fulān, 247–8; ilāh, 245–7, 253, 254, 381; lāh, 253; lāha, 248; lāha/yalūhu, 249–50; walah, 248; see also Allāh
'Allāhu akbar'/takbīr ('God is greater'), 89, 93, 94, 148–9, 164, 224, 267, 301, 315, 321, 343, 351, 384, 385, 388, 439, 431, 440, 447, 448; al-Akbar, 224; prayer and, 436–7, 438, 439
āmīn (amen), 89
ʿĀmir al-Shaʿbī, 342
ʿAmr b. Dīnār, 327
ʿAmr b. Shuʿayb, 114
ʿAmr b. Shuraḥbīl, 277
ʿAmra al-Farghāniyya, 266
analogy (qiyās), 3, 62, 126, 217, 238, 303, 325
Anas b. Mālik, 113, 191, 193, 194, 196, 265, 312, 317, 322–5
'And from You we seek help', 272, 287, 291, 294, 385, 393, 419, 425, 450; exegesis of, 394–7; helplessness without God's protection and help, 394–5; Jabrīs, 395; plural, 402; Q.vii.128: 'Seek help from God', 103, 395; Qadarīs, 395; station of ṭarīqa/path, 290–1, 438; Sūrat al-Baqara and, 414; see also 'You we worship…'
angel, 6, 99, 109, 113, 115–16, 121, 125, 195, 220, 426, 430, 434, 436, 448; 'All praise is for God', 352; angelic Messenger, 413; angels brought near to God, 115–16; angels of the Footstool, 116; Angels of Mercy, 266; Angels of Torment, 266; ascension of elite angels, 431, 432; authority of, 374, 375; bearers of the Throne, 116, 429, 436; duties of, 8; Ezekiel, 439; guardian angels, 265; help from, 139; human angelic-rational essence/ jawhar malakī ʿaqlī, 444, 445; infallibility of, 408; intercession by, 375; Istiʿādha and, 113, 154; making the angels into 'Messengers', 284; nature of, 115, 126; thoughts and, 132; worship, 384, 388; see also Gabriel
anger (ghaḍab), 111–12, 128, 238, 408, 415; God's anger, 238, 409–10
animal, 4, 361, 364, 383, 436; slaughter of, 267, 328
annexation, see iḍāfa
al-Anṣārī, Abū al-Qāsim Salmān, 158
anthropomorphism (tashbīh), 223, 224, 226, 287, 399; refuting anthropomorphism, 440–1
Anushirwan (Khosrau I), 377
Arabic language, linguistic/ grammatical issues, 12, 95; 'All praise is for God', 345–9, 355–6, 450; Allāh, 163, 164, 167, 244, 245–54, 450; Fātiḥa,

299, 317–18; 'Guide us upon the straight path', 400, 401–402; *ilṣāq*/attachment, 3, 10, 50, 147, 149; linguistic enquiries, 10–11, 13; 'Master of the Day of Judgment', 373, 379; *min*, 152–3; reciting the Qur'ān in Arabic or in translation, 329–36; 'The path of those on whom You have bestowed favour', 404; 'You we worship...', 158, 385, 386–9, 394; see also *bā'*; *Basmala*: linguistic/grammatical issues; definite article *al-*; derivation; *iḍāfa*; inflection; *Istiʿādha*: linguistic/grammatical issues; *kalām*; *kalima*; *lafẓ*; letter; *lugha*; noun; particle; *qawl*; verb; vowel

ʿarsh, see Throne

al-Aṣamm, 295, 296, 340

asceticism (*zuhd*), 435, 441

Ashʿarīs, 36, 45, 133, 171, 211, 221–2, 404, 405, 409; *Ahl al-Sunna wa'l-Jamāʿa*, 105, 106, 107

ʿAṭā' b. Abī Rabāḥ, 90–1

al-Awzāʿī, ʿAbd al-Raḥmān b. ʿAmr, 93, 304

ʿazā'im, see incantations

bā', 3, 4, 41, 149–50; attachment/*ilṣāq*, 3, 10, 50, 147, 149; *Basmala*/*bi'smi 'Llāh*, 3, 152, 157, 166, 262, 310, 426; *Istiʿādha*, 10, 147–9; juristic issues concerning the *bā'* of attachment, 150–2; knowledge and, 152; as preposition, 157; usages of, 149, 152; writing, 166; see also *Basmala*; *Istiʿādha*

al-Bāqillānī, Abū Bakr, 124, 305

al-Barā' b. ʿĀzib, 95

Basmala, 3–4, 437–8; ablution and, 265, 266, 328; action of prayer: standing/*qiyām*, 426; *Allāh*, 108, 159, 450; animal slaughtering and, 267, 328; as beginning of the *sūras*, 319–20, 326–7, 328; at the beginning of things, 426; *bi'smi'Llāh*, 3, 160, 166, 314; as the greatest verse in the Qur'ān, 311–12; *ḥadīth* on, 264–5, 266, 277, 307–309, 311, 314–17, 320, 322–5; 'I begin in the Name of God', 259–60; 'In the Name of God', 3n1, 4, 109, 160, 172, 259; 'My servant has glorified Me', 308–309; 'My servant has remembered Me', 420, 422; purity/purification, 306, 314, 328; Q.1.1: 'In the Name of God', 166, 172, 414; remembrance of God, 414, 422; revelation of, 277; *ṣalāh*, 267; spiritual allusions of, 259–67; *Sūrat al-Baqara* and, 414; *tasmiya*, 266, 305–28 *passim*, 379, 416, 426; three Divine Names in, 416, 448–9; as a verse of the *Fātiḥa*, 304, 307–16, 320; as a verse of the Qur'ān, 304–17, 319, 326–7; written, 260, 264, 265, 267, 312–13, 314, 319; see also the entries below for *Basmala*; *al-Raḥīm*; *al-Raḥmān*

Basmala: linguistic/grammatical issues, 157–60, 322; *alif* of *ism*:

removed in *bi'smi 'Llāh*, 166; *Allāh*, pronunciation of, 163, 164, 167; *Allāh*, writing of, 167; *bā'*, 3, 152, 157, 166, 262, 310, 426; *iḍāfa*/annexation, 159, 450; is the verb worthier of being implied, or is the noun?, 157–9; *ism*/Name, 160; *lām*, assimilation of, 164–5; *lām*, doubling in the Name *Allāh*, 163; *lām*, velarised 162–3; *al-Raḥīm*/the Merciful, 165; *al-Raḥmān*/the Compassionate, 165; *al-Raḥmān*, pronunciation of, 164–5; writing, 166–8, 314; see also name

Basmala, recitation: audible/inaudible recitation, 305, 320–6, 327; recitation before any action, 265, 329; recitation before the *Fātiḥa*, 311, 322–4, 327–8; stopping points, 161; *Sunna*, 311, 320, 322, 327, 328

Baṣran grammarians, 80–1, 86, 147, 169–70, 253

al-Baṣrī, Abū ʿAmr b. al-ʿAlā', 68

al-Bayhaqī, Aḥmad b. Husayn, 93, 322, 340

Bedouin, 390, 400; *ḥadīth* of the Bedouin, 91, 301, 330, 338, 341

belief (*īmān*), 2, 38, 199, 287; creed, 413; false beliefs, 135; see also faith

bidʿa, see innovation

Bilāl b. Rabāḥ, 334

Bilqīs, 262, 312–13

body (human body), 4, 256, 363, 418, 428; bodily ascension within the prayer, 432; Divine Names and, 444, 445; perfect wisdom in the creation of, 4, 239; purpose of, 35, 286; resemblance to Hell and nineteen types of Tormentors, 102–103; see also medicine/health-related issues; senses

breath, 7, 35, 79, 126, 255, 256, 265; Satan and, 89; voice/sound and, 11, 21, 34, 41, 68, 70

al-Bukhārī, Muḥammad b. Ismāʿīl, 322

Burayda b. al-Ḥuṣayb, 307

character (*akhlāq*), 8, 128, 241, 292, 397–8, 416, 430

Christianity/Christians, 44, 285, 407; doctrine of Trinity, 207

commands, 8, 33, 38, 45, 221, 390, 437; see also prohibitions

Companions, 95, 185, 298, 301, 310, 312, 330, 336, 340, 342, 343, 390, 401

convention (*iṣṭilāḥ*), 35, 159, 236; meaning by convention, 27, 28, 29, 31, 32, 35–6, 48, 159

cosmology, 360–1; bodies in the universe, 5, 8–9; celestial spheres, 5, 119, 360, 364, 381; heavenly bodies, 132, 360, 364, 384; lofty bodies, 360–1, 383–4; micro- and macro-world, 293, 355; moon, 5, 364; planets, 119, 290; stars, 5, 364; sun, 5, 364; world of spirits and world of bodies, 109, 113; see also Creation

Creation, 4–5, 250, 251; bearing testament to God, 8, 9; Divine

Names and, 241; as God's manifestation, 448; *Isti*ʿ*ādha*, ascending from creation to Creator, 137; pondering upon God's Creation, 423; see also cosmology
creation (process), 4, 26, 30, 80, 189, 283, 284, 380–1; five Divine Names in the *Fātiḥa* and five stages of creation, 449–50; 'God created Adam upon his image', 196–7; man's creation as a favour, 404, 418; place/*makān* and time/*zamān* as greatest and most tremendous of all creations, 434; praise and, 423; Q.XIX.9: 'I did indeed create you before, when you had been nothing', 380, 381; stages of man's creation, 363, 428
the Creator, 133, 159, 184, 192, 200, 213–14, 229, 235, 257, 285, 290, 313, 361, 379, 380, 406; *al-Fāṭir*, 284; *al-Khāliq*, 284; *al-Mūjid*, 212, 213, 251; see also creation; Divine Names

al-Dabūsī, Abū Zayd, 329
al-Ḍaḥḥāk b. Muzāḥim, 93
al-Dāraquṭnī, ʿAlī b. ʿUmar, 339
David, 351
Day of Judgment, 7, 195, 252, 262, 267, 443; *ḥadīth* on, 252; judgment, 7, 379; scale, 252, 267, 377; standing before God, 7, 329, 432; weigh of deeds, 7, 252, 264, 372; see also 'Master of the Day of Judgment'
definite article *al*-, 29, 50, 75, 143, 163, 164, 170, 253, 297; 'All praise is for God', 348–9
derivation (*ishtiqāq*), 17, 27, 38, 202, 253; major/minor derivation, 17, 18, 21; Name/*ism*, 169–70, 174; Satan, 98–9, 144; see also *Allāh*, possible derivations
devil, 143, 361, 430; denying the existence of, 116–20, 130; free will and, 127; *ḥadīth* on, 122–4, 127; nature of, 115, 116, 118–20, 125, 126, 127, 133–4; powers, 133–4; Prophets and, 117–18, 122, 126; Qur'ān on, 122; scholars and, 126, 127; sin and, 119, 127; thoughts and, 132, 133; whispering, 118; see also evil; jinn; Satan
Dhāt, see God's Essence
dhikr, see remembrance of God
disbelief/unbelief (*kufr*), 36, 38, 97, 101, 135, 207, 254, 266, 387; God's favours upon the unbelievers, 404–405; unbelief as cause for destruction, 376; unbelievers/*kuffār*, 407, 409
disobedience, 369, 376
Divine Attributes, 2, 3, 440, 448; Attributes eliminating matters contrary to knowledge, 215; Attributes eliminating matters contrary to power and ability, 216; beneficence/*ikrām*, 177, 180, 229, 230; categories of relative Attributes, 212; denial of, 205–208; deterrent effect of, 142; Divine Essence as cause of Divine Attributes, 178; Divinity/*ilāhiyya*, 435;

'emotional' attributes, 237–8, 408–409; everlasting/*bāqī*, 199–200, 203, 223; evidences of the affirmers of Attributes, 208; greatness/*ʿaẓama*, 224, 225, 435, 440; greatness/*kibriyā'*, 224, 225, 435, 439, 440; knowledge of, 140; majesty/*jalāl*, 177, 180, 185, 229, 230, 233, 435, 440; oneness/*waḥda*, 216; perfection/*kamāl*, 225–6, 230, 231, 247, 353; power and ability/*qudra*, 109, 113, 208, 218–19, 235, 258, 285, 289; pre-eternality/*azal*, 44, 45, 157, 199–200, 201, 203, 206–207, 211, 223, 410; Qur'ān, 200, 237–8; self-subsistent/*qayyūm*, 188; self-sufficiency/*istighnā'*, 137, 216, 231, 353; self-veiling, 250; transcendence, 45, 173, 215, 224, 225–6, 248, 284–5, 440

Divine Names, 2, 3, 93, 259; 4,000 Names, 239; All-Powerful Sovereign, 140, 219; Arabic language, linguistic/grammatical issues, 10, 185–6, 201, 202, 203–204; *al-Arbaʿīn*, 242; Beautiful Names, 123, 172, 173, 185, 237, 239, 240, 440, 449; the Benefactor, 251, 257, 349–51, 353, 355, 359, 360, 362, 386, 427; delimited by revelation or convention, 236–7; *Dhū al-Jalāl wa'l-Ikrām*/the Possessor of Majesty and Beneficence, 180; distinction between name and attribute, 236, 237; five Divine Names denoting mercy, 443; 'God's Greatest Name', 180–1; *ḥadīth* on, 183, 185, 187–8, 189–91, 192, 193–7, 199, 203, 224, 236, 437; *al-Ḥayy al-Qayyūm*/the Living, the Self-subsistent Sustainer, 180–1, 210; infinite number of, 212, 217, 239–40; *al-Jāʿil*/the Maker, 284; *Khudāy*/'He came by Himself '—Persian word, 173, 203; *al-Mujīr*/the Protector, 251; *al-Mu'min*/the Protector, 376; *al-Munʿim*/the Granter of favours, 251; *al-Muṭʿim*/the One Who feeds, 251; Name denoting God's Essence/*Dhāt*, 176–81, 226; name denoting its referent, 181–2; Ninety-Nine Divine Names, 172, 242; praise in, 185, 187, 210; Q.vii.180: 'The most Beautiful Names belong to God…', 172, 173, 185, 237; Q.lv.78: 'Blessed be the Name of your Lord', 172, 173, 435; Qur'ān and, 3, 236–7; *al-Samīʿ*/the Hearing, 92, 93, 99, 111, 184, 222, 263; seeking help through the Divine Name, 158; *Sunna* and, 3; see also the entries below for Divine Names; *Allāh*; the Creator; *Fātiḥa*, five Divine Names in; *al-Mālik*/*al-Malik*; name; pronominal Divine Names; *al-Rabb*; *al-Raḥīm*; *al-Raḥmān*

Divine Names denoting actual Attributes, 183–210; actual Attributes other than existence and its modalities, 205–210; *al-Abadī*, 202; *al-Azalī*/Pre-eternal, 201; *al-Bāqī*, 202; *al-Dā'im*, 203; *al-Dhāt/Essence*, 187–9; *al-Ḥaqq*/Reality, 199; *al-Ḥayy*/the Living, 180–1, 209–10; *al-Inniyya*/Being, 198; *al-Jawhar*/Substance, 197–8; *al-Jism*/Body, 198; *al-Kā'in*/ Entity, 203–204; *Lā awwala lahu*/having no beginning, 201; *al-Māhiyya*/Quiddity, 199; *al-Mawjūd*/Existent, 186–7; *al-Mumtadd*, 202; *al-Mustamirr*, 202; *al-Nafs*/Self, 189–92; Names denoting existence, 183–99; Names denoting modality of existence, 199–204; *al-Nūr*/Light, 192–6; *al-Qadīm*/ Ancient, 201; *al-Sarmadī*, 202; *al-Shakhṣ*/Individual, 192; *al-Shay'*/Thing, 183–5, 187; *al-Ṣūra*/Image, 196–7; terms for 'Everlasting', 202–203; terms for 'Pre-eternal', 201; *Wājib al-wujūd li-dhātihi*/Necessary Existent, 128, 179, 203, 205, 206, 224, 230, 232, 247, 248, 257, 348, 361, 364, 382

Divine Names denoting combinations of actual and relative Attributes, 218–35; *al-Akbar*, 224; *al-Ākhir*/the Last, 222, 434; *al-Aʿlā*/the Most High, 225, 438, 439; *al-Aʿlam*, 219; *al-ʿAlī*/the High, 225, 226, 438, 440; *al-ʿĀlim*, 219; *al-ʿAlīm*/the Knowing, 92, 93, 99, 111, 219, 254; *al-ʿAllām*, 219; *al-Awwal*/the First, 222, 434; *al-Aʿẓam*/the Greatest, 438; *al-ʿAẓīm*/the Great, 224–6, 438, 439, 440; *al-Bāṭin*/the Hidden, 222, 434; *Dhū al-quwwa*, 219; *al-Ilāh*, 223; *al-Kabīr*, 224–6, 440; *al-Laṭīf*, 220; *al-Mālik*, 218; *al-Malik*/the Sovereign, 139, 140, 219; *al-Malīk*, 219; *Mālik al-mulk*, 219; *al-Muqtadir*, 218; *al-Mutaʿālī*, 225; *al-Mutakabbir*, 224; Names connected to hearing/*samʿ* and vision/*baṣar*, 222; Names connected to knowledge/*ʿilm*, 219–20; Names connected to power and ability/ *qudra*, 218–19; Names connected to speech/*kalām*, 220–1; Names connected to volition/ *irāda*, 221–2; Names denoting combinations of relative and eliminative Attributes, 222–3; Names for the Essence along with actual, relative and eliminative Attributes, 223; Names whose denotation is disputed, 223–6; *al-Qādir*, 218; *al-Qadīr*, 218; *al-Qawī*, 219; *al-Qayyūm*/the Self-subsistent Sustainer, 180, 181, 210, 222–3; *al-Shahīd*, 220; *al-Ẓāhir*/the Apparent, 222, 434; see also *Allāh*; pronominal Divine Names

Divine Names denoting eliminative Attributes, 201, 215–17; *al-ʿAzīz*, 217; eliminatives for the actions, 216–17; eliminatives for the Attributes, 215–16, 217; eliminatives for the Essence, 215, 217; *al-Ghaffār*,

217; *al-Ghanī*/Self-sufficient, 215, 217, 234; al-Ḥalīm, 217; *al-Quddūs*/Transcendent, 217, 376; al-Ṣabūr, 217; *al-Salām*/ Peace, 217; *al-Wāḥid*, 217
Divine Names denoting relative Attributes, 211–14; *al-ʿAfū*, 214; *al-Bārī'*, 213; *al-Barr*, 213; *al-Bāsiṭ*, 213, 214; *al-Ḍārr*, 213; existentiation/*takwīn* and the existentiated/*mukawwan*, 211–12; *al-Fātiḥ*, 214; *al-Fāṭir*, 213; *al-Fattāḥ*, 214; *al-Ghafūr*, 214, 443; *al-Jabbār*, 213; *al-Khāfiḍ*, 214; *al-Khāliq*, 213; *al-Laṭīf*, 213; *al-Mubdiʿ*, 213; *al-Mudhill*, 214; *al-Muḥdith*, 213; *al-Muḥyī*, 213, 214; *al-Muʿizz*, 214; *al-Mūjid*, 212, 213, 251; *al-Mukawwin*, 213; *al-Mukhtariʿ*, 213; *al-Mumīt*, 213, 214; *al-Munshi'*, 213; *al-Muntaqim*, 214; *al-Naffāʿ*, 214; *al-Nāfiʿ*, 213, 214; Names for the simple fact of being Creator, 213; Names pertaining to specific acts of creation, 213–14; *al-Qābiḍ*, 213, 214; *al-Qahhār*, 213; *al-Rāfiʿ*, 214; *al-Ra'ūf*, 214; *al-Ṣāniʿ*, 213; *al-Wahhāb*, 214; *al-Wāhib*, 214; see also *al-Raḥīm*; *al-Raḥmān*
divine scriptures, 103, 336, 413, 437; *Fātiḥa* and, 278–9; Gospel, 221, 239, 274, 278–9, 301, 332, 333; Psalms, 239, 274, 278–9, 301; Torah, 162, 190, 239, 274, 278–9, 301, 333; see also Qur'ān
Divinity (*ilāhiyyāt*), 271, 425
divorce, 23–4, 150–1, 173, 297–8
Ḍiyā' al-Dīn ʿUmar (al-Rāzī's father), 9, 158
duʿā', see supplication
dualists (*al-thanawiyya*), 133, 154, 384
duties (*taklīf*), 8, 367, 372, 286

Emigrants, 312, 321, 324
enquiry (*masā'il*/*mas'ala*), 2, 3, 4; linguistic enquiries, 10–11, 13; philosophical enquiries, 11–12
eschatology, see Hereafter
evil, 113, 279, 288–9; envy, 415, 416; evil deeds , 371–2; role of the *Fātiḥa* against seven human evils, 416–17; seven human evils, 415, 416; see also devil; Satan

faith (*īmān*), 356, 371, 404; 'favour' as faith, 406–407; see also belief
al-Fārisī, Abū ʿAlī, 68
al-Farrā', 85
fasting, 300, 374, 445–6
fatalism (*jabr*), 104–106, 271, 287, 399; see also Jabrīs
Fātiḥa (*Sūrat al-Fātiḥa*), 1; actions of the prayer and, 426–8; containing all knowledge of the Beginning, Middle and End, 417–19; eight gates of Paradise and, 432; enquiries on, 9, 12–13; *ḥadīth* on, 274, 275–6, 277, 278, 302, 307–309; *al-ḥamd*, 271; knowledge and, 152; Opening *sūra*, 1, 195; as part of the Qur'ān, 343–4; revelation of, 275, 277–8; role against seven human evils, 416–17; *ṣalāh* and, 274, 275; seven letters absent

from, 279–80; structure of the *sūra*, approaches to, 286–94; superior to other *sūra*s, 302; *Sūrat al-Baqara* and, 414–15; translation of, 334; virtues of, 278–80; words of remembrance and, 384–5; see also the entries below for *Fātiḥa*; 'All praise is for God'; 'And from You we seek help'; 'Guide us upon the straight path'; 'Lord of the worlds'; 'Master of the Day of Judgment'; 'Not of those who incur wrath, nor of those who are astray'; 'The Compassionate, the Merciful'; 'The path of those on whom You have bestowed favour'; 'You we worship…'

Fātiḥa, five Divine Names in, 379, 381–2, 416, 444–8; five aspects of the human being and, 444–5; five pillars of Islam and, 445–6; five senses and, 446; five servant's needs and, 447; five stages of creation and, 449–50; five types of prayer-direction/*qibla* and, 446; five words of remembrance and, 447–8; see also *Allāh*; *al-Mālik*/*al-Malik*; *al-Rabb*; *al-Raḥīm*; *al-Raḥmān*

Fātiḥa, juristic issues, 295–344; Arabic language, linguistic/grammatical issues, 299, 317–18; audible/inaudible recitation, 326, 337, 338, 339, 342; forgetfully missing the recitation, 342; *ḥadīth* on, 295–6, 297, 298–9, 300–301, 303–304, 307–308, 311, 315, 322–4, 330, 337–9, 421; memorisation of, 342–3; order of recitation, 342; recitation of *Fātiḥa* is obligatory in every prayer cycle/*rakʿa*, 320, 340–2; recitation of *Fātiḥa* is obligatory for the follower in prayer, 337–40; recitation of *Fātiḥa* is obligatory in prayer, 295–304, 327, 330, 338, 339, 340, 420–2; *Sunna*, 296–7, 303, 311, 337, 341, 421; see also *Fātiḥa*, verses of

Fātiḥa, other names of this *Sūra*, 271–6; *al-Asās*/the Foundation, 275; *Fātiḥat al-Kitāb*/ Opening of the Book, 271, 275, 277, 278, 299, 300, 301, 303, 304, 307, 309, 331, 337, 340, 341, 354, 421; *al-Kāfiya*/ the Sufficient, 275; *al-Sabʿ al-Mathānī*/the Seven Oft-Repeated, 274–5; *al-Ṣalāh*/the Prayer, 276, 420–1; *al-Shifā'*/ the Cure, 275–6; *al-Su'āl*/the Request, 276; *Sūrat al-Duʿā'*/ Chapter of Supplication, 276; *Sūrat al-Ḥamd*/Chapter of Praise, 271; *Sūrat al-Shukr*/ Chapter of Gratitude, 276; *Umm al-Qur'ān* /Source of the Qur'ān, 271–4, 282; *al-Wāfiya*/ the Complete, 275

Fātiḥa, verses of, 317–19; *Basmala* as a verse of the *Fātiḥa*, 304, 307–16, 320; eight verses, 317; seven verses, 274–5, 307, 308, 310–11, 315–16, 317–19, 416, 422, 426, 428

favour (*niʿma*), 4, 239, 256, 350, 403–406, 410, 419; 'favour' as faith, 406–407; man's creation as a favour, 404, 418; see also 'The path of those on whom You have bestowed favour'
fikr, see thinking
fiqh, see jurisprudence
Footstool (*kursī*), 4, 5, 116, 361, 429, 435
forgiveness, 111, 153, 252, 290, 354, 369–70, 380, 413, 414; 'I ask God's forgiveness'/*astaghfiru Allāh*, 146; see also sin
free will, 2, 36, 127, 399, 419, 424; *Istiʿādha*, 104–108; see also preordainment; voluntarism

Gabriel (Archangel), 93, 111, 123, 261, 263, 274, 396; revelation of the Qur'ān, 277
Galen, 6, 124, 240
Garden, 7, 140–1, 264, 361, 369; people of the Garden, 194; see also Paradise
generosity (*jūd*), 191, 257, 264, 293, 346, 357, 363, 438
genitive case, see *jarr*
gestures, 29, 31, 34, 49
ghaḍab, see anger
al-Ghazālī, Abū Ḥāmid, 128–9, 178, 234–5, 236, 306
glorifiers/glorification (*tanzīh*), 223, 224
gnosis (*maʿrifa*), 163, 177–8, 228, 230, 247, 248, 255; direct gnosis, 178–9; garden of gnosis is better than garden of bounties, 276; 'none knows God except God', 178; see also knowledge
God, 2; God's speech/God's speech is pre-eternal, 43–4, 45; knowledge/wisdom of, 4, 6, 9, 35, 100, 106, 215, 219–20, , 239, 258, 285, 364, 368, 410; longing for, 230–1, 263; manifestation of, 448; seventy veils of light, 429–30; thoughts and, 132, 133; see also Divine Attributes; Divine Names; God's Essence
god/deity, see *ilāh*
'God is greater', see *Allāhu akbar*/*takbīr*
God's Essence (*Dhāt*), 3, 44, 160, 173, 197, 199, 201, 203, 209, 232–3, 248–9, 436, 448; *Allāh*, 181, 422, 448; denial of Attributes and, 205–208; *al-Dhāt*/Essence, 187–9; Divine Essence as cause of Divine Attributes, 178; essential Names/*asmā' al-dhāt*, 226; Name denoting God's Essence, 176–81; Names for the Essence along with actual, relative and eliminative Attributes, 223; pondering upon the Essence of God is impossible, 423; transcendence above location, spatiality and direction, 284–5
good/goodness, 6, 107, 111, 214, 288–9, 313, 321, 346; All praise is for God, 352
guidance (*hidāya*), 8, 292; see also 'Guide us upon the straight path'
'Guide us upon the straight path', 8–9, 276, 318–19, 419, 450; action of prayer: second prostration, 427;

Arabic language, linguistic/grammatical issues, 400, 401–402; exegesis of, 397–403; guidance and knowledge, 294, 318, 398, 425–6; guidance of light to obtain in the heart, 273; guide/*shaykh*, 288; Guide us/plural, 401–402; *mustaqīm*, 400; Paradise, 400; preordainment, 271; prophethood, 271, 398–9; seeking guidance through cleansing and discipline, 8, 9; seeking guidance through evidential methods, 8–9; *ṣirāṭ*, 400; station of *ḥaqīqa*/reality, 291, 438; 'the straight path', 287–8, 398, 400–401, 402–403, 404; *Sūrat al-Baqara* and, 414; 'This is for My servant, and My servant shall have what he requests', 309, 420, 425–6; unveiling and manifestation, 272, 287, 419; see also guidance

ḥadīth: 'All praise is for God', 345, 351–2, 441; *Basmala*, 264–5, 266, 277, 307–309, 311, 314–17, 320, 322–5; Day of Judgment, 252; devil, 122–4, 127; Divine Names, 183, 185, 187–8, 189–91, 192, 193–7, 199, 203, 224, 236, 437; *Fātiḥa*, 274, 275–6, 277, 278, 302, 307–309; *Fātiḥa*, juristic issues, 295–6, 297, 298–9, 300–301, 303–304, 307–308, 311, 315, 322–4, 330, 337–9, 421; *ḥadīth qudsī*, 224, 387; *ḥadīth* as statement, 27; heart, 140, 194, 196; 'I seek refuge in You from You', 108, 109, 115, 131, 189; *Istiʿādha*, 89, 91, 93, 108, 109, 111–15, 138; jinn, 122–4, 265; *kalām* and, 26, 43; 'Master of the Day of Judgment', 372, 373; mercy, 252–3; prayer, 91, 298, 301, 330, 338, 342, 388, 390, 415, 427–8; *qawl*, 20; Qur'ānic recitation, 94, 332; remembrance, 189, 233, 234, 261, 276, 321, 434; Satan, 124, 126, 127; 'The Compassionate, the Merciful', 370–1; worship, 390; see also transmission

al-Ḥallāj, al-Ḥusayn b. Manṣūr, 448–9

Ḥanafīs, 299, 300, 303, 305, 319, 323–4, 336, 337–8

al-Harawī, ʿAbd Allāh al-Anṣārī, 184, 187, 188

Ḥāritha b. al-Nuʿmān, 194

al-Ḥasan b. ʿAlī b. Abī Ṭālib, 114

al-Ḥasan al-Baṣrī, 114, 317, 340

al-Ḥasan b. Ṣāliḥ b. Ḥayy, 295, 327, 340

Ḥashwīs, 44, 45, 171

heart, 128, 251, 256, 257; attachments of, 292, 293–4; believer's heart as the noblest of places, 140–1; detachment, 293; *ḥadīth* on, 140, 194, 196; *Istiʿādha* and, 93, 140; *kalām* and, 26, 36; light and, 194, 196, 229, 251, 273, 389, 446; love of God and, 251; praise expresses an attribute of the heart, 347; purification of, 266; Satan and, 124, 128; 'The heart of the

believer is between two of the fingers of the Compassionate', 396; as wellspring of innate heat, 35, 124; worship alleviates the heart's distress, 391–2
Hell, 7, 279; seven gates of, 274–5, 280; wisdom in creating Hellfire, 367; see also Hereafter
Helpers, 312, 321, 324
Hereafter (*ākhira*), 255, 256, 265, 425, 438; 'Master of the Day of Judgment', 7; reward in, 7; as world of purity, 412; see also Hell, 'Master of the Day of Judgment'; Paradise
Hereafter (*samᶜiyyāt/maᶜād*), 425
hidāya, see guidance
Hishām b. Muᶜāwiya, 81
Hishām b. ᶜUrwa, 196
homonymy (*ishtirāk*), 19, 39, 59, 172
Ḥudhayfa b. al-Yamān, 278
al-Ḥusayn b. ᶜAlī b. Abī Ṭālib, 114
al-Ḥusayn b. al-Faḍl, 278–9
hypocrites (*munāfiqūn*), 26, 263, 347, 407–408

ᶜibāda, see worship
ᶜibāra (expression), 11, 13, 21–2
Iblīs, see Satan
Ibn ᶜAbbās (ᶜAbd Allāh b. ᶜAbbās), 93, 114, 195, 277, 308, 322, 324, 325, 327, 390
Ibn Abī Laylā, 327
Ibn Abī Malīka, 307
Ibn Ḥanbal, Aḥmad b. Muḥammad, 93, 320
Ibn Jinnī, ᶜUthmān, 20–1, 22, 25, 30, 63, 68, 84
Ibn Jurayj, 307
Ibn Masᶜūd, ᶜAbd Allāh, 189, 191, 194, 295, 335–6, 340, 343–4
Ibn al-Mubārak, ᶜAbd Allāh, 307, 327, 337
Ibn al-Mughaffal, ᶜAbd Allāh, 323, 324, 325, 326
Ibn al-Mundhir, 300, 331
Ibn al-Ṣabbāgh, Abū al-Naṣr, 341
Ibn Sīnā, Abū ᶜAlī (Avicenna), 29, 40, 41
Ibn Sīrīn, Muḥammad, 89, 90–1
Ibn ᶜUlayya, 340
Ibn ᶜUmar (ᶜAbd Allāh b. ᶜUmar b. al-Khaṭṭāb), 92, 94, 190, 195, 196, 322, 324, 325, 327
Ibn al-Zubayr (ᶜAbd Allāh b. al-Zubayr), 298, 322
Ibrāhīm b. Adham, 366, 400
iḍāfa (annexation), 9, 61, 75, 78, 193, 254, 450; *Basmala*, 159, 450; 'Lord of the worlds', 5, 364; name and, 171, 172; see also Arabic language, linguistic/grammatical issues
ignorance, 2, 101, 106, 135, 138, 246, 248, 331, 371, 381, 383; mocking is ignorance, 238; people of ignorance, 409
ilāh (god/deity), 142, 167, 361, 383, 393; *al-Ilāh*, 223; as possible derivation for *Allāh*, 245–7, 253, 254, 381; worshipped, 245, 246–7
ilāhiyyāt, see Divinity
ilhām, see inspiration
imagination, 128, 132, 148, 177, 230, 249, 424, 431; see also thoughts
imām (leader), 94, 144, 326, 337, 338, 339, 373, 405

īmān, see belief; faith
ᶜImrān b. al-Ḥuṣayn, 183
Imru' al-Qays b. Ḥujr al-Kindī, 87
incantations (*ᶜazā'im*), 240–1
indicative mood, see *rafᶜ*
inflection (*iᶜrāb*), 66, 80, 153; definition, 66, 71, 72; diptote/*ghayr munṣarif*, 59, 62–3, 73, 75–6, 77–8; inflected noun/*muᶜrab*, 66, 72–4, 167; inflection of verbs, 82–8; inflection vowel, 67, 68, 69–70, 72, 73; triptote/*munṣarif*, 73, 76; types of, 71–2; uninflected word/*mabnī*, 67, 69–71, 74, 78; see also *ṣarf*
innovation (*bidᶜa*), 135, 266, 303, 322, 323, 415, 417
inspiration (*ilhām*), 6, 31, 118, 120, 128, 131, 220, 221
intellect, 9, 112, 115, 231, 232, 233, 321, 382, 430, 431, 448; finitude of, 178; Intellect, 441, 442; 'Master of the Day of Judgment', 7, 8
iᶜrāb, see inflection
irāda, see volition
Isaac, 114
al-Isfarā'īnī, Abū Ḥāmid, 295, 300, 323–4, 340
Isḥāq b. Rāhawayh, 196, 328
Ishmael, 114, 398
ishtirāk, see homonymy
Islam, 194, 266, 306, 400; conversion to, 65, 95, 124, 254, 372; five pillars of, 445
Islamic law, see *sharīᶜa*
ism, see name
Istiᶜādha, 2–3, 432; angels and, 113, 154; *aᶜūdhu*, 82, 98; *aᶜūdhu bi'Llāh*, 10, 13; as disavowal of improper beliefs and actions, 4; Divine Names: the Hearing, the Knowing, 92, 93, 99; *ḥadīth*, 89, 91, 93, 108, 109, 111–15, 138; heart and, 93, 140; 'I seek refuge in God from the rejected Satan', 1, 2, 3; Islamic law, 15; juristic issues related to, 89–97; as obligatory for every recitation, 90–2; Paradise and, 147, 154; prayer and, 90, 91, 92, 93–4, 139, 309; Prophets and saints, 154; Q.XVI.98: 'When you recite the Qur'ān…', 89, 91, 92, 93, 94; Qur'ān, examples from, 110–11; Qur'ānic recitation and, 89–91, 92, 93–4, 138, 144; recited aloud or silently, 92; *Sunna*, 91; theology, 15; time of recitation, 89–90, 92; wording, 92–3, 99, 146; see also the entries below for *Istiᶜādha*
Istiᶜādha: linguistic/grammatical issues, 10, 15, 146, 147; *bā'*, 10, 147–9; derivation, 98–9; *min*, 152–3; see also *Istiᶜādha*
Istiᶜādha, rational enquiries, 98–136; I pillar: seeking of refuge itself/*Istiᶜādha*, 98–108; II pillar: the refuge/*mustaᶜādh bihi*, 98, 108–109; III pillar: the seeker/*mustaᶜīdh*, 98, 110–15; IV pillar: from whom refuge is sought/*mustaᶜādh minhu*, 98, 115–34; V pillar: purpose of seeking refuge/*mustaᶜādh li-ajlihi*, 91, 98, 99, 134–6; every created

being ought to seek refuge in God, 110–15; free will and preordainment, 104–108; knowledge of God, 100–101; need for God in knowledge and action, 101–104; quiddity, 99–101; self-knowledge, 100, 101; see also devil; *Isti*ʿ*ādha*; jinn; Satan
*Isti*ʿ*ādha*, spiritual allusions of, 137–45; admitting the self's impotence and the Lord's omnipotence, 137–8; *Allāh*, 142; ascending from creation to Creator, 137; fleeing from the rejected Satan to the Compassionate and Merciful, 139, 144, 145, 154; obedience, 138, 139; purification, 139, 141, 144; Satan as enemy, 138, 139, 141, 142, 143, 144–5; see also *Isti*ʿ*ādha*
iṣṭilāḥ, see convention

Jābir b. ʿAbd-Allāh b. ʿAmr, 191, 308, 338
jabr, see fatalism
Jabrīs (fatalists), 104, 356, 357–8, 365, 371, 380, 395; see also fatalism
Jacob, 201
Jaʿfar al-Ṣādiq, 144
Jahm b. Ṣafwān, 183, 184
jarr (genitive case), 69, 70, 73, 74–5, 78, 79, 149, 159, 165, 244; annexed genitive, 5, 48, 51
al-Jaṣṣāṣ, Abū Bakr al-Rāzī, 158, 310
jazm (jussive mood), 69, 70
Jesus, 19, 44, 124, 189, 219, 266, 392
Jews, 407
jinn, 98, 361, 420; created from fire, 124; denying the existence of, 116–20; *ḥadīth* on, 122–4, 265; Hell, 279; knowledge of the Unseen/*al-ghayb*, 134; nature of, 115, 116, 118–21, 125, 126; Night of the Jinns, 124; possession by, 125–6, 127; Prophets and, 117–18, 121, 122; Qur'ān on, 121–2; righteous jinns, 116, 118; thoughts and, 132, 133
John, 399
Jonah, 227, 398
Joseph, 110, 391, 426, 446
Jubayr b. Muṭʿim, 89, 93
jūd, see generosity
jurisprudence (*fiqh*), 8, 152, 358
al-Jurjānī, ʿAbd al-Qāhir, 47, 71, 75
jussive mood, see *jazm*
justice, 2, 140, 141, 286, 376–7, 424; *wasaṭ*, 398

Kaʿb al-Aḥbār, 123
Kaʿb b. ʿUjra al-Balawī, 188
Kaʿba, 445, 446
kalām (speech), 11, 13, 18, 65; ability to speak and, 45; definition of, 36; difference between *kalima* and *kalām*, 22–3, 25; Divine Names connected to, 220–1; external speech, 26, 27, 35–6; *ḥadīth* on, 26, 43; heart and, 26, 36; internal speech/ *kalām al-nafs*, 26, 27, 35–6; *kalm*/'to wound and impact', 18, 23, 25; legal implications of the meaning of, 23–4; as meaningful speech, 24; narration on, 26, 43; poetry on,

26; *qawl* and, 25, 26, 27; Qur'ān and, 26; Qur'ān as the speech of God, 43, 44; speech of God, 43–4, 45
kalima (word), 10, 11, 13, 17–39, 109; definition of, 27, 28, 29, 48; difference between *kalima* and *kalām*, 22–3, 25; explaining the term, 18–19; femininity, 73; *lafẓ* and, 27, 28, 48–9; limits of words, 32; meaningful expressions, 28; as meaningful word, 24, 29; onomatopoeia, 30; production of words on the scale of purposes, 35; 'pronounced', 29; Qur'ān and, 19; referents of words, 31, 32, 34, 36, 37, 160; sound and, 24–5, 29; types of words, 46; use of, 19; see also meaning; noun; particle; verb
al-Karkhī, Abū al-Ḥasan, 305
Karrāmīs, 45, 171, 198
Khadīja, 277
al-Khaḍir, 367–8, 399
Khalaf al-Aḥmar, 81
Khālid b. al-Walīd, 123, 266
al-Khalīl b. Aḥmad al-Farāhīdī, 79, 80, 166, 243, 253–4
Khawla b. Ḥakīm al-Sulamiyya, 113
al-Khawzī, Ibrāhīm b. Yazīd, 327
al-Kisā'ī, ʿAlī b. Ḥamza, 169, 374, 378
knowledge, 256, 429; *bā'* and, 152; categories of, 231–2; completion and perfection through knowledge, 419; *Fātiḥa* and, 152; God's knowledge/wisdom, 6, 9, 35, 100, 106, 215, 219–20, 239, 258, 285, 364, 368, 410; guidance and knowledge, 294, 318, 398, 425–6; *ʿilm*, 33, 65, 151, 179, 209, 211; *ʿilm*, Divine Names connected to, 219–20; inductive process, 292–3; knowledge of Lordship, 393, 413, 418, 419, 420, 432; knowledge of the truth and knowledge of goodness, 410, 419; means of, 177; need for God in knowledge and action, 101–104; Qur'ān and, 152; religious knowledge, 272; self-knowledge, 100, 101; seven stations of knowledge, 413–14; see also gnosis
Kūfan grammarians, 77, 80–1, 86–7, 147, 170, 253
kufr, see disbelief/unbelief
kursī, see Footstool

Labīd b. Rabīʿa, 199
ladhdha, see pleasure
lafẓ (utterance), 11, 13, 24; *kalima* and, 27, 28, 48–9; *lafẓ/lafẓa/*word, 28, 29; usage of, 21; used and unused words, 28
language, 31; as divinely inspired/created by God, 31, 37; ways of knowing language, 37; see also *lugha*
leader, see *imām*
leadership, 241; *imāma*, 2, 405–406; *riyāsa*, 103
letter: breath and, 21, 41; consonants, 42; definition of, 41; derivation and, 17–18; *ḥarf/ḥurūf*, 11, 41, 109; inflection, 67; meaningful letter, 29;

meaningful word and, 29; narration on, 43; plosive letter, 68; sound and, 29, 34, 35, 41–2; speech between eternality and temporality, 42–3; thoughts and, 132; voiced/silent letters, 41; see also vowel
liar/lying, 26, 117, 347
'Lord of the worlds', 5–6, 271, 272, 281, 290, 293; *al-ʿālamīn*, 5, 282, 284; bowing/*rukūʿ*, 427; categories of existents, 360–1; divine care, 362, 363–4, 365; exegesis of, 360–6; God's transcendence above location, spatiality and direction, 284–5; *iḍāfa*/annexation, 5, 364; as the most perfect attribute, 364; *murabbī*, 282, 361–2; Oneness of God, 418, 424; praise of God, 362–3; proving God's existence, 281–4; *Rabb*, 5, 284, 361, 365–6, 444; revelation of, 277; world/*ʿālam*, 360
Lordship (*rubūbiyya*), 100, 140, 246, 272, 273, 286, 290, 413, 418–19, 451; Attributes of, 444; Covenant of, 147, 288, 393; knowledge of, 393, 413, 418, 419, 420, 432; *al-Rabb*, 5, 282, 284, 361, 365–6, 376, 379, 381, 416, 417, 444, 445, 447, 448, 449; station of, 422
love: love of God, 251, 429; love of imitation, 292; love of this world, 292
lugha (language), 11, 20–1
al-Lu'lu'ī, al-Ḥasan b. Ziyād, 328
al-Maʿarrī, Abū al-ʿAlā', 5
Magians, 266, 372, 384
Maḥmūd b. al-Rabīʿ, 275, 338
majāz, see metaphor
al-Mālik/al-Malik: five Divine Names in the *Fātiḥa*, 379, 416, 444–8, 449–50; *al-Malīk*, 219; *al-Mālik*/Master, 218, 373–4, 377–8; *Malik*/Sovereign, 139, 140, 219, 373, 374–7, 378; *Malik=Raḥmān*, 417; *Mālik al-mulk*, 219; *Mālik yawm al-dīn*, 381, 382, 445, 446, 447, 448; see also Divine Names; 'Master of the Day of Judgment'
Mālik b. Anas, 91, 122–3, 304, 316, 327, 337, 338, 341
Manicheans, 384
maqāmāt, see stations
Maʿqil b. Yasār, 112
maʿrifa, see gnosis
martyr, 113, 140, 194
Mary, mother of Jesus, 111, 146, 368–9, 392
masā'il/mas'ala, see enquiry
'Master of the Day of Judgment', 7–8, 271, 281, 290, 316, 394, 438; action of prayer: first prostration, 427; Arabic language, linguistic/grammatical issues, 373, 379; evil deeds , 371–2; exegesis of, 371–80; gathering, 7, 379, 418; generosity, 378; good deeds, 371–2; *ḥadīth*, 372, 373; Hereafter, 7, 418, 450; intellect and, 7, 8; Jabrīs, 380; justice, 376–7; mercy, 293, 275–6, 378, 418; *mulk*/dominion, 263, 376,

378; 'My servant has glorified Me', 315, 316, 420, 424; 'My servant has relegated to Me [his affairs]', 309, 420; perfect ability, 273; praise of God, 272, 276, 286; punishment, 380; Qadarīs, 380; resurrection, 7, 379, 418; reward, 371, 380, 424; *Sūrat al-Baqara* and, 414; transmission, 7, 8; *Yawm al-dīn*, 371; see also Day of Judgment; Hereafter; *al-Mālik/al-Malik*
al-Māzinī, Abū ʿUthmān Bakr b. Muḥammad, 70, 76
meaning: impossibility to express some meanings in words, 33–4; meaning of words, 29, 31–2; meaning of words are not inherent, 28, 30; meaning of words by coinage, 28, 30–1, 33, 55, 173–4; meaning of words by convention, 27, 28, 29, 31, 32, 35–6, 48, 159; meaning of words by divine designation/*tawqīf*, 30, 31; meaning of words by reason, 32; as the name for the mental conception, 33; speculation and, 39; wisdom behind words denoting meaning, 34; see also *kalima*
Mecca, 277, 278; Kaʿba, 445, 446; pilgrimage to, 445, 446; Sacred Mosque, 428
medicine/health-related issues, 6, 135, 289
Medina, 123, 278, 312, 321
mercy (God's mercy, *raḥma*), 6–7, 153, 260, 293, 362, 408, 438, 443, 445, 450–1; does anyone besides God have mercy?, 257–8; five Divine Names denoting mercy, 443; five Prophetic names denoting mercy, 443; *ḥadīth* on, 252–3; manifestations of, 256; 'Master of the Day of Judgment', 293, 275–6, 378, 418; Q.vii.156: 'My mercy extends to all things', 362, 443; Q.xxi.107: 'We sent you not but as a mercy for the worlds', 370, 443; see also *al-Raḥīm*; *al-Raḥmān*; 'The Compassionate, the Merciful'
Messenger, 117, 190, 192, 284, 358, 432, 437, 441, 442, 446; angelic Messenger, 413; human Messenger, 413
metaphor (*majāz*), 19, 21, 25, 39, 299
al-Miṣrī, Dhū al-Nūn, 366
monotheism, 243, 248, 383, 384, 386, 392; *tawḥīd*, 100, 235, 437
Moses, 103, 110–11, 121–2, 162, 190, 220–1, 238, 254, 259, 260, 280, 336, 383, 387, 392, 416, 417, 426; al-Khaḍir and, 367–8, 399
mosque, 143, 300, 309, 390, 428
Muʿādh b. Jabal, 111–12, 196–7
Muʿāwiya b. Abī Sufyān, 312, 321, 324
al-Mubarrad, Abū al-ʿAbbās, 153, 169
Mughīra b. Shuʿba, 296
Mujāhid b. Jabr, 278
munāfiqūn, see hypocrites
mushābaha, see similarity
mushrikūn, see polytheists
Muslim b. al-Ḥajjāj, 322
Muslim b. Khālid, 307

Muʿtazilīs, 29, 31, 36, 104–105, 106–107, 125, 133, 171, 205, 211, 222, 356–8, 404, 405, 409

al-Nābigha al-Dhubyānī, 84
Nāfiʿ, 195
nafs, see soul/ego
al-Nakhaʿī, Ibrāhīm b. Yazīd, 89, 316
name (*ism*), 59–60, 73, 160, 169–82; categories of names denoting referents, 174–6; coinage, order of, 173–4; definition of, 171, 174; derivation, 169–70, 174; enquiries based on reason, 171–82; enquiries based on transmission, 169–70; *iḍāfa*/annexation, 171, 172; names of attributes, 174; naming and, 171, 173; referent/*musammā* and, 171–3, 181; *sim*, *simā*, *sum*, *usm*, 169; see also *Basmala*; Divine Names; noun; proper noun
naming (*tasmiya*), 171, 173; see also *Basmala*
naṣb (accusative case, subjunctive mood), 69, 70, 74, 75, 78, 80, 165
al-Naẓẓām, Abū Isḥāq, 40
niʿma, see favour
Noah, 99, 110, 261, 312, 397
nominative case, see *rafʿ*
'Not of those who incur wrath, nor of those who are astray', 9, 273, 291, 318–19, 402, 419, 450; exegesis of, 407–11; God's anger, 409–10; *Sūrat al-Baqara* and, 414; 'those who are astray', 407–408, 409, 411, 419, 438; 'those who incur wrath', 407, 409, 410–11, 419, 438
noun, 12, 13, 159; adjectival noun, 49; annexation and, 75; as a branch, 74; cases for, 78–81; categorisations of, 58–64; coinage, order of, 173–4; compound sentences, 56–7; definite article and, 75; definition of, 46, 48–50, 66, 171, 174; derived noun/*mushtaqq*, 58, 64, 65, 174; generic noun/*ism jins*, 58, 63, 64–5; inflected noun/*muʿrab*, 66, 72–4, 167; *jarr* and, 74, 75; nouns of quiddity/*jāmid* nouns, 64, 174; signs of, 50–1; as subject, 46, 47, 48; verbal noun, 27, 47, 50, 51–2, 53, 54, 74, 82, 98, 170, 204, 219; word combinations, 55–6; see also name; pronoun
nubuwwāt, see Prophethood
al-Nuʿmān b. Bashīr, 188

obedience, 3–4, 8, 261, 272, 322, 340, 356, 376, 398–9, 433; *Istiʿādha* and, 138, 139; the 'Obeyed one', 412–13; people of obedience, 409
Oneness, see *tawḥīd*
oppression, 2, 190, 357, 359, 371, 376, 415

Paradise, 140, 152, 190, 400; eight gates of, 348, 432; *Istiʿādha* and, 147, 154; people of Paradise, 195–6; Qur'ānic recitation and, 94; see also Garden; Hereafter
particle, 13; as accidental state in the quiddity, 66; can be a subject, 46–7, 48; compound sentences, 56–7; definition of, 46, 48, 49,

54; *ḥarf*, 10, 55; meaning, 55; word combinations, 55–6; see also *bā'*
Pen, 361, 436, 440
Persian language, 237, 330, 331, 334–5, 336; *Khudāy*/'He came by Himself', 173, 203
Pharaoh, 110, 226, 260, 383, 416
philosophy/philosopher, 65, 132, 179, 197, 198, 205, 209, 292, 353; practical philosophy/*siyāsāt*, 8
pleasure, 103, 231, 241, 291–2, 393, 397, 412, 424, 429, 445, 446; *ladhdha*, 129–30; *riḍwān*, 189
plural, 73, 74; 'And from You we seek help', 402; broken plural, 50; Divine Names and, 218; dual and sound plural, 50, 72, 75, 87, 254; Guide us, 401–402; *nūn* in *naᶜbudu*/plural, 387–9, 402; as signifier of grandeur, 387, 388
polytheists (*mushrikūn*), 43, 85, 220, 223, 383–4, 387, 407, 431
prayer, 65, 259; as the ascension of the gnostics, 428–34, 446; congregational prayer, superiority of, 388; the *Fātiḥa* as 'the Prayer', 276, 420–1; gift of prayer, 430–2; *ḥadīth*, 91, 298, 388, 390, 415, 427–8; *ḥadīth* of the Bedouin, 91, 301, 330, 338, 341; 'I have divided the prayer between Me and My servant into two halves', 276, 298, 308–309, 315, 338, 419–26; ᶜĪd prayer, 94; *imām*, 94, 144; *Istiᶜādha* and, 90, 91, 92, 93–4, 139, 309; *maghrib*/sunset prayer, 341; night prayers, 93; night prayers of Ramaḍān, 91, 304; non-canonical readings of the Qur'ān and, 96; 'Prayer is the ascension of the believer', 415; Prophet Muḥammad, 390; purpose of prayer is for remembrance to take hold in the heart, 422; Q.VI.72: 'Establish the prayer', 297, 337; Q.XX.14: 'And establish regular prayer for My remembrance', 334, 422; reciting the Qur'ān in Arabic or in translation, 329–36; *ṣalāh*, 65, 90, 139, 267, 274, 275, 295, 297, 315, 369, 420–1; *ṣubḥ*/dawn prayer, 338, 341; *Sunna*, 296–7, 401; see also ablution; *Fātiḥa*, juristic issues; prayer, actions/parts of; *qibla*; supplication
prayer, actions/parts of: approaching the prayer, 435–6; bowing/*rukūᶜ* and prostration/*sujūd*, 302, 320, 321, 327, 427, 433, 438, 439–40; call to prayer/*adhān*, 348; end of the sitting/*tashahhud*, 333; *Fātiḥa* and, 426–8; 'Glory be to my Lord, the Great'/*subḥāna Rabbī al-ᶜAẓīm*, 438; *taḥiyyāt*, 428, 433; *takbīr*, 436–7, 438, 439; see also prayer
preordainment, 2, 36–7, 196, 271, 419, 424; *Istiᶜādha*, 104–108; see also free will
preposition, 10, 50, 56, 86, 159, 364; *bā'*, 157; *lām*, 348; *min*, 152–3
prohibitions, 8, 33, 38, 45, 135, 192; see also commands

pronominal Divine Names, 226–35; *Ana*/I, 226, 227; *Anta*/You, 226, 227; *Huwa*/He, 226, 227–8, 254; longing for God, 230–1; remembrance and *Huwa*/He, 229, 230, 231, 233–4; secrets and benefits of saying *yā Huwa*/'O He', 228–35; 'There is no god but He', 226, 227, 235, 254; 'There is no god but I', 226, 227; 'There is no god but You', 226, 227
pronoun, 49, 72, 85, 86, 87, 228, 230, 244; pronoun occurring before its explicit noun, 83–4; relative pronoun, 50, 167; see also noun; pronominal Divine Names
proper noun (*ʿalam*), 58, 73; agnomen/*kunya*, 59–60, 61; categories of, 59–63; coinage of, 59, 62, 73; constructed proper noun, 61; differences between generic and proper noun, 58–9; generic noun turned into a proper noun, 63; improvised proper noun, 61, 62; indefinite proper noun, 76–7; proper noun for attributes, 62–3; proper noun for essences, 62; simple proper noun, 61; title/*laqab*, 59–60; transferred proper noun, 61–2; see also name; noun
Prophet Muḥammad, 44, 111, 114, 261, 370, 377, 426, 433–4; *Aḥmad* and *Muḥammad*, 442, 443; Ascension/*miʿrāj*, 383, 392, 414–15, 427–30, 431–2; *Fātiḥa*, daily recitation of, 397; five Prophetic names denoting mercy, 443; as the Messenger of God, 26; Night Journey, 123, 383, 392, 428–30; prayer, 390; Q.xxi.107: 'We sent you not but as a mercy for the worlds', 370, 443; revelation of the Qur'ān to, 306, 314, 327, 418; see also *ḥadīth*; *Sunna*
prophethood, 117, 121, 271, 392, 398–9, 430
Prophethood (*nubuwwāt*), 425
Prophets, 8, 111, 312, 313, 394, 402, 448; 'All praise is for God', 352; infallibility of, 408; *Istiʿādha* and, 154; jinns/devils and, 117–18, 121, 122, 126; Q.iv.69: '…the Prophets, the truthful ones…what a beautiful fellowship!', 402, 405, 428
purification, 266, 430, 435–6; *Basmala*, 306, 314, 328; *Istiʿādha*, 139, 141, 144

qadar, see voluntarism
Qadarīs (voluntarists), 104, 356, 365, 371, 380, 395
Qāḍī (judge), 124, 305, 306, 307, 329
qawl (statement), 11, 13, 24, 65; explaining the term, 20; *ḥadīth*, 20; *kalām* and, 25, 26, 27; meaning of words by divine designation, 30; *qāla*/to say, 26; usage of, 25
Qays b. al-Khaṭīm, 273
qibla (prayer-direction), 301; five types of, 446
qiyās, see analogy

Qur'ān, 190, 400; *Basmala* as a verse of Qur'ān, 304–17, 319, 326–7; categories of addressees of, 264; codex, 306, 310, 314, 326; the Criterion, 274, 278–9; Divine Attributes, 200, 237–8; Divine Names in, 3, 236–7; *Fātiḥa* as *Umm al-Qur'ān* /Source of the Qur'ān, 271–4; *al-Furqān*, 278; *kalima*, 19; knowledge and, 152; memorisation of, 332, 335, 342–3; pre-eternality of, 45; purity/purification, 139, 306, 314, 328; purpose of, 271; Qur'ānic script, 306, 310, 313–14, 319; revelation of, 277, 283, 306, 314, 327, 336, 418; as the speech of God, 43, 44; see also the entries below related to Qur'ān

Qur'ānic quotations (repeated appearances in the text): Q.I.1: 'In the Name of God' 166, 172, 414; Q.II.31: 'He taught Adam the names of all things', 30, 219–20; Q.II.152: 'Remember Me; I will remember you', 387, 422; Q.IV.69: '…the Prophets, the truthful ones…what a beautiful fellowship!', 402, 405, 428; Q.IV.115: 'Whoever… follows a path other than that of the believers…', 298, 330, 421; Q.VI.72: 'Establish the prayer', 297, 337; Q.VII.128: 'Seek help from God', 103, 395; Q.VII.156: 'My mercy extends to all things', 362, 443; Q.VII.158: '…and follow him', 91, 296, 311, 313, 329, 337, 341, 421; Q.VII.180: 'The most Beautiful Names belong to God…', 172, 173, 185, 237; Q.VII.205: 'Bring your Lord to remembrance…without loudness in words', 323, 326; Q.XIII.28: 'Without doubt, in the remembrance of God do hearts find satisfaction', 248, 444; Q.XIV.22: 'I had no authority over you except to call you, but you listened to me', 126, 131, 154; Q.XIV.34: 'If you should count the favours of God…', 4, 239, 256, 350; Q.XV.87: 'We have bestowed upon you seven oft-repeated (verses)', 274, 278, 308, 317, 422; Q.XVI.40: 'When We will anything, We but say "Be!" and it is', 26, 109, 216; Q.XVI.98: 'When you recite the Qur'ān…', 89, 91, 92, 93, 94; Q.XVII.110: 'Neither recite your prayer aloud, nor recite it in a low tone', 325, 326; Q.XVII.110: 'Say: Call upon *Allāh*, or call upon *al-Raḥmān*…', 314, 449; Q.XIX.9: 'I did indeed create you before, when you had been nothing', 380, 381; Q.XX.14: 'And establish regular prayer for My remembrance', 334, 422; Q.XXI.107: 'We sent you not but as a mercy for the worlds', 370, 443; Q.XXIV.35: 'God is the light of the heavens and the earth', 192, 193; Q.XXXV.6: 'Satan is an enemy to you: so

treat him as an enemy', 138, 139; Q.LV.78: 'Blessed be the Name of your Lord', 172, 173, 435; Q.LXXIII.20: 'So recite of the Qur'ān what is easy for you', 301–302, 303, 330, 337, 343, 421
Qur'ānic recitation, 44, 69, 89–90, 325; amount of recitation obligatory in prayer, 304; confusion between the letters *ḍād* and *ẓā'*, 95; *ḥadīth* on, 94, 332; *Istiʿādha* and, 89–91, 92, 93–4, 138, 144; mass transmission/*mutawātir*, 96–7; non-canonical readings of the Qur'ān, 96; obligatory in prayer, 295, 330; Paradise and, 94; Q.XVI.98: 'When you recite the Qur'ān…', 89, 91, 92, 93, 94; Q.XVII.110: 'Neither recite your prayer aloud, nor recite it in a low tone', 325, 326; Q.LXXIII.20: 'So recite of the Qur'ān what is easy for you', 301–302, 303, 330, 337, 343, 421; recited with *tartīl*, 94; reciting the Qur'ān in Arabic or in translation, 329–36; reward associated with, 339; *Sunna* and, 94, 95, 329–30; velarised *lām*, 95–6, 162–3; see also *Fātiḥa*, juristic issues
Qur'ānic *sūras*: protection-seeking *sūras*, 336, 343–4; *Sūrat al-Anʿām*, 282–3, 284, 317; *Sūrat al-Aʿrāf*, 111; *Sūrat al-Baqara*, 195, 226, 407, 413–15, 417–18; *Sūrat Fāṭir*, 284; *Sūrat Ḥā Mīm al-Sajda*, 99, 111; *Sūrat al-Ḥashr*, 112–13; *Sūrat al-Ḥijr*, 275, 278, 391; *Sūrat Ibrāhīm*, 244; *Sūrat al-Kahf*, 283; *Sūrat al-Kawthar*, 319, 320; *Sūrat al-Malā'ika*, 284; *Sūrat al-Mulk*, 319; *Sūrat al-Muzzammil*, 226; *Sūrat al-Naḥl*, 92, 225, 226; *Sūrat al-Naml*, 304, 313; *Sūrat Qāf*, 318; *Sūrat al-Qamar*, 318; *Sūrat Saba'*, 283; *Sūrat Ṭā-Hā*, 226; *Sūrat al-Tawba*, 267; *Sūrat Yā-Sīn*, 99
Quraysh, 223, 277–8, 314
al-Qushayrī, Abū al-Qāsim, 158
Qutayba b. Mihrān, 164
al-Qutaybī (Ibn Qutayba, ʿAbd Allāh b. Muslim), 166
Quṭrub, 69

al-Rabb (Lord), 282, 376, 416, 417, 445, 447, 448, 449; five Divine Names in the *Fātiḥa*, 379, 381, 416, 444–8, 449–50; 'Lord of the worlds', 5, 284, 361, 365–6, 444; *Rabb=Raḥīm*, 417; see also Divine Names
Rābiʿa al-ʿAdawiyya, 259
rafʿ (nominative case, indicative mood), 69, 70, 74, 78, 79–80, 244
Rāfiḍīs, 306
al-Raḥīm (the Merciful), 154, 165, 214, 260, 264, 443, 451; being merciful to people at six junctures, 267; derivation, 253; five Divine Names in the *Fātiḥa*, 379, 381, 416, 444–8, 449–50; God is *Raḥīm*, 256, 258; *al-Raḥīm/al-Raḥmān*

distinction, 366, 368, 369, 370; repeated in the *Fātiḥa*, 379–80; salvific function of the Name, 369, 370; three Divine Names in the *Basmala*, 416, 448–9; see also *Basmala*; Divine Names; mercy; 'The Compassionate, the Merciful'
raḥma, see mercy
al-Raḥmān (the Compassionate), 153, 165, 214, 228, 254, 260, 264, 376, 443, 450; derivation, 253; five Divine Names in the *Fātiḥa*, 379, 381, 416, 444–8, 449–50; God is *Raḥmān*, 256, 258; pronunciation of, 164–5; Q.xvii.110: 'Say: Call upon *Allāh*, or call upon *al-Raḥmān*...', 314, 449; *al-Raḥmān*/*al-Raḥīm* distinction, 366, 368, 369, 370; repeated in the *Fātiḥa*, 379–80; salvific function of the Name, 369, 370; three Divine Names in the *Basmala*, 416, 448–9; writing of, 168; see also *Basmala*; Divine Names; mercy; 'The Compassionate, the Merciful'
Ramaḍān: fasting, 300, 374, 445–6; night prayers of, 91, 304
al-Raqqāshī, al-Faḍl b. ʿĪsā, 327
remembrance of God (*dhikr*), 100, 112, 139, 160, 189, 247, 321, 343, 414, 422, 414, 429; *Basmala*, 414, 422; Divine Names and, 241–2; *ḥadīth* on, 189, 233, 234, 261, 276, 321, 434; *Huwa*/He, 229, 230, 231, 233–4; 'If he remembers Me in a gathering...', 189, 234, 434; as the noblest of stations, 234; purpose of prayer is for remembrance to take hold in the heart, 422; Q.ii.152: 'Remember Me; I will remember you', 387, 422; Q.vii.205: 'Bring your Lord to remembrance...without loudness in words', 323, 326; Q.xiii.28: 'Without doubt, in the remembrance of God do hearts find satisfaction', 248, 444; Q.xx.14: 'And establish regular prayer for My remembrance', 334, 422; words of remembrance, 384–5, 447–8
resurrection, 2, 195, 267; Day of Resurrection, 450; 'Master of the Day of Judgment', 7, 379, 418
reward, 2, 139, 187, 391; Hereafter and, 7; 'Master of the Day of Judgment', 371, 380, 424; Qur'ānic recitation and, 339
riḍwān, see pleasure
Rifāʿa b. Rāfiʿ b. Mālik, 300–301, 343
Rightly-Guided Caliphs, 297, 323, 330, 421
rubūbiyya, see Lordship
rūḥ, see spirit

Sabians, 384
Saʿd b. ʿUbāda, 192
Saʿīd b. Jubayr, 308, 327
Saʿīd al-Maqbarī, 307
ṣalāh, see prayer
Salmān the Persian, 334
al-Samarqandī, Abū al-Layth, 329

samʿiyyāt, see transmission
samʿiyyāt/maʿād, see Hereafter
ṣarf (full inflection/nunation), 73, 75, 76, 77; see also inflection
al-Sarī al-Saqaṭī, 354
Satan (Iblīs), 104–108, 124, 125, 126, 154, 384, 386, 405; Adam and, 141, 142; approaches of Satan: appetite, anger, desire, 415–16; breath of, 89; created from fire, 127; derivation, 98–9, 144; as enemy, 138, 139, 141, 142, 143, 144–5, 261; fleeing from the rejected Satan to the Compassionate and Merciful, 139, 144, 145, 154; *ḥadīth* on, 124, 126, 127; heart and, 124, 128; *Istiʿādha*, from whom refuge is sought/ *mustaʿādh minhu*, 98, 115–34; Q.XIV.22: 'I had no authority over you except to call you, but you listened to me', 126, 131, 154; Q.XXXV.6: 'Satan is an enemy to you: so treat him as an enemy', 138, 139; rebellion of, 141, 143, 153; 'Satan runs through the son of Adam like blood', 124, 126, 127; *shayṭān*, 2, 93, 98, 143, 144, 153, 154; sin and, 108, 131, 142, 143–4; as 'stoned'/*rajīm*, 99, 105, 143, 144, 153–4; traps from, 188; whispering, 90, 99, 104–105, 106, 108, 115, 126–31, 138, 141, 154, 251, 415; see also devil; evil
ṣawt, see sound
Ṣayfī b. Aflaḥ, 122
scholars (*ʿulamāʾ*), 3, 54, 197, 204, 224, 277, 278, 397, 401, 403; 'All praise is for God', 352; devils and, 126, 127; *Istiʿādha*, 91, 93
sects, 2–3, 135, 198, 330
senses, 11, 102–103, 117, 128, 129, 230; Divine Names connected to hearing/*samʿ* and vision/ *baṣar*, 222; five Divine Names and five senses, 446; light and, 196; see also body
servanthood (*ʿubūdiyya*), 272, 273, 286, 290, 392–3; attributes of the servant, 444, 446; Covenant of, 147, 288, 393; duties of the servant, 372, 373–4; knowledge of, 393, 413, 418–19, 420, 432; needs of the servant, 447; station of servitude, 113, 250, 391, 392, 422, 451; three states of the servant, 381–2; 'We hear, and we obey', 413
al-Shāfiʿī, Muḥammad b. Idrīs, 92, 93, 149–50, 152, 296, 304, 307, 310, 317, 319, 320, 321, 325, 327, 328, 329, 337, 340, 341, 342, 343, 421
shahāda, see testimony of faith
sharīʿa (Islamic law), 8, 224, 438; *Istiʿādha*, 15; station of *sharīʿa*, 290, 291, 437, 438
al-Shaybānī, Muḥammad b. al-Ḥasan 23, 93–4, 150–1, 304, 305, 328, 329
shayṭān, see Satan
al-Shiblī, Abū Bakr, 227
Shurayḥ al-Qāḍī, 316
Sībawayh, 22, 51, 60, 70, 76, 77–8, 79–80, 149, 165, 243
similarity (*mushābaha*), 19, 21, 48, 73, 92, 95, 253, 412–13

sin, 135, 267, 291, 292, 356; devil and, 119, 127; Satan and, 108, 131, 142, 143–4; sinfulness, 135; sinner, 407, 409; see also forgiveness
Solomon, 122, 134, 261–2, 263–4, 308, 312–13, 314
soul/ego (*nafs*), 4, 7, 118, 230, 256; abstract soul, 120; appetitive ego/*nafs shahwāniyya*, 444, 445; Divine Names and, 241–2, 444–5; heavenly soul, 119; human soul, 118–19, 120, 241; irascible ego/*nafs ghaḍabiyya*, 444–5; lower self, 113; purpose of, 35; satanic ego/*nafs shayṭāniyya*, 444, 445; seeking guidance through cleansing and discipline, 8, 9; self-effacement, 228
sound (*ṣawt*), 29; breath and voice/sound, 11, 21, 34, 41, 68, 70; cause of, 41; definition of, 40; *kalima* and, 24–5, 29; letter and, 29, 34, 35, 41–2; as material, 29; onomatopoeia, 30; thoughts and, 132
speculation (*ẓann*), 38, 39, 134, 306
speech, see *kalām*
spirit (*rūḥ*), 119, 167, 256, 286, 291; spiritual ascension within the prayer, 432
statement, see *qawl*
stations (*maqāmāt*), 109, 139, 158, 167–8, 232, 435–6, 438; longing for God, 230–1, 263; remembrance is the noblest of stations, 234; self-effacement, 228; seven stations of knowledge, 413–14; seven stations in supplication, 414; station of *ḥaqīqa*/reality, 291, 437, 438; station of multiplicity/*takthīr*, 232; station of praise, 423; station of servitude, 113, 250, 391, 392, 422, 451; station of *sharīʿa*, 290, 291, 437, 438; station of *ṭarīqa*/path, 290–1, 437, 438; station of unity/*tawḥīd*, 232; station of witnessing, 227; see also unveiling
'*subḥāna Allāh*' ('Glory be to God'), 89, 327, 332, 353, 384–5, 447, 448
subjunctive mood, see *naṣb*
al-Suddī, Ismāʿīl b. ʿAbd al-Raḥmān, 263
Sufyān b. ʿUyayna, 275
Ṣuhayb b. Sinān b. Mālik, 334
al-Suhrawardī, Abū al-Najīb, 242
Sunna: *Basmala*, 311, 320, 322, 327, 328; Divine Names in, 3; *Fātiḥa*, 296–7, 303, 311, 337, 341, 421; *Istiʿādha*, 91; prayer, 296–7, 401; Qur'ānic recitation, 94, 95, 329–30
supplication (*duʿā'*), 146, 333, 394, 401; seven stations in, 414; see also prayer

Tablet, 239, 361, 436, 440
takbīr, see '*Allāhu akbar*'/*takbīr*
taklīf, see duties
Ṭalḥa b. ʿUbayd Allāh, 309
tanzīh, see glorifiers/glorification
tashbīh, see anthropomorphism
tasmiya, see naming
tawḥīd: monotheism, 100, 235, 437; Oneness, 109, 168, 226, 347, 418, 424; station of unity, 232
testimony of faith (*shahāda*), 19, 252,

254, 261, 369–70, 372, 433, 445; 'There is no god but God', 227, 235, 252, 347–8, 384, 385, 447, 448; see also pronominal Divine Names
Thaʿlab, 169
al-Thaʿlabī, Abū Isḥāq, 273, 275, 277, 278, 307, 308–309, 315
al-thanawiyya, see dualists
al-Thawrī, Sufyān b. Saʿīd, 93, 307, 327, 341
'The Compassionate, the Merciful', 6–7, 161, 271, 272, 281, 290, 418; action of prayer: straightening up/*intiṣāb*, 427; emphasising that God is Compassionate and Merciful, 317; exegesis of, 366–71; *ḥadīth* on, 370–1; Jabrīs on, 371; mercy/*raḥma*, 6, 293, 438; 'My servant has exalted Me', 309, 315, 420, 423–4; praise of God, 272; Q.xxi.107: 'We sent you not but as a mercy for the worlds', 370, 443; Qadarīs on, 371; *Sūrat al-Baqara* and, 414; tales of divine mercy, 366–8; tribulation as mercy, 367; see also *al-Raḥīm*; *al-Raḥmān*
'The path of those on whom You have bestowed favour', 9, 273, 291, 317–19, 399, 444; action of prayer: sitting/*qaʿda*, 427; Arabic language, linguistic/grammatical issues, 404; companions, guards, guides, 450; exegesis of, 403–407; favour/*niʿma*, 403–406, 410, 419; 'favour' as faith, 406–407; people of obedience, 409; Prophets, the truthful, martyrs, the witnesses, the righteous, 288, 402, 405, 428, 438, 450; 'the straight path', 400, 404
theology/theologian, 176–9, 197, 198, 209, 353; difference between *kalima* and *kalām*, 22–3; *Istiʿādha*, 15; meaning of words, 33; proper noun, 58
thinking (*fikr*), 255–6, 437
thoughts, 128, 248; nature of, 132–3; see also imagination
Throne (*ʿarsh*), 4, 5, 116, 190, 194, 198, 225, 277, 361, 435, 438, 439
al-Tirmidhī, Abū ʿĪsā, 338
transmission (*samʿiyyāt*), 7, 8, 39; knowing language by, 37–8; mass transmission/*mutawātir*, 3, 37, 38, 39, 43, 96–7, 123–4, 305, 306, 314, 322; Qur'ānic recitation, 96–7; reliability of, 38–9; solitary reports/*āḥād*, 3, 37, 38, 97, 305–306, 325

ʿUbāda b. al-Ṣāmit, 275, 338, 339
Ubayy b. Kaʿb, 180, 311–12
ʿubūdiyya, see servanthood
ʿulamā', see scholars
ʿUmar b. ʿAbd al-ʿAzīz, 166
ʿUmar b. al-Khaṭṭāb, 26, 98, 265, 297, 322–3, 324, 330, 340, 342; see also Rightly-Guided Caliphs
Umayyads, 324
Umm Salama, 307, 308, 327
unveiling, 115, 168, 230, 272, 276, 279, 283, 287, 288, 291, 293, 419; stages of, 273
ʿUrwa b. Zubayr b. al-ʿAwwām, 390

ʿUthmān b. ʿAffān, 297, 322–3; see also Rightly-Guided Caliphs
utterance, see *lafẓ*

verb, 12, 13, 75; as accidental state in the quiddity, 66; as a branch, 73, 74; can be a subject, 46–7, 48; coinage, order of, 173–4; compound sentences, 56–7; deficient verb, 53; definition of, 46, 51–4, 174; ellipsis of, 148; implied verb, 85; inflection of, 82–8; intransitive verb, 82; non-inflection, 74; object and, 83, 84; subject and, 82–5, 86; transitive verb, 84; two verbs, one conjoined to the other, 85–8; verbal noun, 27, 47, 50, 51–2, 53, 54, 74, 82, 98, 170, 204, 219; word combinations, 55–6
volition (*irāda*), 36, 82, 173, 211, 285, 346, 373, 409; Divine Names connected to, 221–2
voluntarism (*qadar*), 105, 106, 271, 287, 399; see also free will
vowel, 67–8, 70, 78–9; *ḍamma* as the heaviest vowel, 69; explicit vowel, 67; fleeting vowel, 67–8; *ḥaraka*, 42, 67, 70; inflection vowel, 67, 68, 69–70; lengthening and gliding, 68–9; *majārī*/running routes, 70–1; non-pure vowel, 67; nunation, 29, 73, 74, 75, 77; pure vowel, 67; short/long vowels, 42, 67; *sukūn*, 42, 67, 69, 70, 71, 72; uninflected word, 67, 69–71; 'unknown' vowel, 67–8;
vowelled/unvowelled letters, 42, 67, 68, 69, 75, 163; see also letter

Waraqa b. Nawfal, 277
al-Wāsiṭī, Abū Bakr, 351
word, see *kalima*
world: *ʿālam*, 360; corporeal world, 103, 241, 412–13, 429, 449; *dunyā*, 412; love of this world, 292; observed world/*shahāda*, 428, 429, 430; spiritual world/world of spirituality, 103, 412–13, 414, 428–9; Utmost Unseen/*ghayb al-ghayb*, 428, 429, 430; world of spirits and world of bodies, 109, 113; world of the Unseen/*ghayb*, 134, 428, 429, 430
worship (*ʿibāda*), 286; *alaha*, *ilāh*/to worship, worshipped, 245–7; angels, 384, 388; benefits of, 389–90; definition, 380; *ḥadīth*, 390; levels of, 391; meaning, 8; as a trust/*amāna*, 390; worship alleviates the heart's distress, 391–2; see also 'You we worship...'
writing, 34
wrongdoing (*ẓulm*), 96, 127, 142, 260, 372, 415

Yaḥyā b. Saʿīd al-Anṣārī, 123
Yaʿlā b. Munya (Yaʿlā b. Umayya), 195, 310, 327–8
Yaʿlā b. ʿUbayd al-Ṭanāfisī, 305
'You we worship...', 8, 103, 158, 273, 287, 397, 419, 432; action of prayer: sitting between prostrations, 427; Arabic language, linguistic/

grammatical issues, 158, 385, 386–9, 394; effort and striving in servitude, 272; exegesis of, 380–94; free will, 424; God being the object of the creation's worship, 382; 'I/We worship You'/*naᶜbuduka*, 385, 387–8; 'I worship none but You'/exclusivity, 380, 382, 383, 384, 387, 388; *iyyāka naᶜbudu*, 385–7, 388; monotheism, 383–4; *nūn* in *naᶜbudu*/plural, 387–9, 402; preordainment, 271, 424; second person/*khiṭāb*, 394, 449; service and servitude, 272, 273, 276, 286–7, 290–1, 294, 382, 391–3, 394, 418–19; station of *sharīᶜa*, 290, 291, 438; supplication, 394; *Sūrat al-Baqara* and, 414; 'There is no god but God', 384, 385; 'This is [divided] between Me and My servant', 309, 315, 420, 424–5; see also 'And from You we seek help'; worship

al-Ẓāhirī, Dāwūd b. ᶜAlī al-Iṣfahānī, 89
al-Zamakhsharī, Maḥmūd b. ᶜUmar, 27, 48, 51
ẓann, see speculation
Zayd b. Ḥāritha, 263
Zechariah, 399
Zufar b. al-Hudhayl, 23–4
zuhd, see asceticism
ẓulm, see wrongdoing